Keyboarding Formatting Communication Skills Document Production

Complete Course

11th EDITION

COLLEGE KEYBOARDING/ TYPEWRITING

Charles H. Duncan
Professor of Business Education
Eastern Michigan University

S. ElVon Warner
Head, Department of Information Management
University of Northern Iowa

Thomas E. Langford
President, Bay State Junior College
Boston, Massachusetts

Susie H. VanHuss
Professor of Management
University of South Carolina

Copyright © 1985
By SOUTH-WESTERN PUBLISHING CO.
Cincinnati, Ohio

ISBN: 0-538-20750-7

Library of Congress Catalog Card Number: 84-50474

3 4 5 6 7 8 9 10 11 12 13 14 H 2 1 0 9 8 7 6

Printed in U.S.A.

COVER PHOTO: Aetna Life and Casualty Company

PHOTO, p. 6: Location courtesy of Public Library of Hamilton County,
    Mt. Washington Branch

PHOTO, p. 71: Location courtesy of American Express Travel Related Services Co.,
    Cincinnati Office

Published by

T75 **SOUTH-WESTERN PUBLISHING CO.**

CINCINNATI   WEST CHICAGO, IL   DALLAS   PELHAM MANOR, NY   PALO ALTO, CA

CONTENTS

Know your machine: electric typewriter...1
Know your machine: microcomputers...2
Special procedures for nonelectric typewriters...3
Daily get-ready-to-type procedures...4
Daily get-ready-to-type procedures...5

DIVISION 1

LEVEL ONE

LEVEL TWO

DIVISION 2

LEVEL THREE

LEVEL FOUR

LESSONS 114-150. Formatting/typing tables, forms, and reports **214**

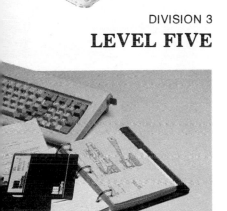

Sections:

DIVISION 3

LEVEL FIVE

LESSONS 151-188. Processing information (staff office simulations) **272**

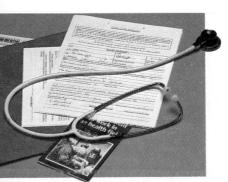

Sections:

LEVEL SIX

LESSONS 189-225. Processing information (service office simulations) **335**

Sections:

PREFACE

College Keyboarding/Typewriting, Complete Course, 11th edition, is the latest revision of a series of learning materials that were first designed specifically for college students over fifty years ago. Since 1930, the various editions of the book have established a reputation for providing college students with those skills and knowledges required for efficient operation of keyboard-activated equipment. In keeping with this tradition, the 11th edition aims specifically at helping students achieve the following personal and professional goals:

1 to operate keyboard-activated equipment rapidly and accurately;
2 to improve their written communication skills;
3 to learn to format rapidly and accurately the kinds of documents most often used in business, professional, and government offices;
4 to develop high-level document production skill;
5 to learn to work and to evaluate their work with little supervision;
6 to become acquainted with terminology, equipment, and procedures of modern offices.

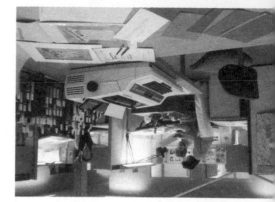

ORGANIZATION

College Keyboarding/Typewriting is divided into three main Divisions and six Levels of learning structured to correspond with student skill-growth patterns. Division 1 introduces students to keyboarding and formatting techniques, teaches them to proofread and make corrections, and develops their basic keystroking speed and accuracy skills. Division 2 builds directly on the competencies developed in Division 1, leading students toward greater speed, improved accuracy, and greater refinement of formatting ability. Division 3 emphasizes vocational application of keyboarding/formatting/editing skills in sections that portray realistic office-like settings that encourage students to perform as if they were at work in real job situations.

SPECIAL FEATURES

Content. The scientifically structured lessons in College Keyboarding/Typewriting are built on the findings of scholars who have researched the areas of keyboarding learning and application.

The lessons, therefore, have a sound psychological as well as topical base that leads to practical achievement.

Goals. To orient and motivate students, learning goals are stated at the beginning of each section of lessons. Intermediate goals are stated periodically throughout the sections to identify the purpose of practice, to indicate how to practice, and to identify expected outcomes.

Skill building. Special sections devoted exclusively to the development and improvement of basic skills are interspersed among application sections. Instructors may use these sections in order of occurrence, group them for intensive emphasis, or select from them to tailor instruction to individual student needs.

Measurement. Sections of lessons that focus on measurement of achievement in basic skill and production power are set midway through each Division and again at its end. Thus, ample opportunities are provided to evaluate intensively and appropriately each student's growth.

Controlled copy. Basic skillbuilding and measurement paragraph copy is triple-controlled to insure uniformity of difficulty. Three factors—syllable intensity, average word length, and percentage of high-frequency words—are simultaneously controlled in each paragraph to assure valid and reliable measures of skill growth. Special keyboarding drills are controlled in other ways to assure "loading" of the factors to be emphasized. Even application problems are controlled so that they progress in length, in complexity, and in vocabulary.

Cycled learning. Each operational presentation (letters, reports, tables, and others) is repeated in cycles of emphasis that provide spaced reviews, assure longer and better retention, and maximize opportunities for transfer.

Input Skills. To provide realism and promote transfer of learning, emphasis is placed on preparing final copy from script and rough-draft source documents.

Directions/illustrations. Complete directions and visual models are used liberally in presenting new learning. The directions-left/copy-right format helps students distinguish operational directions from copy to be typed. As soon as appropriate, students are given a sense of direction, but fewer directions, so that they learn to make necessary decisions about format, spacing, and placement.

Communication skills. Periodic instruction and review to help students develop basic written communication skills are included in many of the lessons. In addition, selected document preparation jobs require students to apply in realistic settings the language skills they have developed. Further, this new edition includes the most up-to-date business terminology and gives specific attention to new procedures and equipment of electronic offices.

ACKNOWLEDGMENTS

The authors gratefully acknowledge the helpful contributions made by instructors who used prior editions of the text, especially those who responded to the national user survey made just prior to the preparation of this new edition. Special recognition is given, also, to Dr. D. D. Lessenberry, the original author of College Typewriting, who for over fifty years set the pattern and pace of typewriting instruction in the United States.

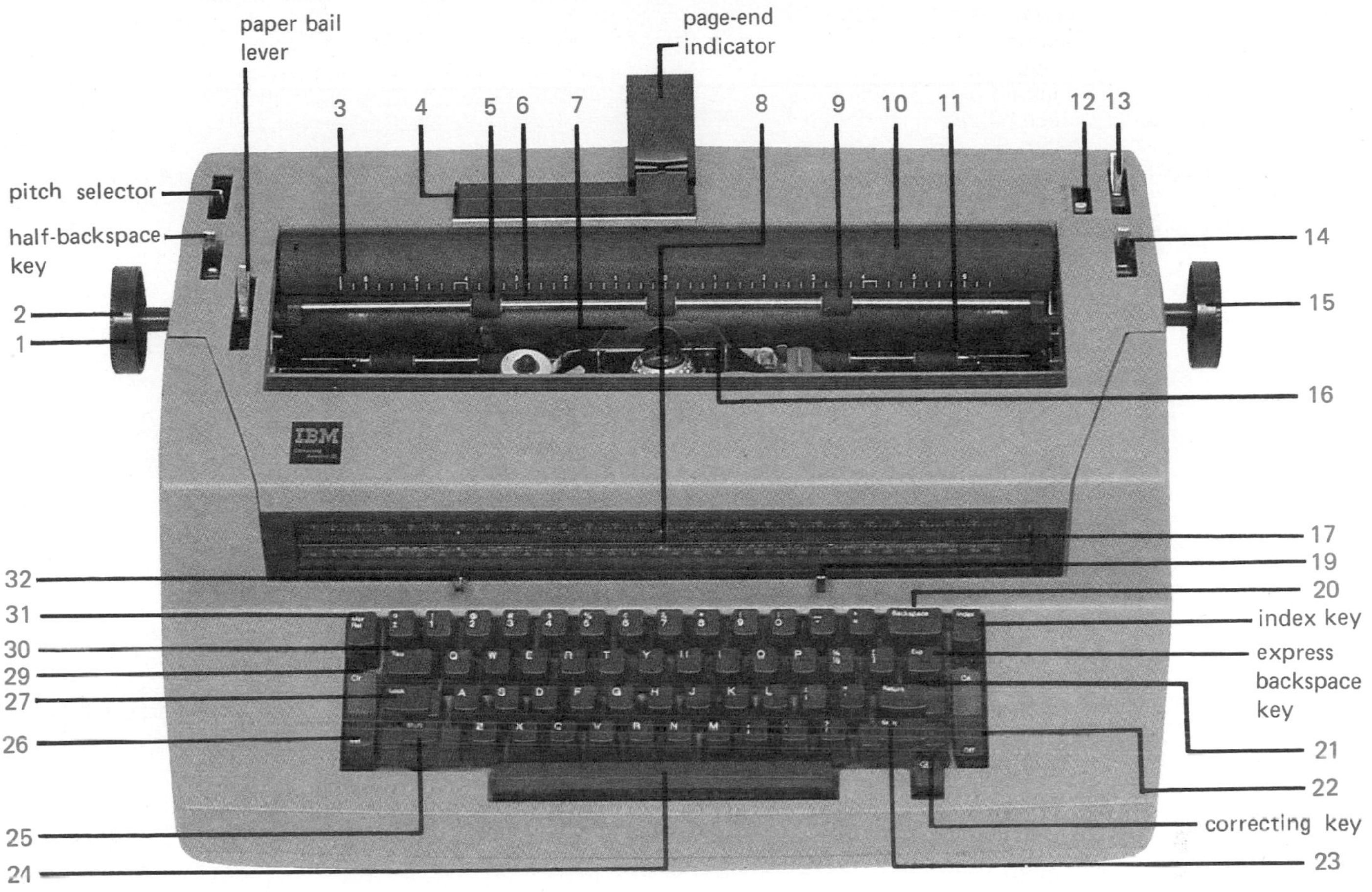

paper bail lever
page-end indicator
pitch selector
half-backspace key
index key
express backspace key
correcting key
1
2
3
4
5
6
7
8
9
10
11
12
13
14
15
16
17
19
20
21
22
23
24
25
26
27
29
30
31
32

The diagram above shows the parts of an electric typewriter. Since typewriters have similar parts, you should be able to locate the parts of your machine from this diagram. However, if you have the instructional booklet that comes with your machine, use it to identify exact locations of these parts.

If you are learning on a non-electric (manual) typewriter, refer to page 3 for those machine parts and keys that differ in location from an electric machine.

Illustrated on page 2 is an array of data/word processing machines to which your keyboarding skills will transfer.

1 Left platen knob: used to activate variable line spacer

2 Variable line spacer: used to change writing line setting permanently

3 Paper guide scale: used to set paper edge guide at desired position

4 Paper edge guide: used to position paper for insertion

5/9 Paper bail rolls: used to hold paper against platen

6 Paper bail: used to hold paper against platen

7 Card/envelope holder: used to hold cards, labels, and envelopes against platen

8 Printing point indicator: used to position element carrier at desired point

9 (See 5)

10 Paper table: supports paper when it is in typewriter

11 Platen (cylinder): provides a hard surface against which type element strikes

12 Line-space selector: sets typewriter to advance the paper (using carrier return key) 1, 2, or (on some machines) 3 lines for single, double, or triple spacing

13 Paper release lever: used to allow paper to be removed or aligned

14 Automatic line finder: used to change line spacing temporarily, then refind the line

15 Right platen knob: used to turn platen as paper is being inserted

16 Aligning scale: used to align copy that has been reinserted

17 Line-of-writing (margin) scale: used when setting margins, tab stops, and in horizontal centering

18 Ribbon carrier: positions and controls ribbon at printing point (not shown—under the cover)

19 Right margin set: used to set right margin stop

20 Backspace key: used to move printing point to left one space at a time

21 Carrier return key: used to return element carrier to left margin and to advance paper up

22 ON/OFF control: used to turn electric typewriters on or off

23 Right shift key: used to type capitals of letter keys controlled by left hand

24 Space bar: used to move printing point to right one space at a time

25 Left shift key: used to type capitals of letter keys controlled by right hand

26 Tab set: used to set tab stops

27 Shift lock: used to lock shift mechanism so that all letters are capitalized

28 Ribbon control: used to select ribbon typing position (not shown—under cover)

29 Tab clear: used to clear tab stops

30 Tabulator: used to move element carrier to tab stops

31 Margin release key: used to move element carrier beyond margin stops

32 Left margin set: used to set left margin stop

On most electric and electronic machines, certain parts may be used for automatic repeat, such as:

20—backspace key
21—carrier return key
24—space bar

Job 2
Unbound report (plain sheet)

Prepare this notice as an unbound report.

Job 3
Topbound report
(plain sheet)

Prepare this notice as a topbound report.

FLEXITIME WORK SCHEDULE

words
5

Effective July 1, our company will initiate a flexi- ~~*Flexitime*~~ time work scheduling procedure. It is a voluntary pro- *employees* gram, and those who wish to remain on their current work schedule should indicate this preference to their department manager.

15

27

40

52

55

Rules and Regulations

64

The following rules ~~and regulations~~ will govern ~~the~~ *our* new flexitime program: (*, including 30 minutes of breaktime*)

71

75

a. All employees must work an 8-hour day. All employees must work between the hours of 10:00 *a.m.* and 2:00 p.m., the core working period.

92

104

110

b. An employee may start work as early as 7:00 a.m. *and work as late as 6:00 p.m.*

122

127

c. An employee must schedule one hour for lunch. The cafeteria will be open from 11:30 a.m. to 1:30 p.m. *accommodate* to ~~serve~~ those who wish to take an earlier *or later* lunch hour.

137

148

162

d. Over time rate and distribution of overtime will be governed by the same regulations as ~~recently~~ *are currently* used in *each* department.

172

183

188

Work Scheduling *es*

195

Each manager will distribute ~~to all employees~~ a flextime scheduling form for each employees to complete. One a daily routine schedule has been agreed upon between the department manager and the employee, any *deviation* ~~variation~~ from that schedule should *occur* ~~happen~~ only for reasons ~~which have been discussed and~~ approved by the department manager.

201

212

223

233

243

248

252

Time schedule
Assembling materials .... 2'
Timed production .... 25'
Final check; compute
    n–pram .... 3'

Job 1
Two-page leftbound report
(plain sheets)

words

COMPUTER-AIDED INSTRUCTION | 5

Computer-aided instruction is the process of having a student interact | 20
with an instructional program that is controlled by a computer. Basically, the | 36
computer presents the information and/or questions about the subject matter to | 51
the student in a systematic manner, usually in small steps from simple to com- | 67
plex. After the computer has supplied the information or question, the student | 83
will study and analyze the material and then will make a response via the | 98
keyboard. At times, the student is permitted an inquiry concerning a specific | 114
question he or she may have about the topic being studied. | 126

Instructional Software | 135

The program which leads the student through the instructional process | 149
may be simple in design or very complex. Most software, however, generally | 164
accepts student responses, checks the responses for accuracy, and then pro- | 179
vides the student with immediate feedback as to the accuracy of his or her | 194
response. The more sophisticated instructional package monitors the student's | 210
progress and may even provide various levels of instruction based upon the | 225
student's understanding of the subject. Most instructional software packages | 240
can be classified into two basic areas: drill and practice or tutorial. | 255

Drill and practice. These types of instructional software packages put the | 274
student through a series of repetitive exercises. One major advantage of these | 290
software programs is that they allow the computer to monitor a student's | 305
progress and provide immediate feedback. One major disadvantage, however, | 320
is that they are usually very structured and provide little deviation from the | 336
step-by-step sequence of the program. | 343

Tutorial. These instructional programs are designed to present new ma- | 359
terial to the student. A good tutorial program will provide for a variety of | 375
responses from the student and then will branch to one of the several different | 391
levels based upon the achievement of the student. | 401

Conclusion | 406

Computer-aided instruction can be a very useful tool in the classroom if | 420
the programs have been carefully developed to provide the student with a | 435
maximum range of options. Even though computer-aided instruction cannot | 449
take the place of a good teacher, it will provide an excellent supplement to the | 466
efforts of the classroom teacher. | 473

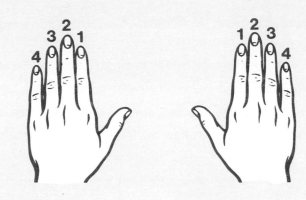

Finger Identification

If you are using a nonelectric (manual) typewriter to learn to keyboard, several of the reaches shown on subsequent pages may be different because of differences in location of the machine part on manual and electric machines. Refer to this page for help in locating these reaches.

Apostrophe

The ' (apostrophe) is the shift of 8. Shift with the left little (fourth) finger; then reach for ' with the right second finger.

k'k k'k k'k it's

Asterisk

The * (asterisk) is the shift of − (hyphen). Depress left shift; then strike * with the right fourth (;) finger.

;−; ;*; ;*; ;*;

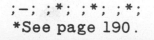
*See page 190.

Backspacer

Reach to the backspace key with the appropriate little (fourth) finger. Depress the key firmly for each backspace desired.

Carriage return

Move the left hand, fingers bracing one another, to the carriage return lever.

Move the lever inward to take up the slack; then return the carriage with a quick inward flick-of-the-hand motion.

Drop the hand quickly to typing position without letting it follow the carriage across the page.

Carriage release

If your typewriter has a movable carriage, depress the right carriage release to move it freely. When you have finished keyboarding for the day, leave the carriage approximately centered.

Exclamation mark

On most manual typewriters (and some electrics), there is no exclamation mark key. To *make* an exclamation mark, strike ' (apostrophe); then backspace and strike . (period).

Oh! I just won!

Quotation marks

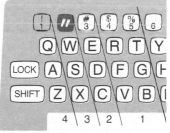

The " (quotation mark) is the shift of 2. Shift with the right little (fourth) finger; then reach for " with the left third finger.

s"s s"s s"s "so"

Tabulator bar

Depress and hold down the tabulator bar with the right first finger until the carriage has stopped.

Tabulator key

Depress and hold down the tabulator key with the nearest little (fourth) finger until the carriage has stopped.

Underline

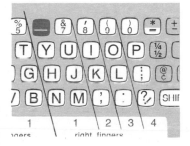

The ___ (underline) is the shift of 6. Shift with the left little (fourth) finger; then reach for ___ with the right first finger.

<u>j j j To Yes</u>

225a ▶ 5
Preparatory Practice

each line 3 times SS (slowly, faster, slowly); DS between 3-line groups; retype selected lines as time permits

alphabet 1 Elizabeth Coxe vowed to make a journey to present a gift to the queen.

fig/sym 2 The room rates are $514.79/double and $268.30/single (plus sales tax).

direct reach 3 My younger brother, who is often hungry, wants rum cake and ice cream.

fluency 4 The city may end the downtown bicycle problem with a sign and penalty.

| 1 | 2 | 3 | 4 | 5 | 6 | 7 | 8 | 9 | 10 | 11 | 12 | 13 | 14 |

225b ▶ 15
Measure straight-copy skill

two 5' writings; record the *gwam* and number of errors for the better writing (LM p. 3)

Difficulty index

all letters used | A | 1.5 si | 5.7 awl | 80% hfw

gwam 1' | 5'

Have you lately attempted to express a significant point, and the 13 | 3 | 64
person to whom you were talking was not paying attention? This behavior 28 | 6 | 67
is not only frustrating for the speaker, but it is also damaging to the 42 | 8 | 69
person listening. Much of our daily time is spent listening to what 57 | 11 | 72
others are saying, and most of the knowledge we gain comes from this 71 | 14 | 75
form of communication. Yet, most of us either do not listen well or 84 | 17 | 78
are passive listeners. It is important that we learn to become good 98 | 20 | 81
listeners. In order to do this, we must become active listeners. 111 | 22 | 83

Important to one becoming an active listener is to show the speaker 14 | 25 | 86
that you are interested in what is being said. Look directly at the 27 | 28 | 89
person who is speaking. Once eye contact has been established, be re- 41 | 30 | 92
sponsive to what the speaker is saying. A nod of the head or a smile 55 | 33 | 94
of agreement can illustrate to the speaker that you are interested. An- 70 | 36 | 97
other way of becoming an active listener is to ask questions that refer 84 | 39 | 100
to the particular topic at hand. Try to avoid asking questions that 98 | 42 | 103
might lead the speaker into areas that have no relationship to the topic 112 | 45 | 106
of discussion. 115 | 45 | 106

Last, it is important to keep an open mind about what the speaker 13 | 48 | 109
is attempting to communicate. Do not interrupt; allow the speaker an 27 | 51 | 112
opportunity to completely make his or her point. Then analyze thoroughly 42 | 54 | 115
the point made before rejecting what has been said or offering an argu- 56 | 57 | 118
ment against it. Being an active listener is a key to knowledge, and 71 | 60 | 120
it is a courtesy we can give to others. 79 | 61 | 122

gwam 1' | 1 | 2 | 3 | 4 | 5 | 6 | 7 | 8 | 9 | 10 | 11 | 12 | 13 | 14 |
5' | 1 | 2 | 3 |

① Adjust paper guide

Line up paper edge guide (4) with zero on the line–of–writing scale (17).

② Insert typing paper

Take a sheet of paper in your left hand and follow the directions and illustrations at the right and below.

1 Pull paper bail (6) forward (or up on some machines).

2 Place paper against paper edge guide (4), behind the platen (11).

3 Turn paper into machine, using right platen knob (15) or index key.

4 Stop when paper is about 1½ inches above aligning scale (16).

5 If paper is not straight, pull paper release lever (13) forward.

6 Straighten paper, then push paper release lever back.

7 Push paper bail back so that it holds paper against platen.

8 Slide paper bail rolls (5/9) into position, dividing paper into thirds.

9 Properly inserted paper.

③ Set line-space selector

Many machines offer 3 choices for line spacing—1, 1½, and 2 indicated by bars or numbers on the line–space selector (12).

Set the line space selector on (—) or 1 to single–space (SS) or on (≡) or on 2 to double–space (DS) as directed for lines in Level 1.

```
1 Lines 1 and 2 are single-spaced (SS).
2 A double space (DS) separates Lines 2 and 4.
3                          1 blank line space
4 A triple space (TS) separates Lines 4 and 7.
5                          2 blank line spaces
6
7 Set the selector on "1" for single spacing.
```

④ Determine type size

Most machines are equipped with pica (10 spaces to a horizontal inch) or elite (12 spaces to a horizontal inch) type size.

Marked intervals on the line–of–writing scale (17) match the spacing of letters on the machine. This scale reads from 0 to 110 or more for machines with elite type, from 0 to 90 or more for machines with pica type.

This is elite (12-pitch) type, 12 spaces to an inch.

This is pica (10-pitch) type, 10 spaces to an inch.

inches					
	1	2	3	4	5

centimeters													
1	2	3	4	5	6	7	8	9	10	11	12	13	14

224b, continued

Job 3
Table with horizontal rulings

Center in exact vertical center on a full sheet. SS body and leave 6 spaces between columns.

DESIRED EMPLOYEE TRAITS

(Employer Survey)

Rank Order	Trait	Percent Responding
1	Skilled	98
2	Responsible	95
2	Honest	95
3	Sincere	91
4	Enthusiastic	87
4	Determined	87
5	Intelligent	84
5	Courteous	84
6	Tactful	82
6	Pleasant	82
7	Neat	80

Job 4
Table with horizontal and vertical rulings and a braced heading

Center in exact vertical center on a full sheet. DS body and leave 4 spaces between columns.

METROPOLITAN PROFESSIONAL BUSINESS ORGANIZATIONS

Organization	Membership		
	Females	Males	Total
Administrative Management Society	65	82	147
American Accounting Association	40	110	150
American Marketing Association	20	55	75
Association for Computing Machinery	19	62	81
Association for Systems Management	13	38	51
National Association of Accountants	30	45	75
Professional Secretaries International	85	10	95

⑤ Plan margin settings

When 8 ½– by 11–inch paper is in-serted into the typewriter (8½–inch end first) with left edge at 0 on the line–of–writing scale (17), center point is 51 (elite) or 42½ (pica). Use 42 for pica center.

To center typed lines, set left and right margin stops the same number of spaces left and right from center point. Diagrams at the right show margin settings for 50–, 60–, and 70–space lines. When you begin to use the warning bell, 5 or 6 spaces may be added to the right margin.

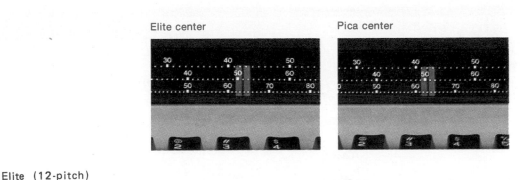

Elite center   Pica center

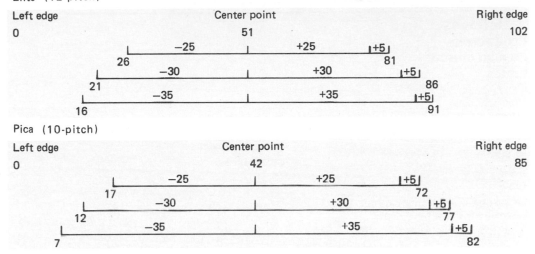

Elite (12-pitch)

Left edge	Center point		Right edge
0	51		102

	−25	+25	+5
	26		81
	−30	+30	+5
	21		86
	−35	+35	+5
	16		91

Pica (10-pitch)

Left edge	Center point		Right edge
0	42		85

	−25	+25	+5
	17		72
	−30	+30	+5
	12		77
	−35	+35	+5
	7		82

⑥ Set margin stops

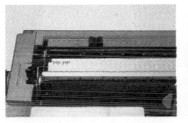

Type A
Push-button set

Adler, Olympia, Remington, Royal 700/870 manuals, Smith-Corona

1 Press down on the left margin set button.

2 Slide it to desired position on the line–of–writing (margin) scale.

3 Release the margin set button.

4 Using the right margin set but-ton, set the right margin stop in the same way.

Type B
Push-lever set

Single element typewriters, such as Adler, Olivetti, Remington Rand, Royal, Selectric

1 Push in on the left margin set lever.

2 Slide it to desired position on the line–of–writing (margin) scale.

3 Release the margin set lever.

4 Using the right margin set lever, set the right margin stop in the same way.

Type C
Key set

IBM typebar, Olivetti electric

1 Move carriage to the left margin stop by depressing the return key.

2 Depress and hold down the margin set (IBM reset) key as you move carriage to desired left margin stop position.

3 Release the margin set (IBM re-set) key.

4 Move carriage to the right mar-gin stop.

5 Depress and hold down the margin set (IBM reset) key as you move carriage to desired right margin stop position.

6 Release the margin set (IBM re-set) key.

Type D
Electronic set

To set margins on some elec-tronic machines, such as Xerox and Silver–Reed, space to the desired margin position and strike the appropriate (left or right) margin key.

On other machines, such as IBM, space to the desired margin position and strike the CODE key and the appropriate (left or right) margin key *at the same time*.

> General information for setting margin stops is given here. If you have the manufacturer's booklet for your typewriter, however, use it; the procedure for your particular model may be slightly different.

224a ▶ 5
Preparatory practice

each line 3 times SS (slowly, faster, slowly); DS between 3-line groups; retype selected lines as time permits

			words

alphabet 1 Zeke Quigley joined a new private karate club for six dollars a month.

fig/sym 2 Policy #12B-43/56 has a monthly premium of $79.80; quarterly, $315.25.

shift key 3 Ask Harvey if he has seen Tom, Jan, Alice, Ron, Pat, Sloan, or Martha.

fluency 4 The eighth amendment is a key proviso for the social work of the town.

| 1 | 2 | 3 | 4 | 5 | 6 | 7 | 8 | 9 | 10 | 11 | 12 | 13 | 14 |

224b ▶ 45
Production measurement: tables
(half sheet and full sheets)

Time schedule
Assembling materials .... 2'
Timed production .... 38'
Final check; compute
n–pram .... 5'

Job 1
Table

Center on half sheet, long side up. DS the body of the table; leave 20 spaces between columns.

words

PRODUCTION — 2

Year		Units	
1980		2,635,269	10
1981	20 spaces here	2,873,621	13
1982		3,050,342	16
1983		3,467,879	19
1984		3,825,771	22
1985		4,276,322	24

(Year / Units header — 7)

Job 2
Table

Center in reading position on a full sheet. DS the body of table; decide intercolumn spacing.

TOP TEN BUSINESS MAJORS			5
Spring 1985			7
Name of Student	Grade-Point Average	Major	11 / 20
Rose Swinton	4.00	Accounting	26
Carlton West	3.98	Office Administration	34
Madge Daugherty	3.96	Marketing	40
Gifford Frette	3.95	Accounting	47
Dwight Rogers	3.94	Business Management	54
Calvin Jennings	3.93	Office Administration	63
Virginia Wong	3.92	Accounting	69
Juanita Lopez	3.91	Marketing	75
Levi Goldberg	3.90	Marketing	81
Maxine Lightfoot	3.89	Office Administration	89

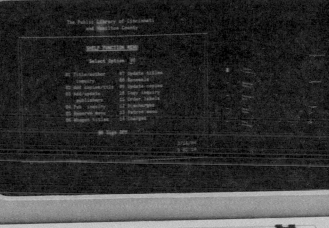

LEVEL ONE

Learning to keyboard and to format personal documents

Your decision to learn to keyboard is a wise one. Just as the 1960's were the decade of the computer and data processing, the 1980's are the decade of microcomputers, text editors, and word or information processing. In business, industry, and the professions, the use of electronic input/output devices is growing at lightning speed. Whether you learn to keyboard on a typewriter or a microcomputer, your keyboarding skill will transfer directly to other data/word processing machines because all use the same standard arrangement of the letter and number keys. In addition, some machines have a 10-key numeric pad arrangement which is the same as that on electronic calculators.

Learning to keyboard with speed and accuracy is only the first step, however. To be able to *use* your skill productively, you must also learn the features of frequently prepared documents (such as letters, reports, and tables) and develop skill in arranging and typing them in their conventional formats.

The purpose of Level 1 (Lessons 1-37), therefore, is to help you develop keyboarding efficiency and to begin teaching you how to format and type documents for personal use. The textbook, like your keyboarding instrument, is only a partner in learning. For your textbook and your machine to help you effectively to learn, you as the third partner must *intend* to learn and must practice intensively to reach your goals.

223b, continued

Job 2
Quitclaim deed
(LM p. 205)

Prepare the quitclaim deed shown at the right using the proper format for legal documents. Use a plain full sheet for second page.

Job 3
Quitclaim deed
(LM p. 207)

Prepare another quitclaim deed using the basic form of Job 2. Substitute the following data:

Party of the first part:
NADINE H. COCKRAN

Party of the second part:
LOWELL B. NEW-COMB

Both live in **Philadelphia, Pennsylvania**

Consideration:
$110,000

Land description:
Lot 28, Tract 245, as per recorded in the Book 331, pages 783-784, in the records of the Philadelphia County Recorder's Office.

Date the document:
July 13, 19--

Total words for Job 3: 438.

Use a plain full sheet for second page.

	words
QUITCLAIM DEED > *spread heading*	3
THIS INDENTURE, made the _23rd_ day of _February_, 19--,	14
between _DEXTER Q. LANDIS_ , of _Pittsburgh,_	22
Pennsylvania, party of the first part, and _JESSICA C._	32
FOWLER , of _Pittsburgh, Pennsylvania_ ,	40
party of the second part, witnesseth:	47

THAT THE PARTY of the first part, for and in consideration 59
of the sum of _Twenty-five Thousand_ Dollars 68
($ _25,000.00_) lawful money of the United States of America, 80
to h_im_ well and truly paid by the party of the second part, at 92
and before the sealing and delivery of these presents, the receipt 106
whereof is hereby acknowledged, has remised, released, and quit- 118
claimed, and by these presents does remise, release, and quitclaim 132
unto the party of the second part, and to h_er_ heirs and assigns, 145
forever, all that parcel: 150

Lot 193, Tract 12, as per recorded in 158
Book 493, pages 329-330, in the records of 166
the Allegheny County Recorder's Office 174

together with all and singular the tenements, hereditaments, and 187
appurtenances thereunto belonging or in anywise appertaining, and 200
the reversions, remainders, rents, issues, and profits thereof; and 214
also all the estate, right, title, interest, property, claim, and 227
demand whatsoever, as well in law as in equity, of the party of 240
the first part, of, in, or to the above-described premises, and 253
every part and parcel thereof, with the appurtenances. 264

TO HAVE AND TO HOLD all and singular the above-named and 275
described premises, together with the appurtenances, unto the 288
party of the second part, h_er_ heirs and assigns, forever. 299

IN WITNESS WHEREOF, the party of the first part, _____ 309
DEXTER Q. LANDIS , hereunto sets h_is_ hand and 318
seal the day and year first above written. 327

_____ (L. S.) 334

Dexter Q. Landis 337

COMMONWEALTH OF PENNSYLVANIA) 343
: ss. 344
County of Allegheny) 349

On this _23rd_ day of _February_ , 19--, before me 358
personally appeared the above-named individual, to me known to 370
be the person described in and who executed the foregoing instru- 383
ment and acknowledged that he/she/they executed the same as his/ 394
her/their own free act and deed. 399

In testimony whereof, I have hereunto subscribed my 410
name at Pittsburgh, Pennsylvania, this day. 418

_____ 425
Notary Public 428
My commission expires on June 30, 19--. 435

Learning goals

1 To master alphabetic reaches.

2 To operate keyboard without looking at your fingers or the keys—"by touch."

3 To type easy paragraph copy.

4 To type or keyboard at a rate of 14 or more gross words a minute (*gwam*).

Machine adjustments

1 Set paper guide at 0.

2 Set ribbon control to type on upper half of ribbon.

3 Set left margin stop for a 50–space line (center − 25); set right margin stop at end of line–of–writing scale.

4 Set line–space selector for single spacing (SS).

Prepare for Lesson 1

1 Acquire a supply of 8½″ by 11″ typing paper of good quality.

2 If your chair is adjustable, raise or lower it to a height that is comfortable for you.

3 If your desk is adjustable, raise or lower it until your forearms parallel the slant of the keyboard when your fingers are placed over asdf jkl;.

4 Follow carefully all directions, both oral and written. Therein lies much of the secret for gaining keyboarding skill.

1a
Get ready to keyboard

1 Clear work area and chair of un-needed books and clothing.

2 Place textbook at right of machine, the top elevated for easy reading; stack paper supply at left of machine.

3 Refer briefly to page 1 of this book where typewriter parts are named, illustrated, and described. In these early lessons, frequent reference is made to these parts; you will need to refer to the illus-trated typewriter on page 1 at those times.

4 Locate on page 5 the type of margin sets that match those on your machine. Set the left margin stop for a 50–space line (center − 25); move the right stop to the ex-treme right end of the line–of–writing scale.

5 Study pages 4 and 5 carefully. If necessary, adjust the paper edge guide (at 0) on your machine. In-sert paper as illustrated.

6 Set line–space selector for single spacing (SS) as directed on page 4.

Preparatory
practice

each line 3 times SS
(slowly, faster, still
faster); DS between
3-line groups; repeat
selected lines as time
permits

alphabet 1 Major Weavers shipped by rail express the quick-frozen fruit packages.

fig/sym 2 Sanders & Johnson (P.O. #3128479) ordered 560 boxes of our #2 pencils.

double letter 3 Her business success occurred suddenly when it hardly seemed possible.

fluency 4 The duty of an auditor is to visit a city and do a formal field audit.

| 1 | 2 | 3 | 4 | 5 | 6 | 7 | 8 | 9 | 10 | 11 | 12 | 13 | 14 |

223b ▶ 45
Production
measurement:
medical and
legal reports
(LM pp. 203–207)

Time schedule
Assembling materials ... 2'
Timed production ...... 36'
Final check; compute
  n–pram .... 7'

Job 1
Medical report
(LM p. 203)

words

E.N.T. Medical Services

OPERATIVE REPORT

Name: *Harold D. Washington*   Case No.: *63241*   5

Date of Surgery: *February 21, 19--*   9

Preoperative Diagnosis: *Pilonidal cyst*   12

Postoperative Diagnosis: *Pilonidal cyst*   15

Operation: *Excision of cyst*   18

Surgeon: *Roberta M. Cunningham, M.D.*   24

PROCEDURE: An elliptical incision was made 33
around the cyst. Also, an incision was made 42
in the midline over the sacrum. The cyst was 51
removed totally. Catgut ligatures were used to 61
control the bleeding. Four interrupted 69
chromic catgut sutures were used to close the 78
subcutaneous tissue. The skin was closed 86
with dermal sutures. For drainage, a small 95
plastic tube was inserted into the wound. A 104
sterile dressing was applied. The patient left 114
the operating room in good condition. 121

1b
Take keyboarding position

1 Sit back in chair, body erect.

2 Place both feet on floor to maintain proper balance.

3 Let your hands hang relaxed at your sides. Your fingers will relax in curved position.

4 From this position, raise the left hand and lightly place the fingertips of your left hand on **a s d f** (home keys). Study the location of these keys.

5 Similarly, lightly place the fingertips of your right hand on **j k l ;** (home keys). Study the location of these keys.

6 Your fingers should be curved and upright; wrists should be low, but they should not touch the frame of the machine.

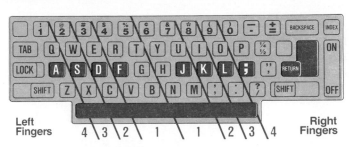

1 Keep fingers curved and upright, wrists low.

2 Keep forearms parallel to slant of keyboard.

3 Keep eyes on copy.

4 Sit back in chair, body erect.

5 Place textbook at right of machine, top raised for easy reading.

6 Keep table free of unneeded books.

7 Keep feet on floor for balance.

1c
Strike home keys, space bar, and return

1 Strike each key with a quick, sharp finger stroke; snap the fingertip toward the palm as the stroke is made.

Type (keyboard):

ffjjffjjfj

2 Strike the space bar with a down–and–in motion of the right thumb.

Type (on same line):

dd kk dd kk dk
space once

3 Keep the fingers well–curved. Concentrate on proper finger action as you keyboard.

Type (on same line):

oo ll oo ll aa ; ;
space once

4 Reach with the little finger of the right hand to the return key and tap it. Then quickly return the little finger to its home position. *Refer to page 3 if your machine is nonelectric.*

Job 3
Letter (LM p. 201)
Use block style with open punctuation.

words

October 18, 19-- — 3

Mr. Leonard I. Owens, President — 10
Owens Office Discount Center — 16
7500 East McDowell Road — 20
Scottsdale, AZ 85257-2229 — 26

Dear Mr. Owens — 29

We have ~~completed our~~ review~~ed of~~ your application for —

a franchise ^ distributorship. We are pleased to welcome you — 48

~~as~~ to our ^ large family of distributors. Within a few days you will — 61

recieve the ~~the~~ sample display kits and a temporary sup- — 72

ply of our special ball-point pens. Please submit your — 83

order within 30 dyas in order to take advantage of our — 94

special "new" distributor discount. — 101

The WINGMATIC new series (Stock #6B-3) is the top of our — 113

ball-point pen line. It features a patented ^ clip mechanism — 125

and a carbide ultrafine ball-point cartridge. In order — 136

to continue to qualify for the special 20 percent ^ discount, however, — 150

you must sell a minimum of ^ 1000 pens per year. — 160

You will ~~be~~ receiving a complete advertising kit — 168

which will include newspaper advertisements, window — 179

dispalys, and a very attractive counter display unit. — 190

If you need additional ^ or help, our advertising department — 201

will be happy to assist you. — 207

Sincerely — 228

Richard V. Turnbull — 232
Vice President, Marketing — 237

Enclosure: Franchise agreement — 243

¶ If you have any questions relating to the — 215
franchise agreement or our products, — 223
please call us. — 226/248

Job 4
Letter (plain sheet)
Retype Job 3 in modified block style with paragraphs indented and mixed punctu- ation.

1d
Learn the home row

1 Strike the return key twice more to leave extra space between the line you have just typed and the lines you will now type.

2 Practice once each line shown at the right. Strike the return key once to single–space (SS) between the two lines of a pair.

3 Strike the return key twice to double–space (DS) between pairs of lines.

4 Strike the return key 3 times to triple–space (TS) after completing Line 6.

5 Repeat the drill.

Technique hint:
Keep fingers well curved; keep wrists low, but do not allow them to touch the typewriter.

Fingers curved

Fingers upright

```
1  fj fj fj dk dk dk sl sl sl a; a; a; fj dk sl a; a;
2  jf kd ls ;a al ak aj sl sk sj dl dk dj fj fk fl f;
```
Return twice to double–space (DS)

```
3  as as ask ask sad sad jak jak fad fad lad lad lass
4  ad ad ads ads jak jak dad dad all all add add fall
```
DS

```
5  a lad; a lass; a jak; all ads; all fall; ask a lad
6  ask dad; all ads; a jak ad; a sad lad; a jak falls
```
Return 3 times to triple–space (TS)

1e
Learn new keyreach: E

1 Find new key on illustrated keyboard; then find it on your keyboard.

2 Study carefully the "Reach technique for **e**."

3 Watch your finger make the *reach* to **e** and back to **d** a few times *without striking the keys*. Keep your fingers curved.

4 Practice the lines once as shown. Keep your eyes on the copy as you keyboard; look only when you "feel lost."

5 If time permits, repeat the drill.

Reach technique for e

Reach *up* with *left second* finger.

Left Fingers   4 \ 3 \ 2 \ 1   1 \ 2 \ 3 \ 4   Right Fingers

all reaches learned
```
1  e ed ed led led lea lea ale ale elk elf eke els ed
2  ed fed fed fled fled kale kale self self lake lake
```
Return twice to double–space (DS)

```
3  e elk ekes leek leak sale dale kale lake fake self
4  sell fell jell sale sake jade sled seek leal deal;
```
DS

```
5  a sled sale; a fake jade; see a lake; a kale leaf;
6  sell a safe; a leaf fell; see a leaf; sell a desk;
```

1f
End the lesson
(standard procedure for all lessons)

1 Raise the paper bail (6) or pull it toward you. Pull the paper release lever (13) toward you.

2 Remove paper with your left hand. Push paper release lever back to its normal position.

3 Turn off the power on an electric or electronic machine. See page 3 if you have a movable carriage typewriter.

Production measurement procedure

1 Remove the appropriate materials from the laboratory manual (LM); have a supply of carbon sheets and plain sheets available.

2 Arrange laboratory materials and plain sheets in the order of need for completing the jobs.

3 Place your correction supplies in a convenient place next to your machine.

4 When you are signaled to begin, make all necessary machine adjustments, insert paper, and begin the first job. Make 1 cc for each job.

5 Before removing your paper from the machine, be sure to proofread and make all necessary corrections.

6 After the time is called to end the measurement, proofread the final job and circle any uncorrected errors.

7 Compute *n–pram* for this measurement.

222c ▶ 37
Production measurement: letters and memos
(LM pp. 199–201)

Time schedule
Assembling materials ...... 2'
Timed production .... 30'
Final check; compute
  n-pram .... 5'

Job 1
Simplified memo
(plain full sheet)

To: **All Managers**
Date: **June 15, 19--**
Subject: **MICROCOMPUTER TRAINING PROGRAM**
From: **Susan Wipple, Training Director**

	words
opening lines	12

(¶) The results of our recent training survey indicated that 85 percent of the company's managers felt a strong desire to have a training seminar devoted entirely to the use of the microcomputer as a business tool.

(¶) We have scheduled a one-day training seminar for August 25. It will be held in the Training Center beginning at 8:30 a.m. The morning will be devoted to basic information about the microcomputer, and the afternoon will be a practical approach to the varied uses of the microcomputer within our organization. You will also be given an opportunity to have some limited hands-on experience at the microcomputer.

(¶) Please notify me by July 1 if you plan to attend this one-day training seminar.

	words
21	
31	
40	
51	
54	
63	
74	
85	
95	
105	
113	
124	
134	
137	
145	
153	
closing lines	159

Job 2
Informal government letter (LM p. 199; no envelope needed)

Date: **September 10, 19--**
Reply to
Attn of: **AFAW**
Subject: **Annual supplies inventory**
To: **U.S. Services Agency**
ATTN: **Mr. Ubaldo Cortez**
7539 Baltimore Drive
Dallas, TX 75225-2331
Signed by: **Anita R. Sanchez, Deputy Chief, U.S. Services Agency**
cc for Official File—AFAW and Ms. Winifred G. Rothchild—AFAX

	words
opening lines	28

Your annual supplies inventory report is due on October 10; therefore, will you please make the necessary arrangements to have a physical inventory taken on September 30 so that our counts will be accurate.

After you have taken the inventory, please complete the necessary forms and submit them to your Agency Deputy Director for approval prior to forwarding them to Washington, D.C.

	words
44	
59	
69	
85	
100	
105	
closing lines	131

2a
Prepare to keyboard
Reread procedures described in
1b, 1c, and 1d, pages 8 and 9.

2b
Preparatory practice
each line twice SS
(slowly, then faster);
DS between 2-line groups

home row 1 `ff jj ff jj dd kk dd kk ss ll ss ll aa ;; aa ;; a;`

e 2 `e el els led ale lea eke lee elf elk eel lake kale`

all reaches
learned 3 `as all ask; a jak ad; ask a lad; a fall fad; a fee`
TS

2c
Learn new keyreaches:
T and O
Use the standard procedure at the
right to learn each new keyreach
in this lesson and in lessons that
follow.

Standard procedure for learning new keyreaches

1 Find new key on illustrated keyboard;
then find it on your keyboard.

2 Study carefully the reach technique illustrated for the key.

3 Watch your finger make the reach to the new key a few times. Keep other fingers curved on home keys. Straighten the finger slightly for an upward reach; curve it a bit more for a downward reach.

4 Practice twice SS the two lines in which the new reach is emphasized. Keep your eyes on the book copy as you keyboard.

5 DS; then learn and practice the next new keyreach according to Steps 1-4.

6 Finally, DS; then practice Lines 5-8 once as shown. If time permits, repeat them. Work for continuity. Avoid pauses.

Reach technique for t

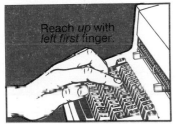

Reach up with *left first* finger.

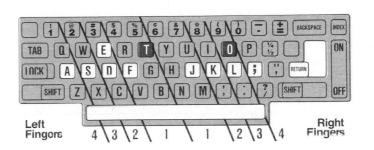

Reach technique for o

Reach up with *right third* finger.

t 1 `t tf tf aft aft tall tall talk talk tale tale task`
t 2 `tf at at aft jet let take tell felt flat slat salt`
DS

o 3 `o ol ol sol sol sold sold of of off off fold folds`
o 4 `ol old sold sole dole do doe does lo loll sol solo`

t/o 5 `to tot tote told dolt toe toes load toad foal soak`
t/o 6 `to too toot lot slot do dot oft loft soft jot jolt`

all letters
learned 7 `to do | to do a lot | take a jet | to let a | to do a task`
8 `so to | so to do | to take a | to tell a joke | left off a`
TS

Measurement goals

1 To select and organize all re–quired materials and supplies.
2 To plan your work carefully and efficiently.
3 To complete a maximum number of jobs in satisfactory form (all errors corrected properly) in the time allowed.

Machine adjustments

1 Set paper guide at 0.
2 Set ribbon control to use upper half of ribbon.
3 Margins: 70–space line for drills and timed writings; as directed (or appropriate) for jobs.
4 Spacing: SS for drills; as ap–propriate for jobs.

222a ▶ 5
Preparatory practice

each line 3 times SS (slowly, faster, slowly); DS between 3-line groups; repeat selected lines as time permits

alphabet	1	A black taxi quickly moved from a parking zone just as a man whistled.
fig/sym	2	Please ship 25 pieces of Stock #3067 (list price $4.98 each) by May 1.
direct reach	3	Barb, my niece, brought many musicians to hear my first cello recital.
fluency	4	The eighty authentic ivory emblems may be downtown in the antique box.

| 1 | 2 | 3 | 4 | 5 | 6 | 7 | 8 | 9 | 10 | 11 | 12 | 13 | 14 |

222b ▶ 8
Measure straight-copy skill

one 5' writing on ¶s combined

Difficulty index

all letters used | A | 1.5 si | 5.7 awl | 80% hfw

gwam 1' 5'

Business organizations now have a new system called electronic mail   14 3 51
for the distribution of documents. With this new system, a letter or   28 5 54
report can be prepared on a word processor and then forwarded within a   42 8 57
few seconds to the addressee. All of this is done without preparing a   56 11 60
hard copy of the document. This new delivery system uses data communica-   71 14 63
tion technology to transmit and receive mail. After a letter or report   85 17 66
is keyed into the system and a file copy saved, the document is then sent   100 20 68
to the addressee's location where it is stored in a computer system.   113 23 71
Then, with just the touch of a key on the terminal, the addressee is   127 26 74
able to see the document on a video screen.   136 27 76

Yet another application of this advanced technology is the use of an   14 30 78
electronic message system within a firm. Much like electronic mail, this   29 33 81
type of message system permits all internal communication, such as memos,   43 36 84
to take place electronically. For example, rather than prepare a memo   58 39 87
on a sheet of paper, a person can enter the message with her or his key-   72 41 90
board and then quickly send it to another person's terminal within the   86 44 93
firm. By using this method, much time and effort is saved, since hard   100 47 96
copy does not need to be prepared.   107 49 97

gwam 1' | 1 | 2 | 3 | 4 | 5 | 6 | 7 | 8 | 9 | 10 | 11 | 12 | 13 | 14 |
     5' | 1 | 2 | 3 |

2d
Practice keystroking technique

each line twice SS; DS between 2-line groups

Technique hints:

1 Concentrate on copy as you keyboard; work slowly, but continuously.
2 Keep your eyes on the book copy as you keyboard; look up only if absolutely necessary.

home row 1 `as ask asks ad ads add jak jaks all fall lass dads`

e 2 `led lead fee feel ell ells elk elks fee fees leads`

t 3 `at kat sat tall talk last fast salt slat task tall`

o 4 `so sol old do ado odd sod of off oaf oak loaf load`

all letters learned 5 `of a | to do | do so | a joke | to lead | odd leaf | ask a lad`
                                                                                                    TS

2e
Practice words/phrases

1 Practice the Level 1 lines once SS at an easy pace.

2 DS; then practice the Level 2 lines in the same way.

3 DS; then practice the Level 2 lines again at a faster pace.

4 If time permits, practice the Level 3 lines once, trying to keep the carrier (carriage) moving steadily.

Note: The 3 sets of lines progress gradually in diffi‑culty.

Goal: *At least* 1 line per minute (10 *gwam*).

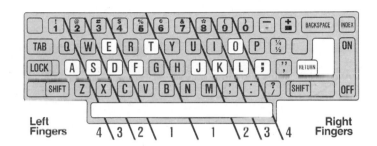

all reaches learned

         1 `a as ask to too foe doe jot jet jak so do sod does`
Level 1 2 `ale ask ode old oak let led ade a at kat take told`
         3 `to see; to a set; ask a lad; lot of tea; ate a jak`

         4 `ale oak jet lot all jak doe too off oft odd dot to`
Level 2 5 `led doe eat let sol ask add eel sad eke see old of`
         6 `do a loaf; a leaf fell; tell a joke; a lot of talk`

         7 `elf self ask asks jet jets lot lots led lead takes`
Level 3 8 `elk elks add adds joke jokes feel feels talk talks`
         9 `to a lake; eat a salad; ask a lass; sell oak desks`

2f
End the lesson
(See page 9 if necessary.)

Remove paper

Turn electric off

221d ▶ 22
Build straight-copy skill

1 Two 1' writings for ac-curacy on each ¶.
2 Two 5' writings for ac-curacy on all ¶s com-bined. Record *gwam* and number of errors (LM p. 3).

Difficulty index

all letters used | A | 1.5 si | 5.7 awl | 80% hfw

	gwam 1'	5'

Most large firms are organized into three levels of management. Each of the levels is responsible for a specific type of decision-making activity. At the top level, the executive officers make all of the stra-tegic plans and long-range goals of the firm. At the middle level, the managers decide the tactics that are needed to carry out the plans and decisions made by the top-level group. The low-level group is opera-tional and puts into action the tactical decisions of the mid-level group. The paragraphs below describe in more detail the functions of the three levels.

13	3
28	6
42	8
57	11
71	14
85	17
98	20
112	22
116	23

The executive officers are charged with the basic duty of guiding and directing the firm to a profitable future. The people who are a part of this top-level group must work with a great deal of uncertainty as they plan. They must not only decide the long-range goals of the firm, but they must also formulate policies and strategies which will cause the goals to be accomplished. In addition to strategic planning, this group must engage in a lot of creative decision-making processes, primar-ily in regard to the introduction of new goods or services.

13	26
28	29
42	32
56	34
70	37
85	40
99	43
111	46

Once the executive officers have set the goals and made the policies and strategies, the mid-level managers must assume the task of carrying out those goals for the firm. Most of the decisions made at this level are tactical; in other words, the managers must have control over the capital, production, budgets, and personnel in order to reach the objec-tives of the firm. Most of the decisions at this level are related to short-term planning and controlling of the required resources needed to do the job.

14	48
28	51
43	54
57	57
71	60
85	63
100	65
102	66

After the tactics of the mid-level managers have been made clear, the supervisors at the lowest level of management must make the day-to-day operating decisions that are vital to get the job done as planned. The supervisors are in charge of all the functional areas, such as manu-facturing, inventory, billing, and payroll, just to name a few. As a result of these duties, the supervisors exercise a great deal of control over the daily operations of the firm.

13	69
27	71
42	74
56	77
70	80
85	83
92	86

gwam 1' | 1 | 2 | 3 | 4 | 5 | 6 | 7 | 8 | 9 | 10 | 11 | 12 | 13 | 14 |
5' | 1 | | 2 | | 3 |

3a
Prepare-to-keyboard checklist

Before you begin to keyboard, check your readiness to begin the lesson.

- ✔ Work area cleared of unneeded clothing and books
- ✔ Book elevated at right of machine

- ✔ Left margin set for 50–space line (center − 25)
- ✔ Right margin set at extreme right end of scale

- ✔ Ribbon control set to type on upper half of ribbon
- ✔ Paper edge guide on correct setting
- ✔ Paper inserted expertly, straightened if necessary

3b
Preparatory practice

each line 3 times SS (slowly, faster, still faster); DS between 3-line groups

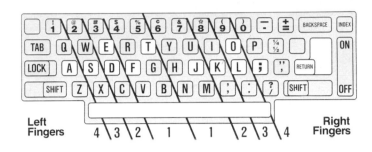

Left Fingers 4 \ 3 \ 2 \ 1 \ 1 \ 2 \ 3 \ 4 **Right Fingers**

home row 1   a; sl dk fj a;sl dkfj all lad as ask fall lass add

e/o/t 2   ol old sold ed fed led ft oft at dot doe let of to

all reaches learned 3   to fold; take a loaf; a lot of; as a joke; at last

TS

3c
Check position and techniques

As you complete the remainder of the lesson, observe the points of good keyboarding position and techniques listed at the right.

- ✔ Seated erect in chair
- ✔ Both feet on floor
- ✔ Fingers relaxed, curved, upright
- ✔ Fingertips touching home keys
- ✔ Wrists low but not touching the machine

- ✔ Slant of forearms parallel to slant of the keyboard
- ✔ Each key struck with a quick stroke of the fingertip
- ✔ Space bar struck with inward motion of the thumb

3d
Practice keystroking technique

each pair of lines SS as shown; DS between 2-line groups; repeat if time permits

Technique hint:
Strike keys at a smooth pace; avoid pauses.

home row 1   a jak; ask dad; as a lad; as a lass; add a fall ad
          2   a fad; as a dad; a fall ad; as all ask; a sad fall

e 3   a doe; led a doe; a sea eel; see a lake; jade sale
  4   a sea; a joke; tell tales; a doe fled; seal a deal

o 5   do so; to do so; odd load; lot of old; sold a sofa
  6   a foe; old oak; jot off a; does a lot; a soft sofa

t 7   to let; to talk; tall tale; eat a lot; told a tale
  8   a tea; to salt; at a late; take a lot; took a seat

TS

221a ▶ 5
Preparatory practice

each line 3 times SS (slowly, faster, slowly); DS between 3-line groups; repeat selected lines as time permits

alphabet	1	Mary Jewel provided the extra cash prize for the best king-size quilt.
fig/sym	2	Check #53 for $1,246.30 (a 7% discount of $93.81 deducted) was mailed.
adjacent key	3	The porter sat by a column eating a pickle as Wes toiled at the stove.
fluency	4	A neighbor may bicycle to the city to visit with the auditor at eight.

| 1 | 2 | 3 | 4 | 5 | 6 | 7 | 8 | 9 | 10 | 11 | 12 | 13 | 14 |

221b ▶ 8
Communication aid: spelling and verb agreement

1 Keyboard and format the paragraph, making any necessary spelling and verb agreement corrections. Check the corrected copy with your instructor.
2 Repeat if necessary.

The Director of Manufacturing, as well as all Production Managers, are well aware of our past procurment problems. They met to intiate procedures to insur that each carton in each shipment arrive in good condition and that a large stock of accesories and materials are always available. The President, in addition to the Baord of Directors, were informed of the new procedures, and everyone knows what needs to be done.

221c ▶ 15
Build statistical-copy skill

1 Two 1' writings for accuracy on each ¶.
2 Two 3' writings for accuracy on both ¶s combined. Record *gwam* and number of errors (LM p. 3).

Difficulty index

all letters/figures used	A	1.5 si	5.7 awl	80% hfw

gwam 1' 3'

	1'	3'
Our revenue from earned interest was approximately 25% higher than	13	4	66
last fiscal year. This year we invested $1,675,000 in 6-month treasury	28	9	71
bills at 8.79%; $2,535,500 in 180-day certificates of deposit at 9.25%;	42	14	75
and $895,000 in a money-market fund at 9.12% for the last 9 months of	56	19	80
the year. The total earned revenue this year from these sources is	70	23	85
$445,984.25; last year's total interest revenue was only $354,387.50.	84	28	89
As we plan for next fiscal year's revenues, our projections indicate	14	33	94
that we should have a sizable increase (17.68%) in earned interest reve-	28	37	99
nue. We will request that a majority of our surplus fund ($3,500,000)	42	42	103
be invested in 180-day certificates of deposit at about 9.35% for the	56	47	108
first 6 months and 9.43% for the last 6 months. The balance of the fund	71	52	113
($2,000,000) will be invested in money-market funds for about 9.3%. The	86	57	118
expected earned interest revenue for next year will be about $521,304.	100	61	123

gwam 1' | 1 | 2 | 3 | 4 | 5 | 6 | 7 | 8 | 9 | 10 | 11 | 12 | 13 | 14 |
    3' | 1 | 2 | 3 | 4 | 5 |

3e
Practice special reach combinations

each line twice SS;
DS between 2-line groups

> **Technique hint:**
> Do not push for speed; work for smooth, fluid keystroking.

as/sa 1 as ask task fast last lass asks sad salt sale sake

lo/ol 2 lo lot lots lode load loaf old fold sold told sole

ed/de 3 led fed deed seed sled fled ode lode ade deal desk

el/le 4 el els sell felt jell self let leak dale dole lest
TS

3f
Practice phrases

1 Practice the Level 1 lines once SS at an easy pace.

2 DS; then practice the Level 2 lines in the same way.

3 DS; then practice the Level 2 lines again at a faster pace.

4 If time permits, practice the Level 3 lines once, trying to keep the carrier (carriage) moving steadily.

Note: The 3 sets of lines progress gradually in difficulty.

Goal: *At least* 1 line per minute (10 *gwam*).

all reaches learned

        1 to let; to set; a jak; to do all of; to a sad lad;
Level 1 2 to set; to do a; fed a doe; ask a fee; ask a lass;
        3 ask a lad; a sad ode; to see a foe; a sad old oak;
DS

        4 to last a; take a jet; tell a tale; take a lot of;
Level 2 5 fall ad; as a set; take a deed; to sell a loaf of;
        6 old jade; to see a; of a sad doll; to seek a deal;

        7 of a flake; to take a salad; to lose a sales deal;
Level 3 8 too stale; to float a; add a total; of a sad tale;
        9 to a; told jokes; soaks a lot; see a lot of lakes;

3g
End the lesson

(See page 9 if necessary.)

220c ▶ 10
Build keystroking precision

each line at least 3 times without error

long words 1 A northwestern congressional representative announced the appointment.

double letters 2 William will cooperate by assigning a room that will accommodate them.

hyphen 3 We hope your mother-in-law and father-in-law have first-class tickets.

word response 4 The busy man may halt work on eight of my maps to visit the city lake.

| 1 | 2 | 3 | 4 | 5 | 6 | 7 | 8 | 9 | 10 | 11 | 12 | 13 | 14 |

220d ▶ 20
Build straight-copy skill

1 Two 1' writings for speed on each ¶.
2 Two 5' writings for speed on all ¶s combined. Record *gwam* (LM p. 3).

Difficulty index

all letters used | A | 1.5 si | 5.7 awl | 80% hfw

	gwam 1'	5'

Each year the cost of operating a business normally rises. Because   14 | 3 | 69
of this, a good business manager must seek constantly for ways to reduce   28 | 6 | 72
his or her firm's operating costs so that there is no need to raise the   43 | 9 | 74
price of goods or services. Many managers look to their expenditure   56 | 11 | 77
accounts to find ways to lower costs. One item often costing more than   71 | 14 | 80
needed is postage. By keeping the following simple guides in mind, post-   85 | 17 | 83
age costs often can be cut significantly.   94 | 19 | 85

Use express mail only for urgent long-distance mailings. First-   13 | 21 | 87
class mail is delivered promptly in most major cities, and a significant   27 | 24 | 90
cost savings will result if the majority of a firm's mail is delivered   42 | 27 | 93
by regular first-class postal service. If first-class mail is deposited   56 | 30 | 96
at the post office prior to noon each day, it is normally delivered   70 | 33 | 99
within a day or two as long as there is frequent air service between   84 | 36 | 101
the point of origin and the destination. When in doubt, check before   98 | 38 | 104
posting an item to be certain that the item sent by express mail will   112 | 41 | 107
actually be delivered faster than if posted by first-class mail.   124 | 44 | 110

Remember also that mail sent on the fifth workday will not be re-   13 | 46 | 112
ceived by the addressee any faster by express mail than by first-class   27 | 49 | 115
mail if the addressee is not at the office on the weekend. Registered   41 | 52 | 118
mail should be used only if the contents have insurable value; otherwise,   56 | 55 | 121
certified mail will give the same service at lower cost. Do not over-   70 | 58 | 124
insure packages; any repayment for a loss is for actual value and not   84 | 61 | 127
for the insured amount. Also, you may realize a notable cost reduction   99 | 63 | 129
in the postage account if you eliminate unnecessary letters.   111 | 66 | 132

gwam 1' | 1 | 2 | 3 | 4 | 5 | 6 | 7 | 8 | 9 | 10 | 11 | 12 | 13 | 14 |
5' | 1 | 2 | 3 |

4a
Prepare-to-keyboard checklist

Check your readiness to begin Lesson 4.

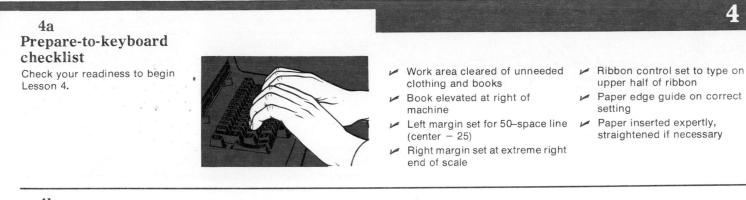

✔ Work area cleared of unneeded clothing and books

✔ Book elevated at right of machine

✔ Left margin set for 50–space line (center — 25)

✔ Right margin set at extreme right end of scale

✔ Ribbon control set to type on upper half of ribbon

✔ Paper edge guide on correct setting

✔ Paper inserted expertly, straightened if necessary

4b
Preparatory practice

each line twice SS (slowly, then faster); DS between 2-line groups

home row 1 `fj dk sl a; jk fd kl ds l; sa as all fad jak dads;`

e/o/t 2 `ed ol tf led old oft ode dot toe doe foe jets fold`

space bar 3 `to do | do so | a foe | to add | a lot | as a joke | to do so;`

all reaches learned 4 `a jak fell; tell a tale; sold a desk; to a sole ad`

TS

4c
Learn new keyreaches: C and H

Reach technique for c

Reach *down* with *left second* finger.

Left Fingers   4 \ 3 \ 2 \ 1 \ / 1 / 2 \ 3 \ 4   Right Fingers

Reach technique for h

Reach to *left* with *right first* finger.

Follow the "Standard procedure for learning new keyreaches" on page 10 (Lines 1–4 twice; lines 5–8 once; repeat 5–8 if time permits).

Technique hint:
Strike the space bar with a down–and–in motion of the thumb.

c 1 `c cd cd cod cod cot cot call call code codes tacks`
2 `cold clod clad coal cola lack lock dock cool cakes`

DS

h 3 `h hj hj he he she she ah ah ha ha lash dash flash;`
4 `oh ho aha the has had hoe that josh shad hall halt`

c/h 5 `ache echo each cash chat chef hack hock tech check`
6 `a chef; a chat; the ache; all cash; check the hack`

all letters learned 7 `had a look | took the jet | josh the ohof | cash a check`
8 `to teach | had the jack | he took half | a cache of food`

TS

Learning goals

1 To increase basic skill on straight, statistical, and script copy.
2 To improve communication skills.
3 To refine keyboarding tech–nique.

Machine adjustments

1 Set paper guide at *0*.
2 Set ribbon control to use upper half of ribbon.
3 Margins: 70–space line for drills and ¶ writings.
4 SS drill lines; DS ¶s.

220a ▶ 5
Preparatory practice

each line 3 times SS (slowly, faster, slowly); DS between 3-line groups; repeat selected lines as time permits

alphabet **1** We have had Jack itemize and ship by air the exact quantity of grills.

fig/sym **2** The discount may be $1,250 (8.36% of $14,950) when paid within 7 days.

third row **3** Roy Roper reported to Pru Tow after the territory dispute was stopped.

fluency **4** A visitor paid the girl for a mantle and a pair of antique ivory pens.

| 1 | 2 | 3 | 4 | 5 | 6 | 7 | 8 | 9 | 10 | 11 | 12 | 13 | 14 |

220b ▶ 15
Build script-copy skill

1 Two 1' writings for speed on each ¶.
2 Two 3' writings for speed on both ¶s com–bined. Record *gwam* (LM p. 3).

Difficulty index

| all letters used | A | 1.5 si | 5.7 awl | 80% hfw |

	gwam 1'	3'
A computer can only run a program that is written in	11	4	60
binary code; this program language is known as machine	22	7	63
language. Because this language is very hard to learn, only	34	11	67
those persons who work directly with the creation of the	45	15	71
hardware use it. Almost all other programmers will use either	58	19	75
an assembly or high-level language to program their jobs.	69	23	79
A program written in machine language can be executed	11	27	83
faster by the computer than can a program that must be	22	30	87
translated from either an assembly or high-level language	33	34	90
into a machine-language program. The use of a translator	45	38	94
to change a program will not result in an object program	57	42	98
that is as unique or as customized as a program written	68	46	102
directly in machine language. However, the small differ-	79	50	106
ence in speed and efficiency is more than made up	89	53	109
by the ease of learning a nonmachine language.	98	56	112

4d
Learn new keyreaches:
R and Right Shift

Reach technique for r

Reach *up* with *left first* finger.

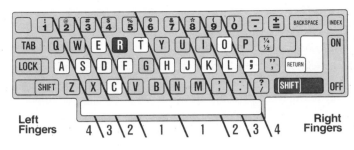

Left Fingers 4 3 2 1 1 1 2 3 4 Right Fingers

Control of right shift key

Reach *down* with *right little* finger; shift, type, release.

Follow the "Standard procedure for learning new keyreaches" on page 10 (Lines 1–4 twice; Lines 5–8 once; repeat 5–8 if time permits).

r

1 r rf rf or or for for fro fro ore ore her her ford
2 roe for oar are fork role tore oral soar rode fort
DS

right shift

3 A; A; Al Al Alf Alf Flo Flo Ed Ed Ted Ted Del Del;
4 Flo Dole; Chad Alte; Alf Slak; Ella Todd; Sol Ekas

r/right shift

5 Alf Roe; Elke or Rolf Dorr; Rose Salk or Dora Ford
6 Sol Ross asked for Ella; Carl Alda rode for Rhoda;

all reaches learned

7 Rose Ford told Cora the joke Ross had told to her;
8 Dot Roe has the oar here; Al left the oar for her;
TS

4e
Practice words/phrases

1 Practice the Level 1 lines once SS at an easy pace.

2 DS; then practice the Level 2 lines in the same way.

3 DS; then practice the Level 2 lines again at a faster pace.

4 If time permits, practice the Level 3 lines once, trying to keep the carrier (carriage) moving steadily.

Note: The 3 sets of lines progress gradually in diffi-culty.

Goal: *At least* 1 line per minute (10 *gwam*).

all reaches learned

Level 1
1 or to do so of he for the she roe toe cod cot coal
2 jak jet hat hot lot jar her car ask lad lass chose
3 Cal had a jar; Rod has a cat; Della has a red hat;

Level 2
4 cod code jet jets for fore ash cash old hold holds
5 are hare ere here car card ale kale rod rode check
6 Al left; Theo has roe; Flo ate cake; Doc had half;

Level 3
7 elf self shelf led sled sleds fed feed feeds chose
8 old fold folds she shed sheds hot shot shots jokes
9 Rolf added a cash ad; Flora called here for Chloe;

Job 5
Prepare form letters from stock paragraphs and variables
(LM pp. 171–181)

To complete your work assignments for Information Processing Services, Inc., Mr. O'Mariety asks you to prepare form letters for Mathas Equipment Company.

CUSTOMER INSTRUCTIONS:

Please prepare form letters for the individuals listed. Use the variable information which is listed after the name and address. Date the letters March 18, 19—.

Dear

It is a pleasure to confirm your order for a new Model (VI--insert number) Mathas (Electronic Printer/Word Processor/Copier). It is scheduled to be installed on (V2--insert date).

Our representative, (V3--insert name), will contact you soon to schedule an appointment to site clear the area for the machine. (He/She) will also check to see that you have adequate supplies for the first month of operation. (She/He) will also be able to answer any questions you may have about the installation.

Our training coordinator, Martha Miller, will schedule operator training for your employees as soon as the equipment is installed. We will be happy to train as many employees as you would like to have trained.

You have selected an excellent (printer/word processor/copier) that will give you many years of dependable service.

Sincerely | Miss Leslie Willis | Customer Service Representative

---

Ms. Amanda Kupier
Dutch Industries, Inc.
2104 Oak Creek Street
Sherman, TX 75090-5310
VI 9051 - Electronic Printer
V2 March 26, 19--
V3 Betsy Jung

Miss Carolyn Luke
Acadiana Rice Company
194 Colonial Drive
Terre Haute, IN 47805-3337
VI 5410 - Word Processor
V2 April 6, 19--
V3 Felix Bernard

Mr. Robert Gregory
Circle R Company
2155 Warren Avenue
Joliet, IL 60162-3330
VI 9401 - Electronic Printer
V2 April 3, 19--
V3 Ken Bishop

Mr. Peter Sheppard
South-West Print Shop
5300 Kenwood Avenue, South
Chicago, IL 60615-3221
VI 9510 - Electronic Printer
V2 March 27, 19--
V3 Rodrigo Gonzalez

Mrs. Mary Thomas
3629 Sunny Lane
Indianapolis, IN 46220-4511
VI 5610 - Word Processor
V2 March 28, 19--
V3 Celia Castillo

Mr. John Burleson
T. J.'s Accounting Service
200 University Place
Evanston, IL 60201-4422
VI 3410 - Copier
V2 April 10, 19--
V3 Lucy Dunlap

5a
Prepare-to-keyboard checklist

Are you ready to keyboard? Check the items listed at the right before you begin. Review 4a, page 14, if you are unsure about any of the items.

- ✔ Work area
- ✔ Book placement
- ✔ Margin stops
- ✔ Ribbon control
- ✔ Paper guide
- ✔ Paper insertion

5b
Preparatory practice

each line twice SS (slowly, then faster); DS between 2-line groups

home row 1   a; as all lad ask add ash fad jak sad has had lash

c/r 2   or ore core jar jars ark lark rock cord lack cross

h/t 3   a hat ate hate the that oath heat halt sloth loath

all reaches learned 4   Ro has a fake jade; ask Cal to let her do the lot;
TS

5c
Learn new keyreaches: W and U

Reach technique for w

Reach *up* with *left third* finger.

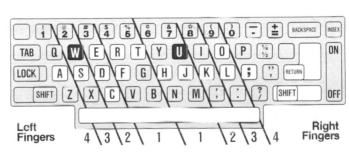

Left Fingers   4 3 2 1   1 2 3 4   Right Fingers

Reach technique for u

Reach *up* with *right first* finger.

Follow the "Standard procedure for learning new keyreaches" on page 10 (Lines 1–4 twice; Lines 5–8 once; repeat 5–8 if time permits).

w
1   w ws ws was was sow sows law laws jaw jaws wow wow
2   ow how owl owe woes cow cows row rows sow sows low
DS

u
3   u uj uj jut jut cut cut us us use use due due fuse
4   cue sue hue rut rude just jute sure lure loud cute

w/u
5   how we do; just a duck; we work out our four cues;
6   we row; use a wok; our used fuse; Sue wore a tutu;

all reaches learned
7   two or four; the cut hurt Wu; a hut for us to use;
8   cut two; Duke had a cake; we just saw Dale at two;
TS

---

printers have been approved for the administrative offices of all ~~each~~ departments. The electronic printer will ~~implement~~ facilitate the forms management program that was piloted and approved for general use.

All forms ~~will be~~ have been stored on an 8-inch floppy disk, and ~~the~~ each form ~~will~~ can now be printed at the same time the information typed on the form is printed. The Vogel printer has type-font flexibility and prints 12 pages per minute. ~~It also can handle computer type graphics.~~

Photocomposition. Photocomposition equipment has not been approved for general use. The pilot study on computer-based type-setting ~~did~~ supported the installation of a small centralized operation. Final management decision is pending.

Purchasing Authority

Final authority for purchasing all office technology rests with the Information Resource Management Committee. Users ~~Staff~~ requesting technology must ~~should~~ conduct a thorough needs analysis, provide complete cost justification, and obtain approval of the department manager prior to submitting ~~before sending~~ the request ~~on~~ to the IRMC.

The Senior Management Committee has the power to overrule any ~~all~~ decisions made at Hudson Advertising Agency. Only in rare circumstances will the Senior Management Committee agree to consider appeals to the decisions made by the IRMC.

5d
Learn new keyreaches:
Left Shift and . (period)

Control of left shift key

Reach *down* with *left little* finger; shift, type, release.

Left Fingers 4 3 2 1 1 2 3 4 Right Fingers

Reach technique for . (period)

Reach *down* with *right third* finger; space twice after . at end of sentence.

Follow the "Standard procedure for learning new keyreaches" on page 10 (Lines 1–4 twice; Lines 5–8 once; repeat 5–8 if time permits).

Period: Space once after a period that follows an abbreviation or an initial, twice after a period that ends a sentence. Do not, however, space after a period at the end of a line.

left shift	1	L La La Lars Lake Ladd Jae Jake Karl Kate Hal Harl
	2	Jae or Jake Kale or Lara Karl or Lars Hart or Ladd
		DS
. (period)	3	. .l .l l.l fl. fl. Dr. E. F. Roe asked for a lot.
	4	Dale has left for Soho. Dr. Sorel saw her at two.
left shift and .	5	Hal saw us. He also saw Joe. He was at the lake.
	6	J. J. does work for us; he used to work for Laura.
all reaches learned	7	Kae used to read to Joe; she works for the Roe Co.
	8	Sr. Jude left for Tulsa; her car was full of food.
		TS

5e
Practice words/sentences

1 Practice the Level 1 lines once SS at an easy pace.

2 DS; then practice the Level 2 lines in the same way.

3 DS; then practice the Level 2 lines again at a faster pace.

4 If time permits, practice the Level 3 lines once, trying to keep the carrier (carriage) moving steadily.

Note: The 3 sets of lines progress gradually in difficulty.

Goal: *At least* 1 line per minute (10 *gwam*).

all reaches learned

	1	rf or of uj us sue use ws ow sow cow ol lo low old
Level 1	2	ed led eke tf to lot dot cd cod doc hj hut hue wok
	3	Jeff used the old wok to cook; Lu added the sauce.
	4	we woe awl cow sow led low for fur let cut our hut
Level 2	5	for fat law saw how use jet jut the work chew fake
	6	Aldo took the saw; Ed has to cut the old jak tree.
	7	we our was wore were just jade josh take sake hour
Level 3	8	that lurk wash four keel chew walk crow talk would
	9	Suella saw the letter that Cora wrote at the lake.

Word) Processors. The Vogel 89̸0 [8 inserted] Word Processor ~~and~~ or the Vogel
890 Information Processor can be purchased by departments that
can
justify~~ing~~ the need and cost of the unit. The Vogel 890 ~~may~~ should
be used by the account ing staff who ~~need to~~ communicate with
major accounts which have devises that use binary syn[s]chron-
80
ous communications. Both the 86̸9̸ and 890 use the Adsearch
Modem to access the Adsearch data base. The Management
made a
Committee commitment to continue the subscription to this
computer-assisted research system.
DS
Personal Computers. The personal computer will be the professional workstation at Hudson Advertising. Any personal com-
i
puter compat[i]ble with our Spreadnet network can be purchased
if justified by need and cost; however, Vogel personal com-
recommended
puters are ~~suggested~~. The Vogel is a 16-bit processor with
256,000 bytes of random access memory.
~~256K RAM~~. The duel disk drive uses 8-inch double-density floppy
disks or rigid disks. The personal computer supports a wide
range of software including word processing, data-base manage-
financial
ment, and electronic spreadsheet ~~type~~ analysis as well as
several programming languages.

Printers. Letter-quality printers are required ~~necessary~~ for all
work which goes out from Hudson Advertising. Dot-matrix
printers (including those with strikeover and multistrike
only
features) may ~~not~~ be used ~~except~~ for graphics, rough-draft
work, and for documents used internally. Daisy-wheel-type
printers with a minimum speed of 40 characters per second
electronic
can be purchased by microcomputer users. Distributed ~~image~~

(Job 4 continued on page 381)

6a
Prepare-to-keyboard checklist

Are you ready? Check the list at the right.

- ✔ Desk and chair
- ✔ Work area
- ✔ Book placement
- ✔ Paper guide
- ✔ Line–space selector (SS)
- ✔ Margin stops

6b
Preparatory practice

each line twice SS (slowly, then faster); DS between 2-line groups

home row 1 `a jak lad as ash ad had add has all fall hash dash`

e/o/t/c 2 `ed ol tf cd led old cot toe eke due lot colt docks`

w/h/r/u 3 `ws hj rf uj we raw hut war who haul hawk rule what`

all reaches learned 4 `Rosela had to cut her rate; Jeff took a weak lead.`

TS

6c
Check keystroking technique

each set of lines twice SS; DS between 3-line groups

Technique hint:
Check the list of techniques at the right; use them as you do the drill lines.

- ✔ Seated erect in chair
- ✔ Both feet on floor
- ✔ Fingertips lightly touching home keys
- ✔ Wrists low, but not touching the machine
- ✔ Slant of forearms parallel to slant of keyboard
- ✔ Each key struck with a quick stroke of the fingertip
- ✔ Space bar struck with inward motion of the thumb

all reaches learned

1 `or do he so of el la ow to she for the fur due row`

words 2 `cue jak foe sod cut doe sow sue all too wood would`

3 `alto also hall fall tall rust dust lark dark jowls`

4 `to do so | he or she | to do the | of all our | as the doe`

phrases 5 `had to do | ask the lad | ate the jak | has the fur coat`

6 `do the work | saw the show | just as she | take the test`

sen-tences 7 `Drew saw the late show.  She had to cut law class.`

8 `Walt was at Olde Lake at two; Joel also was there.`

9 `Kate was at the dock at four to see all of us off.`

TS

6d
Check spacing/shifting technique

each set of lines twice SS; DS between 3-line groups

- ✔ Space with down–and–in motion of the thumb
- ✔ Shift with quick, 1–2–3/ shift–type–release motions
- ✔ Quiet hands; no pauses before or after spacing or shifting
- ✔ Space once after abbreviation period
- ✔ Space twice after a sentence period
- ✔ Space once after a semicolon

Technique hint:
Check the techniques above right; use them as you do the drill.

all reaches learned

1 `ah so he do la of el us to ha for she due cot work`

spacing 2 `to do of us do so a jak the fur for the of all the`

3 `Ask the lad for the oak.  He cut the wood at work.`

4 `Ask for Dr. Lor.  She took a call.  Jae heard her.`

shifting 5 `Todd has to work.  Talk to Jewel; she has the ads.`

6 `Laura left for Duluth.  She took the jet at three.`

Lynn Mitchell has also requested that this report be prepared in final form. Mr. O'Mariety asks you to follow the customer's instructions.

CUSTOMER'S INSTRUCTIONS:

This technology procurement policy must be prepared in the same format as our Policy Manual because it will be incorporated as part of the manual. Please follow these directions carefully.

1 Single–space the body of the report; DS between ¶s.
2 Use 1" side and bottom margins.
3 Place the page number on Line 4 at the right margin; then triple–space. Number the first page 2.3, the second page, 2.4, etc.
4 Please correct any undetected errors which may have been overlooked.

STANDARDS FOR PROCUREMENT OF OFFICE TECHNOLOGY

TS

Hudson Advertising ~~plans to~~ *has to* standardize*d* the purchase of all office technology so that ~~all of the~~ office opera*t*ions ~~may~~ *can* be integrated into one comprehensive system. All purchase*s* ~~for~~ *of office technology* ~~automation~~ must ~~conform~~ *adhere* to the standards described in this policy and ~~should~~ *must* be approved by the information resource management committee.

TS

Technology

Typewriters. The only typewriter*s* which may be purchased is an electronic typewriter with a thin-window display or partial screen, a minimum *memory* capacity of ~~12~~ *15* pages, and ~~also~~ a communi*c*ations protocol option. Department needs must be analyzed carefully; and, if justified, an electronic typewriter with a 5 1/4-inch disk should be purchase*d* to provide ~~greater~~ *unlimited* memory. Up-to-date ~~data~~ *information* on products compatable with the current Hudson system are available from the Information Resource Management Committee

Communication Network. ~~All~~ word and information processing equipment must ~~tie-in~~ *interface* with the Spreadnet Network which have been installed. This network allows point-to-point data communications without the use of a mainframe computer. Communications software operates as a background function allowing text-editing functions and communications to occur *simultaneously*. Applications *include terminal-to-terminal communications* for electronic document distribution and multifunction interfaces. The network is ~~able to~~ support *capable of* ~~some~~ *ing* photocomposition, high-speed printers, micrographics, and optical character recognition devices.

(Job 4 continued on page 380)

7a ▶ 8
Preparatory practice

each line twice SS
(slowly, then faster);
DS between 2-line groups

Note: Beginning with Lesson 7, each lesson part will include in its headings a suggested number of minutes for practicing that activity.

all letters learned 1 Doc took just four hours to row to the south lake.

c/u/r 2 Lou cut the rate cost of our letters to the coast.

w/h 3 Ask Walt Howe to heat the water to wash the shelf.

all reaches learned 4 We saw Jack a lot later; he worked for four hours.
TS

7b ▶ 6
Develop keyboarding fluency

two 30″ writings on each line

Goal: To complete each line in 30″ (14 gwam).

all letters learned

1 Do the oak shelf for the lake dock.

2 She cut half the fuel for the auto.

3 Throw the kale to the cow for Jake.

4 The autos do the work of the world.
TS

7c ▶ 12
Learn new keyreaches: X and I

Reach technique for x

Reach *down* with *left third* finger.

Left Fingers   4 3 2 1   1 2 3 4   Right Fingers

Reach technique for i

Reach *up* with *right second* finger.

Follow the "Standard procedure for learning new keyreaches" on page 10 (Lines 1–4 twice; Lines 5–8 once; repeat 5–8 if time permits).

x 1 x xs xs ox ox axe axe sox sox fox fox hex hex axle
2 xs ax ox tux lox lax sax flex flax flux crux taxed

i 3 i ik ik if if is is it it did did kid kid aid aids
4 ik kit sit fit wit sir lid its side cite kick wick

x/i 5 Felix fixed the six tax rules I asked Exie to fix.
6 I will fix tea for Dixie if she will wax the taxi.

all reaches learned 7 Sid Cox said it was a lax law; Roxie also said so.
8 Jackie will fix the cut foot of the old fox I saw.
TS

Memorandum (full sheet)

Mr. O'Mariety asks you to prepare this memo for Tim Beckel at Mathas Equipment Company. This memo is to accompany the two tables you prepared in Job 1. He instructs you to use the simplified memo style and to date the memo March 16.

CUSTOMER'S INSTRUCTIONS:

Please prepare this memo for photocopying.

To: Sales Staff   From: Tim Beckel

Subject: Status Report on Copiers and Electronic Printers

(¶) Summaries of orders written this month and of equipment cancelled this month are attached.

(¶) The positive side of our sales report is that most of the orders written are for our electronic printers, and most of the cancellation orders are for low-volume copiers. The negative side, however, is that orders are down and cancellations are up. This has been the trend for three months, and it must be reversed.

(¶) Please review the sales situation in your territory carefully and make specific plans for increasing sales for next month. Be sure to identify both copiers and electronic printers that could be in danger of being cancelled. Bring your projections and your action plans for increasing sales to the monthly sales meeting.

Job 3

Memorandum (full sheet)

Mr. O'Mariety hands you a memo from Hudson Advertising, which he just received. He asks you to prepare it for Lynn Mitchell, Sales Manager at Hudson Advertising, and return it to him by early afternoon. He instructs you to use simplified memo style and date the memo March 16.

CUSTOMER'S INSTRUCTIONS:

Please prepare this memorandum for photocopying and return to our office today.

To: Staff   From: Lynn Mitchell

Subject: New Technology Procurement Policy

(¶) The Senior Management Committee has approved a new technology procurement policy which takes effect immediately. Please insert the enclosed policy in your policy manual for future reference.

(¶) It is imperative that we improve our office productivity, and we believe that establishing guides for an integrated office system is a positive step in this direction. The technology market is very dynamic, and this policy will be updated as new technology becomes available and affordable to Hudson.

7d ▶ 12
Learn new keyreaches:
G and N

Reach technique for g

Reach to *right* with *left first* finger.

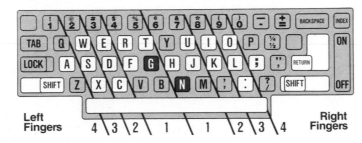

Left Fingers   4 3 2   1   1   2 3   4   Right Fingers

Reach technique for n

Reach *down* with *right first* finger.

Follow the "Standard procedure for learning new keyreaches" on page 10 (Lines 1–4 twice; Lines 5–8 once; repeat 5–8 if time permits).

g
1 g gf gf go go fog fog got got rug rug dog dog frog
2 gf log dug fig wig dig lag tog leg keg jig cog got
DS

n
3 n nj nj an an and and end end hen hen ran ran lend
4 nj on won wan den tan ten can land want rent sends

g/n
5 Gwen longs to sing a grand song she knew in Genoa.
6 Gig noted that one swan wing was green with algae.

all reaches learned
7 Leonor left the show to take a cruise to Calcutta.
8 Just set a fair goal; then work hard to extend it.
TS

7e ▶ 12
Build keyboarding continuity

1 Practice the Level 1 lines once SS at an easy pace.

2 DS; then practice the Level 2 lines in the same way.

3 DS; then practice the Level 2 lines again at a faster pace.

4 If time permits, practice the Level 3 lines once, trying to keep the carrier (carriage) moving steadily.

Note: The 3 sets of lines progress gradually in difficulty.

Goal: *At least* 1 line per minute (10 *gwam*).

Count typewritten words:

Five characters and spaces are counted as one standard typewritten word. The figures in the scale under the copy show the word-by-word count (5 strokes a word) for each line.

all reaches learned

Level 1
1 I will need four to six weeks to work out the act.
2 Janet can ask six of the girls to guide the tours.
3 Ask Nellie to sing one alto aria in our next show.

Level 2
4 He will fix a snack; he will also fix fruit juice.
5 The four girls will use their auto or hire a taxi.
6 Gil has asked six girls to a light lunch in Akron.

Level 3
7 Luann wore a ring and long necklace of green jade.
8 Dixie will send her tax check to the local office.
9 Lex is an officer of high rank in Jackson Tool Co.

| 1 | 2 | 3 | 4 | 5 | 6 | 7 | 8 | 9 | 10 |

To determine words-a-minute rate:

1 List the figure 10 for each line completed during a writing.

2 For a partial line, note from the scale the figure directly below the point at which you stopped.

3 Add these figures to determine the total gross words typed (the same as *gwam* for a 1' writing).

215a-219a ▶ 5
Preparatory practice

each line 3 times SS (slowly, faster, slowly); DS between 3-line groups; repeat selected lines as time permits

alphabet 1 Jack quoted five experts who were trying to formalize a building plan.

fig/sym 2 I ordered 24 blinds (Rx-475/93), but I received 36 shades (Rx-208/16).

combination 3 A bottle with a cork in it rested on the sand at the edge of the lake.

fluency 4 They own the land, and they work in the field when they wish to do so.

| 1 | 2 | 3 | 4 | 5 | 6 | 7 | 8 | 9 | 10 | 11 | 12 | 13 | 14 |

215b-219b ▶ 45
Office job simulation

(LM pp. 171–181)

Job 1

Prepare tables from computer printout (full sheets)

Mr. O'Mariety gives you the first order form from Mathas Equipment Company and asks you to prepare two tables from the computer printout.

CUSTOMER'S INSTRUCTIONS:

Please prepare two tables from the computer printout. Use "Current Orders" as the main heading for the first table and "Equipment Cancellation Orders" for the main heading of the second table. Double–space the columnar items; use full headings in–stead of abbreviations above the columns in the tables. The abbreviations stand for:

Customer Number
CODE Number
Billing Code
Machine Code
Data Unit

```
                    CUST. NO. CODE NO.        B/C        MC        D.U.
    ***ORDERS TAKEN THIS MONTH***
                    641001193 092723          23632      8221      1574
                    087992319 092741          20212      8211      V117


                    641012448 092670          20333      9999      1574
                    641013735 092695          28201      9999      1571
                    641003710 092701          21961      9741      1571
                    641008529 092746          21923      8221      1574
                    857225825 092679          18221      9032      1581
                    093024511 092855          23222      8231      1574
                              092855          23222      8231      1574
                    641012554 092653          23222      9999      1574
                              092653          23222      9999      1574


    ***EQUIPMENT CANCELLATION ORDERS
                    087992319 0927411         20212                V117


                    642231104 2400871         59021                V117
                    092844414 0928851         55722                V117
                    087926713 0928921         20212                H823
                              0928921         20212                H823


                    641001193 092723          23632      8221      1574
```

8a ▶ 8
Preparatory practice

each line twice SS
(slowly, then faster);
DS between 2-line
groups

all letters learned 1 Alexi Garcia had gone to San Juan for three weeks.

x/i 2 I next fixed the axle; then I waxed the six taxis.

g/n 3 Ginger is going to England to sing for Jonah King.

all reaches learned 4 Lex and Rolf saw Luan Ling; Jack had not seen her.

Recall: TS between
lesson parts.

| 1 | 2 | 3 | 4 | 5 | 6 | 7 | 8 | 9 | 10 |

8b ▶ 8
Improve keyboarding technique

each line once as shown;
if time permits, repeat the
drill

all reaches learned

keystroking and spacing
1 ws ik ed ol nj rf uj tf cd .l xs gf hj ec un rg tf
2 if so is do it of an go he el ha ox ah or eh to us
3 as to | we go | at an | we do | as he | see us | get it | ate an

spacing and shifting
4 Ken can win if he will set a goal and work for it.
5 Dorn is now in Rio; Janice is to go there in June.
6 Ann and J. D. Fox had seen Lt. Green at the dance.

| 1 | 2 | 3 | 4 | 5 | 6 | 7 | 8 | 9 | 10 |

8c ▶ 12
Learn new keyreaches: V and , (comma)

Reach technique for v

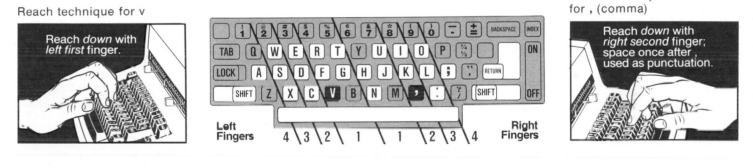

Reach technique for , (comma)

Follow the "Standard procedure
for learning new keyreaches" on
page 10 (Lines 1–4 twice; Lines
5–8 once; repeat 5–8 if time
permits).

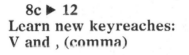

Comma: Space once after a
comma.

v
1 v vf vf vie vie vow vow van van via via five fives
2 vf vf live have dive love vane vain vile view viva

DS

,
3 , ,k ,k kit, kit, Dick, Jane, Nate, and I read it.
4 a rug, a jig, a ski, an igloo, the ring, two songs

v/,
5 Vic, Iva, and Viv dived over and over to save Van.
6 Val, Reva, and Vi voted for Eva; even so, Iva won.

all reaches learned
7 Kevin Nix was a judge at the garden show in Flint.
8 Joan, not Vi, took the jet; Vic also tried for it.

| 1 | 2 | 3 | 4 | 5 | 6 | 7 | 8 | 9 | 10 |

Learning goals

1 To become familiar with the keyboarding/formatting tasks of a word processing office.

2 To learn to produce long docu-ments efficiently.

3 To improve skill in working with form letters.

4 To improve ability to work with minimum instructions.

Machine adjustments

1 Set paper guide at *0*.

2 Set ribbon control to use upper half of ribbon.

3 70–space line for drill lines.

4 Follow customer's instructions for problems.

Office Job Simulation

Read carefully the material at the right before you begin the work in Section 47. Note any standard procedures that you think will save you time in the completion of the word processing activities.

Daily practice plan:

Preparatory practice .... 5'
Work on simulation .... 45'

Work Assignments

You have been assigned by Office Services Temporaries, Inc., to work as a keyboard specialist at Information Processing Services, Inc., a company which provides typing and other office services for a variety of businesses in the Chicago metropolitan area. The com-pany is located at 944 Adella Avenue, Joliet, IL 60433-2212.

Customers can either place their orders via telephone, or they can request pick up and delivery service. You have been assigned to work with materials which have been picked up from the different businesses. Each order will have attached to it instructions stating the procedures that the particular company wishes to have followed. Mr. O'Mariety, your supervisor, will be handing to you these in-structions with the material(s) to be prepared, and you are to follow carefully the procedures indicated.

The procedures manual at Information Processing Services, Inc., specifies that all let-ters are to be formatted with block style and open punctuation unless otherwise indicated by the customer. Closing lines of all letters are to include the typed name of the person for whom the letters are prepared followed on the next line by the person's business title. An en-velope is addressed for each letter unless otherwise stated.

Information Processing Services, Inc., has based its procedures manual on COLLEGE KEYBOARDING/TYPEWRITING, so use your textbook to look up matters of style when in doubt. When a job requires unusual or definite specifications, Information Processing Serv-ices provides them in "Excerpts from the In-formation Processing Manual."

Excerpts from the Information Processing Manual

Information Processing Services, Inc., often uses form letters to reply to orders and corre-spondence. Slightly different procedures are used to prepare form letters on an electric typewriter than on a word processor.

If you are using an electric typewriter, always type a form letter from the letter you have just typed, so that the previous letter will be proofread while you are typing the subsequent letter. All materials prepared should be proofread at least twice to make sure the ma-terial is error free.

On a word processor, if the copy is stored correctly, then you have to proofread only the variable material to make certain that it is error free.

Several different types of form letters may be used. Complete forms are usually printed in bulk. This type of form letter is very imper-sonal. Most companies prefer to use form let-ters which are personalized. The same letter could be prepared on a word processor with only the variable information being the date, letter address, and salutation. Other letters may have one or more items of variable infor-mation in the body of the letter.

Some form letters are prepared from form paragraphs. The date, letter address, and salutation are usually variable information; then the proper form paragraphs are selected. To proofread letters from form paragraphs, proof any variable information and check to make certain that the proper paragraphs were selected.

8d ▶ 12
Learn new keyreaches: Q and Y

Reach technique for q

Reach *up* with *left little* finger.

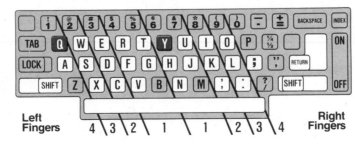

Left Fingers 4 \3 \2 \ 1 \ \ 1 / 2 /3 / 4 Right Fingers

Reach technique for y

Reach *up* with *right first* finger.

Follow the "Standard procedure for learning new keyreaches" on page 10 (Lines 1–4 twice; Lines 5–8 once; repeat 5–8 if time permits).

q
1 q qa qa qu qu quo quo quit quits quad quads quotes
2 qa qu quo quit quad quick quite equal quilt quarts
DS

y
3 y yj yj jay jay you you yet yet day day yell yells
4 yj eye yes rye dye sky cry sly try joy soy yen toy

q/y
5 Jay says Quay is quite young; he is quiet and shy.
6 Troy, Quent, and I are quite glad that Quinn quit.

all reaches learned
7 Frank Cage enjoyed the novel; Jo can read it next.
8 Next, Jacky Quire will leave; she can go in a day.

| 1 | 2 | 3 | 4 | 5 | 6 | 7 | 8 | 9 | 10 |

8e ▶ 10
Build sustained keyboarding power

1 Practice Paragraph (¶) 1 once SS.

2 DS and practice ¶ 2 in the same way.

Technique hints:

1 Keep your eyes on the book copy as you keyboard.

2 Do not pause or look up as you return the carrier or carriage (or cursor on a personal computer).

---

all reaches learned

¶ 1 We often need to choose, and yet it is never easy
to know which of two roads to take.   One can look
exactly like another, yet we are never quite sure
what is involved with each journey or each choice.

¶ 2 However, we do have to choose; and, since we will
not know where the unchosen road would have taken
us, we have to trust that we chose the right road.

| 1 | 2 | 3 | 4 | 5 | 6 | 7 | 8 | 9 | 10 |

In accordance with their limited partnership agreement, the general partners have purchased the limited partner's interest in the J and K Realty Company; therefore, the limited partnership needs to be dissolved. Ms. Adams asks that you prepare this document in final form. All of the partners will come to the office on March 15 to sign the document. Place an appropriate endorsement on the back of the page. A notary statement is not required.

CANCELLATION OF CERTIFICATE OF LIMITED PARTNERSHIP

PURSUANT TO the provisions of the Illinois Limited Partnership Act, the undersigned Partners of the _J and K Realty Company_, a Limited Partnership of Illinois, submit the following statement to cancel the original certificate of Limited Partnership filed of record in the office of the Secretary of State.

THE PARTNERSHIP will not be dissolved but will continue as a General Partnership as all Limited Partners have ceased to be such.

IN WITNESS WHEREOF, this certificate for cancellation of the original certificate of Limited Partnership has been duly executed on behalf of the parties hereto on the day and year set above the signatures of such Partners.

Dated the _15th_ day of _March_, 19__ .

General Partners:

_____
John R. Fowler

Rita L. Kutell
Limited Partner(s):

_____
Terry B. Orton

9a ▶ 8
Preparatory practice

each line twice SS
(slowly, then faster);
DS between 2-line
groups

Recall: TS between
lesson parts.

all letters learned	1	Work quickly, and we can fix the van Janet got us.
v/q/,/y	2	Standing on the quay, Dave, too, felt very queasy.
space bar	3	if it | to do | or he | an ox | for us | to do the | a yen for
easy	4	The city got a quantity of fish for the town lake.

| 1 | 2 | 3 | 4 | 5 | 6 | 7 | 8 | 9 | 10 |

9b ▶ 14
Practice keyreaches

1 Practice each line twice SS;
DS between 2–line groups.
2 Repeat lines that seem most
troublesome.

x	1	Lex next sent six yards of flax to Roxy in a taxi.
g	2	Gwen sang a song as George raised the ragged flag.
y	3	I say Ayn is shy; yet I did enjoy her story a lot.
n	4	For Nana, France was a land of sun, sand, and tan.
v	5	Van ran to visit the levee to view the vast river.
q	6	Quay quickly quoted Queen Arqua. Quent was quiet.

| 1 | 2 | 3 | 4 | 5 | 6 | 7 | 8 | 9 | 10 |

9c ▶ 14
Develop machine parts control

twice as shown; repeat
as time permits

Lines 1-4: Practice each
short line and return without
pausing or looking up.
Lines 5-7: Use space bar efficiently and maintain typing
fluency.
Lines 8-10: Shift smoothly
and rhythmically.

	1	Finish final stroke in the line.
return	2	Reach quickly to the return key.
	3	Hold your eyes down on the text.
	4	Return; start next line at once.
	5	an key fox van vie own hay can jay coy lay rug any
space bar	6	Vote for Gin; Lu is not a good choice. Tell Quin.
	7	Lex, not Tay, has a wagon; he will hang the signs.
	8	Owen Hays and Lil Young will see Neil in New York.
shift keys	9	Cyd, Rod, Susi, and Don will go on to Vienna soon.
	10	J. C. Wort will see Nel Foyt at the Old City Hall.

| 1 | 2 | 3 | 4 | 5 | 6 | 7 | 8 | 9 | 10 |

9d ▶ 14
Build sustained keyboarding power

1 Practice Paragraph (¶) 1 once.
2 DS and practice ¶2 in the
same way.

Technique hint:
Keystroke smoothly, con-
tinuously; avoid pauses.

all reaches learned

¶ 1 There are certain things that each of us wants to
own, and we know there are ways to acquire things
we want. However, there is a flaw in this design.

¶ 2 As soon as we get the thing we want, it loses its
value; so we exchange one want for another. Then
we find that just having does not satisfy wanting.

| 1 | 2 | 3 | 4 | 5 | 6 | 7 | 8 | 9 | 10 |

Job 9
Memorandum of loan and promissory note
(LM p. 167)

You are asked by Ms. Adams to complete this document today because the clients will be in the office tomorrow at 8:30 a.m. This document does not require a notary statement.

MEMORANDUM OF LOAN AND PROMISSORY NOTE

IT IS AGREED between the parties hereto that JAMES R. DOYLE has loaned the sum of Ten Thousand Dollars ($ 10,000.00) to PATRICIA V. LYON , and that the borrower intends to use said sums for the following: as a down payment on purchase of the house at 310 South Grove Avenue, Oak Park, IL 60302-3331.

THE BORROWER, namely PATRICIA V. LYON , hereby agrees to pay to the lender, namely JAMES R. DOYLE , the full amount of the sum loaned as set forth above, together with annual simple/~~compound~~ interest at the rate of 12 % no later than the 14th day of March , 19 94 .

SHOULD THE BORROWER default, either in whole or in part, on this note, the lender shall have the option of claiming an interest in the asset or property purchased with the money in proportion that said money was expended thereon, or to sue for money judgment.

In case suit or action is instituted to collect this note or the asset, the borrower promises to pay to the lender such reasonable attorney's fees and costs as may be fixed by the court.

Dated the 14th day of March , 19-- .

_____
Patricia V. Lyon--Borrower

_____
James R. Doyle--Lender

10a ▶ 8

Preparatory practice

each line twice SS (slowly, then faster); DS between 2-line groups

all reaches learned 1 Yes, Clive took a few quarts; Jan had six gallons.

shift keys 2 The Fortune Five will sing at our Lake Youth Hall.

v/y 3 Every year, I have given Yves five heavy old keys.

easy 4 Diane owns the oak shanty; she also owns the land.

| 1 | 2 | 3 | 4 | 5 | 6 | 7 | 8 | 9 | 10 |

Recall: TS between lesson parts.

10b ▶ 8

Reach for new goals

1 Take a 30–second (30″) writing on Line 4 of 10a above; determine *gwam* (total words typed × 2).

2 From the sentences at the right, choose one that will cause you to aim for 2–3 *gwam* more than your rate in Step 1. (30″ *gwam* for each sentence is shown in Column 2 at the right.)

3 Take two 30″ guided writings on the chosen sentence; try to reach the end of the line each time "Return" is called.

4 If you reach your goal in both 30″ writings, take two 30″ writings on the next sentence. (A total of eight 30″ writings will be given.)

5 Take another 30″ writing on Line 4 of 10a above; determine *gwam* (total words typed × 2).

Goal: An increase of *at least* 2 *gwam* from Step 1 to Step 5.

	words in line	gwam 30″	gwam 20″
1 Nan lent the auto to the girl.	6	12	18
2 Iris did throw a rock at the signs.	7	14	21
3 He did work with vigor to land the fish.	8	16	24
4 Hang the keys to the shanty on the oak chair.	9	18	27
5 The girls wish to visit the city to fix the signs.	10	20	30

| 1 | 2 | 3 | 4 | 5 | 6 | 7 | 8 | 9 | 10 |

10c ▶ 12

Learn new keyreaches: Z and M

Reach technique for z

Reach *down* with left little finger.

Reach technique for m

Reach *down* with right first finger.

Left Fingers 4 \ 3 \ 2 \ 1 \ 1 \ 2 \ 3 \ 4 Right Fingers

Follow the "Standard procedure for learning new keyreaches" on page 10 (Lines 1–4 twice; Lines 5–8 once; repeat 5–8 if time permits).

z 1 z za za az az zoo zoo zed zed jazz jazz lazy crazy
2 za za haze doze zone cozy zany zing zinc size raze

m 3 m mj mj jam jam ham ham may may yam yam make makes
4 mj am me ma man men made must fame dome fume major

z/m 5 Zack was amazed when Mazie came home from the zoo.
6 Lazy Mr. Zym dozed at home in the dim haze of May.

all reaches learned 7 Craving quiet, Jeff mildly dozed; he awoke at six.
8 Zed will move as quickly next June; why, I forget.

| 1 | 2 | 3 | 4 | 5 | 6 | 7 | 8 | 9 | 10 |

Job 7
Letter
(plain sheet)

Ms. Adams asks that you prepare this letter drafted by Mr. Fong for one of his clients. The letter is not officially from Mr. Fong; therefore, this type of letter should be prepared on plain bond paper (like a personal business letter). Be sure to include the appropriate return address on the two lines above the date. The letter is to be addressed to:

Ms. Katherine M. Gajewski
331 North Ridgeland Avenue
Oak Park, IL   60302-3112

The signer of the letter (the client) is:

Mrs. Wanda R. Friedman
635 South Grove Avenue
Oak Park, IL   60304-3314

Mrs. Friedman will come by the office on March 20 to pick up the letter, so date the letter March 20. The letter should be sent **REGISTERED** mail.

Dear Katherine :

Whereas, I am desirous of selling all of my interest in the Partnership of The Book Nook; now, therefore, pursuant to the provisions of Paragraph 7 of the Agreement of Partnership of said Partnership, dated the 10th day of May, 1983, I hereby give you notice of my desire to sell; and I demand that you purchase such interest at a price to be mutually agreed upon within 60 days from the receipt of this notice, or, in default of agreement, at a price to be fixed by arbitration.

Sincerely,

Job 8
Bill of sale
(LM p. 165)

Ms. Adams asks that you prepare this bill of sale. Miss Timms will come to the office on March 14 to sign it. Don't forget to include the acknowledgment (notary statement). Because Mr. Fong wishes this to be a one page document, Ms. Adams asks you to begin the document on Line 10. Place an appropriate endorsement on the back of the page.

BILL OF SALE

ANN H. TIMMS   , in consideration of the receipt by ~~his/~~her~~/them~~ from KIM D. FOX   of Three Thousand Dollars ($3,000)   , the receipt of which is hereby acknowledged, has ~~have~~ transferred and hereby convey(s) to   KIM D. FOX   the following interest, to have and to hold the same unto   KIM D. FOX   , her successors and assigns forever:

Diamond necklace and matching brooch.

ANN H. TIMMS   , for herself   , her heirs, executors, and administrators, warrant(s) and agree(s) to defend the title to such assets subject to all liabilities for the benefit of KIM D. FOX   , her successors and assigns, against all persons.

IN WITNESS WHEREOF, ANN H. TIMMS   , has ~~have~~ signed this Bill of Sale the 14th day of March   , 19 -- , to be effective as of the 25th day of March   , 19 -- .

_____
Ann H. Timms

10d ▶ 12
Learn new keyreaches:
B and P

Reach technique for b

Reach *down* with *left first* finger.

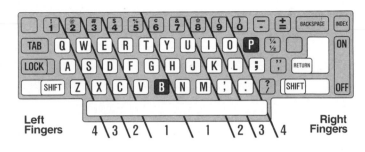

Left Fingers 4 3 2 1   1 2 3 4 Right Fingers

Reach technique for p

Reach *up* with *right little* finger.

Follow the "Standard procedure for learning new keyreaches" on page 10 (Lines 1–4 twice; Lines 5–8 once; repeat 5–8 if time permits).

b
1 b bf bf by by fib fib fob fob bit bit jib jib buff
2 bf by fib fob but rub job rib rob buy tub bid boff
DS

p
3 ; p; p; pa pa pan pan pen pen pad pad pep pep paid
4 up up; cup cup; sip sip; nap nap; map map; ape ape

b/p
5 Pepe bobbed for an apple; Bo jumped rope; I boxed.
6 Pablo Paz paid Barb to probe deeply for old bulbs.

all reaches learned
7 Caleb sipped a cup of pink juice at the Boise Zoo.
8 Five quiet zebus walk up; yet, Drex Marsh jogs on.

| 1 | 2 | 3 | 4 | 5 | 6 | 7 | 8 | 9 | 10 |

10e ▶ 10
Review keyboarding techniques

each line once SS; repeat as time permits

Lines 1-3: Keep wrists low; do not rest palms on machine.

Lines 4-6: Keep unused fingers in home–row position.

Lines 7-9: Move quickly and smoothly from letter to letter and word to word (no pauses).

Spacing review: Strike the space bar with a down–and–in motion of the thumb.

all letters
1 Alice is to speak for the group at the next forum.
2 Dan joined the squad for spring drills last month.
3 Denzyl took a short, fast hike; Bev went with him.
DS

spacing and shifting
4 If it were up to me, I would go for the top prize.
5 Vi, Don, and Jo have yet to win a set in the meet.
6 Ask Dr. Su. She knows O. J.; she once taught him.

easy sentences
7 It is the duty of the firm to fix the eight signs.
8 This land is held by the city to make into a park.
9 If you wish to make a big profit, work with vigor.

| 1 | 2 | 3 | 4 | 5 | 6 | 7 | 8 | 9 | 10 |

Mr. Fong has just completed a marriage contract, or ante-nuptial agreement, for Rex V. Rose and Lea K. Miller. Ms. Adams asks you to review the fill-in form and prepare it in final form. She tells you to include two signature lines on which the parties may sign. Remember to type the signer's name centered below the line. Use a spread heading.

ANTENUPTIAL AGREEMENT

THIS AGREEMENT is made on the 12th day of March _____, 19--, between REX V. ROSE , party of the first part, and LEA K. MILLER , party of the second part,

WHEREAS, a marriage is intended to be entered in-to and solemnized in the near future between the said REX V. ROSE and LEA K. MILLER ;

AND WHEREAS, each of the parties hereto is pos-sessed of considerable property, as set forth in Schedules A and B, annexed hereto, and has made a full and frank disclosure to the other in relation to its character and amount, and each of them has been fully advised as to their respective rights therein in the event of their marriage and in the absence of any agreement between them;

NOW, THIS AGREEMENT WITNESSETH that each of them, the said REX V. ROSE and LEA K. MILLER , hereby declares it to be his or her intention and desire that during their marriage each of them shall be and continue completely independent of the other in regard to the enjoyment and disposal of all property whether owned by either of them at the commencement of the marriage or coming to either of them during the marriage; and each of them hereby agrees with the other, in view and in consider-ation of the said proposed marriage, that so far as is legally possible, by their private act, declaration, and agreement, all property belonging to either of them at the commencement of the marriage or coming to either of them during the marriage shall be and is enjoyed by him or her, and be subject to the dispositions of him or her as his or her separate property, and after the death of either it shall be free from any claim by the other on account of dower, courtesy, or other statutory right in the same man-ner as if the said proposed marriage had never been cele-brated.

AND WHEREAS, it is further agreed by and between the parties hereto that in the event either one of them desires to sell or mortgage any real or personal property owned by either of them respectively, then the other shall sign and join in such deed or mortgage as the case may be in order to make the same legal and effectual.

IT IS FURTHER MUTUALLY AGREED that the terms of this contract shall be binding on the heirs, personal repre-sentatives, executors and/or administrators of the parties hereto.

IN WITNESS WHEREOF, the parties have hereunto set their hands and seals this 12th day of March , 19--.

11a ▶ 8
Preparatory practice

each line twice SS
(slowly, then faster);
DS between 2-line
groups

Recall: TS between
lesson parts.

all letters	1	Have Jeff Pim quickly walk the bridge zone at six.
z/p	2	Pat puzzled Zora; he played a happy piece of jazz.
m/b	3	Bob may remember he was a member of my brass band.
easy	4	The big map firm may make the usual profit for us.

| 1 | 2 | 3 | 4 | 5 | 6 | 7 | 8 | 9 | 10 |

11b ▶ 10
Practice difficult reaches

1 Practice each line once. Place a
check mark on your paper next to
lines that seem difficult for you.
2 Practice at least twice each line
that you checkmarked.

q	1	Quay made a quiet quip to quell a quarrel quickly.
x	2	Knox can relax; Alex gets a box of flax next week.
y	3	Ty Clay may envy you for any zany plays you write.
v	4	Eve and Vera drive the heavy vans every five days.
n	5	Nan danced many a dance, often with Nick and Donn.

| 1 | 2 | 3 | 4 | 5 | 6 | 7 | 6 | 7 | 8 | 9 | 10 |

11c ▶ 12
Learn new keyreaches:
: (colon) and ? (question mark)

Reach technique for : (colon)

Left shift and strike ; key;
space twice after : used
as punctuation.

Reach technique
for ? (question)

Left shift; reach *down* with
right little finger;
space twice after ? at
end of sentence.

Left Fingers 4 \ 3 \ 2 \ 1 / 1 \ 2 \ 3 \ 4 Right Fingers

Follow the "Standard procedure
for learning new keyreaches" on
page 10 (Lines 1–4 twice; Lines
5–9 once; repeat 5–9 if time
permits).

Colon, Question mark:

Hold the left shift key down as
you strike ? and : keys. Except in
rare instances, they are followed
by 2 blank spaces.

:	1 ; :; :; : : To wit: Date: Name: Address: From:
	2 Space twice after a colon, thus: To: No.: Time:
	DS
?	3 ; ?; ?; ? ? Who? When? Where? Who is? Why not?
	4 Did he go? Is she ill? Do I see it? Is it here?
:/?	5 Who is here? I see the following: Joe, Lee, Ray.
	6 Have you a pen? Copy these two words: tier, rye.
	7 When you are puzzled, ask yourself some questions;
all letters	8 for example: Do I have facts? Can I judge? What
	9 options do I have? Who else may be of help to me?

| 1 | 2 | 3 | 4 | 5 | 6 | 7 | 8 | 9 | 10 |

Mr. Fong met with the general partners of The Pottery Shed this morning to draft a certificate of limited partnership. The general partners are returning with their limited partners tomorrow at 2 p.m. to sign the document. Ms. Adams asks you to prepare this document for Mr. Fong. She reminds you to note the three sections that are to be indented to paragraph point and single-spaced. Also, an acknowledgment (notary statement) needs to be included. (See page 369 for sample.)

CERTIFICATE OF LIMITED PARTNERSHIP

THE UNDERSIGNED, desiring to form a Limited Partnership under the Uniform Limited Partnership Act of the State of Illinois, make this certificate for that purpose.

1. The name of the Partnership shall be *The Pottery Shed* .

2. The purpose of the Parnership shall be to *sell hand-crafted pottery articles and pottery supplies* .

3. The location of the Partnership's principal place of business is ___*Cook*___ County, Illinois.

4. The names of the members, and their designation as General or Limited Partners are:

DS →
{ *Gary R. Trotter* — General/~~Limited~~ Partner
{ *Caroline T. Knutzen* — General/~~Limited~~ Partner
SS { *Nadine C. Rhiner* — ~~General~~/Limited Partner
{ *Dennis K. Bascom* — ~~General~~/Limited Partner

DS →
5. The term for which the partnership is to exist is indefinite.

6. The amount of cash and a description of the agreed value of the other property contributed by each Limited Partner are:

SS {
Nadine C. Rhiner, $5,000.00
Dennis K. Bascom, $10,000.00

7. Each Limited Partner may (but shall not be obliged to) make such additional contributions to the capital of the Partnership as may from time to time be agreed upon by the General Partners.

8. The share of the profits which each Limited Partner shall receive by reason of his or her contribution is:

SS {
Nadine C. Rhiner . . . . *10* %
Dennis K. Bascom . . . . *20* %
. . . . ___ %

Signed *March 12* , 19-- .

_____
Gary R. Trotter
_____
Caroline T. Knutzen
_____
Nadine C. Rhiner
_____
Dennis K. Bascom

(Include a notary statement.)

11d ▶ 10
Learn to operate the tabulator mechanism

① **Clear all tab stops**

1 Move carrier to extreme right (or carriage to extreme left).
2 Depress tab clear (29) and hold it down as you return carrier to extreme left (or move carriage to extreme right).

② **Set tab stops**

Move the carrier (or carriage) to the desired position; then depress the tab set (26). Repeat this procedure for each stop needed.

③ **Tabulate (tab)***

Tap lightly the tab key (30), using the nearer little finger; or bar, using the right index finger, and return the finger to home position at once.

* If you are using a nonelectric typewriter, refer to page 3 for tabulating technique.

1 Clear all tab stops as directed.
2 Beginning at the left margin, set 3 tab stops at 5–space intervals from the margin stop.
3 Practice the drill once DS as shown. Begin Line 1 at left margin; tab once for Line 2; twice for Line 3; 3 times for Line 4.

1 It is now time for me to learn to use the tab key.

2 ⟶tab once→ Every tab stop now set must first be cleared.

3 ⟶tab twice→ After that, I set tab stops that I need.

4 ⟶tab three times→ Then I touch the tab key to indent.

11e ▶ 10
Check keyboarding skill

1 Practice the two ¶s once DS. Try to type without looking up, especially at the end of lines.
2 Take two 1' writings on each ¶; determine *gwam*.

Goal: At least 14 *gwam*.

Difficulty index

all letters	E	1.2 si	5.1 awl	90% hfw

gwam 1'

¶ 1   Some people like their music fast; some of us   9
do not. Some people have a taste for certain food   19
that others abhor. Some like flying; some do not.   29

¶ 2   Just why we differ should be quite clear. We   9
set our own example. We try a thing, then we make   19
a choice. Decisions others make need not faze us.   29

| 1 | 2 | 3 | 4 | 5 | 6 | 7 | 8 | 9 | 10 |

Key to difficulty index of timed writings

E = easy
LA = low average difficulty
A = average difficulty
si = syllable intensity
awl = average word length
hfw = high–frequency words

To determine words-a-minute rate

1 Note the figure at the end of the last line of the writing that you completed.

2 For a partial line, note the figure on the scale directly below the point at which you stopped keyboarding.

3 Add these two figures to determine the total gross words a minute (*gwam*) you typed.

Jobs 3 and 4
**Letter and promissory
note** (LM pp. 153–155)

Mr. Fong has edited a draft copy of a letter that is to accompany the promissory note (*shown below*). Ms. Adams asks that you prepare the letter in final form for Mr. Fong's signature. You are also to prepare the promissory note that will be enclosed with the letter. Although the promissory note is very short, you should still prepare it as a full-page legal document. Date the letter **March 11** and address it to:

**Mr. and Mrs. Jeffery T. Hall
1239 North Jackson Avenue
Oak Park, IL 60305-3511**

Mr. Fong's signature block should be:

**Mr. Y. R. Fong
Attorney-at-Law**

Use a spread heading and no acknowledgement for the promissory note. Also correct any undetected errors you may find in the draft letter.

Dear Mr. and Mrs. Hall:

I am enclosing a promissory note for the $80,000 *to* ~~that must~~ be signed by your son, William, upon advancing *him* ~~the~~ funds. As we discussed the *se* funds will be advanced upon an interest-*free* basis to be used to produce necessary income *while he attends college* *to me*.

You have both indicated that you understand the potential tax savings form [*from*] this type of *advance* ~~loss~~. If, however, either of you *has* ~~have~~ additional questions please call me before you*r* consummating *this* ~~of the~~ transaction.

Several aspects of *the* ~~this~~ loan are, ~~quite~~ important. *First,* It must be a demand note; and the note attached is such a note. Secondly, the loan must be bonafide; that is, it must be, in truth, *an actual* a loan. I have stressed to both of you that you must allow william *complete* discretion in the way he invests the money. It would be *wise* ~~sie~~, however, to recomend to him the types of investment*s* which you think most appropriate in view of the fact that he will need *to produce the,* income during the current year. I have discussed with you the major advantages *and disadvantages* of money market *funds*. The majer advantage of this type of investment is that it would give *William* the flexibility of making withdrals [*wa*] whenever *a need occurs* ~~needed~~.

Sincerely,

P R O M I S S O R Y   N O T E

$80,000

1239 North Jackson Avenue
Oak Park, IL 60305-3511

March 11, 19--

FOR VALUE RECEIVED, on demand, the undersigned promises to pay to the order of Mr. and Mrs. Jeffery T. Hall the principal sum of Eighty Thousand Dollars ($80,000) without interest.

_____
William J. Hall

12a ▶ 8
Preparatory practice

each line twice SS
(slowly, then faster);
DS between 2-line
groups

Recall: TS between
lesson parts.

alphabet	1	Biff was to give the major prize quickly to Dixon.
space bar	2	is it me of he an by do go to us if or so am ah el
shift keys	3	Pam was in Spain in May; Roy Bo met her in Madrid.
easy	4	He may sign the form with the name of the auditor.

| 1 | 2 | 3 | 4 | 5 | 6 | 7 | 8 | 9 | 10 |

12b ▶ 15
Develop keystroking technique

1 Practice each line 3
times SS; DS between
3–line groups; place a
check mark on your
paper next to each line
that was difficult for
you.

2 If time permits, repeat each line that was
difficult.

home row	1	Dallas sadly had a salad as Hal had a large steak.
bottom row	2	Can my cook, Mrs. Zockman, carve the big ox roast?
third row	3	The purple quilt is quite pretty where you put it.
1st/2d fingers	4	I took the main route by the river for five miles.
3d/4th fingers	5	Pam saw Roz wax an aqua auto as Lex sipped a cola.
double letters	6	Ann took some apples to school; Dee, a cherry pie.

| 1 | 2 | 3 | 4 | 5 | 6 | 7 | 8 | 9 | 10 |

12c ▶ 15
Reach for new goals

1 Take a 1' writing on Line 4
of 12a above; determine
gwam (total words typed).

2 From the second column
at the right (gwam 30"),
choose a goal that will cause
you to aim for 2–3 gwam
more than your rate in Step 1.
Note the sentence that accompanies that goal.

3 Take two 1' writings on
the chosen sentence; try
to reach the end of the
line each time "Return" is
called (each 30").

4 If you reach your goal on both 1'
writings, take two 1' writings on
the next sentence. (A total of eight
1' writings will be given.)

5 Take another 1' writing on Line 4
of 12a above; determine gwam
(total words typed).

Goals:
12–14 gwam, acceptable
15–17 gwam, good
18–20 gwam, very good
21+ gwam, excellent

		words in line	gwam 30'	gwam 20'
1	I paid for six bushels of rye.	6	12	18
2	Risk a penalty; this is a big down.	7	14	21
3	Did their form entitle them to the land?	8	16	24
4	Did the men in the field signal for us to go?	9	18	27
5	Did she enamel a sign on the auto body with a pen?	10	20	30
6	The ivory emblem is on a shelf in the town chapel.	10	20	30

| 1 | 2 | 3 | 4 | 5 | 6 | 7 | 8 | 9 | 10 |

12d ▶ 12
Check/develop keyboarding continuity

1 Clear tab stops; set a tab for
5–space ¶ indention.

2 Practice ¶ 1 once DS for orientation.

3 Take two 1' writings on ¶ 1; determine gwam on each writing.

4 Use ¶ 2 as directed in Steps 2
and 3.

Goal: At least 14 gwam.

Difficulty index

| all letters | E | 1.2 si | 5.1 awl | 90% hfw |

gwam 1'

¶ 1   What is time? Time is the standard needed to   9
fix in sequence each event that makes up the whole   19
fabric of this effort that we like to call living.   <u>29</u>

¶ 2   Time, we realize, means constant pressure for   9
each of us; it must be used. Our minutes are just   19
tiny sums in a book of account. We are the total.   29

| 1 | 2 | 3 | 4 | 5 | 6 | 7 | 8 | 9 | 10 |

Another client has an appointment with Mr. Fong tomorrow to complete a stock certificate transfer. Ms. Adams asks that you prepare this document with an appropriate acknowledgment (notary statement). Most legal firms have one of their employees as a Notary Public. In this office, Ms. Adams is a Notary Public and is able to execute the notary statements for Mr. Fong's clients. Place an appropriate endorsement on the back of the page.

Indent 9/s 10 spaces

ASSIGNMENT OF SHARE CERTIFICATE

Share Certificate dated: *October 15* , 19 *75*

Issued to: *Rosemary E. Stone*

FOR VALUE RECEIVED, ROSEMARY E. STONE does hereby sell, assign, and transfer unto JARED Q. McGARVEY , *15* shares of the common shares of *Longmont Oil Company* represented by the within certificate numbered *235*, and standing in the name of ROSEMARY E. STONE _____ on the books of said Corporation, and does hereby irrevocably constitute and appoint Y. R. Fong, attorney, to transfer the said shares on the books of the within named Corporation, with full power of substitution.

Dated this the *10th* day of *March* , 19--.

Rosemary E. Stone

STATE OF ILLINOIS)
                  : SS.
County of Cook)

On this *10th* day of *March* , 19-- , before me personally appeared the above-named individual(s), to me known to be the person(s) described in and who executed the foregoing instrument and acknowledged that he/ she/they executed the same as his/her/their own free act and deed.

In testimony whereof, I have hereunto subscribed my name at Oak Park, Illinois, this day.

_____
Notary Public

My commission expires on October 28, 19--.

13

Learning goals

1 To achieve smoother keystrok–ing.

2 To improve use of special machine parts.

3 To develop a relaxed, confident attitude.

4 To increase keystroking speed.

Machine adjustments

1 Set paper guide at 0.

2 Set ribbon control to type on upper half of ribbon.

3 Set left margin for a 50–space line (center point − 25); move right stop to end of scale.

4 Single–space (SS) drills; double–space (DS) paragraphs (¶).

13a ▶ 8
Preparatory practice

each line twice SS (slowly, then faster); DS between 2-line groups

Recall: TS between lesson parts.

alphabet	1	Jacques Lopez might fix the wrecked navy tugboats.
z	2	Liz drove hazardous, zigzag Zaire roads with zeal.
y	3	Kay said you should stay with Mary for sixty days.
easy	4	Their form may entitle a visitor to fish the lake.

| 1 | 2 | 3 | 4 | 5 | 6 | 7 | 8 | 9 | 10 |

13b ▶ 12
Develop keyboarding technique

once as shown; repeat if time permits

Lines 1-2: Reach with fingers; keep hand movement to a mini–mum.

Lines 3-4: Curve fingers over home row.

Lines 5-6: Reach fingers to third–row keys without moving hands.

bottom row	1	Did Cam, the cabby, have extra puzzles? Yes, one.
	2	Do they, Mr. Zack, expect a number of brave women?
home row	3	Gayla Halls had a sale; Jake had a sale last fall.
	4	Gladys had half a flask of soda; Josh had a salad.
third row	5	There were two or three quiet people at our party.
	6	Trudy Perry quietly sewed the four pretty dresses.

| 1 | 2 | 3 | 4 | 5 | 6 | 7 | 8 | 9 | 10 |

13c ▶ 8
Practice difficult reaches

1 Each line once; checkmark any line that you do not keystroke fluently.

2 Repeat each checkmarked line as time permits.

Technique hint:
Work for smoothness and continuity.

v	1	Eva visited every vivid event for twelve evenings.
m	2	A drummer drummed for a moment, and Mimi came out.
p	3	Pat appears happy to pay for any supper I prepare.
x	4	Tex Cox waxed the next box for Xenia and Rex Knox.
b	5	My rubber boat bobbed about in the bubbling brook.

| 1 | 2 | 3 | 4 | 5 | 6 | 7 | 8 | 9 | 10 |

Preparatory practice

each line 3 times SS (slowly, faster, slowly); DS between 3-line groups; repeat selected lines as time permits

alphabet 1 An expert must move quickly to adjust a water gauge before the freeze.

fig/sym 2 The net due on $3,987.46 after a 5.2% discount ($207.35) is $3,780.11.

outside reach 3 A small quail at the local zoo was looking at six gorillas plus a fox.

fluency 4 The sorority girls may go to the island to dig for the ancient emblem.

| 1 | 2 | 3 | 4 | 5 | 6 | 7 | 8 | 9 | 10 | 11 | 12 | 13 | 14 |

209b-214b ▶ 45
Office job simulation

(LM pp. 149–169)

Ms. Adams welcomes you to the office and explains the basic office procedures to you. She suggests that you study carefully the *Legal Office Manual.* She indicates to you that the majority of the jobs in Mr. Fong's office involve the preparation of legal documents. She further informs you that most of the legal documents prepared in this office will be prepared by Mr. Fong on fill-in forms; however, Mr. Fong does not use the preprinted forms as the final legal document. Ms. Adams reminds you to delete the underlining from under the filled-in elements on the preprinted forms when you are preparing final legal documents. For those cases where a fill-in form is not available, Mr. Fong will write out the document in longhand.

Mr. Fong's letters are usually dictated and draft copies are prepared for him to edit. He requests the modified block style with mixed punctuation and indented paragraphs for all his letters. Prepare an envelope for each letter. You begin work today, March 8.

Job 1
Joint purchase agreement
(LM p. 149)

Ms. Adams asks you to prepare this legal document for Mr. Fong. His client will be coming to the office tomorrow to sign the document. You are reminded that the date placed on the legal document is the date the instrument is signed; therefore, you note that Mr. Fong has tomorrow's date on the document. This document does not require an acknowledgment (notary statement).

TS >
JOINT PURCHASE AGREEMENT

RUTH A. FISK and CAROL G. BROWN, who are living in the same house, agree to purchase jointly a car from CENTRAL AUTO COMPANY for a total price, including tax, of $6,543.52.

IT IS AGREED that RUTH A. FISK shall pay toward the down payment the sum of $1,000.00, and CAROL G. BROWN shall pay toward the down payment the sum of $1,000.00. The monthly payments are $212.00. Of this, RUTH A. FISK agrees to pay $106.00 per month, and CAROL G. BROWN agrees to pay $106.00 per month.

IT IS AGREED that this automobile shall be owned by each party equally on a fifty-fifty basis.

IT IS AGREED that should litigation or the use of an attorney be required to enforce this agreement, the defaulting or losing party agrees to pay to the prevailing party such reasonable attorney's fees and costs as may be fixed by the court.

Dated: March 9, 19--

_____
Ruth A. Fisk
_____
Carol G. Brown

13d ▶ 10
Control machine parts
once as shown; repeat if time permits

Lines 1-3: From left margin, set two tab stops at 20–space intervals; tab for second and third sentences in each line.

Lines 4-6: Use space bar with down–and–in motion; space correctly after punctuation marks.

Lines 7-8: Use shift–type–release motions.

tab/return	1	Why not us?	Did she ask?	Is it not?
	2	Who was it?	Will he bid?	Why is it?
	3	Can he see?	Is she well?	Was it he?

space bar 4 an any many am ham them by buy bouy ha ah bah bath
5 to buy | for any | the man | did both | by them | the theory
6 I went; Bo did, too. Is it true? To: Ms. Dudley

shift keys 7 Sofie Lamas visits Al and Mae in Denver, Colorado.
8 Tony lives on Elm Court; he works for K. L. Hains.

| 1 | 2 | 3 | 4 | 5 | 6 | 7 | 8 | 9 | 10 |

13e ▶ 12
Develop keyboarding continuity

1 Clear tab stops; set tab stop for 5–space indention.

2 Practice each ¶ once as shown for orientation.

3 Take three 1' writings on each ¶.

Goal: At least 16 *gwam*.

Technique hint:
Work for smooth, continuous typing, not for high speed.

Difficulty index

all letters used	E	1.2 si	5.1 awl	90% hfw

gwam 1'

¶ 1   If we exert great efforts to do something, it   9

could be true that our effort will bring us higher   19

quality returns to match the work that we put out.   29

¶ 2   Is zeal worth the cost? Some people say that   9

maximum efforts will pay off in real results; even   19

others say the joy of hard work is its own reward.   29

| 1 | 2 | 3 | 4 | 5 | 6 | 7 | 8 | 9 | 10 |

14a ▶ 8
Preparatory practice
each line twice SS (slowly, then faster); DS between 2-line groups

alphabet 1 Kim Janby gave six prizes to qualified white cats.
shift keys 2 Jay Nadler, a Rotary Club member, wrote Mr. Coles.
y 3 Why do you say that today, Thursday, is my payday?
easy 4 Did the girl also fix the cowl of the formal gown?

| 1 | 2 | 3 | 4 | 5 | 6 | 7 | 8 | 9 | 10 |

Approx. 2″ top margin	
Heading centered between ruled lines	ASSIGNMENT OF SHARE CERTIFICATE Share Certificate dated: October 15, 1975 Issued to: Rosemary E. Stone FOR VALUE RECEIVED, ROSEMARY E. STONE does hereby sell, assign, and transfer unto JARED Q. McGARVEY, 15 shares of the common shares of Longmont Oil Company represented by the within certificate numbered 235, and standing in the name of ROSEMARY E. STONE on the books of said Corporation, and does hereby irrevocably constitute and appoint Y. R. Fong, attorney, to transfer the said shares on the books of the within named Corporation, with full power of substitution. Dated this the 10th day of March, 19--. _____ Rosemary E. Stone
Acknowl-edgment SS	STATE OF ILLINOIS)): ss. County of Cook) On this 10th day of March, 19--, before me personally appeared the above-named individual, to me known to be the person described in and who executed the foregoing instrument and acknowledged that she executed the same as her own free act and deed. In testimony whereof, I have hereunto subscribed my name at Oak Park, Illinois, this day. _____ Notary Public
One-page instrument does not need a page number	My commission expires on October 28, 19--.

Assignment of Share Certificate

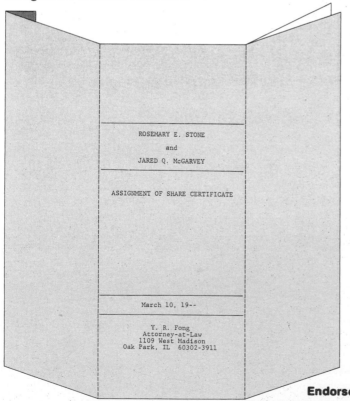

ROSEMARY E. STONE
and
JARED Q. McGARVEY

ASSIGNMENT OF SHARE CERTIFICATE

March 10, 19--

Y. R. Fong
Attorney-at-Law
1109 West Madison
Oak Park, IL 60302-3911

Endorsement on a legal back

Titles on Legal Documents. The title should be in all capital letters, centered between the side margins (vertical rulings). Often a title is s p r e a d. To spread a title or heading, follow these procedures:

1. Backspace from horizontal center point one *backspace for* each stroke in the title or heading (letters, numbers, symbols, and spaces) *except* the last stroke.

2. Enter the title (in all capital letters) with one blank space between characters (letters, numbers, or symbols) and with 3 blank spaces between words in the title.

Example:

Signature Lines. The page on which the signatures of the maker(s) and any witness appear must contain at least 2 lines of the body of the document.

Place the signature lines for the maker or makers of the legal document on the right side of the page. Place the witness' signature, if any, on the left side of the page. Type the first signature line on the third or fourth line below the last line of the document. The actual line upon which the signature is written is about 3″ long. If more than one signature is needed, leave 2 or 3 blank lines between them.

Latin Abbreviations. When a legal document is "under seal," the signature on the document is followed by "L.S." which refers to the Latin phrase *locus sigilli*. Use the abbreviation "ss" for the Latin word *scilicet*, meaning "to wit."

Proofreading. Use the verifying method to proofread all legal documents. In this method, one person reads from the originating material while the other person checks the newly prepared copy. Tricky or unfamiliar words are spelled, and all punctuation marks are also indicated by the person reading aloud.

Endorsements and Legal Backs. The names of the parties, the title of the legal document, the date, and the name and address of the attorney or legal firm appear on the back of legal documents. This information is called the *endorsement*. It may be typed either directly on the back of the last page of the document or on a *legal back* (a heavier and larger paper used to cover the document). If typing the endorsement directly on the back of the legal document, fold the document into thirds and type the endorsement in the middle fold for 8½″ × 11″ paper; fold the document into fourths and type the endorsement on the outer fold for longer, legal-sized paper. If a legal back is used to cover the legal document, prepare it in the following manner for 8½″ × 11″ paper:

1. Fold down the top ½″ and crease it; this fold will later be used to bind the legal document.

2. Fold the remainder into equal thirds (as in folding a business letter).

3. Place the endorsement within the middle section.

Note that most preprinted legal forms have the title of the legal document preprinted on the back and additional information for the endorsement needs only to be typed in the proper place.

14b ▶ 9
Improve response patterns

once as shown; then repeat

Lines 1-2: *Say* and type each word as a unit.

Lines 3-4: Spell each word as you type it; work at a steady pace.

Lines 5-6: *Say* and type short, easy words as units; spell and type longer words letter by letter.

word response	1	he of to if ah or by do so am is go us it an me ox
	2	The corps may pay for the land when they visit us.
stroke response	3	was pop saw ink art oil gas kin are hip read lymph
	4	Sara erected extra seats; Jimmy sat in only a few.
combination response	5	is best | an area | to pump | to join | an acre | he read it
	6	My act forms a base for a tax case with the state.

| 1 | 2 | 3 | 4 | 5 | 6 | 7 | 8 | 9 | 10 |

14c ▶ 9
Control machine parts

once as shown; repeat if time permits

Lines 1-4: Clear tabs; set tab at center point. Tab where indicated.

Line 5: Use correct spacing after each punctuation mark.

Line 6: Depress shift key firmly; avoid pauses.

tab and return	1	———————— tab ————→ Can you work the parts of
	2	your machine?———— tab ——→ Can you work them without
	3	looking at them?———— tab —→ Do you trust your fingers
	4	to do the work you have taught them to do?
space bar	5	We did. Was it here? I saw it; Lois saw it, too.
shift keys	6	Jena visited Washington, D.C., to see Kay and Pat.

| 1 | 2 | 3 | 4 | 5 | 6 | 7 | 8 | 9 | 10 |

14d ▶ 10
Improve keyboarding technique

1 Once as shown; checkmark each line that you do not keystroke fluently.

2 Repeat any line that caused you difficulty.

adjacent reaches	1	Bert read where she could stop to buy gas and oil.
	2	We three are a trio to join the Yun Oil operation.
direct reaches	3	My uncle and my brother have run many great races.
	4	Grace Nurva hunted my canyon for unique specimens.
double letters	5	Jeanne took a day off to see a book show in Hobbs.
	6	Jerry has planned a small party for all the troop.

| 1 | 2 | 3 | 4 | 5 | 6 | 7 | 8 | 9 | 10 |

14e ▶ 14
Reach for new goals

1 Take a 1' writing on Line 2 of 14b above; determine *gwam* (total words typed).

2 From the second column at the right (*gwam* 30"), choose a goal that will cause you to aim for 2–3 *gwam* more than your rate in Step 1. Note the sentence that accompanies that goal.

3 Take two 1' writings on the chosen sentence; try to reach the end of the line each time "Return" is called (each 30").

4 If you reach your goal on either 1' writing, take two 1' writings on the next sentence. (A total of eight 1' writings will be given.)

5 Take another 1' writing on Line 2 of 14b above; determine *gwam* (total words typed).

Goals:
13–15 *gwam*, acceptable
16–18 *gwam*, good
19–21 *gwam*, very good
22+   *gwam*, excellent

		words in line	gwam 30"	gwam 20"
1	The six girls work with vigor.	6	12	18
2	He got the right title to the land.	7	14	21
3	He works a field of corn and rye for us.	8	16	24
4	Row to the big island at the end of the lake.	9	18	27
5	They do their duty when they turn the dials right.	10	20	30

| 1 | 2 | 3 | 4 | 5 | 6 | 7 | 8 | 9 | 10 |

Learning goals

1 To develop knowledge and skill in the preparation of legal documents.

2 To plan your work carefully and to complete your work correctly and efficiently.

Machine adjustments

1 Set paper guide at *0*.

2 Set ribbon control to use upper half of ribbon.

3 Set line–space selector for SS.

4 Set 70–space line for drills.

5 Margins: 2″ top, 1½″ left, ½″ right, and 1″ bottom for legal documents. Other jobs as directed.

Office Job Simulation

Read carefully the material at the right and on page 367 before you begin the work of Section 46. Note any standard procedures that you think will save you time during the completion of the legal office jobs.

Daily practice plan:

Preparatory practice .... 5′
Work on simulation .... 45′

Work Assignment

You have been assigned by Office Service Temporaries, Inc., to work as a legal office assistant for Mr. Y. R. Fong, Attorney-at-Law, 1109 West Madison, Oak Park, IL 60302-3911. One of Mr. Fong's office assistants is on vacation, and you have been hired as a temporary replacement. Ms. Joyce Adams is in charge of office operations and will instruct you on your work assignments.

Mr. Fong has prepared a *Legal Office Manual* that contains both office procedures and examples of document formats. Some of the basic information from this manual has been provided in the "Excerpts from the Legal Office Manual." Mr. Fong has based his office procedures on COLLEGE KEYBOARDING/TYPEWRITING; therefore, use your textbook as a reference guide for all matters of style and placement. Remember to proofread and correct all errors before removing your paper from the machine.

Excerpts from the Legal Office Manual— Preparation of Legal Documents

Top and Bottom Margins. The top margin is usually 2″ (12 blank lines) on each page. The bottom margin should be at least 1″. It is sometimes necessary to leave more than a 1″ bottom margin because the page on which the signature of the maker(s) or any witness appears must contain at least 2 lines of the body of the document.

Side Margins. When using plain paper, set the margin stops for a 1½″ left margin and a ½″ right margin. When using ruled paper, leave one or two spaces between the ruling at the left and the beginning of the line of writing. End the line of writing no closer than one space before the right marginal ruling. In deciding where to end a line, try to avoid hyphenation and to create an overall good appearance.

Spacing. Indent paragraphs 10 spaces. DS the body of the legal document *except* when typing quoted material and land descriptions. Single-space and indent this material 10 spaces from both margins. Also, when used, the witness statement and notary statement should be single-spaced.

Paper. Legal documents may be prepared on preprinted forms, marginal ruled paper, or plain paper. The paper may be either standard-size (8½″ × 11″) or special legal-size paper (8½″ × 13″ or 14″).

Paper with marginal rulings has a double vertical ruling down the left side 1⅜″ from the left edge of the paper, and a single vertical ruling down the right side ⅜″ from the right edge of the paper.

Multiple Copies of Legal Document. Prepare all copies in this office on a photocopy machine. If any corrections have been made on the document, use a photocopy as the "original" document (see *Correcting Errors* below).

Verification of Numbers. Type any important number or sum of money in both numbers and words to provide positive identification of the correct amounts. No legal question would arise if a single digit or letter were corrected provided verification of the amount could be made by the double typing.

Page Numbers. *Except* in a Will, do not number the first page of a legal document. Center the numbers on all subsequent pages between the margins 3 blank lines from the bottom of the page. Type a hyphen before and after the page number; for example, -8-.

Correcting Errors. Correct carefully all important items such as names, sums of money, and numbers. Any obvious corrections on an original legal document should be initialed by all parties concerned to verify agreement of the change or correction. However, if a photocopy of the document is used as the signed "original," neat corrections made with lift-off tape or liquid coverup material would not show on the photocopies; therefore, initialing of corrections would not be necessary on the photocopy.

15a ▶ 8
Preparatory practice

each line twice SS (slowly, then faster); DS between 2-line groups

alphabet	1	Max Jewel picked up five history quizzes to begin.
space bar	2	Did she say she may copy the form in a day or two?
z	3	Liz Zahl saw Zoe feed the zebra in an Arizona zoo.
easy	4	They risk a penalty if he signs their usual forms.

| 1 | 2 | 3 | 4 | 5 | 6 | 7 | 8 | 9 | 10 |

15b ▶ 14
Improve response patterns

1 Once as shown; checkmark three most difficult lines.

2 Repeat the lines you checked as difficult.

3 Take a 1' writing on Line 2, next on Line 4, and then on Line 6. Determine *gwam* on each writing.

word response	1	with they them make than when also work such right
	2	Diana did key work for the city dock for half pay.
stroke response	3	were only date upon ever join fact milk care nylon
	4	Milo acted on only a few tax rebate cases in July.
combination response	5	with were they only them upon than ever when plump
	6	Julio paid the tax on six acres of rich lake land.

| 1 | 2 | 3 | 4 | 5 | 6 | 7 | 8 | 9 | 10 |

15c ▶ 14
Reach for new goals

1 Using your best rate in 15b as a base, choose from the sentences at the right one that will raise your goal by 2–3 *gwam*.

2 Beginning with that sentence, take a series of 1' writings as directed in 14e, page 31.

Goals:

13–15 *gwam*, acceptable
16–18 *gwam*, good
19–21 *gwam*, very good
22+ *gwam*, excellent

		words in line	gwam 30"	gwam 20"
1	This is an authentic ivory antique.	7	14	21
2	Did the cowhand dismantle the worn auto?	8	16	24
3	Is the body of the ancient dirigible visible?	9	18	27
4	If they wish, she may make the form for the disks.	10	20	30
5	Did they mend the torn right half of their ensign?	10	20	30

| 1 | 2 | 3 | 4 | 5 | 6 | 7 | 8 | 9 | 10 |

15d ▶ 14
Check/develop keyboarding continuity

1 Clear tab stops; set a tab for 5-space ¶ indention.

2 Practice ¶ 1 once DS for orientation.

3 Take two 1' writings on ¶ 1; determine *gwam* on each writing.

4 Use ¶ 2 as directed in Steps 2 and 3.

Goal: At least 15 *gwam*.

Technique hints:
Keep the carrier moving at a fairly steady pace. Avoid looking up, especially at line endings.

Difficulty index

all letters used	E	1.2 si	5.1 awl	90% hfw

gwam 1'

¶ 1	To learn to keyboard requires that you simply	9
	allow the skill to form day by day. You may often	19
	be concerned as a result of doubt that the fingers	29
	will do just what you have been told they will do.	39
¶ 2	So the secret is revealed. Typing is not the	9
	hard job it once may have seemed. Now you realize	19
	that what you must do is simply relax and read the	29
	copy carefully; your hands should do all the rest.	39

| 1 | 2 | 3 | 4 | 5 | 6 | 7 | 8 | 9 | 10 |

maxillary and ethmoid sinuses on the right side appear to be clear. There appears to be no involvement of the sphenoids. Some evidence of a soft tissue mass in the left nasal fossa exists; however, there is no destructive bony or fluid level change apparent.

IMPRESSION: A chronic hyperplastic bilateral frontal and left ethmoid sinusitis exists. There is also a left maxillary sinusitis with a dense unaerated left antrum. A pansinusitis on the left may exist. All other sinuses are essentially clear and unremarkable.

Job 10
Pathology report
(LM p. 147)

Dr. Pollei, the Pathologist, dictated his report, and Mr. Moss had another medical assistant prepare the draft copy. After Dr. Pollei checked the draft, he approved it to be typed without making any further corrections. Mr. Moss asks you to prepare the pathology report in final form for the patient's file.

E.N.T. Medical Services

PATHOLOGY REPORT

Name: Andrew G. Konrad	Case No.:	280823
Date: March 5, 19--	Sex: Male	Age: 8
Attending Physician: Susan T. Rosenbloom, M.D.		
Pathologist: Richard B. Pollei, M.D.		
Specimen: Tonsils		

GROSS EXAMINATION: Both tonsils were smooth and ovoid and measured up to 2.3 x 1.9 cm. Both tonsils were partially covered with pitted mucous membrane. The tonsils were homogeneous and not remarkable. A histologic study of several tonsil sections was done.

HISTOLOGIC EXAMINATION: The tonsils had a covering of stratified squamous epithelium. There were some formations of crypts, and within these crypts there were some cellular debris. Also, moderate numbers of bacteria and some collections of coagulated fluid were seen. The coagulated fluid contained fairly numerous polymorphonuclear leukocytes which had infiltrated the lymphoid tissue for short distances; however, no abscesses had formed, and there was no evidence of neoplasm. The base of the tonsils was composed of hyperemic connective tissue with a few glandular lobules.

DIAGNOSIS: Subacute follicular tonsillitis

Learning goals

1 To learn figure keyreaches.
2 To proofread/revise copy.
3 To type statistical copy.
4 To type handwritten copy.
5 To improve stroking continuity.

Machine adjustments

1 Set paper edge guide at 0.
2 Set ribbon control to type on upper half of ribbon.
3 Set left margin for a 50–space line (center point − 25); move right stop to end of scale.
4 SS drills; DS paragraphs.

16a ▶ 7

Preparatory practice

each line twice SS (slowly, then faster); DS between 2-line groups; repeat selected lines if time permits

alphabet	1	We got six quaint bronze cups from heavy old junk.
q/?	2	Did Marq Quin go? Did Quent Quin go? Did Quincy?
z/:	3	To: Zane Mozel, Tempe, AZ From: Ezra A. Lazzaro
easy	4	She may do the work when she signs the right form.

| 1 | 2 | 3 | 4 | 5 | 6 | 7 | 8 | 9 | 10 |

16b ▶ 16

Learn new keyreaches: 3 7 1

Follow the "Standard procedure for learning new keyreaches" on page 10 (Lines 1–6 twice; Lines 7–10 once; repeat 7–10 if time permits).

Under certain circumstances, the small letter l can be used to type the figure 1. Your instructor will tell you which reach to use for daily work.

Reach technique for 3

Reach *up* with *left second* finger.

Reach technique for 7

Reach *up* with *right first* finger.

Reach technique for 1

Reach *up* with *left little* finger.

NOTES ON ABBREVIATIONS

Space once after a period (.) following an initial. Abbreviations such as M.D., B.C., Ph.D., U.S., N.Y., C.O.D., a.m., and p.m. may be typed solid (without internal spacing).

Abbreviations such as mph, rpm, and mg are usually expressed without caps, periods, or internal spacing.

Abbreviations such as ERA, AMA, and TVA are typed in ALL CAPS (without internal spacing).

3	1	d 3d 3d 3 3; 3 did, 3 days, 3 deals, 3 dozen, 3 33
	2	The 33 girls and 3 boys met at 3 p.m. near Gate 3.
7	3	j 7j 7j 7 7; 7 jobs, 7 jets, 7 jacks, 7 jeeps, 7 7
	4	She wrote 7, 7, 7, not 777. She wrote it 7 times.
1	5	a la la l l lla; l arm, l aide, l awl, ll ayes, ll
	6	He bought ll tons of No. l coal on May l at l p.m.
3/7/1	7	Page 371 of Volume 31 states the date as 1737 B.C.
	8	Flight 173, a 737 jet, left on May 31 at 1:31 p.m.
all figures learned	9	Only 3 of the 7 cars clock 71 to 73 mph or better.
	10	Read pages 7, 17, and 37; copy Lines 3, 7, and 31.

| 1 | 2 | 3 | 4 | 5 | 6 | 7 | 8 | 9 | 10 |

Job 8
Consultation report
(LM p. 143)

Mr. Moss gave you a dictation disk and asked you to transcribe Dr. Rosenbloom's consultation report. You have transcribed the report at draft speed and submitted it to Mr. Moss for correction. Dr. Rosenbloom checked the draft and Ok'd it to be finalized without any further corrections. Prepare the report in final form for the patient's file.

E.N.T. Medical Services

CONSULTATION REPORT

Name:	Rowena C. Thompson		Case No.: 283761
Date:	March 4, 19--	Sex: Female	Age: 2

Attending Physician: David E. Randolph, M.D.

Consultative Physician: Susan T. Rosenbloom, M.D.

PRESENT ILLNESS: The child was born with a very unusual midline cleft of the lip with some degree of bifid nose.

PHYSICAL EXAMINATION: a nothing effect of the mucous membrane in the midline of the upper lip is apparent. Also, there is a thinning of the musculature with a very slight depression that extends up near the midline. Her lip is near normal in other respects. Each alar cartilage has separation, and there is a wide depressed cleft tip of the nose; columellas is short and wide. A little midline sulcus is apparent, and there is a very small pocket in the mucous membrane between the incisor teeth. An alveolar margin is connected in the midline.

DIAGNOSIS: The bifid nose as well as the upper lip midline cleft are congenital.

CONCLUSION: Recommend surgery to correct the midline cleft lip and the bifid nose. Dermal skin graft techniques should be used.

Job 9
X-ray report
(LM p. 145)

Mr. Moss hands you this handwritten x-ray report to be finalized. He tells you that the radiologist finds the use of a blank form more useful than the dictation machine. Prepare the final copy for the patient's file.

E.N.T. Medical Services

X-RAY REPORT

Name: Arthur W. Brockbank   Case No.: 289877

Date: March 5, 19--   Sex: Male   Age: 35

Attending Physician: Susan T. Rosenbloom, M.D.

Radiologist: Elizabeth M. Mehmen, M.D.

Examination Requested: Paranasal sinuses

There is a moderate degree of thickening of the mucous membrane in the left frontal area. The left antrum is rather uniformly opaque. The ethmoid on the left is probably involved. Both the

(Job 9 continued on page 365)

16c ▶ 12
Reach for new goals

Follow the directions given for 12c on page 28. Use Line 4 of 16a to determine beginning and ending *gwam*.

Goals:

12–14 *gwam*, acceptable
15–17 *gwam*, good
18–19 *gwam*, very good
20+ *gwam*, excellent

all figures learned

		words in line	gwam 30"	gwam 20"
1	Did the girl hang the 37 maps?	6	12	18
2	She paid Jane to turn the 71 dials.	7	14	21
3	I got 73 burlap panels to make the form.	8	16	24
4	Kent kept 17 worn keys to work the 17 panels.	9	18	27
5	Did they augment the 371 bushels of corn with rye?	10	20	30
6	I did visit a neighbor at 1737 Iris Lane on May 7.	10	20	30
7	Dismantle the 37 chairs in the shanty at 173 Palm.	10	20	30

| 1 | 2 | 3 | 4 | 5 | 6 | 7 | 8 | 9 | 10 |

16d ▶ 7
Improve figure response patterns

each line once DS; repeat Lines 2, 4, and 6

Technique hint:
Control your reading speed. Read only slightly ahead of what you are typing.

all figures learned

1 Flight 371 left Miami at 3:17 on Monday, March 31.

2 *Bill 731 was for 71 boxes of No. 33 bailing brads.*

3 Rico counted 3,711 cartons containing 7,317 tools.

4 *Send Nan 731 No. 3 nails for her home at 771 Anne.*

5 On May 31, Eva drove 373 miles to Denver in Van 7.

6 *Max put 71 extra boxes in the annex at 3731 Parks.*

16e ▶ 8
Improve keystroking technique

once as shown; repeat if time permits

all letters used

1ct finger
1 Bob Mugho hunted for five minutes for your number.
2 Juan hit the bright green turf with his five iron.

2d finger
3 Kind, decent acts can decidedly reduce skepticism.
4 Kim, not Mickey, had rice with chicken for dinner.

3d/4th fingers
5 You will write quickly: Zeus, Apollo, and Xerxes.
6 Who saw Polly? Max Voe saw her; she is quiet now.

| 1 | 2 | 3 | 4 | 5 | 6 | 7 | 8 | 9 | 10 |

17

17a ▶ 7
Preparatory practice

each line twice SS (slowly, then faster); DS between 2-line groups; repeat selected lines if time permits

alphabet 1 Roz Groves just now packed my box with five quail.

b 2 Barb, not Bob, will buy the new bonds at the bank.

figures 3 Try Model 3717 with 7 panels or Model 1733 with 3.

easy 4 Their problems may end when they audit the profit.

| 1 | 2 | 3 | 4 | 5 | 6 | 7 | 8 | 9 | 10 |

DS→

6. I consent to the photographing or televising of the operations or procedures to be performed, including appropriate portions of my body, for medical, scientific, or educational purposes, provided my identity is not revealed by the pictures or by descriptive texts accompanying them.

SS

DS→

7. For the purpose of advancing medical education, I consent to the admittance of observers to the operating room.

SS

DS→

8. I consent to the disposal by hospital authorities of any tissues or body parts which may be removed.

SS

(Center)

TS

(CROSS OUT ANY PARAGRAPHS NOT APPLICABLE)

TS

(Begin at center point) → Signed _____

(Patient or authorized person)

SS

Witness _____

DS Date _____

SS

Move to left margin

Check hospital

_____ Community

_____ Evanston

_____ Saint Francis

Job 7
Composing a memorandum
(LM p. 141)

Mr. Moss asks you to compose a memo from Dr. Rosenbloom to all staff physicians. Notify them that the new patient consent forms will be available after March 10. Ask them to use only the new forms after March 10. They should destroy all copies of the old forms after they receive the new ones. Date the memo March 4.

17b ▶ 16
Learn new keyreaches: 8 4 0

Follow the "Standard procedure for learning new keyreaches" on page 10 (Lines 1–6 twice; Lines 7–10 once; repeat 7–10 if time permits).

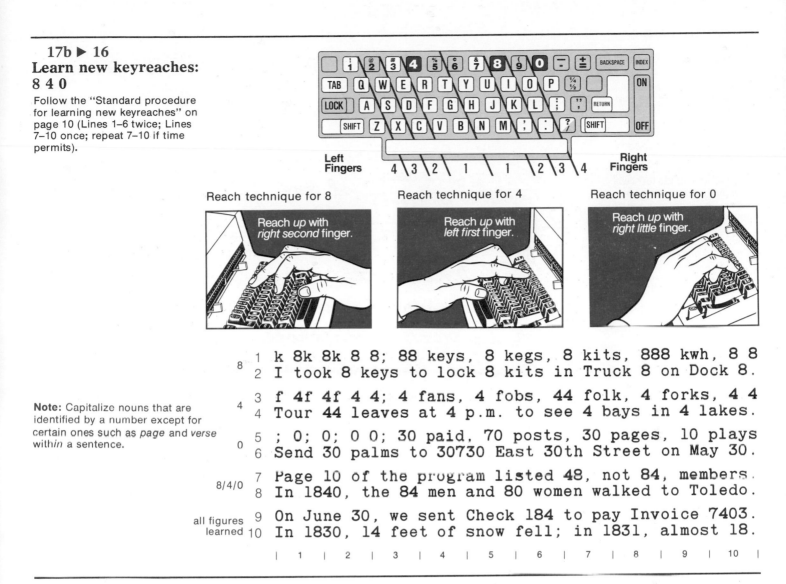

Left Fingers 4 3 2 1 1 2 3 4 Right Fingers

Reach technique for 8
Reach *up* with *right second* finger.

Reach technique for 4
Reach *up* with *left first* finger.

Reach technique for 0
Reach *up* with *right little* finger.

8
1 k 8k 8k 8 8; 88 keys, 8 kegs, 8 kits, 888 kwh, 8 8
2 I took 8 keys to lock 8 kits in Truck 8 on Dock 8.

4
3 f 4f 4f 4 4; 4 fans, 4 fobs, 44 folk, 4 forks, 4 4
4 Tour 44 leaves at 4 p.m. to see 4 bays in 4 lakes.

Note: Capitalize nouns that are identified by a number except for certain ones such as *page* and *verse* within a sentence.

0
5 ; 0; 0; 0 0; 30 paid, 70 posts, 30 pages, 10 plays
6 Send 30 palms to 30730 East 30th Street on May 30.

8/4/0
7 Page 10 of the program listed 48, not 84, members.
8 In 1840, the 84 men and 80 women walked to Toledo.

all figures learned
9 On June 30, we sent Check 184 to pay Invoice 7403.
10 In 1830, 14 feet of snow fell; in 1831, almost 18.

| 1 | 2 | 3 | 4 | 5 | 6 | 7 | 8 | 9 | 10 |

17c ▶ 7
Improve figure response patterns

each line once DS; repeat Lines 2, 4, and 6

all figures learned

1 I live at 418 East Street, not at 418 Easy Street.
2 Memorize pages 137 to 148; omit pages 140 and 141.
3 Tours 478 and 4781 travel to 10 cities in 30 days.
4 Cy will be 18 on May 30; Jo, 17 on May 4 or May 7.
5 English 348 meets in Room 710 at 10 a.m. each day.
6 Memo 7481 says 7 pads and 8 pens were sent May 30.

17d ▶ 8
Improve keystroking technique

each line twice SS; DS between 3-line groups; repeat if time permits

adjacent reaches
1 Teresa knew well that her opinion of art was good.

direct reaches
2 Herb Brice must hunt for my checks; he is in debt.

double letters
3 Anne stopped off at school to see Bill Wiggs cook.

long words
4 Debate concerned parochialism versus universalism.

| 1 | 2 | 3 | 4 | 5 | 6 | 7 | 8 | 9 | 10 |

Mr. Moss has just received a handwritten draft of the new consent form from Dr. Rosenbloom. She wants this form to be prepared in final form today. You are asked to prepare this form on one page; use 1" margins for top and sides so that the form will fit on one page. Follow Mr. Moss's notations on the draft copy.

CONSENT TO OPERATION, ANESTHETICS, AND OTHER MEDICAL SERVICES

DS { 1. I authorize the performance upon

←24 spaces

(myself or patient) of the following operation

←39 spaces to be per-

(state nature and extent of operation)

formed by Dr. _____. ←25 spaces

DS→ 2. I consent to the performance of

SS { operations and procedures in addition to or different from those now contemplated arising from presently unforeseen conditions which the above-named doctor may consider necessary or advisable in the course of the operation.

DS→ 3. I consent to the administration of

SS { such anesthetics as may be considered necessary or advisable by the physician responsible for this service.

DS→ 4. The nature and purpose of the

SS { operation, possible alternative methods of treatment, the risks involved, the possible consequences, and the possibility of complications have been explained to me.

DS→ 5. I acknowledge that no guarantee

SS { or assurance has been given by anyone as to the results that may be obtained.

(Job 6 continued on page 363)

17e ▶ 12
Improve keyboarding continuity

1 Practice the ¶ once for orientation.

2 Take three 30″ writings (30″ *gwam* = words typed × 2).

3 Take three 1′ writings.

4 Determine *gwam*.

Goal: *At least* 14 *gwam*.

Difficulty index

all letters/figures learned | E | 1.2 si | 5.1 awl | 90% hfw

Why did we not all realize that July 17 was a hot day? For 30 days, still summer air had closed in on us. Just to move was an effort; but here we stood, 48 quite excited people, planning our trek.

18

18a ▶ 7
Preparatory practice

each line twice SS (slowly, then faster); DS between 2-line groups; repeat selected lines if time permits

alphabet **1** One judge saw five boys quickly fix the prize elm.

p/x **2** Dixie, please have Pam fix the tax forms Hope has.

figures **3** Is it Channel 3, 8, or 10? Was the score 14 to 7?

easy **4** The girl may enamel the chair for the town chapel.

| 1 | 2 | 3 | 4 | 5 | 6 | 7 | 8 | 9 | 10 |

18b ▶ 16
Learn new keyreaches: 6 2 / (diagonal)

Follow the "Standard procedure for learning new keyreaches" on page 10 (Lines 1–6 twice; Lines 7–10 once; repeat 7–10 if time permits).

Reach technique for 6 — Reach *up* with *right first* finger.

Reach technique for 2 — Reach *up* with *left third* finger.

Reach technique for / — Reach *down* to / with *right little* finger

6 **1** j 6j 6j 6 6; 6 jobs, 6 jugs, 66 jays, 6 jokes, 6 6
2 On July 6, 66 jumpers made 6 jumps of over 6 feet.

2 **3** s 2s 2s 2 2; 2 skis, 2 sons, 22 sites, has 2 signs
4 On May 2, Car 222 delivered 22 tons of No. 2 sand.

/ **5** ; /; /; / /; 1/3; and/or; 4/7/84; 4/14; 8 1/3; / /
6 Type these mixed fractions: 1 3/8; 4 4/7; 1 3/14.

6/2/diag. **7** On May 26, I ordered 2 2/6 yards, not 6 2/6 yards.
8 The recorder, Model 226/62, Serial 626/A, is mine.

all figures **9** Aida was 21 on 3/7/80. Bill will be 21 on 4/6/87.
learned **10** The terms for Invoice 7867/3 are 4/10, 2/30, n/60.

| 1 | 2 | 3 | 4 | 5 | 6 | 7 | 8 | 9 | 10 |

with time and is a result of swelling in this area. Avoid kissing or pursing the lips for the first week. Lipstick can be put on with a brush. When brushing your upper teeth, be careful not to hurt the tissues of the upper lip; overzealous brushing in this area may produce pain and, therefore, is a signal to stop.

EYEGLASSES. Wearing your eyeglasses before six weeks may lead to distortion of the nasal bones. Taping your eyeglasses to your forehead so that they do not rest on your nose is acceptable for those who need eyeglasses to see. Contact lenses can usually be worn the day following surgery.

NASAL CLEANING. Only after the first week can you clean the nostril area. You can use cotton swabs soaked in 3 percent hydrogen peroxide. If done properly, you will have no pain associated with nasal cleaning.

TEMPERATURE. Your temperature should not go above 38.6° C (100°F). If your temperature rises above this limit, contact my office.

SKIN CARE. The skin of the nose and the midface area is usually oily for about one month. Wash this area frequently to avoid pimple infection. Eyebrow plucking should be avoided for two weeks.

INJURY TO NOSE. Please report hard blows to your nose or blows in which your nose bleeds. Four weeks are required before your nose becomes solid enough to withstand moderate trauma. After two weeks, minor trauma should have no effect on moving the nasal bones out of position. Sweaters and T-shirts should not be worn for two weeks, unless the neck opening is sufficiently large not to bump the nose.

Job 5
Composing a memorandum
(LM p. 141)
Dr. Rosenbloom wants all staff physicians to be informed about the new postoperative nasal surgery information sheet. Therefore, Mr. Moss asks you to prepare a memorandum from Dr. Rosenbloom to the staff physicians informing them of this new information sheet. Tell them that it will be available for distribution and use by March 10. Also, inform the staff that they may see a copy in Dr. Rosenbloom's office before next week's distribution. Date the memo March 3.

RESUMPTION OF ACTIVITIES. Rough contact sports must be avoided for four months. Jogging, diving, and waterskiing should be avoided for two months. In any sport (e.g., hockey) in which a major blow to the nose or face can occur, a protective mask should be worn.

HAIR WASHING. If a cast is used, delay hair washing until after the cast has been removed. You should also avoid hot water and hair dryers for two weeks, as they may aggravate the swelling. The use of dry shampoo is recommended when you clean your hair.

DEPRESSION. Some patients feel depressed for two or three days after surgery. Depression is a normal reaction resulting from the bruising and swelling, but it usually passes quickly.

18c ▶ 13
Compare skill: sentences

1 Take a 1' writing on Line 1; de-termine *gwam* and use this score for your goal as you take two 1' writings on Line 2 and two on Line 3.

2 Take a 1' writing on Line 4; de-termine *gwam* and use this score for your goal as you take two 1' writings on Line 5 and two on Line 6.

Goal: To have rates on Lines 2 and 3 and Lines 5 and 6 equal those on Lines 1 and 4.

words in line

1 Did the men enamel emblems on big panels downtown? 10

2 Pay the men to fix a pen for 38 ducks and 47 hens. 10

3 *They blame the chaos in the city on the big quake.* 10

4 Did the amendment name a city auditor to the firm? 10

5 He owns 20 maps of the 16 towns on the big island. 10

6 *Dian may make cocoa for the girls when they visit.* 10

18d ▶ 5
Proofread/revise as you keyboard

each line once DS; correct circled errors as you keyboard; read carefully

1 Court will not (ve) in session again until (august) 6.

2 Put more grass (sede) on the lawn at 307 Elm (Strett).

3 A team is (madeup) of 11 men; 12 were on (t he) field.

4 Liza and/or Dion (willldirect) the choir on (Tuseday).

5 (Theer) were (abuot) 10 or 11 pictures in the gallery.

18e ▶ 9
Improve keyboarding continuity

1 Practice the ¶ once for orienta-tion.

2 Take three 30" writings.

3 Take three 1' writings.

4 Determine *gwam*.

Goal: *At least 14 gwam.*

Difficulty index

all letters/figures learned	E	1.2 si	5.1 awl	90% hfw

Volume 27 is quite heavy. Its weight must be in excess of 10 pounds; yet I realize the only way to complete this type of job is to study 164 pages of Chapter 183 and all of the art in the big book.

Job 4
Job 4
Information sheet
(plain sheets)

Dr. Rosenbloom has just made the final changes on the new postoperative nasal surgery information sheet. Mr. Moss has asked you to prepare it in final form. The format of this information sheet should follow the un-bound manuscript style as far as margins and second–page numbers are concerned. Mr. Moss asks you to use in-verted paragraphs for the body of the information sheet. Show the paragraph headings in ALL CAPS flush with the left margin. Indent all lines except the first in each paragraph 10 spaces from the left margin. Remember, each paragraph should be single–spaced with double spacing between paragraphs. The main heading is:

POSTOPERATIVE NASAL SURGERY INFORMATION

SWELLING. Most of the swelling is gone within two weeks in the majority of patients. The avoidance of lift-ing and bending will help to minimize the swelling. Swelling may also be reduced if you sleep with your head propped up at a 45-degree angle. The swelling around the eyes is often worse on the second day, especially if you lie flat during the night.

DISCOLORATION. You must remember discoloration is tem-porary. The amount of discoloration will vary from patient to patient and is dependent mostly on the amount of surgery needed, the thinness of your skin, and also your tendency to small vessel bleeding.

NOSEBLEEDS AND DISCHARGE. Blood will not likely come from your nose in the postoperative healing period if you avoid all strenuous physical activity inside or outside the home for ten days. This includes such items as exercise and lifting that tend to increase body temperature and blood pressure. There is, however, a bloody mucous discharge that comes from the nose. You must not dab the bottom of the nose, since this may produce a poorer functional and cosmetic result. If you do have a nosebleed, put chipped ice--in a plastic bag--on the bridge of your nose for 15 minutes. If the nosebleed does not stop, please telephone my office or go directly to the hospital where you had the operation.

NASAL BLOCKAGE. Your nose is not usually packed; but if it is, the packing will be removed in the early post-operative period as soon as medically advisable. Inside your nose is a surgical swelling which pro-duces nasal obstruction forcing you to mouth-breathe. Mouth-breathing may give you a dry mouth and throat and cause discomfort. Sips of fluids, hard candies, and mouthwash will be helpful. The nasal blockage usually starts to resolve in two weeks. You should not use any vasoconstrictive spray unless especially instructed to do so.

PAIN. Although there is little pain associated with nasal surgery, there may be pressure and discomfort occasionally that require some medication. A non-prescription drug is useful; but if a stronger drug is required, it will be given to you at the time of hospital discharge.

WEAKNESS. Lightheadedness and cold sweats are quite com-mon in the early postoperative course. These condi-tions will usually clear up without medication.

UPPER LIP DIFFICULTIES. If much surgery has been done at the base of your nose, the upper lip will be stiff and your smile will look strange. This will pass

(Job continued on page 361)

19a ▶ 7

Preparatory practice

each line twice SS (slowly, then faster); DS between 2-line groups; repeat selected lines if time permits

Space once after a question mark when the question is incomplete.

alphabet	1	Mavis Zeff worked quickly on the next big project.
q/?	2	Can you spell queue? quay? aqua? quavered? acquit?
figures	3	If 24 of the 87 boys go on May 10, 63 will remain.
easy	4	Fit the lens at a right angle and fix the problem.

| 1 | 2 | 3 | 4 | 5 | 6 | 7 | 8 | 9 | 10 |

19b ▶ 16

Learn new keyreaches: 9 5 - (hyphen) -- (dash)

Follow the "Standard procedure for learning new keyreaches" on page 10 (Lines 1–6 twice; Lines 7–11 once; repeat 7–11 if time permits).

Hyphen, dash: The hyphen is used to join closely related words or word parts. Striking the hyphen twice results in a dash--a symbol that shows sharp separation or interruption of thought.

Reach technique for 9

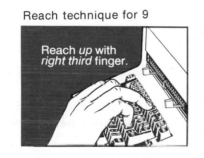
Reach *up* with *right third* finger.

Reach technique for 5

Reach *up* with *left first* finger.

Reach technique for –

Reach *up* to - with *right little* finger.

9
1 l 9l 9l 9 9; 9 left, 9 lost, 9 loans, sell 99 lots
2 On May 9, 99 buyers offered 99 bids for 999 lambs.

5
3 f 5f 5f 5 5; 5 fish, 5 fans, 5 forms, for 55 firms
4 At 5 p.m., the 55 cars, 55 vans, and 5 jeeps left.

-
5 ; -; -; - -- co-op; top-rate; in-depth; up-to-date
6 Use a 5-inch line--50 pica spaces--for lines 1-10.

9/5/-
7 We--all 59 of us--have read pages 59, 95, and 595.
8 All 95 girls--5 did not attend--voted on Item 599.

all figures/ symbols learned
9 Of 13,687 ex-workers, 2,481--or 9/50--had retired.
10 Invoice 347/8--it is dated 2/9, not 2/10--is here.
11 Do Problems 2-27, 8-35, and/or 16-42 before May 9.

| 1 | 2 | 3 | 4 | 5 | 6 | 7 | 8 | 9 | 10 |

Job 3
Operative report
(LM p. 139)

One of the other medical as–sistants prepared a draft copy of an operative report last Friday. Dr. Rosenbloom made the final corrections on it this morning, and Mr. Moss asks you to prepare it in final form for the patient's file.

E.N.T. Medical Services

OPERATIVE REPORT

Name: Carlos X. Biaz   Case No.: 283763

Date of Surgery: March 3, 19--

Preoperative Diagnosis: Esophageal web

Postoperative Diagnosis: Esophageal web with cardiospasm

Operation: esophagoscopy and dilatation

Surgeon: S. T. Rosenbloom, M.D.

PROCEDURE: A general endotracheal anesthesia was given to the patient. A 9-mm. esophagoscope was passed into the esophagus. A slight fibrous constriction of the cervical esophagus was noted. The passage of the esophagoscope corrected this very easily. Otherwise, the esophagus appeared to be normal until about 10 to 15 cm. below the incisor line. The lower esophageal musculature at the cardioesophageal juncture appeared to have a fairly marked spasm. A No. 10 bougie was able to pass through this juncture, but the esophagoscope did not enter the stomach. A nominal amount of bleeding occurred after bougienage. After removal of the 9-mm. esophagoscope, an 8-mm. esophagoscope was used with similar results. No additional lesions were seen. The esophagoscope was removed from the patient, and he left the operating room in good condition.

19c ▶ 7
Improve figure response patterns

each line twice SS; DS between 2-line groups

Technique hint:
Work for continuity. Avoid any pause before or after figures.

all figures used

1 Send immediately 30 Solex cubes, Catalog No. 2748.

2 As of 6/28, your new extension number will be 375.

3 Reserve for me Tape 640. My identification: 819.

4 Date of call: 2/7. Time: 3:30 p.m. No message.

5 Top individual score: 87. Top team average: 46.

19d ▶ 5
Proofread/revise as you keyboard

each line once DS; correct circled errors as you keyboard; read carefully

1 Erin had (s) size 11/12 dress, but it was (two) large.

2 The figure he wrote--475-0 is not a correct answer o

3 All that snow--(mroe) than 5 (feat)--kept her at home.

4 Edna says 936 Valley (Rode) is (here) new home address.

5 He scored 80 on the first (test;he) must do (bet ter).

19e ▶ 5
Improve keystroking technique

each line twice SS; DS between 2-line groups

bottom row 1 Zach, check the menu; next, beckon the lazy valet.

home row 2 Sal was glad she had a flashlight; Al was as glad.

third row 3 Powell quit their outfit to try out for our troop.

| 1 | 2 | 3 | 4 | 5 | 6 | 7 | 8 | 9 | 10 |

19f ▶ 10
Improve keyboarding continuity

1 Practice the ¶ once for orientation.
2 Take three 30" writings.
3 Take three 1' writings.
Goal: *At least 14 gwam.*

Technique hint:
Work with confidence. Set your own "comfortable" rate and try to maintain it.

Difficulty index

| all letters/figures used | E | 1.2 si | 5.1 awl | 90% hfw |

Think with me back to a quite cold morning in

1984. It was just 7:50; I opened my door to leave

for work. Little did I realize that snow had been

expected--2/3 foot of it. I live at 6 Summer Way.

Job 2
Ear, nose, throat examination report
(plain sheet)

Dr. Rosenbloom prepared the E.N.T. examination form last week and placed the hand-written copy in the patient's file folder. Mr. Moss discovered that this report had not been finalized and asks you to prepare it in final form for the patient's file.

E.N.T. MEDICAL SERVICES

EAR, NOSE, AND THROAT EXAMINATION

NAME: Carlos X. Biaz CASE NO.: 283763

DATE: March 2, 19-- SEX: Male AGE: 27

EXAMINING PHYSICIAN: Susan T. Rosenbloom, M.D.

RIGHT EAR: External canal clear. Drum membrane intact. No evidence of suppuration. Hearing, 20/20. Eustachian tube patent.

LEFT EAR: External canal clear. Drum membrane intact. No evidence of suppuration. Hearing, 20/20. Eustachian tube patent.

NOSE: No evidence of obstruction, discharge, or polyps. Nasal septum approximately .5 cm to the right of midline. Turbinate bones normal in size and color.

THROAT: No tonsils. Mucous membrane abnormal in color and size. Evidence of pathology noted.

LARYNX: Epiglottis and ventricular bands normal. Both vocal cords appeared normal in size and color.

DIAGNOSIS: Esophageal web

COMMENT: Recommend an esophagoscopy and dilation procedure be performed.

20

Learning goals

1 To set margins.

2 To determine line endings using the warning bell.

3 To center copy horizontally and vertically.

4 To divide words at line endings.

5 To type short reports and an–nouncements.

Machine adjustments

1 Set paper guide at 0.

2 Set ribbon control to type on upper half of ribbon.

3 Use a 60–space line (center point −30; center point +30).

4 SS drills; DS paragraphs; indent first line of ¶ 5 spaces.

5 Insert half sheets long side first, unless otherwise directed.

20a ▶ 7

Preparatory practice

each line twice SS (slowly, then faster); DS between 2-line groups; repeat selected lines if time permits

alphabet 1 Freda Jencks will have money to buy six quite large topazes.

o/i 2 We take action from our position to avoid spoiling our soil.

figures 3 The 26 clerks checked Items 37 and 189 on pages 145 and 150.

easy 4 She bid by proxy for eighty bushels of a corn and rye blend.

| 1 | 2 | 3 | 4 | 5 | 6 | 7 | 8 | 9 | 10 | 11 | 12 |

20b ▶ 15

Learn to establish margin widths

study copy at right; then do the drills below

Margin release (31)
If the carrier locks, depress the margin release key with the little finger and complete the line.

Know your machine: margin stops

Typewriters (and other keyboarding machines) are usually equipped with one of two type sizes: pica or elite (some with both). Pica (10-pitch) is the larger—10 pica spaces fill a horizontal inch. Paper 8½ inches wide will accommodate 85 pica characters and spaces. Center point for pica type is 42 when left edge of paper is inserted at 0 on line-of-writing scale.

Elite (12-pitch) type is smaller—12 elite spaces fill a horizontal inch. Paper 8½ inches wide will accommodate 102 elite characters and spaces. Center point for elite type is 51 when left edge of paper is at 0 on line-of-writing scale.

Equal margin widths can be had either by (1) setting margin stops an equal distance in inches or spaces from extreme right and left edges of paper or by (2) setting the margin stops an equal distance right and left from center point. In lessons that follow, the second procedure will be used.

Drill 1

exact 60–space line (center − 30; center + 30); DS; make one copy, line for line

Note: A warning bell will sound as you approach the end of each line; listen for it.

If the margins are set correctly, if the paper guide is set at 0, and if you have made no mistakes which affect line length, each of these paragraphs can be typed with right and left margins which are exactly equal in width to each other.

| 1 | 2 | 3 | 4 | 5 | 6 | 7 | 8 | 9 | 10 | 11 | 12 |

Drill 2

exact 50–space line (center − 25; center + 25); DS; make one copy, line for line

If it is not already obvious to you, you will soon find that, while the left edge of a paragraph is even, the evenness on the right edge depends on your ability to decide where and how to end lines.

| 1 | 2 | 3 | 4 | 5 | 6 | 7 | 8 | 9 | 10 |

Preparatory practice

each line 3 times SS (slowly, faster, slowly); DS between 3-line groups; retype selected lines as time permits

alphabet	1	Jorge Willman said to be here at five or six to take the physics quiz.
fig/sym	2	The 8 saucers were $28.56 ($3.57 ea.); 9 cups were $12.60 ($1.40 ea.).
shift key	3	Pamela, Max, Nancy, and Lane ate at Tooele's Club Fourteen Restaurant.
fluency	4	The man paid my neighbor for eight turkeys and eighty bushels of corn.

| 1 | 2 | 3 | 4 | 5 | 6 | 7 | 8 | 9 | 10 | 11 | 12 | 13 | 14 |

203b-208b ▶ 45

Office job simulation

(LM pp. 137–147)

Mr. Moss, the Office Manager, orients you to your new job. He explains that a typical day in a medical office requires an office assistant to perform a variety of jobs. He also informs you that the completion of assigned tasks promptly and accurately is particularly important in any health care service field. A patient's record must be up to date in order to provide the physician with all pertinent information needed to make health care decisions.

Most of the medical reports are either completed by the physician in handwriting or dictated on voice recording equipment. The normal procedure is to prepare in final form any handwritten reports; however, prepare a draft copy of any dictated material and then have the physician make any desired corrections before the final copy is prepared.

Mr. Moss will assign you one job at a time. Upon completion of each job, he will give you another job to do.

Job 1

Letter (LM p. 137)

Mr. Moss asks you to prepare in final form this draft of a letter that Dr. Rosenbloom has corrected.

March 1, 19--

Ruth Anne Collins, M.D.
2352 Dawndale Avenue
Evanston, IL 60201-3333

Dear Dr. Collins:

Ms. Carolyn V. Constantine, your referral patient, was seen by me for the first time on January 3. The complaint was a severe tinnitus in both ears.

¶ A complete ear examination was made and the results were as follows: the right ear hearing was 15/20; the left ear, 13/30. Her Rinne was negative for tuning forks. The audiogram was made which indicated substantial loss of the higher tones. Mrs. Constantine's decreased hearing and severe tinnitus in both ears are caused by the beginning degeneration of her hearing nerve. This conclusion is supported by the audiometric and clinical research findings. Her present hearing problem has been caused by very loud noises at her place of employment.

¶ I have been providing treatment for her for the past 6 weeks, and her hearing has not improved. Her tinnitus also persists.

Sincerely,

Susan T. Rosenbloom, M.D.
Director

20c ▶ 5
Learn to use the backspacer and the margin release

exact 50-space line

Backspacer (20)

Use a quick, light stroke with the little finger. Depress the key firmly for repeated backspace action on an electric or electronic typewriter.

1 At the left margin of your paper, type the first word as it appears in the list at the right.

2 After typing the word, backspace and fill in the missing letter v.

3 Return, then repeat the procedure with each of the remaining words on the list.

lea e

har est

o ens

oli es

sa ings

Left Fingers 4 3 2 1 1 2 3 4 **Right Fingers**

Margin Release (31)

1 Before typing the sentence below, depress the margin release with the little finger and backspace 5 spaces into the left margin.

2 Type the sentence. When the carrier locks, depress the margin release and complete the line.

My typed work should be done neatly, correctly, and quickly.

20d ▶ 13
Learn to end lines

study copy at right; then do Drills 1 and 2

Know your machine: line ending warning bell

Margin stops cause the machine to lock at the point at which they are set. To bypass the lock, you must use the margin release (31), a time-consuming operation if used often.

Lines of a paragraph automatically align at the left margin, but they do not automatically align at the right margin. It is necessary, therefore, that the operator or typist ends lines at the right as evenly as possible.

To help you know when to end a line, a warning bell sounds 7 to 12 spaces before the margin stop is reached. Most typists find that a warning of 5 or 6 spaces (a half inch) is adequate to maintain a fairly even righthand margin. Thus, after setting margins for an exact line length, they move the right margin set 5 or 6 spaces farther to the right.

To use this procedure, set margin stops for an exact line length (50, 60, or 70 spaces); then move the right margin set another 5 or 6 spaces to the right. Doing so allows you to: (1) end a short word or (2) divide a longer one within 5 or 6 spaces after the bell rings.

Drill 1

full sheet; begin on Line 10; DS copy

1 Set exact 60-space line.

2 Move right margin stop 5 or 6 spaces farther to the right.

3 Read the ¶ at the bottom of this page. Then, as you type it, listen for the bell. When it sounds, complete the word you are typing; return immediately. If the machine locks on a long word, operate the margin release, complete the word, and return.

Your typed line endings will not match those in the textbook.

Drill 2

1 After typing Drill 1, return twice.

2 Set machine for a 50-space line with appropriate right margin bell adjustment.

3 Retype the ¶; follow the directions in Step 3 of Drill 1.

When the bell sounds, you must decide just where to end that line and begin a new one. If the word you are typing as the bell rings can be finished within 5 letters, finish it. If it takes more, you may need to divide it. You will learn soon how and when to divide words.

Learning goals

1 To develop knowledge and skill in preparing medical reports and documents.
2 To become familiar with the many administrative support functions within a medical office.

Machine adjustments

1 Set paper guide at *0*.
2 Set ribbon control to use upper half of ribbon.
3 Set line–space selector for SS.
4 Margins: 70–space line for drills; 1" top and side margins for medical reports; as directed for other jobs.

Office Job Simulation

Read carefully the material at the right before you begin the work of Section 45. Note any standard procedures that you think will save you time during the completion of the medical office jobs.

Daily practice plan:

Preparatory practice .... 5'
Work on simulation .... 45'

Work Assignment

You have been assigned by Office Service Temporaries, Inc., to work as a medical office assistant at E.N.T. Medical Services, 1059 Sheridan Road, Evanston, IL 60202-3338. This medical office specializes in ears, nose, and throat cases. E.N.T. Medical Services is a large partnership of 15 physicians, including a pathologist and radiologist. Dr. Susan T. Rosenbloom is the Director of the firm; her regular office assistant is on vacation this week, and you have been hired as a temporary replacement. Most of your work will be for Dr. Rosenbloom; however, all your work will be assigned to you by Reginald R. Moss, the Office Manager.

When a job requires unusual specifications, E.N.T. Medical Services provides them in the "Excerpts from the Medical Office Manual." E.N.T. Medical Services has based its office procedures on COLLEGE KEYBOARDING/TYPEWRITING; therefore, use your textbook as a reference guide for all matters of style and placement. Proofread and correct all errors before removing the paper from the machine.

Excerpts from the Medical Office Manual

Medical Reports. Most medical reports are prepared on preprinted forms.

If a preprinted form is not available, prepare the medical report on plain sheets; follow the illustration below as a general style guide. For medical reports prepared on plain sheets, leave 1" top and side margins on all pages. Leave *at least* a 1" bottom margin for all pages. Center and type the main heading in ALL CAPS and triple-space to the pertinent summary information concerning the patient. Double-space the patient summary information, including the title of the examination, the patient's name, case number, date, sex, age, and name(s) of appropriate physician(s). Triple-space below the patient summary information to the body of the report.

The body of all medical reports should be single-spaced with a double space between paragraphs. Captioned headings in ALL CAPS followed by a colon introduce general topics or areas of examination.

Other Reports. Prepare all other reports as you would a regular business report, following the basic format of an unbound, topbound, or leftbound report.

Letters. Use modified block style with mixed punctuation and indented paragraphs. Close all letters with the name of the person signing the letter, followed on the next line by the person's official title. Prepare *one* carbon copy for the file. Address an envelope for each letter.

```
                              1"

                    E.N.T. MEDICAL SERVICES
                                    TS
         EAR, NOSE, AND THROAT EXAMINATION
         NAME:  Carlos X. Biaz                    CASE NO.:  283763
  1"     DATE:  March 2, 19--      SEX:  Male          AGE:  27      1"
         EXAMINING PHYSICIAN:  Susan T. Rosenbloom, M.D.
                                              TS
         RIGHT EAR:  External canal clear.  Drum membrane intact.  No evi-
         dence of suppuration.  Hearing, 20/20.  Eustachian tube patent.
```

Medical report on plain sheet

20e ▶ 10
Learn to divide words

half sheet; insert (with long side up) to Line 9

1 Read the ¶; it explains basic rules for dividing words.

2 Use a 60–space line, ad–justed for bell warning.

3 As you type, listen for the bell. Complete or divide words as appropriate for a fairly even right margin.

As long as certain guides are observed, words may be divided in order to keep line lengths nearly even. For example, always divide a word between its syllables; as, care-less. Words of one syllable, however long, may not be divided, nor should short words --such as often--of five or fewer letters. The separation of a one- or two-letter syllable, as in likely or across, from the rest of a word must also be avoided.

21a ▶ 7
Preparatory practice

60-space line; each line twice SS (slowly, then faster)

Note: Line 3 has two ALL–CAP items. To type them, find the shift lock (27); depress the key with the left little finger; type the item; release the lock by striking either shift key.

alphabet	1	Jessie Quick belicved the campaign frenzy would be exciting.
figures	2	The 2 buyers checked Items 10, 15, 27, 36, and 48 on page 9.
shift/lock	3	Titles of reports are shown in ALL CAPS; as, DIVIDING WORDS.
easy	4	Did they fix the problem of the torn panel and worn element?

| 1 | 2 | 3 | 4 | 5 | 6 | 7 | 8 | 9 | 10 | 11 | 12 |

21b ▶ 9
Learn to use the warning bell

half sheet; DS; begin on Line 9; 60-space line

Listen for the bell as you type. Make decisions about line endings. Avoid looking at the paper or typewriter as you type.

Learning to use a keyboard is worth our efforts. Few of us do so for the sheer joy of it. When most people type, they have a goal in mind--they want something in return. If we send a letter, we expect a reply--at least a reaction. If it is a job that we are doing for someone, we want approval--maybe payment. If it is for school, we hope for a top grade. What we get, though, will depend on what we give.

21c ▶ 9
Learn to center lines horizontally (side to side)

Drill 1

half sheet; DS; begin on Line 16

1 Insert paper (long side up) with left edge at 0.

2 Move each margin stop to its end of the scale. Clear all tab stops; set a new stop at center point of the page (elite, 51; pica, 42).

3 From center point, backspace once for each two letters, figures, spaces, or punctuation marks in the line.

4 Do not backspace for an odd or leftover stroke at the end of the line.

5 Begin to type where you com–plete the backspacing.

6 Complete the line; return; tab to center point. Type subsequent line in the same way.

Drill 2

half sheet; DS; begin on Line 14; center each line

Drill 1

LEARN TO CENTER LINES

Horizontally--Side to Side

Drill 2

You are invited

to attend the opening

of the new

JONES PUBLIC LIBRARY

Monday, May 3, 10 a.m.

**Build straight-copy
skill**

1 Two 1′ writings for accuracy on each ¶.
2 Two 5′ writings for accuracy on all ¶s com-
bined. Record *gwam* and
number of errors (LM
p. 3).

Difficulty index

all letters used	A	1.5 si	5.7 awl	80% hfw

gwam 1′ | 5′

Every administrator should try to cut the cost of preparing letters 14 | 3
and memos. There are many ways that an organization can reduce the cost 28 | 6
of correspondence; a few of these ways will be discussed at this time. 43 | 9
Perhaps the most efficient way to reduce correspondence costs is just to 57 | 11
write shorter letters. A shorter letter is more effective and takes less 72 | 14
time to prepare. Another way to trim costs is to ask executives to do 86 | 17
all of their dictation at one time; this should be accomplished quite 100 | 20
early in the day, if possible. If a secretary is used to take the dic- 114 | 23
tation, the time used during dictation is a dual expenditure--a cost of 129 | 26
both the executive's and secretary's time. 137 | 28

Form letters can play quite a major part in cutting the cost of 13 | 30
preparing letters and memos. Care needs to be taken to insure that all 27 | 33
form letters are properly prepared and are handy when the need arises. 42 | 36
Not only do form letters save the time of an executive, but the speed 56 | 39
with which a typist can draft a form letter is faster than transcribing 70 | 42
a dictated letter. Of course, many form letters can be prepared on an 84 | 44
electronic typewriter, which will not only type the letters faster than 99 | 47
a typist but will also type them more accurately. The use of preprinted 113 | 50
forms or postal cards for routine replies will cut costs considerably. 128 | 53
The office manager should determine which method of preparing correspon- 142 | 56
dence should be used. 146 | 57

There are many other ways to cut the cost of correspondence. When 13 | 60
it is appropriate, a secretary should be allowed to compose replies to 28 | 62
routine requests and correspondence; just this one item will save a 41 | 65
great deal of an executive's time and will result in a significant cost 56 | 68
savings. The key to cost reduction is planning and reorganizing; if 69 | 71
done properly, a lot of time and effort can be saved. All mail should 84 | 74
be answered the same day as received, if possible; but overtime costs 98 | 76
should not be incurred just to answer routine mail. When a better pro- 112 | 79
cedure is discovered, a long-range cost reduction will result, even if 126 | 82
an immediate cost increase is incurred while the new way is learned. 140 | 85

gwam 1′ | 1 | 2 | 3 | 4 | 5 | 6 | 7 | 8 | 9 | 10 | 11 | 12 | 13 | 14 |
5′ | | 1 | | | 2 | | | 3 | |

**Format a short report
on dividing words**

full sheet; 60-space
line; DS body; begin
on Line 10; TS below
heading; proofread
and circle errors

To TS when machine
is set for DS: DS,
then by hand turn
cylinder (platen) for-
ward one space.

1 Read the report carefully.

2 Center heading on
Line 10; then type the
report.

3 Listen for the warning
bell; decide quickly
about line endings.
Avoid looking up.

4 When finished, examine the margins criti-
cally; proofread your
copy and circle errors.

Proofreading. Con-
scientious keyboard
operators always
check carefully what
they have
keyboarded before
they remove the
paper from the
machine. They
proofread para-
graphs; that is, they
read them for *mean-
ing*, as if they had not
read them before.
They double-check
figures, proper
names, and uncer-
tain spellings against
the original or some
other source.

---

words

DIVIDING WORDS   3
TS

A word may be divided at the end of a line in order to keep   15
the margins as nearly equal in width as possible. Divided words,   28
of course, tend to be more difficult to read than undivided words;   41
so good judgment is needed. The following guides can help you   54
make sound decisions about word division.   62

Words that contain double consonants are usually divided be-   74
tween consonants; as, bal-lots. However, if a word that ends in   87
double letters has a suffix attached, divide after the double let-   100
ters; as, dress-ing or stuff-ing.   107

Words that contain an internal single-vowel syllable should   119
be divided after that syllable; as, miti-gate. If two internal   132
one-letter syllables occur consecutively in a word, divide between   145
them; as, situ-ation or gradu-ation.   153

Compound words that contain a hyphen should be divided only   165
at the hyphen; as, second-class. Compound words written without a   178
hyphen are best divided between the elements of the compound; as,   191
super-market.   194

Two final suggestions: Once you have decided to divide a   205
word, leave as much of that word as you can on the first line; that   219
way, a minimum of guesswork is required of the reader. Further,   232
when in doubt about how to divide a word, remember that a dictio-   245
nary is still the best friend a writer can have.   254

22a ▶ 7

Preparatory practice

60-space line; each line
twice SS (slowly, then
faster); DS between 2-line
groups

alphabet   1   Roxy waved as she did quick flying jumps on the trapeze bar.

shift
keys   2   Yang Woerman hopes Zoe Quigley can leave for Maine in March.

figures   3   Buy 25 boxes, 147 bags, 39 sacks, 68 cartons, and 10 crates.

easy   4   Did the girl make the ornament with fur, duck down, or hair?

| 1 | 2 | 3 | 4 | 5 | 6 | 7 | 8 | 9 | 10 | 11 | 12 |

202a ▶ 5
Preparatory practice

each line 3 times SS (slowly, faster, slowly); DS between 3-line groups; repeat selected lines as time permits

alphabet 1 My quest in Luvungi will be to find an oryx, zebra, hippo, and jackal.

fig/sym 2 We sold consignments #136 for $298 less 5% and #470 for $375 less 10%.

double letter 3 If you succeed in applying the wood filler, you will see good effects.

fluency 4 The panel may blame the firm for toxic clay by the quay on the island.

| 1 | 2 | 3 | 4 | 5 | 6 | 7 | 8 | 9 | 10 | 11 | 12 | 13 | 14 |

202b ▶ 10
Communication aid: capitalization/punctuation

1 Read the ¶ at the right. Type it with correct capitalization and punctuation.
2 Check your corrected ¶ with your teacher. If necessary, repeat the paragraph correcting any errors you made.
3 Take two 1' writings on your corrected copy.

gwam 1'

she remembered her feelings as precisely as she remembered the   13

sights smells and sounds around her as she sang each solo. the crowd   27

which contained a large number of college students had applauded her   41

enthusiastically she had shown no emotion but anxiety and a little   54

nervousness must have been hiding behind the all too cheerful mask   67

of her face.   70

202c ▶ 15
Build statistical-copy skill

1 Two 1' writings for speed on each ¶.
2 Two 3' writings for speed on both ¶s combined. Record gwam (LM p. 3).

Difficulty index

all letters/figures used | HA | 1.7 si | 6.0 awl | 75% hfw

gwam 1' 3'

Our real estate holdings in the area went up by 38 percent during   13 | 4 | 68

the previous fiscal year from $1,785,290 to $2,463,700. This sizable   27 | 9 | 73

increase resulted from the purchase of 15 residential lots ($139,600),   41 | 14 | 77

2 small farms ($298,200), and 1 factory site ($240,610). At the end   55 | 18 | 82

of last fiscal year, the total undeveloped real estate holdings was 70   69 | 23 | 87

percent, or $1,724,590. Included in this category were 13 small farms,   84 | 28 | 91

35 residential lots, and 6 factory sites.   92 | 31 | 94

In addition to the undeveloped real estate, we owned $739,110 of   13 | 35 | 99

developed property. A major segment of this real estate (80 percent or   27 | 40 | 103

$591,288) was fully renovated residential lots which included houses;   41 | 45 | 108

the remaining 20 percent ($147,822) was lots with other kinds of build-   55 | 49 | 113

ings on them that had most deficiencies fixed. There were 20 parcels   69 | 54 | 117

of property with houses and 5 with other buildings in this group. All   84 | 59 | 122

of the developed property was acquired prior to the last fiscal year.   97 | 63 | 127

gwam 1' | 1 | 2 | 3 | 4 | 5 | 6 | 7 | 8 | 9 | 10 | 11 | 12 | 13 | 14 |
3' | 1 | 2 | 3 | 4 | 5 |

22b ▶ 13
Review procedure for horizontal centering

half sheet (long side up); begin on Line 13; DS body; TS below heading; proofread and circle errors

1 Review steps for centering lines horizontally (see 21c).
2 Center each line of the announcement shown at right.

EASTERN HILLS GOLF CLUB
TS
Annual Awards Banquet

The Nineteenth Hole

October 10, 6:30 p.m.

22c ▶ 30
Learn to center copy vertically

half sheet

Study the guides for vertical centering given at the right; then format and type Problem 1 below and Problem 2 on p. 45.

Guides for vertical centering

1 Count all lines and blank line spaces required by the problem (1 blank line space between DS lines; 2 blank line spaces between TS lines).

Note. Both pica and elite type require 1″ for 6 lines of copy.

2 Subtract the total lines required by the problem from the number of lines on the paper (33, half sheet; 66, full sheet).

3 Divide the resulting number by 2 to determine number of lines to be left in top margin. *Disregard any fraction that may result from the division.*

4 From the top edge of the paper, space down 1 more than the number of lines figured for the top margin; begin typing on that line.

5 Center each line of the problem horizontally.

Calculation check

Lines available:	33
Lines required:	12
Lines remaining:	21
Top margin: (20 ÷ 2)	10
(Begin on Line 11)	

This procedure places copy in what is called "exact center."

Problem 1

```
1
2
3
4                              Center
5                                │
6                                │
7                                │
8                                │
9                                │
10                               ▼
11            HISAKO GIBSON HARROW
12                       TS
13
14      will read selections from her book
15                              DS
16            ONE GRAY MORNING
17
18      on Friday evening, August 9, at eight
19
20               in Benjamin Court
21
22        The Art Institute of Jersey City
23
24
25
26
27
28
29
30
31
32
33
```

201c ▶ 10
Improve keystroking precision

each line at least twice without error

left hand	1	The best rewards at a drag race are for the fast cars and eager crews.
right hand	2	I may lend you only my pink pumps, nylon kimono, jumper, or mink muff.
one hand	3	Only Edward Linny saw Lou Street win the awards at the bazaar in Lyon.
long words	4	On examination, an increase in polymorphonuclear leukocytes was shown.

| 1 | 2 | 3 | 4 | 5 | 6 | 7 | 8 | 9 | 10 | 11 | 12 | 13 | 14 |

201d ▶ 20
Build straight-copy skill

1 Two 1' writings for speed on each ¶.

2 Two 5' writings for speed on all ¶s combined. Record *gwam* (LM p. 3).

Difficulty index

all letters used	A	1.5 si	5.7 awl	80% hfw

gwam 1' | 5'

The way in which you assign a task to a worker in your organization — 14 | 3 | 64
can make the difference between the job being accomplished correctly and — 28 | 6 | 67
on time or incorrectly and late. An assignment must be delivered in — 42 | 8 | 70
clear, simple language; and the deadline should be very carefully stated. — 57 | 11 | 73
Also, be sure that the worker feels you have respect for her or him. — 71 | 14 | 75
This respect must be honest and sincere; if it is, you will receive ex- — 85 | 17 | 78
ceptional performance from the worker. — 93 | 19 | 80

Not only must you have respect for the worker, but you must be cer- — 13 | 21 | 82
tain that your expectations are reasonable and that the amount of time — 28 | 24 | 85
allotted is sufficient to perform the assignment. Another technique to — 42 | 27 | 88
create a good attitude on the part of the employee is to present all di- — 56 | 30 | 91
rections in such a way that they appear to be suggestions or requests. — 71 | 33 | 94
Also, follow up on each assigned task. You can be certain that most — 85 | 36 | 97
individuals will feel a job is very important if a routine progress check — 99 | 39 | 99
is made. — 101 | 40 | 100

Another important policy that will help to insure the successful — 13 | 42 | 103
completion of an assigned job is to limit the job to a single goal or — 27 | 44 | 105
objective whenever possible. If a job is to have multiple goals and — 41 | 47 | 108
objectives, however, be sure that all instructions are given in writing — 55 | 50 | 111
to avoid confusion and misunderstanding by the worker. In any case, you — 70 | 53 | 114
should always have the directions repeated to you to make certain they — 84 | 56 | 117
are clear both to you and the employee. If you follow these basic pro- — 98 | 59 | 120
cedures, your employee will do very well on nearly every job. — 111 | 61 | 122

gwam 1' | 1 | 2 | 3 | 4 | 5 | 6 | 7 | 8 | 9 | 10 | 11 | 12 | 13 | 14 |
5' | | 1 | | 2 | | 3 |

22c, continued

Problem 2

half sheet; DS; center each line horizontally and the entire an‑nouncement vertically; proofread; circle errors

Calculation check

Lines on half sheet	33
Lines in announcement	12
Unused lines	21
Top margin	10
(Begin on Line	11)

THE RUGBY SHOP
TS
invites you to attend

a special unadvertised sale

of sweaters, slacks, and shirts

one day only

Saturday, March 13, from 9 to 9

23a ▶ 7

Preparatory practice

60-space line; each line once DS; two 1' writings on Line 4

alphabet 1 Merry will have picked out a dozen quarts of jam for boxing.

d/s 2 Eddie Deeds sold daisy seeds to a student from East Dresden.

figures 3 Your 3:15 p.m. show drew 49 men, 72 women, and 680 children.

easy 4 As usual, Len bid and paid for a quantity of big world maps.

| 1 | 2 | 3 | 4 | 5 | 6 | 7 | 8 | 9 | 10 | 11 | 12 |

23b ▶ 10

Measure straight-copy skill

two 1' writings
two 3' writings

Difficulty index

all letters used	E	1.2 si	5.1 awl	90% hfw

gwam 3'

By this time, you must realize that there are many rules 4

you should learn about line endings and word division. Add 8

to your store of rules those that explain when you ought to 12

avoid dividing a word at the end of a line. Unless you must, 16

for example, you should not divide a figure, a proper name, a 20

date, or the last word on a page. If you learn these rules 24

and combine them with just a little common sense, you will be 28

able to handle problems of word division quickly and wisely. 32

| 1 | 2 | 3 | 4 |

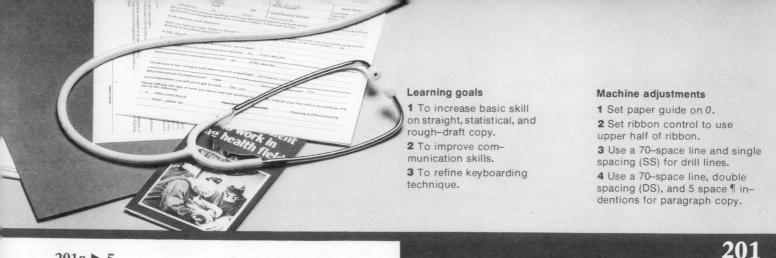

Learning goals

1 To increase basic skill on straight, statistical, and rough–draft copy.

2 To improve communication skills.

3 To refine keyboarding technique.

Machine adjustments

1 Set paper guide on *0*.

2 Set ribbon control to use upper half of ribbon.

3 Use a 70–space line and single spacing (SS) for drill lines.

4 Use a 70–space line, double spacing (DS), and 5 space ¶ in–dentions for paragraph copy.

201a ▶ 5
Preparatory practice

each line 3 times SS; (slowly, faster, slowly); DS between 3–line groups; repeat selected lines as time permits

alphabet	1	Jacqueline publicly visited Zimbabwe after her exile from the kingdom.
fig/sym	2	Invoice #27-386 for $5,941.08 included a trade discount of 2%/10%/10%.
direct reach	3	I am unable to bring the announcement about the municipal celebration.
fluency	4	Their theory may wish to blame the toxic odor on a virus borne by air.

| 1 | 2 | 3 | 4 | 5 | 6 | 7 | 8 | 9 | 10 | 11 | 12 | 13 | 14 |

201b ▶ 15
Build rough-draft skill

1 Two 1' writings for speed on each ¶.

2 Two 3' writings for speed on both ¶s com–bined. Record *gwam* (LM p. 3).

Difficulty index

all letters used	A	1.5 si	5.7 awl	80% hfw

gwam 1'   3'

How would you like to be a good leader? If so, you must learn know   12 | 4 | 60

how to influence another person the behavior of. How do you do this? First,   26 | 9 | 64

communicate your ideas clearly in a manner. Second, coordinate all of the   39 | 13 | 69

activities around the whatever is goal to be achieved. Third, also coop-   52 | 17 | 73

erate with the other person in order to achieve the goal wanted. Fourth,   65 | 22 | 78

correlate any result with the goal end. And fifth, correct any all the   77 | 26 | 82

misteaks you or the other person makes may have made.   87 | 29 | 85

By adhearing to these steps, you will also discover that   10 | 32 | 88

your co-worker the other person will always be up to date on all project   21 | 36 | 92

developments. If a some change in the your plans is expected, or required   34 | 40 | 96

your co-worker friend will know about it well in advance and will accept the   47 | 45 | 101

change with the proper atitude. This type of approach to   57 | 48 | 104

leadership will not eliminate all of the difficulties, but it   68 | 52 | 108

will minimize the number fig of conflicts that can arise.   79 | 56 | 111

23c ▶ 15
Center announcements

Problem 1

half sheet; DS; use exact vertical center; center each line horizontally (not aligned as shown); proofread/circle errors

Problem 2

full sheet; DS; use directions for Problem 1, but center in *reading position*

Reading position

Reading position places data slightly higher on a page than exact vertical center. Find top margin for exact center, then subtract 2 lines. Reading position is generally used only for full sheets (or half sheets with short side up—long edge at the left).

THE ELMIRA CONCERT SOCIETY

proudly presents   TS

the eminent Latin American pianist

Jorge Cabrara

in concert

Saturday afternoon, April 30, at 4:00

Carteret Auditorium

23d ▶ 9
Center data on special-size paper

half sheet, short side inserted first; DS; begin on Line 22; center information requested for each line

---

Finding horizontal center

To find the horizontal center of special-size paper or cards

1 Insert the paper or card into the machine. From the line-of-writing scale, add the numbers at the left and right edges of the paper.

2 Divide this sum by 2. The result is the horizontal center point for that size paper or card.

Your name

Your street address

Your city and state

The name of your college

Current date

23e ▶ 9
Center on a card

use a 5″ × 3″ card or paper cut to size; insert to type on 5″ width; center the data vertically and horizontally DS; proofread/circle errors

Calculation checks

There are 6 horizontal lines to a vertical inch. A 3″ card, therefore, holds 18 lines.

Lines available	18
Lines required	9
Lines remaining	9
Top margin	4
(Begin on Line)	5

John and Mary Dexter

DS

announce the arrival of

Meredith Anne

Born December 8

7 pounds 8 ounces

As Bradley Hubbard is leav-ing the office to meet his last client of the day, he hands you this report and says to you: *I roughed out this staff report very rapidly without correcting errors. You may need to type a draft before typing the final report. Also, please single-space this report because it will accompany other single-spaced documents. DS between paragraphs.*

THE OFFICE ENVIRONMENT--THE SPENCER COMPANY

project team VI ma~~k~~(d)e the initial visit to assess the
present ~~current~~ office facilities *of the Spencer Company*. The present ~~condition of the~~
office ~~environment~~ leaves a great deal to be desired but the poten-
tial for i~~n~~(m)proving the *facility is tremendous.* ~~situation are great.~~ The open-
office conce~~p~~(I)t ~~supposedly~~ was used in ~~layingout~~ *designing* the office~~s~~;
but, *little* ~~no~~ consideration was given to territoriality aesthe~~i~~(t)c
facters, acoustics, lighting, workstation design, or layout.
Worker, *complained* ~~griped~~ most aboyt lack of accoustical privacy. *We*
extimated the articulation index to be over ~~sixty~~ *60* per cent.
The noise, *problem* can be *resolved* ~~elimated~~ by *using* ~~instaling~~ sound-aborbent
materials, minimizing sound-reflective serfaces, and by
workstation arrange~~ment~~ *ing* so that sound~~s~~ are channelled ~~to~~ *in*
directions that cause *the least* ~~little~~ disturbance.
An excessive amount of ~~A lot of peoples~~ movement *by people* was observed ~~in the workplaces~~. ~~None of the~~ workers *did not* complain about workflow, but it, ~~is~~ *seems to be* a major
problem. Task analyses need to be made and work flow, ~~will have to~~ *must* be carefully charted.
Two ~~The~~ cost proposal has been drafted. The first pro-
posal ~~will~~ reconfigure~~s~~ the office and, ~~makes~~ *provides for* minor, changes
~~in design~~ too improve workflow to control noise and to make
the ofice more aesthetically pleasing. The, ~~2nd~~ *second* proposal
provide~~s~~ for, ~~the total~~ *completely* redesigning the interir of the building.
Redesigning the ~~exterior~~ *in* of the building would produce *far* ~~for~~
better results. The cost however is significantly high~~er~~ ~~cost~~.
Cost ~~Justifications~~ are attached. ~~The ultimate~~ *A final* decision on ~~what~~ *which*
proposal to present, *the Spencer Company* must be made soon.

Learning goals

1 To learn symbol keystrokes.
2 To improve facility on figure keyreaches.
3 To improve proofreading and revision skills.
4 To learn proofreader's marks and their uses.
5 To improve keyboarding continuity.

Machine adjustments

1 Set paper edge guide at 0.
2 Set ribbon control to type on upper half of ribbon.
3 Use a 60–space line (adjusted for bell) unless otherwise directed.
4 SS drills; DS paragraphs.
5 Space problems as directed.

24

24a ▶ 6
Preparatory practice

each line twice SS (slowly, then faster); DS between 2-line groups; repeat selected lines as time permits

alphabet	1	John Quigley packed the zinnias in twelve large, firm boxes.
n/m	2	Call a woman or a man who will manage Minerva Manor in Nome.
figures	3	Of the 13 numbers, there were 4 chosen: 29, 56, 78, and 90.
easy	4	An auditor may handle the fuel problems of the ancient city.

| 1 | 2 | 3 | 4 | 5 | 6 | 7 | 8 | 9 | 10 | 11 | 12 |

24b ▶ 12
Learn new keyreaches: $ &

$ − dollars
& = ampersand (and)

Technique hint

Pace your shift–type–release technique when practicing the symbol reaches. Straighten the appropriate finger; avoid as much as you can moving the hands and arms forward.

Reach technique for $

Shift; then reach *up* to $ with *left first* finger.

Reach technique for &

Shift; then reach *up* to & with *right first* finger.

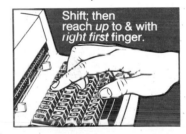

Left Fingers   4 \ 3 \ 2 \ 1 | 1 / 2 / 3 / 4   Right Fingers

Follow the "Standard procedure for learning new keyreaches" on page 10 (Lines 1–4 twice; Lines 5–7 once; repeat 5–7 if time permits).

$	1	$ $ $4 $4, if $4, 4 for $44, her $444 fur, per $4, $4 tariff
	2	The items cost them $174, $184, and $54. They paid $14 tax.
&	3	& & J & J, Jory & Jones, Bern & James, H & U Co., Foy & Hope
	4	We buy pipe from Smith & Jones, Li & Hume, and Clay & Young.
all fingers/ new symbols	5	The $185 check is from J & J. The $192 check is from B & B.
	6	Send $274 to Fish & Heath; deposit $300 with Booth & Hughes.
	7	Hecot & Ryne charged us $165; Carver & Hunt charged us $340.

| 1 | 2 | 3 | 4 | 5 | 6 | 7 | 8 | 9 | 10 | 11 | 12 |

NB:01 Thank you for giving us the opportunity to provide you with information about the design services we offer. We are committed to developing a total office environment which contributes to the productivity, comfort, job satisfaction, and motivation of the employees who work in the environments we design.

NB:02 One of our clients indicated that you are considering moving to new office space soon. If so, you will be interested in the services we can provide for you. Ergonomic Consultants, Inc., is committed to developing a total office environment which contributes to the productivity, comfort, job satisfaction, and motivation of the employees who work in the environments we design.

NB:03 One of our clients indicated you are considering renovating your present office space and may be interested in the services we can provide for you. Ergonomic Consultants, Inc., is committed to developing a total office environment which will contribute to the productivity, comfort, job satisfaction, and motivation of the employees who work in the environments we design.

NB:04 The enclosed booklet describes our approach to helping you design and build new office facilities. It explains how we work with your employees and how we coordinate the activities of other professionals involved in the total building project.

NB:05 The enclosed booklet describes our approach to helping you renovate your present office facilities. It explains how we work with your employees and how we coordinate the activities of other professionals involved in the total renovation project.

NB:06 One of our design specialists will call you in a few days to arrange an appointment at a mutually convenient time. You will be pleased to learn that our services are very cost effective.

NB:07 One of our design specialists would be pleased to visit your office and prepare a proposal for designing your office facilities. You would, of course, be under no obligation. Just return the enclosed card or call us, and a design specialist will arrange an appointment at a mutually convenient time.

24c ▶ 8
Reach for new goals

1 Two 30" writings on each line; try to pace yourself to end each writing just as time is called.

2 Three 1' writings on Line 4; de-termine *gwam* on each writing.

1 The six girls paid $81 to visit the old city.   18

2 Lana paid the man the $94 due for the work he did.   20

3 Coe & Wu may sign the form for the auditor of the firm.   22

4 If Torke & Rush paid $730, then Corlan and Aldorn paid $637.   24

| 1 | 2 | 3 | 4 | 5 | 6 | 7 | 8 | 9 | 10 | 11 | 12 |

24d ▶ 7
Use the warning bell/ divide words

two half sheets; begin on Line 12; once with 70-space line, once with 60-space line

Take time to evaluate your completed work. Look carefully at what you have done. Would you be impressed with it if you were a reader? Is it attractive in form and accurate in content? If it does not impress you, it will not impress anyone else.

24e ▶ 9
Proofread/revise as you keyboard

each line twice SS; DS between 2-line groups; identify and correct the circled errors *as you keyboard*

1 He chose 12 to 14 dozen carda for my all-prupose card shelf.

2 The expert quick ly listed 23 sources of information forher.

3 I drove my new jeep at an average ratt of 56 miles per hour?

4 Minimum spedd on that part of Route 789 is 35 miles an hory.

5 The whit pine frame is 15 x 20 inches; there is no picture.

24f ▶ 8
Improve keyboarding continuity

1 Practice the ¶ once for orienta-tion.

2 Take three 30" practice writings on the ¶. Determine *gwam*: words typed × 2.

3 Take three 1' speed writings on the ¶. Determine *gwam*: total words typed = 1' *gwam*.

Goal: 20 or more *gwam*.

Difficulty index

| all letters used | E | 1.2 si | 5.1 awl | 90% hfw |

We purchased our computer from the Jeff & Zorne Company for $500. That is quite a lot of money; but I think it will be a good investment if I can use the machine and all of the parts--figures and symbols, for example--in the correct way.

25a ▶ 7
Preparatory practice

each line twice SS (slowly, then faster); DS between 2-line groups; repeat selected lines if time per-mits

alphabet 1 Why did the judge quiz poor Victor about his blank tax form?

t/r 2 Bart had trouble starting his truck for a trip to Terrytown.

figure/ symbol 3 Buy 103 ribbons and 45 erasers from May & Muntz for $289.67.

easy 4 Did she rush to cut six bushels of corn for the civic corps?

| 1 | 2 | 3 | 4 | 5 | 6 | 7 | 8 | 9 | 10 | 11 | 12 |

25

Job 5
Design a form for standard information
(full sheets)

After lunch, you find a note from Bradley Hubbard *(shown at right)*. Follow his request.

From the desk of ...   **BRAD HUBBARD**

We have agreed to standardize the Design Project Summary for every project we undertake. Please examine the memo about the Willis Design Project Summary and design a form that we can use to record future summary information.

Be sure to provide space for the following items: name, address, and telephone number of company; names and titles of contact persons; summary information; names of suppliers of the items listed; and names of the design team coordinators. Leave space for the names of additional suppliers that might be needed on some of the projects.   B. H.

Job 6
Prepare letters by using standard form paragraphs
(LM pp. 115–125)

You also receive through company mail a note from Scott Cockrell requesting that you send form letters to potential clients. Attached to his note is the list of form paragraphs you will need to complete the task (see page 350). Date each letter **February 25, 19--**.

From the desk of ...   **SCOTT COCKRELL**

Please send form letters to:

Ms. Connie Bogner, Manager
Bogner Distributors, Inc.
200 Austin Avenue
Skokie, IL 60077-8221
℞s NB:03; NB:05; NB:07

Mr. Mike Goings, Manager
Great Lakes Glass Company
403 Sheridan Road
Evanston, IL 60202-8520
℞s NB:01; NB:05; NB:06

Ms. Mary Fox, Manager
Fox and Associates
1801 Calumet Avenue
Chicago, IL 60616-8541
℞s NB:02; NB:04; NB:07

Miss Annie Cox, Office Manager
Corbett Medical Center
1030 Jackson Avenue
Evanston, IL 60201-8522
℞s NB:01; NB:04; NB:06

Mr. Jack Rutcosky
Rutcosky Enterprises
933 Star Lane
Joliet, IL 60435-8610
℞s NB:02; NB:04; NB:07

Mr. John Smith, Vice President
The Teakwood Company
5629 Fargo Avenue
Skokie, IL 60077-8211
℞s NB:03; NB:05; NB:06

(form paragraphs on next page)

25b ▶ 12
Learn new keyreaches
( )

Follow the "Standard procedure for learning new keyreaches" on page 10 (Lines 1–4 twice; Lines 5–8 once; repeat 5–8 if time permits.)

= number/pounds
( ) = parentheses

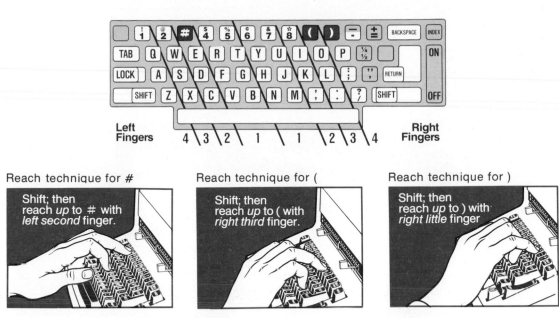

Left Fingers   4 \ 3 \ 2 \ 1 \ 1 \ 2 \ 3 \ 4   Right Fingers

Reach technique for #
Shift; then reach *up* to # with *left second* finger.

Reach technique for (
Shift; then reach *up* to (with *right third* finger.

Reach technique for)
Shift; then reach *up* to) with *right little* finger

1   # # #3 #33 Card #3, File #3, Car #33, #3 grade. Try #3 now.
    2   Memo #169 says to load Car #3758 with 470# of #2 grade sand.

( )   3   (1 (1);); (90) two (2); type (1) and (2); see (8) and (9).
    4   He (John) and his cousin (Lynne) are both the same age (17).

#/( )   5   Pay the May (#34) and June (#54) bills soon (before July 1).
    6   We lease Car #84 (a white sedan) and Car #86 (a blue coupe).

all figures/   7   Our Check #230 for $259 paid Owen & Cobb (auditors) in full.
new symbols   8   Deliver the $78 order (collect) to Fox & Tucker (Room #416).

| 1 | 2 | 3 | 4 | 5 | 6 | 7 | 8 | 9 | 10 | 11 | 12 |

25c ▶ 8
Proofread/revise
as you keyboard

each line twice SS; DS between 2-line groups; correct circled errors as you type

1   I saw them fill the (Baskets) full of (appels) (form) the orchard.

2   None of (use) took that (specal) train to Cincinnati (adn) Dayton.

3   They (paln) an intensive (campaing) for television and/or (raido).

4   (Teh) two leaders (Betty and Luis) left at 2--not 1:30 today.

5   (put) a fork, knife and (sppon) at each informal place setting.

Job 4
Memorandum
(LM p. 113)

After handing you this memo to prepare for distribution to the project teams, Bradley Hubbard instructs you: *Please single-space the memo and double-space above and below listed items. Date the memo February 24, 19--.*

Project teams

Willis DESIGN PROGRAM SUMMARY

An final agreement has been reached on the first phase of the Willis Project. Summary information includes the following:

Floors: 3

Floor space: 145,000 sq. ft.   Average area/floor: 48,000 sq. ft.

Lighting: Task/ambient

Closed/open office ratio: 8:90

Construction cost: #34/sq. ft.

Design/furnishings cost: $25/sq. ft.

HVAC system: Nine 100-ton air cooler chillers

Communication and power: access floor for all cables

We hope to finalize next week the selections of the suppliers for the following items:

alphabetize columnar items

Accessories   General furniture   Shelving

Ceiling   Carpet   Partitions

Lighting   Workstations   Upholstery fabrics

The design team coordinators for the Willis Project have been selected. They are Barb Romero (Interior Design), Ken Davis (Lighting Design), and Joseph Wayne (Landscape).

Tom Fox has developed a new program to predict acoustic noise and will try it on the Willis project. He measures present noise and calculates the difference between the acoustics of the present environment and that of the proposed environment.

25d ▶ 8
Improve keyboarding continuity

1 Practice the ¶ once for orientation.

2 Take three 30″ writings and three 1′ writings.

Goal: At least 14 *gwam*.

```
        .        2        .        4        .        6        .        8        .        10        .
Issue #27 of a recent (1/9/85) magazine told how an ex-
        12        .        14        .        16        .        18        .        20        .        22
ecutive got her first job with a top-level firm (Roe & Roe):
        24        .        26        .        28        .        30        .        32        .        34
She knew how to keyboard. Paid merely $140 a week at first,
        36        .        38        .        40        .        42        .        44        .        46
she moved up quickly; now she is making about $1,360 a week.
```

25e ▶ 15
Review centering an announcement on special-size paper

half sheet; insert short side first; DS; center vertically in reading position; center each line horizontally; proofread/circle errors

Calculation checks:

The page is 8½″ long. There are 6 lines in one vertical inch. 8½ × 6 = 51 available lines.

Lines in problem: 14
Exact top margin: 18
Reading position
   top margin: 16

Add right paper edge reading to left paper edge reading; divide by 2. The result is the center point of the page.

Members of THE CHORALIERS
TS

Arvid Badger

Muriel Ann Bressuyt

Bertram Garrett, Jr.

Wayne L. Jewell

Phillip R. Runyun

Bette Lee Yamasake

26a ▶ 7
Preparatory practice

each line twice SS (slowly, faster); as many 30″ writings on Line 4 as time permits

Goal: Complete Line 4 in 30″.

alphabet 1 Jewel quickly explained to me the big fire hazards involved.

space bar 2 is by it do in be of am my go me an us so if to or ad on and

figure symbol 3 Silva & Stuart checked Items #2346 and 789 (for a $150 fee).

easy 4 The auditor did the rush work right, so he risks no penalty.

```
| 1 | 2 | 3 | 4 | 5 | 6 | 7 | 8 | 9 | 10 | 11 | 12 |
```

Job 2
Compose letter of transmittal
(LM p. 111)

While you were away from your desk, Roberta Tassin left you the note at right. Accompanying it is the file card below, which supplies address information.

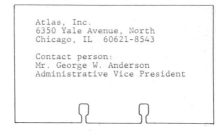

Atlas, Inc.
6350 Yale Avenue, North
Chicago, IL 60621-8543

Contact person:
Mr. George W. Anderson
Administrative Vice President

Job 3
Prepare tables from computer printout (full sheets)

After completing the transmittal, Roberta Tassin gives you the two tables at right, which resulted from a recent research study at Ergonomic Consultants, Inc. She tells you to make the following amendments to the computer printouts: *Do not use abbreviations for column headings. Substitute the following information for the Code Column on both tables:*

Rating

Very frequently
Frequently
Occasionally
Seldom
Never
No answer

From the desk of ...   **ROBERTA TASSIN**

Please prepare a cover letter for my signature to Mr. George Anderson to transmit the Preliminary Design Considerations Report. Date the letter February 23. Confirm our meeting with the Facilities Committee on February 27, at 2:30 p. m. in Conference Room A of our building. We have made arrangements for approximately fifteen people. Invite them to stay for a short reception following the meeting. Ask Mr. Anderson to call me prior to the meeting if he has any questions about the report.   R. T.

Table 1. Eye Strain Experienced By VDT Operators.

CODE	ABSOLUTE FREQ	RELATIVE FREQ (PCT)	ADJUSTED FREQ (PCT)	CUM FREQ (PCT)
1.	124	51.7	58.5	58.5
2.	23	9.6	10.8	69.3
3.	17	7.0	8.0	77.4
4.	15	6.3	7.1	84.4
5.	33	13.7	15.6	100.0
0.	28	11.7	MISSING	100.0
	--------	--------	--------	
TOTAL	240	100.0	100.0	

Table 2. Back Problems Experienced By VDT Operators.

CODE	ABSOLUTE FREQ	RELATIVE FREQ (PCT)	ADJUSTED FREQ (PCT)	CUM FREQ (PCT)
1.	72	30.0	33.6	33.6
2.	15	6.3	7.0	40.7
3.	13	5.4	6.1	46.7
4.	18	7.5	8.4	55.1
5.	96	40.0	44.9	100.0
0.	26	10.8	MISSING	100.0
	--------	--------	--------	
TOTAL	240	100.0	100.0	

26b ▶ 12
Learn new keyreaches: % ' !

% = percent
' = apostrophe/single quote
! = exclamation point

Note: If you are using a nonelectric machine, refer to page 3; see directions for reach to '.

Reach technique for %

Shift; then reach *up* to % with *left first* finger.

Apostrophe (')

Reach to ' with *right little* finger.

Left Fingers 4 3 2 1 1 2 3 4 Right Fingers

Follow the "Standard procedure for learning new keyreaches" on page 10 (Lines 1–4 twice; Lines 5–8 once; repeat 5–8 if time permits).

Exclamation point:

If your machine has an exclamation point key, strike it with the nearest little finger. If it does not, refer to page 3. Space twice after an exclamation point when used after an emphatic interjection or as end–of–sentence punctuation.

% 1 % % 5%, off 5%, if 5%, save 15%, ask 15%, less 50%, 5% force
   2 Mark prices down 15% on coats, 5% on hats, and 10% on shoes.

' 3 ' ' 10's, it's, Bob's, Sec'y, Ok'd; It's summer. I'm going.
   4 It's time for Ann's party. I don't have Melanie's notebook.

! 5 Fire! Ouch! Oh wow! Keep out! They offer a big discount!
   6 Their slogan reads THINK! They used the headline OOPS SALE!

%/'/! 7 Don't give up! Keep on! We're over the top! We have $950!
      8 Uhl & Co. had a 16% profit! Their third quarter showed 20%!

| 1 | 2 | 3 | 4 | 5 | 6 | 7 | 8 | 9 | 10 | 11 | 12 |

26c ▶ 10
Proofread/revise as you keyboard

Errors are often circled in copy that is to be retyped. More frequently, perhaps, the copy is marked with special symbols called "proofreader's marks" which indicate changes desired by an editor.

Some commonly used proofreader's marks are shown at the right. Study them; then type each drill line at least twice, SS; DS between 2–line groups.

Concentrate on copy content as you keyboard.

Proofreader's marks

Symbol	Meaning	Symbol	Meaning
Cap or ≡	Capitalize	#	Add horizontal space
^	Insert	/ or *lc*	Lowercase letters
ℓ	Delete (remove)	⊂	Close up space
⊏	Move to left	∿	Transpose
⊐	Move to right	*stet*	Leave as originally written

1 patience pays; the expert's goal is 1% every day improvement.

2 do today's work today; tommorrow's work will be 100% lighter.

3 One's best is usually enough; Few are expected to give 101%.

4 It's easier to risk 10% than, but return depends on risk.

5 We miss life's pleasures I know because we refuse to sample.

6 I'll be lucky if at anytime I can solve 50% of my problems.

Several factors must be considered before we begin with the preliminary design of the new facilities for Atlas. The following paragraphs summarize the important factors which need to be considered and suggest how to attain desired results.

Access floors. All floors, excluding the executive floor, should be raised a minimum of four inches off the slab to accommodate cables and conduits. Flooring should consist of modular, removable floor panels. Squares of carpet should be laid over the two-foot panels. The power system must be readily accessible to provide flexibility in installing electronic equipment in the workstations.

Energy. The entire building must be energy efficient. Recovering heat generated by office equipment and lighting as well as environmental control is an important factor to consider in the attempt to conserve energy. The influence of technology on ventilation, heat, and air conditioning is another factor which must be determined and controlled.

Office design. All interior office space should be designed with movable wall partitions except the executive office area. Floor-to-ceiling partitions can be used for selected offices.

Lighting. Task/ambient lighting should be used throughout the office area to control glare. The ceiling fixtures should be recessed and should provide soft ambient illumination.

Workstations. Ergonomic design of workstations is crucial. Components must be flexible and must have an effective wire management system. The components must accommodate a wide range of office functions and a wide range of user needs.

Complete documentation for these recommendations will be provided at the initial design planning session.

26d ▶ 11
Reach for new goals

1 Take a 1' writing on Line 1.

2 Take a 1' writing on Line 2, try-ing to type as many lines as on Line 1.

3 Practice each of the other pairs of lines in the same way to im-prove figure/symbol keyboarding speed.

words in line

1	Did the girls make soap in a handy clay bowl?	9
2	They spent $85 on a visit to Field & Co.	8
3	Did the men visit the dismal shanty on the island?	10
4	Form #72 is title to the island (their half).	9
5	I turn the dials on the panel a half turn to the right.	11
6	She may pay me for my work, and I make 40% profit.	10
7	It is a shame he spent the endowment on a visit to the city.	12
8	She paid 20% down for the $18 formal tie; it's apricot.	11

| 1 | 2 | 3 | 4 | 5 | 6 | 7 | 8 | 9 | 10 | 11 | 12 |

26e ▶ 10
Improve keyboarding continuity

1 Practice the ¶ for orientation.

2 Take three 30" writings and three 1' writings.

3 Proofread/circle errors after each writing.

Goal: At least 14 *gwam*.

Avoid looking at the keyboard when you encounter figures and symbols.

Difficulty index

all letters/symbols learned | E | 1.2 si | 6.1 awl | 90% hfw |

Sales Report #38/39 of the modern firm of Wenz & Jelkes states that, if they are to remain in business, they are re-quired to clear a profit of 10% on all sales (net)--or $1 on each $10. They don't expect the figure to change very soon.

27a ▶ 7
Preparatory practice

each line twice SS (slowly, then faster); DS between 2-line groups; take a 1' writ-ing on Line 4 if time per-mits

alphabet	1	Jacky Few's strange, quiet behavior amazed and perplexed us.
shift	2	Lily read BLITHE SPIRIT by Noel Coward. I read VANITY FAIR.
fig/sym	3	Invoice #38 went from $102.74 to $97.60 after a 5% discount.
easy	4	They may go to a town social when they visit the big island.

| 1 | 2 | 3 | 4 | 5 | 6 | 7 | 8 | 9 | 10 | 11 | 12 |

27b ▶ 8
Practice long reaches

each line twice SS; DS be-tween 2-line groups; repeat lines you find most difficult

Keep eyes on copy as you strike figures and symbols.

$	1	He spent $25 for gifts, $13 for dinner, and $7 for cab fare.
( )	2	We (my uncle and I) watched his sons (my cousins) play golf.
%	3	If I add 3% to the company discount of 8%, I can deduct 11%.
&	4	Send the posters to Bow & Held, Mans & Tow, and Wick & Jens.
'	5	It's time to send Hale's credit application to Land's Store.

| 1 | 2 | 3 | 4 | 5 | 6 | 7 | 8 | 9 | 10 | 11 | 12 |

Preparatory practice

each line 3 times SS; DS between 3-line groups; retype selected lines as time permits

alphabet 1 Alex Wajorski apologized for being ill and left the room very quickly.

fig/sym 2 The bill of $1,427.61 ($1,389.40 plus 2.75% interest) is due on May 9.

double letter 3 Jerry and Lynnette will meet at noon to discuss the accounting errors.

fluency 4 A neighbor paid me to go to the island to dig up the bush and burn it.

| 1 | 2 | 3 | 4 | 5 | 6 | 7 | 8 | 9 | 10 | 11 | 12 | 13 | 14 |

195b–200b ▶ 45

Office job simulation

(LM pp. 111–125)

Job 1
Report (full sheets)

Roberta Tassin, Vice President for Ergonomic Consultants, Inc., stops by your desk and tells you: *Please type this report as soon as possible to accompany a transmittal to Atlas, Inc. I think side headings would look better than the paragraph headings I used.*

PRELIMINARY DESIGN CONSIDERATIONS
Atlas, Inc.

The project team recommends, on the basis of its assessment of current Atlas facilities and growth projections of Atlas management, that the new building contain 50,000 square feet. This figure was based on the projected increase in the number of employees, the projected increase in the amount of automation at Atlas, and the 10 percent expansion cushion mandated by the Senior Management Committee.

PRESENT FACILITIES AND FIVE-YEAR PROJECTIONS

Floor	No. of Employees Current	Projected	% Using Terminals Current	Projected	Sq. Ft. Space Current	Projected
1	50	65	40	70	6,200	10,000
2	55	60	60	85	6,800	9,500
3	60	80	45	80	6,500	14,000
4	40	50	20	40	6,000	10,000

The design of the facilities will be impacted heavily by the projected increase in the amount of automation over the next five years. The current facility simply is not designed to accommodate automation. The new facility must reflect the current needs and must be flexible to accommodate future needs.

(Job 1 continued on next page)

Learn new keyreaches:
" __

" = quotation marks
__ = underline

Quotation (")

Shift; then reach to " with *right little* finger.

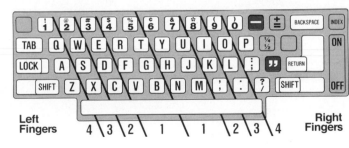

Left Fingers   4 3 2 1   1 2 3 4   Right Fingers

Underline (__)

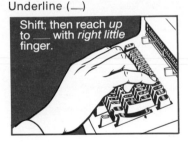

Shift; then reach *up* to __ with *right little* finger.

Follow the "Standard procedure for learning new keyreaches" on page 10 (Lines 1–6 twice; the ¶ once, then again if time permits).

Note: If you are using a non–electric machine, see page 3 directions for reach to ".

To underline: Type the word, backspace to first letter, then strike underline once for each letter in the word.

" 1 ; "; "; James was "Jim"; Mary was "Mo"; and Janis was "Jan."
  2 "We are," he said, "alone." "Wrong," said I, "Lee is here."

__ 3 There is a <u>right</u> way and a <u>wrong</u> way; then there is <u>her</u> way.
  4 I ordered <u>hose</u>, not hoes, and soda for <u>baking</u>, not <u>drinking</u>.

"/__ 5 "This," she stated, "is the <u>antique</u>; <u>that</u> is the facsimile."
  6 She said, "I know that I <u>should</u> go, but I cannot do it <u>now</u>."

Wenz & Jelkes tell us too (in their Report #3) that the margin figure, 10%, is not "very high" for what a major firm makes. The profit this year ($1.5 million) isn't so high as it could have been, but the firm hopes to improve <u>next</u> year.

| 1 | 2 | 3 | 4 | 5 | 6 | 7 | 8 | 9 | 10 | 11 | 12 |

Type a short report

full sheet; DS; 60-space line; 2" top margin; make corrections as you type; proofread/circle errors

words

SOME FACTS TO REMEMBER (Center)   4

TS
one horizontal

Theer are 10 pica and 12 elite spaces to an inch. With   18

size
either style of type, six lines comprise a vertical inch.   30

horizontal   sheet;
To find the center point of a given area add the readings   44

its   edges
for the left and right limits from the line of writing scale;   56

sum
divide the total by 2.   61

determine   for vertical centering
to set top and bottom margins, subtract the number of   79

to format
lines needed for the problem from the number available on the   91

the remaining lines
page; divide by 2 to find exact top margin. Subtract 12 if   107

you desire reading position. After computing lines to be left   120

one line
in the top margin, space down once more and begin the first   133

line of the problem.   137

Learning goals

1 To become familiar with keyboarding/formatting tasks in a technical office.

2 To learn to work with minimum instructions.

3 To improve your ability to work from differing copy sources and to detect and correct errors.

Machine adjustments

1 Paper guide at *0*.

2 Set ribbon control to use upper half of ribbon.

3 Margins: 70–space line and single spacing for drill lines; 6–inch line for copy.

Office Job Simulation

Before you begin the jobs of Section 43, read carefully the information at the right.

Make notes of any standard procedures that you think will save you time during the completion of the production activities in this section.

Daily practice plan:

Preparatory practice .... 5′
Work on simulation .... 45′

Work Assignment

You have been assigned by Office Service Temporaries, Inc., to work for Ergonomic Consultants, Inc., a consulting firm specializing in designing office environments with major emphasis on human factors engineering. In your position, you will be working for: Roberta Tassin, Vice President; Scott Cockrell, Business Manager; and Bradley Hubbard, Design Engineer. The company is located at 300 Simpson Avenue, Chicago, IL 62526-3302.

The Office Procedures Manual for Ergonomic Consultants, Inc., specifies the following standard procedures:

1. A standard 6-inch line is used for all communications unless directed otherwise.

2. Letters are prepared in block style with open punctuation.

3. Reports are double-spaced unless otherwise directed.

4. Copies are made on a photocopy machine.

5. Female consultants use the personal title "Ms." as part of the typewritten signature on communications.

Because you are regarded as both competent and professional, you are not always provided with explicit and detailed instructions. You are expected to use good judgment in setting up communications and in making decisions where detailed instructions are not given.

Because the consultants you are working for are frequently out of the office visiting clients, you will be given instructions primarily by either short, handwritten memos or verbally. A transcript of all verbal communications is provided in italics in the left margin.

Ergonomic Consultants, Inc., has based its Office Procedures Manual and job instructions on COLLEGE KEYBOARDING/TYPEWRITING, so use your textbook to look up matters of style and placement when in doubt. When a job requires unusual specifications or procedures, Ergonomic Consultants, Inc., provides special guides in "Excerpts from the Office Procedures Manual."

Excerpt from the Office Procedures Manual

Standard placement. For all communications, use a 6-inch line length (60 pica spaces; 72 elite spaces) to increase office efficiency. For letters, place the date on a standard dateline, regardless of letter length: Place dateline on Line 13 and leave 3 blank line spaces between the date and the letter address. For memos, use the simplified memo style: Use 1″ top margin for half-page memos and 1½″ top margin for full-page memos. For reports, use 1½″ top margin.

Block style letter with standard placement

Learning goals

1 To achieve smooth, continuous keystroking.
2 To improve ability to concen-trate on copy.
3 To improve proofreading skills.
4 To improve facility with figure and symbol reaches.
5 To type script and rough-draft copy smoothly.

Machine adjustments

1 Set paper guide at 0.
2 Set ribbon control to type on upper half of ribbon.
3 Use 60-space line throughout.
4 SS drills; DS paragraphs.

28

28a ▶ 7
Preparatory practice

each line three times SS (slowly, faster, still faster); DS between 3-line groups; repeat selected lines if time permits

alphabet	1	My wife helped fix a frozen lock on Jacque's vegetable bins.
difficult reaches	2	Beverly sneezed even though she ate a dozen square lozenges.
figures	3	Do Problems 6 to 19 on page 275 before class at 8:30, May 4.
easy	4	Did the form entitle Jay to the land at the end of the lane?

| 1 | 2 | 3 | 4 | 5 | 6 | 7 | 8 | 9 | 10 | 11 | 12 |

28b ▶ 10
Control machine parts

once as shown DS; repeat if time permits

Lines 1-4: Clear all tabs; set tab at center point; tab and type. Keep eyes on book copy.
Line 5: Supply appropriate spac-ing after punctuation.
Line 6: Release margin; back-space 5 spaces into left margin to begin.
Line 7: Depress shift/lock keys firmly.

center

	1	──────────────→ The tab key should be operated
tab and return	2	quickly.──────────→ One quick flick of your finger
	3	should suffice.─────→ Avoid pauses; do not slow down
	4	or look up when you tab.
space bar	5	Was it Mary? Judy? Pam? It was a woman; she wore a big hat.
margin release/ backspacer	6	When you type from copy, elevate the copy to make reading easier.
shift/lock	7	Al read A TALE OF TWO CITIES; Vi read THE MILL ON THE FLOSS.

28c ▶ 10
Improve response patterns

1 Once as shown; checkmark the three most difficult lines.
2 Repeat the lines you checked as difficult.
3 Take a 1' writing on Line 2, next on Line 4, and then on Line 6. Determine *gwam* on each writing.

word	1	Did the antique map of the world also hang by the oak shelf?
	2	Did they pay the auditor the duty on eighty bushels of corn?
stroke	3	Holly tests fast race cars; we get oil at my garage in Juno.
	4	Johnny erected a vast water cascade on my acreage in Joplin.
combination	5	She paid the extra debt and the taxes on their land in Ohio.
	6	Lynn sewed the nylon flaps on the six burlap bags with care.

| 1 | 2 | 3 | 4 | 5 | 6 | 7 | 8 | 9 | 10 | 11 | 12 |

Job 6, continued

Job 7
Title page
(full sheet)

Mr. Rutledge has asked that the report prepared in Job 6 be finished by preparing an appropriate title page.

The title page should contain the following:

GOVERNMENT LETTER STYLES

Mr. Terence J. Rutledge
U.S. Services Agency
February 19, 19—

Job 8
Composing an informal government letter (LM p. 107)

Ms. Sanchez asks that you prepare a letter for distribution to the office staff informing them of the decision to adopt the new letter styles. A copy of the report will accompany each copy of the letter. Provide whatever information that you feel is appropriate. Ms. Sanchez will sign the letter. Date the letter **February 20.** Prepare the rough draft on plain paper and the final draft on letterhead.

Job 9
Informal government letter with window envelope (LM p. 109)

Ms. Sanchez has drafted a letter to the Los Angeles branch office informing the staff about the adoption by the Chicago branch of the government letter styles. Prepare a letter to the Deputy Director in Los Angeles. Date the letter **February 20.** Use as a subject line: **Adoption of new letter styles.** Correct any undetected errors.

DS body of report

Special Style Characteristics

 Style. For formal government letters, use the block style with a salutation, complimentary close, and mixed punctuation. For informal government letters, use block style with necessary headings to the right of the preprinted captions. Exclude the salutation and the complementary close in the informal letter.

 Stationery. In addition to the letterhead, the sationery for the informal letter must have the captions "Date:", "Reply to Attn of:", "Subject:", and "To:" preprinted in the left margin.

 Dateline. Place the dateline on the 7th line at the left margin in a formal letter; place to the right of the "Date:" cation in the informal letter.

 Sender's reference. In an informal letter the official symbol of the sender (e.g., AFAW) is placed flush with the left margin in line with the "Reply to Attn of:" caption. Use only / Place

 Special mailing instructions. Place a special mailing notation (e.g., EXPRESS MAIL) on the ninth line at the left margin for the formal style; place mailing notations on the same lien as the sender's reference, starting at the horizontal center, in the informal style.

Subject line. Place the subject on the 11th lien in both styles.

 Address. The address begins on the fourteenth lien in the formal letter. In an informal letter, the address begins on the same line as the "To:" caption.

The chicago Branch office will adopt next month on February 28 the two basic government letter styles recommended by the Gen. Services Adm. Pehaps your branch will aslo want too consider adopting these letter styles as well. ¶ The general format styles for both the formal and informal letters are very similar, and keyboard specialists Your typists should find them easy to learn. I am enclosing a brief report that we prepared for our office staff to help familiarize them with these two letter styles. Also, under separate cover, I am sending to you a copy of the U.S. Government Correspondence Manual. ¶ Arnold, I am sure confident you will like appreciate the simplicity of these both letter styles. If you would like to have a copy of our new correspondnece training materials, please let me no, and I will send a copy to you.

**Improve keyboarding
continuity**

full sheet; DS; 60-space line;
1½" top margin

1 Prepare the report once, making
the corrections designated by the
proofreading symbols.

2 Correct any new errors using
proofreader's marks.

3 Prepare a final copy from your
marked paragraphs; proofread;
circle errors.

words

my ARIZONA HIDEAWAY   4

TS

In arizona, there is a small hotel that is locatd near   15

six ~~high~~ green and white mountains. I like it there, for I   27

enjoy the quite of that palce. The morningview is special,   40

and each day there i feel better that I felt the day before.   52

The six mountains are quite high, green just so far up;   63
then they turn white. They reach into the azure beyond like   75
human hands; and when a cloud appears, it seems as if one of   88
the hands has flung a small piece of vapor into the heavens.   100

Rates are excellent. The hotel provides two (2) large-   111

size rooms and a tasty dinner for just $65 daily. The hotel   123

has only 134 rooms; therefore, I call early for reservations   136

when I visit this area--as I did last April 7, 8, 9, and 10.   148

29

29a ▶ 7

Preparatory practice

each line twice SS (slowly,
then faster); DS between
2-line groups; 1' writings
on Line 4 as time permits

alphabet   1   Bob realized very quickly that jumping was excellent for us.

fig/sym   2   Ann's 7% note (dated May 23, 1985) was paid at 4690 J Drive.

double
letters   3   Will Buzz and Lee carry the supplies across the street soon?

easy   4   He paid for the endowment, and he owns the giant coal field.

| 1 | 2 | 3 | 4 | 5 | 6 | 7 | 8 | 9 | 10 | 11 | 12 |

29b ▶ 10

**Improve symbol
keyreaches**

each line twice SS; DS between 2-line groups; repeat
lines that seemed difficult

Keep eyes on copy; keep keystroking smooth and continuous.

'   1   Ray's brother didn't plan for the day's work; it's not done.

-   2   A pay-freeze plan on so-called full-time jobs is well-known.

()   3   All of us (including Vera) went to the game (and it rained).

"   4   They read the poems "September Rain" and "The Lower Branch."

$ 5   His weekly checks totaled $128.35, $96.20, $114.80, and $77.

/   6   The Sr/C Club walked and/or ran 15 1/2 miles in 6 3/4 hours.

Body. *or message* Begin the body or message of the letter at least two lines below the last line of the address or on the twentieth line if a window envelope is used. Begin the main paragraphs flush with the left margin, and single-space the lines of the paragraphs. Double-space between the paragraphs in the body. Number or letter all subparagraphs, and indent the first line of each subparagraph five spaces; begin all succeeding lines in the subparagraph flush with the left margin. If the body of the letter consists of a single paragraph *of fewer than ten lines* double-space the body.

Enclosure(s). Place the work "Enclosure(s)" a double space below the signature element, if needed. If no specific reference to an enclosure is made in the body, a listing of all enclosures--single-spaced and each one flush with the left margin--should be made below the word "Enclosure(s)."

Signature element. Place the signers name *flush with* at the left margin in ALL CAPS on the fourth line space below the last line of the body or complimentary close. Place the signers title flush with the left margin on the next line.

Material sent Under Separate Cover. If any material is *to be* sent under separate cover, list each item--single-spaced and *each item* flush with the left margin--below the words "Separate cover."

Copy and identification notations. *These* Notations are not shown on the original *copy*; they appear *only* on the file copies.

Window envelopes. If a window envelope is used, the address should not contain more than five lines. Each line of the address should *no* be longer than 4 *sp.* inches. If any part of an address must be divided, indent the second line 2 *sp.* spaces from the left margin. After the adress *has been* is completed, space down to the 20th *sp.* line to begin the body *of the letter*.

(Job 6 continued on next page)

29c ▶ 5

Develop concentration with fill-ins

each line once DS; proofread and mark with proofreader's marks any errors you make; retype from your edited copy

1 Rent in the amount of $185 is payable the 5th of each month.

2 In response, refer to Invoice #187-3 and the date, April 21.

3 Plant seedlings 3 inches deep, 12 inches apart, after May 1.

4 On 3-17-85 Bands 7746-7789 were used to band Canadian geese.

5 Shipments left Dock 15 via Atlantic Express May 29 at 3 p.m.

29d ▶ 6

Improve response patterns

once as shown; repeat if time permits

Lines 1-2: Say and type each word as a unit.

Lines 3-4: Spell each word as you type it letter by letter at a steady pace.

Lines 5-6: Say and type short, easy words as units; spell and type longer words letter by letter.

word
1 Their goal is to do social work downtown for a city auditor.
2 Did the men cut the eight bushels of corn down by the field?

stroke
3 He acts, in my opinion, as if my cards gave him greater joy.
4 Jimmy deserves my extra reward; few cars ever tested better.

combination
5 Based on my theory, she decreased that quantity of protozoa.
6 They sign with great care several of their formal abstracts.

| 1 | 2 | 3 | 4 | 5 | 6 | 7 | 8 | 9 | 10 | 11 | 12 |

29e ▶ 9

Improve keystroking technique

each line twice SS; DS between 2-line groups; keep wrists low, eyes on copy

bottom row
1 Did six brave, zany exhibitors and/or bakers climb Mt. Zemb?

home row
2 Sada and Jake had a dish of salad; Gail had a glass of soda.

3d row
3 At her party, a quiet waiter poured tea as I wrote a letter.

figures
4 On June 24, Flight 89 left at 1:30 with 47 men and 65 women.

| 1 | 2 | 3 | 4 | 5 | 6 | 7 | 8 | 9 | 10 | 11 | 12 |

29f ▶ 13

Measure skill growth: straight copy

60-space line; DS

three 1' writings

three 3' writings

Goal:

1'—25 or more *gwam*

3'—21 or more *gwam*

Difficulty index

| all letters used | E | 1.2 si | 5.1 awl | 90% hfw |

gwam 3'

Do we care about how people judge us? Most of us do.   4 | 26

We hope and expect that other people will recognize quality   8 | 30

in what we do, what we say, and the way we act. Is it not   12 | 34

true, though, that what others think of us results from some   16 | 38

image that we have created in their minds? In other words,   20 | 42

are we not really our own creation?   22 | 44

gwam 3' | 1 | 2 | 3 | 4 |

(Job 6 continued on next page)

Job 5
Informal government letter
(LM p. 105)

Now that the final decision has been made to adopt the GSA letter styles, Ms. Sanchez has assigned Mr. Rutledge to write a letter for her signature to the agency's purchasing agent to order the needed correspondence manuals.

Mr. Rutledge gives you the letter to prepare in final form. Because February 28 is only about two weeks away, you are asked to mail this letter by express mail.

The subject of the letter is: **Immediate order for correspondence manuals.** Date the letter **February 17, 19--;** address the letter to:

**Mr. Anthony Thomaswick
Purchasing Agent
U.S. Services Agency
Washington, DC 20469-5514**

(¶) A decision has been made to adopt new letter styles for all written communications within our branch office. The decision also was made to implement the new written communication procedures on February 28.

(¶) We do not have very much time to inform our personnel and to provide our keyboard specialists with the necessary training materials and correspondence manuals. Therefore, will you please expedite the preparation of the purchase order for these correspondence manuals. I am confident we can receive the manuals within seven days if the purchase order is sent immediately.

(¶) Order the manuals from the Superintendent of Documents, U.S. Government Printing Office, Washington, DC 20402-5541. The title of the manual is: U.S. Government Correspondence Manual (U.S. Printing Office Stock Number 022-000-00129-9). Please order 25 copies at $3.80 each.

(¶) I will be out of the office on official business on February 23-28. Mr. Terence J. Rutledge, Assistant Deputy Director, will be in charge of the office while I am away. Please send a copy of the purchase order confirmation to him.

Job 6
Three-page report (full sheets)

Mr. Rutledge has been assigned to draft a report about the government letter styles that the branch will adopt on February 28. He asks that you prepare this report in final form as an unbound manuscript.

Copies of this report will be distributed to all branch office personnel and to the other agency branches.

Heading for the report is:
GOVERNMENT LETTER STYLES
Correct any undetected errors that Mr. Rutledge may have overlooked.

The Gen. Services Adm. has developed the U.S. Government correspondence Manual which includes two basic letter formats: formal and informal. the basic styles characteristics of the two formats are presented first, and then the special style characteristics of each format are noted.

Basic Style Characteristics

Stationery. Official agency letterhead should be printed on the standard 8 1/2" x 11" paper.

Subject line. The first letter of the first word and all proper nouns are capitalized in the subject line. If more than one line is needed for the subject, single space and place the succeeding line flush with the left margin.

Margins. The side margins on al government correspondence should be 1 inch. The bottom margin should not be less than 1 inch on any page

Attention line. An attention line, when needed, is placed as the second line of the address. The caption "attn:" should preceed the name of the person to whose attention the letter is called

30

Learning goals

1 To prepare personal letters in block and modified block styles.
2 To correct keyboarding errors.
3 To improve ability to keyboard unedited copy.
4 To address envelopes.
5 To align and type over words.

Machine adjustments

1 Position desk and chair at com—fortable heights.
2 Elevate book.
3 Set ribbon control to type on upper half of ribbon.
4 Use 60–space line for drills; 50–space line for letters.
5 SS drills; DS paragraphs.
Materials: monarch–size sheets and envelopes; plain sheets; supplies for correcting errors.

30a ▶ 7
Preparatory practice

each line 3 times SS (slowly, faster, slower); DS between 3-line groups; re-peat if time permits

alphabet	1	Jayne Coxx puzzled over the workbooks required for geometry.
a/s	2	This essay says it is easy to save us from disaster in Asia.
figures	3	The box is 6 5/8 by 9 1/2 feet and weighs 375 to 400 pounds.
easy	4	The city auditor paid the proficient man for the fine signs.

| 1 | 2 | 3 | 4 | 5 | 6 | 7 | 8 | 9 | 10 | 11 | 12 |

30b ▶ 43
Prepare personal letters in block style

7¼″ × 10½″ personal station-ery [Laboratory Materials pp. 17-19]; 50-space line; 2″ top margin; proofread/circle errors

If personal–size stationery or plain paper cut to size is not available, use full sheets (8½″ × 11″); 50–space line; 2½″ top margin.

1 Study the explanatory para–graphs at the right. Refer to the style letter on page 58 for further illustration.
2 Prepare the letter illustrating the block style shown on page 58. Follow spacing directions given on the letter.
3 On a plain full sheet, do two 1′ writings on the opening lines (return address through saluta–tion) and two 2′ writings on the closing lines (last 3 ¶s through complimentary close).
4 Retype the letter; omit ¶3.

Letter placement information

Many personal letters are prepared on personal-size stationery; and Style Letter 1, page 58, is shown with pica (10-pitch) type on that size stationery.

Good letter placement results from the ability to make judgments based on the length of letter, style of stationery, and size of type. Therefore, while it is suggested that letters in Section 7 be started on Line 13 when personal stationery is used (which al-lows approximately a 2″ top margin) or on Line 16 if full sheets are used (approxi-mately a 2½″ top margin), the starting point can be raised for a longer letter or lowered for a shorter one if you believe it is wise to do so.

Every letter must have a return address. On business stationery, the return address is part of the letterhead. When personal stationery is used, a return address must be typed as part of the letter. The most appro-priate place for this address, according to common usage, is on the two lines imme-diately above and aligned with the date.

It is standard procedure to operate the return 4 times, leaving 3 blank line spaces between the date and the letter recipient's address. This procedure is repeated after the complimentary close, leaving 3 blank line spaces for the signature to be written between the complimentary close and the writer's typed name. (For a personal letter, a typed name is not necessary.) These placement procedures should be followed with all letters in Section 7.

For smaller personal stationery, side margins should be no less than 1″ and no more than 1½″. A 50-space line, pica or elite, fits within this standard. It is recom-mended, therefore, that a 50-space line be used with Section 7 letters regardless of type size.

Job 3
Composing an informal government letter (LM p. 101)

Job 4
Formal government letter (LM p. 103)

Ms. Sanchez has asked Mr. Rutledge to prepare a thank you letter to **Mr. Roberto V. Sebastian, Director of Special Services, General Services Administration, Washington, D C 20405-5512.**

Mr. Sebastian was very helpful to the branch office during the decision–making process concerning the adoption of the new government letter styles. She wishes to express her appreciation to him and to inform him of the decision to adopt the GSA letter styles.

You need to prepare only 1 carbon copy for the official file. Correct any undetected errors. Ms. Sanchez will be the signer of this letter. Date the letter **February 16, 19--.** Use the subject: **Decision to adopt the GSA letter styles.**

Ms. Sanchez asks that you compose an informal letter that will be duplicated and distributed to the Chicago branch office staff.

The subject is: **Out-of-town schedule for February 23-28.**

For future reference, remember that the office symbol for the Chicago branch is AFAW.

Ms. Sanchez wants you to include the following information in the letter:

1 The purpose of her trip.
2 The dates and places she will visit.
3 The fact that Mr. Terence J. Rutledge, Assistant Deputy Director, will be directing the office while she is away.

Two copy notations should be made, one for the Official File—AFAW, and one for Mr. Terence J. Rutledge—AFAW.

Note: All correspondence should have 1 cc for the Official File—AFAW.

Date the letter **February 16, 19--.**

Prepare a rough draft on plain paper, final copy on letterhead.

Dear Mr. Sebastian :

Thankyou for assisting our agency in it's recent decision-making process to standardize the letter styles used in the Chicago branch of the U. S. Services Agency.

The two government letter styles that the General Services Administration has developed for use in U. S. Government offices provide the needed flexibility between informal and formal communications. Also, the two styles are very easy four are keyboard specialists to learn.

Effective February 28, our brench office will begin using two official goverment letter styles for all of our enternal and external written communications. However, as you can see, I am using the new letter styles now so that I will become familiar with them prior to our adoption of them.

Our order for copies of the correspondance manual will be sent directly to the U. S. Government Printing Office as you suggested.

Sincerely,

gwam 1' (total words)

gwam 2'

Return
address
Dateline

101 Kensington Place   Line 13
Brockton, MA ⌐ 02401-5372
August 3, 19-—⌐ 2 spaces

           Operate return
            4 times

4
9
12

Letter
address

Ms. Viola Bargas
6776 Heidelberg Street
Durham, NC 27704-4329
          DS

15
20
25

Salutation

Dear Viola
    DS

27

Body
of
letter

It will be great to have you living in Brockton
again. Your promotion to vice-president of the
marketing division is certainly well deserved.

36
46
55

You will find that our town has changed considerably since your last visit three years ago. It is
still a small, close-knit community; but the newly
established Arts Commission has begun to promote
the efforts of many local artists. As a result,
our little village has taken on a bohemian air.

65
75
86
95
105
115

Let me show you one way that Brockton has changed.
I should like you to be my guest on August 23 when
the local theater group presents SCHOOL FOR SCANDAL
at the Whitmore Playhouse. Two of our sorority
members are directing the production.

125 5
135 10
146 15
155 20
163 24

As you requested, I shall meet you at the airport
(Gate 11) on August 23 at 8:25 a.m. You can spend
the afternoon apartment hunting, and you can relax
in the evening during dinner and the play.

173 29
183 34
193 39
202 44

I am very eager to see you, Viola!
        DS

209 47

Complimentary
close
Signature

Cordially

Amanda

211 48

This letter is typed with
"open" punctuation; that is,
no punctuation follows the
salutation or complimentary
close.

Style letter 1: personal letter in block style

189a-194a ▶ 5
Preparatory practice

each line 3 times SS (slowly, faster, slowly); retype selected lines as time permits

alphabet	1	Both judges gave my wax sculpture of a quail the coveted king's prize.
fig/sym	2	Please pay Invoice #1937 for $26,450 (less 8% discount) by November 3.
bottom row	3	Seven members of the city zoning council have condemned six buildings.
fluency	4	The name of the neighbor also may be on the title of the antique auto.

| 1 | 2 | 3 | 4 | 5 | 6 | 7 | 8 | 9 | 10 | 11 | 12 | 13 | 14 |

189b-194b ▶ 45
Office job simulation
(LM pp. 97–109)

Job 1
Itinerary with braced headings (full sheet)

Ms. Sanchez received her flight confirmations yesterday for her upcoming trips to the agency branch offices in New Orleans and Los Angeles. She will also go to Washington, D.C. in order to report to Ms. Jean Carson, Chief of the U.S. Services Agency, and discuss with her the visits to the branch offices.

She requests that you prepare her itinerary as a boxed table, DS. Center the table horizontally and vertically in reading position. Leave 2 spaces between the columns. Add heading: **ANITA R. SANCHEZ;** Add subheading: **Itinerary for February 23-28, 19—.**

Job 2
Informal government letters
(LM pp. 97–99)

Ms. Sanchez asks that you prepare the following letter for the branch Deputy Directors in the New Orleans and Los Angeles offices informing them of her on-site visits at the end of the month. To insure fast mail service, be sure to send the letters by express mail.

The address for the Los Angeles Deputy Director is:

Mr. Arnold V. Stucki
Deputy Director
U.S. Services Agency
11000 Wilshire Blvd.
Los Angeles, CA 90024-3105

If you were using information word processing equipment, you would need to key the data only once, and then change only the variable data (name and address) for each subsequent letter printed.

Date	Departure City	Time	Flight	Arrival City	Time
23	Chicago	10:45 a.m.	EA 925	New Orleans	12:50 p.m.
25	New Orleans	1:38 p.m.	DL 132	Los Angeles	5:05 p.m.
27	Los Angeles	7:28 a.m.	TW 630	Washington	2:05 p.m.
28	Washington	6:45 p.m.	UA 496	Chicago	7:09 p.m.

Date: February 15, 19-- | Sender's reference: AFAW | Special Mailing Instructions: EXPRESS MAIL | Subject: Confirmation of on-site visit | Address: Ms. Nicole Goulet | Deputy Director | U.S. Services Agency | 569 Loyola Avenue | New Orleans, LA 70113-2211

(¶) Ms. Jean Carson, Chief of the U.S. Services Agency, has assigned me to visit each branch office for the following purposes:

a. Audit the branch's affirmative action records for the past year to verify compliance with the Agency's Affirmative Action Plan.

b. Audit the employee attendance records to verify that proper documentation was obtained to support all sick leaves, personal leaves, and vacation periods.

c. Deliver and discuss with you the Agency's budget plans for the next fiscal year.

(¶) Please have all documentation readily available and the necessary records up to date prior to my arrival.

(¶) A copy of my itinerary is enclosed. Please have someone meet me at the airport when I arrive. Also, will you please make a hotel reservation for me at the most convenient location.

ANITA R. SANCHEZ | Deputy Chief, U.S. Services Agency | Enclosure | cc: Official File--AFAW | Ms. Jean Carson--AFAC | AFAW:ARSanchez:xx 2-15---

31a ▶ 7
Preparatory practice

each line twice SS (slowly, faster, slower); DS between 2-line groups; then as many 30″ writings on Line 4 as time permits

alphabet 1 Max Jurez worked to improve the quality of his basic typing.

adjacent reaches 2 Bert quickly pointed to where onions grew in the sandy soil.

fig/sym 3 Veronica bought 16 7/8 yards of #240 cotton at $3.59 a yard.

easy 4 The formal gowns worn by the girls hang in the civic chapel.

| 1 | 2 | 3 | 4 | 5 | 6 | 7 | 8 | 9 | 10 | 11 | 12 |

31b ▶ 15
Correct errors

1 Read the information at the right.

2 Keyboard the lines below the information exactly as they appear DS; correct the errors *after* you have typed each line.

Truly finished work contains no errors. Most individuals rely upon an "inner sense" to tell them when they have made an error, and they stop keyboarding at once and correct it. This "inner sense," however, is fallible; and even an expert typist should carefully proofread completed work for undetected mistakes while the paper is still in the machine. Correcting errors before the paper is removed is easier than reinserting paper and trying to realign lines of copy.

There are several acceptable methods that can be used to correct errors, and they are explained below. Whichever one of them is used, one should keep in mind that an error must be repaired skillfully enough so that neither the error nor evidence of the correction can be observed.

Automatic correction

If your machine is equipped with an automatic correcting ribbon, consult with your instructor or the manufacturer's manual for operating instructions.

Correction paper ("white carbon")

1 Backspace to the error.

2 Place the correction paper in front of the error, coated side toward the paper.

3 Retype the error. The substance on the correction paper will cover the error.

4 Remove the correction paper; backspace; type the correction.

Correction fluid ("liquid paper")

1 Be sure the color of the fluid matches the color of the paper.

2 Turn the paper forward or backward to ease the correction process.

3 Brush the fluid on sparingly; cover only the error, and it lightly.

4 The fluid dries quickly. Return to correction point and make the correction.

Rubber eraser

1 Use a plastic shield (to protect surrounding type) and a typewriter (hard) eraser.

2 Turn the paper forward or backward in the typewriter to position the error for easier correction.

3 To keep bits of rubber out of the mechanism, move the carrier away from the error (or move carriage to the extreme left or right).

4 With a sharp edge of the eraser, erase ink from the paper. Move the eraser in one direction only to avoid cutting the paper.

1 Concentrate when you type; fongers can "telegraph" an error.

2 Just as soon as a mistade is made, it ought to be corrected.

3 It pays to be sure that you find evrey error and correct it.

4 Proofread carefully; then remove your work from the nachine.

Formal government letter

Informal government letter

Blind Carbon Copy Procedure. To exclude information from the original copy: (1) turn the cylinder (platen) knob toward you—rolling the carbon pack backward; (2) insert a half sheet of fairly transparent paper in front of the original to cover the area where the notations are to be placed; (3) turn the carbon pack back to the position of the notation; (4) type the notations in their proper order.

Blind Photocopy Procedure. You may add information to the file copies by (1) omitting these notations from the original copy; (2) photocopying the original and then reinserting the photocopy and typing the notations in their proper order; (3) making the needed number of file copies.

Special Style Characteristics for Formal and Informal Style Government Letters

Formal Government Letters. Use the block style with a salutation, complimentary close, and mixed punctuation. Other special style characteristics are as listed:

Dateline on Line 7 at the left margin.

Special Mailing Instructions such as SPECIAL DELIVERY, REGISTERED, CERTIFIED, or EXPRESS MAIL on Line 9 at the left margin.

Subject Line on Line 11 at the left margin.

Address begins on Line 14 at the left margin. Arrange the lines in block style single-spaced. (See *Window Envelopes*, p. 337, for further directions.)

Informal Government Letters. Use the block style with the necessary headings placed to the right of the preprinted captions. Other special style characteristics of the informal style are:

Sender's Reference is the official symbol of the sender (e.g., AFAW). Place the official symbol flush with the left margin in line with the "Reply to Attn of:" caption (placed a double space below the dateline). An office that does not have an official symbol uses an abbreviation of the office name.

Special Mailing Instructions such as SPECIAL DELIVERY, REGISTERED, CERTIFIED, or EXPRESS MAIL should be placed on the same line as the sender's reference, starting at the horizontal center of the letterhead. If the sender's reference line extends to or beyond the center of the line, begin the special mailing notation 3 spaces to the right of it. Note: Special mailing instructions are placed on the letter *only* if the keyboard specialist does not prepare the envelope.

Address begins at the left margin in line with the "To:" caption. Arrange the lines in block style single-spaced. (See *Window Envelopes*, p. 337, for further directions.)

31c ▶ 28
Personal letters in block style

3 personal-size sheets [LM pp. 21-25] or plain paper; see pages 57 and 58 for guides to letter placement; proofread/ correct errors

Postal authorities recommend using 2–letter state abbreviations (always with ZIP Code). For a complete list of such abbrevia– tions, see the Reference Guide, p. iv at the back of this book.

Problem 1   words

900 Beecher Street | Montgomery, AL 36108-4473 | May 18, 19-- | 12
(Operate return 4 times) | Mr. Lymon S. Bohn | 890 Crestview   18
Drive | Rockford, IL 61107-2317 | DS | Dear Lymon | DS   26

(¶) This morning I talked with Debra Tredsaw, a member of the   38
school reunion committee; and I heard a bit of great news--that   51
you plan to attend our class reunion next month.   61

(¶) More great news! Herb Dobynski will also be here, and he   72
and I want to play a little golf that afternoon. Can you arrange   85
to be in town early enough to join us? Maybe I can persuade   98
Jimmy Geddes or Ted Oxward to make it a foursome.   108

(¶) Let me know when you are arriving, Lymon. I'll be glad to   120
pick you up at the airport or to make any other arrangements for   133
you.   133

Cordially | (Operate return 4 times) | Mike Stavros   138

Problem 2

890 Crestview Drive | Rockford, IL 61107-2317 | May 25, 19-- | Mr.   12
Michael Stavros | 900 Beecher Street | Montgomery, AL 36108-   24
4473 | Dear Mike   26

(¶) I do indeed plan to attend the Monroe High reunion of the   38
Class of '78. I wouldn't miss it--nor would I pass up a chance to   51
give you and Herb a drubbing on the golf course.   61

(¶) The trip to Montgomery will also involve taking care of some   74
business. I shall drive down, arriving there during the late   86
afternoon or early evening of the 16th. I have made reserva-   98
tions at the Graymoor for three days. I'll call you when I get in.   112

(¶) I'm really looking forward to this trip, Mike, and to the oppor-   125
tunity to visit many old friends.   131

Cordially | Lymon Bohn   135

Problem 3

900 Beecher Street | Montgomery, AL 36108-4473 | May 27, 19-- | 11
Mr. Herbert Dobynski | 8098 Fairwater Drive | Norfolk, VA   23
23508-6172 | Dear Herb   27

(¶) I have tried to reach you several times by phone, but I have   39
not been successful; hence, this brief note.   48

(¶) Lymon Bohn has confirmed that he'll be in town for the re-   60
union on June 17, and he has agreed to join us for golf that after-   73
noon. Ted Oxward will also join us.   81

(¶) Because I expect things might be hectic at my club that day,   93
I called the pro, Jill Nyles, today and asked her to save us a   105
tee-off time of 1 p.m. If for any reason this time is not good   118
for you, let me know.   123

Cordially | Mike Stavros   127

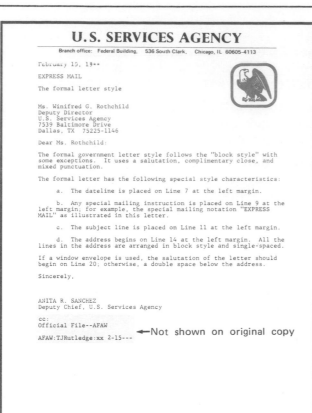

Formal government letter

Informal government letter

Enclosures. When needed, place the word "Enclosure " a double space below the signature element. If more than 1 item is enclosed, use the plural form and indicate the number of enclosures; for example: "3 enclosures." When specific references to all enclosures are not made in the body of the letter, list each enclosure on a separate line below the word "Enclosure:"; single-space enclosure lines flush with the left margin.

Material Sent Under Separate Cover. If material that is to be sent under separate cover is mentioned in the letter, place the words "Separate cover:" flush with the left margin, a double space below the signature element or the enclosure notation (if there is an enclosure notation). List the material to be sent under separate cover, whether or not it is identified in the body, below the words "Separate cover:", single-spaced, and flush with the left margin. For example:

> Separate cover:
> Copy of bid form
> Bidding packet

Information Not Shown on Original Copy. *The Distribution of Copies* and *Identification of Office, Writer, and Keyboard Specialist* elements are shown *only* on file copies.

Distribution of Copies. This notation is shown only on the file copies. Place the *Distribution of Copies* notation a double space below the signature element or enclosure notation or the separate cover listing. List the names of all recipients one below the other with their corresponding office symbol when appropriate:

> cc:
> Official File--AFAW
> Reading File--AFAW
> RTBrown--AFAX

Identification of Office, Writer, and Keyboard Specialist. This notation is shown only on the file copies. Place the office symbol of the preparing office, the writer's initials and surname, the keyboard specialist's initials, and the date on this line a double space below the last line used and flush with the left margin. For example:

> AFAW:RJFranz:cv 4-19-85

Note: In some cases the writer of the letter is not the signer of the letter; therefore, the writer's name should be placed in the identification line instead of signer's name.

Window Envelopes. When a window envelope is used, the address should be 5 lines or fewer, and no address should be more than 4 inches wide. If a line must be divided, begin the second line 2 spaces from the left margin. The body (message) of the letter should start on Line 20.

32a ▶ 7
Preparatory practice

each line three times SS
(slowly, faster, slower); DS
between 3-line groups; repeat if time permits

alphabet 1 Jim Kable won a second prize for his very quixotic drawings.

shift 2 Zora and Donald Pace flew over Byrd Peak six times in March.

fig/sym 3 I said, "My check for $739.50 (#184) is not dated April 26."

easy 4 The ancient oak on the quay is visible to an island visitor.

| 1 | 2 | 3 | 4 | 5 | 6 | 7 | 8 | 9 | 10 | 11 | 12 |

32b ▶ 10
Improve concentration: typing from unedited copy

60-space line; DS

1 Find and correct errors in the
copy as you type the paragraph.
2 Proofread/correct final copy
while it is still in the machine.

words

What causes you eraser to erase? There is no thing spe- 11
cial about it. When you type, the element forses ink into the 24
fibers of the paper. If you type some thing wrong, therefore, 36
the fibers under the error must be remover. Such removal is 48
best accomplished by confining the erasing to a small area 60
and by moving the eraser in just one direction, an action that 73
removes just one layer of inked fibbers. 81

32c ▶ 13
Personal letter in block style

1 personal-size sheet [LM p.
27] or plain paper; SS ¶s; DS
between ¶s; proofread/correct
errors

1 Format the letter at the right,
making corrections as marked.

2 For special parts, use:

Return address and date

334 Pittman Street
Olathe, KS 66061-1678

March 22, 19--

Letter address

Miss Evelyn Guione
1352 Pilgrim Place
Pasadena, CA 91108-3307

Salutation **Dear Evelyn**

Closing lines

Sincerely

(Return 4 times)

Trevor Hunter

Save your typed letter to
use in 33c, p. 63.

words

opening lines 20

¶ AS I told you I might, I have changed my plans. I shall be 38
taking several morning classes, there at the University during 52
July and August. 55

¶ My expenses would be eased considerably if I could find a 67
part-time job where I might work afternoons or evenings. 78
So, would you be kind enough to let me know if you should 89
learn of such a position? May I use your name as a reference if I make the 104
application? 106

¶ I value you friendship, Evelyn; and I shall be very gratful 119
for any assistance that you may provide. 127

closing lines 129

Learning goals

1 To develop knowledge and skill in preparing government corre—spondence.

2 To plan your work and complete it correctly and efficiently.

Machine adjustments

1 Set paper guide at *0*.

2 Set ribbon control to use upper half of ribbon.

3 Set line-space selector for SS.

4 Margins: 70–space line for drills; 1" side margins for government letters.

189-194

Office Job Simulation

Read carefully the material at the right and on pages 337–38 before you begin the work in Section 42. Note any standard procedures that you think will save you time during the completion of the government office activities.

Daily practice plan:

Preparatory practice .... 5'
Work on simulation .... 45'

New Location

Your parents recently moved to Chicago, and you decided to relocate with them. You asked Ms. DeSoto if you could be reassigned to work through the Chicago office of Office Service Temporaries, Inc. She has agreed and has transferred your file to the Chicago office. You are requested by the Office Manager of the Chicago office to report to work for a first assignment on February 15.

Work Assignment

You have been assigned by Office Service Temporaries, Inc., to work as a keyboard specialist with the U.S. Services Agency, an agency of the U.S. Government. You will work directly for Ms. Anita R. Sanchez, Deputy Chief, Chicago Branch, U.S. Services Agency, Federal Building, 536 South Clark Street, Chicago, IL 60605-4113.

Ms. Sanchez orients you to your work assignment the morning you arrive. She informs you of the decision to adopt the government letter styles recommended by the General Services Administration. Although the Chicago branch will not officially adopt the new letter styles until February 28, she has requested that all of her correspondence be prepared using these new formats. She also requires that 1 carbon copy of each government letter be prepared, unless otherwise instructed.

The U.S. Services Agency bases most of its keyboarding and formatting preparation on COLLEGE KEYBOARDING/TYPEWRITING; therefore, if you have questions regarding style or format, refer to your textbook. Ms. Sanchez has a copy of the *U.S. Government Correspondence Manual* for you to use as a reference. Excerpts from the manual are given at the right and on pages 337-38 for quick reference.

Excerpts from the U.S. Government Correspondence Manual

The U.S. Services Agency has adopted both the formal and informal government letter styles.

Basic Style Characteristics for Formal and Informal Government Letters

Style. The basic style of both formal and informal government letters is essentially "block with some exceptions."

Stationery. Official agency letterhead is printed on 8½" × 11" paper. Stationery for the informal government letter will have the following captions preprinted in the left margin: "Date:", "Reply to Attn of:", "Subject:", and "To:" (see illustration on page 337 or 338).

Margins. Side margins on all government correspondence are 1". A 1" left margin in the informal government letter should leave about 2 spaces between preprinted captions and the typed headings. The bottom margin should not be less than 1".

Subject Line. Capitalize only the first letter of the first word and all proper nouns. When more than 1 line is needed for the subject, single-space and begin each succeeding line flush with the left margin.

Attention Line. If needed, place the attention line as the second line of the address. Precede the name of the person to whose attention the letter is called with the "ATTN:" caption.

Body (Message). Begin the message of the letter at least 2 lines below the last line of the address or salutation. Begin the main paragraphs flush with the left margin single-spaced; double-space between paragraphs. Indent the first line of numbered or lettered subparagraphs 5 spaces; begin all succeeding lines in subparagraphs flush with the left margin. If a letter consists of a single paragraph of fewer than 10 lines, double-space the body.

Signature Element. Place the name of the signer flush with the left margin in all capital letters on the 4th line space below the last line of the body or complimentary close. Place the signer's title on the next line, flush with the left margin. If more than 1 line is needed for the signer's title, place the succeeding lines flush with the left margin. The entire signature element (name and title) should be 4 lines or fewer.

32d ▶ 12
Address envelopes

1 Addressing envelopes is entirely a matter of visual placement. Read the following guides and study the illustrations to help you with the placement of addresses.

2 Type in United States Postal Service (U.S.P.S.) style a Monarch envelope (No. 9) and in standard style a small envelope (No. 6¾) for each address [LM pp. 29–33]. Use your own return address; proofread/circle errors.

Letter address

Vertically: Visualize a line drawn from side to side across the vertical center of the envelope. Begin the first line of the address just below such an imaginary line.

Horizontally: Visualize a line drawn from top to bottom across the horizontal center of the envelope. Align an address from 5 (for larger envelopes) to 10 (for smaller envelopes) spaces to the left of such an imaginary line.

Return address

Type the writer's name and address SS in block style in the upper left corner. Start about 3 spaces from the left edge on Line 2.

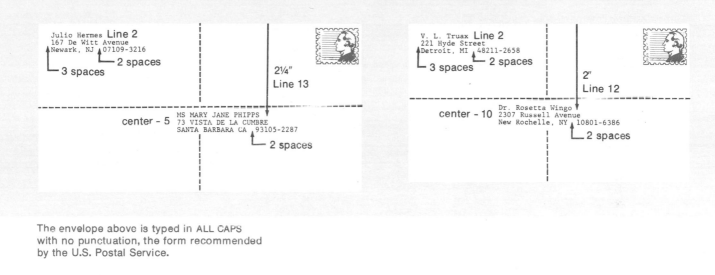

The envelope above is typed in ALL CAPS with no punctuation, the form recommended by the U.S. Postal Service.

Mrs. Arthur T. Werther
1321 Fairbanks Road
Concord, NH 03301-1789

Miss Grace Carveck
35 Fox Mill Lane
Springfield, IL 62707-7133

Mr. Brett Reymer
94 Mercer Street
Paterson, NJ 07524-5447

32e ▶ 8
Fold and insert letters

Study the illustrations below. Practice folding 8½" × 11" paper for small envelopes and 7¼" × 10½" paper for Monarch envelopes.

The folding procedure for Monarch envelopes is also used for large (No. 10) business envelopes.

Folding and inserting letters into small envelopes

Folding and inserting letters into Monarch envelopes

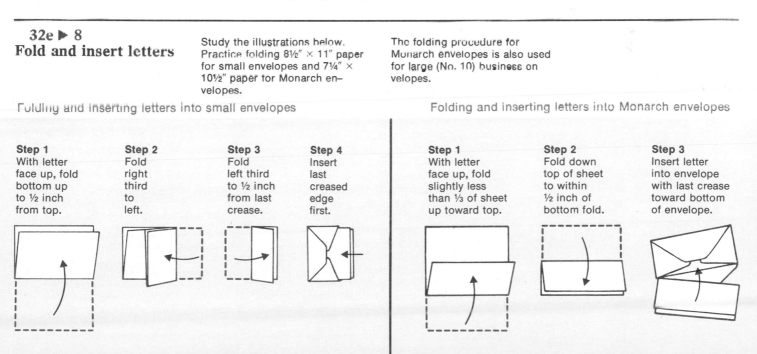

Step 1
With letter face up, fold bottom up to ½ inch from top.

Step 2
Fold right third to left.

Step 3
Fold left third to ½ inch from last crease.

Step 4
Insert last creased edge first.

Step 1
With letter face up, fold slightly less than ⅓ of sheet up toward top.

Step 2
Fold down top of sheet to within ½ inch of bottom fold.

Step 3
Insert letter into envelope with last crease toward bottom of envelope.

LEVEL SIX
Processing information (service office simulations)

This level of Advanced Keyboarding/Formatting Skills is designed to provide you with the opportunity to develop your production skills in a variety of simulations that are commonly found in government, medical, legal, consulting, and information processing offices.

A secondary purpose of this level is to help you continue to improve your basic speed and accuracy skills. In addition to the daily Preparatory Practice, two sections are devoted almost entirely to speed and accuracy development.

The final section of Level 6 is a measurement section that tests both your basic speed and accuracy skills and your production skills. Your two major performance goals in Level 6 are the same as those for Level 5. They are:

- To develop a keen responsibility for high-quality work.
- To develop the ability to make decisions without direct supervision.

This level provides for about 20 percent of your classroom time to be devoted to basic speed and accuracy development and 80 percent to simulated production activities.

335

33a ▶ 7
Preparatory practice

each line 3 times SS (slowly, faster, still faster); DS between 3-line groups; repeat if time permits

alphabet	1	Perry might know I feel jinxed because I have missed a quiz.
figures	2	Buy 147 fish, 25 geese, 10 ponies, 39 lambs, and 68 kittens.
hyphen	3	He won the first-class ribbon; it was a now-or-never effort.
easy	4	The neighbor owns a fox, six foals, six ducks, and six hens.

| 1 | 2 | 3 | 4 | 5 | 6 | 7 | 8 | 9 | 10 | 11 | 12 |

33b ▶ 10
Align and type

It is sometimes necessary to reinsert the paper to correct an error. The following steps will help you learn to do so correctly.

1 Type this sentence, but do not make the return:

I can align this copy.

2 Locate aligning scale (16), variable line spacer (2), and paper release lever (13) on your machine.

3 Move the carrier (carriage) so that a word containing an i (such as align) is above the align-

ing scale. Note that a vertical line points to the center of i.

4 Study the relation between top of aligning scale and bottoms of letters with downstems (g,p,y).

Get an exact eye picture of the relation of typed line to top of scale so you will be able to adjust the paper correctly to type over a character with exactness.

5 Remove paper; reinsert it. Gauge the line so bottoms of letters are in correct relation to top of aligning scale. Operate the variable line spacer, if necessary, to move paper up or down. Operate paper release lever to move paper left or right, if necessary, when centering the letter i over one of the lines on the aligning scale.

6 Check accuracy of alignment by setting the ribbon control (28) in stencil position and by typing over one of the letters. If necessary, make further alignment adjustments.

7 Return ribbon control to normal position (to type on upper half of ribbon).

8 Type over the characters in the sentence, moving paper up or down, to left or right, as necessary to correct alignment.

33c ▶ 10
Address envelopes; fold letters

1 sheet plain paper

Refer to page 62 as needed.

Use your letter from 32c, page 61, or plain paper cut to size.

NOTE: If you typed the letter of 32c on standard typing paper, fold it for insertion into a large envelope in the same way the personal-size letter is folded for a Monarch envelope.

1 Address a Monarch envelope to the address below right; use your return address.

2 Fold the letter you typed in 32c, p. 61, for insertion into the envelope.

3 Open the folded paper. Is the typed side facing you?

4 Mark an X at the top edge of a plain sheet, then fold for insertion into a small envelope.

5 Open the folded paper. Is the X facing you?

MISS EVELYN GUIONE
1352 PILGRIM PLACE
PASADENA CA   91108-3307

33d ▶ 23
Prepare personal-business letters in modified block style

1 sheet personal-size paper [LM p. 35] or plain paper; envelope

*From this point on, the last figure in the word count column includes the envelope address.

Study the letter in modified block style illustrated on page 64. Notice the change in position of the return address, date, complimentary close, and typed name.

2 Clear tab stops; set a new stop at center point.

3 Type the letter. Proofread/correct errors.

4 Type an envelope; correct errors.

5 Fold the letter for insertion into envelope.

Job 3
Balance sheet
(full sheet)

Format and type the bal—
ance sheet. Leave a 1" top
margin; leave 8 spaces be—
tween Columns 1 and 2 and
2 spaces between Columns
2 and 3.

COLEMAN REAL ESTATE COMPANY				6
Balance sheet				8
June 30, 19--				11
Assets				14
Current assets:				17
Cash			$ 45,650	20
Accounts receivable	$ 42,000			26
Less reserve for bad debts	1,500		40,500	34
Office supplies			3,500	38
Fixed asset:			175,000	41
Land			~~176,300~~	44
Building _accumulated_	$150,000			47
[Less] depreciation	75,000		75,000	59
Office equipment	$ 85,000			64
Less accumulated depreciation	25,000		60,000	75
Total assets			#399,650	81
TS→ Liabilites				85
Current liabilites:				89
Accounts payable	$ 20,000			94
Notes payable	35,000	$ 55,000		102
Long-term liabilities:				107
Mortgage payable		50,000		113
Total liabilities		$105,000		119
Owner's Equity				125
Capital:				127
Capital stock	$280,000			131
Retained earnings	14,650	$294,650		142
Total liabilities and				146
owner's equity		$399,650		154

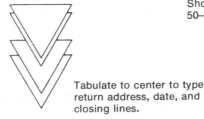

Shown in pica type
50–space line

Tabulate to center to type
return address, date, and
closing lines.

<table>
<tr><td>Return address</td><td>Line 13</td><td>4885 Crescent Avenue, N.</td><td>3</td><td>5</td></tr>
<tr><td></td><td></td><td>Chicago, IL 60656-3781</td><td>5</td><td>10</td></tr>
<tr><td>Dateline</td><td></td><td>April 6, 19--</td><td>6</td><td>13</td></tr>
</table>

Operate return
4 times

<table>
<tr><td>Letter address</td><td>Ms. Alice Trent-Rockler</td><td>9</td><td>17</td></tr>
<tr><td></td><td>Personnel Manager</td><td>11</td><td>21</td></tr>
<tr><td></td><td>Leisure Life Inns</td><td>12</td><td>25</td></tr>
<tr><td></td><td>1000 East Lynn Street</td><td>15</td><td>29</td></tr>
<tr><td></td><td>Seattle, WA 98102-4268</td><td>17</td><td>34</td></tr>
</table>

DS

Salutation   Dear Ms. Trent-Rockler   19   38

DS

The Placement Office at Great Lakes College tells   5   48
me that your company has employment available this   10   58
summer for students.   12   63

I am now in my junior year as an economics major.   17   73
Although my educational background has been mostly   22   83
in the liberal arts, I have learned to keyboard;   27   93
and I have taken two accounting courses. In past   32   103
summers I have worked successfully at a variety of   37   113
jobs; in fact, I have accepted responsibility for   42   123
most of my college expenses. I travel as much as   47   133
I can; I like to meet new friends; and I have a   52   143
friendly, outgoing personality.   56   149

Your interest in providing summer employment for   5   159
students is much appreciated, Ms. Trent-Rockler.   10   169
I am sure I would enjoy working at Leisure Life   15   178
Inns. May I send you a complete resume and a list   20   189
of my references?   21   192

DS

Complimentary close   Sincerely yours   23   195

Operate return
4 times

Lance J. Mykins

Typed name   Lance J. Mykins   25   198

232

gwam 2'   total words

Style letter 2: personal-business letter in modified block style,
open punctuation

188a ▶ 5
Preparatory practice

each line 3 times SS
(slowly, faster, top
speed); DS between
3-line groups; repeat
selected lines as time
permits

alphabet 1 An expert adjustment by Virge was made quickly before the pipes froze.

fig/sym 2 In the fall (9/20/86), we purchased 357.4 metric tons of #1 red wheat.

shift lock 3 A mailing notation--REGISTERED or HOLD FOR ARRIVAL--should be in caps.

fluency 4 She may sight a whale if she pays a visit to the downtown island dock.

| 1 | 2 | 3 | 4 | 5 | 6 | 7 | 8 | 9 | 10 | 11 | 12 | 13 | 14 |

188b ▶ 45
Production measurement

(LM p. 95; full sheets)

Time schedule

Assembling materials . 2'
Timed production ..... 38'
Final check; compute
  n-pram .... 5'

Job 1
Invoice (LM p. 95)

Format and type the invoice
given at the right; prepare 1
cc on plain half sheet;
proofread carefully; correct
errors neatly.

words

Invoice

Brown & Row Publishers
200 Malvern Avenue
Cleveland, OH 44116-0032

Terms *Net 30 days*

Date July 12, 1986 — 7
Our Order No. M-3211-005 — 13
Cust. Order No. Z-511-250 — 23
Shipped Via UPS — 26

Quantity	Description	Unit Price	Total	
25	File folders (9⅜" × 11¾")--A1593	.40	10.00	37
2	MLZ microfiche readers--M-7821	304.20	608.40	47
3	Computer terminal tables(oak finish)--			55
	S-5502	56.20	168.60	60
1	Portable changeable letterboard			68
	(with color panel)-- Z-4559	84.65	84.65	76
			871.65	77

Job 2
Agenda (full sheet)

Prepare for left binding the
agenda shown at the right.
Leave a 2" top margin.

RUSSELL DISTRIBUTORS, INC.
Agenda for Meeting of the Board of Directors } DS
November 13, 19-- TS

5
14
18

1. Call to order . . . . Percy Kolstad — 30

2. Minutes of Last meeting . . . . Raymond Kofer / ~~Fred Kuker~~ e — 42

3. Special reports — 46
   Manufacturer's Liaison . . . . Carol Sizes — 57
   Retailer's Division . . . . Tim Rathe — 67
   Special Promotions . . . . Renee High — 76
   Land Acquisition Committee . . . . . . Martha Seely — 87

4. Discussion of Special reports . . . . . Percy Kolstad — 99

5. Declaration of Dividend . . . . Rebecca / ~~Ruth~~ Nettle — 111

6. Other business . . . . Percy Kolstad — 123

7. Adjournment — 126

34a ▶ 7
Preparatory practice

each line twice SS (slowly, then faster); DS between 2-line groups; then 30" writings on Line 4; repeat if time permits

Goal:
Finish Line 4 in 30".

alphabet	1	Buddy Jackson is saving the prize money for wax and lacquer.
figures	2	He moved from 823 West 150th Street to 794 East 66th Street.
space bar	3	Mr. Han may go to Cape Cod on the bus, or he may go by auto.
easy	4	Do throw a bit of light on their theory of dual entitlement.

| 1 | 2 | 3 | 4 | 5 | 6 | 7 | 8 | 9 | 10 | 11 | 12 |

34b ▶ 10
Improve concentration: typing from unedited copy

60-space line; DS

1 Correct errors in the copy as you type the paragraph.

2 Proofread/make final corrections before you remove paper from the machine.

words

Two kinds of erasers can be help ful to a typist: A 10
soft eraser, like the one on a pencil, is use to remove ink from 24
hard-surfaced, erasable paper; to take off carbon smudges; and 36
fro erasing carbon copies. The harder, more abrasive typing 49
erase is used to remove ink that is embedded in paper. Typing 61
erasers are abailable in both "wheel" and "pencil" forms and 74
with or without a brushh. 78

34c ▶ 33
Personal-business letters in modified block style

Problem 1

personal size sheet [LM p. 37]; address envelope; proofread/correct errors

5601 Sharp Lane | Denver, CO 80239-3618 | October 15, 19-- | 11
Mrs. Barbara Arbee | 4445 George Drive | Lubbock, TX 79416- 23
6841 | Dear Barbara | 26

(¶) I am delighted to hear that you have finished your courses 38
and are ready to accept that "just right" position. All of 50
your friends are, I know, proud of you; and they all say that 62
you will be a great asset to any company that hires you. 74

(¶) Might you consider moving to a new location? If so, I hope 86
you'll consider moving to Colorado--maybe even to Denver. I 98
know of several places where your talents would match what I 110
consider genuine opportunities. 117

(¶) I shall, of course, be very pleased to have you use my name 129
as one of your references. Thank you for asking. Please let 141
me know if I can be helpful in other ways. 149

Sincerely | Ms. Fusako L. Kimura 155/**179***

*From this point on, the last figure in the word count column includes the envelope address.

187a ▶ 5
Preparatory practice

each line 3 times SS (slowly, faster, slowly); DS between 3-line groups; repeat selected lines as time permits

alphabet	1	Ask Quincy Janze if he expects good work to be accomplished every day.
fig/sym	2	My building sold for $157,363, 14% less than its valuation ($182,980).
shift–key	3	Nathan will go to Spain from Italy; Larry will go to Egypt from India.
fluency	4	Due to the virus problem, it is their civic duty to suspend the visit.

| 1 | 2 | 3 | 4 | 5 | 6 | 7 | 8 | 9 | 10 | 11 | 12 | 13 | 14 |

187b ▶ 45
Production measurement: tables

(2 half sheets and full sheet)

Time schedule

Assembling materials .... 2'
Timed production .... 38'
Final check; compute
   n–pram .... 5'

Job 1
Unruled table

half sheet, long side up; SS body of table; 6 spaces between columns

words

MICROELECTRONICS, INC.   5
(Annual Sales Comparison by District)   12

District	1987	1986	
			16 / 21
Eastern	$2,138,265	$2,022,035	27
Central	1,962,820	1,826,250	33
Northern	862,210	851,928	38
Southern	432,025	425,632	43
Western	2,041,632	1,989,281	49 / 53
Totals	$7,436,952	$7,115,126	55 / 57 / 59

Job 2
Ruled table

full sheet, reading position; DS body of table; 4 spaces between columns

Job 3
Boxed table

Retype Job 1 as a boxed table on a half sheet, long side up. Center the following braced heading above Columns 2 & 3: **June 30.** SS columnar material; leave 6 spaces between columns. (Add 36 words for braced heading and rules.)

words

PETERSON-BROWN EQUIPMENT COMPANY   7

(Summary of Female/Male Employees)   14

Year	Number of Men Employees	Percentage of Total Employees	Number of Women Employees	Percentage Of Total Employees	Total Number of Employees	
						28 / 42 / 51 / 60 / 71 / 85
1981	64	40	96	60	160	89
1982	67	40	99	60	166	93
1983	75	43	98	57	173	98
1984	70	37	120	63	190	102
1985	70	37	120	63	190	106 / 120

34c, continued
Problem 2

personal–size sheet [LM p. 39]; SS ¶s; DS between ¶s; address envelope; proofread/correct errors

4445 George Drive | Lubbock, TX 79416-6841 | October 27, 19-- | 12

Ms. Fusako Kimura | 5601 Sharp Lane | Denver, CO | 21

80239-3618 | Dear Fusako | (¶) Thank you for your | 30

kind note filled with words of praise and | 38

encouragement. (¶) You teased me just enough | 46

with your comments about opportunities in | 55

Colorado that I must insist upon more | 62

information. Yes, I might move. Yes, I | 71

might move to Colorado under the right | 78

circumstances. Now, tell me more. (¶) You | 86

know me well enough, Fusako, to give | 94

me the kind of advice I need; and I'm | 101

going to rely on you to be frank about | 109

such a move. | Sincerely | Mrs. Barbara Arbee | 117

141

35a ▶ 7
Preparatory practice

each line twice SS (slowly, then faster); DS between 2-line groups, then type 30″ writings on Line 4; repeat if time permits

Goal: Finish Line 4 in 30″.

alphabet 1 Loquacious, breezy Hank forgot to jump over the waxed floor.

figures 2 Must he add the fractions 2/3, 3/4, 4/5, 5/6, 7/8, and 9/10?

shift keys 3 Ready to cross the Pacific, Commander Law boarded HMS JAMES.

easy 4 It is a shame to make such emblems of authentic whale ivory.

| 1 | 2 | 3 | 4 | 5 | 6 | 7 | 8 | 9 | 10 | 11 | 12 |

35b ▶ 10
Build speed on problems

Use Style Letter 2, page 64. Take five 1′ writings on the opening lines of the letter. At the signal to begin a 1′ writing, insert the paper to the point where the return address is to be placed. Type it and the date, and then space forward and type the letter address and salutation. Make completion of the salutation your goal; ignore all errors temporarily.

35c ▶ 33
Personal-business letters

3 personal-size sheets; [LM pp. 45-49]; envelopes; proofread/correct errors

1 Format/type each of the letters on page 67 in the style indicated.
2 Prepare an envelope for each letter; use the appropriate address and return address.
3 Fold each letter for insertion into an envelope.

Production measurement:
reports

(full sheets)

Time schedule

Assembling materials .... 2'
Timed production .... 30'
Final check; compute
  n–pram .... 5'

Job 1
Leftbound
manuscript

Prepare the report shown at
the right in leftbound style. The
report is to be photocopied, so
make corrections very neatly.

Job 2
Unbound
manuscript

Using the leftbound report you
have just typed, prepare it un–
bound style. Copying from
your leftbound manuscript will
provide you with an additional
opportunity to detect errors.

	words
INFORMATION PROCESSING SYSTEM	6

Introduction

11

When a decision was reached last year to install information processing
equipment in our home office, a target date of July 1 was established to have the
system in full operation. The following report summarizes the changes and
results of this new system.

25
42
57
63

History

66

Before the installation of the information processing equipment last
March, the word processing department consisted of one supervisor, five cor-
respondent secretaries, one administrative secretary, and a clerk-typist. The
workload was provided mainly by middle-management personnel.

79
95
110
123

The same workload is now performed in our home office by four information processing employees. Supervision is now handled by the information
processing supervisor.

136
152
156

New Information Processing System

170

The new system operates with three text-editors connected directly with
our mainframe computer. The text-editor consoles allow the operators to
keyboard copy at increased speeds and to make necessary corrections when
needed. As the information is keyboarded, it is recorded on the auxiliary storage device at our central computer center. Once the information has been
saved on disk storage, it can be retrieved for future reference. The stored
information can be used with information from other departments to produce
letters or reports. The ability of this system to store and to integrate various
data from different departments provides many new and exciting applications
that before installation were too difficult to achieve.

184
199
213
229
244
260
275
291
306
317

Future Applications

325

We are now beginning to install information processing input equipment
in all departments so that the collection of critical data from the various
departments can be achieved with a minimum of time and effort. As soon as
this phase of the system has been fully implemented, the information processing system will have the capacity to retrieve, sort, and merge information from
all departments within our company. Also, with the upgrading of our data base
management system, we shall have all information stored and updated continuously to provide a base for timely management decisions and reports.

339
354
369
384
400
416
430
445

Long-Range Goal

452

The private consulting firm that we hired to design and install our present
information processing system has been retained to provide us with an evaluation of ongoing information processing needs. Twice a year, the consultants
will review our system and make recommendations of needed changes within
the system. We anticipate that our system will continue to change with our
company's growth.

467
482
498
512
528
531

35c, continued

Problem 1
modified block style
Goal: 9 minutes

778 Diamond Street | Wilkes Barre, PA 18704-8121 | February 11
10, 19-- | Mr. Marvyn Hyatt | 303 King Edward Trail, SW | Atlanta, 24
GA 30331-5749 | Dear Marv | 28

(¶) I'm sorry my memory was so nonfunctional when I spoke to 40
you Saturday about my current stock holdings. 49

(¶) As soon as I returned to Wilkes Barre, I checked my files; the 62
stock I wanted to mention to you was Allied Plastics common 74
stock. Its present quotation, I see, is 16 3/8. 84

(¶) I enjoyed having lunch with you and wish we could have 95
arranged to have more time to talk about your portfolio. 106

(¶) I'll call you again next month when I am in Atlanta. 117

Sincerely yours | Brad Bruhnsen 124/**148**

Problem 2
block style
Goal: 12 minutes

248 Brooklyn Avenue | Salt Lake City, UT 84101-6112 | September 12
12, 19-- | Ms. Cluny Lee Brinks | 465 Fulkerson Street | St. Joseph, 25
MO 64504-3783 | Dear Ms. Brinks | 31

(¶) I have read with much interest the manuscript you propose to 43
submit to AMERICAN TECHNOLOGY. I think it is a very fine 55
piece of writing, and I encourage you to submit it right away. 68

(¶) Your approach to methods for gradual changeover to word 79
processing by small companies will be helpful, I am sure, to 91
many readers. I commend especially your nontechnical ap- 102
proach to what can be a very technical problem. 112

(¶) Your manuscript will be returned in a few days; my few 123
criticisms will accompany it. Should you believe it might be 135
helpful, mention to Adele Abt, the editor, that you sent the manu- 148
script to me to read. 153

Cordially | Miss Joyce Ashmyre 158/**185**

Problem 3
style of your choice
Goal: 9 minutes

2120 Uhle Street, S. | Arlington, VA 22204-4961 | May 24, 19-- | Ms. 13
Cara Ann Babbett | 42 Quebec Street, S. | Arlington, VA 22204- 25
4975 | Dear Cara Ann | 29

(¶) Thank you for your note reminding me that the Lilac Valley 41
Golf League is making plans for the opening of league play next 53
month. 55

(¶) Unfortunately (or, on the other hand, fortunately), I have 67
accepted a position as research assistant during the summer 79
months with Dr. Eunice Guzman; therefore, I shall not be able 91
to participate in league play this year. 99

(¶) I shall miss playing. Perhaps I can join you again next year, 112
Cara Ann. Please keep my name on your list just in case. 123

Cordially | Miss June Dupois 129/**154**

186a ▶ 5
Preparatory practice

each line 3 times SS (slowly, faster, slowly); DS between 3-line groups; repeat selected lines as time permits

alphabet	1	Jack Weylan received inquiries about a zoological exhibit performance.
fig/sym	2	Yung & Marx, Inc., 3168 Oak Ave. (Suite #97) paid $2,450 for the vase.
outside reaches	3	Last, he hopes people will analyze all quizzes and express an opinion.
fluency	4	Firms may make the profit they wish if they handle the city's problem.

| 1 | 2 | 3 | 4 | 5 | 6 | 7 | 8 | 9 | 10 | 11 | 12 | 13 | 14 |

186b ▶ 8
Measure straight-copy skill

one 5' writing on ¶s combined; record *gwam* and number of errors (LM p. 3)

Difficulty index

| all letters used | A | 1.5 si | 5.7 awl | 80% hfw |

gwam 1' | 5'

Data processing can be divided into three basic steps. First, data — 14 | 3 | 76
must be obtained or collected. The collected data are called source — 27 | 6 | 79
documents. Although a source document can vary depending on the needs — 42 | 8 | 81
of the collector of the data, a common source document may be a cash — 55 | 11 | 84
register tape, a sales slip, a purchase order, or a time card. Once — 69 | 14 | 87
the data are obtained, they must be loaded or entered into a data pro- — 83 | 17 | 90
cessing system (usually a computer). The usual manner of entry into the — 98 | 20 | 93
system is through a keyboard. — 104 | 21 | 94

The second basic step is manipulation of the data. Many procedures — 14 | 23 | 97
may be required to produce an end result, depending on the information — 28 | 26 | 99
desired and the source documents that have been obtained. The data may — 42 | 29 | 102
have to be sorted into some logical order, such as a numeric or alpha- — 56 | 32 | 105
betic list. They may also have to be adjusted into classifications, such — 71 | 35 | 108
as grouping employee time cards by last name. Calculations using one or — 86 | 38 | 111
more of the arithmetic functions may have to be performed on the data. — 100 | 41 | 114
Results may have to be stored temporarily for later use, such as storing — 115 | 44 | 117
data of an employee's gross pay, retirement deduction, and various taxes — 129 | 47 | 120
to be used later to compute his or her net pay. Last, the data must be — 144 | 49 | 123
reduced to a size that can be easily handled. — 153 | 51 | 124

The third and final operation includes output and storage of the — 13 | 54 | 127
data. After the data have been manipulated and processed, the results — 27 | 57 | 130
must be presented in a form that is easily understood. For example, a — 41 | 59 | 133
printed report of an employee's gross pay with various amounts deducted — 56 | 62 | 136
for taxes and other deductions may be given to the employee with his or — 70 | 65 | 138
her paycheck. This printed report is called hard copy. If the results — 85 | 68 | 141
of the data processing need to be kept for future reference, they may — 99 | 71 | 144
be stored on tapes, disks, or in the form of hard copy. — 110 | 73 | 146

gwam 1' | 1 | 2 | 3 | 4 | 5 | 6 | 7 | 8 | 9 | 10 | 11 | 12 | 13 | 14 |
5' | 1 | 2 | 3 |

36

Learning goals

1 To evaluate problem formatting and keyboarding skills.

2 To measure statistical–copy keyboarding speed.

3 To measure straight–copy keyboarding speed.

Machine adjustments

1 Set paper guide at 0.

2 Set ribbon control to type on upper half of ribbon.

3 Use a 60–space line for drills and writings; a 50–space line for let–ters.

4 SS drills: DS paragraphs.

Materials: Monarch–size sheets and envelopes; plain sheets.

36a ▶ 7
Preparatory practice

each line three times SS (slowly, faster, slower); DS between 3-line groups; repeat selected lines as time permits

alphabet	1	Jim was able to liquify frozen oxygen; he kept it very cold.
figure	2	Sue moved 720 boxes, 395 of which went to Rooms 146 and 188.
i/e	3	Neither friend believes she received benefits from the diet.
easy	4	Do they blame us for their dismal social and civic problems?

| 1 | 2 | 3 | 4 | 5 | 6 | 7 | 8 | 9 | 10 | 11 | 12 |

36b ▶ 12
Measure skill growth: statistical copy

three 3′ writings; determine *gwam*; circle errors

Difficulty index

all letters/figures used	E	1.2 si	5.1 awl	90% hfw

	gwam 3′	5′
As you might know, the size of the liability to which a	4	2
car insurance firm limits itself is expressed in three fig-	8	5
ures; as, 10/20/5. The first figure in this group, 10, means	12	7
that a limit of $10,000 has been set for one person hurt in	16	9
one accident; the 20 means that $20,000 has been set for all	20	12
persons who are hurt in one accident--subject, of course, to	24	14
the limit of $10,000 a person--and the last figure (5 here)	28	17
is for loss due to other damage up to $5,000 in value. What	32	19
you might not know is that if you were to look at 70 or 80	36	22
car insurance contracts of the kind that were used 20 years	40	24
ago in the 1960's, you might find that just 3 out of 4 had a	44	26
liability clause in them. Such clauses are now required in	48	29
each of the 50 states.	49	30

gwam 3′ | 1 | 2 | 3 | 4 |
5′ | 1 | 2 | 3 |

36c ▶ 31
Measure skill application

Materials needed:
2 half sheets
1 full sheet

Time schedule:

Assembling materials .... 2′
Timed production .... 25′
Proofread; circle errors ..... 4′

Production measurement procedure

For each production measurement activity in this section, follow the procedures at the right.

1 Remove whatever stationery is supplied in the laboratory materials (LM); have plain full sheets available, also.

2 Arrange stationery and plain paper in the order of need for completing the jobs.

3 Place correction supplies in a convenient location.

4 When the signal to begin is given, insert paper and make machine adjustments for the first job. Type as many jobs as you can in the time allowed.

5 Proofread each job and make needed corrections before removing it from the typewriter.

6 When time is called, proofread the final job and circle any uncorrected errors.

7 Compute *n–pram*.

185c ▶ 37
Production measurement: letters and memo

(LM pp. 91–95)

Time schedule

Assembling materials .... 2'
Timed production .... 30'
Final check; compute
  n–pram .... 5'

Job 1
Rough-draft letter (LM p. 91)

AMS style; 1cc; address envelope. Use current date; address the letter to:

Columbia Computers, Inc.
Attention Ms. Karen T. Gammill
7504 Oak Street, N.E.
St. Petersburg, FL 33702-7714
Send the letter **SPECIAL DELIVERY**

Enclosures
  CP/M Product List
  CP/M Order Forms
cc to **Mr. Roland V. Upchurch**

Job 2
Letter (LM p. 93)

Use the finished copy of Job 1, and retype it in Modified Block style with indented ¶s and mixed punctuation. Use subject line and appropriate salutation and complimentary close; address envelope. (Add 6 words for salutation and complimentary close.)

	words
	opening lines 36

NEW CP/M SOFTWARE FOR MICROCOMPUTERS — 43

¶ Our company *has* recently acquired *, through a merger,* the ~~good and~~ well-established — 58

Joplin Micro Software Company. ~~Because~~ *As a result* of the merger, we *is* — 70

are ~~able~~ *now in a position to* offer *to our dealers* a much broader range of software packages — 88

for nearly all makes and models of microcomputers on the — 99

market. *r today* — 102

¶ *Now that* Most of the microcomputers have a CP/M based operating system — 116

available, we are ~~finding~~ *discovering* that more computer users are asking — 129

for CP/m based software. As a further advantage of our mer- — 141

ger, we are able to offer some very exciting new CP/M programs — 154

to meet these requests. *Because you are* ~~As~~ one of our preferred ~~customers~~ *dealers*, — 168

we can offer to you--for a 30-day period--*only* the opportunity to — 181

order any CP/M package at an additional 20 percent discount. — 193

Our new CP/M product list and special CP/M order forms are — 205

enclosed for your convenience *in placing your order.* — 215

¶ We are ~~sure~~ *confident* that you will be *completely* satisfied with this new line of — 231

CP/M software. *As always,* ~~We will continue to~~ appreciate your input as — 245

to how we can improve ~~the~~ *or change a* product line to better seve our — 257

users. — 258

CARLOS J. FERNANDES, SALES MANAGER — 265

closing lines 280/**305**

Job 3
Memorandum

(LM p. 95)

Prepare the memorandum at the right; address a company mail envelope. (Add 5 words if prepared on plain paper.)

TO: Sylvester Throckmorton, Accounting Supervisor FROM: Virginia Ashton, — 13
Director of Training DATE: Current date SUBJECT: Information Processing — 24
Seminar — 25

(¶) The information processing seminar planned for Friday at 3 p.m. will be held — 41
in the Training Room rather than in the Main Floor Seminar Room. Please — 55
announce this change to those employees in your department who are planning — 71
to attend. xx — 73/**85**

36c, continued

When the signal to begin is given, begin with Problem 1. Prepare the problems in sequence until the signal to stop is given. Do Problem 1 again if you have finished Problem 3 and time has not been called.

Problem 1

half sheet (insert long side up); DS; exact center

Problem 2

half sheet (insert long side up); DS; center the problem in exact vertical center; center each line horizontally

Problem 3

Repeat Problem 1 in reading position on full sheet; DS.

	words
The committee	3
for the reelection of	7
JOAN E. SHEARD	10
as county commissioner	15
respectfully solicits your support	22
on election day	25
Tuesday, November 7	29

Mr. J. Drew Munger	4
cordially requests your presence	10
at dinner	12
Saturday evening, March 23	18
at eight o'clock	21
One Hunter Cross, Sturgis	26

37a ▶ 7
Preparatory practice

each line 3 times SS (slowly, faster, still faster); DS between 3-line groups; repeat selected lines as time permits

alphabet 1 Avoid lazy punches; expert fighters jab with a quick motion.
fig/sym 2 Hunt & Moya's $623.75 check (#1489) was delivered on May 10.
adjacent reaches 3 We sat talking by ruined columns prior to an opera overture.
easy 4 The big men paid their own firms for the eight enamel signs.

| 1 | 2 | 3 | 4 | 5 | 6 | 7 | 8 | 9 | 10 | 11 | 12 |

37b ▶ 12
Measure skill growth: straight copy

three 3' writings; determine *gwam*; circle errors

Difficulty index

| all letters used | E | 1.2 si | 5.1 awl | 90% hfw |

gwam 3'

How easy it is to become discouraged, especially after | 4 | 35

we did what we thought was the best we could do with a job; | 8 | 39

and we still did not quite win the specific prize we had in | 12 | 43

mind. It is often difficult for us to realize that what we | 16 | 47

think is our best is not really our best at all. Few of us | 20 | 51

ever approach our maximum potential at what we do. There's | 24 | 55

always another path to try, another step that can be taken. | 28 | 59

The wise among us just knuckle down and take that next step. | 02 | 03

gwam 3' | 1 | 2 | 3 | 4 |

Measurement goals

1 To select and organize all needed materials and supplies quickly for efficient use.

2 To plan your work and make machine adjustments efficiently.

3 To complete a maximum number of jobs acceptably (errors neatly corrected) in the production time allowed.

Machine adjustments

1 Set paper guide at *0*.

2 Set ribbon control to use upper half of ribbon.

3 Margins: 70–space line for drills and ¶ writings; as directed (or appropriate) for problems.

4 SS drills lines; DS ¶s; space jobs as directed (or appropriate).

185a ▶ 5
Preparatory practice

each line 3 times SS (slowly, faster, slowly); DS between 3-line groups; repeat selected lines as time permits

alphabet	1	After hearing an expert witness, Merv Zoleck was acquitted by a judge.
fig/sym	2	June sales for Model #243 are $1,348,602 (15,395 units at $87.60 ea.).
bottom row	3	Mountain climbers examined unexpected phenomena in an amazing crevice.
fluency	4	The visit to the ancient map in the town chapel may amend the problem.

| 1 | 2 | 3 | 4 | 5 | 6 | 7 | 8 | 9 | 10 | 11 | 12 | 13 | 14 |

185b ▶ 8
Measure straight-copy skill

one 5' writing on ¶s combined; record *gwam* and number of errors (LM p. 3)

Difficulty index

all letters used | A | 1.5 si | 5.7 awl | 80% hfw

	gwam 1'	5'
Our modern-day computers are less than forty years old. In this	13	3	55
short period of time, three generations of computers have been devel-	27	5	58
oped. The first computers were large in size, often filling a whole	41	8	61
room; they were hard to run, and if compared to computers today, they	55	11	64
were also very slow. Made up of thousands of vacuum tubes, these ma-	68	14	66
chines often overheated; and this caused many systems to fail. As a	82	16	69
result of these traits, the first computers were not very effective.	96	19	72
The next generation of computers were more reliable because of the	13	22	75
use of the transistor. These very small and low heat-producing units	27	25	77
took the place of the large vacuum tubes. Because of the transistors,	42	27	80
the actual size of the machine was smaller, and more data could be stored	56	30	83
in the main storage area. These computers were small, fast, and reli-	70	33	86
able; yet, there were still some jobs that would need an even greater	84	36	89
reduction in the size of the central processing unit.	95	38	91
As a result of our space-age needs, the silicon chip was developed;	14	41	94
and the modern-day computer was ushered into being. Thousands of tran-	28	44	96
sistors were put in a single one-fourth inch square chip, and millions	42	47	99
of data items could be held in the central unit. The third generation	56	49	102
machines were very small, very fast, and more reliable than the previous	71	52	105
generations.	73	53	106

| gwam 1' | 1 | 2 | 3 | 4 | 5 | 6 | 7 | 8 | 9 | 10 | 11 | 12 | 13 | 14 |
| 5' | | 1 | | 2 | | 3 | |

37c ▶ 31
Measure skill application

2 Monarch sheets [LM pp. 51-53]
2 Monarch envelopes

Reference pages

Block style letter, p. 58
Modified block style
letter, p. 64
Envelopes, p. 62

Time schedule:

Assembling materials . . . . 2'
Timed production . . . . 25'
Proofread; circle errors . . . . . 4'

When the signal to begin is given, insert paper and begin with Problem 1. Prepare the problems in sequence until the signal to stop is given.

Begin Problem 1 again if you have finished Problem 2 and time has not been called.

You are not necessarily expected to finish all problems within the time limit. Do your best, not your most; and you will have better results.

words

Problem 1
Personal-business letter

modified block style; address envelope

890 Congress Street | Stamford, CT 06902-6417 | November 6, 11
19-- | Mr. Ezra M. Rhyne, Jr. | 6331 Shell Point Place | Tampa, 23
FL 33611-5121 | Dear Mr. Rhyne 29

(¶) Thank you for your note about the rental of your condo- 40
minium. My husband and I plan to be in Tampa on December 1 52
and should like to take occupancy then. As I have done in past 65
years, I shall give you the full rental amount for two months 77
($1,200) as soon as we arrive. 83

(¶) Thank you, too, for inquiring about our daughter, Katren. She 96
will visit with us only during the holidays this year. Katren has 109
accepted a position as consultant with the Bowers, Roos, & 121
Arensberg investment firm and is their first unsighted em- 133
ployee. They seem to be pleased with her work, for she was 145
promoted in October. 149

(¶) Fred and I are looking forward to our annual visit to Florida 161
and the renewal of old friendships. 168

Very sincerely | Mrs. Kate Murphy 175/200

Problem 2
Personal-business letter

block style; center the speech topic on a separate line with a DS above and below it; address envelope

2452 Shadetree Drive | Cincinnati, OH 45242-4377 | January 24, 12
19-- | Mrs. Lucia Bravo | 1551 Geranium Avenue, E. | St. Paul, MN 24
55106-1721 | Dear Lucia 29

(¶) I have a note from my good friend, Theresa Ogden, the noted 41
ornithologist from Cleveland, saying that she will be in St. Paul 54
during the entire first week of June. She has been invited to 67
speak before the combined Kiwanis Clubs on the subject | (DS) 78
ECOLOGY: WHERE NOW? (DS) | 82

(¶) This is exciting news, because her visit coincides with our 94
national convention that week. If you think there might be a 106
place on our program for Tess, I'll be happy to make the request. 120

Cordially | Edward T. Baer 124/150

Build rough-draft copy skill

1 One 1' writing for accuracy.

2 Two 3' writings for accuracy; record *gwam* and number of errors for more accurate writing (LM p. 3).

Difficulty index

| all letters used | A | 1.5 si | 5.7 awl | 80% hfw |

gwam 1' | | 3'

On display at several of the offices *in our city* is a small sign that   14 | 5 | 54

displays a very important ~~message~~ *word*. The sign says ~~appropriately~~ *quite simply*   26 | 9 | 58

"think." Busy workers *and customers* quickly look at the sign, and it is inter-   40 | 13 | 63

esting to ~~wander if~~ *conjecture that maybe* the sign says something a little bit differ-   55 | 18 | 68

ent to every one *who reads it*. to some, for example, it might ~~say~~ *portend that* they should   73 | 24 | 74

exercise greater caution in their work; to others, it *could* offers the   87 | 29 | 79

encouragement to attack *a pressing* problems that need solving; ~~another~~ *while a third* group   103 | 34 | 84

might ~~think~~ *interpret* it to be a note of stimulation. *to expand creativity* That a five-letter   121 | 40 | 90

word printed on a sign could, like a tiny, mystical beacon, flash   134 | 45 | 94

an individualized a message to all who read it, is itself thought provoking.   149 | 50 | 99

Build straight-copy skill

1 One 1' writing for accuracy on each ¶.

2 Two 5' writings for accuracy on both ¶s combined. Record *gwam* and number of errors for more accurate writing (LM p. 3).

Difficulty index

| all letters used | A | 1.5 si | 5.7 awl | 80% hfw |

gwam 1' | | 5'

In the years ahead, the office must be planned for flexibility of   13 | 3 | 55

space, furniture, and equipment. The time has passed when the needs and   28 | 6 | 57

demands of the office setting could be predicted for a decade. The of-   42 | 8 | 61

fice must be designed to enable it to be adjusted quickly and efficiently   57 | 11 | 64

to any change that might come, whether that change be some progress in   71 | 14 | 67

high technology or some new technique. Most of the changes that come   85 | 17 | 70

may impact on space needs, on related needs for furniture and equipment,   100 | 20 | 72

or on both. Perhaps one of the better approaches to office layout is   114 | 23 | 75

the new open architectural concept; this is an approach that uses por-   128 | 26 | 78

table walls to separate the office into its designated areas.   140 | 28 | 81

Also, the office of the future must provide for modular office fur-   13 | 31 | 83

niture. Whenever the office layout needs to be changed, there is a cor-   28 | 34 | 86

responding need to be sure that the office furniture will continue to be   42 | 37 | 89

functional in the new space arrangement. The office furniture that will   57 | 39 | 92

most surely continue to be useful for decades to come will be those items   72 | 42 | 95

that can be made to fit the size of any new office layout that is re-   86 | 45 | 98

quired. The trend also may be to increase the number of leases for high   100 | 48 | 101

technology equipment; to lease equipment may be needed to hedge against   115 | 51 | 103

the high probability of obsolescence.   122 | 53 | 105

gwam 1' | 1 | 2 | 3 | 4 | 5 | 6 | 7 | 8 | 9 | 10 | 11 | 12 | 13 | 14
5' | 1 | 2 | 3

LEVEL TWO

Formatting/typing basic communications

Let's be elemental. A keyboard is made up of several rows of buttons, or keys, which, when struck, operate your machine. This activity of striking is called keyboarding.

Keyboarding certainly seems commonplace enough. It takes on added meaning when you consider that your keyboard is identical to those used to operate an increasingly large number and variety of technical machines, such as computers, microcomputers, word processors, and electronic typewriters. As part of such equipment, the keyboard becomes the instrument through which are transmitted thoughts and ideas, facts and figures, and all sorts of business, academic, social, and scientific data.

How efficiently any machine functions, of course, depends directly upon how skillfully the operator uses it. Its utility increases in ratio to a user's knowledge about it and ability to operate it rapidly and accurately.

By successfully completing Level 1 work, you have gained ability to keyboard by touch and to enter data attractively on a page. Now you are ready to begin a new level of learning, one in which you will learn to put these important skills to professional use.

You will learn, for example, to format and input business correspondence, tables, data sheets, and reports; and you will gain more experience using printed, rough-draft, and handwritten input materials.

In addition, as you enter the practice and problem data, your keyboarding speed should increase; and, with concentrated effort, your accuracy should also improve.

Learning to keyboard and format with skill is a significant accomplishment. From now on, you should realize that future output from equipment you use depends on the input abilities you develop now.

184a ▶ 5
Preparatory practice

each line 3 times SS
(slowly, faster,
slowly); DS between
3-line groups; repeat
selected lines as time
permits

alphabet 1 Jodie Cozzel anxiously requested that the workers' group be very firm.

fig/sym 2 My legal fees were $3,109.75, a 6.84% increase over estimate ($2,897).

3d row 3 Prior to your proprietorship, I was the housekeeper of the properties.

fluency 4 If the city auditor is right, she may halt the audit and sue the firm.

| 1 | 2 | 3 | 4 | 5 | 6 | 7 | 8 | 9 | 10 | 11 | 12 | 13 | 14 |

184b ▶ 10
Communication aid:
functional punctuation

1 Study the 3 groups of
sentences and note the
punctuation that is used
in each sentence.

2 Type each sentence
twice; DS between
4-line groups.

3 Compose 3 sen-
tences, using one
of the types of
functional punctu-
ation in each sen-
tence.

separate
ideas

1 Your instructions were correct, but they were not very well presented.

2 You should plan to leave by six o'clock, and they should leave by ten.

enclose
parenthetic
expressions

3 The new accounting instructor, Dr. Wilma Williamson, arrives tomorrow.

4 Our letter of June 1 (a copy is attached) should answer the questions.

give
special
emphasis

5 They need to leave--right now--before another accident happens to you.

6 This textbook--newly revised--is now available at the local bookstore.

184c ▶ 10
Communication aid:
proofreading for meaning

1 Read the paragraphs at the
right carefully, noting changes
that must be made to correct the
material.

2 Type the paragraphs, making
the necessary changes as you
type.

3 Remove the paper from your
machine and proofread, making
any additional corrections with
proofreader's marks.

4 If necessary, retype the paragraphs, making all corrections.

words

Most of us want to make sure are own well fair is being taken care 13
of properly. This need embraces such items as job security, fringe bene- 28
fits, and final retiremint. Their are dozens of other items that could 42
be listed under personal well fair, but we can cope with these other 55
items if the basic three are covered. Four individuals, personal well 69
fair means more than acquiring the mirror basics of life--food, clothing, 84
and shelter; we also want two be able to afford a few luxuries. 96

Job security, two some, is thought to be the single most criticle 109
item of all on the list. If your do not possess good job security, you 123
may not have adiquate fringe benifits nor a sufficient retiremint pack- 137
age. If you are like mose people, you expect a job that is pleasant and 151
financially rewarding as will; but a good environment is oftimes of more 166
importance than wages too some people. Your hole outlook on life 179
cam be more positive when their is not significant concern about you job 194
security. 196

Learning goals

1 To improve understanding of the place and function of capital letters.
2 To strengthen ability to spell.
3 To improve decision making.
4 To increase keystroking skill.

Machine adjustments

1 Set chair and desk adjustment and placement.
2 Set paper guide at *0*.
3 Set ribbon control to type on upper half of ribbon.
4 Use a 70–space line unless otherwise instructed.

38a ▶ 7
Preparatory practice

each line 3 times SS (slowly, faster, slower); DS between 3-line groups; repeat if time permits

alphabet	1	Would a lazy executive manage to finish his job quickly and properly?
figures	2	Polly Wertze moved from 479 East 125th Street to 328 West 60th Street.
adjacent keys	3	We condemn her notion that we can buy rewards with excellent behavior.
easy	4	The sorority did work with vigor for the goals of the big civic corps.

| 1 | 2 | 3 | 4 | 5 | 6 | 7 | 8 | 9 | 10 | 11 | 12 | 13 | 14 |

38b ▶ 14
Review/improve communication skills: capitalization

full sheet; DS; 1½" top margin; set a tab 5 spaces to right of center point

1 Keyboard the data as shown; tab to type each example.

2 Proofread carefully and correct errors.

3 Study each line and its example from your copy.

Note: Some literary titles may be underlined or shown in all capital letters.

USING CAPITAL LETTERS

TS

words

4

9

Capitalize

the first word of a complete sentence:	She put the car in the garage.	23
the first word of a direct quotation:	Tio said, "That is my valise."	37
titles that precede personal names:	Introduce me to Senator Reese.	50
main words in literary titles:	I saw Anne of a Thousand Days.	67
adjectives derived from proper nouns:	We always enjoy Italian opera.	81
weekdays, months, and holidays:	Sunday, April 1, isn't Easter.	94
political and military organizations:	The Democrat left by Navy jet.	109
names of specific persons or places:	Jo jogs daily in Central Park.	123
nouns followed by identifying numbers:	They were assigned to Room 14.	137

TS

144

Do not capitalize

compass directions not part of a name:	I drive due north to Leesport.	158
a page if followed by a number:	Did he quote Milton on page 9?	171
a title that follows a name:	LeCare is captain of the ship.	183
commonly accepted derivatives:	Put french toast on the china.	196
geographic names made plural:	I sail on Moon and Fish lakes.	209
seasons (unless personified):	Sweet Summer gave way to fall.	221
generic names of products:	Try Magic Mugg instant coffee.	232

183d ▶ 10
Build statistical-copy skill

1 One 1' writing for speed on each ¶.

2 Two 3' writings for speed on both ¶s combined. Record *gwam* on (LM p. 3).

Difficulty index

all letters/figures used | HA | 1.7 si | 6.0 awl | 75% hfw

gwam 1' | 3'

On October 26, 1985, Americana Consolidated, Inc., requisitioned from | 14 | 5 | 57
us 30 metric tons of Idaho potatoes. However, the invoice stated 30 tons | 29 | 10 | 62
at $74 per ton, but the $74 rate is for a regular ton--2,000#; the rate | 43 | 14 | 67
for a metric ton (2,200#) is $82. Therefore, will you please have the | 57 | 19 | 71
invoice department make the required changes and issue a new invoice for | 72 | 24 | 76
the correct amount. | 76 | 25 | 78

Also, the Jamison Cozy invoice needs to be changed because of an | 13 | 30 | 82
error in the amount shipped. The purchase order dated October 2, 1985, | 27 | 34 | 87
requested 760# of cornmeal; the shipping documents examined on October 13 | 42 | 39 | 92
specify that the 760# were shipped by Zippo Express, but the invoice | 56 | 44 | 96
indicates that only 460# were billed. Please make the necessary changes | 71 | 49 | 101
and forward Jamison Cozy a copy of the new invoice. | 81 | 52 | 105

gwam 1' | 1 | 2 | 3 | 4 | 5 | 6 | 7 | 8 | 9 | 10 | 11 | 12 | 13 | 14 |
3' | 1 | 2 | 3 | 4 | 5 |

183e ▶ 15
Build straight-copy skill

1 One 1' writing for speed on each ¶.

2 Two 5' writings for speed on both ¶s combined. Record *gwam* on (LM p. 3).

Difficulty index

all letters used | A | 1.5 si | 5.7 awl | 80% hfw

gwam 1' | 5'

Data processing is the manipulation of facts, ideas, or concepts | 13 | 3 | 54
for the purpose of producing some useful and desired results. These | 27 | 5 | 57
results are known as information or output. In data processing, you | 41 | 8 | 60
must know the category of output you are looking for before you can | 54 | 11 | 62
begin the process. The data placed into the system--the input--is de- | 68 | 14 | 65
cided by the results--the output--that you desire. After the input and | 83 | 17 | 68
output formats have been formalized, the details of the way in which the | 97 | 19 | 71
data are to be processed can be specified. When data are processed using | 112 | 22 | 74
a computer system, the entire operation can be performed in just a frac- | 126 | 25 | 77
tion of the time required if a mechanical system were used. | 138 | 28 | 79

The speed in which a data processing application can be executed | 13 | 30 | 82
is related directly to the speed of the computer and the manner in which | 28 | 33 | 85
the program is written. The speed of a computer cannot be altered, but | 42 | 36 | 88
the way in which a program is written can often be improved to increase | 56 | 39 | 90
the speed with which it executes. There is a variety of programming | 70 | 42 | 93
languages; some are better suited for specific jobs, but the programmer | 85 | 45 | 96
must know a language very well in order to have the program execute in | 99 | 48 | 99
an efficient manner. Poor programming can cause an application to take | 113 | 50 | 102
much longer to execute. | 118 | 51 | 103

gwam 1' | 1 | 2 | 3 | 4 | 5 | 6 | 7 | 8 | 9 | 10 | 11 | 12 | 13 | 14 |
5' | 1 | 2 | 3 |

38c ▶ 17
**Review/improve
communication skills:
forming plurals**

full sheet; SS, DS between ¶s,
listed items, and examples; 1"
top margin; 5-space ¶ indention; set a tab 10 spaces to left
of center point to type examples

1 Prepare the data as shown; tab
to type each example.
2 Proofread and correct errors.
3 Study the rules from your typed
copy.

Note: The abbreviation e.g. may
be used in place of the phrase *for
example*.

FORMING PLURALS
TS

To achieve the regular plural form for most nouns, simply add s to the singular form; e.g., hats. Some nouns, such as men and oxen, take an irregular plural form. These nouns have to be memorized. A few nouns, such as deer and sheep, have no plural form at all. To achieve the plural form for still other groups of nouns, certain guidelines, some of which are given below with exam-ples, should be followed. In every instance of doubt, of course, consult a dictio-nary.
DS

1. To form the plural of a noun ending in y preceded by a consonant sound or a consonant (any letter except a, e, i, o, or u), change the y to i and add es.

husky--huskies
hobby--hobbies
colloquy--colloquies

2. To form the plural of a noun ending in y preceded by a vowel, just add s.

attorney--attorneys
decoy--decoys
holiday--holidays

3. To form the plural of most nouns ending in o, add es.

tomato--tomatoes
hero--heroes
mosquito--mosquitoes

4. To form the plural of nouns ending in o preceded by a vowel, add s to the singular.

cameo--cameos
ratio--ratios
taboo--taboos

5. For singular nouns ending in sis, change the sis to ses to form the plural.

basis--bases
analysis--analyses
crisis--crises

6. To form the plural of most nouns ending in s, ss, ch, sh, or x, add es.

kiss--kisses
box--boxes
lash--lashes
match--matches

Learning goals

1 To increase basic skill on straight, statistical, and rough-draft copy.

2 To increase expertise in communication and proofreading skills.

3 To refine keyboarding technique.

Machine adjustments

1 Set paper guide at *0*.

2 Set ribbon control to type on upper half of ribbon.

3 Margins: 70-space line for drills and ¶ writings.

4 SS drill lines; DS ¶s.

183a ▶ 5
Preparatory practice

each line 3 times SS (slowly, faster, slowly); DS between 3-line groups; repeat selected lines as time permits

alphabet	1	We realize that providing quick excuses for poor jobs may not be wise.
fig/sym	2	The 1985/86 price ($67.23) increased by over 10% to $74.56 in 1986/87.
double letter	3	According to a letter from personnel, these layoffs will be necessary.
fluency	4	The title to an antique auto is held by a rich man down on the island.

| 1 | 2 | 3 | 4 | 5 | 6 | 7 | 8 | 9 | 10 | 11 | 12 | 13 | 14 |

183b ▶ 8
Communication aid: active/passive voice

Each sentence is identified by the voice in which it appears; type each sentence, changing the voice from active to passive or passive to active.

Note: A passive verb is a form of *be* and a past participle. All other verbs are active.

active	1	The First National Bank of Reno, Nevada, employs Ms. Jessica Goldberg.
passive	2	The amounts reported in the report were thoroughly checked by Phillip.
active	3	The students studied the major modern authors in the literature class.
passive	4	The company's annual report was approved by the senior vice president.
passive	5	The new customer was asked by the store manager to return later today.

| 1 | 2 | 3 | 4 | 5 | 6 | 7 | 8 | 9 | 10 | 11 | 12 | 13 | 14 |

183c ▶ 12
Communication aid: proofreading/combining sentences

1 Type the paragraph, making necessary corrections. Use connectives (and, or, but, however, etc.) to join some of the short choppy sentences.

2 Remove paper from the machine and proofread, correcting the copy with proofreader's marks.

3 Retype the paragraph from your corrected copy.

Every person in the world depend on having access to energy. We use en ergy to keep warm cook food, provide light, and run the machines that make our products or serve us. In the past few centurie, the population of the world has increased drammatically. So has the demand for energy. At the present rate of demand the minerall resources of the earth will soon be depletted. Efforts at conservation are making our machines more energy efficient. We must also makes more use of renewable energy resources. If human civilization is to continue with out radical change, we must practice conservavtion of nonrenewable energy sources. We must make greater use of wind, solar and other renewable energy sources.

38d ▶ 12
Improve keyboarding continuity

1 Type the ¶ once for orientation. Be aware of spelling and word usage.
2 Take two 3′ writings.

Goal: 22 or more *gwam*

Difficulty index

all letters used	LA	1.4 si	5.4 awl	85% hfw

gwam 1′ | 3′

Just where does responsibility lie? I recall a day last fall when   13 | 4 | 39

I had a date to meet with two attorneys to discuss a crisis our firm   27 | 9 | 43

was having. It was in October. The night before my meeting, my young   41 | 14 | 48

nephew called to remind me that I had said I would go to his school's   55 | 18 | 53

Halloween party the next day. I apologized and told him why I could   69 | 23 | 58

not be there. While he said he understood, I learned quickly that re-   83 | 27 | 62

sponsibility has two bases--emotional and economical--and that it is   97 | 32 | 67

sometimes hard to separate the two.   104 | 35 | 69

gwam 1′ | 1 | 2 | 3 | 4 | 5 | 6 | 7 | 8 | 9 | 10 | 11 | 12 | 13 | 14 |
3′ | 1 | 2 | 3 | 4 | 5 |

39a ▶ 7
Preparatory practice

each line three times SS (slowly, faster, still faster); DS between 3-line groups; repeat if time permits

alphabet   1 We have begun our quiz in journalism; do not make a copy for the exam.

fig/sym   2 Han's Policy #718426 for $49,300 has been renewed for another 5 years.

third row   3 We were quite ready to prepare a report for our quiet trio of workers.

easy   4 Hand me a bit of cocoa, a pan of cod, an apricot, and a bowl of clams.

| 1 | 2 | 3 | 4 | 5 | 6 | 7 | 8 | 9 | 10 | 11 | 12 | 13 | 14 |

39b ▶ 11
Improve keystroking technique

60-space line; type 2 times SS; DS between 3-line groups

Technique hint:
Concentrate on each word as you type it.

direct reaches

1 ice cede gun herb deck mute nut shy grunt hunt hymn jump sun

2 Cecelia Haynes and John Lunce hunt in Greece every December.

3 A group of shy, hungry gnus munched on green jungle grasses.

adjacent reaches

4 folk three lion port trite quit pods ankle oil yule were art

5 Opal is prepared to buy gas and oil for her sporty roadster.

6 Tio has a new poncho for sale; it has beading and silk trim.

double letters

7 door veer err skiing lass committee odd off all success inns

8 Ella successfully crossed the creek at the foot of the hill.

9 Deer need access to green grass, weeds, and trees in summer.

Job 11
Retained earnings statement
(full sheet)

Mr. Murtha has only one audit statement remaining to be processed for the Chula Vista audit. He asks that you prepare the retained earnings statement. Follow the basic procedures that you have followed on the previous statements.

all CAP (Chula Vista Manufacturing, Inc.) } DS

Retained Earnings Statement

For the Year Ended December 31, 19-- } TS

Retained earnings, beginning of year $35,310

SS { Add net income for year 28,037

$63,347 } SS

Less dividends declared 7,500

Retained earnings, end of year $55,847

Job 12
Chart of accounts
(full sheet)

Ms. Skopec has accepted a new client who is organizing a wholesale produce distributorship. This is the first client she has had in this particular business; therefore, she has prepared a chart of accounts that may be used when preparing an audit for this type of business. She has given the job to Mr. Murtha to complete, and he has asked that you prepare this chart of accounts as your last job this week. He asks that you do the following:

1 Prepare the chart as shown in 2 columns; leave a 2" top margin and 1" side margins.

2 Insert the handwritten accounts in their proper order.

3 The left–hand column should include all accounts under the headings of assets, liabilities, stockholders' equity, and income.

4 The right–hand column should include only the expense accounts.

5 Only the first letter of the first word in the account title should be capitalized.

WHOLESALE PRODUCE SUPPLIERS
Chart of Accounts

ALL CAP
Assets: DS

101	Cash in bank
106	Petty cash
130	Produce Inventory
142	Security Deposits Paid
153	Furniture, Fixtures, and Equipment
154	Accumulated Depreciation-- Furniture, Fixtures, and Equipment
181	Organization Expense

ALL CAP ← TS
Liabilities: DS

201	Accounts Payable
205	FICA and FIT Payable
206	State Withholding Payable
207	Sales Tax Payable

← TS
STOCKHOLDERS' EQUITY:

350	Capital Stock
DS 360	Retained Earnings

← TS
INCOME:

401	Sales, Taxable
DS 410	Miscellaneous Income

109 *Investments*

131 *Supplies inventory*

157 *Leasehold improvements*

158 *Accumulated depreciation-- leasehold improvements*

409 *Interest income*

EXPENSES: DS

501	Cost of Produce Sold
511	Advertising
513	Cash short (over)
514	Casual Labor
517	Contributions
519	Depreciation
520	Dues & Subscriptions
521	Equipment Rental
529	Insurance
530	Interest
532	Laundry
535	Legal & Accounting
536	Miscellaneous
540	Office Supplies
542	Payroll Taxes
544	Rent
548	Repairs & Maintenance
550	Sanitation & Hauling
555	Spoilage Loss
557	Supplies
560	Taxes, Permits, & Licenses
561	Telephone
564	Travel & Entertainment
574	Utilities
590	Wages--Officers
591	Wages--Others

592 *Employee benefits*

39c ▶ 20
Reach for new goals

1 Take a 1' writing on ¶1. Note your *gwam* base rate.

2 Add 4 words to base rate to set a new goal. Note your ¼' subgoals below.

3 Take a ½' writing on ¶1, guided by ¼' guide call. Try to reach your ¼' goal as each guide is called.

4 Take a 1' writing on ¶1, guided by ¼' guide call. Try to reach your ¼' goal as each guide is called.

5 Take two more ½' and two more 1' writings as directed above. If you reach your 1' goal, set a new one.

6 Type ¶2 as directed in 1–5.

7 Take a 3' writing on both ¶s without the call of the guide.

gwam	¼'	½'	¾'	Time
16	4	8	12	16
20	5	10	15	20
24	6	12	18	24
28	7	14	21	28
32	8	16	24	32
36	9	18	27	36
40	10	20	30	40
44	11	22	33	44
48	12	24	36	48

Difficulty index

all letters used | LA | 1.4 si | 5.4 awl | 85% hfw

gwam 3'

Who is happier, a person with much education or one with little? 4

Which of the two is better adjusted, more satisfied, and better able to 9

realize goals? These are not easy questions. Education is no magic 14

elixir. It is only a tool that can help us to use knowledge to win out 19

over problems. The answer lies in how we use that tool. 22

Education will not bring about happiness any more than a hammer will 27

bring about a house. Yet we can use what we learn, through experience as 32

well as through school, to build the kind of lifestyle that will enable 37

us to recognize those values that have great significance for us. We can 41

use them in our best judgment to find the satisfaction we all seek. 46

gwam 3' | 1 | 2 | 3 | 4 | 5 |

39d ▶ 12
Make decisions

1 Decide what size paper to use and how to place the announcement attractively on the page; then prepare the copy.

2 Check the appearance of your completed copy. Note your comments on the bottom of your typed copy.

THE WAREHAM GRADUATE SCHOOL OF BUSINESS

announces its winter graduation ceremonies

to be held January 5

in the Bristol-Callister Memorial Auditorium

Processional begins promptly at 2 p.m.

40a ▶ 7
Preparatory practice

each line three times SS (slowly, faster, still faster); DS between 3-line groups; repeat if time permits

alphabet 1 Two exit signs jutted obliquely above the beams of a razed skyscraper.

figures 2 The test on March 26 will cover the contents of pages 14-59 and 70-83.

capitalization 3 Do Max and Kay Pasco expect to be in breezy Vera Cruz, Mexico, in May?

easy 4 Did the visitor on the bicycle signal and turn right at the cornfield?

| 1 | 2 | 3 | 4 | 5 | 6 | 7 | 8 | 9 | 10 | 11 | 12 | 13 | 14 |

40b ▶ 17
Reach for new goals:

Repeat 39c, above.

Mr. Riech's assistant has prepared a rough draft of the Chula
Vista balance sheet. Mr. Murtha
gives you this draft and asks you
to prepare the final copy for the
audit report.

First column indentions are
the same as for the other statements you have prepared. Place
8 spaces between Columns 1
and 2, and 2 spaces between
Columns 2 and 3.

CHULA VISTA MANUFACTURING, INC.

Balance Sheet

December 31, 19--

add remaining leaders

Assets

Current assets:			$ 27,150
Cash			
Accounts receivable		$ 57,056	
Less allowance for bad debts		9,346	47,710
Inventories			
Raw materials		$ 16,822	
Work in process		7,477	
Finished goods		39,299	63,598
Prepaid expenses			
Factory supplies on hand		$ 3,738	
Office supplies on hand		1,869	
Prepaid insurance		935	6,542
Total current assets			$ 145,000
Long-term assets:			
Machinery and equipment		$ 105,240	
Less accumulated depreciation		24,299	80,941
Total assets			$ 225,941

Liabilities and Stockholders' Equity

Current liabilities:			$ 6,542
Accounts payable			9,346
Wages payable			935
Interest payable			15,888
Income taxes payable			
Total current liabilities			$ 32,711
Long-term notes payable			37,383
(9%, due 5 years hence)			
Total liabilities			$ 70,094
Stockholders' equity:			
Common stock, $10 par value,			
authorized and issued:			
10,000 shares		$ 100,000	
Retained earnings		55,847	155,847
Total liabilities and stockholders' equity			$ 225,941

40c ▶ 13
Review/improve communication skills: spelling

70-space line; decide size of paper (full or half sheet), top margin (1″, 1½″, or 2″), and spacing (SS or DS)

1 Clear tab stops; set two new tab stops, one 29 spaces from left margin and one 58 spaces from left margin.

2 Type the first word at left margin as shown; tab and type the word again; then tab and type it a third time, this time without looking at the word in the book or on the paper.

3 Repeat this procedure for each word on the list. Proofread care—fully; correct errors.

4 Use the completed copy as a study list and for future reference.

5 Make comments about your placement decisions on the bot—tom of your typed copy.

SPELLING DEMONS

absence	absence	absence
accumulate		
already		
benefited		
convenience		
develop		
embarrass		
guarantee		
judgment		
likable		
noticeable		
parallel		
receive		
seize		
surprise		
vacuum		
yield		

40d ▶ 13
Proofread/revise as you keyboard

half sheet; 1″ top margin; DS

1 Cover the answer key at the bottom of the column. After keyboarding, check your answers.

2 As you keyboard each line, decide whether each circled word is correct accord—ing to rules of form, spelling, or capitaliza—tion. If it is not correct, make the correction.

Key: 1 and, china **2** analyses, hobbies **3** huskies, winter, north, parks **4** already, seize, yield **5** parties, attor—neys, Room, Hall **6** convenient, vacuum, lobbies **7** judgment, embarrass, absence **8** Fall, Winter's, De—cember **9** Put, to—matoes, potato, holi—days **10** accumulate, receive, surprise

1 Lay my copy of The King and I on the shelf beside the old china bowls.

2 Dr. Thu gave several analysis of why a person needs some good hobbies.

3 To see huskeys at work in winter, go North to Whaler or Glacier parks.

4 The enemy had already tried to sieze the tower; Kroma would not yield.

5 The partys will meet with their attornies in Room 27 of Yorkton Hall.

6 When it is convient, please vacuum the carpets in the front lobbies.

7 In my judgment, I did not embarass her; her abscence spoke for itself.

8 Demure fall trembled before winter's icy breath. It was now december.

9 He said, "put a few tomatoes in your potatoe salad for these Holidays."

10 If we accumulate enough points, we shall receive three surprise gifts.

Job 9
**Cost of goods manufactured
statement** (full sheet)

Mr. Murtha asks you to prepare the final copies of some of the Chula Vista audit report state‒ments. He hands you the form containing the cost of goods manufactured information. Pre‒pare the statement following the basic procedures that you have followed previously. Leave 8 spaces between Columns 1 and 2, and 2 spaces between Col‒umns 2 and 3. Remember to use a 1″ top margin for the Chula Vista audit statements.

CHULA VISTA MANUFACTURING, INC.

DS > Cost of Goods Manufactured Statement

DS > For the Year Ended December 31, 19--

TS >

Beginning work in process inventory . . .		$ 5,607
Raw materials used:		
Beginning inventory	$ 9,346	
Materials purchased (net)	106,542	
Transportation charges	1,869	
Cost of materials available . .	$117,757	
Less ending inventory	16,822	
Cost of raw materials used . .		100,935
Direct labor		75,701
Factory overhead:		
Administrative salaries	$ 14,019	
Depreciation on equipment	5,607	
Factory supplies used	12,150	
Indirect labor	42,991	
Insurance	1,869	
Rent on furniture and fixtures . .	7,477	
Rent on plant facilities	22,430	
Repairs and maintenance	7,477	
Utilities	14,953	
Total factory overhead		128,973
Total manufacturing cost . . .		$311,216
Less ending work in process inventory		7,477
Cost of goods manufactured . .		$303,739

41a ▶ 6
Preparatory practice

each line 3 times
SS (slowly, faster, slower);DS between 3-line groups; repeat if time permits

alphabet 1 One gray antique zinc box was the most favored object kept on display.

figures 2 Please turn to page 350 and answer Questions 2, 4, 6, 7, 8, 9, and 17.

hyphen 3 Pam thinks we have an up-to-the-minute plan for our out-of-town sales.

easy 4 When risk is taken by a giant firm, signs of visible profit may ensue.

| 1 | 2 | 3 | 4 | 5 | 6 | 7 | 8 | 9 | 10 | 11 | 12 | 13 | 14 |

41b ▶ 10
Compose at the keyboard

2 half sheets; 1″ top margin; 5-space ¶ indention; DS

1 Keyboard the sentences in ¶ form, inserting the needed information. Do not correct errors.
2 Remove the paper and make pencil corrections. Retype the ¶s. Proofread; correct errors.

(¶ 1) **My name is** (your name). **My home address is** (your complete home address, including ZIP Code). **I am a student at** (name of your school) **in** (city and state), **where I am majoring in** (major area of study). **My school address is** (street address, dormitory name, or other). (¶ 2) **The brand name of the typewriter I use is** (brand name). **I type at approximately** (state the rate in figures) **gwam. My greatest difficulty now seems to be** (name one, as: too many errors, not enough speed, poor techniques, lack of confidence).

41c ▶ 34
Format business letters in block style

plain full sheets

1 Read the special information at the right; then study the style letter on page 78.
2 Prepare a copy of the letter, following directions given on the letter. Correct errors.
3 Take three 2′ writings on opening lines and ¶1. Begin with paper out of the machine. Estimate placement of the date; move quickly from part to part to improve your speed.

Business letter placement information

Letter styles used for business letters are similar to styles used for personal letters, but note the following differences.

When letterhead paper (with a printed return address) is used, the return address is not typed above the date; begin the letter by typing the date.

If the letter is signed by a woman, the personal title she prefers (Ms., Miss, or Mrs.) may be included on the typed signature line. No title, personal or professional, is needed if the writer is male.

The writer's official title may be typed directly beneath the typed signature line.

The initials of the typist may be shown at the left margin a DS below the typed name or title. (In Section 10 letters, reference initials are indicated by xx; you should substitute your own initials.)

If an enclosure notation is used, type it a DS beneath the reference initials.

An attractive appearance is as essential for business letters as for personal letters. Proofreading and correcting must be done well if a letter is to have its desired effect.

The business letters in Section 10 are of average length; such letters fit well on a 60-space line. The date is usually typed on about Line 15, or 2½″ from the top of the page. This placement is recommended for all letters to be typed in Section 10.

Job 7
Payroll report with braced heading (full sheet)

Mr. Murtha has finished the weekly payroll for the week of January 11–15. He has made a draft of the payroll report that he must submit to Ms. Skopec each Friday before the checks are signed by her. He asks that you prepare the final copy of this payroll report. If you have any questions about how to do a braced heading, refer to the Office Procedures Manual (see the excerpt on page 315).

As a temporary office worker, you are paid directly by OSTI; therefore, you are not included on the regular payroll report.

Center the table in reading position; allow 4 spaces between columns and an extra ½" in the left margin for binding purposes.

DENISE SKOPEC, CPA
Payroll Report
Week of January 11–15, 19—

| Name | Gross Pay | Deductions | | Net Pay |
		F.I.T.	F.I.C.A.	
Stanley Riech	480.75	65.00	33.65	382.10
Rosetta Lopez	423.00	78.00	29.61	315.39
Jose Murtha	288.00	28.00	20.16	239.84
Stella Dernovich	250.00	32.00	17.50	200.50
Jimmy Woo	180.00	18.00	12.60	149.40
Totals	1,621.75	221.00	113.52	1,287.23

Job 8
Auditor's opinion statement (full sheet)

Mr. Riech has just completed his audit of Chula Vista Manufacturing, Inc. He has submitted the entire audit report in draft form to Mr. Murtha to be processed. Mr. Murtha hands you a copy of the standard unqualified opinion statement that is used for all audits that do not have to be qualified in any way.

Prepare this statement in the form of a letter; use **December 31** as the examination date in the body of the letter. Date the letter **January 14, 19—**, and address it to:

**Mr. Walter P. Lewis,
Chairperson
Chula Vista Manufacturing, Inc.
1035 Del Mar Avenue
Chula Vista, CA 92011-3115**

This letter will be bound in the client's audit report; therefore, leave an additional ½" in the left margin for binding.

UNQUALIFIED OPINION STATEMENT

We have examined the balance sheet of the _____ _____ (a California corporation) as of _____, 19___, and the related statements of earnings and retained earnings and changes in financial position for the year then ended. Our examination was made in accordance with generally accepted auditing standards and, accordingly, included such tests of the accounting records and such other auditing procedures as we considered necessary in the circumstances.

In our opinion, the accompanying financial statements referred to above present fairly the financial position of the _____ as of _____, 19___, and the results of their operations and changes in their financial position for the year then ended, in conformity with generally accepted accounting principles applied during the period.

Communications Design Associates

348 INDIANA AVENUE
WASHINGTON, DC 20001-1438
Tel: 1-800-432-5739

total words | gwam 2'

Dateline February 14, 19-- Line 15 — 4 | 2

Operate return 4 times

Letter Mr. Harvey B. Barber — 8 | 4
address Sunstructures, Inc. — 12 | 6
2214 Brantford Place — 16 | 8
Buffalo, NY 14222-5147 — 21 | 10
DS

Salutation Dear Mr. Barber — 24 | 12
DS

Body of This letter is written in what is called "block style." It — 36 | 18
letter is the style we recommend for use in your business office for — 48 | 24
reasons I shall detail for you in the following paragraphs. — 61 | 30

First, the style is a very efficient one. Because all lines — 73 | 6
(including the date) begin at the left margin, time is not — 85 | 12
consumed in positioning special parts of each letter. — 96 | 18

Second, this style is an easy one to learn. New employees — 107 | 23
should have little difficulty learning it, and your present — 119 | 29
staff should adjust to it without unnecessary confusion. — 131 | 35

Third, the style is sufficiently different from most other — 143 | 41
styles that it can suggest to clients that your company is a — 155 | 47
creative one. The style is interesting. It gains attention. — 168 | 54

I am pleased to enclose our booklet on the subject of letter — 180 | 6
styles and special features of business letters. — 190 | 11
DS

Complimentary Sincerely yours — 193 | 13
close Operate return 4 times

Kathryn E. Bowers

Typed name Ms. Kathryn E. Bowers — 197 | 15
Official title Senior Consultant — 201 | 17
DS

Reference xx — 202 | 17
initials DS

Enclosure Enclosure — 203 | 18
notation

Shown in pica type
60–space line

Style letter 3: business letter in block style, open punctuation

If an accounting or tax client must pay an estimated quarterly income tax, a form is completed for the client that contains both filing instructions and the amount of the quarterly tax payment.

Mr. Murtha gives you a rough–draft copy of a new instruction sheet that Ms. Lopez has prepared and asks that you prepare it in final form for duplication.

Leave a top margin of 2″ and side margins of 1½″. Leave 4 spaces between columnar items. Correct any undetected errors.

Instructions for Payment
of
19-- Estimated Federal Income Tax

You and your spouse should sign and date voucher #1 and forward it not later than April 15.

Make your check payable to Internal Revenue Service in the amount indicated below.

Place your social security number on the check for identification.

Mail Voucher and Check to:

Director
Internal Revenue Servise
Fresno, Calif. 93888-3401

Mail Voucher #1 separately from your 1040 tax return.

We suggest you mark your calendar with the date when your estimated taxes will be due. The Internal Revenue Service does not send notices to remind you of due dates. Estimated taxes for future dates are provided below.

Fill in the dates paid and bring this record to us when we do your next year's tax returns.

Voucher	Due	Amount	Date Paid
#1	April 15	$_____	_____
#2	June 15	$_____	_____
#3	Sept. 15	$_____	_____
#4	Jan. 15	$_____	_____
Total		$_____	

Your estimates are based on last year's tax due. If your income, expenses credits, or witholdings will be appreciably different this year, please discuss amending these figures with us.

42a ▶ 6
Preparatory practice

each line 3 times SS (slowly, faster, still faster); DS between 3-line groups; repeat if time permits

alphabet 1 Jim Bond quickly realized that we could fix the pretty girl's vehicle.

fig/sym 2 Serial #815-47 was stamped on the engine; Model #209(36) was below it.

combina-tion 3 Look for the fastest racer to get a big treat at the end of the races.

easy 4 Both of the towns bid for the giant quantity of coal down by the dock.

| 1 | 2 | 3 | 4 | 5 | 6 | 7 | 8 | 9 | 10 | 11 | 12 | 13 | 14 |

42b ▶ 10
Compose at the keyboard

2 full sheets; 2" top margin; DS

1 Center your name horizontally, then TS.

2 Answer the questions at the right in complete sentences.

3 Make pencil corrections on your copy, then retype it. Proofread; correct errors.

1 What is the name and address of the high school from which you were graduated?

2 In what year were you graduated from high school?

3 How long have you been studying at your present school?

4 Have you attended any other postsecondary schools?

5 When do you plan to complete your formal schooling?

42c ▶ 12
Determine line endings

2 half sheets; insert long edge first; 2" top margin; divide words as needed; proofread; correct errors

1 Type ¶ SS, 60-space line.
2 Type ¶ DS, 70-space line.

words

Composing at the typewriter can be helpful 9
to you, for you should be able to get your thoughts 19
and ideas onto paper more quickly with a typewriter 29
than with a pencil or pen. Concentrate on your sub- 40
ject and let ideas flow to the page; ignore for the 50
present any typographical mistakes. Use double 60
spacing so that proofreader's marks can be easily 70
used. Rewrite your composition as many times as 80
you think necessary. 84

Job 4
Income statement (full sheet)

Mr. Murtha assigns you to continue finalizing the financial statements for Nick's TV Service. You are handed the income statement form to process, which will be part of the final bound audit report. Follow the specific markings on the form. Indentions in the first column are the same as the indentions used for the balance sheet in Job 3. Place 8 spaces between Columns 1 and 2, and 2 spaces between Columns 2 and 3. Place the two depreciation expense items on 2 lines each (be sure to indent the second line an additional 3 spaces). Remember to allow an extra ½–inch in the left margin for binding purposes.

NICK'S TV SERVICE
Income Statement

For the Year Ended December 31, 19--
                              TS

Income:

    Service fees $61,205
                TS

Operating expenses:

    Rent expense $ 4,800

    Wages expense   10,964

    Advertising expense   602

    Depreciation expense-- delivery truck   1,205

    Depreciation expense--testing equipment   598

    Utilities expense   964
    Delivery expense   2,048
    Supplies and parts expense   4,578
        Total operating expenses   25,759

        Net income for the year $35,446

Job 5
Statement of owner's equity (full sheet)

Mr. Murtha still has one of Nick's TV Service statements yet to be processed. He asks you to process it following the same basic procedures as in the previous two statements. In this statement, place 10 spaces between the 2 columns.

NICK'S TV SERVICE
Statement of Owner's Equity   <DS
For the Year Ended December 31, 19--
                                            <TS
Nicholas Dominic, capital
    January 1, 19-- $25,000

Add: <DS
    ~~Capital contributed this year;~~
    Net income for year   35,446
                                                 $60,446

                                                 <DS
Less:
    Capital withdrawn during year   26,400
                                                 <DS
Nicholas Dominic, capital
    December 31, 19-- $34,046

43

42d ▶ 22
Format business letters in block style

2 plain full sheets; 60-space line; begin on Line 15

Problem 1

Prepare the letter; proofread and correct your copy before removing it from the machine.

	words
(Current date)	Mr. Herbert B. Wymore, Jr.	Millikin & Descartes, Inc.	800	15
Hazel Court	Denver, CO 80204-1192	Dear Mr. Wymore		25

(¶) In answer to his request, I am very happy to write a letter of recommendation for Mehti K. Boromand, who worked with our company for about fourteen months. — 40, 55, 56

(¶) Mr. Boromand's responsibilities, while he was employed here with us, involved carrying important documents and packages from building to building. He was responsible, prompt, and virtually tireless; cheerful, polite, and very friendly; and above all, discreet and reliable. He was absolutely trustworthy. — 71, 86, 102, 118

(¶) He left our employ at the end of last summer to begin college studies, but he will be welcomed back to our staff at any time that we have an opening in which he might be interested and for which he might be qualified. — 134, 150, 161

Sincerely | Miss Kim L. Schuyler | Assistant Vice President | xx — 173

Problem 2

Follow directions given for Problem 1.

(Current date) | Mrs. Lynn Martinez | 431 Poplar Lane | Annapolis, MD 21403-2261 | Dear Mrs. Martinez | — 15, 19

(¶) Our Credit Department informs me that you recently returned to us for credit a Wilcox Model 24 toaster. It appears from the report that some question was raised about the condition of the toaster when it was returned and that you objected to certain statements made at the credit counter. — 33, 49, 65, 77

(¶) I apologize if in any way the routine return of this toaster was questioned. As you know if you are a longtime shopper in our store, we guarantee our merchandise to be satisfactory in every way. If you, the customer, are not satisfied, then we, the store, are not satisfied either. — 93, 108, 125, 134

(¶) I assure you, Mrs. Martinez, that we have properly adjusted your account to reflect credit for the return. If you have any further questions about this matter, please contact me personally. — 150, 166, 173

Sincerely yours | Myles J. Longano, Head | Customer Relations | xx — 185

43a ▶ 6
Preparatory practice

each line 3 times SS (slowly, faster, slower); DS between 3-line groups; repeat if time permits

alphabet	1	Ben Jackson will save the money required for your next big cash prize.
fig/sym	2	The 7 1/2% interest of $18.68 on my $249.05 note (dated May 3) is due.
double letters	3	Dell was puzzled by the letter that followed the offer of a free book.
easy	4	In Dubuque, they may work the rich field for the profit paid for corn.

| 1 | 2 | 3 | 4 | 5 | 6 | 7 | 8 | 9 | 10 | 11 | 12 | 13 | 14 |

Job 3
Balance sheet (full sheet)

Ms. Lopez has just completed the year–end closing and financial statements for Nick's TV Service, an accounting service client. Whenever possible, financial statement forms have been prepared to make the accountant's job a little easier. Ms. Lopez has filled in the financial statement forms and submitted them to Mr. Murtha for final processing. You have been assigned to prepare the balance sheet and put it in final form. Ms. Lopez has indicated on the form for you to use leaders.

Mr. Murtha reminds you that all financial statements are bound in a report for the client. Therefore, all financial statements have an extra ½–inch in the left margin for binding purposes. Use a 1″ top margin for all statements that are to be bound in a report; use center point for a leftbound report. Indent items at intervals of 3 spaces. SS the body of the document, unless otherwise indicated. Leave 4 spaces between Columns 1 and 2 and 2 spaces between Columns 2 and 3. Correct any undetected errors you may find.

DS {

NICK'S TV SERVICE
Balance Sheet
For the Year Ended December 31, 19--

TS

Add remaining leaders

Assets
DS

Cash		$15,227
Accounts receivable		2,915
Supplies and parts on hand . .		1,235
Testing equipment	$ 5,250	
Less accumulated depreciation	1,794	3,456
Delivery truck	17,500	
Less accumulated depreciation	3,012	14,488
DS> Total assets		$37,321

TS
Liabilities

Accounts payable	$ 2,230	
Utilities	85	
Wages payable	225	
Service fees unearned	735	
DS> Total liabilities		$ 3,275

Owner's Equity

Nicholas Dominic, capital		34,046
DS> Total liabilities and owner's equity		$37,321

43b ▶ 10
Compose at the keyboard

2 full sheets; decide top
margin and spacing

1 Read the questions at the right.

2 Compose an answer for each
question in one or two sentences.
Join the sentences into para–
graphs to make a short essay.
Center the title **MY CAREER** over
the paragraphs.

3 Proofread; mark errors. If time
permits, retype the copy in final
form.

1 What is your career goal as you now see it?

2 What led you to make this career choice?

3 In what part of the world do you think you would like to live
and work?

4 Why do you want to live and work there?

5 Do you see yourself following any other career path in the
years ahead?

43c ▶ 12
Address large envelopes

3 large (No. 10) envelopes
[LM pp. 55-57]

1 Read carefully the special
placement information.

2 Address a large envelope to
each addressee listed below;
proofread; circle errors.

3 Fold a sheet of blank 8½″ ×
11″ paper for insertion into a
large envelope. Use the folding procedure shown for the
Monarch envelope on page
62.

Placement information

Some businesses use small
envelopes for 1-page letters
and large envelopes for letters
of 2 or more pages or letters
with enclosures. Many firms,
however, use large envelopes
for all correspondence.

Study the placement of the
letter address on the large envelope illustrated below. Set a
tab stop about 5 spaces to the
left of center or about 4″ from
the left edge of the envelope.
Space down about 14 lines
from the top edge of the envelope and begin typing at the
tab stop, thus positioning the
address in approximately vertical center and slightly below
the horizontal center. Learn to
visualize this position so that
you can type envelope ad-
dresses without special settings or measurements.

Type special messages for
the addressee (*Please forward, Hold for arrival, Personal,* etc.) a TS below the return address and 3 spaces
from the left edge of the envelope. Underline or type in
ALL CAPS

Type special mailing notations (such as REGISTERED,
SPECIAL DELIVERY, etc.) in ALL
CAPS below the stamp position.

MR MILO K DECKER PRESIDENT
POPULAR TOOL COMPANY
528 ESSEX LANE
DAVENPORT IA 52803-4163

BERA WALLPAPERS INC
7747 MC ARTHUR CIRCLE
EVANSVILLE IN 47714-3821

Ms. Barbara B. Treece
Breummer & Joyner
6234 Reynolds Avenue
Columbus, OH 43201-6822

Fairfield Manufacturing, Inc.
4320 Aldine Drive
San Diego, CA 92116-2307

TS

Hold for arrival

└─3 spaces

SPECIAL DELIVERY

center-5   MS TERESA ATGOOD   about Line 14
            524 JUHL DRIVE NE
            CEDAR RAPIDS IA 52402-8193

Office job simulation
(LM p. 83)

Job 1
Confirmation of audit visit
(LM p. 83)

As your first keyboarding job, Ms. Skopec hands you a hand–written draft of a letter she has written in order to confirm an audit visit to Office Interiors, Inc.

Date the letter **January 11** and address it to

Ms. Constance Pettiford, President
Office Interiors, Inc.
2385 Broadway
San Diego, CA 92102-3306

Ms. Skopec requests that you prepare a photocopy (pc) for Mr. Stanley Riech. She also wants her name and title typed as fol–lows on all letters:

MS. DENISE SKOPEC, CPA

CONFIRMATION OF AUDIT VISIT

Mr. Stanley Riech, our Senior Auditor, and I will begin the annual audit of your financial records at 9:00 a.m. on Monday, January 21. Our schedule is to spend five working days at your office.

To assist us in being as efficient as possible, will you please do the following prior to our arrival:
1. Arrange for us to have a private office with two desks and a telephone.
2. Notify all officers and employees who need to know of our visit.
3. Complete all year-end financial statements.

If there are any problems with the planned audit dates or in completing needed financial statements, please notify our office as soon as possible.

Job 2
Simplified Memo (plain full sheet)

Ms. Skopec has assigned you to be supervised by Office Manager Jose Murtha. In order to clarify workload assignments, Ms. Skopec has drafted a memo to be sent to Stanley Riech, Senior Auditor, and Rosetta Lopez, Senior Accountant. You have been asked to prepare the simplified memo in final form. Date the memo **January 11, 19—**. Use the subject line: **TEMPORARY OFFICE WORKER EMPLOYED**. Correct any undetected errors that Ms. Skopec may have missed.

I have contracted with office Service Temporaries, Inc., to provide us with a temporary ofice worker for the next six days. This new employee is (insert your name). (She/He) has excellent keyboarding and formating skills and should be of great assistance to us during our peak workload period.

I have asked our Office Manager, Jose Murtha, to supervise the workload of this temporary office worker. Please continue to submit all keyboarding work directly to Jose for processing.

43d ▶ 22
Format business letters in block style

2 plain full sheets; 60-space line; date on Line 15

Problem 1

Make a corrected copy of the letter at right. Insert longer changes as numbered.

Problem 2

Follow the directions for Problem 1, but address the letter to

Mr. George B. Glackmun
406 Rathbun Avenue
White Plains, NY 10606-3642

Use an appropriate salutation. In ¶2, change office layout to office hours.

① for consideration
② has been accepted by them,
③ adoption and
④ amount of money

June 16, 19--   3

Mr. Olin N. Werger   7
1640 Barnes Lande   10
White Plains, NY 10604-3719   16

Dear Mr. Werger   19

inform ①
It is my happy opportunity to ~~tell~~ you that the sug-   30
gestion you recently submitted ~~has been studied~~ by   40
our Management Board, and they have recommended to me   56
its immediate implementation. ②   65

③ *your*
I, too, have studied ~~the~~ suggestion, and I must tell   74
you that I am extremely enthusiastic about it. Your   85
explanations makes it quite obvious that by making   95
the changes in office layout you recommend our com-   105
pany should be able to save a substantial ~~expense~~. ④   117

Will you attend a brief ceremony to be held in my   127
office next Friday morning at 13? At that time it   137
will be my pleasure to award to you a check in the   147
amount of $4500 in appreciation of your excellent   157
money-saving recommendation.   163

Accept my sincere congratulations.   170

Sincerely yours   173

Mrs. Cecelia P. Barbette   178
President   180

xx   181

44

44a ▶ 6
Preparatory practice

each line 3 times SS (slower, faster, slower); DS between 3-line groups; repeat if time permits

alphabet	1	The explorer questioned Jack's amazing story about unknown lava flows.
figures	2	I am sending 2,795 of the 4,680 sets now and the remainder on June 13.
capitali-zation	3	Is the notation on this memorandum Bob's, Edna's, Ralph's, or Myrna's?
easy	4	Work with vigor to shape a theory to make visible and audible signals.

| 1 | 2 | 3 | 4 | 5 | 6 | 7 | 8 | 9 | 10 | 11 | 12 | 13 | 14 |

Learning goals

1 To develop knowledge about and skills in preparing accounting documents.

2 To become familiar with the various tasks performed in an accounting office.

3 To plan your work efficiently and to complete it correctly.

Machine adjustments

1 Paper guide at *0*.

2 Ribbon control set to use upper half of ribbon.

3 Margins: 70–space line for drills; as appropriate for letters, memorandums, reports, and tables.

4 Space job tasks as directed (or appropriate). .

Office Job Simulation

Before you begin the jobs of Section 39, read carefully the material at the right.

Make appropriate notes of any procedures that will save you time as you complete the job activities of this accounting office simulation.

Daily practice plan:

Preparatory practice .... 5'
Work on simulation .... 45'

Work Assignment

You have been assigned by Office Service Temporaries, Inc., to work for Ms. Denise Skopec, a certified public accountant who heads an accounting firm in Chula Vista. Her address is 633 Alpine Avenue, Chula Vista, CA 92010-3040.

Ms. Skopec's office procedures manual specifies that all letters are to be prepared using the AMS simplified letter style. All financial statements are to be bound, unless otherwise indicated. Therefore, leave an extra ½" in the left margin for these financial statements. All documents are to be photocopied; thus, no carbon copies are required to be made of any work done in the office. All work must be proofread carefully and all errors corrected before removing the document from the machine.

Ms. Skopec has based her office procedures manual on COLLEGE KEYBOARDING/TYPEWRITING, so use the Reference Guide and the index of your textbook to look up matters of style and placement when in doubt. When a job requires unusual specifications, she provides them in "Excerpts from the Office Procedures Manual."

When specific job instructions are qiven, follow them carefully. When specific instructions are not given, make appropriate decisions on the basis of your knowledge and experience. If Ms. Skopec (or your teacher) considers some of your decisions unacceptable, learn from her or his suggestions—just as you would do in any business office.

Excerpts from Office Procedures Manual

Braced Headings. A heading which is centered over 2 or more columns is called a braced heading. This type of heading is found generally in a table that has both horizontal and vertical rulings. However, a braced heading is sometimes used both in a ruled table or in a simple table that has no rulings.

In a table with horizontal rulings, a braced heading will be found within the column heading area—between the double ruling below the main heading and the single ruling below the column headings. Generally, the braced heading is separated from the column headings (or another braced heading) by a horizontal ruling.

As a rule, double-space above and below the double horizontal ruling which follows the main heading. Single-space above and double-space below a single horizontal ruling.

The illustration below shows the placement of a braced heading.

| | INVENTORY REPORT | | | | |
		DS			
Stock No.	Received*		Shipped*	DS SS	Balance on Hand
	Date	Qty	Date	Qty DS SS	

*braced heading

Preparatory practice

Type as many times as you can in 5' at the beginning of each class period in this section.

alphabet	1	My exceedingly well-known jazz quintet plays before the lively groups.
fig/sym	2	Sales this year are up 10.6% ($229,872) from $2,168,603 to $2,398,475.
direct reach	3	My brother, the grocer, often hums a tune as he unpacks the groceries.
fluency	4	The quantity of fish at my lake may also be a problem for the visitor.

| 1 | 2 | 3 | 4 | 5 | 6 | 7 | 8 | 9 | 10 | 11 | 12 | 13 | 14 |

44b ▶ 12
Improve concentration

1 Cover the answer key at the bottom of the column. When you have finished keyboarding, check your answers.

2 Prepare a copy of the ¶ DS. Unscramble the underlined words as you keyboard.

3 Using your corrected copy, take 1' writings as time permits.

Key: down, what, will, this, them, Then

Difficulty index

all letters used	A	1.5 si	5.7 awl	80% hfw

gwam 1'

When you sit <u>donw</u> at your typewriter to compose, the first problem   13
to be conquered is deciding <u>waht</u> to write about. For a school paper,   27
however, this problem does not exist; the subject <u>lliw</u> likely have been   42
assigned. Therefore, the primary need in <u>hist</u> situation is to organize   56
mentally your facts and ideas and type <u>mhet</u> in somewhat logical order   70
as they occur to you. <u>Tehn,</u> the process is one of continual refinement.   85

gwam 1' | 1 | 2 | 3 | 4 | 5 | 6 | 7 | 8 | 9 | 10 | 11 | 12 | 13 | 14 |

44c ▶ 12
Use carbon paper

Materials needed:

1 original sheet
2 second sheets
2 carbon paper sheets
1 firm (5"×3") card

70–space line; DS; 2½" top margin; correct errors

1 Study the information and illustrations at the right.

2 Assemble a carbon pack and make an original and 2 carbon copies of the ¶ shown below the illustrations.

Assembling a carbon pack

1 Assemble letterhead, carbon sheets (uncarboned side up), and second sheets as illustrated below. Use one carbon and one second sheet for each copy desired.

2 Grasp the carbon pack at the sides. Turn it so that the letterhead faces away from you, the carbon sides of the carbon paper are toward you, and the top edge of the pack is face down. Tap the sheets gently on the desk to straighten.

3 Hold the sheets firmly to prevent slipping; insert pack into typewriter. Hold pack with one hand; turn platen with the other.

Many companies no longer make carbon copies; of those that do, some do not erase errors on them. If you need to do so, pull the original forward and place a firm card in front of the carbon sheet. Erase the error on the original with a typewriter eraser; erase the carbon copy with a soft pencil eraser. For additional carbon copies, use the card to protect them by placing it between the sheet being erased and the next sheet of carbon paper.

44d ▶ 20
Format business letters in modified block style

2 plain full sheets; copy sheets

1 Study the special information at the right, then study Style Letter 4 on page 84.

2 Type a copy of the letter; proofread; correct errors.

3 Type another copy of letter. Make one carbon copy.

As you study Style Letter 4, page 84, note that the block style has been "modified" by moving the dateline and the closing lines from block position at the left margin. In the modified block style, these lines begin at the center point of the page.

Because stationery with printed letterhead is either used or assumed, the dateline will be the first item typed in these letters. As all letters in Section 10 are of average length, it is correct to type the dateline on about Line 15 and to use a 60–space line for all of them.

Spacing between letter parts is the same as was used with the block style. This spacing is standard for all business letters.

Job 14
Prepare a quality control report (LM p. 81)

Duane Elkins, Quality Control Coordinator, prepares every Monday a report summarizing the activity of the quality control staff during the past week and indicating the current status of software under development. He gives Ms. Fillmore his handwritten report for the week ending January 8; she assigns you the task of preparing the report in final form for photoduplication and distribution.

To distinguish a zero from a capital letter O in stock numbers, Ms. Fillmore suggests that you strike a diagonal (/) through the 0 (zero) as you prepare the report.

WEEKLY QUALITY CONTROL REPORT

Week Ending _January 8, 19--_

Computer Operator	Stock No.	Disk No.	Pass No.	Date Completed	Hours	Approved for Duplication
Hernandez	CØ46	1	4	Jan. 2	3:30	Yes
		2	3	2	3:45	No
	CØ47	1	2	3	3:00	Yes
		2	1	3	4:15	No
		3	1	4	6:30	No
	K1Ø2	1	4	5	7:00	Yes
	E21Ø	2	3	6	6:45	No
King	CØ46	3	2	Jan. 2	4:25	No
	F137	1	5	2	3:00	Yes
	E21Ø	2	3	3	7:00	No
	M212	1	2	4	6:45	No
		2	1	5	7:00	No
	CØ47	1	2	6	3:15	Yes
		2	1	6	4:00	No
Yamuri	CØ46	2	3	Jan. 2	3:00	No
		1	4	2	3:45	Yes
	A11Ø	3	5	3	6:30	Yes
		4	3	4	6:45	No
	DP1Ø	1	2	5	7:00	No
	WP2Ø	1	4	6	6:30	Yes

Total Quality Control Hours _103:40_

Communications Design Associates

348 INDIANA AVENUE
WASHINGTON, DC 20001-1438
Tel: 1-800-432-5739

Tabulate to center to type
date and closing lines

Dateline   Line 15 November 28, 19--   4

Operate return 4 times

Letter   Mr. Otto B. Bates, President   9
address   Third Bank and Trust Company   15
          9080 Reservoir Avenue   20
          New Brunswick, NJ 08901-4476   26
                                        DS

Salutation Dear Mr. Bates   28
                    DS
Body of   This letter is written in what is called the "modified block   41
letter   style." It is the style we recommend for use in your office   53
          for reasons I shall detail for you in the paragraphs below.   65

          First, the style is a fairly efficient one that requires only 77
          one tab setting--at center point--for positioning the current 90
          date, the complimentary close, and the typed signature lines. 102
          All other lines begin at left margin.   110

          Second, the style is quite easy to learn. New employees will 123
          have little difficulty learning it, and your present staff can 135
          adjust to it without unnecessary confusion.   144

          Third, the style is a familiar one; it is used by more busi-   156
          ness firms than any other. It is conservative, and customers 168
          and companies alike feel comfortable with it.   178

          I am happy to enclose our booklet on the subject of letter   189
          styles and special features of business letters.   199
                                                             DS
Complimentary   Sincerely yours   202
close   Operate return 4 times

                       Kathryn E. Bowers

Typed name   Ms. Kathryn E. Bowers   206
Official title   Senior Consultant   210
                                        DS

Reference xx   211
initials   DS
Enclosure Enclosure   213
notation

Shown in pica type
60-space line

Style letter 4: modified block style, block paragraphs, open punctuation

Job 12
Prepare an Invoice (LM p. 77)

Ms. Fillmore hands you an order taken by one of the sales representatives. She asks you to check the accuracy of extensions and the total and then to prepare an invoice (in duplicate) to be sent to the customer as soon as the confirming purchase order is received and the order has been shipped. She gives you the following additional information:

1. Date: **January 4.**
2. Our Order No.: **B4015627.**
3. Terms: **Net 30 days.**

TauTronics Corp.   (619) 877-4000
1051 Graves Avenue
El Cajon, CA 92021-3001

ORDER FORM

Purchase order No. *PS 705-2841L*

Date *January 2, 19--*

Ship Via *UPS*

Portland Learning Center
2811 NE Holman
Portland, OR 97211-3245

Process order; hold shipment for receipt of purchase order.

Quantity	Cat. No.	Description	Price	Total
15 sets	TO16-3	Lamda MicroType 1 (4-disk)	195.00	2,925.00
15 "	TO17-3	Omicron ElectroType 1	89.95	1,349.25
10 "	TO17-4	Omicron ElectroType 2	115.00	1,150.00
10 "	EO18-3	Lamda MicroEnglish Lab 1 (5-disk)	240.00	2,400.00
1 set	MO19-5	Sigma Math-Pac 1 (Network)	875.00	875.00
				8,699.25

_____
Sales Representative

Leonora Phillips
Purchasing Agent

Job 13
Prepare a purchase order
(LM p. 79)

Ms. Fillmore asks you to prepare Purchase Order No. **PO493-2305** to order the items listed in the note at the right. She asks that you figure and enter the extensions in the total column and determine and enter the grand total of the order.

January 4, 19--

Order from Sigma Computer Store, Pacific Design Center, 8687 Melrose Avenue, Los Angeles, CA 90069-3281:

2   No. *8511-1*   Looseleaf diskette binders, 5 1/4" inserts, at *$8.95* each

1   No. *4207*   Sigma printer stand, 30 x 30 x 26 1/2", at *$220*

5 boxes   No. *3481*   Sigma diskettes, 5 1/4", at *$38.95* per box

1   No. *207*   HeatPruf diskette storage cabinet, 19 1/2 x 20 x 22", at *$1,038.95*

Sigma's terms of sale are 2/10, net 30. Have order shipped by Pacific Express.

J. F.
Judith Fillmore

45a ▶ 6
Preparatory practice

each line 3 times SS (slowly, faster, still faster); DS between 3-line groups; repeat if time permits

alphabet	1 Douglas quickly won several junior prizes at the Foxburgh swim trials.
figures	2 Flight 372 will leave at 9:58 a.m. and arrive in Buffalo at 10:46 a.m.
left shift	3 Jenny and I are going to Maryland in May, but Jane is going to Norway.
easy	4 They may also dismantle the eight authentic antique autos in the town.

| 1 | 2 | 3 | 4 | 5 | 6 | 7 | 8 | 9 | 10 | 11 | 12 | 13 | 14 |

45b ▶ 6
Proofread/revise as you keyboard

1 Cover the answer key at the bottom of the column. When you have finished keyboarding, check your answers.

2 Provide needed capitals for each of the five sentences.

Key: 1 Lee, Room, He, Chapter **2** You, New York **3** They, Thursday's **4** Jan, Mo, I, Chicago, Thanksgiving **5** Did, Shaw, Caesar, Cleopatra, I, Memphis

1 lee left his history book in room 27. he must study chapter 15 today.

2 you will reach the new york state line if you drive east for 21 miles.

3 they announced their fall hosiery sale on page 15 of thursday's paper.

4 jan said, "mo and i should arrive in chicago on thanksgiving evening."

5 did shaw write "caesar and cleopatra"? i saw it at a memphis theater.

45c ▶ 18
Keyboard letter parts

Lines 1-3: Take three 1' writings on each line. Try to finish each line at least once in the time allotted.

Lines 4-6: Take two 45" writings on Lines 4-6, arranging them in 3-line address format.

Goal: To complete each address in Lines 4-6 in 45".

> **Technique hint:**
> Type at a controlled, but constant rate. Do not pause before typing figures.

1 123 Brandy Street; 459 Reynolds Drive; 650 River Road; 78 Osage Avenue

2 Erie, PA 16511-4478; Brooklyn, NY 11227-2785; Dayton, OH 45410-3367

3 April 29, 19--; May 18, 19--; June 27, 19--; July 26, 19--; January 17

4 Ms. Deirdre Ann Beebe | 262 Orient Boulevard | Wichita, KS 67213-4976

5 Mrs. Rosetta Hayman | 595 Singingwood Drive | Torrance, CA 90505-3047

6 Mr. Angelo Ybarra | 341 Demunda Avenue | Niagara Falls, NY 14304-8259

| 1 | 2 | 3 | 4 | 5 | 6 | 7 | 8 | 9 | 10 | 11 | 12 | 13 | 14 |

Job 11
Sales analysis report
(full sheets)

Mr. Lambert hands Ms. Fillmore a rough draft of a sales analysis report that he wants prepared in final form for photocopying. Ms. Fillmore asks you to prepare the report in unbound style.

She cautions you to look for unmarked errors and to correct any you find. She asks you to add the side heading

Comments and Projections

between the fourth and fifth paragraphs of the report.

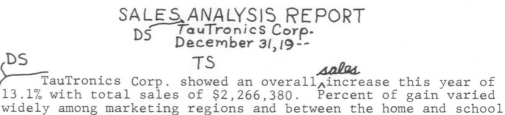

SALES ANALYSIS REPORT
DS TauTronics Corp.
December 31, 19--
TS

DS

TauTronics Corp. showed an overall *sales* increase this year of 13.1% with total sales of $2,266,380. Percent of gain varied widely among marketing regions and between the home and school market segments. *Sales by Regions* <TS

The Western region lead in total dollar sales with sales of $7/6,325. The North-Central Region was second with totla sales of $500,325¢. *Each* All of the ③ other regions (Eastern, Mountain-Plains, and Southern) *posted* had sales of over $300,000.

The greatest percentage of total sales increase was enjoyed by the Southern region with a 20.3% gain, followed by the Western Region with 15.6%, the Mountain-Plains Region with 13.8%, the North *-Central* Region with 9.1%, and the Eastern Region with 7.0%.

TS
Sales by Market Segment

The sales leader in both home and school markets in terms of dollar volume was the Western Region. The greatest percentage of sales gain in the school market, however, was the Southern Region (38.2%), with the Mountain-Plains Region running a *distant* poor second (18.9%). In the home market, the Western Region lead with a 16.8% sales gain, with the North-Central Region *posting* showing an 11.2% increase. School sales over-all increased by 15.3%; *whereas,* home sales *increased by* jumped 11.7%.

Overall, the year just *past* passed was a successful one. Our goal for next year is to increase *total* sales by *at least* 15%, with no region or market segment falling below a 10% gain. ¶Plans already in place should help us attain our goal. Contracts with *new* home suppliers in the *and Southern* Eastern regions should boost sales there dramatically. Pending school adoptions in the Eastern and *North-* Central regions should have a major postive impack on *school* sales in those regions.

The addition of sales *representatives* reps in the Eastern and North-Central Regions, combined with the positive *conditions just mentioned,* above should help us to generate *at least* the projected 15% increase in the coming year.

45d ▶ 20
Review business letters in modified block style

2 letterheads and envelopes [LM pp. 59-61]; carbon paper; copy sheets

60-space line; begin on Line 15

Problem 1

Prepare the letter; make one carbon copy. Proofread and correct your copy before re–moving it from the machine. Address an envelope.

words

August 28, 19-- | Miss Noriko Harada | 9580 Evelyn Way | Reno, NV 89502-4839 | 14
Dear Miss Harada   18

(¶) Thank you for your recent letter inquiring about admission to our School of   33
Graduate Studies. I hope the following information will be helpful.   47

(¶) Admission here depends upon several factors. The applicant, for example,   62
must have completed an appropriate undergraduate degree at an accredited   76
institution with a cumulative grade point average of 2.75 or better on a 4-point   93
scale.   94

(¶) Further, each applicant's transcript is examined to determine whether   108
additional background courses will be required. The background courses   123
necessary for admission are set by each of the various areas of study. The   138
applicant must also complete satisfactorily any admission test that may be   153
required by the area of study for which admission is sought.   165

(¶) I am enclosing an application form for your use. Please let me know if I can   181
help you again.   184

Sincerely | Derek J. Wertz, Ph.D. | Dean, Graduate Studies | xx | Enclosure   197/208

Problem 2

Follow directions given for Problem 1.

July 29, 19-- | Mr. Hyman J. Greathouse | President, Apex Motors | 5600 El Avado   15
Avenue | Lincoln, NE 68504-3976 | Dear Mr. Greathouse   25

(¶) Thank you for your kind comments about my presentation before the Lincoln   40
Chamber of Commerce. It was a pleasure for me to be there to describe our   55
company's fringe benefits program.   62

(¶) You asked about my allusion to our company's physical fitness program. We   77
have a good one, I believe. Each year in March, for example, every employee is   93
encouraged to have a complete physical examination by a personal physician at   108
our expense.   111

(¶) We maintain a company membership in a fitness facility, which we urge our   126
employees to use for swimming, racquetball, and other forms of exercise.   141

(¶) We engage in team and league sponsorship when a substantial number of our   156
employees are involved.   161

(¶) As you can see, we are strong advocates of healthy minds and bodies for   175
people who work for us. This program is mutually advantageous and makes   190
very good business sense to us.   196

Cordially yours | Mrs. Frances Trewes Baxter | Executive Vice President | xx   210
  228

Job 9
Regional sales comparison
(full sheet)

Mr. Jerome Lambert, National Director of Marketing, has put together a comparison of sales by regions. Ms. Fillmore asks you to prepare final copy for photocopying; SS data for each region; DS between regions.

REGIONAL SALES COMPARISON

TauTronics Corp.
December 31, 19--

Region	Last Year	This Year	% Increase
Eastern			
Home Market	$186,750	$198,470	6.3%
School Market	132,690	143,285	8.0
Mountain-Plains			
Home Market	162,585	178,605	9.8
School Market	105,990	126,040	18.9
North-Central			
Home Market	271,590	301,920	11.2
School Market	187,045	198,460	6.1
Southern			
Home Market	175,140	189,520	8.2
School Market	118,490	163,755	38.2
Western			
Home Market	398,410	465,200	16.8
School Market	264,715	301,125	13.7
	$2,003,405	$2,266,380	13.1%

Job 10
Letter response to new product proposal
(LM p. 75)

After the committee meeting to discuss the Jackson–Williams proposal, Dr. Calo composed a letter to the authors. Ms. Fillmore asks you to prepare the final copy and gives you these directions:

1 Date: **January 3, 19—**
2 Address:

Dr. Hilda Jackson
Department of Office Systems
Southern California College
1112 E. Artesia Boulevard
Compton, CA 90221-3009

3 Correct any errors in spelling, punctuation, and capitalization you find.
4 Indicate that a photocopy of the letter is being sent to Dr. Mark Williams.

New
Members of our/Products Evaluation Comitee meet yesterday to discuss your Keyboarding letter-pac proposal. The reactions were positive and I received approval to work with you in attempting getting the block letter segment ready for field testing.

For field testing we shall need in final try-out form all materials dealing with the modified block style letter; diskette, source document booklet with asignments and directions and all material for the instructional leader's guide.

Only after the results of field testing is are available will we be able to decide whether to procede in the development of the complete product. We at TauTronics are optomistic that field test results will be positive.

with us
If you and dr. Williams are willling to work/in this way I would like to suggest meet with the two of you soon to discuss some suggestions that we believe will help in the refinement process.

46a ▶ 6
Preparatory practice

each line 3 times SS (slowly, faster, still faster); repeat if time permits

alphabet 1 Gwendolyn Post lives in a quiet area just six blocks from the old zoo.

figures 2 The 1983 edition of this book had 5 parts, 40 chapters, and 672 pages.

hyphen 3 Here is an up-to-date reference for those out-of-this-world questions.

easy 4 The rich man paid half of the endowment, and this firm also paid half.

| 1 | 2 | 3 | 4 | 5 | 6 | 7 | 8 | 9 | 10 | 11 | 12 | 13 | 14 |

46b ▶ 10
Improve concentration

1 Cover the answer key at the bottom of the column. When you have finished, check your answers.

2 Prepare a copy of the ¶ DS. Unscramble the underlined words as you keyboard.

3 Using your corrected copy, take 1' writings as time permits.

Key: make, been, good, very, read, with, more

Difficulty index

| all letters used | A | 1.5 si | 5.7 awl | 80% hfw |

gwam 1'

Many people mkac fast work of their letter writing. They com- 12
pose letters on their typewriters. Such a letter has not always bene 26
considered doog form; but now even etiquette experts, whose judgments 40
are accepted by some, recognize and accept typed letters--and for ervy 55
good reasons. A typed letter is easier to rade than a handwritten one; 69
and, as a typist can more easily keep pace hitw his or her thoughts, a 83
typed letter seems to be erom coherent, interesting, and conversational. 98

gwam 1' | 1 | 2 | 3 | 4 | 5 | 6 | 7 | 8 | 9 | 10 | 11 | 12 | 13 | 14 |

46c ▶ 10
Compose at the keyboard

2 full sheets; 2½" top margin; 70-space line

1 Compose three brief ¶s, each beginning with the words shown at the right.

2 Make pencil corrections; retype edited copy.

¶ 1 One of my favorite

¶ 2 However, I must say that I dislike

¶ 3 Therefore, whenever I can I

46d ▶ 24
Improve production skill

2 plain full sheets

1 Using Style Letter 4, p. 84, take a 10' writing. Proofread and circle errors. Calculate g–pram.

2 Take a second 10' writing. Proofread; circle errors. Calculate g–pram. Work to improve either speed or accuracy on the second writing.

Use the following formula to calculate *g–pram* (gross production rate a minute):

$$g\text{–}pram = \frac{total\ words\ typed}{time\ (10')}$$

Job 7
Letter response to inquiry
(LM p. 71)

Ms. Dorinda Chagall, Assistant Manager, Marketing, has drafted a letter in response to an inquiry. Ms. Fillmore asks you to format and type it in final form. Address the letter to:

Mrs. Maria Munoz, Head
Office Training Center
Rocky Mountain College
1514 Cleveland Place
Denver, CO 80202-3005

Job 8
Adapt a letter
(LM p. 73)

Ms. Chagall asks to have the Munoz letter adapted to answer another inquiry. Ms. Fillmore assigns the job to you and gives you a paragraph to substitute for Paragraph 1. Use the same date and address the letter to:

Mr. John Kirk, Manager
Word Processing Center
Johnson Manufacturing Co.
6503 E. Ocean Boulevard
Long Beach, CA 90803-3007

(The substitute paragraph is shown at right.)

December 30, 19--

¶ Your decision to begin replacing electromechanical typewriters with electronic typewriters and microcomputers is both wise and timely. Increasingly, applicants for jobs in modern offices have a decided advantage if they have had training on these kinds of equipment and on more sophisticated word and data processors. This is especially true of graduates of 2- and 4-year colleges.

¶ TauTronics is a leader in the development of educationally sound printware and software for training office personnel. Most of our electronic instructional packages are available for use on the three most popular personal computers. We also have training materials available for use on selected makes of electronic typewriters. The enclosed catalog describes each of the learning packages that are currently available.

¶ Some of our courseware requires only 32K of memory; some packages require 48K; others, 64K. The memory requirement is given for each product in our catalog. Most new products are programmed for 64K minimum.

¶ After you have had an opportunity to review the enclosed catalog, I would like to arrange an appointment for one of our representatives to demonstrate those products in which you are interested.

¶ Just remove, fill in, and return the information form on on page 15 of the catalog. Leave the rest to me.

¶ Thank you for requesting information about our electronic education packages for possible use in your in-service training programs. The following information and the enclosed catalog may be helpful.

47a ▶ 6
Preparatory practice

each line 3 times SS (slowly, faster, still faster); DS between 3-line groups; repeat if time permits

alphabet	1	Does Frank expect to solve the jigsaw puzzle more quickly than before?
fig/sym	2	Model #S6-713 (20″ screen) sells for $359; with a 27″ screen, $468.20.
long words	3	Automatic typewriters are highly effective with repetitive procedures.
easy	4	Pay the right girl to work with them as a tutor with the ancient maps.

| 1 | 2 | 3 | 4 | 5 | 6 | 7 | 8 | 9 | 10 | 11 | 12 | 13 | 14 |

47b ▶ 11
Measure skill growth: straight copy

a 3′ and a 5′ writing; determine gwam; proofread and circle errors

Difficulty index

all letters used | A | 1.5 si | 5.7 awl | 80% hfw

gwam 3′ | 5′

Diogenes, quaint little light in hand, journeyed out night after night looking for an honest man. We don't know exactly how Diogenes intended to recognize honesty, but he was very serious about his effort. He really thought he would know such a person when he met one. — 4/3, 9/5, 14/8, 18/11

Just as a matter of conjecture, do you wonder whether Diogenes, if he were living today, might look for an educated person? If he were to undertake such a search, would an educated person be recognizable? If so, how? What qualities might you expect an educated person to have? — 22/13, 27/16, 32/19, 37/22

The idea poses interesting questions. Just what is education? Is it a mental thing? Can it be recognized in the actions or reactions of a person? Is it backed up by a diploma? Or is it more? Does it perhaps include such unscholarly elements as experience and observation? — 41/25, 46/28, 51/30, 55/33

Diogenes might find that an educated person is one, for example, who has more questions than answers, is more puzzled than positive, is aware that more is not known than is known, yet is better able to solve problems with value judgments than with memorized formulas. — 59/36, 64/38, 69/41, 73/44

gwam 3′ | 1 | 2 | 3 | 4 | 5 |
5′ | 1 | 2 | 3 |

47c ▶ 33
Measure skill application: business letters

Time schedule:
Assembling materials .... 2′
Timed production .... 25′
Final check; proofread;
  compute g–pram .... 6′

Materials needed:
3 letterheads and envelopes [LM pp. 63–67] or plain paper
60–space line; begin on Line 15

When the signal to begin is given, insert paper and begin typing Problem 1. Keyboard the problems in sequence until the signal to stop is given. Prepare a large envelope for each letter. Do Problem 1 again on a plain sheet if you have finished Problem 3 and time has not been called. Proofread all problems; circle errors. Calculate g–pram.

$$g–pram = \frac{total\ words\ typed}{time\ (25')}$$

Job 3
Memorandum (LM p. 67)

Dr. Calo has drafted a memo requesting cost estimates from Miss Arlene Simms. Ms. Fillmore asks you to format and type the memo on a memo form. Correct any undetected errors you may find.

Jobs 4 and 5
Adapt a memorandum
(LM pp. 67–69)

Dr. Calo has asked Ms. Fillmore to have the rough-draft memo modified to request that Kevin Marx estimate the sales potential of Letter-Pac in the school market and that he send his report to Jerome Lambert by the end of the week. Be sure to inform him of the upcoming meeting on Letter-Pac and its purpose.

He also wants the memo modified and sent to Ms. Sheila Prentiss for an estimate of the sales potential of the new product in the home market. She will need to be informed of the upcoming meeting also.

Ms. Fillmore asks you to prepare both memos.

Job 6
Tentative agenda (full sheet)

Dr. Calo has roughed out a tentative agenda for the meeting of the New Products Evaluation Committee. Ms. Fillmore asks you to format and type it in the final form for photocopying.

TO: Arlene Simms

FROM: Dru Calo

DATE: *December 23, 19--*

SUBJECT: PRODUCTION COST ESTIMATE**S** FOR JACKSON-WILLIAMS PROJECT

A meeting of the New Products *Evaluation* Committee is ~~set~~ *scheduled* for *2 p.m.* December ~~29~~ *30*, 19--, to discuss the development *and marketing* of Jackson and Williams *H*Letter-Pac proposal. Before that meeting you *will need to* ~~must~~ provide production cost *information* ~~data~~ to Jerome Lambert, who sets product prices. I am *enclosing* ~~attaching~~ a copy of the proposal and prototype *materials* as a basis for *your cost* ~~you~~ estimate. Mr. Lambert *wants* ~~will need~~ your cost estimate by the end of *this* ~~the~~ week.

TENTATIVE AGENDA
New Products Evaluation Committee Meeting
2 p. m., December 30, 19--

1. *Introductory Comments* . . . . *Jerome Lambert*
2. *Presentation of Letter-Pac Proposal* . . . *Dru Calo*
3. *Special Reports*
   Production Costs . . . . *Arlene Simms*
   Estimate of School Sales Potential . . *Kevin Marx*
   Estimate of Home Sales Potential . . *Sheila Prentiss*
4. *Discussion of Proposal* . . . . *Committee Members*
5. *Summary of Discussion: Pros and Cons* . . *Jerome Lambert*
6. *Call for Vote* . . . . *Dru Calo*
7. *Adjournment*

words

Problem 1
block style

(Current date) | Mr. Lonny L. Johnson, Director | The House by the Side of the   15
Road | 679 Truman Street | Abilene, TX 79601-5739 | Dear Mr. Johnson   28

(¶) The Executive Board of The House by the Side of the Road has instructed me   43
to express to you how deeply it regrets your resignation as House Director.   58
(¶) The Board recognizes that you have served as Director for 18 years. Your   73
leadership, loyalty, and perseverance will be missed; and finding another Direc-   89
tor to take your place will not be easy.   97
(¶) Therefore, the Board also asks me to express its special thanks for your   112
willingness to continue to serve as Director until we find a replacement.   126
(¶) We shall, of course, begin a search for a new Director right away; but, in the   142
meantime, please let us know of any assistance we can provide.   155
Sincerely yours | Dale L. Berger | Secretary | xx   163/**184**

Problem 2
modified block style

(Current date) | Mr. Byung Chung, Manager | Nikki's Paris Shop | 1890 San Luis   15
Street | Las Vegas, NV 89110-7241 | Dear Mr. Chung   24

(¶) This letter introduces Gale Senter, our Nevada representative for Cleo   38
Sportswear. Gale will stop at your shop in a day or two to show you samples of   54
our new spring line.   59
(¶) One of the features you should look for in Cleo clothes--and stress to your   74
customers--is the basic, uncluttered look of each style. Our designers fashion   90
clothes that do not have faddish elements that outdate them after one or two   105
seasons.   107
(¶) Also, examine carefully the fine cloth used to make our Cleo line. All our   122
fabrics are washable and do not need ironing. Easy care and long wear are Cleo   138
hallmarks. Notice our wide range of color choices, which allows customers to   154
pick colors that complement personality as well as please the eye.   167
(¶) Gale will be happy to discuss availability and terms of purchase with you.   181
You'll be glad she called.   187
Sincerely yours | Miss Celia Murtagh | Sales Manager | xx   197/**215**

Problem 3
style of your choice

(Current date) | Miss Molly Bester | 3724 Mumford Road | Macon, GA 31204-4493 | 15
Dear Miss Bester   18

(¶) It is difficult for us to express adequately our regret for the recent error we   34
made in your telephone order. Mistakes like this rarely occur; when they do, it   50
is not easy to make them right.   57
(¶) We understand that you ordered a pound box of chocolates to be sent gift   71
wrapped for your mother's birthday. All our records confirm this. We do not   87
know why a box of cigars was sent.   94
(¶) We can understand your acute embarrassment when your mother opened   108
your gift and found a box of cigars. Immediately upon hearing of our error, we   124
sent by special messenger a 5-pound box of our deluxe chocolates with a note of   140
apology to your mother. We hope she will understand.   150
(¶) We do not ask that you pay for the chocolates. We do not ask that you return   166
the cigars. We do ask you to forgive us.   174
Sincerely yours | Leonard J. Anhut | Vice President | xx   184/**196**

Office job simulation

(LM pp. 67–81)

Job 1
New product proposal (full sheets)

Ms. Fillmore gives you a new product proposal prepared by Dr. Dru Calo, Director of New Products. Dr. Calo wants the material formatted and typed in unbound manuscript style DS. It will later be duplicated for distribution to members of the New Products Evaluation Committee.

Ms. Fillmore asks you to identify and correct any unmarked errors you find in addition to those that have been marked by Dr. Calo.

Job 2
Compose a simplified memo
(plain full sheet)

Dr. Calo has asked Ms. Fillmore to have a cover memo composed to accompany the new product proposal. She assigns you the job with these instructions:

1 Use simplified memo style.

2 Date the memo December 23.

3 Address the memo to: Jerome Lambert, Jena Fox, and Ronald Simons.

4 Use the product proposal title as the subject line.

5 Indicate that a copy of the new product proposal, sample storyboards, and diskette are attached.

6 Request a meeting a week from December 23 to discuss the proposal.

7 Use Dr. Calo's name as the originator of the memo.

PROPOSAL FOR NEW PRODUCT:
KEYBOARDING LETTER-PAC

The feedback *reports* to our school products division ~~have~~ *is* show, *clearly* that teachers want computer-aided instructional matrials that go beyond our basic keyboard learning packages. We have been exploring the *possibility* ~~idea~~ of extending computer-aided instruction to the formating and production of documents frequently processed in business offices.

Dr. Hilda Jackson, *and Mark Williams have* ~~has~~ been working on a microcomputer program to teach students how to fromat and produce letters, using the microcomputer *first* as a tutor to teach format *and procedure* and ~~also~~ *then* as the tool *or medium* for processing letter communications. They have submitted for our consideration some sample storyboards, *and a correlated diskette* They propose the development of a package of materials that consists of:

1. To diskettes
2. A source document printware item of perhaps 64 pages
3. An instructional leader's guide of about 16 pages *plus solutions*

The program is menu driven, giving the operator options in terms of the letter style to be used, preprogrammed formats, and operator-controlled formats. The operator works first from model copy, than from semiarranged and unarranged copy The operator is first led step by step through the process and is given adequate guidance and frequent prompts. In the learning process, the computer provides evaluation feedback. Later in the production process where the operator does the formatting, the operator (or an instructional leader) evaluates the finsihed products for acceptability. Evaluation of format features is made by comparison with a model in the printware item.

Production costs *data* are being put together by Arlene Simms. An estimate of sales potential for the school market is being prepared by Kevin Marx; for the home market, by Sheila Prentiss. All three reports will be submitted to Jerome Lambert, who will determine a viable cost/price structure.

Among the proposals we have *received* ~~seen~~, this one by Jackson and Williams appears to have the greatest potential for acceptance. Although their original work is on the Sigma Personal Computer, they plan to convert it to other propular microcomputers as soon as the Sigma package is completed. It is my recomendation that we give the proposal serious consideration, provided the cost/price information is compatable with that of our other comparable products.

Learning goals

1 To improve use of numbers in data.
2 To strengthen ability to spell.
3 To improve ability to make deci–sions.

Machine adjustments

1 Set paper guide at *0*.
2 Set ribbon control to type on upper half of ribbon.
3 Use a 70–space line unless otherwise instructed.

48a ▶ 7
Preparatory practice

each line twice DS (slowly, then faster); DS between 2-line groups; then 1' writings on Line 4; repeat if time permits

alphabet	1	Why did an oval jet-black onyx ring blaze on the queen's plump finger?
figures	2	Bob moved 395 cardboard boxes, 146 of which went to Rooms 270 and 188.
home row	3	Hals had half a glass of soda as Jihad had half a dish of fresh salad.
easy	4	A cow, six roan foals, six turkeys, and a duck amble to the cornfield.

| 1 | 2 | 3 | 4 | 5 | 6 | 7 | 8 | 9 | 10 | 11 | 12 | 13 | 14 |

48b ▶ 13
Review/improve communication skills: number usage

half sheet; 74-space line; 1" top margin; SS sentences; DS between groups

1 Cover the answer key at the bottom of the column. When you have finished keyboarding, check your answers.

2 Study guides for number usage.

3 Keyboard guide number 1a. (with period), space twice, and keyboard review sentence(s), noting guide applications.

4 Keyboard apply sentence(s), correcting errors in number usage as you prepare the copy.

Key: 1b. Eight 2c. three, seven 2d. 7 3b. four, 20, two, four 4b. forty, two thirds 5b. Eighty–five 5c. thirty–one

Express as words

1. A number which begins a sentence even if figures are used later in the sentence.

2. Numbers ten and lower unless they are used in close proximity to numbers higher than ten, which are expressed as figures.

3. One of two adjacent numbers. Preferably the smaller number should be spelled for efficiency.

4. Isolated fractions and indefinite numbers.

5. Use a hyphen to separate compound numbers between twenty-one and ninety-nine that are spelled out, whether they stand alone or as a part of a number over one hundred.

review	1a.	Six players were cut from the 37-member team.
apply	b.	8 altos and 21 sopranos filled the front row of the stage.
review	2a.	We saw five or six wild ducks swim away; three were mallards.
review	b.	All but 5 of the 15 lamps were turned on.
apply	c.	Andrew took 3 sweaters and 7 shirts to the cleaning service.
apply	d.	The librarian repaired the loose bindings on seven of the 25 books.
review	3a.	The six 200-gallon drums are in the truck.
apply	b.	Cora bought 4 twenty-cent stamps; she used only 2 of the 4 stamps.
review	4a.	About fifty women registered, but only one half stayed for the meal.
apply	b.	Close to 40 attended the meeting; 2/3 offered to help.
review	5a.	Seventy two of the four hundred fifty-eight pages were about Brahms.
apply	b.	Eighty five of the one hundred forty-six entry forms were submitted.
apply	c.	Out of the one hundred thirty one varieties, sixty-two were hybrids.

Excerpts, continued

Business Forms. Business forms such as purchase requisitions, purchase orders, and invoices can be typed quickly and efficiently if the following procedures are observed by the typist.

1 Set the left margin stop for typing the name and address block.

2 Set a tab stop for aligning the items in the information section to the right of the address block.

3 Set additional tab stops for aligning and typing the columnar entries.

Note: Well-designed business forms permit the left margin stop to be used for positioning both the address and one column of entries beneath the address block (usually the first column). Often, too, the tab stop set for the information section may be used to position the items in one of the columns beneath the information section.

4 Position columnar entries (except Description items) so that they are in the approximate horizontal center of their respective columns. Begin the Description items 2 spaces to the right of the vertical rule.

5 SS the columnar entries when there are 4 or more single-line items. DS the items in the body of the form when there are 3 or fewer single-line items.

6 If an item in the body of the form requires more than 1 line, SS the item and indent the second and succeeding lines 3 spaces.

7 Underline the last figure in the Total column; then DS before typing the total amount.

8 Tabulate and type *across* the form rather than typing all items in the first column.

Properly arranged and typed business forms are illustrated at the right.

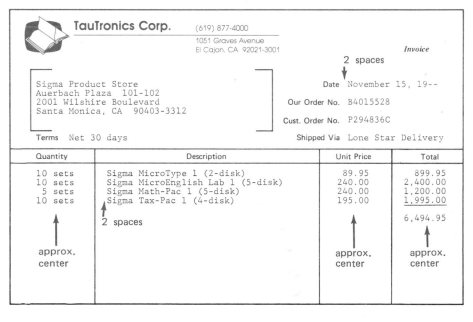

Properly typed purchase order

Properly typed invoice

171a-176a ▶ 5

Preparatory practice

Type as many times as you can in 5′ at the beginning of each class period in this section.

alphabet	1	Joseph Zbornak meets every degree requirement of six western colleges.
fig/sym	2	On 6/15/85, Kenny & Anderson, Inc., received a 9.4% discount ($2,730).
adjacent key	3	Children on vacation trips like our very popular ice-cream sandwiches.
fluency	4	The box is right for the antique bowl, the panels, or the eighty maps.

| 1 | 2 | 3 | 4 | 5 | 6 | 7 | 8 | 9 | 10 | 11 | 12 | 13 | 14 |

**Review/improve
communication skills:
number usage**
Follow directions given in
48b.
Key: 1b. 43 2c. One 3b.
18 4d. 9 4e. 23d 5b. cor–
rect 6b. ⅛

Express as figures

1. Numbers which are preceded by nouns.
2. House numbers (except house number One) and street names (except ten and under). When both the street name and house number are expressed as figures, place a dash (--) between them.
3. Numbers that precede an abbreviation such as *a.m., lbs., in., and tsp.*
4. Dates followed with *d* or *th* when the date precedes the month and is sepa-

rated from the month by words. When the day follows the month, express the day in cardinal figures (4, 5, etc.) without *th* or *d* after the number. When the month is not given, the day may be written with figures followed by *th* or *d*; or, if it is ten or lower, it may be spelled.
5. Sums of money preceded by a dollar sign.
6. Fractions in a series.

review 1a. The Treaty of Ghent is covered in Chapter 9 of the history text.
apply b. Cesar went to Room forty-three and delivered his application.

review 2a. Pick up the parcel at One Elm Way and take it to 4729 Fifth Avenue.
review b. The new address of the Museum of Modern Art is 2647--56th Street.
apply c. The taxi stopped at 1 Sixth Street and 234--42d Street.

review 3a. At 8 a.m. the chef simmered the 3 lbs. of beef in the kettle.
apply b. Their carton (14 in. × 14 in. × eighteen in.) was mailed.

review 4a. She will arrive in Boston between the 2d and the 4th of January.
review b. On May 13 we shall attend the opening of the art exhibit in Richmond.
review c. I shall arrive on the 15th. He will leave Mexico on the 12th.
apply d. Victoria arrived on the 12th of April, and she left on June 9th.
apply e. The cast had a rehearsal on the twenty-third.

review 5a. Maxine earned $68 last week for her work at the local garden store.
apply b. This antique vase, which is made of porcelain, is valued at $400.

review 6a. What is the sum of 1/2, 3/4, and 4 2/3?
apply b. The tailor cut 2 2/3, 1 1/4, one-eighth, and 4 5/8 yards of fabric.

**Improve keyboarding
continuity:
statistical copy**

1 Keyboard the ¶ once for orientation. Be especially aware of number usage as you prepare the copy.
2 Take two 3' writings; de-termine *gwam*.
Goal: at least 22 *gwam*.

Difficulty index

all letters/figures used	LA	1.4 si	5.4 awl	85% hfw

gwam 3'

We started to manufacture Dixie Real Tractors in the back of a small   5
plant at 3720 First Avenue in Quantico, Virginia; and in that first year   9
of 1968, we actually completed only five or six of these small-size 9 hp.   14
machines. Today, in our big, modern factory at One 45th Avenue, we find   19
it hard to realize that we turn out about seventy of our machines in just   24
one day and that our profit for last year was over $1 million.   28

gwam 3' | 1 | 2 | 3 | 4 | 5 |

Learning goals

1 To become familiar with the keyboarding/formatting tasks in a firm that produces/markets educational software.

2 To learn selected terms frequently used in word processing.

3 To improve your ability to work from differing copy sources and to detect and correct unidentified errors.

Machine adjustments

1 Paper guide at *0*.

2 Set ribbon control to use upper half of ribbon.

3 Margins: 70–space line for drills and ¶ writings; 1″ standard side margins for reports and correspondence; as appropriate for tables and forms.

4 Space job tasks as directed (or appropriate).

Office Job Simulation

Before you begin the jobs of Section 38, read carefully the information at the right and on page 307.

Make notes of any standard procedures that you think will save you time during the completion of the document production activities.

Daily practice plan:

Preparatory practice .... 5′
Work on simulation .... 45′

Work Assignment

You have been assigned by Office Service Temporaries, Inc., to work in the word processing unit of TauTronics Corp. TauTronics develops, publishes, and markets computer-aided educational products for both school and home markets. The company is located at 1051 Graves Avenue, El Cajon, CA 92021-3001. Your work assignments from various members of the staff will be made by Ms. Judith Fillmore, Supervisor, Word Processing Unit.

TauTronics' word processing manual specifies that all company letters are to be formatted in block style with open punctuation. Closing lines of all letters include the typed name of the person for whom the letters are prepared, followed on the same line by that person's business title. An envelope is addressed for each letter. All documents are prepared for photocopying except business forms which require the preparation of one carbon copy.

When specific job instructions are given, follow them carefully. When specific instructions are not given, make appropriate decisions on the basis of your knowledge and experience. If your supervisor (your instructor) considers some of your decisions unacceptable, learn from her or his suggestions—just as you would do in a business office.

TauTronics Corp. has based its word processing manual and job instructions booklets on *COLLEGE KEYBOARD-ING/TYPEWRITING*, so use the reference Guide and the index of your textbook to look up matters of style and placement when in doubt. When a job requires unusual specifications, TauTronics provides special guides in "Excerpts from the Word Processing Procedures Manual."

Excerpts from the Word Processing Procedures Manual

Leaders. Leaders, which are a series of periods (. . .) that are typed between two items in tabular material, are used to make reading easier. They "lead the reader's eye" from one columnar item to another. They are primarily used when the distance between certain items in two columns is so great that matching columnar items is difficult.

Leaders are made by alternating the period (.) and a space. The lines of leaders should be aligned in vertical rows and should end at the same point at the right.

To align leaders, type all periods on either the odd or the even numbers on the line-of-writing scale guided by their position in the first line of leaders. Begin the first line of leaders on the second space after the first item in the column and end the leaders 2 or 3 spaces to the left of the beginning of the next column.

An agenda is one example of a business document that makes use of leaders. TauTronics Corp. uses the *non*justified format for agendas (all items in Column 2 begin at the same horizontal point). Study carefully the agenda shown below.

```
                    TAUTRONICS CORP
         Agenda for Meeting of the Board of Directors
                     February 8, 19--

1.  Call to Order . . . . . . . . . . . . . .  Andrew B. McDaniels
2.  Minutes of Last Board Meeting . . . . . .  Charles L. Black
3.  Special Reports
       Foreign Suppliers . . . . . . . . . .  Kathy Stetson
       Domestic Suppliers  . . . . . . . . .  Carl W. Handley
```

Leaders in *non*justified agenda

49a ▶ 7
Preparatory practice

each line twice SS (slowly, then faster); DS between 2-line groups; then 1' writings on Line 4; repeat if time permits

alphabet	1	Put my five boxes in with the dozen jugs of quick-drying blue lacquer.
fig/sym	2	Hunt & Carte's $623.75 check (Check 1489) was delivered on January 10.
1st/2nd fingers	3	As Frederick Vertman hinted, they were regarded as tame but untrained.
easy	4	Did a city auditor handle the formal audit of both firms for a profit?

| 1 | 2 | 3 | 4 | 5 | 6 | 7 | 8 | 9 | 10 | 11 | 12 | 13 | 14 |

49b ▶ 8
Review/improve communication skills: number usage

Follow directions given in 48b.

Key: 1b. 40 percent 1c. 37 percent, 15% 2c. 75 cents

Express as figures

1. Definite numbers with a (%) sign; percent (spelled) is used with formal writing and with approximations.

2. Large round numbers in the millions or higher with their word modifiers, such as 25 *million* or 63 *billion*; use with or without a dollar sign. Use the word *cents* after figure amounts of less than one dollar.

Note

To avoid confusion or error, businesses commonly use figures for all numbers except those which begin a sentence.

review	1a.	Attendance is about 97 percent. The interest rate soared to 17%.
apply	b.	Nearly 40% of the 86% increase came from charitable donations.
apply	c.	The firm reinvested close to 37% of last year's 15 percent profit.
review	2a.	They budgeted $12 million for highways and $10 million for parks.
review	b.	She took $25 from her savings account; now she has only 14 cents.
apply	c.	The group collected $1 million; some donations were only 75¢.

49c ▶ 10
Proofread/revise as you keyboard

half sheet; 74-space line; 1" top margin; DS

1 Cover the answer key at the bottom of the column. When you have finished keyboarding, check your answers.

2 Keyboard the guide number (with period), space twice, and type the sentence.

3 As you keyboard each line, decide if the sentence is correct according to the guides for number usage. If the sentence is not correct, make the appropriate correction as you keyboard.

Key: 1. 2 **2.** seven **3** cents **4.** three, eight **5.** $25 million **6.** forty–six, 3d **7.** 9 **8.** One, 231–– 18th **9.** correct **10.** ¼, ½

1. A recipe containing two lbs. of veal won Al the 20th annual contest.

2. About 7 20-ounce containers of milk were on the counter yesterday.

3. He gave the clerk $5 and waited for the 25¢ change.

4. Yoko stacked 3 books and 8 magazines on the shelf.

5. Nearly two thirds of the $25,000,000 was spent on medical research.

6. Six hundred forty six graduates receive diplomas on the third of June.

7. Julio read Rule nine and then applied the principle to the problem.

8. We sent the gifts to 1 Laurel Avenue and 231 18th Street.

9. The company increased productivity by approximately 20 percent in May.

10. What is the sum of 2 1/8, one fourth, and one half?

**Build rough-draft
copy skill**

1 One 1' writing for accuracy.
2 Two 3' writings for accuracy; record *gwam* and number of errors for more accurate writing (LM p. 3).

Difficulty index

all letters used	A	1.5 si	5.7 awl	80% hfw

	gwam 1'	3'
When you go to ̲O̲n̲ a job interview, the first few minutes are the most impor-	15	5	48
tant. The interview*er's* first impressions of you will be more ~~impor-~~	27	9	52
~~tants~~ *detailed* than what you ~~put,~~ *have written* on your resume. Remember, *to* smile sin-	42	14	57
cerely, have a hearty handshake, dress pro͝perly, and ~~put forth~~ *exhibit*	54	18	61
a pleasant personal͝ity. Look confident and be positive about	66	22	65
what you, *as an employee,* have to offer the organization. Be careful that you do	83	28	70
not give the impression that you are interested only in ͝what	95	32	74
you can get from the f͝irm. If you can, *also* art͝iculate you*r* answer*s*	109	36	79
to the *interview* questions, you will have a much better chance to have	123	41	84
a job offer*s extended to you.*	128	43	86

**Build straight-
copy skill**

1 One 1' writing for accuracy on each ¶.
2 Two 5' writings for accuracy on both ¶s combined. Record *gwam* and number of errors for more accurate writing (LM p. 3).

Difficulty index

all letters used	A	1.5 si	5.7 awl	80% hfw

	gwam 1'	5'
Today, most data and text are input into a computer system through a	14	3	55
keyboard. Therefore, any individual who will be working with a computer	28	6	58
will need to have some basic keyboard skill. The level of keyboarding	43	9	61
skill needed is dependent upon the frequency with which a person must	57	11	64
work with a computer and the amount of data or text required to be input.	72	14	67
For example, a manager who only works on a terminal once in a while and	86	17	69
then uses just a few keystrokes does not need to develop the same high	100	20	72
skill level that is required of a word processing operator. Obviously,	115	23	75
the individual who is required to input large volumes of data or text	129	26	78
must develop very good keyboarding skills.	137	27	80
The keyboard is divided into two major parts: alphabet and numbers.	14	30	82
Many keyboard operators need to develop good skill on both types of key-	28	33	85
boards, since they are required to input large volumes of both numeric	42	36	88
data and text material into the computer. A person who must input such	57	39	91
large quantities of text material will need to spend a great deal of	71	42	94
time and effort to learn the alphabet keyboard by the touch method. To	85	44	97
learn the number keyboard does not require nearly the time and effort,	99	47	99
since there are not as many number keys to learn and since the organiza-	113	50	102
tion of the number keys are in a sequential pattern.	124	52	104

gwam 1'		1		2		3		4		5		6		7		8		9		10		11		12		13		14	
5'					1						2						3													

49d ▶ 13
Measure straight-copy skill

1 Keyboard the ¶s once for orientation. Pay attention to spelling and usage.
2 Take two 3′ writings.
Goal: 26 or more *gwam*.

Difficulty index

all letters used	LA	1.4 si	5.4 awl	85% hfw

	gwam 1′	3′
Being able to communicate can truly help us to realize success in	13	4 | 51
both our private and business lives. We can write, and we can quickly	29	9 | 56
read what is written. We can speak, and we can hear what is said; but	42	14 | 61
hearing is not exactly the same as listening. Hearing means using the	56	19 | 65
ears and sound waves; listening is using the mind and making judgments.	70	23 | 70
Listening requires an active mind, not a lazy, closed one. Those	13	28 | 74
of us who want to be good listeners must work for it, not just expect	29	32 | 79
that it will come. Good listening always begins with a real desire to	42	37 | 84
understand what others are trying to tell us; it increases when we are	56	42 | 89
patient and objective while they explain to us their thoughts and ideas.	70	47 | 93

gwam 1′ | 1 | 2 | 3 | 4 | 5 | 6 | 7 | 8 | 9 | 10 | 11 | 12 | 13 | 14 |
3′ | 1 | 2 | 3 | 4 | 5 |

49e ▶ 12
Make decisions: keyboarding a personal letter

1 plain full sheet

1 Make decisions about the line length and appropriate placement of the personal letter, and then type it.
2 Examine the letter carefully when you have finished it, and correct errors. Note your comments about it at the bottom of the page.
If necessary, refer to page 57 for assistance.

	words
1225 Seventh Street | Bakersfield, CA 93304-9012 | February 2, 19-- | Mr. Bertram	15
B. Heck | 2521--112th Street, W. | Kansas City, MO 64131-7144 | Dear Bert	29
(¶) Good news! I found your copy of _Analyses_. It was behind a drape where you	46
often sat by the window to read. You may have set the book on the floor, and the	62
wheel of your chair pushed it behind the drape.	72
(¶) I shall mail the book back to you in four or five days. Why the delay? I must	88
confess that when I reexamined the book and discovered it was written by an	103
ex-worker with the Peace Corps, I became fascinated with it. Forgive me, good	119
friend; but I must read it before I return it. I shall have it in your hands, though,	130
before the 14th, when I know you are leaving for Chicago.	148
(¶) I hope your trip home was a pleasant one, Bert.	157
Cordially | Lu Chi	160

50

50a ▶ 7
Preparatory practice

each line twice SS (slowly, faster, still faster); DS between 2-line groups; then take a 1′ writing on Line 4; repeat if time permits

alphabet	1	Some obviously deaf, unknown organists composed the six jazz quartets.
fig/sym	2	Interest accumulated to $270.56 in 1984 (when the rate increased 13%).
long words	3	Their accumulated analyses provided reliable estimates of probability.
easy	4	Did the visitor to the city handle the authentic enamel dish and bowl?

| 1 | 2 | 3 | 4 | 5 | 6 | 7 | 8 | 9 | 10 | 11 | 12 | 13 | 14 |

50b ▶ 13
Measure straight-copy skill

Repeat 49d, above.

170a ▶ 5
Preparatory practice

each line 3 times SS (slowly, faster, top speed); DS between 3-line groups; repeat selected lines as time permits

alphabet 1 Max Culp knew every answer on today's quiz; he must enjoy being first.

fig/sym 2 The note #65731 (dated 2/09/85 with interest at 14.3%) is due 2/09/89.

shift lock 3 Two typing texts were CENTURY 21 TYPEWRITING and COLLEGE KEYBOARDING.

fluency 4 The title to the land is the endowment held by the panel for the city.

| 1 | 2 | 3 | 4 | 5 | 6 | 7 | 8 | 9 | 10 | 11 | 12 | 13 | 14 |

170b ▶ 10
Communication aid: subject/verb agreement

1 Type the paragraph and make the necessary verb agreement corrections. Check the corrected copy with your instructor.
2 Repeat if necessary.

The date and time of the department meeting has not been decided; but the director and her assistant is trying to make a decision. Either of them are capable of making the decision; however, neither she nor her assistant know which date to select. Consequently, I was told that one of us were to be responsible for the final decision--after all, someone has to take responsibility.

170c ▶ 10
Build statistical-copy skill

1 One 1' writing for accuracy on each ¶.
2 Two 3' writings for accuracy on both ¶s combined. Record *gwam* and number of errors for more accurate 3' writing (LM p. 3).

Difficulty index

all letters used | HA | 1.7 si | 6 awl | 75% hfw

gwam 1' | 3'

The Area Micro Store, Limited, sold 1,031 personal computers during 14 5 67
the second quarter of 1985. The hardware sales (including all peripheral 28 9 72
kits) were $1,870,947, or 78% of the total sales; and software sales were 43 14 77
$527,703, or 22% of the total sales. Total revenues for the second per- 58 19 82
iod were $2,398,650; sales are up over 23% over the 1984 second quarter 72 24 86
period. 73 25 87

The major reason for the extremely large increase in total revenues 14 29 91
was that the organization, during the 1984 fourth quarter, had expanded 28 34 96
into 11 states and had increased the number of retail outlets from 12 42 39 101
to 21. The average gross revenue per retail outlet during this second 56 43 106
quarter was $113,220, up 35.4% over the previous second quarter. The 70 48 110
exceptional growth was due in part to the establishment of five new re- 84 53 115
tail outlets in large metropolitan areas. These five new outlets pro- 98 57 120
duced an average of $160,840 per outlet or 58% of the total increased 112 62 124
sales. 114 62 125

gwam 1' | 1 | 2 | 3 | 4 | 5 | 6 | 7 | 8 | 9 | 10 | 11 | 12 | 13 | 14 |
3' | 1 | 2 | 3 | 4 | 5 |

50c ▶ 15
Review/improve communication skills: spelling

70-space line; decide size of paper, top margin, and spacing

1 Clear tab stops; set two new tab stops, one 30 spaces from left margin and one 59 spaces from left margin.

2 Keyboard the first word at the left margin; tab and type the word again; then tab and type it a third time, this time without looking at the word in the book or on the paper.

3 Repeat this procedure for each word on the list.

4 Study your completed copy. Correct errors. Note your com—ments about placement at the bot—tom of the copy.

SPELLING DEMONS

accessible	accessible	accessible
achieve		
analyze		
comparative		
definitely		
disappoint		
forty		
harass		
leisure		
maintenance		
occurrence		
privilege		
recommend		
separate		
truly		
weird		

50d ▶ 15
Proofread/revise as you keyboard

1 Cover the answer key at the bottom of the column. After keyboarding, check your answers.

2 As you keyboard each line, decide whether each circled word or figure follows the rules of form, spelling, or capitalization. If an item is incorrect, make the correction.

Key:
1. accessible, achieve, disappoint
2. privilege, eight, nine, 2d
3. Plaza, Cinema, rec—ommended, 40
4. 50, Chapter, achievement
5. 40, truly, weird, lei—sure
6. comparatively, 3
7. 100, ten—cent, 1245—125th
8. recommend, analyze, separate, maintenance
9. Harass, definitely, five
10. 30, percent

1 The goal was (accessable). I did not (achieve) it. Did I (disappoint) you?

2 It was a (privilege) to meet (8) or (nine) students on the (second) of August.

3 The (plaza) (cinema) (reccommended) that we sit in the (forty) reserved seats.

4 The (50) questions from (chapter) 9 were included on the (acheivement) test.

5 They walked (forty) miles--(truly) a (weird) way to use their (liesure) hours.

6 It was (comparitvely) simple to find a place to sit at the May (3rd) meet.

7 Send the (100) (ten-cent) gifts to 125 Fifth Avenue or (1245--125th) Street.

8 I (recommend) that you (analyze) costs and (seperate) (maintenance) from rent.

9 (Harras) me no further; I (definitely) will not set places for (five) of us.

10 Approximately (thirty) (percent) of the profit is designated for salaries.

Build rough-draft copy skill

1 Two 1' writings for speed.
2 Three 3' writings for speed; record *gwam* (LM p. 3).

Difficulty index

| all letters used | A | 1.5 si | 5.7 awl | 80% hfw |

gwam 1' | 3'

Most ~~firms want~~ *companies need* workers who ~~can type~~ *are able to prepare* different types of / 14 | 5 | 45

tables; ~~the~~ *therefore,* good typists need to ~~understand~~ *know* the different / 26 | 9 | 49

formats of tables and there basic ~~traits~~ *characteristics*. As a rule, any / 39 | 13 | 53

table used in business will be *one* of three basic types: simple, / 53 | 17 | 58

rule*d*, or boxed. The simple table usually has just a *main* heading / 66 | 22 | 62

and one-line headings above each ~~of the~~ column *of the table*. A ruled / 80 | 27 | 67

or boxed table is more difficult than a simple table to type. / 93 | 31 | 71

Both ~~They~~ have horizontal rules above *and below* the column headings and the *below* / 108 | 36 | 76

body. in addition, a boxed table requires vertical ~~ones~~ *rulings*. / 120 | 40 | 80

Build straight-copy skill

1 One 1' writing for speed on each ¶.
2 Two 5' writings for speed on both ¶s combined. Record *gwam* (LM p. 3).

Difficulty index

| all letters used | A | 1.5 si | 5.7 awl | 80% hfw |

gwam 1' | 5'

Advances in technology have caused many of the changes that have | 13 | 3 | 58
taken place in both equipment and procedures in the modern office. Some | 28 | 6 | 61
of the changes have had a positive impact on the levels of production | 42 | 8 | 63
in the office. One of the first changes came with the arrival of the | 56 | 11 | 66
copy machine. If a file copy was desired, the copier ended the need to | 70 | 14 | 69
use carbon paper or to retype the job. Now that an electronic photo- | 84 | 17 | 72
copier is placed in most organizations and the cost per copy is low, | 98 | 20 | 75
there is little need for carbon copies. Another change came with the | 112 | 22 | 77
arrival of the electronic calculator which could perform any calculation | 126 | 25 | 80
many times faster than a mechanical machine. | 135 | 27 | 82

Changes also have been made in the typing area. The use of the | 13 | 30 | 85
magnetic-tape typewriter was the beginning of a new period for repeti- | 27 | 32 | 87
tive typing jobs. The office staff no longer was required to type the | 41 | 35 | 90
same material over and over again; the machine mechanically typed the | 55 | 38 | 93
item as many times as was needed. The next change was the word proces- | 69 | 41 | 96
sor with its many text-editing functions. The person who uses a word | 83 | 44 | 99
processor is able to enter, correct, change, and print data with a mini- | 98 | 47 | 102
mum of rekeying. However, for those who do not want a complete word | 111 | 49 | 104
processor, there is an electronic typewriter which has only a few of the | 126 | 53 | 107
automatic functions and has a limited amount of internal storage space. | 140 | 55 | 111

gwam 1' | 1 | 2 | 3 | 4 | 5 | 6 | 7 | 8 | 9 | 10 | 11 | 12 | 13 | 14 |
5' | 1 | 2 | 3 |

Learning goals

1 To prepare topical outlines.
2 To prepare unbound reports.
3 To prepare a data sheet.
4 To keyboard spread headings.
5 To develop greater awareness of copy content.
6 To improve ability to think and compose at the keyboard.

Machine adjustments

1 Set paper guide at 0; remove all tab stops.
2 Set ribbon control to type on upper half of ribbon.
3 Use a 70–space line unless otherwise directed.

51a ▶ 6
Preparatory practice

each line 3 times SS (concentrate on copy); DS between 3-line groups; repeat selected lines if time permits

alphabet	1	Dixie Vaughn acquired the prize job with a large firm just like yours.
figures	2	The ad said to call 964-5781 before 3 p.m. to order 20 sheets on sale.
shift	3	Rosa and Lazaro spent April in Connecticut and May and June in Hawaii.
easy	4	The eight auto firms may pay for a formal field audit of their profit.

| 1 | 2 | 3 | 4 | 5 | 6 | 7 | 8 | 9 | 10 | 11 | 12 | 13 | 14 |

51b ▶ 14
Compose at the keyboard

2 full sheets; 1½" top margin; DS

1 Compose a four- or five-line paragraph in which you describe yourself.

2 Proofread the ¶; make changes with proofreader's marks.

3 Make a final copy. Center the title **A SELF PORTRAIT** over the ¶.

51c ▶ 14
Preapplication drill: format/type an outline

1 Study the information and the sample outline at the right.

2 Because the lines of the outline are short, set for a 40–space line (center point −20/center point +20); SS; 4-space indentions; 1½" top margin.

3 Use **PREPARING OUTLINES** as a main heading; TS; prepare a copy of the outline.

Preparing outlines

It is important that students and others interested in organizing data be able to use a standard form of outline. As you study and keyboard the example at right, note:

• that 4-space indentions separate divisions and subdivisions of various orders.

• that first-order divisions are typed in all capitals; second-order divisions have main words capitalized; third- and subsequent-order divisions have only the first word capitalized.

• that single spacing is used except before and after first-order divisions.

• that there must be at least two parts to any division.

• that all Roman numerals other than I, V, and X necessitate the use of the margin release and backspacer.

• that the line length used must accommodate the longest line in the outline but not exceed a 70–space line.

I. FIRST-ORDER DIVISION
               DS

  A. Second-Order Division
  B. Second-Order Division
    1. Third-order division
    2. Third-order division
  C. Second-Order Division
               DS

II. FIRST-ORDER DIVISION

  A. Second-Order Division
    1. Third-order division
    2. Third-order division
      a. Fourth-order division
      b. Fourth-order division
    3. Third-order division
  B. Second-Order Division

Learning goals

1 To increase basic skill on straight, statistical, and rough–draft copy.

2 To improve communication skills.

3 To refine keyboarding technique.

Record results where indicated and compare them to the results recorded in Section 33.

Machine adjustments

1 Set paper guide at 0.

2 Set ribbon control to type on upper half of ribbon.

3 Margins: 70–space line for drills and ¶ writings; as directed (or appropriate) for problems.

4 SS drill lines; DS ¶s; space problems as directed (or appropriate).

169a ▶ 5
Preparatory practice

each line 3 times SS (slowly, faster, slowly); DS between 3-line groups; repeat selected lines as time permits

alphabet	1	If we arrive too quickly tonight, our expectations may be jeopardized.
fig/sym	2	Do you know how to calculate this: 5230 × (14 − 6) / 8 × (397 − 392)?
bottom row	3	Recent bank embezzlements now exceed the maximum government estimates.
fluency	4	The ivory box with an ancient owl emblem is also an authentic antique.

| 1 | 2 | 3 | 4 | 5 | 6 | 7 | 8 | 9 | 10 | 11 | 12 | 13 | 14 |

169b ▶ 15
Build statistical-copy skill

1 Two 1' writings for speed on each ¶.

2 Two 3' writings for speed on both ¶s combined. Record *gwam* (LM p. 3).

Difficulty index

all letters used	A	1.5 si	5.7 awl	80% hfw

gwam 1' | 3'

During 1985, the Jacques Renee Company had net profits after federal — 14 | 5 | 75
income taxes of $2,476,302. The Board of Directors has declared a divi- — 28 | 10 | 80
dend of $14.00 per share of common stock for the stockholders of record — 43 | 14 | 85
as of 7/01/85. The total amount of dividends to be paid is $1,500,000; — 57 | 19 | 90
this represents an annual return on investment of about 12.5%, which is — 72 | 24 | 94
3.75% more than the previous year. With the Board's recent decision to — 86 | 29 | 99
invest $1,000,000 of the net profits in new equipment, the outlook for — 100 | 33 | 104
the future is very good. — 105 | 35 | 106

The Board of Directors' 1985 capital investment in export markets — 13 | 39 | 110
will begin to show a sizable increase in gross profits as early as 1987. — 28 | 44 | 115
The Jacques Renee Company's forecast is for gross sales of exports to — 42 | 49 | 120
increase by 3% by the end of 1986; then in 1987, export gross sales — 56 | 53 | 124
should increase by over 12.5%. Of course, the operating costs will — 69 | 58 | 129
also increase during this period, but at a much lower percentage. The — 83 | 63 | 133
1987 net profit after federal income taxes is expected to be at least — 97 | 67 | 138
$2,826,200, which is a 9.7% increase over 1985. — 107 | 71 | 142

gwam 1' | 1 | 2 | 3 | 4 | 5 | 6 | 7 | 8 | 9 | 10 | 11 | 12 | 13 | 14 |
3' | 1 | | 2 | | 3 | | 4 | | 5 |

51d ▶ 16
Format/type
an outline
full sheet; 1½″ top margin; 70-space line; center heading

UNBOUND REPORTS
TS

3

I. MARGINS — 6

  A. Top Margins — 9

    1. First page: pica, 1 1/2″; elite, 2″ — 17

    2. Other pages: 1″ — 21

  B. Side and Bottom Margins — 27

    1. Left and right margins: 1″ — 33

    2. Bottom margin: 1″ — 38

II. SPACING — 40

  A. Body of Manuscript: Double — 47

  B. Paragraph Indentions: 5 or 10 Spaces Uniformly — 57

  C. Quoted Paragraphs — 62

    1. Four or more lines — 66

      a. Single-spaced — 70

      b. Indented 5 spaces from each margin — 78

      c. Quotation marks not required — 84

    2. Fewer than 4 lines — 89

      a. Quotation marks used — 94

      b. Not separated from text or indented from text margins — 105

III. PAGINATION — 109

  A. Page 1: Usually Not Numbered, but Number May Be Centered 1/2″ from Bottom Edge — 122 / 125

  B. Other Pages: Number Typed at Right Margin, 1/2″ from Top Edge of Paper Followed by a Triple Space — 139 / 146

52

52a ▶ 6
Preparatory
practice
each line 3 times SS; (concentrate on copy); DS between 3-line groups; repeat selected lines if time permits

alphabet 1   Our unexpected freezing weather quickly killed Joann's massive shrubs.

figures 2   Invoices 625, 740, and 318 were dated June 5, 1984; and all were paid.

br 3   Brad's brother, Bruce, broke my bronze brooches and brass bric-a-brac.

easy 4   Did the roan foal buck, and did it cut the right elbow of the cowhand?

| 1 | 2 | 3 | 4 | 5 | 6 | 7 | 8 | 9 | 10 | 11 | 12 | 13 | 14 |

52b ▶ 14
Align at the right
half sheet; 40-space line; exact vertical center; SS

1 Space forward from left margin 20 spaces; set tab; space forward 20 more spaces; set second tab.

2 Keyboard first column at left margin; backspace from tab stops to type second and third columns.

words

1.	I.	one	2
2.	II.	two	4
3.	III.	three	7
4.	IV.	four	9
5.	V.	five	12
6.	VI.	six	14
7.	VII.	seven	17
8.	VIII	eight	20
9.	IX.	nine	22
10.	X.	ten	24

Job 12
Letter on executive-size stationery (LM p. 55)

Mrs. Wiseman asks you to prepare a letter to Mr. James Wolfe, Solicitor, which she has written this morning. You have Mr. Wolfe's address card in your rotary address file. Add remaining closing lines and enclosure notations for:

Check #26500 for $750.00
Check #26501 for $8,225.00

Send a blind photocopy to Mrs. Carolyn Gosset.

```
Wolfe, James (Mr.)

Mr. James Wolfe, Solicitor
21, Fleet Street
LONDON   TA449FB
ENGLAND
```

December 13, 19--

add name and address

Dear Mr. Wolfe:

We have hired Carolyn Gosset as the Branch Manager of our Foreign Regional Office, and she should be arriving in London on January 15. I have wired a fund transfer of #100,000 to the London account for the initial office expenses. Please confirm its arrival and make necessary arragements with the bank to have mrs. Gosset's name added to the account

It is important that you act soon on the Lease arrangements which we discussed last week via telephone. I have wired John Thatcher, the Rental agent for Jacqus Rental Agency, and have told him that you will deliver the Lease Agreement as well as the enclosed checks for the rental fees and rental deposit by December 23. Please call my office and confirm completion of these matters.

I will be in London on January 16 and will call you upon my arrival. I look forward to seeing you at that time.

Sincerely,

Job 13
Letter on executive-size stationery (LM p. 57)

To follow up the night letter, Mrs. Wiseman asks you to prepare this letter and send it to Mr. Thatcher, Rental Agent, to confirm the fact that Mr. Wolfe will be coming to his office with the rental fees and deposit and to give the date of Mrs. Gosset's expected arrival in London. Date the letter December 13, 19—. Add closing lines. Send a carbon copy to Carolyn Gosset. You have Mr. Thatcher's address card in your rotary address file.

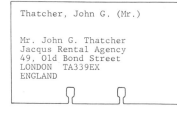

```
Thatcher, John G. (Mr.)

Mr. John G. Thatcher
Jacqus Rental Agency
49, Old Bond Street
LONDON   TA339EX
ENGLAND
```

(¶) I have written James Wolfe, Solicitor, and have requested that he stop by your office with the rental deposit and lease agreement. He will also be paying your rental agency fees.

(¶) Also, our Branch Manager, Mrs. Carolyn Gosset, will be arriving in London on January 15. I will have Mrs. Gosset contact you upon her arrival to make all necessary arrangements to take possession of the new office space.

(¶) I appreciate the fine job which your agency has done in helping Centek locate the property which we needed. I plan to be in London in January, and I will make an appointment to visit you when I arrive.

Sincerely, add remaining closing lines

52c ▶ 30
Format/type outlines

Problem 1

full sheet; 1½″ top margin

1 Set a line length that will accommodate the longest line.

2 Set tab stops at 4-space intervals.

3 Center the heading and type the outline.

Problem 2

full sheet; 1½″ top margin; reset margins to accommodate longest line

1 Type the second part (II) of Problem 1 as a total outline.

2 Change the first division **FORMAT ADAPTATIONS** to a centered heading.

3 Adapt all other parts of the outline to a form appropriate to their division.

	words
LETTER FORMATS AND ADAPTATIONS	6
I. LETTER FORMATS	10
A. Line Length (for Average Length Letter): 60 Spaces	21
B. Date Placement: Approximately Line 15 (2 1/2 Inches)	33
C. Common Formats (or Styles):	39
1. Block	41
a. All lines flush left	46
b. SS; DS between paragraphs	52
2. Modified Block	56
a. Most lines flush left	61
b. Certain lines begin at center point	69
(1) Date	71
(2) Closing lines	75
(a) Complimentary close	79
(b) Typed name	82
(c) Official title (when used)	88
c. SS; DS between paragraphs	94
II. FORMAT ADAPTATIONS	99
A. Personal Letter	103
1. Return address above date	109
2. Reference initials usually omitted	117
3. Enclosure notation usually omitted	125
B. Business Letter	129
1. Return address usually printed (letterhead)	139
2. Reference initials used	144
3. Enclosure notation used when appropriate	153
C. Personal Business Letter	159
1. Address typed above date	165
2. Reference initials usually omitted	173
3. Enclosure notation used when appropriate	182

53

53a ▶ 6
Preparatory practice

each line 3 times SS (work for fewer than 3 errors per group); DS between 3-line groups; repeat selected lines if time permits

alphabet	1	With a fixed goal in mind, quickly size up a job before making a move.
fig/sym	2	Items 318-325 cost $690, which is 75% (or 3/4) of the $920 sale price.
double letters	3	Three little batters slugged a ball across the deep and narrow valley.
easy	4	Did the men fight a duel, or did they go to the chapel and sign a vow?

| 1 | 2 | 3 | 4 | 5 | 6 | 7 | 8 | 9 | 10 | 11 | 12 | 13 | 14 |

Job 10
Itinerary (full sheet)

Mrs. Wiseman has checked and approved the handwritten draft itinerary you have prepared for her. All of the flights have been confirmed for her business trips for the month of January. Prepare her itinerary in final form in reading position. Place 2 spaces between columns. Be sure to include the horizontal ruling between each horizontal line of copy.

ITINERARY
Regina B. Wiseman
January 2 to January 26, 19 - -

| | | Depart | | Arrive | |
Date	City	Time	Flight No.	City	Time
Jan. 2	San Diego	8:04 a.m.	WA 632	Los Angeles	8:45 a.m.
Jan. 4	Los Angeles	12:15 p.m.	UA 415	Kansas City	4:40 p.m.
Jan. 7	Kansas City	9:20 a.m.	OZ 592	St. Louis	10:15 a.m.
Jan. 10	St. Louis	3:20 p.m.	EA 192	Atlanta	5:15 p.m.
Jan. 13	Atlanta	10:35 a.m.	DL 481	New York	12:30 p.m.
Jan. 16	New York	8:00 a.m.	TW 702	London	10:40 p.m.
Jan. 25	London	8:30 a.m.	TW 771	Chicago	12:30 p.m.
Jan. 26	Chicago	3:00 p.m.	TW 235	San Diego	6:45 p.m.

Job 11
Compose a night letter (plain full sheet)

Because it is important that leasing arrangements be made quickly on office space for the new London office, Mrs. Wiseman asks you to compose a night letter to Mr. John G. Thatcher at Jacqus Rental Agency, who is handling the rental. Tell Mr. Thatcher that a Branch Manager has been hired and that Centek will be leasing the property located at 30 McGuire Square beginning January 1, 19—. Also, explain that Centek's Solicitor, James Wolfe, will be requested to bring to Jacqus Rental Agency the lease agreement and rental deposit by December 23. If there are any problems, Mr. Thatcher is asked to contact Mrs. Wiseman immediately. Date the letter December 12, 19—, 5:45 p.m.

Mr. Thatcher's address is in the rotary address file on your desk.

```
Thatcher, John G. (Mr.)

Mr. John G. Thatcher
Jacqus Rental Agency
49, Old Bond Street
LONDON   TA339EX
ENGLAND
```

53b ▶ 12
Improve concentration

1 Keyboard a copy of the ¶ DS. Where a blank space occurs, insert either the word **they** or **that**.

2 Using your corrected copy, take as many 1' writings as time permits.

Difficulty index

all letters used | A | 1.5 si | 5.7 awl | 80% hfw

gwam 1'

Typically, women and men who are successful give the best _____ can   13

give. _____ do not do this just because _____ have the personality makeup   28

_____ demands it; _____ do so because _____ are seemingly oriented to be   42

achievers. Quite simply, _____ expect to succeed; and _____ refuse to   56

recognize any effort, including theirs, _____ is not top rated.   68

gwam 1' | 1 | 2 | 3 | 4 | 5 | 6 | 7 | 8 | 9 | 10 | 11 | 12 | 13 | 14 |

53c ▶ 32
Format/type reports/ spread headings

Problem 1

full sheet; DS; 1" side margins; 5–space ¶ indention.

1 Read carefully the guides for preparing reports.

2 Follow these guidelines as you keyboard.

Preparing reports

Before you prepare any report, determine whether or not there are specific instructions for its format. In the absence of such instructions, the guides given here are generally accepted for reports that are not to be bound. Follow these guidelines for the reports in Section 12.

• Use a 1½" top margin (pica) or 2" (elite) for the first page; otherwise, use 1" margins for all four sides.

• Use double spacing.

• Do not number the first page.

• Number the second and all subsequent pages in the upper right corner, ½" (Line 4) from the top of the page.

• Enclose short quotations in quotation marks. Indent longer quotations 5 spaces from each margin; omit quotation marks, and use single spacing.

words

SIMPLE REPORT FORMAT   4
TS

It is important that students who prepare term papers, themes, and other   19
forms of academic writing know the procedures for typing reports.   32

In the previous sections, your typed work has been set to a stated line   46
length of 50, 60, or 70 spaces, regardless of whether your machine was equipped   62
with pica- or elite-size type. Here in Section 12 you will be asked to prepare formal   79
reports that require placement in accordance to the number of inches in top,   95
bottom, and side margins rather than to the number of spaces in the writing   110
line.   111

Because of the difference in type size, pica and elite solutions will differ   127
somewhat. When 1-inch side margins are used, a pica line will contain 65   141
spaces; an elite line will contain 78 spaces. Both sizes of type, of course, will   158
accommodate 6 line spaces to a vertical inch.   167

When side margins of 1 inch are used, 10 pica spaces should be allowed in   182
each margin; on the other hand, users of elite type should allow 12 spaces.   197

Job 9
News release
(plain full sheet)

Mrs. Wiseman asks that you pre–
pare the news release to an–
nounce the opening of the new
office in the Foreign Region. Use
2" top margin; 1½" side margins;
DS the body; TS above and below
the main heading; indent ¶s. Correct any undetected errors.

December 11, 19--
FOR IMMEDIATE RELEASE

CENTEK OFICE SYSTEMS, INC.
OPENS FOREIGN OFFICE

¶ Centec Office Systems, Inc., announced today the opening of its new branch office in London, England. The London office will handle sales, service, and installation of it's microcomputer systems throughout the British Isles and Europe. Also, the London office will serve as the main headquarters for European sales if the current plan to open a Berlin or Munich office materialize.
¶ With the main headquarters located in San Diego, this company has had tremendous growth over the past twelve years since its founding. The company now has five service regions and assets in excess of $18 million. With the opening of the London Office, European sales are expected to assure Centeks success as a leader in micro-computer design in the British Isles and Europe.
¶ The new office is to be located at 30 McGuire Square, London, England. The new office should be operative by June 30.

53c, continued

Problem 2

half sheet; 2″ top margin; center each heading at the far right as a spread heading, as shown in the first heading.

Center spread headings

1 To center a spread heading, backspace from the center point once for each letter, character, and space except for the last letter or character in the heading.

2 From this point, type the heading, spacing once after each letter or character and 3 times between words.

	words
S P R E A D H E A D I N G S	6
SIMPLE REPORT FORMAT	10
SOURCE FOOTNOTES	14
PREPARING AN OUTLINE	18

Problem 3

full sheet; refer to page 98 for for—mat directions if necessary

Repeat the report in Problem 1 page 98. Use a spread heading.

54

54a ▶ 6
Preparatory practice

each line 3 times SS (work for fewer than 3 errors per group); DS between 3-line groups; repeat selected lines if time permits

alphabet 1 We have printed just sixty dozen meal tickets for the banquet meeting.

fig/sym 2 Room #476 is $39 a day, but call 615-2890 (before 2 p.m.) for 7% less.

hyphen/dash 3 Hyphenate a multiword modifier preceding a noun--a hard-and-fast rule.

easy 4 The town may wish to blame us for the auditory problems in the chapel.

| 1 | 2 | 3 | 4 | 5 | 6 | 7 | 8 | 9 | 10 | 11 | 12 | 13 | 14 |

54b ▶ 12
Improve concentration

1 Prepare a copy of the ¶ DS. Where a blank space occurs, insert either the word **that** or **your**.

2 Take 1′ writings as time permits. Use your corrected copy.

Difficulty index

all letters used	A	1.5 si	5.7 awl	80% hfw

gwam 1′

When ———— job requires you to use the telephone, use it well. A   13

caller cannot see you; so you should realize ———— ———— words have to   27

express the same cordiality, sincerity, and interest ———— you would show   41

if you were talking to the caller face to face. You can project a posi-   56

tive image for ———— company with polite answers and a helpful, consider-   70

ate attitude.   73

gwam 1′ | 1 | 2 | 3 | 4 | 5 | 6 | 7 | 8 | 9 | 10 | 11 | 12 | 13 | 14 |

54c ▶ 5
Keystroke the * (asterisk)

The * (asterisk) may be used to refer to a footnote. Find the loca-tion of the * on your machine; watch your finger practice the reach; then type the drill line twice.

* ** * I may use * and ** to indicate the first and second footnotes.

**Job 8
Letter on executive-size
stationery** (LM p. 53)

Mrs. Wiseman dictated a letter to you and asked that you type a rough-draft copy so that she could edit it and make changes, if necessary. Now she has edited the letter and asks that you prepare a final copy for her signature on executive-size stationery. Correct any errors she may have missed. Remember that this letter has enclosures.

Mrs. Gosset's address is in the rotary address file on your desk.

Gosset, Carolyn (Mrs.)

Mrs. Carolyn Gosset
1432 Cape Cod Way
Rochester, NY 14623-1433

Send Special Delivery

December 10, 19--

Dear Mrs. Gosset:

Thank you for coming to San diego to visit with us about the position of Branch manger in England. If you will send us a statement of expenses, we will send you a reimbursement check immediately. Our executive committee has approved my recommendation that we hire you to fill the Branch Manager position and has authorized me to offer you this position at an annual salary of $50,000. If you wish to accept this offer, you should plan to be in San Diego by January 4.

Please complete the enclosed contracts and employment forms and return them to our San Diego office by December 20. At this time, we can discuss in details the operations of the London office and make specific arrangements for your move to London.

We hope that you will accept this offer and that we may have a long successful association with you as the Branch manager of our Foreign Region.

Sincerely,

In addition to the annual salary, our normal fringe benefits package includes a housing and automobile allowance, educational allowances for each child in the family, complete medical and life insurance coverage, and a four-week vacation outside of London.

Format/type a report with a footnote

full sheet; refer to pages 96 and 98 for format guidelines if necessary

words

F O O T N O T E S   4
TS

Formal reports are usually written to put forward some point of view, to   18

convince readers, and/or to convey information in such a way that it will be   34

relied upon, accepted, or believed. To substantiate the contents of a report and 50

to give it greater weight of authority, a writer often cites evidence that other   66

people support his or her conclusions. Sources for such support are then shown   82

as footnotes at appropriate places within the report.   93

Citations for all such opinions or statements of fact spoken or written by   108

someone other than the writer should be documented. This procedure is simply   124

a matter of fair play, of "giving credit where credit is due." Whenever a writer 140

paraphrases or quotes directly from the work of someone else, credit should be   156

given.   158

Footnotes are also frequently used to clarify points, provide additional   172

information, or add other forms of editorial comment that the writer may wish   188

to make. For whatever reason a footnote is included, it must be done with the   204

idea of assisting a reader.   209

Footnotes may be placed at the end of a report, or they may be placed at the   224

foot of the page on which reference to them is made.* In either case, the   239

footnotes are typed in sequential order and numbered consecutively throughout   255

the report. Footnotes on a partially filled page may immediately follow the last 271

line of the text, or they may be placed to end one inch from the bottom of the   287

page.   288

1½" underline —————— SS ——————   291
                              DS

* Footnotes at the foot of the page are usually preferred for academic   305

writing.   307

55a ▶ 6
Preparatory practice

each line 3 times SS (work for fewer than 3 errors per group); DS between 3-line groups; repeat selected lines as time permits

alphabet	1	The objective of the tax quiz was clarified by checking samples of it.
fig/sym	2	Ship the $567 order for 29 1/3 grams of X8-D40 (8% solution) tomorrow.
shift	3	Will Pamela Forsman be quite happy visiting Kansas and Alaska in July?
easy	4	In the land of enchantment, the fox and the lamb sit down by the bush.

| 1 | 2 | 3 | 4 | 5 | 6 | 7 | 8 | 9 | 10 | 11 | 12 | 13 | 14 |

Sales for the Western Region were well over $6.85 million last year. A major part of the Western Region's growth is the result of opening a branch office in Los Angeles two years ago. The Los Angeles office accounted for over $3.5 million of the Western region's sales volume last year.

make this # 6

foreign

As noted in the introduction of this report, plans have been formalized for the official opening of our Foreign Region next month. The location of the branch office will be in London, England. This branch office will serve primarily the British Isles and Europe. In addition, plans are under way to evaluate the need for establishing a branch office in either Berlin or Munich.

make this # 4

Southern

The Southern Region was opened at the same time as the Eastern Region three years ago. The branch office is located in Atlanta, Georgia. Although the sales in this region has been relatively good in the past, a leveling off has occurred during the past six months. In spite of the leveling of sales volume, the total sales for the last fiscal year were still in excess of $3 million.

Preapplication drill: format/type source footnotes

1 Study carefully the guides and models for preparing footnotes.

2 Using the appropriate model (pica or elite) below, type the final lines of a page and its source footnotes. Use 1″ side margins. (Note: Since 19 typed and blank lines are needed to complete the 66–line page, begin typing on Line 48.)

3 Compare the appearance and content of your finished product with the model in the textbook.

Format/type source footnotes

Preparing footnotes correctly takes skill, knowledge, and careful planning. The guidelines below will help you to plan and type the footnotes in Section 12.

• Footnotes should be placed at the foot of the page on which reference to them is made.

• Use a superior figure (raised a half line) in the text as reference to the footnote; repeat the superior figure with the footnote.

• Separate footnotes from the body of the report with a single underline 1½″ (18 elite or 15 pica spaces); SS before the line and DS after it.

• SS footnotes; DS between them if more than one occurs on a page.

• When one or more footnotes must appear at the foot of a page, allowances must be made for a 1″ (6 lines) bottom margin, 3 or 4 lines for each footnote, and 2 lines for the dividing line. As can be seen, it is important to know when to stop keyboarding and when to begin the footnotes.

---

pica   formats as discussed by Guffey and Erickson[1] (business reports)   48
                                                                          49
and Hashimoto, Kroll, and Schafer[2] (academic reports).   50
    SS _____   51
    DS   [1]Mary Ellen Guffey and Lawrence W. Erickson, Business Office 52
                                                                          53
Practices Involving the Typewriter with Implications for Business   54
Education Curricula, Monograph 136 (Cincinnati: South-Western   55
Publishing Co., 1981), pp. 17, 27, and 28.   56
    DS   [2]Irvin Y. Hashimoto, Barry M. Kroll, and John C. Schafer,   57
                                                                          58
Strategies of Academic Writing: A Guide for College Students   59
(Ann Arbor: The University of Michigan Press, 1982), p. 1.   60
    1″ (6 lines)   61
    bottom margin   62
                                                                          63
                                                                          64
                                                                          65
                                                                          66

---

elite   formats as discussed by Guffey and Erickson[1] (business reports) and Hashimoto,   48
                                                                                          49
Kroll, and Schafer[2] (academic reports).   50
    SS _____   51
    DS   [1]Mary Ellen Guffey and Lawrence W. Erickson, Business Office Practices   52
                                                                                          53
Involving the Typewriter with Implications for Business Education Curricula,   54
Monograph 136 (Cincinnati: South-Western Publishing Co., 1981), pp. 17, 27,   55
and 28.   56
    DS   [2]Irvin Y. Hashimoto, Barry M. Kroll, and John C. Schafer, Strategies of   57
                                                                                          58
Academic Writing: A Guide for College Students (Ann Arbor: The University of   59
Michigan Press, 1982), p. 1.   60
    1″ (6 lines)   61
    bottom margin   62
                                                                                          63
                                                                                          64
                                                                                          65
                                                                                          00

Job 7
Long report (full sheets)

Mrs. Wiseman hands you a two-page report and asks you to prepare it in leftbound format. Note that after originally typing it, Mrs. Wiseman added two paragraphs at the end, which she wants inserted. Put the paragraphs in their proper order while typing. Also, correct any undetected errors Mrs. Wiseman may have missed.

ANNUAL REGIONAL REPORT

~~Introduction~~

The ~~countrye~~ *United States* is divided into four ~~territories;~~ *service regions:* Eastern, (Southern, /Central,) and Western. ~~Also,~~ plans are *under way* to open a foreign office, which should be opened within *the next* sixty days. At present all foreign sales hare handled by the *home office in the* Western Region. *(and fully operative by June)*

Eastern TS

The Eastern ~~territory~~ *Region* was opened three years ago with an *branch* office in Philedelphia and (we have been experiencing phenomenal growth. In the first year of operation, the Eastern ~~territorye~~ *Region* had over $1.5 million ~~is~~ *in* sales; ~~the~~ *this* past fiscal year, sales were in excess of $4.2 million. *Thus far,* ~~During~~ the current year the Eastern ~~territory~~ *Region* is continuing to experience *substantial* growth. *(Since the introduction of our electronic office systems in the eastern part of the country,)*

Central

This *regional* branch office has been in existence for *nearly* five years and it continues to be one of our ~~best offices and~~ top producers. With two offices *-- St. Louis and Kansas City --* are ability to serve a wider geographic area has improved *considerably* ~~a great deal~~. This region accounted for $\overset{3}{\not2}$.8 million in sales last year, ~~and~~ if the trend *of the past few months* continues, the sales volume for this year will exceed last year by *nearly* 15 percent.

Western TS

~~This region has been in existence for over twelve years and continues to dominate the sales picture of the Company~~
The Western Region is the home office of ~~the~~ Centek, and all sales for this region come through the San Diego office. Total

make this # 5

Job 7 continued on page 297

55c ▶ 27
Format/type the second page of a report

full sheet; refer to pages 96 and 98 for format directions if necessary

line 7 Today, much of the movement for technological change involves the   14
search for efficiency; that is, shortcutting time and energy, especially as they   30
touch upon the flow of information. Langford says, "Society today is an infor-   45
mation society. Information is what office operations produce."[1] In today's   61
highly competitive business world, accurate information must be readily avail-   76
able; and it is this need, of course, that has given us word processing.   91

Sociologists say that society does not adopt new technology until con-   105
ditions, always changing, make it ready to do so; then it assimilates change very   121
rapidly. The automobile, for example, was invented years before its acceptance   137
as a popular method of transportation. It seems, therefore, that as technology   153
becomes available, society needs pioneers with foresight who will work for its   169
acceptance. Speaking of word processing, Will and Dake say,   181

In order to keep up with technological change and at the same   194
time address human factors, those involved in setting up and run-   206
ning word processing systems must be change agents. Change   218
agents know where to find information on the constant changes in   231
the industry and how to utilize it advantageously.[2]   242

Other "agents of change" must function to prepare a consuming society   256
to trust change; to support it financially; and, above all, to use it. Perhaps the   273
greatest challenge involving technology is not to create change, but to learn to   289
live with it.   292

296

[1] Floyd Langford, "Systems Concept," The Changing Office Environ-   314
ment (Reston: National Business Education Association, Yearbook No. 18,   329
1980), p. 31.   332

[2] Mimi Will and Donette Dake, Concepts in Word Processing: The Chal-   353
lenge of Change (Boston: Allyn and Bacon, Inc., 1981), p. v.   368

56a ▶ 6
Preparatory practice

each line 3 times SS (work for fewer than 3 errors per group); DS between 3-line groups; repeat selected lines as time permits

alphabet 1 Jenny Saxon left my squad a week after giving back the disputed prize.

fig/sym 2 I paid $1.95 for 2% milk and $3.87 for 60 rolls at J & D's on June 14.

long words 3 A probability study is particularly helpful for effective forecasting.

easy 4 At a signal, he may sign a name and title at the end of the amendment.

| 1 | 2 | 3 | 4 | 5 | 6 | 7 | 8 | 9 | 10 | 11 | 12 | 13 | 14 |

Job 5
Memorandum (LM p. 49)

Mrs. Wiseman hands you a sheet of paper on which she has written a memo. She asks you to prepare the memo and send it to Sylvia Phillips, who is the Personnel Director. Today is December 9. The subject of the memo is: **Training Program for Computer Service Technicians.**

Sylvia Phillips, *Personnel Director*

REgina Wiseman, *Executive Vice President*
December 9, 19--

The Executive committee ~~held a meeting~~ met yesterday afternoon ~~to discuss and~~ to consider your recommendations concerning the training program of our computer service technicians. They felt that your recommendations will greatly improve the current program, and they have approved them *with only a few minor changes.* ~~In particular,~~ They felt that your ~~idea about~~ *suggestion that* a course on computer theory be added to the present curriculum was a fine one. Also, your recommendations that the initial on-the-job training program be extended *from* one year to 16 months was approved ~~without hesitation~~ and will be implemented ~~soon~~ *within six months.*

Ms. Anna Russo will be visiting you to /d/scuss changes.

 # The Executive Committee wishes to congratulate you for your outstanding work. Over the past two years, the training program has improved substantially as a result of your diligent efforts.

Job 6
Compose a memorandum (LM p. 51)

Mrs. Wiseman asks you to compose a memorandum to all administrative heads from the sketchy notes shown at the right. The required number of copies will be made on the photocopy machine. Date the memo **December 9, 19—.** The subject of the memo is: **Staff Meeting for Administrative Heads.**

The staff meeting for administrative heads will be held December 20 at 1 p.m. in Room 304. Proposed program enclosed (updated program to be distributed on December 16).

Purpose: present and discuss changes in the training program for computer service technicians, which will be implemented over the next six months.

Ms. Sylvia Phillips, Personnel Director, to give formal presentation concerning changes. Any administrative head who cannot attend meeting to inform Mrs. Phillips by December 17.

56b ▶ 44
Format/type a two-page report with footnotes

2 full sheets; standard unbound report format; SS and indent enumerated items 5 spaces from each margin; number second page in upper right corner

1 Review unbound report format on page 96 for placement of unbound report.

2 Format and type the report at right as an unbound report.

3 Proofread; correct errors.

preparing REPORTS: THE PROFESSIONAL TOUCH   < TS — 9

Both the writer and keyboard operator, or compositor, share — 21

a mutual concern for the preparation and for the ultimate suc- — 30

cess of a report, but usually the writer must accept final — 42

accountability. The compositors contribution, however, is an a — 54

extremely vital one; and she or he should porceed with great — 62

caution ously. For example, even before they starting to prepare a — 73

final copy of a report, the compositor should proceed with — 82

determinthe e — 84

1. the specified purpose of the report and whether some par- — 96
ticular format is required; — 102

2. the number, kind, and grade of cpies required(1) and — 113

3. deadliens for completion. — 119

Thekeyboard operator should be prepared to work k from the — 130

script, rough-draft, or printed copy and yet give the report a — 143

final presentation that is) as professional as it is functional. — 156

< TS before a side heading — 164
"Tricks of the Trade"

Those with experience in preparing reports have found that — 176

there are special procedures they can use to simplify their — 188

lc tasks. The following paragraphs contain samples of some pro- — 200

cedures that can be especially (eh)lpful to a person who has not 5 — 212

prefiously keyboarded reports. (Anyone who pahns to prepare — 224

more that a few reports ,however, should read several good books on the subject.) n — 241

Right margins. Attractive right margins result result when — 254

good judgment is used exercised. Using the warning bell judiciously — 267

ensures right margins that approximate left margins in width. — 279

SS { _____ — 283

{ [1] For further information see The Chicago Manual of Style, — 300

{ 13th ed. (Chicago: The Universint of chicago Press, 1982), — 312

SS { p. 40. — 314

(continued on page 104)

Job 3
Leftbound report (full sheets)

Mrs. Wiseman typed a copy of a report on her typewriter at home, which is to be distributed to the Marketing Department. She asks you to finalize the report by typing it in appropriate report format for a leftbound report.

Job 4
Unbound report (full sheets)

Mrs. Wiseman asks that you retype the report (Job 3) as an unbound report because she will be having it duplicated for distribution by the company's sales representatives.

MEDICAL MICRO-OFFICE SYSTEM

Introduction

The new electronic information processing system designed especially for small medical centers (those staffed by fewer than twelve doctors) was released for promotion and installation on October 30, 19--. This new system is referred to as "Medical Micro-Office System."

Hardware Components

The Medical Micro-Office System is comprised of a 256K microcomputer with a 50-megabyte hard-disk storage system. Up to four terminals and two printers may be connected to the system. The terminals have a standard selectric-type keyboard with a 10-key numerical pad and fifteen special purpose control keys. The terminal display is a 12-inch green phosphorous screen. The printers may be either spinwriters (with tractor feed or automatic sheet feeder) or matrix printers.

Each system is supplied with either an 8-inch floppy disk drive or a tape drive to be used as a backup. The floppy disk has a 1.25 megabyte capacity on each side; the tape drive has a 50-megabyte capacity.

Software Package

A comprehensive package of medical software is provided with each Micro-Office System. All accounting, billing, insurance forms, appointments, and patient records are handled efficiently with the software package provided with the Medical Micro-Office System. Most operators can learn to use the system productively with approximately six hours of training.

Pre-Installation Study

A complete study of office operations in each medical center should be completed by our qualified service representative before a prospective customer places an order. After the office operations of a particular medical center have been analyzed, recommendations for smooth transition to our system should accompany all orders.

Installation and Delivery

Once an order has been authorized, delivery will occur within six weeks from the date of authorization. Installation should take approximately two weeks. The Medical Micro-Office System is guaranteed operational within ten days after installation is completed.

words

2   314

<u>Reference characters</u>. To keystroke a superior figure,   329

turn the platen back half a line and type the figure. Aster-   341

isks and other refrence symbols requires no such adjustment.   353

Keyboards equipped with special symbol keys for report writing are also   367

available for regular use.   369

<u>Page endings</u>. A few very simple guides become important when-   383

ever a report has more than one page. For example, never end a   396

page with a hyphenated word. Farther, do not leave a single   408

line a of paragraph at the bottom of a page or at the top of a   420

page (unless the paragraph has only one line, of course).   432

<u>Footnote content</u>. Underline titles of complete publica-   446

tions; use quotation marks with parts of publications. Thus,   460

the name of a magazine will be underlined, but the title of an   472

article within the magazine will be placed in quotation marks.   485

Months and locationla words, such as <u>volume</u> and <u>number</u>, may be   500

abbreviated.   503

<u>Penciled guides</u>. A light pencil mark can be helpful to   517

mark approximate page endings, planned placement of page numbers,   530

and potential foot note locations. When the report has been   542

finished, of course, erase any visable pencil marks.   553

TS

<u>Conclusion</u>   557

With patience and skill, the keyboard operator can give a   560

well-written report the porfessional appearance it deserves. Says   582

Lesikar,   584

Even with the best typewriter available, the fin-   594
ished work is no better than the efforts of the typist.   605
But this statement does not imply that only the most   616
skilled typist can turn out good work. Even the the   626
inexperienced typist can produce acceptable manuscripts   637
simply by exercising care.   642

646

Raymond V. Lesikar, <u>Basic Business Communcation</u> (Homwood: 657
Richard D. Irwin, Inc., 1979), p. 364.   665

Preparatory practice

Type as many times as you can in 5' at the beginning of each practice session during this section.

alphabet	1	A vexing blitz of a very quick opponent was the major cause of defeat.
fig/sym	2	Interest (18.5%) starts today (7/23/85) if bill ($460.79) is not paid.
outside reach	3	Paula and Pasquale always fix pizzas with a lot of sauces and peppers.
fluency	4	The man in the auto and my neighbor on the bicycle both work downtown.

| 1 | 2 | 3 | 4 | 5 | 6 | 7 | 8 | 9 | 10 | 11 | 12 | 13 | 14 |

163b-168b ▶ 45

Office job simulation

(LM pp. 45–57)

Job 1

Memorandum (LM p. 45)

Mrs. Wiseman hands you a sheet of notepaper on which she has written a memo. She asks you to prepare the memo and send it to **Sylvia Phillips, Personnel Director.** Today is **December 9.** The subject of the memo is: **Need to Hire Computer Service Technicians.** Remember, Mrs. Wiseman prefers to have her title typed after her name on all memos for which the business title is typed after the name of the addressee. Correct any undetected errors Mrs. Wiseman may have made while writing the memo.

¶ After our discussion yesterday I have again reviewed very thoroughly the personel report that you gave me. I agree with your conclusion that we must actively begin to recruit three people to fill the computer service technician positions. ¶ Please begin the recruiting proces immediately, keeping in mind that these people will need to be hired before the end of the current fiscal year. The candidates should have at least two years of post-high school training in basic electronics or electrical engineering. it would also be perferable if the candidates had one or two years of on-the-job training, especially in the area of installation.

Job 2

Letter (LM p. 47)

Mrs. Wiseman asks you to prepare this letter and send it to a client to confirm installation of one of their microcomputer systems. Send a blind photocopy (bpc) to Victor B. Ruiz. Use executive–size stationery.

December 9, 19-- | Dr. Rudolf Heinz, Director | Dixie Medical Center | 325 Main Street | St. George, UT 84770-1245 | Dear Dr. Heinz | Installation Phase of Micro-Office System

(¶) This letter is to confirm our telephone conversation of this morning concerning the installation of your micro-office system. After consulting with the design engineer for your project, we are now able to give you a firm date when the installation of your new system will begin.

(¶) All system components will arrive at your office on or before December 28. Our installation personnel will be in St. George to begin the installation on the morning of January 4. As per our agreement, the system will be installed and operational within ten days from the beginning date of the installation.

(¶) If you have any further concerns, please do not hesitate to phone me at any time.

57a ▶ 6
Preparatory practice

each line 3 times SS (work for fewer than 3 errors per group); DS between 3-line groups; repeat selected lines as time permits

alphabet	1 Wilma thinks freezing prices at fixed levels for July is questionable.
fig/sym	2 A grant of $12,367.50 won't fund 10% of the studies; it is $948 short.
direct reaches	3 No doubt my brother Cecil served as an umpire on that bright June day.
easy	4 A fox lay in an island lair; a girl dug a quantity of pale lake worms.

| 1 | 2 | 3 | 4 | 5 | 6 | 7 | 8 | 9 | 10 | 11 | 12 | 13 | 14 |

57b ▶ 14
Compose at the keyboard

full sheet; 1½" top margin; DS; 1" side margins

1 Compose a four- or five-line paragraph in which you describe one or two hobbies you enjoy or wish you could enjoy.

2 Proofread the ¶; make changes with proofreader's marks.

3 Type a final copy. Center a spread heading **H O B B I E S** over the ¶.

57c ▶ 15
Format/type a bibliography

full sheet; use standard unbound report format; 1½" top margin recommended

1 Read the guides at the right; study the illustrated bibliography.

2 Keyboard the bibliography; make one carbon copy.

Guidelines for preparing a bibliography

A bibliography is a list of works cited or used in some way in the preparation of a report. Bibliographical entries are distinctive from footnotes, as can be noted in the following items:

- A bibliography is the final part of a report.
- The first surname of an entry is identified first, allowing the list to be arranged in alphabetic order.

- The first line of an entry is placed flush left; all succeeding lines of the entry are indented five spaces.
- Reference characters are not used.
- Items are made more incisive with the elimination of most parentheses and commas.
- Specific page numbers used in a footnote may be omitted.

BIBLIOGRAPHY

pica type

Langford, Floyd. "Systems Concept." The Changing Office Environment. Reston: National Business Education Association. Yearbook No. 18, 1980.

Lesikar, Raymond V. Business Communication: Theory and Application. 4th ed. Homewood: Richard D. Irwin, Inc., 1980.

Will, Mimi, and Donette Dake. Concepts in Word Processing: The Challenge of Change. Boston: Allyn and Bacon, Inc., 1981.

Learning goals

1 To become familiar with the work in an executive office.

2 To plan and organize your work in an efficient manner.

3 To complete your work neatly and correctly.

4 To integrate your skills and knowledge.

Machine adjustments

1 Set paper guide at *0*.

2 Set ribbon control to type on upper half of ribbon.

3 Margins: 70–space line for drills and ¶ writings; as directed (or appropriate) for problems.

4 SS drill lines; DS ¶s; space problems as directed (or appropriate).

Office Job Simulation

Read carefully the material at the right before you begin the work in Section 36. Make notes of any procedures that you think will save you time during the completion of the production activities of this section.

Daily practice plan:

Preparatory practice .... 5'
Work on simulation .... 45'

Work Assignment

You have been assigned by Office Service Temporaries, Inc., to work for Centek Office Systems, Inc., an organization that designs and installs electronic, microcomputer-based office systems. The address where you are to report to work is 300 Lorenz Avenue, San Diego, CA 92114-3002. Your immediate supervisor while working for Centek will be Mrs. Regina Wiseman, Executive Vice President.

The firm's office manual specifies that all company letters are to be typed in the modified block style with mixed punctuation. The closing lines of all letters should include the typed name of the person for whom the letters are typed followed on the next line by the person's business title. All letters and memorandums require one photocopy (pc) for the file. Some letters require a blind photocopy (bpc) or a blind carbon copy (bcc). Address appropriate envelopes for all letters.

Proofread all work carefully before removing it from your machine; correct all errors. All work that is to leave the company should be "mailable"—technically correct with all errors corrected neatly. All work to be used *within* the company should be "usable"—content correct but with minor "flaws" in format and placement permitted.

When specific job instructions are given, follow them carefully; however, when specific instructions are not given, make appropriate decisions on the basis of your knowledge and experience. If your employer (your teacher) considers some of your decisions unacceptable, learn from her or his suggestions—as you would need to do in any business office.

Centek Office Systems, Inc., has based its office manual on COLLEGE KEYBOARDING/TYPEWRITING; therefore, use the Reference Guide and the index of your textbook to check matters of placement and style when you are in doubt. When a job requires unusual specifications, Centek provides them in "Excerpts from the Office Procedures Manual."

Excerpts from the Office Procedures Manual

Executive-size stationery. The size of the paper is 7¼" by 10½". When you use stationery that is narrower than the standard 8½", use 1" side margins. Begin the dateline on Line 11. The center point is 36, pica; 43, elite.

Blind photocopy notation. If you want to send a photocopy of a letter to someone without disclosing the fact to the addressee of the letter, type a notation on the photocopy but not on the original. This notation, called *blind photocopy notation* (bpc), is typed at the left margin a double space below the last typed line, for example: bpc Mr. John Howard.

Blind carbon copy notation. The originator of a letter may wish to send a copy of a letter to someone without disclosing this fact to the addressee of the letter. When such a copy is sent, omit the notation from the original copy of the letter. A notation—called *blind carbon copy*—is typed at the left margin a double space below the last typed line on each carbon copy requiring the notation. To type the blind carbon copy notation, insert a heavy piece of paper between the ribbon and the original (first) sheet. Then type the notation, for example: bcc Mr. John Howard. The notation will appear on the inserted paper and the carbon copies but not on the original letter.

If any carbon copy should not have the blind carbon copy notation, insert a piece of paper behind the carbon sheet and in front of the carbon copy lacking the notation; type the notation; it will not appear on the original or any copy for which you inserted a piece of paper.

57d ▶ 15
Format/type footnotes as a bibliography

full sheet; 1½" top margin; 1" side margins

1. Center the heading **BIBLIOGRAPHY.**

2 Adapt the copy in footnote format at the right to appear as entries in a bibliography.

Refer to 57c, page 105, as necessary.

---

[1] Chicago Manual of Style, 13th ed., (Chicago: The University of Chicago Press, 1982), p. 40.

[2] Irvin Y. Hashimoto, Barry M. Kroll, and John C. Schafer, Strategies of Academic Writing: A Guide for College Students, (Ann Arbor: The University of Michigan Press, 1982), p. 1.

[3] William C. Himstreet and Wayne M. Baty, A Guide to Business Communication, (Homewood: Learning Systems Company, 1981), p. 161.

58a ▶ 6
Preparatory practice

each line 3 times SS (work for fewer than 3 errors per group); DS between 3-line groups; repeat selected lines as time permits

alphabet	1	Melva Bream required exactly a dozen jackets for the long winter trip.
fig/sym	2	Carter & Unter's check for $679.20 (Check #1348) was cashed on June 5.
one hand	3	You deserved, in my opinion, a reward after you started a faster race.
easy	4	Did he sit in a chair and do sleight of hand for the prudish visitors?

| 1 | 2 | 3 | 4 | 5 | 6 | 7 | 8 | 9 | 10 | 11 | 12 | 13 | 14 |

58b ▶ 12
Improve concentration

1 Make a copy of the ¶ DS.

2 Where a blank space occurs, insert a common 4 letter word that fits the context.

3 Using your corrected copy, take 1' writings as time permits.

Key: that, more, must, from, know

Difficulty index

all letters used | A | 1.5 si | 5.7 awl | 80% hfw |

gwam 1'

Men and women who succeed seem to realize _____ genuine success is   13

much _____ than just turning in one star performance after another. To   27

acquire actual success, they tell us, we _____ measure our achievements   42

by our own standards of excellence. Success truly stems _____ a belief   56

in ourselves and a determination to do well what we _____ we can do.   69

gwam 1' | 1 | 2 | 3 | 4 | 5 | 6 | 7 | 8 | 9 | 10 | 11 | 12 | 13 | 14 |

58c ▶ 32
Format/type a personal data sheet

full sheet; 1" top and side margins; set tab stop at center point

1 Read the information about data sheets at the right.

2 Keyboard a copy of the data sheet on page 107.

Developing personal data sheets

A personal data sheet is a summary of pertinent, personal facts, organized for quick reading. Data can be categorized in a number of ways, and the writer should use a form that will best display her or his qualifications. Note the following suggestions:

• The data sheet is accompanied by a well-worded letter of application.

• The appearance of the data sheet is as important as what it says.

• Complete sentences are rarely used.

• The data sheet should stress capabilities, not just aspirations.

• The data sheet should be as brief as possible but as long as necessary. Try not to exceed one page.

Job 11
Table (full sheet)

Mr. Tullane wants all office personnel in the company to have a copy of the two–letter ZIP abbreviations for ready reference at their desks. You have been asked to prepare an approval copy of a table using the tabular material at the right. Arrange the table attractively on the page. The main heading is **TWO-LETTER ZIP AB-BREVIATIONS**, and the secondary heading is **(For Use with Zip Code)**. Correct any undetected errors as you prepare the table.

AL	Alabama	MT	Montana
AK	Alaska	NE	Nebraska
AZ	Arizona	NV	Nevada
AR	Arkansas	NH	New Hampshire
CA	California	NJ	New Jersey
CO	Colorado	NM	New Mexico
CT	Connecticut	NY	New York
DE	Delaware	NC	North Carolina
DC	District of Columbia	ND	North Dakota
FL	Florida	OH	Ohio
GA	Gorga	OK	Oklahoma
GU	Guam	OR	Oregone
HI	Hawaii	PA	Pennsylvania
ID	Idaho	PR	Puerto Rico
IL	Illinois	RI	Rhode Island
IN	Indiana	SC	South Carolina
IA	Iowa	SD	South Dakota
KS	Kansas	TN	Tennessee
KY	Kentucky	TX	Texas
LA	Louisiana	UT	Utah
ME	Main	VT	Vermont
MD	Maryland	VI	Virgin Islands
MA	Massachusetts	VA	Virginia
MI	Michagan	WA	Washington
MN	Minnesota	WV	West Virgina
MS	Mississippi	WI	Wisconsin
MO	Missouri	WY	Wyoming

Job 12
Compose an evaluation report (full sheets)

Now that you have completed your first assignment for OSTI, Mrs. DeSoto, Office Manager of OSTI, requests that you prepare a short evaluation report for her files. She asks you to include in the report a description of the typing and office tasks performed, a summary of which activities you liked and disliked and why, and last, a self–evaluation of your performance. Prepare as an unbound report with title page that includes the information shown at right.

EVALUATION REPORT

of

(your name)

Prepared for

Mrs. Silvia DeSoto
Office Service Temporaries, Inc.
San Diego, California

Introducing

3

SALLY ANN DUPOIS
123 Poinciana Road
Memphis, Tennessee 38117-4121
(901-365-2275)   TS

6
10
16
19

<u>Present Career Objective</u>

28

Eager to accept part-time position that provides opportunities for
additional training and potential for full-time employment.
                                                     TS

42
54

<u>Personal Qualifications</u>

63

Cheerful, outgoing personality; dependable, cooperative worker
Very interested in retailing work; find it challenging
Excellent health; participate in golf, racquetball, and tennis

76
87
100

<u>Experience</u>

104

1985--present	The Toggery, 100 Madison Avenue, Memphis, TN 38103-4219; Assistant Manager
1984 (summer)	Chobie's, 1700 Poplar Avenue, Memphis, TN 38104-2176; Inventory Clerk and Cashier
1983 (summer)	Todds, 1450 Union Avenue, Memphis, TN 38104-5417; Clerk and Assistant to the Buyer
1982 (summer)	Chobie's, 1700 Poplar Avenue, Memphis, TN 38104-2176; Salesperson and Utility Helper

117
122
135
141
154
161
174
181

<u>Education</u>

185

Junior, Marketing, Memphis State University, Memphis, Tennessee
AA degree (associate degree/advertising; honors), State Technical
Institute, Memphis, Tennessee
Graduate (honor student), East High School, Memphis, Tennessee

198
211
217
230

<u>References</u>

233

Mrs. Evelyn J. Quinell
Manager, Chobie's
1700 Poplar Avenue
Memphis, TN 38104-2176

Professor Aldo R. MacKenzie
Department of Marketing Management
Memphis State University
Memphis, TN 38114-3285

244
255
263
273

Ms. Lanya Roover
The Toggery
100 Madison Avenue
Memphis, TN 38103-4219

Mr. Robert E. Tindall, Jr.
Attorney-at-Law
1045 Quinn Avenue
Memphis, TN 38106-4792

282
287
294
304

Job 9
Leftbound report with justified right margin
(full sheet)

Mr. Tullane has asked that you prepare the copy at the right as a leftbound report with justified right margin. The title of the report is **COMPANY PUBLICATIONS,** and the finished report will be added to the <u>Office Procedures Manual</u> as an illustration. You are to have Mr. Tullane check the report before copies are made for the manual.

In the body of the report are two 4–line examples of material to be justified on a 46–space line; be sure to center the 46–space line when typing these two examples. Type them as is, once with the diagonals for extra spaces and once justified.

Note: Many businesses today have word processing equipment that will automatically justify the right margins of reports and other publications. However, Fairfield Manufacturing has not yet purchased such equipment, so the process described in the report and on page 284 for justifying right margins by hand will have to be used.

(¶) All publications of Fairfield Manufacturing, Inc., are prepared and duplicated in our office. Because we want all our publications to have the appearance of a printed page, you should become expert in justifying the right margin.

(¶) A professional-looking effect is achieved by having a right margin that is evenly aligned. Although the procedure for justifying the right margin is time consuming, we feel that it is worth the additional time and expense incurred.

(¶) As you type a line to be justified, come as close to the right margin as possible (without extending beyond the margin). To determine how many extra spaces will be needed in the line, type a diagonal (/) in every space remaining until you reach the right margin. For example, the following material is typed on a 46-space line:

```
All the cards in a card index file should be//
typed in the same form.  Uniformity of style//
facilitates the filing and finding operations.
```

(¶) After you have typed the material the first time, then retype the material and evenly distribute the extra blank spaces throughout the line. For example, the illustration above could be retyped as follows:

```
All the cards in  a card index  file should be
typed  in the same form.   Uniformity of style
facilitates the filing and finding operations.
```

(¶) Please read thoroughly the procedures as outlined in the new <u>Office Procedures Manual</u>.

Job 10
Compose a letter (LM p. 43)

Mr. Tullane gives you a letter he received from an associate; the body of the letter is shown at the right. He asks you to compose a reply to the letter and instructs you to include a copy of the report you completed above to furnish the information requested. Date the letter **December 6, 19—,** and address it to **Mrs. Sylvia Perry, Office Manager, Ripple, Ripple, and Carey, Attorneys-at-Law, 8505 Black Canyon Highway, Phoenix, AZ 85201-6943.**

Dear Duncan:

We are preparing a new <u>Procedures Manual</u> for our employees at Ripple, Ripple, and Carey. I remember discussing some of our mutual problems last May when we were at the International AMS Conference.

I recall that your company had decided to use the justified right margins for all in-house publications. Could you give me a brief summary of the procedures that a typist should follow when preparing copy with the right margin justified. Perhaps a statement of rationale (at least the major advantage) for using the procedure would be of help to me.

Sincerely,

59a ▶ 6
Preparatory practice

each line 3 times SS (work for fewer than 3 errors per group); DS between 3-line groups; repeat selected lines as time permits

alphabet 1 June Wilcox printed five dozen banquet tickets for my seventh meeting.

figures 2 Please turn to page 350 and answer Questions 2, 4, 6, 7, 8, 9, and 17.

double letters 3 Lynn's committee supplied food and coffee for the Mississippi meeting.

easy 4 We may augment with an eighth element the fuel for the busy dirigible.

| 1 | 2 | 3 | 4 | 5 | 6 | 7 | 8 | 9 | 10 | 11 | 12 | 13 | 14 |

59b ▶ 10
Measure skill growth

Take one 3' and one 5' writing; determine *gwam*; proofread and circle errors.

Difficulty index

| all letters used | A | 1.5 si | 5.7 awl | 80% hfw |

gwam 3' | 5'

Usually, writing a report does not seem quite so difficult if the 4 | 3
writer breaks the task down into smaller jobs. Before even starting to 9 | 5
write, for example, a writer must know exactly what is to be written, 13 | 8
for whom, and why; and a request for a report ought to have specific 18 | 11
directions with it. The next step is to build a working outline that 23 | 13
summarizes the report. The outline can later be changed to a skeleton 28 | 17
report with statements of purpose and main headings, subheadings, and 32 | 19
paragraph headings that will in time grow into a completed report. 37 | 22

Solutions to the problem under study must be found and analyzed; 41 | 25
and supporting data can be found, among other sources, by observation, 46 | 28
by experimentation, in books, with a questionnaire, with interviews, 50 | 30
and by examining all kinds of records. Each bit of data can be jotted 55 | 33
on a file card, along with a complete citation of its source. As a 60 | 36
last step, these data are added to the skeleton report; the citations 65 | 39
are the footnotes. Then all that is needed are the final touches that 69 | 41
produce a report that is usable, complete, to the point, and readable. 74 | 44

gwam 3' | 1 | 2 | 3 | 4 | 5 |
5' | 1 | 2 | 3 |

59c ▶ 34
Measure skill application

Time schedule

Assembling materials .... 2'
Timed production .... 26'
Final check; compute
  g-pram .... 6'

Materials needed

3 full sheets

When the signal to begin is given, insert paper and begin Problem 1. Format/type the problems in sequence until the signal to stop is given. Do Problem 1 again if you have finished Problem 3 and time has not been called. Proofread all problems; circle errors. Calculate *g-pram*.

$$g\text{-}pram = \frac{\text{total words typed}}{\text{time (26')}}$$

Form letter (LM pp. 35–41)

Mr. Tullane has received from Mr. Romain duPont, Vice President of Marketing, this letter which must be sent to the individuals on the cards he has handed to you. Date the letter December 5, 19—. Correct any undetected errors.

```
Cruze, Stephen R.

Mr. Stephen R. Cruze
2403 East Calle Concordia Street
Tucson, AZ  85704-4307
```

```
Montgomery Office Furniture Company

Montgomery Office Furniture Company
510 College Street
Santa Rosa, CA  95404-4207
```

```
LaRouge, Vivian T. (Mrs.)

Mrs. Vivian T. LaRouge
Landmark Office Systems, Inc.
48 Intervale Road
Bridgeport, CT  06611-5101
```

```
Advanced Office Systems

Advanced Office Systems
3709 Potomac Street
St. Louis, MO  63116-3263
```

Note: If you are using an electric or manual typewriter, the form letter will have to be typed for each individual to whom it is addressed. If a word processor is available, you need to type the letter only once, store it in memory, and type only the variables (the inside address and salutation, in this case) for each succeeding letter.

ANNOUNCING THE NEW APACHE EXECUTIV DESK ← subject line

We are *proud* ~~happy~~ to announce that our deluxe Apache Executive Desk will ~~soon~~ be avilable for shipment to our dealers *within thirty days.* ~~next month.~~ We are *confident* ~~sure~~ that this *new* product will be come one of our biggest sellers to date.

When we first introduced this ~~new~~ desk *concept* last fall *we had* ~~there was~~ a very good response from our d*a*elers. Those dealers who have now *s*een the finished*#*product are even more enthusiastic. *Further,* For a limited time, we are offering to our dealer*s* a special introductory discount of 20 percent on all orders ~~which~~ *received before March 1.* ~~we receive.~~ A brochure has been enclosed. Please take a moment to review the brochure, and then place an order with*#*us for several of these *revolutionary* desks. Once your customer*s have* ~~has~~ a chance to see this *new* desk, you will *understand* ~~know~~ why we are so enthusiastic about this new product.

Sincerely

Romain duPoint

xx

Enclosure

P. S.
↳ Remember, this introductory ofer will continue only until March 1. Don't delay. Place your order today.

for your to review the specifications of the Apache

Problem 1

Second page of an unbound report

Use standard unbound report format; number as page 2; place footnotes on foot of page.

words

2   0

adds to profits. To be profitable, Cecil says that business offices must "aim for   17
the most efficient method to generate, record, process, file, and distribute in-   33
formation."[2] It is in the quest for this goal that word processing has developed.   50

    Word processing involves people, procedures, and highly technical   63
equipment, all of which are scientifically interposed between originating   78
thoughts (in words) and the production of the same thoughts in some physical,   93
functional form.   97

    <u>People</u>. The people involved in word processing need specialized training.   113
They should be able to manipulate a keyboard with facility; be sure in their   129
knowledge of language, especially spelling and grammar; have managerial   143
skills; and /or understand word processing concepts, procedures, vocabulary,   158
and equipment.   163

    <u>Procedures</u>. The procedures of word processing are not really new, but   178
they have new importance. They include such operational tasks as formatting,   193
or giving form to documents; editing and proofreading copy; and keyboarding,   209
or activating equipment.   214

    <u>Equipment</u>. Types of word processing equipment vary; Anderson reports   230
that there are more than a hundred companies manufacturing word processing   245
equipment and supplies.[3] A list of recent equipment, though, will likely include   261
stand-alone display text editors, optical character readers, central dictation   277
systems, intelligent printers, electronic typewriters, and sophisticated storage   293
media.   295

   298

    [2] Paula B. Cecil, <u>Word Processing in the Modern Office</u>, 2d ed. (Menlo   320
Park: The Benjamin/Cummings Publishing Company, 1980), p. 3.   332

    [3] Ruth I. Anderson, "Word Processing," <u>The Changing Office Environ-</u>   351
<u>ment</u> (Reston: National Business Education Association, Yearbook No. 18,   365
1980), pp. 56-57.   369

Job 7
Cost sheet (full sheet)

Mr. Tullane asks that you prepare a cost sheet for duplication. Make a first copy for his approval. Have him check it; if he suggests any changes, retype the cost sheet.

Center the cost sheet on a full sheet; leave 4 spaces between columns; make the rules under the column headings and in the total columns 8 spaces wide.

FAIRFIELD MANUFACTURING, INC.

Cost Sheet

Product:
Product Code No.:

Material costs:

Operation	Code	Quantity	Cost	Total
1	___	___	___	___
2	___	___	___	___
3	___	___	___	___
4	___	___	___	___
Total				$ ___

Variable costs:

Operation	Hours	Cost	Total
1	___	___	___
2	___	___	___
3	___	___	___
4	___	___	___
Total			___

Fixed costs:

Operation	Hours	Cost	Total
1	___	___	___
2	___	___	___
3	___	___	___
4	___	___	___
Total			___

Total standard cost per unit $ ___

59c, continued

Problem 2

Outline

50–space line: 1½″ top margin; spread heading; use standard outline format

	words
M E X I C O	2
I. LAND AREA	5
A. Approximately 761,600 Square Miles	13
B. Temperate to Tropical Climate	19
II. HISTORY	22
A. Early Advanced Indian Cultures	29
1. Mayans	31
2. Toltecs	34
3. Aztecs	36
B. Conquered by Spanish in 1521	43
C. Independence from Spain in 1821	50
III. GOVERNMENT	53
A. Federal Republic (President Elected)	61
B. Federal District and 31 States	68
C. Capital: Mexico City	73

Problem 3

Unarranged outline

Use Problem 2 format with a solid (not spread) heading; add designation numerals and letters for each order; use correct capitalization and spacing.

	words
WORD PROCESSING SYSTEM	5
origination	8
thoughts reduced to some communicable form	17
written	20
spoken	22
transmitted into system	27
production	31
placed in semi-final form	37
formatted	39
keyboarded	40
placed in final form	47
edited	50
printed	52
reproduction	56
number of desired copies produced	63
photocopy or mechanical process	71
distribution	74
dissemination of data as planned/directed	83
hard copy or electronic mail medium	91
retention	94
hard copy file	98
soft copy file	102
floppy diskette	106
archival disk	109
winchester disk	113

Job 4
Ruled table (full sheet)

Mr. Tullane asks you to format a table that he received from the Inventory Control Department. The normal procedure for formatting tables is to use horizontal rulings. Because the table is not very long, format the table DS in reading position. Follow any markings on the copy.

INVENTORY CONTROL ← DS
Executive Desk Components ⟩ SS
(Model #6372)
December 4, 19-- ← DS

Component	In Process	Finished	Total
Tops	216	172	388
Center drawer	193	210	403
Top drawer	401	312	713
Middle drawer	210	221	431
Bottom drawer	178	272	450
File drawer	116	227	343
Cabinet	110	290	400
Legs	450	320	770

Job 5
Compose a letter (LM p. 31)

As Mr. Tullane was leaving the office, he stopped by your desk and asked you to take a few notes and compose a letter. Use subject line: Our Purchase Order #C–3629. He quickly gave you the following facts:

Data shown on file card:

Roth Office Products Company
535 South Broadway
Wichita, KS 67202–2212

Office
Manager: Miss Thelma Round

December 4, 19-- Write letter to Roth-- Attn. Office Manager; Inquire about P.O. #C-3629 sent 2 weeks ago. No confirmation received. We are low on paper. Must have order in 2 weeks (or partial order) or we must cancel. Send duplicate copy of order. Ask for acknowledgement by return mail.

Job 6
Preparing index cards (LM p. 33)

Mr. Tullane maintains a current file of all approved suppliers. The name of each supplier is typed on a 5″ × 3″ index card. You will notice on the sample card that the first line contains the transposed name of the individual if an individual's name is the first line.

Mr. Tullane has given you the names of 4 new suppliers to be added to the file. (See the list below.) You are to prepare an index card for each supplier and arrange the cards in alphabetical order.

```
                    TS
Frankhauser, Paul L. (Mr.)
                    TS
Mr. Paul L. Frankhauser
954 Cabrillo Drive
Hayward, CA  94545-8091
```

1. Ms. Carlotta Ciminero
   18632 Vale Street
   Santa Ana, CA 92705-1704

2. Bolivar Paper, Inc.
   208 International Way, W
   Seattle, WA 99201-7012

3. Tucson Fabrication Company
   809 North Arcadia Avenue
   Tucson, AZ 85711-4023

4. Mr. Faramarz Samadi
   5724 Wandering Way
   Austin, TX 78754-3067

Learning goals

1 To gain skill in improving data input.

2 To strengthen ability to spell.

3 To understand better the functions and usage of the period and the question mark.

4 To improve ability to format materials.

Machine adjustments

1 Set paper guide at 0; remove all tab stops.

2 Set ribbon control to type on upper half of ribbon.

3 Unless otherwise appropriate, use a 70–space line.

60a ▶ 6
Preparatory practice

each line 3 times SS (slowly, faster, still faster); DS between 3-line groups; repeat selected lines if time permits

alphabet 1 Please have Dorothy get four dozen quarts of lemon juice by next week.

fig/sym 2 Duggan & Ford's catalog lists Item #93276 at $845 (less 10% for cash).

shift/lock 3 Send Marshall & Filarb ten copies of THE NEW LOOK by Hahn and Ostgard.

easy 4 Theodosia paid them to go downtown to bid on the authentic enamel owl.

| 1 | 2 | 3 | 4 | 5 | 6 | 7 | 8 | 9 | 10 | 11 | 12 | 13 | 14 |

60b ▶ 14
Improve keystroking continuity

1 Take two 1' writings on each ¶, then two 3' writings on both ¶s.

2 Proofread; circle errors; determine *gwam*.

3 Try to add one additional word to your *gwam* on each successive writing.

Difficulty index

| all letters used | A | 1.5 si | 5.7 awl | 80% hfw |

gwam 1'　3'

It has been said that human intelligence is the ability to acquire　13　4　60
and retain the kind of knowledge that will permit a person to respond　27　9　64
quickly and successfully to new and different problems. It is also the　42　14　69
ability to use mental power and sound judgment to recognize problems　56　19　74
we face and resolve them. In other words, it is the driving force that　70　23　79
moves our bodies from place to place, like moving game-board pieces.　84　28　83

Education teaches us to use intelligence. How shall we use it?　13　32　88
That question is partly answered for us when we realize that we need to　27　37　92
be bright enough to earn a livelihood, coexist with others, and make　41　42　97
contributions to our society and our environment. Beyond that, we must　56　46　102
decide for ourselves just how we use our intelligence, how different we　70　51　107
want to be from the other moving pieces on the game board.　82　55　110

| gwam 1' | 1 | 2 | 3 | 4 | 5 | 6 | 7 | 8 | 9 | 10 | 11 | 12 | 13 | 14 |
| 3' | | 1 | | 2 | | 3 | | 4 | | 5 | | | | |

Office job simulation
(LM pp. 27–43)

Job 1
Memorandum (LM p. 27)

Mr. Tullane has asked you to prepare this memorandum for direct–copy duplication. It will be sent to all office employees. Proofread and correct errors before you remove the memo from the machine.

Job 2
Spirit master

After you have finished Job 1, you discover that the photocopy machine is not working. The technician indicated that it will be tomorrow before the machine will be working again. After checking with Mr. Tullane, you prepare the memo on a spirit master. Remember to type the headings for the memo.

All Office Staff | Duncan G. Tullane, Office Manager | December 3, 19-- | Integration of Information Processing Equipment

(¶) Many of you are already aware that the company has made the decision to implement the recommendation of the consultants to install a new information processing system. This new system will merge many of the present data processing systems and word processing functions. Also affected will be our records management department and our company's resource center.

(¶) The planned implementation schedule shows a conversion to the new system over the next six months. The first phase will be to convert the present company records to a computer compatible medium; in our case, that media will have two large capacity storage disks. The second phase will be the orientation and training of all office personnel on the new information processing equipment. Over the period of three months, we will have present word processing equipment replaced by a more sophisticated system. The third and final phase will be an evaluation of the system. Although this phase is scheduled for a two-month period, the evaluation will be an ongoing one for many months.

(¶) If any of you would like to discuss the implementation schedule of our new information processing system, please come and visit me. xx

Job 3
Letter (LM p. 29)

The general office does most of the correspondence for the various departments within the company. Mr. Tullane has asked that you type this letter he has written for Mrs. Jacobsen, a design engineer for Fairfield Manufacturing.

December 4, 19-- | Baton Rouge Petrochemicals, Inc. | Attention Mr. Henry I. Franklin | 7899 Jefferson Highway | Baton Rouge, LA 70809-1403 | Ladies and Gentlemen

(¶) Mrs. Anna Jacobsen, our Desk Design Engineer, has asked that I write to you concerning the estimated delivery date for the new plastic laminate product that you recently announced (Shipment No. #A-386).

(¶) Your announcement indicated that the product should be ready for distribution prior to April 1. Mrs. Jacobsen would like to know if a firm date has been established, since one of her major decisions on whether to use the mar-proof top for a new executive desk is dependent upon the date that this new product will be available to us. Would you please let us know within 10 days if your delivery schedule will permit a March 1 shipment to us.

(¶) We appreciate your recent performance of providing us with top-quality products for our office furniture and equipment.

Sincerely | Duncan G. Tullane | xx

Improve keystroking technique

70-space line; keyboard each line 3 times SS; DS between each 2-line group

1st/ fingers

1 Those 456 heavy black jugs have nothing in them. Fill them by June 7.
2 A youth of just over 6 or 7 years of age ran through the orange grove.

2d/ fingers

3 Mike Deak, who was 38 in December, likes a piece of ice in cold cider.
4 Eddie decided to crate 38 pieces of cedar decking behind the old dock.

3d & 4th/ fingers

5 Polly made 29 points on that quiz; Wex made 10 points. Did they pass?
6 Zone 12 was impassable; we quickly roped it off. Did you wax Zone 90?

| 1 | 2 | 3 | 4 | 5 | 6 | 7 | 8 | 9 | 10 | 11 | 12 | 13 | 14 |

60d ▶ 20

Review/improve communication skills: period and question mark

1 Make decisions about placement of the copy. A full sheet and a 1½" top margin are suggested.

2 Proofread carefully; correct errors.

3 Note your comments about your placement decisions at the bottom of the page.

4 Study the rules and examples from your copy.

THE PERIOD AND THE QUESTION MARK

1. Use a period after a complete sentence; follow the period with two blank spaces.

Examples: Buy the books. She will use them later.
I know Don. He is a member of our club.

2. Use a period after an abbreviation. Space once after periods used after abbreviations unless the abbreviation is made up of letters that are combined to represent more than one word; in that case, space only after the final period.

Examples: Mr. Ogden will be graduated with a Ph.D.
Mrs. Sipe arrived at 6 a.m. last Monday.

3. Use periods to form an ellipsis. Ellipsis periods, commonly three in number, represent the omission of words from quoted data. Use four periods when an ellipsis ends a sentence. Space once between ellipsis periods.

Examples: The economy . . . has not yet responded.
We agree the general won the war . . . .

4. Use a question mark after a direct question--not after an indirect question. Space twice after a question mark that is used to terminate a question.

Examples: Where is he? I wonder if he had dinner.
Did she go? I asked if she had tickets.

5. A request that is phrased as a question is usually terminated with a period.

Examples: Will you please bring me a glass of tea.
Will you kindly mail that letter for me.

6. Use a question mark after each of a series of short questions that are related to a single thought. Capitalize the first word of each of the questions only if it is a complete sentence. Space once after all but the final question mark.

Examples: Was it birds? squirrels? rabbits? ducks?
Who wrote this? Was it Lee? Was it Dale?

Spirit Duplication. The spirit duplication process is generally used for runs of 10 to 100 copies, although up to 300 copies can be made from a single spirit master. The spirit master set consists of two basic parts: a master sheet and a sheet of special car–bon (see illustration at the right). The use of a backing sheet will improve the consistency of the type impression. As you type, the carbon copy will be on the *back* of the master sheet.

The following steps should be followed when preparing a spirit master:

1 Prepare a model copy of the material to be typed on the master. Check the copy for accuracy of format and keyboarding.

2 Clean the type. The ribbon should be lightweight to prevent broad impressions and filled-in characters.

3 Use a firm, even stroke on a nonelectric typewriter. On an electric or electronic typewriter, one of the lower pressure settings is better.

4 If you make an error, scrape off the letter or word on the back of the master sheet with a knife or razor blade. Rub the scraped area with a correction pencil. Then place a small piece of carbon (torn from an unused section of the spirit master) under the area to be retyped; place the glossy side toward you. Type the correction over the incorrect letter or word. Remove the piece of carbon as soon as you have corrected the error.

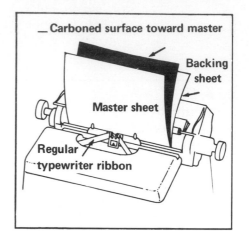

Memo Headings on Plain Paper. If a printed memo form is not available, or if a memo is to be prepared for duplication on a spirit master or a stencil, the memo headings TO:, FROM:, DATE:, and SUBJECT: must be typed as a part of the memo. Note the placement of the headings in the illustrations below.

```
              1½" on full sheet
              1" on half sheet


       TO:     All Office Secretaries
                                      DS
       FROM:   Duncan Tullane, Office Manager
1"
       DATE:   December 5, 19--                        1"

       SUBJECT: Typing Memo Headings
                                   TS
       Occasionally it is necessary to type an interoffice memorandum on
       a spirit master, a stencil, or a plain sheet of paper.  In such
       cases, the headings which are preprinted on our memo form must be
```

or

```
              1½" on full sheet
              1" on half sheet


         TO:   All Office Secretaries
                                    DS
         FROM: Duncan Tullane, Office Manager
1"
         DATE: December 5, 19--                        1"

         SUBJECT: Typing Memo Headings
                                    TS
       Occasionally it is necessary to type an interoffice memorandum on
       a spirit master, a stencil, or a plain sheet of paper.  In such
       cases, the headings which are preprinted on our memo form must be
```

157a-162a ▶ 5
Preparatory practice

Type as many times as you can in 5′ at the beginning of each class period in this section.

alphabet	1	Major Pluvicky quizzed six officers about their losses during the war.
fig/sym	2	The total is $1,841.71 (sales, $1,762.40; and 4.5% sales tax, $79.31).
shift key	3	Is this Agnes', Ron's, or Jane's new computer? No, it is Carma Lou's.
fluency	4	The chair of the island city panel is to handle the amendment problem.

| 1 | 2 | 3 | 4 | 5 | 6 | 7 | 8 | 9 | 10 | 11 | 12 | 13 | 14 |

61a ▶ 6
Preparatory practice

each line 3 times SS
(slowly, faster, still
faster); DS between
3-line groups; re-
peat selected lines
as time permits

alphabet 1 Pamela Becker recognized the excellent quality of this silver jewelry.

figures 2 Walford reported on the following rooms: 6, 10, 25, 37, 129, and 148.

double
letters 3 Will Scott attempt to sell his three bookkeeping books to Ellis Leeds?

easy 4 Orlando did vow to fight for his right to work as an auditor for them.

| 1 | 2 | 3 | 4 | 5 | 6 | 7 | 8 | 9 | 10 | 11 | 12 | 13 | 14 |

61b ▶ 17
Review/improve communication skills: suffixes

1 Set for 70–space line. Use a 1½″ top margin.

2 Center the heading, TS, and keyboard the first column as shown. Indent examples 5 spaces from left margin.

3 Reset left margin 4 spaces to the right of center point. Keyboard the second column. Indent examples 5 spaces from left margin.

4 Study carefully your finished copy. Correct errors.

ADDING SUFFIXES TO WORDS ENDING IN E OR Y

1. The e is usually dropped if the suffix begins with a vowel.

    like--likable
    pursue--pursuant
    sue--suing
    drive--drivable

2. The e is usually retained if the suffix begins with a consonant.

    care--careful
    nice--nicely
    rare--rareness
    case--casement

3. The e is usually retained before the ous or able when the root word ends in ce or ge.

    change--changeable
    notice--noticeable
    outrage--outrageous
    advantage--advantageous

4. The e is usually retained when the word ends in oe.

    shoe--shoeing
    canoe--canoeing
    hoe--hoeing

5. When a word ends in y preceded by a consonant, the y is usually changed to i before adding a suffix.

    lovely--loveliness
    economy--economical
    plenty--plentiful
    drowsy--drowsiness

6. Of course there are always exceptions that have to be remembered.

    oboe--oboist
    malice--malicious
    judge--judgment
    argue--argument

Learning goals

1 To become familiar with the work of a general office.

2 To plan your work and complete it efficiently.

3 To integrate your knowledge and skills in completing office work acceptably.

Machine adjustments

1 Set paper guide at *0*.

2 Margins: 70–space line for drills and ¶ writings; as directed (or ap–propriate) for problems.

3 Set ribbon control to use the upper half of ribbon.

4 SS drill lines; DS ¶s; space prob–lems as directed (or appropriate).

Office Job Simulation

Read carefully the material at the right and on page 285 before you begin the work of Section 35. Note any standard procedures that you think will save you time during the completion of the production activities.

Daily practice plan:

Preparatory practice .... 5'
Work on simulation .... 45'

Work Assignment

You have been assigned by Office Service Temporaries, Inc., to work for Fairfield Manufacturing, Inc., a firm that manufactures office furniture. The address where you are to report to work is 4320 Aldine Drive, San Diego, CA 92116-2307. Your immediate supervisor will be Mr. Duncan G. Tullane, Office Manager.

The company style manual at Fairfield Manufacturing specifies that all company letters are to be formatted in block style with open punctuation. The closing lines of all letters should include the typed name of the person for whom the letters are prepared followed on the next line by that person's business title. All letters and memorandums require *one* carbon copy for the file. Address appropriate envelopes for all letters.

Proofread all work carefully before removing it from your machine; correct all errors. All work that is to leave the company should be "mailable"—technically correct with all errors corrected neatly. All work to be used *within* the company should be "usable"—content correct but with *minor* "flaws" in format and placement permitted.

When specific job instructions are given, follow them carefully. When specific instructions are not given, make appropriate decisions on the basis of knowledge and experience. If your supervisor (teacher) considers some of your decisions unacceptable, learn from his or her suggestions—just as you would do in a business office.

Fairfield Manufacturing, Inc., has based its office manual and job instruction booklets on COLLEGE KEYBOARDING/TYPEWRITING, so use the Reference Guide and the index of your textbook to look up matters of style and placement when in doubt. When a job requires unusual specifications, Fairfield Manufacturing provides them in "Excerpts from the Office Procedures Manual."

Excerpts from the Office Procedures Manual

Justifying the Right Margin. The process of justifying the right margin gives the finished copy the appearance of a printed page with the right margin evenly aligned. Except for the last line of a paragraph, the words in each line are carefully spaced so that the right margin will be even. When using a standard manual or electric typewriter, all material must be typed twice. The first typing is used to determine how many extra spaces must be added to each line during the final or second typing. The normal procedure is to type as close to the end of the line as possible and then fill the remaining spaces with diagonals.

First typing
```
A major obstacle to communica-/
ting on a worldwide level lies/
in differences in languages.///
People who can't read, write,//
```

Second typing
```
A major  obstacle to communica-
ting on a worldwide level  lies
in  differences  in  languages.
People who  can't read,  write,
```

When typing the material in final form, you must use good judgment in distributing the unused spaces throughout the line so they are least noticeable. If you are keyboarding on a computer or electronic typewriter, consult the operator's manual to automatically justify the right margin.

Direct-Copy Duplication. The direct-copy process is used primarily for making from one to ten copies. Copy machines are especially useful in making additional copies of incoming documents such as customers' orders and bills of lading. They may also be used when a few copies of correspondence are needed.

In preparing materials for copy machines, follow these guides:

1 Clean the type; use a good ribbon.

2 Prepare the material to be copied on plain paper, letterhead, or special form.

3 Erase or correct errors neatly before making the additional copies.

Measure straight-copy skill

two 3′ writings; proofread; determine *gwam*; circle errors

Difficulty index

| all letters used | A | 1.5 si | 5.7 awl | 80% hfw |

gwam 1′   3′

Just recently an acquaintance of mine was complaining about how 13 | 4 | 50
quickly papers accumulated on her desk; she never seemed able to reduce 27 | 9 | 54
the load down to ground zero. There appeared to be some law working, 41 | 14 | 59
she explained, that continued to increase the stack each day by exactly 56 | 19 | 64
the amount she had reduced it the day before. 65 | 22 | 67

My friend ought to be better organized. She should schedule activi- 14 | 26 | 72
ties so that work is attended to daily. Any paper that requires only a 28 | 31 | 76
glance, a decision, and swift, final action should get just that. Any 42 | 36 | 81
paper that must for some reason get closer attention should be subject 56 | 40 | 86
to a fixed schedule for completion. Self-discipline is the key to order. 71 | 45 | 91

gwam 1′ | 1 | 2 | 3 | 4 | 5 | 6 | 7 | 8 | 9 | 10 | 11 | 12 | 13 | 14 |
3′ | 1 | 2 | 3 | 4 | 5 |

61d ▶ 17
Make decisions: format a business letter

plain full sheet

1 Make decisions about the style and placement of the letter, then keyboard it.
2 Examine the letter carefully when you have finished it. Correct errors. Note your comments about your deci-sions at the bottom of the page.

If necessary, refer to pages 78 or 84 for assistance.

words

August 1, 19-- | Mr. Frederick K. Barnum | 4748 Jarvis Drive | Corpus Christi, 15
TX 78412-2346 | Dear Mr. Barnum 21

(¶) Thank you for your letter requesting information about one of our personalized 37
Name Pictures for your grandson. I hope the following description will be 52
helpful. 54

(¶) The Name Picture is an original hand-painted design featuring the name of a 69
child--in this case your grandson's name--in bold artist's print. Three or four 85
little boys or girls in colorful outfits are portrayed in playful situations as a part 102
of each picture. As a finishing touch, each picture is matted and framed in a 118
12″ by 16″ anodyzed aluminum frame. It sells for $30. 129

(¶) The enclosed order form specifies clearly the information we need to complete 145
the picture for you. Please allow us six weeks for delivery. 158

Sincerely yours | Miss Brenda Weaster | Sales Manager | xx | Enclosure 170

62a ▶ 6
Preparatory practice

each line 3 times SS (slowly, faster, still faster); DS between 3-line groups; re-peat selected lines if time permits

alphabet 1 Max perhaps realized that jet flights can quickly whisk us to Bolivia.
figures 2 Our latest inventory includes 958 rings, 3,064 pins, and 172 brooches.
hyphen 3 Oki thinks we have an up-to-the-minute plan for our out-of-town sales.
easy 4 Clement and eight neighbor girls wish to visit this cornfield at dusk.

| 1 | 2 | 3 | 4 | 5 | 6 | 7 | 8 | 9 | 10 | 11 | 12 | 13 | 14 |

62b ▶ 10
Measure straight-copy skill

Repeat 61c, above.

154b-156b, continued
Preemployment testing, Part II (continued)
Problem 3
Table (full sheet)
exact vertical center; DS between entries; 4 spaces between columns

					words
JOB SATISFACTION					3
RATINGS FOR SECRETARIAL TASKS					9
(% of Secretaries)					13
Task	Like Very Much	Like Somewhat	Dislike Somewhat	Dislike Very Much	18 / 35
Receive Visitors	78%	20%	2%	0%	41
Write Letters for Executive	73	22	4	1	44 / 48
Type	70	27	3	0	51
Arrange Meetings	70	25	4	1	57
Schedule Appointments	66	29	5	0	63
Make Travel Arrangements	64	30	5	1	66 / 70
Attend Meetings	62	33	4	1	75
Take Shorthand/ Rapid Note Taking	49	35	12	4	79 / 84
Answer Telephone/ Route Calls	46	36	14	4	88 / 93
Open/Sort Mail	35	53	10	2	98

Source: "The Evolving Role of the Secretary in the Information Age," — 117

The Secretary (April 1983), p. 12. — 125

Job 4
Employee Record Form (LM p. 25)

Mrs. DeSoto has informed you that you have passed OSTI's preemployment testing program. She asks you to type the Employee Record Form which will be kept in the files of Office Service Temporaries, Inc. Prepare the Employee Record Form, supplying information about yourself.

OFFICE SERVICE TEMPORARIES, INC.

EMPLOYEE RECORD FORM

An Equal Opportunity Employer

Last Name	First	Middle Initial	Home Phone	Business Phone

Street Address	City	State	Zip	U.S. Citizen ☐ yes ☐ no

Social Security No.	Days Available (circle) M T W T F S S	Hours of Day Available

EXPERIENCE AND SKILLS (Type an X in the square opposite each area in which you have had experience; fill in blanks where appropriate.)

Secretarial Support

☐ administrative   ☐ medical
☐ general   ☐ shorthand
☐ executive   ☐ machine transcription

Word Processing

specific machines used:

62c ▶ 16
Review/improve communication skills: spelling

full sheet; DS; 1½" top margin; 70-space line

1 Clear tab stops; set two new tab stops, one 28 spaces from left margin and one 56 spaces from left margin.

2 Type the first word at left margin; tab and type the word again; then tab and type it a third time—this time, do not look at the word in the book or on the paper.

3 Repeat this procedure for each word on the list.

4 Study your completed copy; correct errors.

			words
	SPELLING DEMONS		3
accommodate	accommodate	accommodate	10
acknowledgment			19
argument			25
congratulate			33
conscience			39
description			46
eligible			52
grammar			57
irresistible			64
license			69
miscellaneous			78
pamphlet			83
questionnaire			91
ridiculous			98
similar			103
usable			107
whether			112

62d ▶ 18
Proofread/revise as you keyboard

full sheet

1 Use the copy at the right as the body for a personal letter. (See page 58 if needed.)

2 Make changes as marked and those needed changes that have not been marked. Proofread carefully.

3 Incorporate the additional information below.

Return address:
485 Burgundy Drive
Flint, MI 48506-4789

Date: **January 15, 19—**

Letter address:
Mr. Guy Baggett
1845 Berent Street
Flint, MI 48529-2973

Salutation: **Dear Guy**

Complimentary close: **Cordially**

Signer: **Terri Vreede**

opening lines 25

¶ Congradulations on your superb talk. The fact you gave us 37

from the Ph. D. questionnaire were not at all similar to those 49

we heard last year. You make an interesting argument that 61

both women and men should be eligible for the jobs that you 73

describe. it is ridiculous to beleive otherwise, and people 85

of good conscience will find your logic irrefutable. ¶ A pam- 97

phlet about the research would be very useable, beleive me. 109

Would you consider publishing such a pamphlet? If so, may I 121

help? Would it be advantageous to work for us in the office 133

in my basement? or in Buell Hall? or in your study at home? 146

I wonder if Mrs. Shewerr would help us with grammer and punc- 158

tuation. ¶ Let me hear from you soon, Guy. 166

closing line 168

Preemployment testing, Part II
(continued)

Problem 2
Unbound, unedited report
(full sheet)

Using correct format, prepare the copy at the right as an un-bound report DS. Correct any errors as you type.

words

EMPLOYEE BENEFITS   4
OFICE SERVICE TEMPORARIES, INC.   10

<u>Payed Holidays</u>   16

As a OSTI employ you may be eligible to be   25
paid for any of the following holidays: new year's day, 36
memorial day, independence day, labor day, thanks-   46
giving day, and Christmas day. To qualify for each   57
paid Holiday you muts have work 300 hours in the 60 day 69
period imediately preceeding the holiday In addition   80
you must have worked the working day imediately   90
before and the one immediately after the holliday.   100

Vaccation Pay   105

Your eligible for vacation pay when you have   114
werked 1600 ours. Your vacation pay'll be for forty hours 126
at your most resent hourly rate. Once you rech 1600   137
hours and receive vacation pay you begin acumulatin   148
your nest 1600 hours. You must nottify the OSTI ofice   159
manager each time you became eligable.   167
<u>Special Compinsation</u>   175

Your fuly covered by the OTSI workers compen-   185
sation plan if your enjured or killed as a result of   196
an acident that is work related. If you aer injured   207
in a nonwork related accident you maybe eligable   218
for a $1,500 cash benafit. If you are hospitalyzed as a 229
result of such an accident you may qualify for   239
reimbursement of $25 per day — up to a mapimum   248
of $1,000 in anyone calender year.   255

(Problem 3 is on next page)

Learning goals

1 To type tables in exact center and in reading position.
2 To type main, secondary, and column headings.
3 To align figures, decimals, and dollar signs in columns.
4 To center announcements horizontally and vertically.

Machine adjustments

1 Set paper guide at 0; remove tab stops.
2 Set ribbon control to type on upper half of ribbon.
3 Use a 70–space line.
4 SS drills; DS paragraphs.

63a ▶ 6
Preparatory practice

each line 3 times SS (work for fewer than 2 errors per group); DS between 3-line groups; repeat selected lines as time permits

alphabet	1	Jack may provide a few extra quiz questions or problems for the group.
figures	2	We can try to add these fractions: 2/3, 3/4, 4/5, 5/6, 7/8, and 9/10.
shift/lock	3	THE LAKES TODAY, published in Dayton, Ohio, is issued in June or July.
easy	4	Enrique may fish for cod by the city docks, but he may risk a penalty.

| 1 | 2 | 3 | 4 | 5 | 6 | 7 | 8 | 9 | 10 | 11 | 12 | 13 | 14 |

63b ▶ 16
Compose at the keyboard

Make all format decisions.

1 Read the ¶ thoughtfully.
2 Compose a second ¶ of five or six lines in which you express your ideas about success. Begin with the word **Personally.**
3 Proofread your ¶.
4 Type a final copy of both ¶s. Center a title over the ¶s.

Each of us is building a road that is to lead to some ultimate place known as "success." We construct our highway in stages, passing from one objective to another, expecting in time to reach our goal--to be successful. But how shall we recognize success when we reach it? What is success? When is a person successful?

Personally, (Compose the remainder of the second paragraph.)

63c ▶ 28
Format/type centered announcements

3 half sheets

Review centering procedures shown at the right, then type the three announcements on page 117.

Vertical centering

1 Count the lines to be centered.
2 Subtract counted lines from total lines available (66 for a full sheet and 33 for a half sheet).
3 Divide the remaining lines by 2 and distribute these lines as top and bottom margins. Ignore fractions.
4 Space down from the top edge of the paper 1 more line than the number of lines figured for the top margin.

Horizontal centering

1 Move margin stops to ends of the scale.
2 Clear all tab stops.
3 From the center point, backspace *once* for each 2 letters, figures, spaces, or punctuation marks in the line to be centered. Do not backspace for a leftover stroke at the end of a line.
4 Begin to keyboard where you complete the backspacing. If all lines are of the same length, set a margin stop; if not, repeat Steps 3 and 4 for each subsequent line.

Preemployment Testing, Part II

After completing Part I of the employment test, Mrs. DeSoto asks you to complete Part II (Problems 1–3). Mrs. DeSoto allots you 45' to take Part II of the test. She suggests that you use 15' of this time to set up problems and to proofread and correct errors.

Problem 1
Rough-draft letter
(plain full sheet)

block style, open punctuation; use **December 2, 19—** for the current date

words

Current date — 3

~~[~~10 Manning Lane   *Use your personal title and name* — 6 / 9
San Diego, CA 92154-2221 — 14

Dear ← — 18

Thank you for your *recent inquiry about* ~~letter concerning~~ employment opportunities — 31
with Office Service Temporaries, Inc. — 39

OSTI is one of the largest temporary office *support* service sup- — 52
pliers in *the* San Diego area. We maintain a ~~working~~ staff of — 63
over ~~more than~~ 600 temporary office *workers* ~~people~~ whose qualifications — 74
fit them for assignment to jobs *in areas* ranging from general office — 88
~~work~~ to executive offices, from legal offices to medical cen- — 99
ters. We *currently* have people on assignment in more than 350 companies — 114
and institutions in San Diego. — 120

Because our personel must substitue for regular employees —
who happen to be away for several days at a time, our temporar- —
ies must be able to adjust quickly to different office systems —
and working conditions —

I would be ~~more than~~ pleased to have you come to my office — 130
to discuss your qualifications. This will give us the *opportunity* ~~chance~~ — 143
to assess how we might give *you* ~~one~~ the variety of experiences — 155
you want and at the same time provide our clients with the — 167
office skills they temporarily need. — 175

Sincerely yours — 224

Ms. Silvia DeSoto, *Office Manager* — 230

xx — 231

Enclosed is a brochure which explains in greater detail how — 187
OSTI functions and lists the steps in our employment pro- — 198
cedure. Please use one of the telephone numbers given on — 210
page 8 of the brochure to arrange for an appointment. — 220

(Problem 2 is on next page)

63c, continued
Problem 1

Use a half sheet (insert long side first). Center the problem verti-cally; center each line horizon-tally; DS.

words

ARS MUSICA 2

under the direction of Serge Chomentikov 10

will present its 14

Annual Spring Concert 18

Friday evening, April 24, at eight o'clock 27

Taer Recital Hall 30

Problem 2

Follow directions given for Prob-lem 1. The left margin will not be even, as shown.

Dr. Grace G. Gregory 4

announces the relocation of her 11

dental practice 14

to the Professional Arts Building 21

2300 Plymouth Avenue 25

541-8500 27

Effective August 1 30

Problem 3

Follow directions given for Prob-lem 1.

Ambassador and Mrs. Jorge Samoya 7

request the honor of your presence 14

at dinner 16

Wednesday, October 15, at seven 22

1424 Hemlock Road 26

R. S. V. P. 00

Job 1
Letter of inquiry
(plain full sheet)

Your school advisor has given you an example of an inquiry letter which another student has recently sent to a temporary office service agency. Format and type the sample inquiry letter. Use modified block style with mixed punctuation and indented paragraphs.

Job 2
Compose a letter of inquiry (plain full sheet)

Study your copy of the inquiry letter you prepared in Job 1. Compose your own inquiry letter, using pertinent information about yourself. Use modified block style, indented paragraphs, and mixed punctuation. Date the letter **December 1, 19—;** address it to:

Mrs. Silvia DeSoto
340 Dominican Dr.
San Diego, CA 92128-4411

Job 3
Application form (LM p. 23)

Mrs. DeSoto responds to your letter of inquiry with a return letter and an application form, which she asks you to fill out, supplying pertinent information about yourself. You are to bring the completed application form with you to OSTI for an initial interview and pre-employment testing.

Preemployment testing, Part I
(full sheet)

Mrs. DeSoto asks you to take the first part of the job application test. Take one 5' writing on the copy at the right for accuracy; record *gwam* and number of errors on the top of your paper.

	words
211 Asbury Court	San Diego, CA 92109-2113	May 14, 19--	Mrs. Delores Cuen,	15
Personnel Manager	Temporary Office Personnel Center	30 Ballinger Avenue		29
San Diego, CA 92119-2210	Dear Mrs. Cuen	37

(¶) I will soon complete the course requirements for an associate degree at   52
Coronado College. My major is office systems and administration with a minor   67
in personnel management. I have been on the Dean's List each term, and I need   83
only three more courses to complete my degree.   93

(¶) In addition to taking courses in concepts and principles relating to office   108
systems and administration, I have taken several hands-on courses in the use of   124
office automation equipment. I am also proficient in shorthand, although I have   140
not used the skill in a work setting.   148

(¶) To help me decide the kind of business or office in which I may want to seek   163
long-term employment, I would like to become an office temporary worker for   179
the next several months and to take evening classes to finish my degree. Dr.   194
Fremont Fisher, one of my professors, suggested that I contact you about this   210
kind of employment.   214

(¶) Will you please send me information about your agency and tell me how I can   229
become one of your temporary office personnel staff.   240

Sincerely yours | Roger K. Dastrup   246

Difficulty index

all letters used | A | 1.5 si | 5.7 awl | 80% hfw

gwam 5'

When people in the office work force write in longhand, type on a   3 | 47
standard typewriter, or use an electronic typewriter, they are processing   6 | 50
words. The volume of copy that must be produced in the office of today   8 | 53
continues to grow, and there is more and more a need to simplify and   11 | 56
speed up the handling of words. In order to keep pace with the need to   14 | 59
produce copy more efficiently, office personnel often use more complex   17 | 62
word processing equipment that can record and store the typed material.   20 | 65
Once the material is stored, it may be retrieved and printed rapidly.   23 | 67

Not only does sophisticated word processing equipment allow stored   25 | 70
data to be reprinted quickly, it also provides a very simple way to edit   28 | 73
and correct typewritten material without the need to retype the entire   31 | 76
document on a typewriter. Any size document that needs to be revised   34 | 79
may be retrieved from a file or tape, and only those parts that need to   37 | 81
be corrected are changed. The typist can make the needed changes and   40 | 84
print the new document in just a fraction of the time that it would take   42 | 87
to retype the entire document on a standard typewriter.   45 | 89

5' | 1 | 2 | 3 |

64a ▶ 6
Preparatory practice

each line 3 times SS (work for fewer than 2 errors per group); DS between 3-line groups; repeat selected lines as time permits

alphabet 1 The wizard quickly converted six pert frogs into small bags of jewels.

figures 2 In 1980, their company had 64 drivers; in 1983, 273; and in 1985, 310.

direct reaches 3 Bryce obtained many junk pieces dumped by Marvyn at my service center.

easy 4 Viviana, hand me the element so I may fix the problems with the robot.

| 1 | 2 | 3 | 4 | 5 | 6 | 7 | 8 | 9 | 10 | 11 | 12 | 13 | 14 |

64b ▶ 9
Preapplication drill: tabulation

1 Clear all tab stops. Set a tab stop at center point.
2 Type the drill 3 times as shown SS; DS between drills. Keep your eyes on the book while you keyboard.

———————————— tab ⟶ Centering columns is not a totally

new procedure to you.———— tab ⟶ Center the line for columns as you

center a continuous line.———— tab ⟶ Backspace for blank spaces just as

for typed characters.———— tab ⟶ Backspace for the whole line, then

set the left margin stop.———— tab ⟶ Backspace one for two; set margin;

space forward one for one.———— tab ⟶ Set tab stops as needed.

64c ▶ 35
Center tables

3 half sheets

Guidelines for centering columns horizontally

1 Take preparatory steps

a Move margin stops to ends of scale. Clear all tabulator stops.
b Move carrier (carriage) to center point.
c If spacing is not given, estimate spacing for intercolumns (the area between columns)—preferably an even number of spaces (4, 6, 8, 10, or 12, for example).

2 To set left margin stop

Check the longest item in each column. Then from the center point, backspace *once* for each 2 characters and spaces in the longest items in each column then for each 2 spaces to be allowed for the intercolumns. Set the left margin stop at this point.

If the longest item in one column has an extra character, combine the extra character with the first letter in the next column. If one stroke is left over after back spacing for all columnar items, disregard it.

Study the illustration below used to center two items and a 10-space intercolumn for the first table on p. 119.

3 To set tabulator stops

After setting the left margin stop, space forward once for each character in the longest item in the first column, then for each space to be allowed for the first intercolumn. Set tab stop at this point. Follow this procedure for each subsequent column and intercolumn.

backspace once for each two characters ⟶ | 1 | 1 | 1 | 1 | 1 | 1 | 1 | 1 | 1 | 1 | 1 | 1 | 1 | 1 | 1 | 1 | 1 | 1 | 1 | 1 | 1 | 1 | 1 |
Ca | ro | ly | n | Ly | nn | C | ar | ve | re | Vi | ce | P | re | si | de | nt | 1-2 | 3-4 | 5-6 | 7-8 | 9-10 |

Learning goals

1 To prepare a letter of inquiry for job placement.
2 To complete properly a job application form for a temporary office service agency.
3 To complete a job applicant testing program.
4 As time permits, to complete properly an employee record form.

Machine adjustments

1 Set paper guide at *0*.
2 Set ribbon control to type on upper half of ribbon.
3 Use a 70–space line and single spacing for drills; use a 70–space line and double spacing for timed writings; prepare jobs as directed.

Office Job Simulation

Before you begin work in Section 34, read carefully the material at the right.

Daily practice plan:

Preparatory practice .... 5'
Office work simulation ...... 45'

Introduction

You have been searching for just the right job for the past several weeks. You consult with your advisor at school who suggests that you seek employment through a temporary office service agency. According to your advisor, working through such an agency will give you a variety of office experiences, will help you decide the kind of office in which you may wish to work after graduation, and may lead to a permanent position with one of the firms to which you will be assigned.

After making the decision to work as a temporary office worker, you make inquiries about what temporary office help agencies exist in your city. You compile information and send letters of inquiry to the leading agencies in your area. Office Service Temporaries, Inc., (OSTI), sends you a brochure describing the various services it offers and invites you to come in to the office for an interview. You decide to go to OSTI to seek temporary employment.

At the end of the initial interview, the office manager of OSTI, Mrs. Silvia DeSoto, asks you to take an application form home, complete it in typewritten form, and bring it back the next day. Mrs. DeSoto explains that this completed form will help Office Service Temporaries match your qualifications to any of the positions currently available.

Because of your strong qualifications, OSTI decides to have you undergo the final step in its application process. Mrs. DeSoto asks you to undergo OSTI's complete testing process. The test requires you to take a straight-copy timed writing test and to format and prepare a letter, a report, and a table. Your ability to proofread and correct errors will also be observed.

After taking the test, OSTI decides that they can use your services. They ask you to type the Employee Record Form for their files so that they can match your qualifications with specific job skills temporarily required by various firms in your community.

154a-156a ▶ 5
Preparatory practice

each line 3 times SS (slowly, faster, top speed); DS between 3-line groups; repeat selected lines as time permits

alphabet	1	Zachary and Jim, both fine young explorers, quickly wanted adventures.
fig/sym	2	Corn is $2.504/bu. (down 13 cents); beans are $6.718/bu. (up 9 cents).
third row	3	Your top priority was to equip your territory people with typewriters.
fluency	4	The auditor may handle the six problems for the firms at half the pay.

| 1 | 2 | 3 | 4 | 5 | 6 | 7 | 8 | 9 | 10 | 11 | 12 | 13 | 14 |

		words
CALUMINEX BOARD OF DIRECTORS		6
TS		

Margin stop ↓   Tab stop ↓

Muriel E. Bouhm	President	11
R. Grady Atgood	Vice President	17
Alonzo J. Cruz, Sr.	Secretary	23
Carolyn Lynn Carvere	Treasurer	29
Myron A. Moilion	Member	34
Sara Harley Beck	Member	39

Key | *Carolyn Lynn Carvere* | *10* | *Vice President* |

64c, continued

Center the tables vertically and horizontally on half sheets.

Problem 1

Study the information on page 118 and the illustration above; then format and type the illustrated problem on a half sheet (insert long side first); SS; exact center; 10–space intercolumn.

Problem 2

Format/type the illustrated prob–lem again. Use the same direc–tions as for Problem 1, but change SS to DS.

Problem 3

Format/type the problem at the right on a half sheet (insert long side first); SS; exact center; 14–space intercolumn.

		words
CALUMINEX BRANCH MANAGERS		5
TS		
Gertrude F. Schuyler	Albuquerque	12
Albert C. Chung	Allentown	17
Dale T. O'Hargran	Birmingham	23
F. Samuel Montgomery	Denver	28
Rose B. Shikamuru	Honolulu	34
Myrle E. Bragg	New Haven	39
Margret G. Bredeweg	St. Louis	45
Trace J. Brecken	San Diego	50
Jose J. Morales	San Juan	55
Myrna Lee Targliff	Seattle	60

Key | *Gertrude F. Schuyler* | *14* | *Albuquerque* |

Inventory production skills

Time schedule

Assembling materials .... 2'
Timed production .... 23'
Final check; compute
n–pram .... 5'

Job 1 (half sheet)
Table with rulings

Center table on half sheet, long side up; insert horizontal rulings as you type; DS body of table; leave 4 spaces between columns.

Job 2 (half sheet)
Boxed table

Center table on half sheet, long side up; insert horizontal and vertical rulings; SS body of table; SS column headings; divide the main heading into two lines; leave 8 spaces between columns.

Job 3 (full sheet)
Rough-draft table

Center table in reading position; DS body of table; leave 4 spaces between columns; do not use rulings. Use main heading: **EMPLOYEES OF THE SANCHEZ MANUFACTURING COMPANY**; use secondary heading: **(Years of Employment)**.

QUARTERLY SALES REPORT

(January–March, 19--)

Salesperson	January	February	March	Total	
					22
					35
					44
					57
Lois R. Andrus	$ 3,840	$ 3,911	$ 4,870	$12,621	66
Charles A. Cummings	2,130	3,731	2,986	8,847	75
Leslie Q. Owens	4,210	4,560	4,874	13,644	83
Stephanie E. Scott	3,830	3,924	3,870	11,624	92
Jane Y. Zwick	2,870	2,710	3,870	9,450	99
					112
Totals	$16,880	$18,836	$20,470	$56,186	120
					133

CHECKLIST OF OUTSTANDING TRAITS OF SUCCESSFUL EMPLOYEES

(19-- Local Survey)

Order of Importance	Outstanding Traits Mentioned	Percent of Employers	
1	skilled	98	64
2	responsible	95	67
2	honest	95	70
3	sincere	91	72
4	enthusiastic	87	75
4	determined	87	78
5	intelligent	84	82
5	courteous	84	84
6	tactful	82	87
6	pleasant	82	89
7	neat	80	91
			102

words in heading   14

Employees of Less Than 1 Year	Employees of 1 to 5 Years	Employees of 6 to 10 Years	Employees of 11 to 15 Years	
				24
				47
Robert Sawyer	Peter Dunne	Jon Larsen	Sue Patrick	57
Patricia Jones	Jolynn Kohler	Frank Lopez	Juan Gomez	68
Waku Mori	George McMurdie	Dedra West	Joseph Rozales	78
Jack DeWitt	Mary Hendrix	Jimmy Von Herman	Richard Washington	90
Richard petersen	Margaret Black	Irma Hardy	Douglas Berry	101

65a ▶ 6
Preparatory practice

each line 3 times SS (work for fewer than 2 errors per group); DS between 3-line groups; repeat selected lines as time permits

alphabet	1	The king and queen brought dozens of expensive jewels from the colony.
fig/sym	2	Check #4690 for $1,375, dated February 28, was sent to O'Neill & Sons.
adjacent reaches	3	As Louise Liu said, few questioned the points asserted by the porters.
easy	4	He may fish for a quantity of smelt; he may wish for aid to land them.

| 1 | 2 | 3 | 4 | 5 | 6 | 7 | 8 | 9 | 10 | 11 | 12 | 13 | 14 |

65b ▶ 9
Preapplication drill: realigning/aligning items

twice as shown DS; 14-space intercolumn

Realigning items at the left

After setting the left margin as usual, adjust it to the right (in this instance 3 spaces) to accommodate the most common line setting. Use the margin release and backspacer for longer lines.

Aligning items at the right

Since spacing forward and backward will be needed to align items at the right, adjust the tab setting for the item length that requires the least forward and backward spacing.

District 9	tab ↓
Reset margin → Almont	27
Belden	Backspace once → 150
District 10	
Erie	85
Lamberg	Space forward once → 9
District 11	
Orville	46
Racine	9

Key | District 10 | 14 | 150 |

65c ▶ 35
Format/type tables: realign/align columns

Problem 1

full sheet; DS; reading position; 20–space intercolumn (see p. 46 to review reading position, if necessary)

ALLOCATION OF MICROCOMPUTERS

		words
ALLOCATION OF MICROCOMPUTERS		6
Eastern Region		12
Allentown	51	14
New Haven	112	17
Southern Region		24
Birmingham	65	29
San Juan	121	31
Midwestern Region		38
St. Louis	14	41
Denver	7	43
Western Region		49
Albuquerque	35	52
Honolulu	9	54
San Diego	115	57
Seattle	25	59

Key | Midwestern Region | 20 | 112 |

Continue with Problem 2, page 121.

153a ▶ 5
Preparatory practice

each line 3 times SS (slowly, faster, slowly); DS between 3-line groups; repeat selected lines as time permits

alphabet 1 Max Verbeck set the quartz jewel in antique gold for the lucky person.

fig/sym 2 Please write to us at Box 847, R.R. #1, or phone us at (319) 268-4705.

double letter 3 Access to the accounts will alleviate the need for conferring with me.

fluency 4 The haughty visitor is to pay for the memento and then cycle downtown.

| 1 | 2 | 3 | 4 | 5 | 6 | 7 | 8 | 9 | 10 | 11 | 12 | 13 | 14 |

153b ▶ 15
Inventory/build straight-copy skill

1 One 5' writing for accuracy; on LM p. 3, record *gwam* and number of errors.
2 Two 1' writings on each ¶ for speed.

Difficulty index

| all letters used | A | 1.5 si | 5.7 awl | 80% hfw |

gwam 1' | 5'

The computer age has arrived in the classrooms of many schools in — 13 | 3 | 64
the United States. The advent of the microcomputer, which is small, — 27 | 5 | 67
self-contained, and inexpensive to run, has done much to bring about — 41 | 8 | 70
this change. Microcomputers offer a way for teachers to introduce stu- — 55 | 11 | 73
dents to machines which may do much to shape their careers. Students — 69 | 14 | 76
who learn how to keyboard on these machines will have an advantage over — 83 | 17 | 79
others in a world that is finding more and more uses for the computer. — 97 | 20 | 81

A new type of microcomputer has been increasing in popularity be- — 13 | 22 | 84
cause it can be used by people without the specialized training that — 27 | 25 | 87
made the old-style microcomputers so difficult to use. This new micro- — 41 | 28 | 90
computer is equipped with a "help" key that can aid the user in operating — 56 | 31 | 93
any function on the machine. The user simply pushes the help key and — 70 | 34 | 95
indicates that aid is needed to perform a specific activity. The com- — 84 | 36 | 98
puter responds by giving a series of prompts, at the end of which it — 98 | 40 | 101
offers the answer to the user's problem. — 106 | 41 | 103

Changes in software are also making microcomputers very easy to use. — 14 | 44 | 105
Before the changes, it was often necessary to have large files of floppy — 29 | 46 | 108
disks, each used for a particular job activity. The user had to change — 43 | 49 | 111
the disks as he or she went from one job activity to another. New soft- — 57 | 52 | 114
ware packages are so nearly linked that by simply pressing a key the — 71 | 55 | 117
operator can change from one job activity to another. This ends the — 85 | 58 | 119
need to change software modules between jobs and to deal with new command — 100 | 60 | 122
modes for each business operation. — 107 | 62 | 124

gwam 1' | 1 | 2 | 3 | 4 | 5 | 6 | 7 | 8 | 9 | 10 | 11 | 12 | 13 | 14 |
5' | 1 | 2 | 3 |

65c, continued

Problem 2

half sheet (enter long side first); SS; exact center; 14-space inter-column; SS the heading

TIME DIFFERENCES AT NOON		
EASTERN STANDARD TIME		9

		words
Albuquerque	10:00 a.m.	14
Allentown	12:00 noon	18
Birmingham	11:00 a.m.	23
Denver	10:00 a.m.	26
Honolulu	7:00 a.m.	30
New Haven	12:00 noon	34
St. Louis	11:00 a.m.	38
San Diego	9:00 a.m.	42
San Juan	12:00 noon	46
Seattle	9:00 a.m.	50

Key | *Albuquerque* | *14* | *10:00 a.m.* |

(TIME DIFFERENCES AT NOON = 5 words; EASTERN STANDARD TIME = 9 words)

Problem 3

half sheet (enter long side first); DS; exact center; 12-space inter-column

To align a column of words at the right (as in the second column), backspace as usual to set left margin. When spacing forward, set the tab at the end of the second column rather than at the beginning; backspace once for each character in the second column to position for keyboarding.

PROPOSED BANQUET AGENDA		words
		5
	Tab stop ↓	
Preliminary remarks	Ellen Prater	11
Introductions	Grant Dubin	17
Speaker	Rosalyn Booth	21
Commentary	Drake Eppingham	26
Closing remarks	Ellen Prater	32

Key | *Preliminary remarks* | *12* | *Drake Eppingham* |

66

66a ▶ 6

Preparatory practice

each line 3 times SS (work for fewer than 2 errors per group); DS between 3-line groups; repeat selected lines as time permits

alphabet	1	Qualified judges will have to analyze our club performances next week.
fig/sym	2	The 7 1/2% interest of $18.68 on my $249.05 note (dated May 3) is due.
1st row	3	Can this excited man, Mr. Zinc, visit the monument to an Indian brave?
easy	4	If he burns the sign, the odor of the enamel may form a toxic problem.

| 1 | 2 | 3 | 4 | 5 | 6 | 7 | 8 | 9 | 10 | 11 | 12 | 13 | 14 |

66b ▶ 14

Compose at the keyboard

Make all decisions about format.

1 Assume that you have agreed to run for president of the student body at your college. Compose a four- or five-line paragraph in which you set forth some of the changes you would attempt to inaugurate.

2 Proofread the ¶; make changes with proofreader's marks.

3 Type a final copy. Center the title **MY PLATFORM**.

**Inventory
production skills**

Time schedule

Assembling materials 2′
Timed production ... 18′
Final check; compute
  n-pram .... 5′

Job 1
Leftbound manuscript

(full sheets)

Job 2
Unbound manuscript

(full sheets)

words

DS   employee cost and productivity   6

Perhaps

The greatest challenge facing employees today is not the cost   20
of recruiting and training an employee, but keeping the productive   34
employee once he or she is hired. Employers must be able to   46
recruit efficiently and hire employees who can be quickly trained   60
to work at a productive level. More importantly, however, the   72
employers must be able to keep these employees working at a pro-   85
ductive level for an extended period of time. Expert who make   98
hiring decisions all agree that the ability of a company to keep   110
its employees productive justifies the cost involved. monetary   123

Much of the costs in hiring new employees is obvious: trips,   137
Recruiting

placement fees, and advertising expenses are more costly now than ever.   152

recruiting, even when successful and relatively free of complica-   165

tions, accounts for only part of the cost. Lower productivity of   178
new

the employee while he or she is being trained is a hidden cost   191

fact. or the time lag between when a person is hired and when that   236

person actually becomes productive may extend to six or seven months.   250

As expensive as the cost of recruiting and training is, the investment   264
ultimately

is worthwhile if an employee is kept productive and remains with   280

the company. There are, however, a large number of dissatisfied   293

employees who stay on the job but remain uninspired about their   305

Such people

positions. Employees become "retirees in residence." These mar-   319
may feel

ginal workers, who think that their expectations have not been   332
begin to

realized, do just enough to get by and find their greatest   346
discovering their

challenge and fulfillment in finding new ways to avoid work   360
in accomplishing

rather than doing their production goals. An employer who can   374
the employee   cost

motivate and keep one satisfied will realize a price benefit in   389
the

increased productivity of that employee. As expensive as the   401
ultimate

cost of recruiting and training an employee is, the final goal   414
or him

should be retaining an employee and keeping her productive. The   429
ting

cost of recruiting and training, like any investment, will be high   442
the   of the employee

or low according to long-range productivity.   455

Just because an experienced engineer or secretary has been
hired does not mean that the person can walk into a company
and become productive immediately.

66c ▶ 30
Format/type columns with main and secondary headings

Problem 1

full sheet; DS; reading position; 20–space intercolumn

A TS usually separates a main heading from a table; when a sec–ondary heading is used, DS after the main heading and TS after the secondary heading.

For columns with dollar signs, use the dollar sign only with the top figure and the total (when one is shown). Keystroke $ one space to the left of horizontal beginning point of the longest line in the col–umn. It should be typed again in the same position when a *total line* appears in the table.

		words
CALUMINEX		2
DS		
Branch Office Sales for March		8
TS		
Albuquerque	$ 32,791	12
Allentown	47,781	16
Birmingham	60,898	19
Denver	4,558	22
Honolulu	8,432	25
New Haven	104,932	28
St. Louis	13,166	32
San Diego	89,005	35
San Juan	113,364	39
Seattle	21,539	43
	$496,466	45

Problem 2

full sheet; DS; reading position; 16–space intercolumn

		words
SOUTH AMERICAN COUNTRIES		5
Approximate Area in Square Miles		12
Argentina	1,072,067	16
Bolivia	424,162	19
Brazil	3,286,470	22
Chile	292,256	25
Colombia	439,512	28
Ecuador	105,685	31
Peru	496,222	34
Uruguay	72,172	37
Venezuela	352,143	40

Problem 3

1 Read the guidelines for deciding intercolumn spacing.

2 Repeat Problem 1. Use a half sheet; exact center; SS. Set a new width for the intercolumn.

Guides for deciding intercolumn spacing
These guidelines will help you decide on the number of spaces to use for inter-columns.

● The body of a table should be wider than its main and secondary headings.

● To center a table, backspace for columns first, intercolumns last.

● Backspace for intercolumns until an appropriate place for setting the left margin has been reached. Set the margin stop; space forward as usual.

152a ▶ 5
Preparatory practice

each line 3 times SS (slowly, faster, top speed); DS between 3-line groups; repeat selected lines as time permits

alphabet	1	Jacques Kipman was excited to see the zebra and giraffe arrive safely.
fig/sym	2	You may borrow $1,349.52 on Policy #6-B90287; the interest rate is 9%.
direct reach	3	Any unnecessary waste of aluminum is in our view economically unsound.
fluency	4	Their ivory sorority emblem is of an island chapel, a fox, and an owl.

| 1 | 2 | 3 | 4 | 5 | 6 | 7 | 8 | 9 | 10 | 11 | 12 | 13 | 14 |

152b ▶ 10
Inventory communication skills

1 Set margins for a 60–space line.
2 Type each set of words across page, making changes as directed. SS drill lines; TS between sets.

Set 1	Change to plural	analysis soprano premise copy stencil niece century basis calf footnote brother-in-law frogman bypass hero
Set 2	Change to past tense	check circumvent answer mail punish commit leave offend pay send transmit prescribe prove collect
Set 3	Add ing	appraise rattle enclose get put mark dine cross choose run permit chase forget love

---

152c ▶ 10
Inventory/build rough-draft copy skill

1 Two 3' writings for inventory; circle errors. On LM p. 3, record *gwam* and number of errors for the more accurate of the two writings.
2 One 1' writing on each ¶ to improve speed.

Difficulty index

all letters used	A	1.5 si	5.7 awl	80% hfw

	gwam 1'		3'

Today, business firms Many organizations have a great many jobs to offer give to people those who want to accept the unique challenge of trying to solving solve some of the foremost greatest problems facing opposing the business world. The fields disciplines of science, insurance, finance, sales, medicine and law, to name just a few, offers business-related jobs. however, iregardless of the area of business in which you decide to work certain factors must be considered if you wish to be a success.

Your Inherent talent and your education are two of the # primary factors needed for sucess. Success rarely comes happens to those with no training or little no ability. Also, most almost all of the personel experts in the field will agree that your interest in business plays a major role in determining your job success. Success comes more easily to those who if you are properly equpped and i like the who are zealous about the work that they do.

gwam 1' / 3':
11 | 4 | 60
23 | 8 | 64
33 | 11 | 67
46 | 15 | 71
59 | 19 | 76
70 | 23 | 79
83 | 27 | 84
86 | 29 | 85
13 | 33 | 89
25 | 37 | 93
36 | 40 | 97
50 | 45 | 101
66 | 51 | 107
83 | 56 | 112

67a ▶ 6
Preparatory practice

each line 3 times SS (work for fewer than 2 errors per group); DS between 3-line groups; repeat selected lines as time permits

alphabet	1	Julie began to study the six chapters on vitamins for her weekly quiz.
figures	2	I will send 2,795 of the 4,680 sets now and the remainder on the 13th.
one hand	3	I refereed only a few cases; I regarded waste water as a greater case.
easy	4	May I also fix the shape of the right hand and elbow of the clay form?

| 1 | 2 | 3 | 4 | 5 | 6 | 7 | 8 | 9 | 10 | 11 | 12 | 13 | 14 |

67b ▶ 12
Improve concentration

1 Type a copy of the ¶. Provide capitalization and terminal punctuation as needed.

2 Compare your typed copy with the ¶ in 63b, page 116. Correct errors.

3 Use the corrected copy for 1' writings as time permits.

Reminder

Type periods inside quotation marks.

Difficulty index

all letters used | A | 1.4 si | 5.4 awl | 80% hfw

gwam 1'

each of us is quietly building a road that is to lead to some ulti-   13
mate place known as "success" we construct our highway in stages, pass-   28
ing from one objective to another, expecting eventually to reach our   42
goal--to be successful   but how shall we recognize success when we   56
reach it   what is success   when is a person successful   67

| 1 | 2 | 3 | 4 | 5 | 6 | 7 | 8 | 9 | 10 | 11 | 12 | 13 | 14 |

67c ▶ 10
Preapplication drill: center column headings

half sheet; DS; 10 spaces between columns

1 Read the information about centering column headings.

2 Type the drill below; center headings over the columns. Underline the headings.

Guides for centering columnar headings

● A column heading is typed a double space above a column centered over the longest item in the column.

a To determine the center point of the longest item in a column, space forward from the starting point of the column *once* for every *two* strokes or spaces in the longest item. Disregard a leftover stroke.

b The point where the forward spacing stops is the center point of the column. Backspace *once* for each *two* strokes in the heading; disregard a leftover stroke. Starting at the place where backspacing ended, type the heading.

● You may prefer to type column headings after you type the columns. After typing the table headings, space down to the approximate position for the first line of the table, leaving the column heading line vacant. After the columns have been typed, you may enter the column headings.

● If the column heading is longer than its column, use the heading as the longest item in the column for horizontal placement purposes. Then, center the column under the column heading.

Book	Author
Jane Eyre	Bronte
Oliver Twist	Dickens
The Great Gatsby	Fitzgerald
Showboat	Ferber

Key | *The Great Gatsby* | 10 | *Fitzgerald* |

151d ▶ 25
Inventory
production skills

Time schedule

Assembling materials	2'
Timed production	18'
Final check; compute	
n-pram	5'

Job 1
Letter (LM p. 17)

modified block style with in–dented ¶s, mixed punctuation

July 23, 19-- | Ms. Juanita Rosini | 7302 East Forest | Detroit, MI 48214-2010 | Dear   16

Ms. Rosini   18

(¶ 1) On July 20, the Board of Directors declared a cash dividend of   30
$2.50 per share of common stock. This dividend will be payable after   44
September 1 to stockholders of record as of July 1, 19--.   56

(¶ 2) The dividend is equal to a 13.9 percent return on the par value   69
investment. The company's profits after taxes for the past fiscal year   83
were $23,987,500, which was a 10.5 percent increase over the previous   97
year.   99

(¶ 3) Your dividend check will be mailed to you on September 1. (92)   110

Sincerely | Ahmad Z. Farouk | President | xx   118

Job 2
Memorandum (LM p. 19)

TO: Robert P. Jones | FROM: Carolyn D. Tew | DATE: November 13, 19-- | 14
SUBJECT: Thanksgiving Holiday Hours   21

(¶ 1) As Personnel Manager, will you please announce to our employees that the   36
office will be closed from noon on Wednesday, November 22, until 8 a.m. on   51
Monday, November 27.   55

(¶ 2) The following policy has been established for any employees who do not   69
have an excusable absence. Office personnel must report for work on Wednes-   84
day morning in order to qualify for the Wednesday afternoon paid holiday.   99
Employees who do not report to work on Wednesday morning will be charged   114
with a full day's vacation for that day.   122

(¶ 3) Please see that the employees are made aware of the policy which has been   137
described above.   140

xx   141

Job 3
Letter with tabulation
(LM p. 21)

block style, open punctuation;
SS and center tabular material
in two columns; allow 4 spaces
between columns

Note: If time permits, redo Job
1 on a plain full sheet.

April 6, 19-- | Anderson Lumber Company | Attention Mr. Ricardo Lopez | 3905   14
North Diamond Mill Road | Dayton, OH 45246-3210 | Ladies and Gentlemen   28

(¶ 1) Your order dated April 1 has been filled and shipped with the exception of   43
the following two items: oak paneling, Stock #32-124, and birch paneling, Stock   59
#87-331. We no longer handle these two items; however, we do have the follow-   75
ing two items which are excellent substitutes in stock: 86

Stock #32-X124	Oak Paneling (4' × 8')	93
Stock #87-X331	Birch Paneling (4' × 8')	101

(¶ 2) Enclosed is a brochure which describes these two items. Please let us know   116
if you would like to substitute these items, and we will ship them to you im-   132
mediately. (106)   134

Sincerely | Miss Loretta V. Conrad | Sales Manager | xx | Enclosure   146

67d ▶ 22
Format/type tables with column headings
Problem 1

full sheet; reading position; DS; decide intercolumn spacing

		words
PRINCIPAL WORLD LANGUAGES		5
Language	Millions	12
Arabic	155	14
Bengali	151	16
English	397	19
French	107	21
German	119	23
Hindi	254	25
Japanese	119	28
Malay-Indonesian	115	32
Mandarin Chinese	726	36
Portuguese	151	39
Russian	274	42
Spanish	258	44

Problem 2

half sheet (insert long side first); exact center; SS; decide inter—column spacing

		words
THE SPRINGARN MEDAL		4
Selected Winners		7
Recipient	Year	13
Ralph J. Bunche	1948	17
Jack Roosevelt Robinson	1955	22
Martin Luther King, Jr.	1956	20
Edward (Duke) Ellington	1958	33
Leontyne Price	1964	37
Sammy Davis, Jr.	1967	41
Henry Aaron	1974	44
Andrew Young	1977	48
Coleman Young	1980	51

68

68a ▶ 6
Preparatory practice

each line 3 times SS (work for fewer than 2 errors per group); DS between 3-line groups; repeat selected lines as time permits

alphabet 1 May the judge quiz the clerks from Iowa about extensive profit-taking?

figures 2 Flight 374 will leave at 10:46 a.m. and arrive in Buffalo at 9:58 p.m.

double letters 3 The school committee will do well to pass on all the Tennessee offers.

easy 4 It is a duty of the civic auditor to aid a city firm to make a profit.

| 1 | 2 | 3 | 4 | 5 | 6 | 7 | 8 | 9 | 10 | 11 | 12 | 13 | 14 |

Inventory goals

In Section 33, you will take a series of tests to prepare yourself to take an employment test in Section 34. You will determine:

1 Your present straight–copy skill on 5–minute timed writings.

2 Your present production skill performance level. Record the results when indicated.

Machine adjustments

1 Set paper guide at *0*.

2 Set ribbon control to type on upper half of ribbon.

3 Use a 70–space line and single spacing (SS) for drill lines.

4 Use a 70–space line, double spacing (DS), and 5–space ¶ indentions for paragraph copy.

151

151a ▶ 5
Preparatory practice

each line 3 times SS (slowly, faster, slowly); DS between 3-line groups; repeat selected lines as time permits

alphabet	1	Judge Kerrwick explained very carefully both city zoning requirements.
fig/sym	2	We must pay $2,495 interest (13.8%) on the $18,080 note dated 6/07/85.
adjacent key	3	After we stopped for a look at the poor lions, we pondered about them.
fluency	4	The auditor is to blame for the chaotic problem of the city endowment.

| 1 | 2 | 3 | 4 | 5 | 6 | 7 | 8 | 9 | 10 | 11 | 12 | 13 | 14 |

151b ▶ 10
Inventory capitalization and punctuation

1 Read the ¶ at the right. Type it line for line with correct capitalization and punctuation.

2 Check your corrected ¶ with your instructor. Use your corrected copy to type two 1' writings.

gwam 1'

eleven people participated in the recent trip to the eiffel tower   13

in paris france the following number were from the united states   27

one was from boise three were from chicago of the remaining seven   41

one was from quayaquil two were from rio de janeiro three were from   55

vienna and one insisted that she was from reykjavik.   66

| 1 | 2 | 3 | 4 | 5 | 6 | 7 | 8 | 9 | 10 | 11 | 12 | 13 | 14 |

151c ▶ 10
Inventory/build script-copy skill

1 Two 3' writings for inventory; circle errors. On LM p. 3, record *gwam* and number of errors for the more accurate writings.

2 Two 1' writings to improve speed.

Difficulty index

all letters used	A	1.5 si	5.7 awl	80% hfw

	gwam 1'	3'
A person begins to learn the art of production typing	11	4	36
by first recognizing the basic rules for the placement	22	7	40
and balance of any typing job, whether it is a letter,	33	11	44
manuscript, or table. At first, the typist must have	44	14	47
something concrete upon which to construct a sound	54	18	51
production skill. After a while, improvement is per-	64	21	54
ceived; and the typist is able to format a job without	75	25	58
the exact adherence to rule requirements. Later, the per-	87	29	62
son may not need to refer to the placement rules at all.	98	33	65

68b ▶ 14
Compose at the keyboard

Make all decisions about format.

1 Read carefully the report in 55c, page 102. Then, in a four- or five-line ¶, summarize what you believe to be the main thoughts of the report.

2 Proofread the ¶; make changes with proofreader's marks.

3 Type a final copy. Center a title over the ¶.

68c ▶ 30
Format tables

1 Make all decisions about the format of the two tables below, then type them.

2 Examine each of the tables carefully for correct placement and attractive appearance. Repeat the tables if they do not appear to you to be of high quality.

Guidelines for formatting a table

To format a table attractively, certain questions must be answered appropriately; as:

- Single or double spacing? Double spacing is more attractive and easier to read, but it may require more space than you have available.
- Full or half sheet? Consider how the table will be used and how much space is available. If more than 20 lines are required, use a full sheet.
- Reading position or exact center? Reading position is recommended for a full sheet, exact center for a half sheet.
- Number of intercolumn spaces? Backspace for columns. Then backspace once for each two spaces to be left between columns (leave an even number of spaces between columns). Be sure the body of the table will be wider than the table heading.

Problem 1

Notes:

For Column 3, set the tab for the longest number in the column; then backspace one space to type the dollar sign.

Many electronic typewriters and microcomputers have a decimal tab which automatically aligns copy at the decimal.

			words
THE ALGONQUIN CLUB			4
Operating Budget, 19--			8
Committee	Chairperson	Budget	19
Business Affairs	C. Villeneuve	$310.50	27
Conservation	D. Treece	95.00	33
Finance	A. Perez	8.50	37
International Relations	F. Heckman	85.00	46
Program	I. Breece	375.00	51
Projects	G. Muncey	500.00	56
Youth and Aging	E. Runyan	200.00	62

Problem 2

CALUMINEX			2
Branch Managers' Home Telephones			9
Manager	Branch	Number	14
Gertrude F. Schuyler	Albuquerque	505-821-0147	23
Albert C. Chung	Allentown	215-640-9226	31
Dale T. O'Hargran	Birmingham	413-468-7308	39
F. Samuel Montgomery	Denver	396-386-8469	48
Rose B. Shikamuru	Honolulu	808-104-5580	56
Myrle E. Bragg	New Haven	203-401-5691	63
Margret G. Bredeweg	St. Louis	314-575-3773	72
Trace J. Brecken	San Diego	714-757-4812	80
Jose J. Morales	San Juan	809-039-2934	87
Myrna Lee Targliff	Seattle	846-913-1055	95

Continue with Problem 3, page 126.

LEVEL FIVE
Processing information (staff office simulations)

This level of Advanced Keyboarding/Formatting Skill is designed to provide you with ample opportunity to develop your information processing skills in a variety of situations commonly found in sales offices, general offices, accounting offices, and executive offices.

Although the primary emphasis in Level 5 is on the development of your production competence, you should continue to improve your basic speed and accuracy skills. This level of the textbook provides you with two sections that are devoted almost entirely to speed and accuracy development.

In addition, the final section is a measurement section that tests both your production skills and your speed and accuracy skills. Your two major performance goals are:

- To develop a keen responsibility for high-quality production work.
- To develop the ability to make decisions without direct supervision.

This level provides for about 23 percent of your classroom time to be devoted to basic speed and accuracy development and 77 percent to production activities.

			words
	CALUMINEX		2
19--	Representatives of the Year		9
Region	Representatives	Sales	20
Eastern	Polly Murger	$ 357,214	26
Southern	Brent Ortega	542,168	32
Midwestern	Rick Hyatt	497,135	38
Western	Mika Shibasaki	568,900	44

69

69a ▶ 6
Preparatory practice

each line 3 times SS (slowly, faster, slowly); DS between 3-line groups; repeat selected lines as time permits

alphabet	1	I quickly explained the grave fire hazards of the job to two managers.
fig/sym	2	Order #7849-0 (date 3/16) must be shipped by May 25 to Spahn & Erven.
long words	3	Evaluators ordinarily acknowledge routine performance characteristics.
easy	4	Claudia may make a hand signal to this man with the auditory problems.

| 1 | 2 | 3 | 4 | 5 | 6 | 7 | 8 | 9 | 10 | 11 | 12 | 13 | 14 |

69b ▶ 10
Measure skill growth: straight copy

one 3' and one 5' writing; determine *gwam* for all writings

Difficulty index

all letters used | A | 1.5 si | 5.7 awl | 80% hfw |

gwam 3' | 5'

Almost everyone is conscious of a renewed concern about quality-- 4 | 3
quality of life; of goods; and, yes, of people. Behind this concern, 9 | 5
which borders on anxiety, lies a realization that we live in a world in 14 | 8
which we must totally depend on other people to produce the items that 19 | 11
are essential to our daily living. The quality of such production is, 23 | 14
justifiably we believe, a matter of some importance to each of us. 28 | 17

We expect superior workmanship in the goods and services we acquire 32 | 19
from other people. However, we ought to realize that we are in a real 37 | 22
sense those "other people." In theory at least, we produce as well as 42 | 25
consume; and just as we expect excellence from others, we should be pre- 47 | 28
pared to provide it for them. In an economy wherein people are mutually 51 | 31
dependent, no one is exempt from making a best-possible contribution. 56 | 34

The element of quality results from a mixture of skill, judgment, 60 | 36
knowledge, and energy. These ingredients, however, blend well only 65 | 39
in the presence of an important catalyst--pride. Pride is the attitude 70 | 42
that places great value on doing the job, not just on getting the job 74 | 45
done; the worth of the finished product is viewed in terms of the work 79 | 47
put into it. The real return for quality work is a very personal one 84 | 50

gwam 3' | 1 | 2 | 3 | 4 | 5 |
5' | 1 | 2 | 3 |

Problem 2
Leftbound report
DS the report given at the right.

RECOMMENDATION FOR IMPROVING EMPLOYEE BENEFITS PLAN 10

Serious consideration should be given to establishing a thrift plan for 25
all employees of your company. A thrift plan is a voluntary supplemental 40
retirement plan that encourages employees to save part of their earnings. 55
Encouragement comes in the form of matching contributions by the employer. 70
Most plans allow limited withdrawals or borrowing to meet emergencies or 84
long-term savings plans for purposes such as the accumulation of equity or the 100
financing of a child's education. 107

A typical thrift plan would allow employees to contribute a maximum of 6 122
percent of salary. Employee contributions would be matched at the rate of fifty 138
cents from the employer for each dollar from the employee. The best plans 153
have employer contributions that match those of employees on a dollar-for- 168
dollar basis. 171

Vesting typically occurs faster in thrift plans than in pension plans. A 186
typical plan would have no vesting for five years and would then give 100 200
percent vesting. Vesting refers to the point at which an employee does not 216
forfeit the right to employer contributions in the event of termination of his or 232
her employment. 235

REFERENCES 238

Hess, Mary. "Thrift Plans." Class handout in Business Administration 487, 253
   Central University, 1985. 258

Pritchett, Stephen A. "Employee Benefits Plans." Consultant's Report, 273
   Columbia, South Carolina, 1985. 279

Problem 3
Second page of an unbound report

Prepare the material given at the right as the second page of an unbound report.

DS   The *true* value of a*n* evaluation program lies in *its* being continu*o*us 14
and functional. One or more persons involved in the initial 26
evaluation should be ~~given~~ *assigned* the respons*i*bility of administering 39
the program *for your company* on a continuing basis. The experience and ~~training~~ *stet* 55
given the *members of the* Job Evaluation Committee (qualify uniquely) them to 70
administer ~~such~~ *the* a program. ¶ The f*or*ms, manu*a*ls, and ~~other~~ 80
records contain*ed* in th*is* report reflect step-by-step proce*d*ures 93
to *be* follow*ed* and provide ~~the~~ *all* data needed to administer the program. 107

69c ▶ 34
Measure skill application: tables

Time schedule

Assembling materials .... 3'
Timed production .... 25'
Final check; proofread;
  compute *g–pram* .... 6'

Materials needed

1 full sheet
2 half sheets

Problem 1

full sheet; DS; reading position;
6–space intercolumns

			words
CHIEF JUSTICES OF THE SUPREME COURT			7
as of 1984			9
Justice	State	Term	16
John Jay	New York	1789-1795	22
Oliver Ellsworth	Connecticut	1796-1800	30
John Marshall	Virginia	1801-1835	36
Roger B. Taney	Maryland	1836-1864	43
Salmon P. Chase	Ohio	1864-1873	49
Morrison R. Waite	Ohio	1874-1888	56
Melville W. Fuller	Illinois	1888-1910	64
Edward D. White	Louisiana	1910-1921	71
William H. Taft	Ohio	1921-1930	77
Charles E. Hughes	New York	1930-1941	85
Harlan F. Stone	New York	1941-1946	91
Fred M. Vinson	Kentucky	1946-1953	98
Earl Warren	California	1953-1969	104
Warren E. Burger	Virginia	1969-	111

Problem 2

half sheet (enter long side first);
SS; exact center; decide inter–
column spacing

			words
FAMOUS AMERICAN PAINTINGS			5
Painter	Title	Size	12
Mary Cassatt	After the Bath	26″ × 39″	20
Willem de Kooning	Woman I	76″ × 58″	27
Winslow Homer	The Gulf Stream	28″ × 49″	35
Jackson Pollock	Number 27	11′ × 24′	42
Robert Rauschenberg	Tracer	84″ × 60″	50
John Singer Sargent	Madame X	82″ × 43″	57
Grant Wood	American Gothic	30″ × 25″	66
Andrew Wyeth	Christina's World	32″ × 48″	73

Problem 3

half sheet; make all decisions for
placement of copy

			words
THE UNITED NATIONS			4
Small-Nation Members			8
Country	Admitted	Est. Pop.	18
Belize	1981	146,000	22
Dominica	1978	80,000	26
Grenada	1974	108,000	31
Maldives	1965	150,000	35
St. Lucia	1979	124,000	40
St. Vincent and the Grenadines	1980	120,000	48
Sao Tome and Principe	1975	90,000	55
Seychelles	1976	70,000	60
Vanutu	1981	112,700	64

150a ▶ 5
Preparatory practice

each line 3 times SS (slowly, faster, slowly); DS between 3-line groups; repeat selected lines as time permits

alphabet 1 Wakui analyzed the complex questionnaire just before he gave it to us.

figure 2 The 375 scouts sold 29,648 boxes of good cookies in less than 10 days.

one hand 3 Phillip was in tears at noon; Lynn gave him a red lollipop as a treat.

fluency 4 I am busy, but I may go to the lake and do the usual work on the dock.

| 1 | 2 | 3 | 4 | 5 | 6 | 7 | 8 | 9 | 10 | 11 | 12 | 13 | 14 |

150b ▶ 45
Measure production: reports

full sheets

Time schedule
Assembling materials ... 3'
Timed production ...... 35'
Final check; compute
n–pram .... 7'

1 Arrange supplies for easy handling.

2 When directed to begin, work for 35'. If you complete all three problems in less than 35', start over.

3 Correct errors neatly as you work.

4 Compute n–pram (see p. 171)

Problem 1
Unbound report

Prepare the material given at the right as a short unbound report; DS.

Problems 2 and 3 are on the next page.

words

CATEGORY III JOB EVALUATION   5

A comprehensive study was made of all office posi-   15
tions in Category III. Two major facets of the study were   27
to conduct a complete job evaluation and to estab-   37
lish a salary classification system for all positions in   48
Category III. The objective of the job evaluation was   59
to determine the relative value of individual posi-   69
tions. The objective in developing a new salary   79
classification system was to ensure that all   88
employees are paid equitable and competitive wages.   98

Data were gathered from all Category III employees   108
and their supervisors. Data from the questionnaires   119
and the interviews were used to write job descrip-   129
tions and specifications. The job descriptions and   139
specifications were evaluated by the Job Evalu-   148
ation Committee. Jobs were ranked on the basis   158
of points ascribed to each of the compensatory fac-   168
tors. Present wages, wages of benchmark positions in   179
competitive industries, and point evaluations were   189
used to determine salary ranges.*   196
                                                                           199

*A copy of all forms, a summary of the data,   208
and the salary scale are included in the Appendix.   218

Learning goals

1 To improve keystroking con–tinuity and control.

2 To review principles of typing letters, tables, outlines, an–nouncements, and reports.

3 To improve control of straight, rough–draft, and statistical copy.

Machine adjustments

1 Set paper guide at 0.

2 Set ribbon control to type on upper half of ribbon.

3 Set a 70–space line.

4 SS drills; DS paragraphs.

70

70a ▶ 5
Preparatory practice

each line 3 times SS (work for errorless lines); DS between 3-line groups; repeat selected lines as time permits

alphabet 1 Place the five dozen gloves in the box quickly before John moves away.

figures 2 The 1984 edition of this book has 5 parts, 30 chapters, and 672 pages.

shift 3 Dora will make a quick flight to La Paz, Bolivia, next March or April.

easy 4 The girls, sick and shaken with dyspepsia, kept to their work in town.

| 1 | 2 | 3 | 4 | 5 | 6 | 7 | 8 | 9 | 10 | 11 | 12 | 13 | 14 |

70b ▶ 14
Improve basic skill

two 3' writings
one 5' writing

proofread; circle errors

Goal: at least 27 *gwam* with fewer than 6 errors on 3' writing.

Difficulty index

| all letters used | A | 1.5 si | 5.7 awl | 80% hfw |

	gwam 3'	5'

i remember so well my first encounter in the employment interview | 4 | 3

arena. It was one beautiful morning in early June; but although when the | 9 | 5

interviewer smiled and shook my hand when we met, I knew at once that I | 14 | 8

was pitted against a strong character who would quickly and zealously | 19 | 11

explore for any chinks in my professional and personal armor. | 23 | 14

The interviewer, who seemed to be totally relaxed, quickly scanned over | 27 | 16

my personal data sheet. The then questions began. What experience had | 32 | 19

I had? Why did I want this specific job? What career goal had I set | 37 | 22

for myself? But I was not caught offguard. I had anticipated many | 41 | 25

questions, and my short answers contained all the data asked for. | 45 | 27

Next, my references came under cold, quiet scrutiny. Had I asked | 50 | 30

permission to use the names? Could they be contacted? Yes, I replied, | 55 | 31

still a step ahead. I relaxed; I had started to enjoy this experience. | 59 | 36

Finally, the interviewer smiled, stood, and took my hand again; and I | 64 | 38

realized the contest was over. she offered me a job. We both had won! | 69 | 41

Section **15** | **Preparing for measurement** | Lessons 70-72

128

149b, continued

Problem 3
Invoice (LM p. 195)

Prepare on an invoice form the invoice given at the right.

words

		DATE	Current	3
SOLD TO	The Sports Shop			6
	735 Alexandria Drive	OUR ORDER NO.	SW86127	10
	Macon, GA 31210-3567			16
		CUST. ORDER NO.	3570	17
TERMS	2/10, n/30	SHIPPED VIA	Bulldog Express	22

QUANTITY	DESCRIPTION	UNIT PRICE	TOTAL	
24	Champ I racquetball racquet	74.99	1,799.76	30
10	Champ II racquetball	46.75	467.50	38
12	Racquetball bag	21.42	257.04	44
6	Tetherball set	26.49	158.94	49
24	Champ I soccerball	19.25	462.00	55
12	Badminton set	33.90	406.80	60
24	Champ I tennis racquet	94.50	2,268.00	69
			5,820.04	71
	Sales tax		291.00	76
			6,111.04	78

Problem 4
Four-column table

full sheet; DS; exact vertical center; 6 spaces between columns

SCHEDULE OF EXPENDITURES FOR 19--   7

(City Manager's Office)   12

Code	Account Classification	Expended	Budgeted	
101	Salaries	$46,680	$51,480	45
210	Printing and Binding	1,597	2,400	52
211	Postage	238	400	55
212	Office Supplies	1,269	2,000	61
214	Memberships and Dues	726	950	67
215	Professional Development	1,584	1,900	74
217	Automobile Expenses	1,111	1,000	80
218	Depreciation Expense	1,508	1,510	87
221	Telephone	738	850	91
226	Maintenance and Contracts	1,843	750	101
	Total	$57,294	$63,240	105

70c ▶ 31
Review letters

2 letterheads, 1 Monarch sheet [LM pp. 73-77]; 1 large, 1 small, 1 Monarch envelope; carbon paper, copy sheet

Format and type Problems 1, 2, and 3 for 26 minutes as in-structed below; begin each letter on Line 15; circle errors; compute *g–pram*.

Problem 1
business letter

block style; 60–space line; small envelope

March 26, 19-- | Mr. Charles Onehawk | 4570 Virginia Avenue, W. | Phoenix, AZ   14
85035-6231 | Dear Mr. Onehawk   20

(¶ 1) As a member of a select group of responsible people who have substantial   35
equity in their homes, you should know about our revolutionary new concept in   51
homeowner liquidity. Now you can have instant access to large amounts of cash   67
at low interest rates.   71

(¶ 2) Our EQUITY LOAN SERVICE can put $10,000 to $100,000 at your instant   85
disposal, for this line of credit lets you borrow up to 70 percent of the value of   101
your home at less than current market rates.   111

(¶ 3) Once your loan application is approved, you'll receive a personalized   125
checkbook that you can use to write your own loans; you won't even have to go to   141
the bank.   143

(¶ 4) I invite you to apply for the EQUITY LOAN SERVICE by returning the en-   157
closed application blank. Do it now and put your idle assets to work for you.   172

Sincerely | Amy E. Wilkes | President | xx | Enclosure   182/**195**

Problem 2
business letter

modified–block style; 60–space line; large envelope

August 30, 19-- | Ms. Barbara B. Brahms | 2457 Washington Avenue | Columbus,   14
GA 31906-4226 | Dear Ms. Brahms   20

(¶ 1) Your letter asking for my comments about "easy loan plans" came this   34
morning. I hope the following information is helpful as you write your paper.   50
Quote from this letter as you wish.   58

(¶ 2) It is a well-accepted fact that our economy thrives on credit. Credit replaces   74
cash and adds to purchasing power, but it leads to inflation if used heavily. Few   90
of us, however, could live the kind of lives we enjoy if it were not for credit.   107
Establishing and maintaining a healthy personal credit rating is beneficial to   122
each of us.   125

(¶ 3) Credit, however, must be used cautiously; for it enables us to satisfy   139
wants--and our wants are insatiable. Credit makes getting the things we want--   155
from a sink to a mink--easy; paying for them, an eventuality easily dismissed, is   171
not always easy.   175

(¶ 4) Have available as much credit as you need; use as little of it as you can. Your   191
credit rating will be healthier for it--and so will your pocketbook.   205

Sincerely yours | Andrew W. Mayhouse | President | xx   214/**228**

Problem 3
personal letter

block style; 50–space line; Monarch envelope

Reference pages

block style letters: 77, 78
modified–block
style letters: 83, 84
personal letters: 57, 58
Monarch/small
envelopes: 62
large envelopes: 81

---

45 Reed Avenue | Springfield, OH 45505-3971 | October 15, 19-- | Miss J. E.   14
Murgraff | 545 Saint Johns Lane | New York, NY 10013-2106 | Dear Janelle   28

(¶ 1) I have some great news. My company has asked me to be in New York on   42
November 10, 11, and 12 to attend a conference at the St. Regis Hotel. I shall be in   59
your town for three whole days.   66

(¶ 2) I am sure my evenings will be free while I am there; and I should very much   81
like to see a show, dine at some special place, and enjoy a very long chat with you.   98
Why don't you choose the evening(s), make the reservations, get the tickets--   114
whatever--and I'll reimburse you. This time it's my treat.   126

(¶ 3) Much has happened since I last saw you in July; we have a lot of real   140
catching up to do. Let me know if your schedule is clear or if it can be cleared for   157
these days in November.   162

Very sincerely | Lex Bynum   166/**179**

149a ▶ 5
Preparatory practice

each line 3 times SS (slowly, faster, slowly); DS between 3-line groups; repeat selected lines as time permits

alphabet	1	Joanne Quinn moved four young azalea plants next to the back sidewalk.
figure	2	We ordered 29 lamps, 36 tables, 15 mirrors, 48 rugs, and 705 ashtrays.
adjacent key	3	They were pleased the government responded quickly to help the people.
fluency	4	Did she blend the fuel with dye to make the flame visible at the lake?

| 1 | 2 | 3 | 4 | 5 | 6 | 7 | 8 | 9 | 10 | 11 | 12 | 13 | 14 |

149b ▶ 45
Measure production: tables and invoice

(LM p. 195 and full sheets)

Time schedule

Assembling materials .... 3'
Timed production .... 35'
Final check; compute
  n–pram .... 7'

1 Arrange supplies for easy handling.

2 When directed to begin, work for 35'. If you complete all four problems in less than 35', start over on plain paper.

3 Correct your errors neatly as you work.

4 Compute n–pram (see page 171).

Problem 1
Three-column table

full sheet; DS; reading position; 6 spaces between columns

words

BENEFITS COMPARISON FOR CATEGORY III EMPLOYEES			9

Type	Regional Average*	Company Average	
			23
Term life insurance	$ 3,000	$ 5,000	30
Disability (monthly)	528	550	35
Medical (maximum)	50,000	100,000	41
Dental (yearly maximum)	750	500	47
Retirement (yearly maximum)	4,800	5,000	54
Educational (yearly maximum)	500	500	61
Payment for vacation	500	575	66
Payment for holidays	450	525	71
			75
*Source: Regional Survey by Fred Walters.			83

Problem 2
Four-column table

full sheet; DS; reading position; 4 spaces between columns

PROPOSED SALARY CLASSIFICATION				6
(Category III Employees)				11

Grade	Number of Employees	Present Range	Proposed Range	
				31
17	6	4.60-6.60	6.00-7.00	36
16	8	4.27-6.50	5.65-6.65	41
15	12	4.52-6.28	5.30-6.30	46
14	34	4.01-5.40	4.95-5.95	51
13	108	3.80-5.09	4.60-5.60	56
12	76	3.45-5.01	4.25-5.25	61
11	69	3.35-4.70	3.90-4.90	66
10	2	3.35-4.25	3.55-4.55	71

Problems 3 and 4 are on the next page.

71a ▶ 5
Preparatory practice

each line 3 times SS
(work for errorless
lines); DS between
3-line groups

alphabet 1 The value of a quality work-experience program has just been realized.

figures 2 Will my summary report on Senate Bill 7635-48 be due the 19th or 20th?

one hand 3 In my opinion, a few plum trees on a hilly acre create no vast estate.

easy 4 The men at the dock may wish to shape the rock in the form of a whale.

| 1 | 2 | 3 | 4 | 5 | 6 | 7 | 8 | 9 | 10 | 11 | 12 | 13 | 14 |

71b ▶ 8
Improve keystroking control

each line twice SS;
proofread and circle
errors before typing
the next line; DS be-
tween 2-line groups
Type at a steady rate;
concentrate on the copy.

1st row 1 Uncle Xavier mines zinc, cobalt, and silver on vacant land in Bavaria.

2d row 2 As she dashed to Dad's lake last fall, Sarah had half a glass of soda.

3d row 3 Terrie, try to work quietly if you operate our out-of-date typewriter.

4th row 4 A 4-act play, to be given June 17, 26, and 30, will begin at 8:59 p.m.

fingers 1/2 5 Trudy knew by her voice that Martha had broken the hush of the jungle.

fingers 3/4 6 Polly was puzzled by six quaint wax dolls in an antique dealer's shop.

| 1 | 2 | 3 | 4 | 5 | 6 | 7 | 8 | 9 | 10 | 11 | 12 | 13 | 14 |

71c ▶ 12
Improve basic skill: statistical copy

three 3' writings

Proofread carefully; circle errors.

Goal: at least 28 *gwam* with fewer than 6 errors.

Difficulty index

	A	1.5 si	5.7 awl	80% hfw
all letters used				

gwam 3' | 5'

According to a 1984 publication, our 50-state nation is a country　　4　3
of interesting extremes. First of all, it is a nation of considerable　　9　5
size, including within its borders approximately 3,623,537 square miles　14　8
of land and water. Its largest state, Alaska, alone extends across a　19　11
territory of 491,004 square miles, while its smallest, Rhode Island,　23　14
has an area of just 1,212 square miles. The lowest town in the country　28　17
is Calipatria, California, which is 184 feet below sea level. (Death　33　20
Valley, which is uninhabited, is 383 feet below sea level.) If, on the　37　22
other hand, we talk of high points, Mount McKinley must be mentioned;　42　25
it has a height of 20,320 feet. The rainiest place is an area in Hawaii　47　28
that has an annual average rainfall of 480 inches--1.315 inches a day.　52　31
The strongest surface wind occurred in New Hampshire, where a measure-　56　34
ment of 231 miles an hour is on record. The deepest well, for those who　61　37
might be interested in such a figure, is a gas well in Oklahoma that　66　40
goes down 31,441 feet.　67　41

gwam 3' | 1 | 2 | 3 | 4 | 5 |
5' | 1 | 2 | 3 |

148b ▶ 45
Measure production: administrative communications

(LM pp. 191–193 and plain full sheet)

Time schedule

Assembling materials ... 3'
Timed production ...... 35'
Final check; compute
n–pram .... 7'

1 Arrange supplies for easy handling.

2 When directed to begin, work for 35'. If you complete all three problems in less than 35', start over on plain paper.

3 Correct your errors neatly as you work.

4 Compute n–pram (as page 171).

Problem 1
Full-page memo (LM p. 191)

Prepare the memo given at the right.

Problem 2
Full-page memo

(plain full sheet)

Repeat the memo in Problem 1 on a plain full sheet, making the following changes:

1 Add **New Orleans** to enumerated Item No. 1.

2 Delete enumerated item No. 2.

3 Change Item No. 3 to Item No. 2. Total words: 206.

Problem 3
Message/reply memo

(LM p. 193)

Format the memo given at the right on a message/reply form.

	words
TO: Board Members	3
FROM: Elizabeth Hughes, President	9
DATE: Current	12
SUBJECT: Conference Site Selection	17

(¶ 1) The final decision on the site of next year's Youth Club Conference must be made within two weeks. I have reviewed suggestions that were submitted by members of the Youth Club. Our staff has also made suggestions for the site. The following information should be helpful in making our decision: — 32 / 47 / 62 / 77

1. Pittsburgh, Chicago, New York, and San Antonio have been eliminated from consideration because conferences have been held in those cities recently. — 92 / 107

2. New Orleans is still being considered even though we met there three years ago. New Orleans really appeals to the members. — 123 / 133

3. Jacksonville, St. Petersburg, and Newport News were suggested most frequently by the members. Waterfront Inns has an inn in each city and will give us reduced rates. — 149 / 163 / 168

(¶ 2) Please call me and let me know how you rank these cities. You may add other cities to the list if you wish to do so. Messages may be left with my secretary if I am out of the office at the time you call. I will let you know the site of next year's conference when we have made a decision. — 182 / 197 / 214 / 226

xx — 227

(Message for Problem 3) — words

TO Frank Lopez | Facilities Manager — 6 / 7

DATE Current — 10

SUBJECT Problems with Electronic Equipment — 15 / 17

MESSAGE (¶ 1) We experienced problems with most of our electronic equipment during the electrical storm we had last week. It was my understanding when we purchased superior wiring and placed the wires underground that this type of problem would not occur. — 21 / 28 / 34 / 41 / 47 / 54 / 61 / 65

(¶ 2) Please have one of our best-trained electrical supervisors check the wiring and report to me. — 71 / 78 / 84

SIGNED Alma Thomas, Vice President — 89

(Reply for Problem 3) — words

DATE Tomorrow's date

REPLY (¶ 1) The problems you experienced during the electrical storm last week are of great concern to us. Bob Bishop and I both checked the wiring today, and we located the cause of the problem. Water seepage caused a short in Transformer #2. — 92 / 96 / 102 / 109 / 117 / 125 / 132 / 139

(¶ 2) We are trying to work out solutions to the problem with the contractor who installed the wiring. As soon as we agree on the best solution, we will schedule the work and see that it is done properly. — 140 / 146 / 153 / 161 / 169 / 176

SIGNED Frank Lopez — 181

183/**189**

71d ▶ 25
Review reports
2 full sheets

Format and type the report at the right in appropriate report form for 20 minutes as directed in Problems 1 and 2 below; circle errors; compute *g–pram*.

Goal: 12 *g–pram* or more.

Problem 1

as first page of a report
margins:
  top: 1½″ (pica) 2″ (elite)
  sides: 1″
bottom: 1″

Problem 2

as second page of a report; omit main heading; subtract 5 from total word count

Reference pages:

reports: 96, 98
footnotes: 101
second page: 96, 98

words

THE CONSTANCY OF CHANGE — 5

A wise philosopher reflects in one of his books that "There is nothing new — 20 under the sun." Form may change, he tells us, but substance does not. Life — 35 consists of functions and rituals that are vital parts of living; once we accept the — 52 inevitability of these constants, there is, indeed, nothing new under the sun. — 68

Changes! Will they never stop? Is there nothing constant we — 81 can count on in this world? To the many who are currently asking — 94 such plaintive questions, the answer is no; change is the only thing — 108 that is permanent.[1] — 112

Today, we do all those things that humans have historically done; this — 126 is the constancy of life. We have just learned to do them differently; and this is — 143 change. We do not change what we do; we change how we do. We tell time by — 159 glancing at our digital watches, not at the sun, a candle, a sundial, or an — 175 hourglass. — 177

Change occurs slowly, persistently. Each generation creates its quota — 191 of change--little enough to digest in its lifetime, big enough to revolutionize its — 208 way of life. The typewriter, telephone, automobile, airplane, radio, television, — 224 and computer are changes that truly exemplify the generations that created — 239 them. — 241

Change is not always beneficial, it does not always last, and it is not always — 257 easy to accept; but it is always taking place. The well-adjusted person expects — 273 change, tries it, and adopts from it what seems to serve her or him best in the — 289 pursuit of a "way of life." By the way, what are your thoughts about a home — 305 robot? — 306

— 310

[1] "The Pressures of Change," The Royal Bank Letter, The Royal — 322 Bank of Canada 63 (July/August 1982), p. 1. — 331

147c ▶ 30
Measure production: business letters

(LM pp. 185–189)

Time schedule

Assembling materials ...	3'
Timed production	20'
Final check; compute n–pram	7'

1 Arrange supplies for easy handling.

2 When directed to begin, work for 20'. If you complete all three problems in less than 20', start over on plain paper.

3 Correct your errors neatly as you work.

4 Address envelopes.

5 Compute n–pram (see page 171).

Problem 1
Block style letter

open punctuation

Problem 2
Modified block style letter

mixed punctuation; indented ¶s

Problem 3
Block style letter

Prepare the letter in Problem 2 a second time in block style, open punctuation. Substitute in the appropriate places the information given at the right.

Current date | Mrs. A. W. Marshall | Route 1, Box 258 | Moreauville, LA 71355-5478 | Dear Mrs. Marshall · · · 15 / 20

(¶ 1) Thank you for attending the Klienwood Community Council meeting. We were pleased with the participation of so many citizens. · · · 34 / 45

(¶ 2) The public hearing was held to assure to all of our citizens the right to make their wishes known to the Council. The proposed zoning regulations to upgrade the 200 block of Broad Street from B3 to 04 will affect many people, and we want to consider all of the issues carefully before making a decision. · · · 61 / 77 / 92 / 106

(¶ 3) As you know, the comments ranged from strongly in favor of the regulations to strongly against them. We will review all comments to determine what is in the best interest of the community. (122) · · · 119 / 134 / 143

Sincerely | C. Ralph Walker | Secretary | xx · · · 151

Current date | Mr. Gregg White | 126 Pleasant Street | Claremont, NH 03743-3256 | Dear Mr. White · · · 15 / 18

(¶ 1) This letter is to notify you that your automobile, Serial Number 3X7R9M4720561, must be taken to one of our authorized dealers for an inspection of the safety system. · · · 31 / 46 / 51

(¶ 2) We have reason to believe that part of the safety system is not our standard equipment. If standard equipment was not used in the manufacturing process, it is our responsibility to change it. Any repair or replacement of equipment by an authorized dealer will be completed at our expense. · · · 66 / 81 / 99 / 110

(¶ 3) Please accept our apology for this factory error. Our authorized dealer in your area will do the work at your convenience. (114) · · · 125 / 134

Sincerely | Ms. Deborah Burge | Customer Care Manager | xx · · · 145

Current date | Miss Sharon Long | Box 257C, Roberts Hill Road | Rye Beach, NH 03871-5386 | Dear Miss Long · · · 15 / 20

Serial Number 6K85T2B951403 · · · total words 147

148a ▶ 5
Preparatory practice

each line 3 times SS (slowly, faster, slowly); DS between 3-line groups; repeat selected lines as time permits

alphabet	1	Zed believes the quarterback was injured long before the complex play.
fig/sym	2	My $762.59 check (No. 304-8) for the June 1 dinner for 25 is enclosed.
direct reach	3	My great uncle and my great aunt brought us both nice and funny gifts.
fluency	4	Did Jane rub the clay to shape it, or did she make the bowl in a form?

| 1 | 2 | 3 | 4 | 5 | 6 | 7 | 8 | 9 | 10 | 11 | 12 | 13 | 14 |

72a ▶ 5
Preparatory practice

each line 3 times SS (work for errorless lines); DS between 3-line groups; repeat selected lines as time permits

alphabet 1 We have quizzed Joy about a family with whom she is expecting to work.
figures 2 Our store has three locations: 36040 Grand; 6275 Maywood; 1890 Olive.
3d row 3 Perry, you were to type quietly the two erudite reports that were due.
easy 4 He may make a profit on corn, rye, yams, and hay if he works the land.

| 1 | 2 | 3 | 4 | 5 | 6 | 7 | 8 | 9 | 10 | 11 | 12 | 13 | 14 |

72b ▶ 8
Improve keystroking control

each line twice SS; proofread and circle errors before typing the next line; DS between 2-line groups; repeat selected lines as time permits

direct reaches 1 My brother, Mervyn, has my army carbines; Bernice has my breechloader.
adjacent reaches 2 Three guides loped in a column as we stalked over trails after a lion.
double letters 3 Lynn will see that Jill accepts an assignment in the office next week.
long words 4 Governmental departments encourage associations to photocopy booklets.
shift 5 In May, Don, Sonia, and Jason Halls left for Italy, Spain, and Turkey.
quotation marks 6 "Have 'sunglow' all winter," I typed, "with the all-new Polk sunlamp."

| 1 | 2 | 3 | 4 | 5 | 6 | 7 | 8 | 9 | 10 | 11 | 12 | 13 | 14 |

72c ▶ 12
Improve basic skill: straight copy

two 5' writings; proofread carefully; circle errors; compute *g-pram*

Goal: at least 29 *gwam* with fewer than 6 errors.

Difficulty index

| all letters used | A | 1.5 si | 5.7 awl | 80% hfw |

gwam 3' | 5'

I'm a prospective employee. I want to work; indeed, for various   4 | 3
practical reasons, I need to work. I want a job that provides me with   9 | 5
opportunities to earn sufficient income to live a comfortable life.   13 | 8
I want a chance for promotion as quickly as possible. I want to realize   19 | 11
what I believe is my potential for success. Probably of most signifi-   23 | 14
cance, I want a job that I will enjoy doing; I cannot spend a lifetime   28 | 17
dreading Monday mornings.   30 | 18

I'm a prospective employer, but I'm reluctant to hire just one more   34 | 20
worker. I want a team member. I expect to pay well, but I also expect   39 | 23
something in return. I want a person who is promotable and who will   44 | 26
dazzle me to get it. Probably of most significance, I want an employee   48 | 29
who does not add to my absenteeism problems, who takes pride in the   53 | 32
quality of individual output, and who associates personal achievement   58 | 35
with company growth.   59 | 36

gwam 3' | 1 | 2 | 3 | 4 | 5 |
      5' | 1 | 2 | 3 |

Measurement goals

1 To demonstrate your best straight–copy keyboarding skill.

2 To demonstrate your best skill in formatting communications, in–cluding letters, memos, tables, forms, and reports.

Machine adjustments

1 Paper guide at 0.

2 Margins: 70–space line for ¶ writ–ings; as directed for problems.

3 DS ¶ writings; as directed for problems.

4 Indention: 5 spaces for ¶ writ–ings; as appropriate for problems.

147a ▶ 5
Preparatory practice

each line 3 times SS (slowly, faster, slowly); DS between 3-line groups; repeat selected lines as time permits

alphabet	1	Can we analyze the next problem quickly and just give a frank opinion?
figure	2	Please request 2,675 copies of Form 8139 and 1,500 copies of Form 462.
outside reach	3	Vasquez was at a park and was puzzled by games he saw Maxwell playing.
fluency	4	Did she pay for the eight enamel emblems or for the six antique bowls?

| 1 | 2 | 3 | 4 | 5 | 6 | 7 | 8 | 9 | 10 | 11 | 12 | 13 | 14 |

147b ▶ 15
Inventory/build straight-copy skill

Two 5′ writings for accu–racy; circle errors; determine *gwam*.

Difficulty index

all letters used	A	1.5 si	5.7 awl	80% hfw

gwam 1′ 5′

	1′	5′
Retrieving records is more difficult than filing records. One	13	2	60
reason that records are hard to locate is that they may be requested	27	5	63
under a number of different words or names. Workers who maintain man-	41	8	66
ual record systems often are told to label each file with adequate in-	55	11	69
formation to facilitate easy retrieval of the file. In some cases,	69	14	72
cross-references are placed on the file label. The idea seems to be	83	17	75
that the more data provided, the easier it will be to find the file	97	20	78
that has been ordered. Of course, many other procedures are used to	111	23	81
help locate records in manual record systems. Color codes, indexes,	125	26	84
cross-references, and a wide range of other techniques may be used to	139	29	87
assist the file worker.	144	30	88
Will the same techniques work in computerized records systems?	13	33	91
The idea of labeling the file with as much data as possible will not	27	36	94
work in many electronic filing systems. Most word processing systems	41	39	97
limit the field or amount of space that is available to label a record.	56	42	100
Some systems just assign a number to each record, and an index of all	70	45	103
records is kept. Almost all systems provide space for naming a docu-	84	48	106
ment; but, in many cases, the name can have only a limited number of	98	51	109
characters. In some systems, the number is eight. The procedure used	112	54	112
to shorten the name is called truncating. For example, quarterly may	126	57	115
be written as QTR.	130	58	116

gwam 1′ | 1 | 2 | 3 | 4 | 5 | 6 | 7 | 8 | 9 | 10 | 11 | 12 | 13 | 14 |
     5′ | 1 | 2 | 3 |

72d ▶ 25
Review tables and outlines

2 full sheets
1 half sheet

Format and type Problems 1, 2, and 3 for 20 minutes as directed below; compute *g–pram*.

Problem 1
table

half sheet (enter long side first); SS; 6–space intercolumns

Problem 2
outline

full sheet; 1½" top margin; 40–space line; add designation numerals and letters for each order; use correct capitalization and spacing

Problem 3
table

repeat Problem 1; full sheet; DS; reading position; 6–space intercolumns

Reference pages:

Centering
   Vertical: 116
   Horizontal: 116
   Columns: 118
Outlines: 95, 96

			words
BEAUX ARTS CONCERTS			4
Classical Series			7
Date	**Presentation**	**Hall**	16
October 1	Elton Kunter, violinist	Harvard Auditorium	27
October 25	Grieg Chamber Group	Harvard Auditorium	37
November 1	Los Angeles Ballet	Cluny Center	45
November 10	Alice Humphrey, pianist	Harvard Auditorium	56
November 16	Marta Ruiz, cellist	Cluny Center	65
February 4	Brett Luxward, tenor	Cluny Center	74
February 15	Minneapolis Players	Harvard Auditorium	84
March 8	John Lo, pianist	Cluny Center	92
March 25	Toledo Symphony	Cluny Center	100
April 4	Rose Kunzel, soprano	Harvard Auditorium	109

	words
COMPENSATION FOR EMPLOYMENT	6
forms of compensation	10
hourly wage	12
regular time	15
overtime	17
straight salary	20
piece rate	22
commission	24
bonus	26
combination	28
deduction from compensation	34
federal income tax	38
federal insurance contributions act	45
other	46
income tax	48
state	49
city	50
dues and assessments	55
health insurance	58
medical	60
dental	61
voluntary items	64

Measure communication skills

plain sheet; 70-space line; 1½″ top margin; DS copy

1 Read the ¶, noting typographical errors as well as corrections that must be made in capitalization, punctuation, word usage, grammar, and spelling.

2 Format and type the ¶; proofread; retype the ¶ if necessary.

lynn we are prepare to except your advise on the type of printer we should by for our model 10 supertron microcomputer. however before we precede with the perparation of the perchase order we want to make sure the printer will except lose sheets of stationary as well as continous roles of stationary. in edition its necessary for us to handle various waits of papers. we will not do nothing until we here from you. we hope that you can give us you response within the next to or three days because our personnell is eager to have the new electronic printer.

146d ▶ 15
Inventory/build statistical-copy skill

1 One 5′ writing on both ¶s combined to determine base rate; circle errors; determine *gwam*.

2 Two 3′ writings on both ¶s combined to build speed; circle errors; determine *gwam*.

Difficulty index

all letters/figures used	A	1.5 si	5.7 awl	80% hfw

	gwam 3′	5′
Developing fair and equitable expense policies for the 3,796 sales	4	3	60
representatives we employ is very hard to do. Over 85 percent of our	9	6	63
sales force drive more than 48,000 miles a year. The outlay for main-	14	9	66
taining a fleet of 4,215 cars is significant. About 74 percent of our	19	12	69
travel budget is consumed by automobile costs. The most equitable way	24	15	72
of paying automobile expenses for a very mobile sales force is to give	29	18	75
a company automobile to each person who drives at least 18,000 miles	34	21	78
a year for sales work and to pay for the operating costs. Represen-	38	24	81
tatives who drive 17,999 or fewer miles a year are paid 23 cents a mile	43	27	84
for driving their own vehicles.	45	28	85
Developing a fair way of paying for other travel expenses is more	49	31	88
difficult. The company must follow tax laws and must minimize costs.	54	34	91
About 46 percent of our representatives are away from home at least 12	59	37	94
nights a month. Hotel costs range from $30 to $175 a night. Actual	64	40	97
hotel costs are paid, but a valid receipt must accompany the expense	69	43	100
report. If the charge exceeds $79 per night, it must be approved by a	74	46	103
sales manager. Meal costs vary widely. A typical lunch in a large	79	49	106
city may be $7.25 with the gratuity. The same lunch in a small town	84	52	109
may be only $3.85 with the gratuity. Representatives will be asked to	89	55	112
justify excessive meal and entertainment costs.	92	57	114

gwam 3′ | 1 | 2 | 3 | 4 | 5 |
5′ | 1 | 2 | 3 |

Measurement goals

1 To demonstrate ability to type at acceptable levels average–difficulty writings in straight, rough–draft, and statistical copy for 3' and 5'.

2 To demonstrate ability to type letters, tables, and reports in proper format from semi–arranged copy, according to specific direc–tions.

Machine adjustments

1 Check chair and desk adjust–ment and placement of copy for ease of reading.

2 Set ribbon control to type on upper half of ribbon.

3 Set paper guide at 0.

4 Set 70–space line.

Materials. Letterheads, full, half, Monarch, and copy sheets; large, small, and Monarch envelopes.

73a ▶ 5
Preparatory practice

each line 3 times SS (slowly, faster, slowly); DS between 3-line groups; repeat selected lines as time permits

alphabet 1 Jack is becoming acquainted with an expert on Venezuelan family names.

fig/sym 2 Our #38065 pens will cost Knox & Brady $12.97 each (less 4% discount).

direct reaches 3 June obtained unusual services from a number of celebrated decorators.

easy 4 It is a problem; she may sue the city for a title to the antique auto.

| 1 | 2 | 3 | 4 | 5 | 6 | 7 | 8 | 9 | 10 | 11 | 12 | 13 | 14 |

73b ▶ 11
Measure skill growth: straight copy

a 3' and a 5' writing; determine *gwam*

Difficulty Index

all letters used | A | 1.5 si | 5.7 awl | 80% hfw

gwam 3' | 5'

Clothes do not "make the person." Agree? Still, clothes form an | 4 | 3

integral part of impressions we have of others. Whenever we first meet | 9 | 6

people, for example, we quickly look them over (and they us), and we | 14 | 8

mentally categorize each other. Inexpert as these conclusions may be, | 19 | 11

we all justify them in our own minds on the basis that clothing is the | 23 | 14

only evidence of personality we have. | 26 | 16

Clothes are, of course, quite practical; we need them for modesty | 30 | 18

purposes and to protect us from the hazards of extreme weather. Yet, | 35 | 21

clothes are also decorative; they should, beyond just looking nice, | 40 | 24

reflect a personality, a mood, and a natural coloring--but not a finan- | 44 | 27

cial status. Clothes should be part of a picture--a picture of a per- | 49 | 29

son--and the person should be the central part of the picture. | 53 | 32

Clothes do serve a purpose. They always make a direct statement | 57 | 34

about a person; so they should be suitable, and they should be fresh. | 62 | 37

High style (but not quality) is out for usual business occasions, as | 68 | 40

is excessive jewelry and tantalizing scents. A good mirror and a bit | 71 | 43

of common sense can indicate to a person what clothes are appropriate. | 76 | 46

gwam 3' | 1 | 2 | 3 | 4 | 5 |
5' | 1 | 2 | 3 |

146a ▶ 5
Preparatory practice

each line 3 times SS (slowly, faster, slowly); DS between 3-line groups; repeat selected lines as time permits

alphabet 1 Quincy will visit Kalamazoo next week to be the judge for the parades.

figure 2 She bought a Model 2430A, but it cost $1,963.27 more than Model 9582X.

shift lock 3 Why did they learn COBOL and FORTRAN before learning BASIC and PASCAL?

fluency 4 Did their auditor fight for the right to sign an amendment to the bid?

| 1 | 2 | 3 | 4 | 5 | 6 | 7 | 8 | 9 | 10 | 11 | 12 | 13 | 14 |

146b ▶ 15
Inventory/build straight-copy skill

1 One 5' writing on both ¶s combined to determine base rate; circle errors; determine *gwam*.

2 Two 3' writings on both ¶s combined to build speed; circle errors; determine *gwam*.

Difficulty index

all letters used | A | 1.5 si | 5.7 awl | 80% hfw

	gwam 3'	5'
Power is a fascinating concept. Power is simply the ability to	4	2	60
act or to get others to act. Many people define power as using one's	9	5	63
position to exploit or to manipulate others. Power can be used to	13	8	66
exploit or to manipulate, but that view of power is somewhat narrow.	18	11	69
Each person in an organization has or can acquire power. The amount	23	14	72
of power and the source of that power will vary widely. Persons in	27	17	75
positions of high rank and persons who perform jobs that make signifi-	32	20	78
cant contributions to the profits of a company are said to be in "power"	37	23	81
positions.	38	24	82

Anyone who has the ability to reward or to punish a worker has power over that worker. A supervisor who can fire a person, give a raise, or take action that affects an employee has power. Knowledge can also generate power. A person who has information that other people require is said to have expert power. Patients follow the advice of a physician because they believe the physician is an expert in a particular field. The person who possesses qualities that people admire or want to imitate has a type of power that is called referent power. Perhaps the strongest power is the ability to convince others that what they do can have a significant impact on others. The famous quotation, "Ask not what your country can do for you, but what you can do for your country," is an illustration of this charismatic type of power.

gwam 3' | 1 | 2 | 3 | 4 | 5 |
5' | 1 | 2 | 3 |

73c ▶ 34
Measure skill application: letters

Time schedule

Assembling materials .... 3'
Timed production .... 25'
Final check; compute
g–pram .... 6'

Materials needed

Letterheads and Monarch sheet [LM pp. 87–91]; copy sheet; carbon paper; large, small, and Monarch envelopes

Format and type as many problems as you can in 25'. Type Problem 1 again if you finish Problem 3 before time has been called. Proofread all problems; circle errors.

Problem 1
Business letter (letterhead)

block style, 1 carbon copy, large envelope; 60–space line; begin on Line 15

Problem 2
Business letter (letterhead)

modified–block style, small envelope; 60–space line; begin on Line 15

Problem 3
Personal letter (Monarch sheet)

modified–block style; Monarch envelope; 50–space line; begin on Line 15

words

June 9, 19-- | Ms. Debra V. Wynn | 80005 Grand Central Pkwy. | Jamaica, NY | 14
11435-6071 | Dear Ms. Wynn | 19

(¶ 1) Word power! It's important to most people. It's absolutely indispensable 34
to a businessperson like you. Word power commands recognition; it smooths 49
the way to promotion and higher salary; and it brings much personal satisfac- 64
tion. 65

(¶ 2) Vocabulary is a good place to start, of course; but knowing how to choose 80
words, pronounce and spell them, and fit them together to make meaningful 95
sentences is the added knowledge that makes vocabulary work. This is word 110
power. And it can take a lifetime to achieve it. 120

(¶ 3) SPEAK OUT by Guy Hunter brings you a shortcut to word power. This 133
175-page book will help you to build your word power and give you confidence 148
to put your thoughts and ideas to work for you. Your copy of SPEAK OUT is on 164
our "save shelf." You can pick it up at your convenience. It's only $17.95. 180

Sincerely | Cesar J. Strongbow | Manager | xx   188/201

October 28, 19-- | Mrs. L. L. Sangtry, President | United Casings, Inc. | 1600 14
Kirby Street, W. | Shreveport, LA 71103-4923 | Dear Mrs. Sangtry 27

(¶ 1) Last Tuesday afternoon, a shipment of rubber casings from your company 41
arrived at our receiving dock. It had been rushed to us as requested, and we 57
were grateful. 60

(¶ 2) We were not so grateful when we discovered that the shipment was not 74
complete, and I telephoned your sales staff to tell them so. The young lady who 90
answered the telephone listened patiently while I exploded in her ear. Then she 106
went to work. 109

(¶ 3) She asked exactly what was missing and what was happening to our pro- 123
duction schedule. She apologized for the mistake and promised to rush the 138
missing casings to us. I bid her a very doubtful goodbye. 150

(¶ 4) The parts arrived this morning, just 36 hours after I called. 162

(¶ 5) Mrs. Sangtry, I am impressed with the way your firm handled this very 176
serious problem. To have an error handled promptly and courteously was a 191
pleasant surprise. We shall order from you again. 201

Sincerely yours | Ms. Phyllis E. Trerrett | Purchasing Director | xx   214/234

---

543 El Caprice Avenue | Hollywood, CA 91605-7168 | August 19, 19-- | Miss Felicia 15
Wymore | 278 Fryman Place | Hollywood, CA 91604-4811 | Dear Felicia | 28

(¶ 1) You asked me to write to you about the interviews and tests I took at 42
the Brewer Publishing Company. I spent most of yesterday morning in the 57
company's personnel office. The tests were intensive--mostly keyboarding, 72
composing, editing, spelling, grammar, and vocabulary. 83

(¶ 2) The interviewer asked about my in-school and out-of-school activities, 97
what magazines I regularly read, and what books I had read recently. We also 113
discussed current events. 118

(¶ 3) Frankly, Felicia, I am excited about the prospects of working for Brewer. 133
I'll let you know when I have more news. Thanks for your encouragement. 148

Yours sincerely | Steve Merrewether   151/176

145c ▶ 15
Measure communication skills

plain sheet; 70-space line; 1½"
top margin; DS

1 Correct spelling and typographical errors as you keyboard.

2 As your teacher reads the paragraph correctly, note any corrections you must make; if necessary,
repeat the paragraph, correcting
all errors.

The standard turnaround time for our word processing center is one
day, but we try to accomodate rush jobs. A principle submitting work should
complete a seperate from to indicate that the word needs to be given prioritie.
On many occasions, our turnaround time has been less then fourty-five minutes
on short documents. Of coarse, we prefer to have adequate time to proofread
hour work carefully.

145d ▶ 15
Build/measure rough-draft skill

1 Two 1' writings on each
¶ for speed; circle errors;
determine *gwam*.

2 One 5' writing for control on all ¶s combined;
circle errors; determine
gwam.

Difficulty index

all letters used	A	1.5 si	5.7 awl	80% hfw

gwam 1' | 5'

Do you thing of yourself as a negotiator? Most people do not. Most
people think of negotiation as a process that is often used
only to resolve major conflict such as labor problems, political issues, and salary matters. The truth is that each person negotiates dozens of situations every day of the year. Each
time you try to gain something that you want from somebody else,
you negotiate.

You cannot negotiate with an other person unless you and the
other person both have something to gain and something to
lose. Why bother to negotiate if you can not gain something you
want? Why modify your position if it satisfies you and you have
nothing to lose by maintaining it? What each individual wants is to
satisfy his or her own needs. The key question is whether both individuals can meet their needs. Most, but not all people, enter
a negotiation expecting to win. You are
more likely to win if the other person also wins. just because one individual wins doesnot mean the other individual loses.
The important thing is to discover what the other person
really wants and assist that individual to get it so that at the
same time you can get what you really desire. This approach to negotiating is called
"win-win" strategy.

1'	5'
14	3	48
25	5	50
37	7	52
49	9	54
62	11	56
76	13	58
78	14	59
12	16	61
24	18	63
37	20	65
50	22	67
64	25	70
78	28	73
82	29	74
15	32	77
27	34	79
41	37	82
52	39	84
65	41	86
82	44	89
86	45	90

74a ▶ 5
Preparatory practice

each line 3 times SS (work for smooth, continuous rhythm); DS between 3-line groups; repeat selected lines as time permits

alphabet	1	Max queried Parker about having a jewel box for the many huge zircons.
figures	2	Are those last-minute reports on Bill 3657-84 due on October 19 or 20?
shift/lock	3	Ping-ying Fu typed the notations REGISTERED and CERTIFIED in ALL CAPS.
easy	4	The auditor may laugh, but the penalty for such chaotic work is rigid.

| 1 | 2 | 3 | 4 | 5 | 6 | 7 | 8 | 9 | 10 | 11 | 12 | 13 | 14 |

74b ▶ 11
Measure skill growth: statistical copy

a 3' and a 5' writing; determine *gwam*

Difficulty index

all letters used | A | 1.5 si | 5.7 awl | 80% hfw

gwam 3' | 5'

	3'	5'
According to a special report of NEWSWEEK (January 17, 1983), the	4	3
makeup of the American work force is making some sharp adjustments.	9	5
Extracting data from the 1980 census, NEWSWEEK says that the median age	14	8
of workers dropped from 39 in 1970 to 34 in 1981. Quite a large number	19	11
of women have entered the force--67 percent of women between the ages	23	14
of 18 and 34 are working. In fact, a total of 46.8 million women--an	28	17
amazing 52 percent of the female population--work.	31	19
Fewer men are now working, explains the magazine. Consequently,	36	21
their portion of the work force has come down since 1951 from 87.3 per-	40	24
cent to just 77 percent, due perhaps to better disability benefits and	45	27
early retirement. The departure of males begins at the age of 25 and	50	30
speeds up at the age of 45. Of males 65 and older, the portion has de-	55	33
clined from 44.6 percent in 1955 to 19.9 percent in 1981.	58	35
The magazine also quotes some extraordinary figures about the	62	37
situation of males and females who are 75 years old and older and who	67	40
have continued to work. A total of 451,000 of them remained active in	72	43
the 1981 labor force, and the unemployment rate was just 2.8 percent.	77	46

gwam 3' | 1 | 2 | 3 | 4 | 5 |
5' | 1 | 2 | 3 |

74c ▶ 34
Measure skill application: reports

Time schedule

Assembling materials .... 3'
Timed production .... 25'
Final check; compute
  g-pram .... 6'

Materials needed

2 full sheets

When the signal to begin is given, insert paper and begin typing the problem on page 137, as directed. Type until the signal to stop is given. Begin the problem again if you finish before time is called. Proofread all problems; circle errors. Compute *g-pram*.

145a ▶ 5
Preparatory practice

each line 3 times SS (slowly, faster, slowly); DS between 3-line groups; repeat selected lines as time permits

alphabet	1 Alvarez might be back next week to join your friends for a quick trip.
figure	2 We will need 2,750 copies of Form 8436 and 12,500 copies of Form 6289.
shift key	3 Janice, Tommy, Pamela, and Marta left for La Paz, Bolivia, on Tuesday.
fluency	4 The neighbor may chant the ancient anthem at the chapel on the island.

| 1 | 2 | 3 | 4 | 5 | 6 | 7 | 8 | 9 | 10 | 11 | 12 | 13 | 14 |

145b ▶ 15
Measure/compare progressive straight-copy skill

1 Three 1' writings on ¶1. Use the highest rate as the base rate for the next writings.
2 Three 1' writings on ¶2. Try to equal or exceed the base rate established on ¶1.
3 One 5' writing on both ¶s. Try to maintain the ¶1 base rate on both ¶s.

¶1 Difficulty index — all letters used — E | 1.2 si | 5.1 awl | 90% hfw

¶2 Difficulty index — HA | 1.7 si | 6.0 awl | 75% hfw

gwam 1' | 5'

The robot is often thought of as an aid for blue-collar workers, but it is a key aid for white-collar workers, too. The robot is, in a number of cases, being used to do the work that at one time was done by people. What types of work can be done by robots? No one can give the answer to that question because new ways to use robots are being found each day. The use of robots is having a big impact on many different types of industries. One example is the machine tool industry. Machine tools are not tools as most people think of them, but are machines that make parts for other machines. Many of the machine tools that are used today run with little or no help from people. They take their orders from computers.

Initially, robots were developed to do hazardous and boring jobs that did not appeal to workers. Today, robots are being programmed to do a wide variety of tasks. When a task done by a robot is no longer necessary, the robot can be reprogrammed to do other tasks that may be drastically different. In a number of industrial operations, robots are taking certain types of jobs away from workers because robots are more productive and more cost effective. On the other hand, the use of robots is creating a number of new jobs. Technicians are needed to program and to maintain these computerized industrial "workers." Training programs in robotics are critical in filling these new jobs.

gwam 1' | 1 | 2 | 3 | 4 | 5 | 6 | 7 | 8 | 9 | 10 | 11 | 12 | 13 | 14 |
5' | 1 | 2 | 3 |

Format and type the prob–
lem as a 2–page report.
Center the heading; use a
1½″ (pica) or 2″ (elite) top
margin; 1″ side and bot–
tom margins.

BUSINESSPEOPLE WITH A SENSE OF HUMOR?

8

Is there a place in the hurly-burly world of business for humor? Some   22

businesspeople--perhaps even some successful executives--seem to believe not.   38

Business is a very serious undertaking, they say; and there is not much time to   54

be lighthearted about it. Smiles are all right, but only on the way to the bank.   70

On the other hand, Businesspeople With a Sense of Humor--BWSH we   83

can call them--disagree. They say that the best recipe for business success   99

calls for equal parts of dedication and humor.   108

The BWSH know that business does not thrive on a devil-may-care   121

attitude; they know that it does not thrive on melancholy either. For them, a   137

sense of humor creates a "middle" attitude that tells them how to be con-   151

cerned and smile at the same time.   158

The BWSH are champions of the smile. They know that regardless of how   173

critical things become, a smile helps to ease pain and pressure. A millisecond of   189

life is lived only once, they say; and it can be relived only in retrospect. Nothing   206

will change those spent milliseconds, so the BWSH try to be as positive about   222

the disastrous milliseconds as they are about the more fortuitous ones.   236

A sense of humor is what gets BWSH through such calamities as the   250

last-minute Christmas rush, the over-order for 100 mechanized dolls, and the   265

front door that can't be unlocked on the day of the Big Sale. These problems   280

are truly not laughing matters, but how they are viewed determines how they   206

will be handled. With typical good humor, the BWSH keep business moving   310

positively ahead and on the right track.   319

The BWSH know also that a sense of humor helps build their ability   332

to communicate. To paraphrase a daily newspaper item,   343

If a business executive can speak to people with a little   355
warmth and humor, then those people will be more responsive   367
in listening. If they're paying attention to hear what the speaker   381
says next, he or she will have a better chance to communicate   393
effectively.*   396

Businesspeople With a Sense of Humor? Why not? Why not, indeed?   409

413

* Detroit Free Press, May 22, 1983, p. 3b.   421

Measure communication skills

plain sheet; 70-space line, 1½"
top margin; DS

1 Correct errors in word usage
and grammar as you keyboard.

2 As your teacher reads the paragraph correctly, note any corrections you must make; if necessary,
repeat the paragraph, correcting
all errors.

Default standards are basic format characteristics that are preprogrammed on a word processing system. Default standards specifies the conditions
that apply unless the operator change them. The effect of default standards is
to save a operator from having to set margin, tab stops, and other parameter
each time a document is prepare. Some firms even adopt there style guides to
conform to the default standards of there word processing equipment.

144d ▶ 15
**Build/measure
script-copy skill**

1 Two 1' writings on
each ¶ for speed;
circle errors; deter-
mine *gwam*.

2 One 5' control writing on all ¶s com-
bined; circle errors;
determine *gwam*.

Difficulty index

all letters used	A	1.5 si	5.7 awl	80% hfw

gwam 1' | 5'

¶ Most men and women in executive positions accept travel as   12 | 2 | 43
a part of corporate life. At the same time, executives try to keep   26 | 5 | 46
time spent on the road to a minimum. Top management usually   38 | 7 | 48
supports the efforts to reduce travel time as long as effective-   51 | 9 | 50
ness is not jeopardized. One of the reasons for this support is   64 | 11 | 52
that it is quite expensive for executives to travel. Other   76 | 13 | 54
reasons are that traveling can be tiring and frequently   87 | 15 | 56
causes stress.   90 | 16 | 57

¶ One suggestion to reduce travel is to find alternatives that   12 | 18 | 59
will accomplish the objectives of the outing so that no one   24 | 20 | 61
has to leave the office. In some instances, a letter or telephone   37 | 23 | 64
call may be appropriate; but a letter or telephone message may   50 | 25 | 66
not be effectual in many situations. It is much easier to   62 | 27 | 68
communicate when you can see the person with whom you are   74 | 29 | 70
talking.   76 | 30 | 71

¶ The technology that is on the market today makes it   10 | 32 | 73
feasible for executives to hold meetings with people in   21 | 34 | 75
other sections of the state or country without leaving the   33 | 36 | 77
office. Teleconferencing with two-way video enables mem-   44 | 38 | 79
bers of a group to see and hear each other even though   55 | 40 | 81
they may be great distances apart.   62 | 41 | 82

75a ▶ 5
Preparatory practice

each line 3 times SS (work for smooth, continuous rhythm); DS between 3-line groups; repeat selected lines as time permits

alphabet	1	Meg was not packed to fly to Zanesville to inquire about her next job.
figures	2	Dial 649-4718 or 469-5709 to obtain your copy of this 32-page booklet.
long words	3	Buyers are ordinarily knowledgeable about performance characteristics.
easy	4	Due to the rigor of the quake, the city may dismantle the old chapels.

| 1 | 2 | 3 | 4 | 5 | 6 | 7 | 8 | 9 | 10 | 11 | 12 | 13 | 14 |

75b ▶ 11
Measure skill growth: rough-draft copy

a 3' and a 5' writing; determine *gwam*

Difficulty index

all letters used	A	1.5 si	5.7 awl	80% hfw

gwam 3' | 5'

A lot of people (surprisingly,) measure job potential primarily no ... 4 | 3
the basis of the size of the pay check involved. it would be foolish ... 9 | 5
to argue that money should not play an essential part in job selection and ... 14 | 8
career planning, but money alone is not an accurate test to use ... 18 | 11
when considering a possible career or looking for that first job. ... 23 | 14
There is a very subtle difference in philosophy between the person who ... 27 | 16
is "hunting for a job" and another who is "beginning a career". These ... 32 | 19
position itself, however, is not central to this discussion. Rather ... 36 | 22
the divergence lies in the approach to the job by each applicant. One ... 41 | 25
is attracted by what the job brings; the other, by what it takes ... 45 | 27
we must acknowledge that everybody, or almost everybody, is required ... 50 | 30
to work to purchase the necessities of life; money is essential to that ... 55 | 33
extent. but when we calculate that we will each spend a third of our life- ... 60 | 36
times preforming that work, it follows that whatever we do should be ... 64 | 39
enjoyable, allowing us to make a contribution and help us grow. ... 68 | 41

75c ▶ 34
Measure skill application: tables and outlines

Time schedule

Assembling materials .... 3'
Timed production .... 25'
Final check; compute
  g-pram .... 6'

Materials needed

half sheet; 2 full sheets
When the signal to begin is given, insert the paper and begin typing Problem 1 as directed. Type the problems in sequence until the signal to stop is given.

Type Problem 1 again if you finish before time is called. Proofread all problems; circle errors. Compute *g-pram*.

Learning goals

1 To increase basic skill on straight, script, rough–draft, and statistical copy.
2 To improve proofreading skills.
3 To improve composition and grammar application skills.

Machine adjustments

1 Paper guide at 0.
2 Margins: 70–space line for drills and ¶s; as directed for com–munication skill problems.
3 SS line drills; DS ¶s; as directed for communication skill problems.

144a ▶ 5
Preparatory practice

each line 3 times SS (slowly, faster, slowly); DS between 3-line groups; repeat selected lines as time permits

alphabet	1	Leonor asked how we can justify the very expensive but equitable plan.
figure	2	I added $93.62 tax and $15.04 shipping charges to the $1,872.43 total.
space bar	3	He did go to work on the bus; and in the city, he did do the big jobs.
fluency	4	Dorman may go to the city with them, or he may go to the lake with us.

| 1 | 2 | 3 | 4 | 5 | 6 | 7 | 8 | 9 | 10 | 11 | 12 | 13 | 14 |

144b ▶ 15
Build/measure straight-copy skill

1 Two 1' writings on each ¶ for speed; circle errors; determine *gwam*.
2 One 5' control writing on all ¶s combined; circle errors; determine *gwam*.

Difficulty index

all letters used	A	1.5 si	5.7 awl	80% hfw

gwam 1' | 5'

Business, government, and industry spend huge sums of money each — 13 | 2 | 55
year to create and to maintain records. A major portion of the records — 27 | 5 | 58
are kept in paper-based filing systems. Payment for time and for space — 41 | 8 | 61
accounts for the bulk of the cost of manual systems for storing records. — 56 | 11 | 64
Equipment, supplies, and overhead account for most of the remaining — 70 | 14 | 67
cost. The volume of paper to be filed seems to expand each year. — 83 | 16 | 69

Organizations concerned with the increase in the volume of paper to — 14 | 19 | 72
be filed and with the increase in the cost of keeping paper records are — 28 | 22 | 75
looking at automated systems as a solution to the problem. One system — 42 | 25 | 78
that is attracting a great deal of attention is electronic filing. Elec- — 56 | 28 | 81
tronic filing merges the use of a computer with the use of microfilm. — 70 | 31 | 84

The main advantage of using microfilm is that a large amount of — 13 | 34 | 87
space can be saved. Only a small portion of the space used for paper — 27 | 37 | 90
files is needed for files kept on microfilm. The main advantage of — 41 | 40 | 93
using the computer is that time can be saved. Manual systems require — 55 | 43 | 96
a great deal of time to sort, file, and find records. Electronic — 68 | 46 | 99
filing provides fast access to records. The combination of time saved — 82 | 49 | 102
and space saved makes electronic filing a good alternative for companies — 96 | 52 | 105
with large numbers of office workers. — 103 | 53 | 106

gwam 1' | 1 | 2 | 3 | 4 | 5 | 6 | 7 | 8 | 9 | 10 | 11 | 12 | 13 | 14 |
5' | 1 | | 2 | | 3 |

75c, continued

Problem 1

two-column table

half sheet (enter long side first)

Center and type SS the table in vertical and horizontal center; use a 10–space intercolumn.

words

LEADING AMERICAN MAGAZINES		5
In 1981		7
Magazine	Circulation	15
Reader's Digest	17,926,542	20
TV Guide	17,670,543	24
National Geographic Magazine	10,861,186	32
Better Homes & Gardens	8,059,717	39
Family Circle	7,427,979	44
Modern Maturity	7,309,035	49
Woman's Day	7,004,367	53
McCall's	6,266,090	59
Ladies' Home Journal	5,527,071	65
Good Housekeeping	5,425,790	71

Problem 2

three-column table

full sheet

Center and type DS the table in reading position; decide inter-column spacing.

EARLY AMERICAN COLLEGES			5
With Dates of Establishment			10
College	State	Year	15
Brown	Rhode Island	1764	20
Columbia	New York	1754	25
Harvard	Massachusetts	1636	30
Moravian	Pennsylvania	1742	36
Pennsylvania	Pennsylvania	1740	42
Princeton	New Jersey	1746	47
Rutgers	New Jersey	1766	52
William and Mary	Virginia	1693	58
Yale	Connecticut	1701	62

Problem 3

outline

full sheet

3″ top margin; 40–space line; add designation numerals and letters for each order; use correct capitalization and spacing

PLANTING LAWN GRASS | 4

clear the area | 8

    turn over and break up the soil | 15

        hand implements | 19

        power implements | 23

    remove old roots and stems | 29

    spread nutrients over area | 36

prepare the seedbed | 40

    level high and low places | 46

        drag | 48

        light roller | 52

    rake to loosen lumps and clods | 59

plant | 61

    sow seeds | 64

    add protective cover | 69

        straw | 71

        burlap | 73

    wet thoroughly to set seed | 79

143c, continued

Problem 3
Employee record
(LM p. 181)

Prepare the employee record given at the right.

Note: The information contained in this record can be requested after an employee has been hired but cannot be asked for on an application form.

The extra lines for the address and telephone number provide space for updating when an employee moves.

The position history section contains the employee's record with this company only. Information is added to the form as the employee moves to different positions within the company.

The termination record is completed when the employee leaves the company.

words

EMPLOYEE   RECORD

EMPLOYEE _Michi Nitobe_ SOCIAL SECURITY NUMBER _398-84-9085_

STREET _2213 R Street_ CITY _Ft. Smith_ 5

STATE _Arkansas_ ZIP _72904_ TELEPHONE _(501) 555-6453_ 9

STREET _____ CITY _____ 14

STATE _____ ZIP _____ TELEPHONE _____

DATE OF BIRTH _September 6, 1962_ SEX _Female_ U.S.A. CITIZEN _X_ OTHER (NAME) _____

MARITAL STATUS _Married_ SPOUSE _Robert Sumida_ NUMBER OF DEPENDENTS _0_ 19

IN EMERGENCY NOTIFY _Robert Sumida_ RELATIONSHIP _spouse_ 24

ADDRESS _same_ TELEPHONE _____ 28

EDUCATION: HIGH SCHOOL _Sterling Academy_ COLLEGE _Eastern Shores Community College_ 29

DEGREE _Associate of arts_ MAJOR _Office systems management_ 39

SPECIAL SKILLS _Fluent in Japanese and Chinese_ 48

54

COMPANY TRAINING _Orientation and supervisory development_

62

SECURITY CLEARANCE _____

POSITION   HISTORY

DATE _March 5, 19--_ POSITION _Word Processing Coordinator_

DEPARTMENT _Administrative Services_ SALARY _$16,850_ 70

DATE _____ POSITION _____ 76

DEPARTMENT _____ SALARY _____

DATE _____ POSITION _____

DEPARTMENT _____ SALARY _____

DATE TERMINATED _____ WOULD WE REHIRE _____

REASON FOR TERMINATION _____

LEVEL THREE

Formatting/typing business correspondence

Now that you have reached a basic competency in keyboarding and achieved a basic understanding of the formatting of business forms, you are now ready to build on this foundation.

In addition to the continued emphasis on speed and accuracy, the 38 lessons that comprise Level 3 are devoted to developing your expertise in solving a wide variety of communication activities. Communication aids that influence the "sound" of communications are combined with the technical aspect of letter formats, special features, and writing styles that influence the "appearance" of the finished product. This careful melding of skill, knowledge, and practical application is a vital link in making your typing ability an integral part of your total education.

Directions and sample solutions are provided throughout Level 3 to give you a feel for acceptable business correspondence and communication. However, the directions leave you flexibility for making decisions in designing, implementing, and producing acceptable business communications. When performed in a dedicated and timely manner, your work on tables, letters, memos, manuscripts, and resumes will result in more efficient production at the keyboard.

140

143a ▶ 5
Preparatory practice

each line 3 times SS (slowly, faster, slowly); DS between 3-line groups; repeat selected lines as time permits

alphabet 1 Vasquez bought expensive jewelry for his mother when he visited Clark.

fig/sym 2 We were given a 45% discount ($381.92) on Invoice #607-25A1 yesterday.

double letter 3 Lee and Ann will see us before the committee meeting tomorrow at noon.

fluency 4 The auditor got the panel to focus on the dual problems in the manual.

| 1 | 2 | 3 | 4 | 5 | 6 | 7 | 8 | 9 | 10 | 11 | 12 | 13 | 14 |

143b ▶ 10
Measure communication skills

plain sheet; 70-space line, 1½" top margin; DS copy

Read the ¶, noting corrections in capitalization and punctuation that must be made. Format and type the ¶; proofread; retype the paragraph if necessary.

president smith said to henry you will receive state of the art equipment good software and ergonomic furniture and you will be given adequate training on the equipment. the vice president of the human resources division is responsible for scheduling and coordinating the training program. although the training program will be conducted by the vendor it will be held in our facilities.

143c ▶ 35
Prepare follow-up letters and an employee record

Problem 1
Follow-up letter
full sheet

Prepare the letter given at the right in an appropriate letter style.

words

1802 Madison Avenue | New York, NY 10028-5743 | February 19, 19-- | Mrs. Selma 15
Parker | Ozark Insurance Company | P.O. Box 8910 | Ft. Smith, AR 72906-6431 | 29
Dear Mrs. Parker 32

(¶ 1) Thank you for giving me the opportunity to talk with you about the position 47
of word processing coordinator of Ozark Insurance Company. 59

(¶ 2) The tour of your facilities was quite impressive, and I was especially 74
pleased with the satellite-center approach to word processing that you are 89
planning at Ozark. You will be able to take advantage of the productivity of 104
dedicated word processing operators; and, at the same time, you will minimize 120
the control and logistical problems inherent in large, centralized word process- 136
ing centers. 139

(¶ 3) Mrs. Parker, I look forward to hearing from you; and I hope you will give 153
me the opportunity to utilize my word processing supervisory skills as coor- 169
dinator of your satellite word processing centers. (146) 179

Sincerely | Ms. Michi Nitobe 184

Problem 2
Follow-up letter
full sheet

Using the information given at the right, compose and type a follow–up letter.

In Lesson 142b, Problem 3, on page 256, you wrote a letter of application for a position for which you feel qualified. Today, you had an interview for that position. You spoke with the same person to whom you had addressed the letter of application. Now prepare a follow-up letter. You were given a tour of the facilities as part of the interview. You were impressed with the company, the position, and the facilities. Confirm your interest in the position. Your letter should be short, friendly, and sincere.

Learning goals

1 To improve basic skill on straight, statistical, and rough–draft copy.

2 To demonstrate ability to use the operative parts.

3 To improve technique of striking the keys.

4 To demonstrate understanding of proofreader's corrections.

Machine adjustments

1 Paper guide at *0*.

2 Margins: 70–space line for drills and ¶ writings; as directed for problems.

3 Spacing: SS drills; DS ¶ writings; as directed for problems.

4 Indention: 5 spaces for ¶ writings; as appropriate for problems.

76a ▶ 5
Preparatory practice

each line 3 times SS (slowly, faster, slowly); DS between 3-line groups; repeat selected lines as time permits

alphabet	1	Jack asked seven pertinent questions before he analyzed my wage taxes.
figures	2	Between 1985 and 1992, we may open 43 offices and hire 16,078 workers.
fig/sym	3	The deposits of $958 and $1,476 ($2,434 total) were made at 11:30 a.m.
fluency	4	Sue and Henry may wish to fish by the dock when they visit the island.

| 1 | 2 | 3 | 4 | 5 | 6 | 7 | 8 | 9 | 10 | 11 | 12 | 13 | 14 |

76b ▶ 20
Inventory/build straight-copy skill

1 Two 5' writings; proofread and circle errors; determine *gwam*.

2 Two 1' writings on each ¶ to improve speed.

Difficulty index

all letters used	A	1.5 si	5.7 awl	80% hfw

gwam 1'   5'

Traffic jams, deadlines, problems at work, and squabbles at home	13	3 | 55
are some ways in which tension is created. When our tension is about	27	6 | 58
to reach the boiling point, what do people usually tell us? In most	41	9 | 61
cases, they urge us to relax. But relaxation is not always easy to ac-	55	12 | 64
complish. We frequently think we cannot find the time for this impor-	69	15 | 67
tant part of our daily activity.	75	16 | 68
To understand how relaxation works for us, we must realize how the	13	19 | 72
stress of contemporary existence works against us. Developed for sur-	27	22 | 75
vival in a challenging world, the human body reacts to a crisis by get-	41	25 | 78
ting ready for action. Whether we are preparing for a timed writing or	55	28 | 81
for an encounter on a dark street, our muscles tighten and our blood	69	31 | 84
pressure goes up. After years of this type of response, we often find	83	34 | 87
it difficult to relax when we want to.	91	35 | 88
Now think about the feeling which is the opposite of this turmoil.	14	38 | 91
The pulse slows down, the breath comes slowly and calmly, and the ten-	28	41 | 94
sion leaves the body. This is total relaxation. And if it sounds good,	43	44 | 97
consider how good it must actually feel. Our bodies are already pre-	57	47 | 100
pared to relax; it is an ability all individuals have within themselves.	72	50 | 103
What we have to practice is how to use this response.	83	52 | 105

gwam 1'| 1 | 2 | 3 | 4 | 5 | 6 | 7 | 8 | 9 | 10 | 11 | 12 | 13 | 14 |
5'| 1 | 2 | 3 |

142a ▶ 5
Preparatory practice

each line 3 times SS (slowly, faster, slowly); DS between 3-line groups; repeat selected lines as time permits

alphabet 1	Jacob suggested a good way to formalize the complex plan very quickly.
figure 2	The salaries range from $9,705 to $36,841; but the average is $14,264.
direct reach 3	The injection my nurse gave me hurt and left a large bruise on my arm.
fluency 4	She may go to the island with a neighbor to fish and to dig for clams.

| 1 | 2 | 3 | 4 | 5 | 6 | 7 | 8 | 9 | 10 | 11 | 12 | 13 | 14 |

142b ▶ 45
Apply for employment

Problem 1
Letter of application

full sheet

Read the advertisement given at the right; then prepare in an appropriate letter style the letter that follows it.

Problem 2
Help-wanted ad

half sheet, long side up

Compose and type a help-wanted ad for a full-time position for which you feel qualified. Place the ad attractively on the half sheet.

Problem 3
Letter of application

full sheet

Compose and type, in an appropriate style, a letter of application in response to the help-wanted ad you have just written.

EMPLOYMENT OPPORTUNITY—FULL-TIME

Need experienced word processing supervisor to establish and to coordinate three satellite word processing centers. Must be familiar with the insurance industry. Send data sheet to Mrs. Selma Parker, President; Ozark Insurance Company; P.O. Box 8910; Ft. Smith, AR 72906-6431

---

words

1082 Madison Avenue | New York, NY 10028-5743 | February 8, 19-- | Mrs. Selma   15
Parker | Ozark Insurance Company | P.O. Box 8910 | Ft. Smith, AR 72906-6431 | 29
Dear Mrs. Parker   32

(¶ 1) Your ad in today's <u>Ft. Smith News</u> described a position for an experi-   49
enced word processing supervisor who is familiar with the insurance industry. I   65
feel that my background in business administration and my experience super-   80
vising a word processing center in an insurance company make me an ideal   95
candidate for the position.   101

(¶ 2) As a word processing technician, I operated three different brands of word   116
processors and both impact and nonimpact printers. After two years as an   130
operator, I was promoted to supervisor of the center. Recently, I was respon-   146
sible for the evaluation and selection of new software for our information pro-   162
cessors. This experience and my other experiences summarized on the   177
enclosed data sheet will be extremely valuable in setting up new centers.   191

(¶ 3) Our family is scheduled to move to Ft. Smith on March 1; however, I could   205
come for an interview prior to that time. Please give me the opportunity to   221
demonstrate to you that my qualifications are a perfect match for the position   237
you advertised. You may call me at (212) 555-6034 to suggest a convenient time   253
for an interview. (219)   256

Sincerely | Ms. Michi Nitobe | Enclosure   263

Inventory operative parts control

If you do not understand the use of any proofreader's mark shown at the right, see 78c, page 145, for an explanation of proofreader's marks and their meanings.

Format the material at the right with a 2″ top margin. Set margin stops for an exact 70-space line. Type the first side heading "Margin Release Key" as it is shown at the right. Then reset the left margin stop 12 spaces to the right to format the first ¶; SS ¶s, DS between them. Format each ¶ and then do as it directs before proceeding to the next ¶; proofread finished copy and correct errors.

words

USING THE OPERATIVE PARTS — 5

Margin Release Key
If the carrier (carriage) locks before you completely — 18
finish a word, press the margin release key and com- — 28
plete the word. After you double-space at the end of — 39
each paragraph, depress the margin release key, back- — 50
space 21 spaces into the left margin, and place the — 60
side heading at the top left of the paragraph as shown — 71
above, on this page — 74

Bell and Margin Lock
After you finish the ending line of this paragraph, — 88
space forward until the bell rings. Then count the no. — 99
of strokes between the ringing of the bell and the a lock- — 110
ing of the machine. Subtract 5 from this number and — 122
add the difference to the figure at which the right- — 132
hand margin stop was set for a 70-space line. Reset — 143
the right marginal stop. — 146

Variable Line Spacer
When you complete this paragraph, operate the — 160
variable line spacer and turn the cylinder forward — 170
about 2 inches. Then depress the variable line spacer — 181
again and return as accurately as you can to the last — 192
line of this paragraph; then release the variable line — 202
spacer. Repeat the line, typing over the original copy — 214

Tab Clear Key
When you complete this practice paragraph and the — 226
side heading, move the carrier to the extreme right — 237
(or the carriage to the extreme left). Depress and — 247
hold down the tab clear key as you return the carrier — 258
to the extreme left (or the carriage to the extreme — 268
right) to all remove of the tab stops. Some machines — 279
have a mechanism that clears all stops, at once — 288

Tab Set Key
Move the carrier (carriage) to the centerpoint — 300
of your paper; then depress the tab set key. — 309

Tabulator; Backspace Key
Tabulate to the center of the paper. Using the — 323
backspace-from-center method, center the title given — 333
below. Place the title two line spaces below on your — 347
paper. this paragraph — 349
KNOW YOUR MACHINE — 352

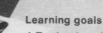

Learning goals

1 To develop skill in preparing a personal data sheet and other employment communications.

2 To improve ability to compose communications used in the employment process.

Machine adjustments

1 Paper guide at 0.

2 Margins: 70–space line for drills; as directed for problems.

3 Spacing: SS drills; follow directions outlined for each problem.

141a ▶ 5
Preparatory practice

each line 3 times SS (slowly, faster, slowly); DS between 3-line groups; repeat selected lines as time permits

alphabet 1 James Waverly placed the bronze plaques next to the drinking fountain.

figure 2 We mailed 96,372 brochures; 410 personal letters; and 685 invitations.

adjacent key 3 We were walking quickly to avoid the people trying to view a big fire.

fluency 4 Their enchantment with the robot is a sign they may make a bid for it.

| 1 | 2 | 3 | 4 | 5 | 6 | 7 | 8 | 9 | 10 | 11 | 12 | 13 | 14 |

141b ▶ 45
Prepare personal data sheets

plain sheets

Problem 1
Personal data sheet

The data sheet given at the right illustrates one acceptable style for formatting a data sheet. Prepare the data sheet in the style illustrated, using a 2" top margin and 1" side margins. Indent ¶s 5 spaces from left margin.

Problem 2
Personal data sheet

Use your own data and the format you used for a data sheet in Problem 1 to prepare a personal data sheet.

words

MICHI NITOBE 3
1082 Madison Avenue 7
New York, NY 10028-5743 12
(212) 555-6034 15

CAREER OBJECTIVE 18

Career in administrative office management in the insurance 30
industry. 32

MAJOR QUALIFICATIONS 36

Knowledge of office management and related areas of business 49
administration. Experience in the insurance industry. 60

EDUCATION 62

Associate in arts degree, Eastern Shores Community College, 74
June, 1985. Majored in office systems management. Courses 86
in office management, accounting, word/data processing, records 98
management, and management of the automated office. 109

High school diploma, Sterling Academy, June, 1983. Majored 121
in business and mathematics. 127

EXPERIENCE 129

Supervisor, Word Processing Center, Hobbs Insurance Company, 141
from June, 1985, to present time. Responsible for supervis- 153
ing 12 employees, analyzing and evaluating work, developing 165
procedures manuals, training technicians, and coordinating 177
with users. Productivity of the Center has increased 20 per- 189
cent, and costs have remained constant under my supervision. 202

REFERENCES 204

References, including present employer and former instructors, 217
will be provided upon request. 223

Preparatory practice

			words
alphabet	1	Jack quickly thawed five big boxes of frozen shrimp to make the salad.	
figures	2	Holes 9, 10, and 11 had yardages of 378, 526, and 450 for a par of 13.	
fig/sym	3	One calculator (used) at $16.84 and a chair at $59.36* came to $76.20.	
fluency	4	The ivory tusk, if authentic, is the key to the ancient island ritual.	

| 1 | 2 | 3 | 4 | 5 | 6 | 7 | 8 | 9 | 10 | 11 | 12 | 13 | 14 |

77b ▶ 30

Inventory report skills

Problem 1

Format the copy at the right in unbound manuscript style: top margin 1 ½″ for pica, 2″ for elite; side margins 1″; DS the first ¶; then reset margins so that the numbered ¶s are indented 5 spaces from both right and left margins; SS the body of each numbered ¶ and DS between the numbered ¶s; center the title **DIVIDING WORDS** above the report.

Problem 2

Reformat the copy at the right as the second page of an unbound report; place the page number in the appropriate place; omit the main heading.

	words
	title 3

A word may be ~~broken~~ *divided* at the end of a line in order to   14

keep right margin as even and attractive as possible. When   26

in dout about the proper division of a work, consult a dic-   38

tionery or a word-division guide. The following rules will   50

be helpful: 52

1. If you decide that you must divide a word, ~~then~~   61
   divide it between syllables, as <u>your-self</u>, <u>con-</u>   73
   <u>flict</u>, <u>dif-fer-ent</u>. Even though they may have   86
   two or more syllables, never divide words of   95
   five or fewer letters, as <u>offer</u>, <u>onto</u>.   104

2. Divide words between two vowels if each is a   114
   separate syllable, as <u>situ-ations</u>, <u>evalu-ation</u>.   128
   Hyphenated compounds should be divided only at   137
   the point of the hyphen, as <u>know-how</u>, <u>cross-</u>   148
   <u>file</u>, <u>son-in-law</u>.   155

3. When the single-letter syllable <u>a</u>, <u>i</u>, or <u>u</u> is   166
   followed by the ending syllable <u>ble</u>, <u>bly</u>, <u>cle</u>,   177
   or <u>cal</u>, the two ending syllables should be   186
   joined when carried over to the next line, as   195
   <u>cur-able</u>, <u>favor-ably</u>, <u>mir-acle</u>, or <u>cler-ical</u>.   211

4. Regardless of the length of the word, do not   221
   divide a one-letter syllable at the beginning   230
   of it, as <u>e-nough</u>, or a one- or two-letter   240
   syllable at the end of a word, as <u>read-y</u> or   250
   <u>ghast-ly</u>. Words of one syllable cannot be   260
   divided, as <u>thought</u>, <u>trained</u>, or <u>straight</u>.   273

5. Divide words after a prefix or before a suffix   283
   if possible, as <u>pre-scribe</u>. Words should be   294
   divided between double consonants unless the   303
   root word ends in a double letter, as <u>strip-</u>   313
   ping or <u>process-ing</u>.   320

**Problem 2
Leftbound report
with footnotes**
Format the report DS.

words

TRANSPARENCIES AFFECT SUCCESS OF MEETING   8

Communication experts believe that audiovisual aids help make a busi-   22
ness meeting more successful. These devices add to what is being said, help   37
listeners understand complex concepts, and maintain interest and attention.[1]   52
Tables and graphs presenting statistical data are among the most commonly   67
used visual aids.   70

Results of the Wharton study indicate that overhead transparencies have   84
a positive impact on business meetings. Presenters who used overhead trans-   99
parencies in presentations were perceived as significantly better prepared,   114
more professional, more persuasive, more credible, and more interesting than   129
presenters who did not use overhead transparencies.[2]   139

Transparencies must be used effectively if they are to make a positive   153
impact on a meeting. Each participant must be able to read easily the informa-   169
tion that is projected. The information presented on each transparency should   185
be limited. A good transparency uses a few well-chosen words to make one   200
point only. A simple, uncluttered transparency is more effective than a com-   215
plex, cluttered one. Projectors must be turned on only when the attention of the   231
audience is being directed to the screen.   239

_____   242

[1]Allan D. Frank, Communicating on the Job. Glenview, Illinois: Scott,   261
Foresman and Co., 1982, p. 300.   267

[2]"How to Present More Effectively--and Win More Favorable Responses   281
From More People in Less Time." A summary of the Wharton Report. Audio   296
Visual Division/3M, 1981.   301

**Problem 3
Title page**

Prepare a title page for Problem 2. Use the information given at the right.

TRANSPARENCIES AFFECT SUCCESS OF MEETING   8

Cynthia Jackson, Training Director   15

Human Resources Department   20

February 8, 19--   23

77c ▶ 15
Inventory/build statistical-copy skill

1 Two 3' writings; proofread and circle errors; determine *gwam*.
2 Two 1' writings on each ¶ to improve speed.

Difficulty index

| all letters/figures used | A | 1.5 si | 5.7 awl | 80% hfw |

gwam 1' | 3'

The number of women in the labor force of our nation has been ris- 13 | 4
ing steadily from 18.2 percent in 1890 to around 51 percent by 1980. 27 | 9
This indicates that in 1980, 51 percent of all women over the age of 41 | 14
16 held jobs. In addition, the number of fields which women pursue 55 | 18
has slowly risen. New technology has brought about new career areas, 69 | 23
and women are performing jobs today that had never been open to them 83 | 28
previously. These new opportunities offer pursuits to women of all 97 | 32
skills and job backgrounds. 102 | 34

Women are now gaining experience to help them in developing careers. 14 | 39
In 1974, just 1,000 of the 200,000 coal miners in our land were women. 28 | 44
Nowadays, over 6,000 female miners are employed. Even as recently as 10 43 | 49
years ago, relatively few women operated heavy equipment. Now roughly 57 | 54
1/5 of 1 percent of the women in the work force use apparatus of this 71 | 59
size. In 1975, just 26 percent of bank managers were women. By the 85 | 63
early 1980's, that figure had grown to 33 percent. 95 | 66

gwam 1' | 1 | 2 | 3 | 4 | 5 | 6 | 7 | 8 | 9 | 10 | 11 | 12 | 13 | 14 |
3' | 1 | 2 | 3 | 4 | 5 |

78a ▶ 5
Preparatory practice

each line 3 times SS (slowly, faster, slowly); DS between 3-line groups; repeat selected lines as time permits

alphabet 1 Luckily, we packed just the required number of frozen vegetable boxes.
figures 2 The following 4 classrooms are still unusable: 69, 150, 354, and 728.
fig/sym 3 Helen's 13% note (matures May 25, 1987) will yield a return of $4,690.
fluency 4 The spry buck and the big doe may be visible in the field by the lake.

| 1 | 2 | 3 | 4 | 5 | 6 | 7 | 8 | 9 | 10 | 11 | 12 | 13 | 14 |

78b ▶ 15
Inventory technique

each pair of lines 3 times SS at a controlled rate; DS between 6-line groups

double letters 1 Many employees will attend the annual meeting to support their issues.
2 Their accounting staff will need supplies in approximately three days.

adjacent reaches 3 Portia asked that we talk to various teachers about the ruined chairs.
4 A reasonable understanding was quickly developed joining both parties.

direct reaches 5 Many hungry soldiers brought much of the food which they had received.
6 The survey continued to project gradual gains for many technical jobs.

shift-key reaches 7 Janette and Tommy will probably meet Harriet on Sunday in Kansas City.
8 Today, the Boston Red Sox played the Toronto Blue Jays in Fenway Park.

| 1 | 2 | 3 | 4 | 5 | 6 | 7 | 8 | 9 | 10 | 11 | 12 | 13 | 14 |

139b ▶ 45
Sustained production: prepare reports

Time schedule:

Assembling materials .... 3'
Timed production .... 35'
Final check; compute
   n–pram .... 7'

1 Make a list of problems to be prepared.
page 244, 133b, Problem 1
page 246, 134c, Problem 1
page 247, 134c, Problem 2
page 252, 138c, Problem 2

2 Arrange plain paper and supplies for easy handling. When directed to begin, work for 35'. Follow directions given for each problem. Correct errors neatly. Proofread carefully before remov–ing each page from your machine.

3 Start over with the first problem if you complete all problems be–fore time is called.

4 Compute *n–pram* (see page 171).

140a ▶ 5
Preparatory practice

each line 3 times SS (slowly, faster, slowly); DS between 3-line groups; repeat selected lines as time permits

alphabet	1	Quincy apologized for the lack of objectivity in your complex reviews.
figure	2	Did 387 people pay $695 to attend the training program on April 14-20?
outside reach	3	We saw Wally Maxwell quickly swim past Alex in a show at the zoo pool.
fluency	4	Susie did sign both of the forms, and she did pay half of the penalty.

| 1 | 2 | 3 | 4 | 5 | 6 | 7 | 8 | 9 | 10 | 11 | 12 | 13 | 14 |

140b ▶ 45
Measure production on reports and title page

plain sheets

Time schedule:

Assembling materials ...... 3'
Timed production .... 35'
Final check; compute
   n–pram .... 7'

Problem 1
Unbound report with reference citations

Prepare the report given at the right DS.

	words
LENDING POLICY FOR COUNTY BANK	6
Limits of Authority	10

The President of the bank is authorized to make loans up to $100,000 on   24
a secured basis and up to $50,000 on an unsecured basis. Any request for a line   40
of credit in excess of the limit specified for the President must be approved by   56
at least two members of the Loan Committee other than the President. These   71
lending limits are in agreement with recommended standards (Burge, 1985).   86

The President shall delegate authority to make loans to the senior officers   101
of the bank. Senior officers may approve loans up to $50,000 on a secured basis   117
and up to $25,000 on an unsecured basis. The President may delegate authority   133
to make loans to other officers. Authority delegated to officers other than the   149
senior officers shall not exceed $10,000 and shall be for secured loans only. This   166
policy is based on recommended guides (White, 1985).   176

REFERENCES   178

Burge, S. Michael. "General Lending Policy." South-Western Banking Associa-   189
    tion Report. March 12, 1985, p. 8.   198

White, Deborah B. "Guides for Delegating Lending Authority." Class handout   213
    in Bankers' School, Central University, 1985.   222

78c ▶ 10
Review proofreader's marks

Sometimes typed or printed copy may be corrected with proofreader's marks. The keyboard operator must be able to interpret these marks correctly in reformatting the corrected copy, or *rough draft*, as it may be called. The most commonly used proofreader's marks are shown at the right.

Read the ¶s of 78d below and compare the use of the symbols shown there to the illustrations at the right.

Proofreader's Marks

Capitalize	Insert space	Move up; raise
≡ or *Cap*	# or /#	
Close up	Insert apostrophe	Set in lowercase
	∨	*lc* or /
Delete	Insert quotation marks	Paragraph
ℓ	∨∨ ∨∨	#
Insert		Spell out
∧	Move right	*sp*
Insert comma	Move left	Let it stand; ignore correction
∧		*stet*
Insert period	Move down; lower	Transpose
⊙		∿ or *tr*
		Underline or italics

78d ▶ 20
Inventory/build rough-draft skill

1 Two 5' writings; proofread and circle errors; determine *gwam*.

2 Two 1' writings on each ¶ to improve speed.

Difficulty index

all letters used	A	1.5 si	5.7 awl	80% hfw

	gwam 1'	5'
Believe it or not, stress maybe good for ~~you~~ us. Without	11	2	43
it stress, we would be a less productive society. we would have	23	4	45
fewer ~~less~~ ulcers, headaches, and heart seazures, ~~and~~ but we would find	36	6	47
it difficult to work. Why the paradox? Actually, stress itself	49	9	50
is not ~~isn't~~ good or bad, but our reactions ~~feelings~~ to pressure situations can	62	12	53
be positive or negative.	67	13	54
On the positive side, stressful situations ~~things~~ force us to ~~do~~ complete	13	16	57
our tasks. if we didnot have dead lines and schedules,	24	18	59
many ~~most~~ of us would put of until latter what could be	34	20	61
handled immediately ~~quickly~~. Deadlines give us certain times for	46	22	63
completing our activities. We all require just enough	57	24	65
stress to stimulate ~~push~~ us to reach our goals. Thus, stress can ~~will~~	69	26	67
be a positive force in our lives ~~life~~.	76	27	68
But stress can also have a negative aspect. Dead lines	11	29	70
are not necessarily ~~really~~ realistic. sometimes we have, many goals too to	25	32	73
achieve at once, too many requirements to ~~do~~ complete. At these times,	39	35	76
we often feel uncomfortable ~~nervous~~ because we are under too much pressure.	53	38	79
All of us must learn how much stress we need ~~can take~~ in our daly ~~life~~ lives.	66	41	82

138c ▶ 35
Prepare an unbound report and a bibliography
plain sheets
Problem 1
Unbound report

Prepare the material at the right in unbound report form on a full sheet. Compose an appropriate title page for the report. Use your name, your title (Manager of Technical Services), and the current date.

words

ELECTRONIC PRINTING   4

    We are presently considering using electronic printing in our company.   28
Products are now available which combine several technologies. These   42
technologies include digital computers with the capacity of handling informa-   57
tion at high rates of speed, lasers with the ability to create high-resolution   73
images, and xerography with the capability of producing high-quality printed   88
output. The new systems can scan photographs or designs and convert them   103
into digital images.   107

    Numerous office automation references have been reviewed to determine   121
the different applications of electronic printing technology in our company.   137
One application which is being analyzed carefully is forms control. Forms can   153
now be printed at the same time that they are filled with information. Logos and   169
signatures can be reproduced. Artwork can be digitized and merged into text.   184

Problem 2
Bibliography

Prepare the material at the right with the same margins as you need for the unbound report in Problem 1. Use a full sheet.

Note: Articles or news stories for which no author is given are reported in a bibliography starting with the first words in the title (disregard *a*, *an*, or *the*).

BIBLIOGRAPHY   3

Crawford, T. James, et al. <u>Basic Keyboarding and Typewriting Applications</u>.   28
    Cincinnati: South-Western Publishing Co., 1983.   38

"Electronic Printing Hits Its Stride." <u>Xerox World</u> (Summer 1982), pp. 11-15.   56

Hess, M. Elizabeth. Printing Manager, Effective Office Systems, New Orleans,   72
    Louisiana. Interviewed by Lois Walker, March 20, 1985.   83

Ray, Patrick V. "Electronic Printing Applications." Class handout in BADM   98
    487, Central University, 1985.   104

Toffler, Alvin. <u>The Third Wave</u>. New York: William Morrow and Company,   121
    Inc., 1980.   123

139a ▶ 5
Preparatory practice

each line 3 times SS (slowly, faster, slowly); DS between 3-line groups; repeat selected lines as time permits

alphabet 1   Jeffy was lucky to be given a deluxe bronze plaque by his soccer team.

fig/sym 2   Diana sold 863 tickets to 241 people for $9,057.68 in a 30-day period.

space bar 3   Kay can own the land if she can pay them for it by the end of the day.

fluency 4   My goal is to make eight bushels of corn on the land to make a profit.

| 1 | 2 | 3 | 4 | 5 | 6 | 7 | 8 | 9 | 10 | 11 | 12 | 13 | 14 |

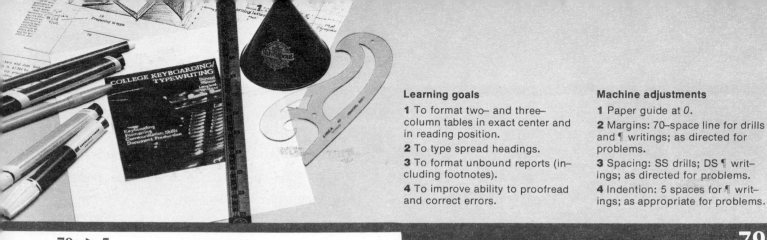

Learning goals

1 To format two– and three–column tables in exact center and in reading position.

2 To type spread headings.

3 To format unbound reports (including footnotes).

4 To improve ability to proofread and correct errors.

Machine adjustments

1 Paper guide at *0*.

2 Margins: 70–space line for drills and ¶ writings; as directed for problems.

3 Spacing: SS drills; DS ¶ writings; as directed for problems.

4 Indention: 5 spaces for ¶ writings; as appropriate for problems.

79a ▶ 5

Preparatory practice

each line 3 times SS (slowly, faster, slowly); DS between 3-line groups; repeat selected lines as time permits

alphabet	1	My objectives were analyzed quickly during the corporate proxy fights.
fig/sym	2	The value of my stock ($185/share) has increased $7,364.20 since 1985.
long words	3	Numerous organizations established special conditions for future work.
fluency	4	Helen, the usual tutor, is sick; but the six girls may do the problem.

| 1 | 2 | 3 | 4 | 5 | 6 | 7 | 8 | 9 | 10 | 11 | 12 | 13 | 14 |

79b ▶ 10

Inventory/build script-copy skill

1 Two 3' writings; proofread and circle errors; determine *gwam*.

2 One 1' writing on each ¶ to improve speed.

Difficulty index

all letters used | A | 1.5 si | 5.7 awl | 80% hfw

	gwam 1'		3'
To buy on impulse is just that--going into a store,	10	3	53
seeing an item we like, and purchasing it quickly.	20	6	56
Dealers aid this type of buying by displaying	29	9	59
numerous whimsical items at various checkout	38	12	62
points. This makes it easy for us to engage in	48	15	65
such buying. Many people are against such buying	58	18	68
because it often wrecks a well-planned and well-	68	21	71
ordered budget and may lead to financial problems.	78	24	74
By contrast, planned buying is rational de-	8	27	77
cision making by consumers. While it may lack	17	30	80
spontaneity, such action does have the advantage	27	33	83
of safety if it is in line with expendable resources.	38	36	86
As a rule, people will not overstep their incomes	48	39	89
if they plan carefully to keep in line with pre-	57	42	92
sent or anticipated income. But we must also	66	45	95
realize that even the best made plans can	74	48	98
go wrong.	76	50	100

137a ▶ 5
Preparatory practice

each line 3 times SS (slowly, faster, slowly); DS between 3-line groups; repeat selected lines as time permits

alphabet 1 Fran, a great quarterback, emphasized six major ways to avoid a blitz.

figure 2 Make 248 permits for Lot 9178, 356 for Lot 9102, and 480 for Lot 9765.

fig/sym 3 The total for Invoice #85748 is $695.81; and the terms are 2/10, n/30.

fluency 4 I do risk half of the profit I make to own a key island in a big lake.

| 1 | 2 | 3 | 4 | 5 | 6 | 7 | 8 | 9 | 10 | 11 | 12 | 13 | 14 |

137b ▶ 45
Prepare a report, title page, and memo

plain sheets

Problem 1

Repeat 136c in leftbound report form with reference citations. In the reference section at the end of the report, the Hersey and Blanchard citation occurs on pages 193–197 and the Reber and Van Gilder citation occurs on pages 41–42.

Problem 2

Compose a title page for the leftbound report you prepared in Problem 1. Use your name, your title (Manager of Human Resources), and the current date.

Problem 3

Compose a simplified memo to all supervisors from you. The memo will be sent to each supervisor with a copy of the report you have just prepared. Ask each supervisor to read the report and be prepared to discuss it at the staff meeting scheduled one week from today at 2:00 p.m. Use today's date and an appropriate subject line.

138a ▶ 5
Preparatory practice

each line 3 times SS (slowly, faster, slowly); DS between 3-line groups; repeat selected lines as time permits

alphabet 1 Felix Jiminez hopes to fly back to Quebec to visit with great friends.

figure 2 I ordered 3,750 labels, 1,984 pencils, 625 legal pads, and 95 folders.

double letters 3 Anne will accept the offer and discuss fully the process that applies.

fluency 4 Akeo may go to the big city on the bus to visit with the busy auditor.

| 1 | 2 | 3 | 4 | 5 | 6 | 7 | 8 | 9 | 10 | 11 | 12 | 13 | 14 |

138b ▶ 10
Preapplication drill: prepare a bibliography

plain sheet

1 For this drill, use the same margins that you would use for the first page of an unbound report.
2 Start the first line of each entry at the left margin; indent the second and subsequent lines 5 spaces. SS each entry; DS between entries.

BIBLIOGRAPHY

Gates, Calvin. The Micro-Editor. Cincinnati: South-Western Publishing Co., 1983.

Rosen, Arnold, and Rosemary Fielden. Word Processing. 2d ed. Englewood Cliffs: Prentice-Hall, 1982.

Will, Mimi, and Donette Dake. Concepts in Word Processing: The Challenge of Change. Boston: Allyn and Bacon, Inc., 1982.

79c ▶ 35
Inventory problem skills: outline and report
Problem 1
Outline

full sheet; 2" top margin; 1" side margins; center heading **MAN-AGEMENT WORKSHOP OUTLINE**

	in heading 5
I. GETTING THE DESIRED RESULTS	11
A. Characteristics of a Productive Manager	20
B. Problem Analysis	24
1. Identifying the real problem	30
2. Sorting symptoms from causes	36
C. Assigning Work Effectively	42
1. When and how to delegate	48
2. How to maintain control	53
II. IMPROVING COMMUNICATION SKILLS	60
A. How to Deal with Employees in Face-to-Face Situations	71
B. Developing a Rapport with Subordinates	79
C. Recognizing and Overcoming Communication Barriers	90
D. Giving Negative Feedback Effectively	98

Problem 2
Unbound manuscript with footnote

full sheet; top margin 2" elite, 1½" pica; sides 1"; bottom approximately 1"; DS; footnote at bottom of page

words

CORPORATIONS
2

Most of us take for granted the "Inc." that normally appears after the 16
legal name of many business firms. Yet not all business enterprises are corpo- 30
rations. Law firms and many other professional-service businesses custom- 45
arily work as partnerships. Some businesses that are set up in one individual's 61
name may operate as a sole proprietorship. However, the fact remains that 70
corporations are the dominant force in American business. In fact, although 91
corporations account for only 15 percent of all business enterprises, they col- 107
lect 77 percent of all business earnings.[1] 115

The law governing incorporation is complex and varies from state to 129
state. But any corporation has three fundamental features: limited liability, 145
eternal life, and greater capital. 152

Basically, limited liability means that a corporation is liable for only as 107
much money as it has "capitalized." The corporation may go bankrupt, but the 183
individuals who started it can lose no more than they have invested. Eternal life 200
means the corporation lives on and on, and the corporation's life doesn't 215
depend--as with a partnership or proprietorship--on the life or death of any 230
person or group of people. Third, a corporation can raise capital by selling 246
stock. Through the sale of corporate stock, firms are able to raise large 261
amounts of capital funds. 266

270

[1] William H. Cunningham, Ramon J. Aldag, and Christopher M. Swift, 283
Introduction to Business (Cincinnati: South-Western Publishing Co., 1984), 304
p. 63. 305

You see, really and truly, apart from the things any-   137
one can pick up (the dressing and the proper way of   147
speaking, and so on), the difference between a lady   157
and a flower girls is not how she behaves but how   167
she's treated. I shall always be a flower girl to   177
Professor Higgins, because he always treats me as a   187
flower girl, and walays will; but I know I can be a   197
lady to you, because you treat me as a lady, and al-   207
ways will (Livingston, 1969, 81-84).   214

Livingston found in his research that some managers *tend to*   226
treat subordinates ina manner that improves performance. *Other*   239
Managers unintentionally follow Professor Higgins and treat   251
employees in a way that *leads to* lowers performance. The way a man-   264
ager *treats* handles an employee is often based on the expectations   276
the that manager has for the employee. High expectations *tend to* lead to   290
high productivity. Low expectations tend to *lead to* cause lower worke   301
productivity. Employees can tell *sense* how the superior *supervisor* feels about   313
their there potential. These workers may then perform *in* as the role   325
in which they think they *h* nave been cast. *Thus,* So, a manager's   337
behavior toward an employee can have a long-range effect on the   350
employees job performance.   355

The term "effective *y* cicle" refers to the *phenomenon* phemonenen that   366
occurs happens when empollyees respond to the high expectations of their   379
managers with high performance (Hersey and Blanchard, 1982).   391
Managers *concerned with* worred about developing the talents of all *their*   403
employees need to very carefully examine the expectations they   415
hold for *each* every employee. *Stating* Saying what you think an employee can   427
do is not enough. You have to believe it.   435

TS

REFERENCES   437

TS

Hersey, Paul, and Kenneth H. Blanchard. Management of Organiza-   454
tional Behavior: Utilizing Human Resources. 4th ed.   474
Englewood Cliffs: Prentice-Hall, Inc., 1982. DS   483
Livingston, J. Sterling. "Pygmalion in Management." Harvard   497
Business Review, July-August 1969, pp. 81-84. DS   509
Reber, Ralph W., and Gloria Van Gilder. Behavioral Insights   525
for Supervision. 2d ed. Englewood Cliffs: Prentice-Hall,   540
Inc., 1982.   542

80a ▶ 5
Preparatory practice

each line 3 times SS (slowly, faster, slowly); DS between 3-line groups; repeat selected lines as time permits

alphabet 1 Jack surmised a biology quiz was given during fifth and sixth periods.

fig/sym 2 I believe the 15% discount stated on Invoice #804 amounted to $326.97.

long words 3 Considerable thought and understanding were involved in the decisions.

fluency 4 Their oak workbox on the chair by the door in the shanty is authentic.

| 1 | 2 | 3 | 4 | 5 | 6 | 7 | 8 | 9 | 10 | 11 | 12 | 13 | 14 |

80b ▶ 45
Inventory communication skills

full sheets; unbound report style

1 Write numbers 1–48 down the left margin of a ruled or plain sheet of paper.

2 Read and note (line for line on the numbered sheet) any additional corrections you need to make in the report beyond those marked for correction.

3 Format and type the report, correcting all errors—those marked and those you detect in the copy.

4 Proofread your copy and mark for correction any errors you find.

5 If time permits, prepare a final copy from your marked copy with all errors corrected.

words

1   Processing data by Machine   *TS*   5

2   Since the beginning of history, ~~people~~ *recorded men and women* have felt the   19

3 need to handle data. *and process* Early people ~~have~~ left records of   32

4 their processing *of data* carved into rocks, baked into clay tab-   45

5 lets, and drawn on papyrus. Regardless of the process used,   57

6 processing data was laborious and time-consuming. as time   69

7 passed, however, new ~~discoveries~~ *inventions* made date processing easier.   82

8 Rocks, clay tablets, and paprus gaveway to vellumn which   95

9 gaveway ~~for~~ *to* paper. quills were given up for pans, which in   107

10 turn were given up for *the* type writers. In the second 1/2 of   119

11 the twentieth-century, the ease and speed of processing data   131

12 *stet increased* ~~have speed up~~ tremendously with the ~~discovery~~ *invention* of various ~~new~~   143

13 electro-mechanical and electronic processing ~~ideas~~ *systems*.   153

                                  TS

14 Mechanical Processing   161

15   Mechanical proscessing of data involves people using   171

16 machinery to process. *the data* for instance, a typewriter one kind   185

17 of mechanical processor can be used to prepare bills, pur-   197

18 chase orders and other business records. ~~But~~ *However* each piece of   210

19 data must be processed ~~one at a time~~ *individually* and be filed by hand.   222

                        TS

20 Electro-mechanical processing   233

21   An electromechanical processor is a machine, that   243

22 can operate automatically. The ~~usual~~ *most common* electromechanically   255

continued on p. 149

135c ▶ 37
Prepare title pages and reports

plain sheets

Problem 1
Title page for unbound report

Prepare the title page illustrated at the right for an unbound report; center each line horizontally; use the title **FEASIBILITY OF CENTRALIZED COPY CENTER**; the author is **Thomas Kishpaugh, Operations Manager**, and the date of the report is **August 14, 19--.**

Problem 2
Title page for leftbound report

You are the personnel manager of a corporation. Prepare a title page for your annual progress report on your corporation's affirmative action program. Compose a title; use today's date.

Follow the illustration above right for the title page of a leftbound report; center each line over the line of writing for a leftbound report.

Problem 3
Leftbound report

Prepare the report given at the right.

Problem 4
Title page for leftbound report

Prepare an appropriate title page for the report in Problem 3. The report was written by **Marjorie Sullivan, Vice President of Marketing**. Use today's date.

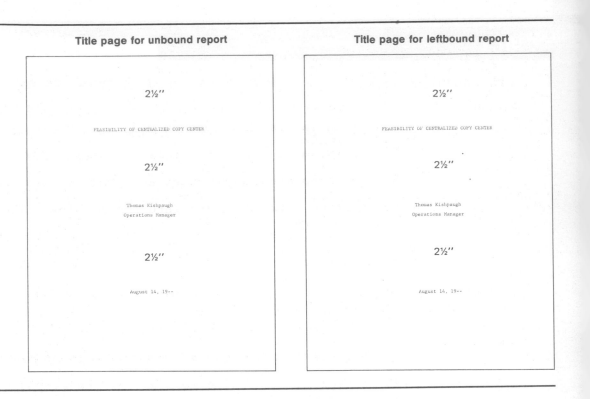

Title page for unbound report

Title page for leftbound report

2½"

FEASIBILITY OF CENTRALIZED COPY CENTER

2½"

Thomas Kishpaugh
Operations Manager

2½"

August 14, 19--

	words
CUSTOMER SERVICE DEPARTMENT PERFORMANCE	8

¶ The performance of the Customer Service Department for the — 20
second quarter was evaluated. Data were compared to the — 31
existing company standards and to the departmental per- — 42
formance for the past 12 quarters. The individual performance of — 55
each customer service representative was also evaluated. — 66

¶ Performance met and exceeded every standard except that the — 78
complaint ratio increased by 38 percent this quarter. Birsner — 91
and Balsley recommend an investigation any time complaint — 103
activity increases radically.* An increase of 38 percent — 115
is a major increase and merits further study. — 124

— 127

*E. Patricia Birsner and Ronald D. Balsley, _Practical_ — 140
Guide to Customer Service Management and Operations — 160
(New York: AMACOM, 1982), p. 180. — 167

81a ▶ 5
Preparatory practice

each line 3 times SS (slowly, faster, slowly); DS between 3-line groups; repeat selected lines as time permits

alphabet	1	Many judges were very anxious to quiz four key couples about the case.
fig/sym	2	Order #5972 from Baker & Bird totaling $16,401.03 was shipped July 18.
direct reach	3	He doubts my secretary can be certain any amount collected is correct.
fluency	4	A giant whale by the dock is a visitor to the island, and she is sick.

| 1 | 2 | 3 | 4 | 5 | 6 | 7 | 8 | 9 | 10 | 11 | 12 | 13 | 14 |

81b ▶ 10
Review/apply communication skills: capitalization

full sheet; 1″ top margin; 74-space line

1 Cover the answer key at the bottom of the column.

2 Study carefully each guide under *Capitalize* presented at the right.

3 To assure understand– ing, read and then type each *review* and *apply* sentence, including the guide number, to which the communication guide applies.

4 Check your corrected sentences. Make any additional corrections in pencil or pen.

5 Repeat any *apply* sen– tence containing an error, correcting the error as you type.

Key: 1b. This 2b. Shakespearian, Elizabethan 3b. Jove, Maurice Building 4b. Memorial Day, Monday, May 5b. Street, Company 6b. to the, Lenox Theater

Capitalize

1 The first word of a sentence or of a complete direct quotation, and the first word after a colon if the word introduces a complete sentence.

2 Proper nouns and their derivatives or names or nicknames that designate a par- ticular person, place, or thing.

3 Names of organizations, clubs, build- ings, and brand names, but usually not the commodity they identify.

4 Words that indicate time, such as days of the week, months, holidays, historical events or periods; seasons of the year only if personified.

5 Street, avenue, company, etc., when used with a proper noun.

6 The first and all other important words in the titles of books, articles, periodicals, headings, plays, movies, songs, and works of art, but not the conjunctions, articles, or prepositions having four or fewer letters.

review	1a.	Amy announced, "They drove south to Peoria to attend a meeting."
apply	b.	Leo spoke confidently: "this is the only way to Central Plaza."
review	2a.	Moving the large painting by Manet required a Herculean effort.
apply	b	The shakespearian actor performed in the elizabethan drama.
review	3a.	The Chamber of Commerce held a fund raiser in the Endicot Complex.
apply	b.	The jove electrical outlets were installed in the maurice building.
review	4a.	This fall, Thanksgiving Day occurs on Thursday, November 24.
apply	b.	We celebrated memorial day on monday, may 30.
review	5a.	The J. A. Tempe Company, located on Iris Avenue, gave prompt service.
apply	b.	One Locust street is the new address of the Hammersmith company.
review	6a.	The Last of the Mohicans is an early adventure novel by Cooper.
apply	b.	I saw The Road To The Republic at the lenox theater last Sunday.

81c ▶ 25
Inventory problem skills: tables

Problem 1
Table with main heading

half sheet, long side up; DS; 10 spaces between columns

ROSTER OF NEW EMPLOYEES		words
		5
Administrative Assistant	Maria Georgiopoulos	14
Assistant Registrar	Robert Parks	20
Controller	Cleopatra Sophios	25
Dean of Students	Mary Cadigan-Jones	32
Director of Health Services	Arline Keefe	40
Personnel Administrator	Wally Wong	47
Purchasing Administrator	Marylou Shumski	55
Staff Nurse	James Spanks	60

Problem 2
Unbound report
with footnote

Follow the guides given in the outline on page 245 for an unbound report.

words

INTEGRATING MAIL PROCESSING WITH WORD PROCESSING 10

The mailroom is the major bottleneck in the handling of 21
correspondence in your company. The volume of mail currently 33
handled by the mailroom averages 28,000 pieces per day. The bulk 46
of the processing is being done manually. Handling large volumes 59
of mail is a time-consuming and costly operation. 69

Mailing systems are available which streamline office 80
efficiency and enable organizations to concentrate more time on 93
improving communications.* A cost analysis will be made to 105
determine which system is feasible for your company. 115
118

*David Duke, "Mailing Machines Complete Word Processing 129
Cycle," Word Processing & Information Systems (July 1982), p. 35. 149

135a ▶ 5

Preparatory
practice

each line 3 times SS
(slowly, faster,
slowly); DS be-
tween 3-line groups;
repeat selected lines
as time permits

alphabet 1 Maxwell brought good quality black pajamas in five sizes for children.
fig/sym 2 My $1,098 raise (22.75%) was excellent; the average was $654 (10.35%).
, (comma) and figure 3 Should the figure be $13,234,987 rather than the $9,256,087 indicated?
fluency 4 Jane may go to the city to work with the audit panel on the amendment.

| 1 | 2 | 3 | 4 | 5 | 6 | 7 | 8 | 9 | 10 | 11 | 12 | 13 | 14 |

135b ▶ 8

Preapplication drill:
center heading in a
leftbound report

plain sheet; top margin: 1½"
for pica, 2" for elite; left margin: 1½"; other margins same
as for unbound

Read the guides contained in the drill at the right. Then prepare the drill, following the guides pre-sented.

words

GUIDES FOR CENTERING HEADINGS IN LEFTBOUND REPORTS 10

Main headings in leftbound reports are centered over the line of writing. 25
Follow these guides to center the main heading in this report and in other 40
leftbound reports. 44

1. Set the margins for the report. Use a 1½" left margin and a 1" 58
   right margin. 61

2. Determine the horizontal center of the line of writing by adding 75
   the scale number at both margin stops and dividing by 2. 86

3. Backspace from the horizontal center in order to center the 99
   heading. 101

Problem 2
Table with main, secondary, and column headings

full sheet; DS; reading position; 12 spaces between columns

Note: In Column 2, align the numbers at the right and include the letters after the numbers as part of the column.

			words
EVENING DIVISION CLASSROOM SCHEDULE			7
Thursday Evening Classes			12
Class	*Room*	*Instructor*	20
General Chemistry I	355R	Tourangeau	27
Typewriting I	31	Parks	31
Management	41	Sandberg	35
Literature	353F	Diepstra	39
Accounting	362R	Zabocki	44
English Composition	23	Costello	50
Marketing	356F	Foster	54
Psychology	310R	da Costa	58

81d ▶ 10
Inventory proof-reading/correcting skills

full sheet; DS; 2″ top margin; 1″ side margins; format the copy shown at the right, making the corrections indicated; BE ALERT there are at least 4 additional corrections that have *not* been indicated

	words
The ~~Nature of~~ Computers SOCIETY	4
Without a doubt, the computer has become a major force in	16
our society. Schools, corporations, government agencies, and	28
small business firms rely on computers on a daily basis. Com-	40
puter have even entered our personal lives with home computers	53
and electronic games--and that is just the begining. As the	65
costs for computer equipment continues to go down, computers	77
will became an even more integral part of our daily lives.	89
Most people have a fear of the unknown, therefore, they view com-	102
puters as electronic marvels with mystical powers. In reality,	115
a computer's abilities and capabilities are directly related to	128
the imagination of people. Therefore, it becomes essential that	141
people gain a basic under standing of computer functions. ~~knowledge,~~	152

134a ▶ 5
Preparatory practice

each line 3 times SS (slowly, faster, slowly); DS between 3-line groups; repeat selected lines as time permits

alphabet 1 The quarterbacks utilized very good judgment except for a few minutes.

fig/sym 2 The reference manual (Stock No. 2476*) was dated 1983 and cost $10.50.

long number groups 3 437-62-8072; (803) 787-7404; 15,342,679; #21376; 29206-6559; 777-60412

fluency 4 Did she visit the man to sign the form and to pay for the six bushels?

| 1 | 2 | 3 | 4 | 5 | 6 | 7 | 8 | 9 | 10 | 11 | 12 | 13 | 14 |

134b ▶ 15
Preapplication drills: prepare superscript and subscript figures and footnotes

plain sheets

Drill 1

70–space line; DS; do the drill twice

Drill 2

Assume this unbound report ended on Line 20. Place the footnote at the bottom of the page.

To type a superscript (superior figure), operate the automatic line finder; turn platen backward (toward you); type the figure or symbol; then return the automatic line finder and platen to normal position. Follow the same procedures to type a subscript, except turn platen forward (away from you).

To place footnotes at the bottom of a partially filled page, count the number of lines needed for the footnotes, plus 2 lines for the divider, and 6 lines for the bottom margin. Count from bottom of page to determine the placement of the footnotes.

Drill 1 Statistics quoted were from Xerox,[29] IBM,[30] Apple,[31] and Dictaphone.[32]

Table 2 gives values of critical points: $F_{.90}$, $F_{.95}$, $F_{.975}$, and $F_{.99}$.

Drill 2 _____

[4] Nancy DeMars, "Today's Professional Secretary," The Balance Sheet (September/October 1981), pp. 9-11.

134c ▶ 30
Prepare reports with footnotes

plain sheets

Problem 1
2d page of leftbound report

Prepare the material given at the right as the 2d page of a leftbound report. Follow the guides given in the outline on page 245 for a leftbound report.

words

The preliminary survey of all mid-level and top-level managers in our company 16

indicates that some resistance to the installa- 25

tion of desk-top computers can be expected. Approximately 40 percent of 40

our midlevel managers, and over 60 percent of our top-level managers 52

said they did not need a terminal. Management 59

consultants report similar findings in other companies. 73

Many corporate executives are not comfortable 82

with the thought of working with a computer. Executives are often 95

intimidated by the keyboard but they are not honest enough to 108

admit that[4] they are afraid of it 115

118

[4] Alexander L. Taylor, III, "Dealing with Terminal Phobia," 130
Time (July 19, 1982), p. 82. 136

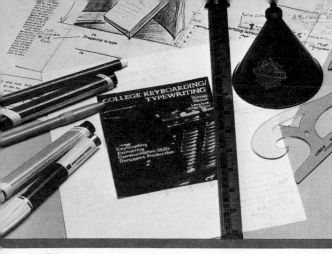

Learning goals

1 To improve basic skill on straight, rough–draft, and statistical copy.

2 To format personal–business letters in block and modified block styles.

3 To format business letters in block and modified block styles.

Machine adjustments

1 Paper guide at 0.

2 Margins: 70–space line for drills and ¶ writings; as directed for problems.

3 Spacing: SS drills; DS ¶ writings; as directed for problems.

4 Indention: 5 spaces for ¶ writings; as appropriate for problems.

82a ▶ 5
Preparatory practice

each line 3 times SS (slowly, faster, slowly); DS between 3-line groups; repeat selected lines as time permits

alphabet	1	Jack anxiously grabbed the dazed visitors from within their aquaplane.
fig/sym	2	A&N placed Order #4361, totaling $859.10, which was shipped August 27.
shift key	3	Jan and Kaye Vogt played golf at the Appomattox Country Club last May.
fluency	4	A fight may halt the amendment to rid the downtown zone of toxic odor.

| 1 | 2 | 3 | 4 | 5 | 6 | 7 | 8 | 9 | 10 | 11 | 12 | 13 | 14 |

82b ▶ 15
Build/measure straight-copy skill

1 Two 1' writings on each ¶ (1 for speed, 1 for control).

2 One 5' writing; proofread and circle errors; determine *gwam*.

Difficulty index

all letters used	A	1.5 si	5.7 awl	80% hfw

gwam 1' | 5'

You have probably noticed that money seldom stays in your pocket 13 | 3 | 57
for very long. The fact is, money never stays in any one location for 27 | 6 | 60
very long. Cash deposited in a bank is immediately put to work in the 41 | 9 | 63
form of loans and investments. When you buy merchandise at a business 55 | 12 | 66
establishment, your money travels on to pay employees, wholesalers, and 64 | 15 | 69
anyone else to whom the proprietor has an obligation. The role of money 79 | 18 | 72
is to circulate through the economy. 86 | 19 | 73

Money is required by companies of any size. Working with the fi- 13 | 22 | 76
nances of a firm means always thinking about assets and liabilities. 27 | 25 | 79
Assets are the items of value that a firm owns. Money held by a company 42 | 28 | 82
is one of its assets. Liabilities are debts, the money that the firm 56 | 31 | 85
owes to other people or groups. By subtracting the liabilities from the 71 | 34 | 88
assets, company officials can judge the financial strength of their firm. 86 | 37 | 91

Company financial managers must know how to regulate the movement 13 | 40 | 94
of money into and out of the firm. The fiscal operation of an organi- 27 | 43 | 97
zation is quite a complex area. A small business venture may have one 41 | 46 | 100
person directing its financial matters. But in a large firm, a whole 55 | 49 | 103
department is occupied with keeping track of the flow of funds and the 69 | 52 | 106
optimum ways to acquire and invest money. 77 | 54 | 108

gwam 1' | 1 | 2 | 3 | 4 | 5 | 6 | 7 | 8 | 9 | 10 | 11 | 12 | 13 | 14 |
5' | 1 | 2 | 3 |

Problem 2
Outline

2 full sheets; top margin on first page: 1½" for pica or 2" for elite; top margin on second page: 1"; side margins: 1"; bottom margin: approximately 1"; use main heading **GUIDES FOR KEYBOARDING REPORTS OR MANUSCRIPTS**; TS after main heading

1 Space forward once from left margin to type Roman numeral *I*. Reset left margin 2 spaces to the right of the period following *I*. The margin is now set at the point at which subheading *A* begins.

2 Set 3 tab stops: one 4 spaces, one 8 spaces, and the third 12 spaces from the left margin set for subheading *A*. You will use the margin release and backspace when you come to *II* and *III*.

3 Place the page number for the second page on Line 4, even with the right margin. Begin typing on Line 7.

4 Use a page–end indicator or a light pencil mark about 1½" from the bottom edge of the page to alert you to leave a 1" bottom margin. If you use a light pencil mark, be sure to erase it. A page–end indicator (page–line gauge) is provided on LM p. 6.

words
in heading 9

```
I.   MARGINS, SPACING, AND PAGINATION                              16
     A.  Unbound Reports                                           20
         1.  Margins                                               22
             a.  First page:  1 1/2" pica or 2" elite top margin; 1"  33
                 side and bottom margins for pica and elite.       42
             b.  Subsequent pages:  1" top and side margins and at 53
                 least 1" bottom margin for pica and elite.        61
         2.  Spacing                                               63
             a.  Body:  double-space; 5-space paragraph indentions;  74
                 leave at least 2 lines of a paragraph at top and  84
                 bottom of page.                                   87
             b.  Quoted material:  single-space quotes of 4 lines or  98
                 more; indent 5 spaces from both margins.          106
         3.  Pagination                                            109
             a.  First page:  center number 1/2" from bottom or omit  120
                 number.                                           121
             b.  Subsequent pages:  number on Line 4 at right margin.  132
     B.  Topbound and Leftbound Reports                            139
         1.  Margins                                               141
             a.  Topbound:  2" pica or 2 1/2" elite top margin for  152
                 first page; 1 1/2" top margin for subsequent pages;  162
                 same side and bottom margins as for unbound reports.  172
             b.  Leftbound:  1 1/2" left margin; other margins same  183
                 as for unbound.                                   186
         2.  Spacing                                               188
             a.  Topbound:  same spacing as for unbound.           197
             b.  Leftbound:  same spacing as for unbound.          206
         3.  Pagination                                            209
             a.  Leftbound:  number pages as for unbound reports.  220
             b.  Topbound:  number first page (or omit) and subse-  230
                 quent pages 1/2" from bottom; center number.      239
II.  HEADINGS AND SUBHEADINGS                                      245
     A.  Main and Secondary Headings                               251
         1.  Main:  format in ALL CAPS; center over line of writing;  263
             leave 1 blank line space between main and secondary   273
             headings or 2 blank line spaces between main heading and  284
             body if secondary heading is not used.                292
         2.  Secondary:  center over line of writing; capitalize im-  304
             portant words; leave 2 blank line spaces between the  315
             secondary heading and the body.                       321
     B.  Side Headings (Marginal Headings)                         328
         1.  Triple-space below text to type side heading.         338
         2.  Place side heading at left margin; use no terminal punc-  350
             tuation; capitalize important words; underline.       359
         3.  Leave 1 blank line space below side headings.         369
     C.  Paragraph Headings (Run-in Headings)                      377
         1.  Place at paragraph indention point; follow with period;  389
             underline.                                            391
         2.  Capitalize the first word of each heading.            400
III. DOCUMENTATION                                                 404
     A.  Footnotes                                                 407
         1.  Number consecutively; identify by superscript figures in  419
             body of report and in footnotes.                      425
         2.  Separate from body of text by a single space and a 1 1/2"  437
             divider line; DS below divider line.                  444
         3.  Indent first line of footnotes; single-space footnotes;  456
             double-space between footnotes.                       462
     B.  Explanatory Notes                                         466
         1.  Reference one note with asterisk or number in order.  477
         2.  Follow the same spacing guides as used for footnotes. 488
```

82c ▶ 30
Inventory/build letter skill

3 plain full sheets

Problem 1
Inventory personal-business letter

modified block style, open punctuation; date on Line 19; 60–space line

Note: Refer to page 64 to review proper format of a personal–business letter in modified block style.

words

132 Parkside Crescent | Rochester, NY 14617-7337 | June 13, 19-- | Mr. Paul   15
Perine | 308 Myrtle Avenue | Syracuse, NY 13204-4876 | Dear Paul   27

(¶ 1) Today I received my renewal form for season football tickets from the   41
Alumni Relations Office. I hope that you have received yours, also. It would be   57
great to get seats all together this year.   65

(¶ 2) I think it would be a good idea to sign up for seats right on the 40-yard line.   81
Mary and I have requested seats 20A and 21A. Maybe you could get seats 22A   96
and 23A.   98

(¶ 3) Mary and I are eager to see you and Carolyn again. Perhaps we can spend a   113
few weekends together this year!   119

Sincerely | William Sutton   124

Problem 2
Build personal-business letter skill

block style, open punctuation; date on Line 19; 60-space line

Note: Refer to page 58 to review proper format of a personal–business letter in block style.

532 Lemar Avenue | Evanston, IL 60201-5425 | October 29, 19-- | Mrs. Ann   14
Etowski | Alumni Relations Director | Underwood College | Palatine, IL 60067-   29
6325 | Dear Mrs. Etowski   32

(¶ 1) Thank you for writing to me about the Underwood College Alumni Giving   46
Campaign.   48

(¶ 2) I fondly remember my days on campus at Underwood. I received an edu-   62
cation there from which I have benefited all my life; furthermore, I took full   78
advantage of the extracurricular activities that Underwood offered during my   93
four years at the school.   98

(¶ 3) I want current and future students to enjoy the outstanding academic and   113
extracurricular advantages of Underwood College. Therefore, I am happy to   128
make my pledge to support Underwood in the coming year.   139

Sincerely | Ms. Sandra A. Brown   145

Problem 3
Build personal-business letter skill

use block or modified block style as you prefer, open punc–tuation; date on Line 19; 60–space line

Compose and format a response to the letter in Problem 1, using the current date. Express your interest in attending games and visiting for the weekend. Make any necessary corrections and retype the letter in final form.

83

83a ▶ 5
Preparatory practice

each line 3 times SS (slowly, faster, slowly); DS between 3-line groups; repeat selected lines as time permits

alphabet 1 Goff quickly realized his express bus ticket was good just this month.

fig/sym 2 General T & T (common stock) had sales of 5,936,067 shares at 142 5/8.

double letters 3 Bonnie and Sally will recommend acceptance at your next press meeting.

fluency 4 Nan Cox may wish to dismantle the bicycle for the visit to the island.

| 1 | 2 | 3 | 4 | 5 | 6 | 7 | 8 | 9 | 10 | 11 | 12 | 13 | 14 |

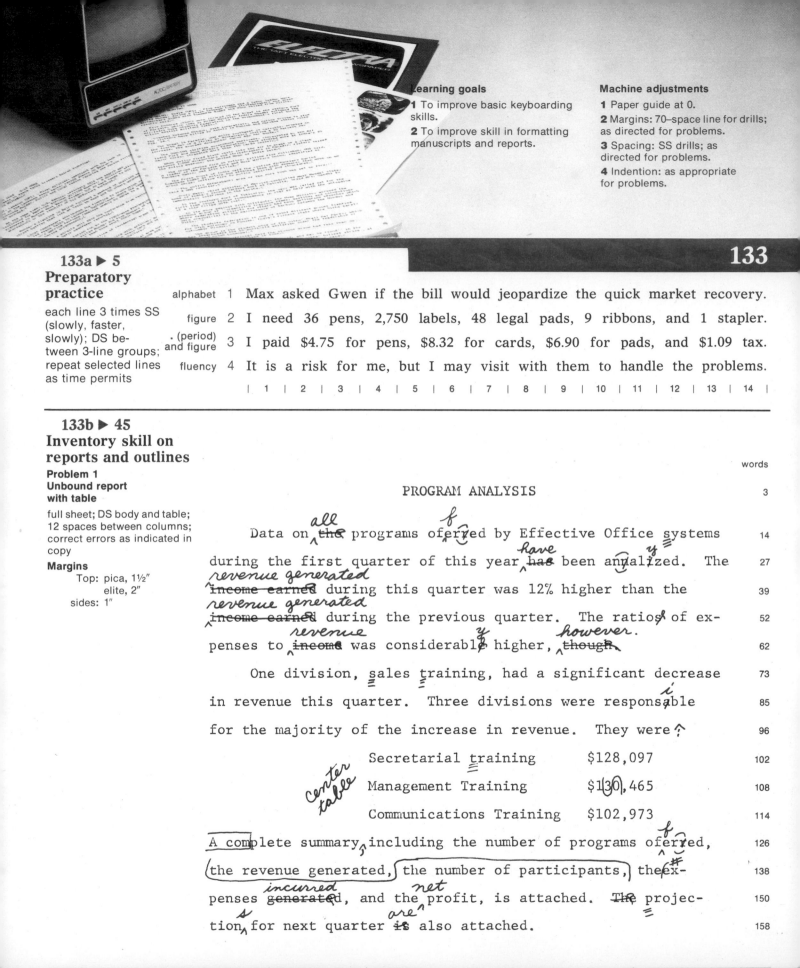

133a ▶ 5
Preparatory practice

each line 3 times SS (slowly, faster, slowly); DS between 3-line groups; repeat selected lines as time permits

alphabet 1 Max asked Gwen if the bill would jeopardize the quick market recovery.

figure 2 I need 36 pens, 2,750 labels, 48 legal pads, 9 ribbons, and 1 stapler.

. (period) and figure 3 I paid $4.75 for pens, $8.32 for cards, $6.90 for pads, and $1.09 tax.

fluency 4 It is a risk for me, but I may visit with them to handle the problems.

| 1 | 2 | 3 | 4 | 5 | 6 | 7 | 8 | 9 | 10 | 11 | 12 | 13 | 14 |

133b ▶ 45
Inventory skill on reports and outlines

Problem 1
Unbound report with table

full sheet; DS body and table; 12 spaces between columns; correct errors as indicated in copy

Margins
    Top: pica, 1½"
           elite, 2"
    sides: 1"

words

PROGRAM ANALYSIS   3

Data on all programs offered by Effective Office systems   14
during the first quarter of this year have been analyzed. The   27
revenue generated during this quarter was 12% higher than the   39
revenue generated during the previous quarter. The ratios of ex-   52
penses to revenue was considerably higher, however.   62

One division, sales training, had a significant decrease   73
in revenue this quarter. Three divisions were responsible   85
for the majority of the increase in revenue. They were: 96

center table

    Secretarial training $128,097   102
    Management Training $130,465   108
    Communications Training $102,973   114

A complete summary, including the number of programs offered,   126
the revenue generated, the number of participants, the ex-   138
penses incurred, and the net profit, is attached. The projec-   150
tions for next quarter are also attached.   158

Learning goals
1 To improve basic keyboarding skills.
2 To improve skill in formatting manuscripts and reports.

Machine adjustments
1 Paper guide at 0.
2 Margins: 70–space line for drills; as directed for problems.
3 Spacing: SS drills; as directed for problems.
4 Indention: as appropriate for problems.

**Build/measure
rough-draft skill**

1 Two 1' writings on each ¶
(1 for speed, 1 for control).

2 One 5' writing; proofread
and circle errors; determine
gwam.

Difficulty index

all letters used	A	1.5 si	5.7 awl	80% hfw

gwam 1' 5'

Everybody has goals, not matter how clearly this maybe de-   13 | 3 | 61
fined. For example, we understand that all in but a few excep-   25 | 5 | 63
tional cases, the main purpose of most individuals is happy.   39 | 8 | 66
So to reach this objective, we set various goals. A goal may   53 | 11 | 69
be to get done with college or to find the right job or to re-   64 | 13 | 71
dieve a salary increase or to head something.   74 | 15 | 73

Another know fact is that most people change there goals   12 | 17 | 75
from time to time. In fact, experts who specialize in getting   25 | 19 | 77
others plan for the futeur often urge that goals should be   37 | 21 | 79
made for the short, intermedate, and long term, and that these   50 | 23 | 81
goals should be rethoughts often. We usually resets our goals   62 | 25 | 83
when we acquire new confidence about our own, or new information   77 | 28 | 86
about this world.   82 | 29 | 87

We must come up with plans to accomplish our goals. We   11 | 31 | 89
must decide what goals to achieve first and put the goals into   24 | 33 | 91
properorder. Short-term goals should really point to longer   38 | 36 | 94
term goals. For example, as a student new to college, achieving   52 | 39 | 97
the short-term goal of finding a part-time job maybe necessary   65 | 41 | 99
before i can develop a course schedule that will take me to my   78 | 44 | 102
longer term goal, a collage education.   86 | 45 | 103

It may look like conscientious planing of our goals would   12 | 47 | 105
prevent us from enjoying spontaneity in our life But having   25 | 49 | 107
a set of plans doesn't mean that we cannot change or postpone   38 | 51 | 109
projects. We canstill have spur-of-the-moment activities. But   52 | 54 | 112
making plans and sticking to them will help us to make the most   65 | 56 | 114
of our abilities and to accomplish our goals.   74 | 58 | 116

Communication skills checkup: choose the right word

half sheet, long side up; 1″ top margin; 74-space line

Keyboard and format as directed in 127d, p. 234.

Key: 1. accept, advising, principal 2. It's, past, advise, personnel, affect 3. personnel, cited, per–sonal, principles 4. site, except 5. further, farther, passed

1. Who must (accept/except) the responsibility for (advicing/advising) the (principal/principle) stockholders of the loss?

2. (Its/It's) in the minutes of (passed/past) meetings that the president will (advice/advise) stockholders and company (personal/personnel) of any changes that (affect/effect) our financial position.

3. The (personal/personnel) director was (cited/sited/sighted) for (personal/ personnel) integrity and high (principals/principles).

4. The (cite/site/sight) is excellent (accept/except) for the cost.

5. After (farther/further) consideration, the motion to move (farther/further) from the airport was (passed/past).

132d ▶ 15
Build/measure statistical-copy skill

1 Two 1′ writings on each ¶ for speed; circle errors; determine *gwam*.

2 One 5′ control writing on all ¶s combined; circle errors; determine *gwam*.

Difficulty index

all letters used	A	1.5 si	5.7 awl	80% hfw

	gwam 1′	5′
More and more women are employed today. In 1965, less than 40	13	3 | 60
percent of women participated in the labor force. In 1982, the rate	27	6 | 63
had risen to 52 percent. The rate is predicted to rise to 65 percent	41	9 | 66
by 1995. Roughly 50 percent of all married women with children under	55	12 | 69
six years old maintain jobs outside the home. Over 40 percent of all	69	15 | 72
families are two-income families. The typical two-income family earns	83	18 | 75
about 27 percent more than the typical one-income family.	94	20 | 77
Salaries for women lag behind salaries for men by about 35 percent.	14	23 | 80
Several studies have shown that women make about 59 cents for every dol-	28	26 | 83
lar men make. Many women today are choosing careers in areas that were	42	29 | 86
once thought of as jobs for men. In fact, about 33 percent of women	56	32 | 89
now entering the work force choose jobs traditionally held by men. These	71	35 | 92
women say they are choosing jobs in order to maximize their incomes.	85	38 | 95
The changing role of women has had a significant effect on society.	14	41 | 98
Changes are reflected in consumer buying, in voting, in the division of	28	44 | 101
duties of caring for home and children, and in many other ways. Day-	42	47 | 104
care centers are quite common today, but they cannot accommodate the	56	50 | 107
13,000,000 children who are 13 years old and under. Many firms have	70	53 | 110
had to adjust working hours or to offer flexible time to help working	84	56 | 113
parents.	86	57 | 114

gwam 1′ | 1 | 2 | 3 | 4 | 5 | 6 | 7 | 8 | 9 | 10 | 11 | 12 | 13 | 14 |
5′ | 1 | 2 | 3 |

83c ▶ 30
Inventory/build letter skill
3 plain full sheets

Note: Refer to page 78 to re-view proper format for busi-ness letters in block style.

Problem 1
Inventory business letter

block style, open punctuation; date on Line 19; 60–space line

May 15, 19-- | Mr. George Fox | 200 Old Tappan Road | Old Tappan, NJ 07675- | 15
3126 | Dear Mr. Fox | 19

(¶ 1) Although you were notified that Vantage Motor Homes, Inc., has placed | 33
your account with us for collection, we at Colby Financial Association have | 48
received no response from you to our previous request for payment. | 61

(¶ 2) In order to avoid taking further steps to collect this account, it is necessary | 75
that we receive the full payment of $345.89 by May 28. | 86

(¶ 3) Please make your check payable to Colby Financial Association and send it | 101
immediately. If you have any questions about this matter, please direct them to | 117
Mr. Robert Wilson, Credit Manager at Vantage Motor Homes, Inc. | 129

Yours very truly | Joseph Brennan | Collection Manager | xx | 140

Problem 2
Build business letter skill

block style, open punctuation; date on Line 16; 60–space line

Current date | Ms. Sylvia Perez | 415 East Plaza Drive | Westmont, IL 60559-8736 | | 17
Dear Ms. Perez | 20

(¶ 1) You will soon be receiving your Redi-Cash Card. Your card will make it | 34
possible for you to enjoy our All Hours Banking Service. | 45

(¶ 2) In order to operate the All-Hours machine, you must utilize your personal | 60
identification code. This confidential code must be entered into the keyboard | 76
before any machine transaction can be completed. | 86

(¶ 3) Never carry the code in written form in the same purse or billfold with | 100
your card. If your card were lost or stolen, you would not want the code to be | 116
available also. Immediately report any lost or stolen card to your bank. | 131

(¶ 4) You will receive your Redi-Cash Card within the next few days. Several | 146
days later, your personal identification code will come in the mail. We at First | 162
National Bank hope that you will use and enjoy our All-Hours Banking Service. | 177

Yours very truly | Mrs. Karen Myers | New Accounts Manager | xx | 189

Problem 3
Build personal-business letter skill

block style, open punctuation; date on Line 19; 60–space line

Compose and type a short response to the letter in Problem 1, using the date May 17 of the current year. Use the following elements in your letter: (1) express concern that you have received a notice from the collection agency even though the bill has been paid; (2) state that you sent a check for the full payment of $345.89 to Vantage Motor Homes on May 5; (3) address the letter to **Mr. Robert Wilson** at the following location: **Vantage Motor Homes, Inc., 501 Main Street, Old Tappan, NJ 07675-5235.** Type the title **Credit Manager** under Mr. Wilson's name in the address.

132a ▶ 5
Preparatory practice

each line 3 times SS (slowly, faster, slowly); DS between 3-line groups; repeat selected lines as time permits

alphabet 1 We did ship six blue, blazer-style jackets to Farmington very quickly.

figure 2 The numbers on Lines 9 and 16 should be 437-621-8071 and 803-252-4593.

symbol 3 Please order 4 new carts, #A-6467 (Size 32″ × 30″ × 20″), at $75 each.

fluency 4 Did the busy civic auditor pay for the big field work on the key land?

| 1 | 2 | 3 | 4 | 5 | 6 | 7 | 8 | 9 | 10 | 11 | 12 | 13 | 14 |

132b ▶ 15
Build/measure straight copy skill

1 Two 1' writings on each ¶ for speed; circle errors; determine *gwam*.

2 One 5' control writing on all ¶s combined; circle errors; determine *gwam*.

Difficulty index

| all letters used | A | 1.5 si | 5.7 awl | 80% hfw |

gwam 1' | 5'

People spend far more time listening than they spend communicating   14 | 3 | 70
in any other way, but only a very few people have developed good listen-   27 | 6 | 73
ing skills. There is a big difference between hearing and listening.   41 | 9 | 76
Hearing does not require major effort, but listening is hard work. One   55 | 12 | 79
of the problems with listening is that we can listen about three times   68 | 15 | 82
faster than most people speak. We are able to hear what the speaker   81 | 18 | 85
is saying and still have extra time for our minds to wander to other   94 | 21 | 88
things.   95 | 22 | 89

An active listener utilizes the difference between the listening   13 | 25 | 92
and the speaking rates to make mental summaries of the conversation.   27 | 28 | 95
One way to listen actively is to try to anticipate the next point that   41 | 31 | 98
the individual will make. It is also important to clarify in your own   55 | 34 | 101
mind what is being said. Generally, people try to assume too much. A   69 | 37 | 104
good listener will let the person explain in her or his own words ex-   83 | 40 | 107
actly what she or he would like to say. Paraphrasing is a good way to   97 | 43 | 110
confirm that the message is understood.   115 | 45 | 112

A person who has developed good listening skills will not interrupt   14 | 48 | 115
the person who is speaking. The problem is that most people prefer to   28 | 51 | 118
speak than to listen. Sometimes it takes a considerable amount of   41 | 54 | 121
effort to give the person an opportunity to get the message across.   55 | 57 | 124
Showing that you are interested in what is being said helps to put the   69 | 60 | 127
speaker at ease. It is not enough just to listen; you also have to look   84 | 63 | 130
like you are listening. The effective use of body language enhances   98 | 66 | 133
listening.   100 | 67 | 134

gwam 1' | 1 | 2 | 3 | 4 | 5 | 6 | 7 | 8 | 9 | 10 | 11 | 12 | 13 | 14 |
5' | 1 | 2 | 3 |

84a ▶ 5
Preparatory practice

each line 3 times SS (slowly, faster, slowly); DS between 3-line groups; repeat selected lines as time permits

alphabet 1 My dazed quarterback was very jumpy and frightened from a taxing blow.

fig/sym 2 Their newest model (XL-264) is selling at $1,853.79 less 10% for cash.

adjacent keys 3 In Luis' opinion, a few assets were reported in excess of their value.

fluency 4 She may go with them to the downtown firm to sign the authentic title.

| 1 | 2 | 3 | 4 | 5 | 6 | 7 | 8 | 9 | 10 | 11 | 12 | 13 | 14 |

84b ▶ 15
Build/measure statistical-copy skill

1 Two 1' writings on each ¶ (1 for speed, 1 for control).

2 One 5' writing; proofread and circle errors; determine *gwam*.

Difficulty index

all letters/figures used | A | 1.5 si | 5.7 awl | 80% hfw

gwam 1' 5'

Women in the United States continue to gain power in the day-to- 13 | 3 | 64
day activities of business and government. Part of this power shift is 27 | 5 | 67
attributable to the changing numerical balance between men and women. 41 | 8 | 70
In 1950, for the first time in history, there were more women than men 56 | 11 | 72
in this country. Presently, our nation has nearly 6 million more fe- 69 | 14 | 75
males than males; and a Census Bureau projection reveals that the gap 83 | 17 | 78
could widen to 7.2 million by the year 2000. 93 | 19 | 80

To examine the numbers in another manner, we can state that in 13 | 21 | 82
1910 there were 106 males for every 100 females, but that in the year 27 | 24 | 85
2000 there will be only 95 males for every 100 females. Throughout 40 | 27 | 88
history, more boys than girls have come into the world--the ratio has 54 | 29 | 91
been approximately 105 baby boys per 100 baby girls. However, the mor- 68 | 32 | 94
tality rate of infant boys is always higher than that of infant girls. 83 | 35 | 96
This discrepancy in the survival rate more than makes up for the greater 97 | 38 | 99
number of boys born. 102 | 39 | 100

Women have consistently had lower mortality rates than men at all 13 | 42 | 103
stages of life. Girls born in 1900 could expect to outlive boys by 27 | 44 | 104
less than 3 years. For people born in 1977, women are anticipated to 41 | 47 | 108
outlive men by about 8 years. During the same 77-year period, life 54 | 50 | 111
expectancies at birth grew 29 years for women (from 48 in 1900 to 77 68 | 53 | 114
in 1977) while increasing just 23 years for men (rising from 46 to 69 82 | 55 | 117
years). The greater number of women and their lengthier life spans 96 | 58 | 119
will be significant in all aspects of commerce and government in fu- 109 | 60 | 122
ture decades. 112 | 61 | 123

gwam 1' | 1 | 2 | 3 | 4 | 5 | 6 | 7 | 8 | 9 | 10 | 11 | 12 | 13 | 14 |
5' | 1 | 2 | 3 |

131c ▶ 10
Communication skills checkup: choose the right word

half sheet, long side up; 1″ top margin; 74-space line

Keyboard and format as directed in 127d, p. 234.

Key: 1. principal, passed, personnel 2. past, personal, principle

passed — (verb) past tense of pass	past — (adjective) ended, gone by (noun) time gone by
personal — (adjective) private, individual	personnel — (noun) employees
principal — (adjective) main (noun) leading person; head of a school	principle — (noun) basic truth, rule

1. The (principal/principle)(passed/past) out the report but referred questions to the director of (personal/personnel).

2. The manager was out for the (passed/past) five days conducting (personal/personnel) business and, as a matter of (principal/principle), would not disclose the nature of the business.

131d ▶ 15
Build/measure rough-draft skill

1 Two 1′ writings on each ¶ for speed; circle errors; determine *gwam*.

2 One 5′ writing for control on all ¶s combined; circle errors; determine *gwam*.

Difficulty index

all letters used	A	1.5 si	5.7 awl	80% hfw

gwam 1′ | 5′

It is ~~necessary~~ important that ~~every~~ each employee learns how to make   11 | 2 | 50

wise decisions. an ~~employee~~ worker who helps to make a decision   22 | 4 | 52

about her or his job is much more likely to support that decision   35 | 7 | 55

than is an employee who is not given the chance to make   46 | 9 | 57

job-related decisions. Decisions made by a group ~~or~~   56 | 11 | 59

~~groups~~ of ~~employees~~ workers will normally be better than deci-   65 | 13 | 61

sions made by one person. ~~Group~~ cooperative decision making pro-   77 | 15 | 63

duces a synergistic effect. Synergy ~~is~~ means working ~~together~~   82 | 16 | 64

cooperatively. A synergistic effect produces out comes   15 | 19 | 67

that are far greater than the sum of all the separate   26 | 21 | 69

actions. ~~Every~~ Each person who analyzes a problem brings to   37 | 23 | 71

the problem-solving process a ~~different~~ unique view of the ~~thing~~ problem   48 | 25 | 73

and how to solve it. The idea that one worker may bring   59 | 27 | 75

to discuss with the group may cause others workers to think of   71 | 29 | 77

some thing else that is related.   77 | 30 | 78

Workers can not be expected to make wise decisions   10 | 32 | 80

unless they are taught ~~how to make decisions~~ the process of decision making. The first   23 | 35 | 83

step is ~~to try~~ to identify the basic problem. The second   33 | 37 | 85

step is to ~~look for~~ seek all of the feasible ways to solve ~~it~~ the problem.   46 | 40 | 88

The third step is to analyze each ~~of the~~ alternatives in   56 | 42 | 90

an objective fashion. Then the fourth step is to decide   67 | 44 | 92

which of the various alternatives would be ~~a good~~ the best possible solution to   92 | 47 | 95

the problem.   94 | 48 | 96

**Inventory/build
letter skill**

3 plain full sheets

Note: See page 84 to review proper format of a business letter in modified block style.

**Problem 1
Inventory business letter**

modified block style, open punctuation; date on Line 16; 60–space line

words

June 27, 19-- | Mr. Jerry Donahoe | President | Woodall Manufacturing Corpora- 15
tion | 2345 Fifth Avenue | Atlanta, GA 30354-4752 | Dear Mr. Donahoe 28

(¶ 1) Do you have security problems at your plant? You may be amazed to read 42
this: Many industrial buildings which house extremely costly equipment 56
nevertheless lack an adequate security system. In many cases, security gaps 71
exist even though highly sensitive and expensive protective devices have been 87
installed. 89

(¶ 2) Open-plan facilities such as those at your company are especially vulner- 104
able. We in the commercial security field are becoming more and more aware of 120
the losses that can result from open work environments. 131

(¶ 3) Continental Protection is eager to help you protect your facilities. I hope 146
that you will contact us soon so that we can visit your plant and describe to you 163
the types of security systems we can set up at Woodall. I am sure that Con- 178
tinental can provide you with peace of mind about your important and valuable 194
industrial assets. 198

Sincerely yours | Mrs. Margaret Ann Roth | Industrial Representative | xx 212

**Problem 2
Build business
letter skill**

modified block style, open punctuation; date on Line 16; 60–space line

September 9, 19-- | Mr. Charles Sauder | 89 East Avenue | Rochester, NY 14604- 15
6983 | Dear Mr. Sauder 19

(¶ 1) As a high-school senior interested in enrolling at Underwood College, you 34
are cordially invited to attend the Fall Open House to be given by the school. 50
The open house is scheduled for Saturday, November 1, from 11 a.m. to 4 p.m. 66
This event will include all departments on campus. In addition, students who 82
are considering enrolling in the science, engineering, music, and business cur- 98
ricula may attend special programs in these areas. 108

(¶ 2) If you would like to participate in the Fall Open House, please write and let 124
us know by October 15. A detailed schedule of events, along with a map and 139
directions to the campus, will be sent to you upon receipt of your reply. 154

(¶ 3) We appreciate your interest in Underwood College and know that you will 168
find the open house informative and stimulating. We look forward to welcom- 183
ing you to our campus and community on Saturday, November 1. 195

Sincerely yours | Ms. Karen Schwarzwalder | Public Relations Director | xx 209

**Problem 3
Build personal-
business letter skill**

modified block style, open punctuation; date on Line 19; 60–space line

Compose and format a short response to the letter in Problem 2, using the date of **September 12, 19—**, and these elements: (1) you wish to attend the open house; (2) the business curriculum interests you; (3) you would like information on expenses at Underwood. Address the letter to **Ms. Karen Schwarzwalder**, who is the **Public Relations Director** at **Underwood College, Palatine, IL 60067-6325.**

131a ▶ 5
Preparatory practice

each line 3 times SS (slowly, faster, slowly); DS between 3-line groups; repeat selected lines as time permits

alphabet	1	Glenda Schatzer just came back from a very quick trip to a wax museum.
figure	2	Please change Stock Numbers 3231-A and 62987-C to 4865-A and 147009-C.
direct reach	3	My brothers found a large piece of medium grey and light green fabric.
fluency	4	Andy paid for work on eight maps of the lake and six maps of the town.

| 1 | 2 | 3 | 4 | 5 | 6 | 7 | 8 | 9 | 10 | 11 | 12 | 13 | 14 |

131b ▶ 20
Measure/compare progressive straight-copy skill

1 Three 1' writings on ¶1. Use the highest rate as the base rate for the next writings.

2 Three 1' writings on ¶2. Try to equal or exceed the base rate established on ¶1.

3 Three 1' writings on ¶3. Try to equal or exceed the base rate established on ¶1.

4 One 5' writing on all ¶s. Try to maintain the ¶1 base rate on all ¶s.

all letters used

¶1 Difficulty index	¶2 Difficulty index	¶3 Difficulty index
E 1.2 si 5.1 awl 90% hfw	A 1.5 si 5.7 awl 80% hfw	HA 1.7 si 6.0 awl 75% hfw

gwam 1' 5'

Just who is a leader? Could you learn to be a leader if you wanted 14 3 60
to be one? A number of people have done studies on the traits of lead- 28 6 63
ers and on leadership style. For many years, studies were done to see 42 9 66
if traits could be found in people who were leaders that were not found 56 12 69
in people who were not leaders. Not a single one has been found that 70 15 72
can be used to separate persons who are leaders from persons who are 84 18 75
not. 85 19 76

Recent studies seem to focus on style of leadership. One way to 13 22 79
define leadership is that it is a means of influencing the actions or 27 25 82
behavior of others in an effort to reach a goal. A leader, thus, must 41 28 85
care about working with others and about getting a job done. Concern 55 31 88
about working with others is called relationship behavior. Concern 69 34 91
about getting a job done is called task behavior. Both kinds of be- 82 37 94
havior are very important. 87 38 95

Effective use of leadership style requires a leader to vary the 13 41 98
leadership style depending on the situation that exists. Some situ- 26 44 101
ations call for a leadership style that is relationship oriented; some 40 47 104
call for a leadership style that is task oriented; and others call for 54 50 107
a leadership style that is a combination of the two. Varying the style 68 53 110
is not easy because each person in an organization tends to feel more 82 56 113
comfortable with a given style. 87 57 114

| gwam 1' | | 1 | 2 | 3 | 4 | 5 | 6 | 7 | 8 | 9 | 10 | 11 | 12 | 13 | 14 | |
| 5' | | | | 1 | | | | 2 | | | | 3 | | | |

Learning goals

1 To format business letters in the acceptable styles illustrated.

2 To improve basic keyboarding and proofreading skills.

3 To address two sizes of envelopes in an acceptable manner.

Machine adjustments

1 Paper guide at 0.

2 Margins: 70–space line for drills and ¶ writings; as directed for problems.

3 Spacing: SS drills; DS ¶ writings; as directed for problems.

4 Indention: 5 spaces for ¶ writings; as appropriate for problems.

85a ▶ 5
Preparatory practice

each line 3 times SS (slowly, faster, slowly); DS between 3-line groups; repeat selected lines if time permits

alphabet 1 Jackie reported sixty-four valuable quartz watches missing on Tuesday.

fig/sym 2 Did their Invoice #9264 for $1,037.88 include a 5% discount of $51.89?

adjacent key 3 Her appointment to the new position pleased many leaders in education.

fluency 4 Do we both wish to work with the panel to enrich the authentic ritual?

| 1 | 2 | 3 | 4 | 5 | 6 | 7 | 8 | 9 | 10 | 11 | 12 | 13 | 14 |

85b ▶ 10
Improve keyboarding technique

each pair of lines 3 times SS; DS between 6-line groups; work at a controlled rate

direct reach 1 They agreed a maximum number of payments for service must be received.

2 We doubt a great many officers must renounce their service agreements.

adjacent keys 3 What equipment do we need to record her weekly news talks on the radio?

4 We outlined for you the six important points in the government report.

double letters 5 A traffic officer suggested we needed three additional gallons of gas.

6 Book orders for all college classes this summer must be submitted now.

shift keys 7 Donna's itinerary included New York, Boston, Los Angeles, and Chicago.

8 Mary Ann attended River College after graduation from Lee High School.

| 1 | 2 | 3 | 4 | 5 | 6 | 7 | 8 | 9 | 10 | 11 | 12 | 13 | 14 |

85c ▶ 7
Learn letter format

plain sheets; 60-space line; begin on Line 14

1 Using Style letter 5, page 159, format and type the opening lines and the first line of the body. Leave proper spacing between parts.

2 Space down to Line 48. Format and type the last 3 lines of ¶4 and the closing lines, leaving proper spacing between them.

3 On another sheet of paper, take a 1' writing on the opening lines and ¶1; a 1' writing on ¶s 2 and 3; and a 1' writing on the last 3 lines of ¶4 and closing lines.

85d ▶ 28
Improve business letter skill

60-space line; begin on Line 13

Note: From this point, LM page references refer to the second workbook, *Laboratory Materials*, stock number T771.

Problem 1 (plain sheet)
Format and type the letter illustrated on page 159.
  Proofread; use standard proofreader's marks to indicate needed corrections.

Problem 2 (LM p. 11)
Using your corrected copy, prepare a final copy of the letter, making the corrections indicated in your copy.

Problem 3 (plain sheet)
If time permits, take a 5' writing on the entire letter. Determine *gwam* by dividing total words typed by 5.

Improve keyboarding technique

each pair of lines 3 times SS at a controlled rate; DS between 6-line groups

letter response
1 Kinuyo, in my opinion, deserves only a few bad grades on tests in art.
2 We regret Lynn started at only minimum wage in a union garage in July.

word response
3 The amendment to their bid is a civic problem for the towns to handle.
4 The auditor did the work, and the firms paid the city with the profit.

combination response
5 We did imply they may have to limit the work they do on the editorial.
6 Ted plans to visit with the vendor to look at the quality of the loom.

| 1 | 2 | 3 | 4 | 5 | 6 | 7 | 8 | 9 | 10 | 11 | 12 | 13 | 14 |

130d ▶ 15

Build/measure script-copy skill

1 Three 1' writings on each ¶ for speed; circle errors; determine *gwam*.
2 One 5' control writing on both ¶s combined; circle errors; determine *gwam*.

Difficulty index

all letters used	A	1.5 si	5.7 awl	80% hfw

	gwam 1'	5'
We hear a tremendous amount about the negative side	10	2 | 45
of stress, but we do not hear very much about the	20	4 | 47
positive side. Stress can be very healthful. It can be a	32	6 | 49
motivating or an energizing force. It is important to	43	8 | 51
learn to control our frustrations and to incorporate	54	10 | 53
some satisfying activities into our work. Before we can	65	12 | 55
manage our stress, we must identify the cause of	75	14 | 57
it. Identifying the cause of a problem is not always	86	16 | 59
simple. Frequently, we deal with symptoms rather	96	18 | 61
than the actual problem.	101	19 | 63
It might be necessary to alter our life-style sig-	10	21 | 65
nificantly if we wish to manage stress effectively.	21	23 | 67
We cannot separate stress caused by our work from	31	25 | 69
that caused by other factors in our lives. The first	42	27 | 71
step is to reassess our priorities in life. We should	53	29 | 73
question ourselves seriously about those things in	63	31 | 75
life that are most precious to us. The second step	73	33 | 77
is to examine carefully our job priorities. Then we	84	35 | 79
can work to balance the two. Trying to do too	93	37 | 81
much causes most of the pressures we experience.	103	39 | 83
We need to recognize the things that are most	112	41 | 85
important and put our emphasis on those things.	121	43 | 87

Pennsylvania Junior College Association

1500 Academy Street
Harrisburg, PA 15906-4532
(717) 555-1490

	words	in parts	total

Dateline   June 15, 19--   3   3

Letter   Mr. Dana Fox, President   8   8
address   York Community College   12   12
            West Seventh Avenue   16   16
            York, PA 17404-5436   20   20

Salutation   Dear Mr. Fox: 23   23

Body   The annual meeting of the Pennsylvania Junior College   34   34
of letter   Association will take place on Thursday, September 9, at the   46   46
            Plaza Hotel, Philadelphia, Pennsylvania.   55   55

                A stimulating program has been developed by the program   11   66
            committee, chaired by Susan Walker, Dean, Community College   23   78
            of Philadelphia. This year's speaker will be John Winston,   35   90
            Assistant Dean of Education, Syracuse University Graduate   47   101
            School of Education. His address is entitled "Education in   59   113
            a Time of Change."   63   117

                Dr. Winston's teaching, research, and administrative   73   128
            activities focus on lifelong learning, professional develop-   85   140
            ment, and administration of postsecondary education. He cur- 98   152
            rently serves as education chairperson of the Institute for   110 164
            the Development of Lifelong Education.   118 172

                We are certain that you will find this meeting timely   183
            and informative. Please call (717) 281-4339 to register and   195
            get any additional information you may desire. The $25 reg-   207
            istration fee covers the cost of the meeting, refreshments,   12   219
            and luncheon. We look forward to seeing you on September 9   24   231
            at the Plaza Hotel.   28   235

Complimentary   Yours very truly,   31   239
close

Signature   *Pamela Strombom*

Typed name   Pamela Strombom, Ph.D.   36   243
Official title   President   38   245

Reference   xx   39   246
initials

In *mixed punctuation*, a colon follows
the salutation and a comma follows
the complimentary close.

Style letter 5: modified block style with indented paragraphs and mixed punctuation

Learning goals

1 To improve basic skill on straight, script, rough–draft, and statistical copy.
2 To improve proofreading skills.
3 To improve composition and grammar application skills.

Machine adjustments

1 Paper guide at 0.
2 Margins: 70–space line for drills and ¶ writings.
3 Spacing: SS drills; DS ¶ writings.
4 Indention: 5 spaces for ¶ writings.

130a ▶ 5
Preparatory practice

each line 3 times SS (slowly, faster, slowly); DS between 3-line groups; repeat selected lines as time permits

alphabet	1	Kevin may be required to utilize six large units on the wharf project.
figure	2	Maria said 827 men, 934 women, and 1,056 children attended the picnic.
adjacent key	3	Are you going to shop there because pop art and coins are on sale now?
fluency	4	Eight of the downtown firms paid for the city to do the work for them.

| 1 | 2 | 3 | 4 | 5 | 6 | 7 | 8 | 9 | 10 | 11 | 12 | 13 | 14 |

130b ▶ 15
Build/measure straight-copy skill

1 Two 1′ writings on each ¶ for speed; circle errors; determine *gwam*.
2 One 5′ control writing on all ¶s combined; circle errors; determine *gwam*.

Difficulty index

all letters used | A | 1.5 si | 5.7 awl | 80% hfw

	gwam 1′	5′

At one time it was thought that managers were the primary employees · 14 · 3 | 62
who needed to be able to cope with occupational stress. Today, however, · 29 · 6 | 65
research has shown that blue-collar workers and office employees are · 43 · 9 | 68
also victims of job pressures and tensions. In fact, these two groups · 57 · 12 | 71
are rated on many scales as having very high-stress jobs. Companies · 71 · 15 | 74
are spending a major amount of time and money to help workers in these · 85 · 18 | 77
jobs learn how to manage job pressure. · 93 · 20 | 79

One factor that seems to have an effect on the amount of stress a · 13 · 23 | 82
person experiences at work is the perception the individual has of how · 27 · 26 | 85
the requirements of the job match her or his ability. A person who · 41 · 29 | 88
perceives a poor fit between his or her ability and the job require- · 55 · 32 | 91
ments seems to experience more stress than a person who believes his or · 69 · 35 | 94
her ability matches the job. A challenging position is not necessarily · 83 · 38 | 97
a stressful position. · 88 · 42 | 101

Another factor that appears to have an effect on the amount of · 13 · 45 | 104
stress a worker experiences on the job is the amount of control that she · 28 · 48 | 107
or he can exert over the work. Those individuals who have the chance · 42 · 51 | 110
to help make decisions that affect their jobs seem to encounter fewer · 56 · 54 | 113
problems than individuals in organizations that do not permit them to · 70 · 57 | 116
take an active part in making job-related decisions. · 80 · 59 | 118

gwam 1′ | 1 | 2 | 3 | 4 | 5 | 6 | 7 | 8 | 9 | 10 | 11 | 12 | 13 | 14 |
5′ | 1 | 2 | 3 |

86a ▶ 5
Preparatory practice

each line 3 times SS (slowly, faster, slowly); DS between 3-line groups; repeat selected lines if time permits

alphabet	1 The six zany jokers might have had backup plans they quickly followed.
fig/sym	2 The bid by Lee & Fox for $28,746 was 9% lower than our bid of $31,590.
direct reach	3 Reserving my doubts should end a great number of technical objections.
fluency	4 The problem is with their firm, so he may sue to enrich the endowment.

| 1 | 2 | 3 | 4 | 5 | 6 | 7 | 8 | 9 | 10 | 11 | 12 | 13 | 14 |

86b ▶ 10
Review envelope format

Postal recommendations

1 Format the address lines in block style (even left margin) in the area on the envelope that the scanner is programmed to read.

2 For a large (No. 10) envelope, begin the address vertically on Line 15 and horizontally about 5 spaces left of the center point.

3 For a small (No. 6¾) envelope, begin the address vertically on Line 12 and horizontally about 10 spaces left of the center point.

4 In the address, capitalize all letters and eliminate all punctuation.

5 Use the standard 2-letter ZIP Code abbreviation for the state. State abbreviations for use with ZIP Codes appear on page iv of the Reference Guide.

6 Place the name of the city, 2-letter state abbreviation, and ZIP Code on the last line of the address. The space below the address must be completely clear.

7 Long city names and street designators may be abbreviated, using the abbreviations found in the *National ZIP Code Directory* or *Customer Service Publication 59* (both available from the U.S. Postal Service).

Recommended placement of additional information

1 When an address contains such notations as *Personal* or *Confidential*, underline them or use all capital letters. Place these notations 3 lines below the return address and aligned with the left edge of the address.

2 Use all capital letters for mailing directions such as SPECIAL DELIVERY or REGISTERED MAIL. Place these directions below the space for the stamp.

3 When an address contains an *attention line*, type it as the second line of the address.

General information

1 If the ZIP Code of an address is not available, use either the state name in full or the traditional abbreviation. You may format this address in either capital and lowercase or all capitals.

2 As a mark of courtesy, always use an appropriate personal title on a letter, envelope, or card addressed to an individual. When a woman's preferred title is unknown, use Ms. as the personal title.

3 Some companies use No. 10 envelopes as a standard practice. Others use No. 10 envelopes for all original copies on 8½" × 11" stationery and No. 6¾ envelopes for half-size stationery or onionskin sheets.

4 Although the U.S. Postal Service recommends the use of ALL CAPS and no punctuation in envelope addresses, many companies continue to use cap and lowercase style with punctuation as illustrated on the No. 6¾ envelope below.

Examples

MISS MELANIE MILLER
BOX 422
WHITTIER CA 90608-4223

MR SUMIO TANAKA
JACKSON ELECTRIC COMPANY
2408 GROVER STREET
OMAHA NE 68105-3542

HANDEL DRY GOODS INC
ATTENTION MS ANN HANDEL
1300 PACIFIC STREET
PORTLAND OR 97232-5235

Mr. Jonathan Becker
RR 4 Box 120
Woronoco, Mass.

(When ZIP Code is not available)

Large envelope (No. 10) 9½" × 4⅛"

Continental Industries, Inc.
204 West Madison Street
Chicago, IL 60606-3313

TS
PERSONAL

SPECIAL DELIVERY

——— Center -5 ———▶ MS MARIANNE WHITNEY Line 14
SCHUBERT REALTY INC
2121 STATE STREET
TAMPA FL 33606-2928

Small envelope (No. 6¾) 6½" × 3⅝"

John B. Scott
78 Monroe Street
Ann Arbor, MI 48104-3742
TS
HOLD FOR ARRIVAL

└— 3 spaces

REGISTERED

——— Center -10 ——▶ Mr. Anthony Fields Line 12
Colonial Hotel
1269 Washington Boulevard
Ogden, UT 84404-5722

Style of addressing envelope used above is recommended by U.S. Postal Service to aid mechanical mail sorting.

Problem 3
Invoice

				words
SOLD TO	The Cook's Nook	DATE	January 15, 19--	6
	235 Adams Street	OUR ORDER NO.	Rm-160472	11
	New Orleans, LA 70118-5723	CUST. ORDER NO.	C-351908	18
TERMS	2/10, n/30	SHIPPED VIA	Palmetto Express	23

QUANTITY	DESCRIPTION	UNIT PRICE	TOTAL	
6	Espresso maker, #PO16	86.95	521.70	29
24	Bird's nest fryer, large, #9R6	14.39	345.36	37
12	Soda siphon, chrome, #7N29	37.95	455.40	42
6	Silver decanter label sets, #J5	41.75	250.50	48
9	Beverage warmer, #G243	27.89	251.01	55
			1,823.97	57
	Sales tax		72.96	61
			1,896.93	63

Problem 4
Statement of account

DATE	February 28, 19--				3
TO	The Gourmet Shop				6
	214 Burnett Drive				9
	Baytown, TX 77520-4891				14

DATE	ITEMS	DEBITS	CREDITS	BALANCE	
February 1	Balance			694.28	19
7	Invoice L-6174	285.79		980.07	24
11	Invoice L-6923	410.80		1,390.87	30
15	Payment on account		550.00	840.87	36
18	Credit Memo 752		39.98	800.89	42

Problem 5
Inventory of equipment

DEPARTMENT	Sales	DATE	December 31, 19--	4
MANAGER	L. A. Matthews	TELEPHONE	555-2918	8

LOCATION	ITEM	SERIAL NUMBER	EMPLOYEE RESPONSIBLE	
122	Telecopier	8942R64	D. Steranka	14
122	Photocopier	628150JT	D. Steranka	19
122	Electronic typewriter	RM62943	D. Steranka	28
122	Shredder	1240635	D. Steranka	34
124	Word processor	X860-29	V. Johnson	41

86c ▶ 35
Format envelopes and business letters

Problem 1
Envelopes

3 No. 10 and 3 No. 6¾ envelopes (LM pp. 13–17)

Address 3 No. 10 envelopes for the 3 addresses given at the top right and 3 No. 6¾ envelopes for the 3 addresses given below them (see p. 160 for directions).

Mr. Harold Jackson
4740 Jerald Drive
Monroe, LA 71203-5868

Ms. Brenda S. Gara
7800 Carousel Lane
Miles, VA 23114-4692

Dr. Robert Friend
325 Brook Road
Boston, MA 02187-1493
(Confidential)

MRS ROBERTA KING
17027 BIHL AVENUE
TOLEDO OH 43619-8275

MISS JO ANN WHEELER
WESTGAGE PLAZA HOTEL
1641 W 16TH STREET
CHICAGO IL 60608-5993

MR LOU KELLY
SAWYER SCHOOL
917 MAIN STREET
ROCHESTER NY 14605-4458

Problem 2
Letter in modified block style, indented paragraphs, mixed punctuation

plain sheet; 60–space line; begin on Line 19

	words
Current date	Mr. Wayne Blanton	Assistant to the President	Telstar Industries,	17
Inc.	1141 State Street	Bowling Green, KY 42101-2643	Dear Mr. Blanton:	32

(¶ 1) Thank you for giving us the opportunity to assist you in filling your Admin- 47
istrative Assistant position. 53

(¶ 2) As we discussed, all positions secured through our agency are on an em- 67
ployer fee-paid basis. If the employee ceases employment in your company 82
within the first 14 days, we will refund the fee. Unless you notify us in writing, 99
acceptance of our referrals will constitute acceptance of this agreement. 114

(¶ 3) Thank you again, Mr. Blanton, for accepting our assistance in filling your 129
personnel requirements. 134

Very truly yours, | Ms. Sharon Burgin | Placement Counselor | xx 146

Problem 3
Letter in block style, open punctuation

plain sheet; 60–space line; begin on Line 19

Current date | Ms. Linda Dodge | 1939 Lincoln Drive | Annapolis, MD 21401-7396 | 16
Dear Ms. Dodge 19

(¶1) Thank you for calling us about our summer study and cultural tour of 33
Southern Spain. Our next tour is planned for June 21 through July 12 and will 49
include visits to Cadiz, Seville, Granada, and Valencia. 60

(¶2) The tour is open to all college students who wish to continue the study of 75
Spanish and to all high-school seniors who have studied Spanish for a minimum 91
of two years. 94

(¶3) Please contact me should you have any questions or wish further informa- 108
tion about this tour. 112

Sincerely yours | John C. Sacora | Tour Director | xx 122

87a ▶ 5
Preparatory practice

each line 3 times SS (slowly, faster, slowly); DS between 3-line groups; repeat selected lines if time permits

alphabet	1	Many bold jockeys were fighting for a quick view to examine the prize.
fig/sym	2	Wilson & Son pay $238,645 annually on a 7-year lease expiring in 1990.
double letters	3	We cannot arrange to add personnel in each territory as you suggested.
fluency	4	Mandy may wish to make a rigid audit of the eight firms by the eighth.

| 1 | 2 | 3 | 4 | 5 | 6 | 7 | 8 | 9 | 10 | 11 | 12 | 13 | 14 |

Measure production: business forms

Time schedule
Assembling materials . 5'
Timed production ..... 30'
Final check; compute
  n–pram .... 10'

1 Arrange forms (LM pp. 165–173) and supplies for rapid handling.

2 When directed to begin, work for 30'. Make 1 cc of each problem.

3 Erase and correct errors; proofread carefully; compute n–pram.

Problem 1
Purchase requisition

words

FILLMORE recording specialists. inc.
2335 IOWA AVENUE
OGDEN, UT 84401-5332
(801) 555-3238

PURCHASE REQUISITION

Deliver to: M. C. Luke
Location: Front Showroom
Job No. 57398

Requisition No. 59374 — 3
Date April 27, 19-- — 8
Date Required As soon as possible — 12

Quantity	Description	
1	Quartz guitar tuner	15
12	Battery, 9 volt	18
6	AC adaptor, 12 volt	21
1	Record cleaner, #J7328	25
1	Stylus care kit, #ST157	29

Requisitioned by: _____

Problem 2
Purchase order

The Music Center
555 Capitol Boulevard
Nashville, TN 37219-4273 (615) 555-5700

PURCHASE ORDER

Orneduff Guitars
4829 Patrick Road
Memphis, TN 38114-3724

Purchase order No. JT5143 — 1
Date May 5, 19-- — 6
Terms Net 30 — 11
Ship Via Sunshine Express — 19

Quantity	Cat. No.	Description	Price	Total	
6	746MTX	Folk guitar	52.91	317.46	25
2	619MHU	Concert folk guitar	84.23	168.46	33
12	423MHU	Jumbo western guitar	125.75	1,509.00	42
8	570MLB	Deluxe 30-bracket banjo	145.99	1,167.92	51
4	216MTX	Model 55 amplifier	180.32	721.28	60
				3,884.12	62

By _____ Purchasing Agent

87b ▶ 10
Improve keyboarding technique

each pair of lines 3 times SS; DS between 6-line groups; work at a controlled rate

adjacent keys	1	He said new government funds were required for the proposed buildings.
	2	A few people support the view that government needs more taxing power.
double letters	3	Their committee may soon recommend that all new agreements be written.
	4	My immediate need appears to be getting agreement on all staff issues.
direct reach	5	My annual service contract was brought to the central council offices.
	6	My company must urge larger payments to serve these doubtful accounts.
shift lock	7	A contract will be awarded to WJAR-TV in Chicago or WWRN-TV in Boston.
	8	Bill Smythe will enter ROTC at SMU, USC, VMI, or UCLA later this year.

| 1 | 2 | 3 | 4 | 5 | 6 | 7 | 8 | 9 | 10 | 11 | 12 | 13 | 14 |

87c ▶ 10
Learn to use a letter placement table

Study the letter placement table and other information given at the right and below in preparation for completing the following letters.

LETTER PLACEMENT TABLE*

Letter Classification	5-Stroke Words in Letter Body	Side Margins	Dateline Position	Placement of Second Page Heading
Short	Up to 125	2″	19	Type the first line
Average	126–225	1½″	16	of second and fol-
Long	226–325	1″	13	lowing page headings
Two–page	More than 325	1″	13	on 7th line from top
Standard 6″ line for all letters**	As above for all letters	1¼″	As above for all letters	edge. TS below head- ing and continue letter.

*As determined from extensive research conducted on business letters by L. W. Erickson, UCLA.
**Use only when so directed. Some business firms use a standard 6″ line for all letters.

Stationery

Business letters are usually typed on 8½″ × 11″ letterhead paper. For a multipage letter, plain paper of the same size, color, and quality as the letterhead is used after page 1. Onionskin or manifold paper is used for carbon copies.

Margins/vertical placement

Some offices use a set line length for all letters. Others vary the margins according to the letter length.

The placement table given here will help you place letters properly. Use the table as an aid; discontinue using it as soon as possible.

For the rest of Division 2, a number in parentheses will appear at the end of the body of each letter to indicate the number of 5–stroke words in the body of the letter. This will serve as an aid in determining letter placement. Estimate letter length, and place letters by judgment. Your ability to judge will be vital.

Adjustment guides

As you learn to judge letter placement, consider two factors.

(1) Is your type size pica or elite and (2) does the letter contain extra opening and closing lines, a table, or a list? Allow for these extra lines by raising the dateline from 1 to 3 lines.

If the letterhead prevents typing the date on the designated line, type it on the second line below the last letterhead line.

87d ▶ 25
Format business letters

Problem 1
Block style, open
(LM p. 19)

Determine margins and letter placement from the table above. The number of 5–stroke words in the body of the letter is indicated by the number in parentheses at the end of the body of the letter. Correct errors.

	words
Current date	Mr. Alexander Powers	Sturmer School of Business	2101 South	16
Hamilton Road	Columbus, OH 43227-3757	Dear Mr. Powers	27

(¶ 1) Our company is a distributor of computer equipment and supplies available from over one hundred manufacturers. We have offices in nine states and plan offices in two more states in the near future. — 41 / 57 / 67

(¶ 2) The products we distribute include over twenty mainframe microcomputers, over one hundred input and output devices, software packages from over two hundred software companies, and any microprocessor books which might be needed. — 81 / 96 / 111 / 113

(¶ 3) Please add our company to your bid list. We can fill your needs for computers and electronic equipment for use in accounting, computer-assisted instruction, student record keeping, text editing, and document preparation. (130) — 128 / 143 / 158

Sincerely | Soledad Volcy | Sales Manager | xx — 167

128a ▶ 5
Preparatory practice

each line 3 times SS (slowly, faster, slowly); DS between 3-line groups; repeat selected lines as time permits

alphabet 1 Alvarez keeps saying the good scores on the basic exam were justified.

fig/sym 2 Of the group, 30% (74,928) earned less than $24,650 each in 18 months.

shift lock 3 Type PIP and press RETURN to copy the disk; then press CTRL&C to exit.

fluency 4 The auditor may pay for mementos for the work the eight big firms did.

| 1 | 2 | 3 | 4 | 5 | 6 | 7 | 8 | 9 | 10 | 11 | 12 | 13 | 14 |

128b ▶ 10
Communication skills checkup: choose the right word

half sheet, long side up; 1" top margin; 74-space line

Keyboard and format as directed in 127d, p. 234.

Key: 1. It's, site, affect 2. cite, effect, its 3. sight, its, affected 4. It's, effect, site

affect — (verb) to influence; to change

effect — (noun) result; (verb) to produce a result; to cause

cite — (verb) to quote
site — (noun) place; location
its — (pronoun) possessive of it

sight — (noun) view; (verb) to see

it's — (contraction) it is

1. (Its/It's) **certain that the** (cite/sight/site) **selected will** (affect/effect) **attendance.**

2. **Did the manager** (cite/sight/site) **the** (affect/effect) **of the hotel's not having** (its/it's) **own parking lot?**

3. **The** (cite/sight/site) **of the canyon with** (its/it's) **majestic view** (affected/effected) **all of us.**

4. (Its/It's) **true that the** (affect/effect) **of moving to the new** (cite/sight/site) **will be an increase in rental costs.**

128c ▶ 35
Build sustained business form production skill

Time schedule
Assembling materials .... 3'
Timed production .... 25'
Final check; compute
  n-pram .... 7'

1 Make a list of problems to be typed for this assignment:
  page 228, 123c, Problem 2
  page 230, 124c, Problem 2
  page 231, 125c, Problem 2
  page 232, 126b, Problem 2
  page 233, 127c, Problem 2

2 Arrange forms (LM pp. 155–163) and supplies for rapid handling.

3 When directed to begin, work for 25'. Make 1 cc of each problem. Erase and correct errors. Compute *n-pram* (see p. 171)

129a ▶ 5
Preparatory practice

each line 3 times SS (slowly, faster, slowly); DS between 3-line groups; repeat selected lines as time permits

For Line 3, leave 3 spaces between number groups.

alphabet 1 Meg quickly asked if the annexation project was criticized very badly.

figure 2 I need $1,536.70 and a 48-hour notice before I can begin Project 2819.

long numbers 3 437-62-8072   803-787-7404   29163   903-41-5862   318-842-528   94545

fluency 4 Jana may go with them to the lake at dusk to sit on the dock and fish.

| 1 | 2 | 3 | 4 | 5 | 6 | 7 | 8 | 9 | 10 | 11 | 12 | 13 | 14 |

87d, continued

Problem 2
**Modified block style,
mixed**

letterhead and envelope (LM
p. 21); use the letter placement
table on page 162; correct errors

Note: The total word count is
shown as 115/**128**: the first figure is the letter count; the second is the letter plus the envelope.

Current date | Mr. Walter Anderson | 550 Old Country Road | Hicksville, NY   15
11801-8653 | Dear Mr. Anderson: 21

(¶ 1) Congratulations on the purchase of your new home. As you know, your   35
home has been schematically prewired for burglar and fire alarms.   48

(¶ 2) When you decide to install your security system, all you have to do is call   63
us. We will be pleased to quote you prices and options to secure your invest-   81
ment.   82

(¶ 3) We will also be happy to send you a list of our services, as well as a few of   98
our many references. (79)   102

Sincerely yours, | Miss Susan K. Patseas | Security Consultant | xx   115/**128**

88a ▶ 5
Preparatory
practice

each line 3 times SS
(slowly, faster,
slowly); DS between
3-line groups; repeat
selected lines if time
permits

alphabet 1 My chief executives were pleased by the quarterly junkets I organized.

fig/sym 2 Model #TRX-590 has sales of $864,132 or 14% higher than Model #RXL-77.

double
letters 3 Employees were happy to support the official committee recommendation.

fluency 4 She may wish to suspend the formal audit if the firm pays the penalty.

| 1 | 2 | 3 | 4 | 5 | 6 | 7 | 8 | 9 | 10 | 11 | 12 | 13 | 14 |

88b ▶ 45
Learn to format
multipage letters

1 Study the information at the
right and the illustrations below.

2 Format and type the problems
that follow (LM p. 23). Make 1 cc
and address an envelope for Problem 1.

3 Proofread and circle errors.
Check placement of second-page
headings.

**Second and subsequent pages of
a letter:** For the second and subsequent pages of a multipage letter, use plain paper of the same
color and quality as the letterhead.

Do not end a page with a divided
word. If possible, leave at least 2
lines of a paragraph at the foot of a
page and carry at least two lines to
the next page.

Place the first line of second-
and subsequent-page headings
on the 7th line from the top edge.
TS after heading and continue typ-

ing. Use the same side margins as
for the first page.

If the horizontal style is used for
the heading of the second page,
center the page number and make
sure the dateline ends at the right
margin.

Before starting the first page of
any long letter, draw a light pencil
line 1½" to 2" from the bottom
edge of the page as a page-end
warning. You can then judge
where to end the page if the letter
is too long for the page.

```
                        1"


Mrs. Carmen Quintana
Page 2
May 9, 19--
                 TS
If you have any additional questions concerning our facilities,
please feel free to contact me.

Sincerely
```

Block style heading for second page

```
                        1"

Mrs. Carmen Quintana             2             May 9, 19--
                                                       TS
If you have any additional questions concerning our facilities,
please feel free to contact me.

                              Sincerely
```

Horizontal style heading for second page

Problem 1

Two-page letter in block
style, open punctuation,
with block second-page
heading.

words

Current date | Mrs. Carmen Quintana | 3013 Fountain View Drive | Houston, TX   16
77057-8423 | Dear Mrs. Quintana   22

(¶ 1) Thank you for your recent letter requesting clarification of our provisions   37
for the disabled at International Airport. We welcome the opportunity to ac-   52
quaint the public with our provisions for mobility-limited travelers, whether   68
physically handicapped or elderly, and with the many services and facilities   83

(continued on next page)

Problem 3
Credit application

Prepare the credit appli–
cation shown at the
right.

words

APPLICATION FOR CREDIT
(INCORPORATED BUSINESSES)

DATE _February 6, 19--_   3

COMPANY NAME _Burleson Records, Inc._   8

STREET _1955 Admiral Street_ CITY _Portland_   14

STATE _Oregon_   ZIP CODE _97201-3562_ TELEPHONE _(503)555-5206_   20

LINE OF BUSINESS _Production and distribution of records to retailers_   30

PRESIDENT _Eula Ule_   TREASURER _Fred Busch_   34

SECRETARY _Floyd Langley_   37

BANK REFERENCE _Oregon National Bank_ TELEPHONE _(503)555-2700_   44

ADDRESS _4200 S.E. Evergreen, Portland OR 97206-3354_   53

TRADE REFERENCE _Ladner & Babb Associates_ TELEPHONE _(503)555-9287_   61

ADDRESS _4991 Foster Road, Portland OR 97206-6235_   70

TRADE REFERENCE _Bridges & Servat, Inc_ TELEPHONE _(503)555-4183_   77

ADDRESS _8225 S.E. Main Street, Portland, OR 97216-6534_   87

REPRESENTATIVE TAKING APPLICATION _Harriet Overley_   90

COMMENTS: _Has been in business in Portland for 15 years_   97
and is a leading distributor of records and tapes.   107

127d ▶ 10
Communication skills checkup: choose the right word

half sheet, long side up; 1″ top
margin; 74-space line

1 Cover the answer key at the bot–
tom of the column. When you have
finished keyboarding, check your
answers.

2 Study the definitions of the
closely related words at the right.
Then type the sentences, selecting
the appropriate word from the
words in parentheses. Include the
sentence numbers in the 74-space
line.

Key: 1. accept, advice, further
2. except, farther, advised
3. further, accept, advice

accept — (verb) to receive; to agree

advice — (noun) counsel; suggestion

farther — (adverb) more remote (distance)

except — (verb) to exclude; (preposition) with the exclusion of

advise — (verb) to give counsel

further — (adverb) to a greater degree (thought)

1. Did he (accept/except) her (advise/advice) to study the matter (farther/further)?

2. All of us (accept/except) John traveled (farther/further) than we were (adviced/advised) to travel in one day.

3. Jane said she would question Tom (farther/further), but she did not think she could (accept/except) his (advice/advise).

which are available for their convenience. We also encourage your comments   98
and suggestions regarding these facilities.   107

(¶ 2) Specific policies or requirements with regard to transporting mobility-   121
limited travelers aboard aircraft may differ according to the individual airline.   138
If you have specific questions regarding facilities aboard aircraft or if you   154
desire additional information, call the respective airline you plan to use.   169

(¶ 3) If wheelchair assistance is needed, every major scheduled airline operat-   183
ing at International Airport can provide such assistance. We recommend that   198
you reserve the wheelchair by calling your travel agent or airline in advance of   214
the particular flight arrival or departure. You may find it easier to make all   230
arrangements for special assistance or wheelchair reservations when making   245
your original travel arrangements.   252

(¶ 4) You may also arrange for wheelchair assistance at the airline ticket coun-   267
ters. You can arrange for wheelchair and skycap to meet you within minutes of   283
your arrival at the terminal front curbside or at the airline gate. No charge or   299
deposit is required. Airlines do, however, require a skycap to accompany the   315
wheelchair and passenger to the destination point in the terminal. Gratuity for   331
the skycap's service is at the discretion of the individual.   343

(¶ 5) Airlines Transportation Company, located at the ground level of the termi-   358
nal, operates limousines and vans that can accommodate handicapped travelers   373
proceeding to the downtown area. Van service for groups up to 12 and private   390
lift-van service for wheelchair-bound travelers is available with a minimum   405
one-day advance notice by calling 803-4652.   414

(¶ 6) If you have any additional questions concerning our facilities, please con-   429
tact me.   431

Sincerely | Ms. Betty Nielsen | Director, Department of Aviation | xx   444/**458**

Problem 2
Modified block style

Format the material given at the right as the second page of a two-page letter using horizontal second-page heading.

Dr. Yolanda Ball | 2 | Current date   7

Positions are available both at our plant site near Berwick and at our Allentown   23
headquarters. If your graduates have degrees in mechanical, electrical, civil,   39
or nuclear engineering, we would like to hear from them.   50

Sincerely yours, | Peter A. Stimson | Placement Director | xx   62

89

89a ▶ 5
Preparatory
practice

each line 3 times SS (slowly, faster, slowly); DS between 3-line groups; repeat selected lines if time permits

alphabet 1 Roy realized a pair will beat a queen, jack, five, or six in the game.

figures 2 The 89-unit mall built on a 205-acre site can accommodate 37,146 cars.

adjacent key 3 Quickly make three copies of the sales invoice for my equipment parts.

fluency 4 An ancient burial ritual of the island town is the theme of the chant.

| 1 | 2 | 3 | 4 | 5 | 6 | 7 | 8 | 9 | 10 | 11 | 12 | 13 | 14 |

127a ▶ 5
Preparatory practice

each line 3 times SS (slowly, faster, slowly); DS between 3-line groups; repeat selected lines as time permits

alphabet 1 Mercedes was just given the deluxe bronze plaque for her charity work.

figure 2 My telephone number was changed from 392-0174 to 853-6927 on March 18.

shift key 3 Jan, Don, Tom, and May wrote "Bonn on Less than $10 Per Day" for Life.

fluency 4 A neighbor owns key land downtown, and she also owns a dock on a lake.

| 1 | 2 | 3 | 4 | 5 | 6 | 7 | 8 | 9 | 10 | 11 | 12 | 13 | 14 |

127b ▶ 10
Preapplication drill: tabulate columns of figures

half sheet, long side up; SS; center vertically and horizontally; set margins and tab stops according to key; repeat if time permits

73920	17305	82065	27569	21097	10638	03927
82084	14730	65843	02395	30816	86402	27504
21074	38612	90361	73294	52819	38275	36571
20074	65034	19576	30750	56328	10935	64728
46031	83183	65872	27193	42860	37924	18675

| 5 | 4 | 5 | 4 | 5 | 4 | 5 | 4 | 5 | 4 | 5 | 4 | 5 |

127c ▶ 25
Prepare statements of account and a credit application

(LM pp. 149–153)

Problem 1
Statement of account

Prepare the statement of account shown at the right; make 1 cc.

Problem 2
Statement of account

Repeat Problem 1, adding the information at the right. Compute balances; make 1 cc.

words

Statement of Account

King Manufacturing Co.
3

625 Allerton Avenue
Milwaukee, WI 53221-4723
(414) 555-7225

Date   April 30, 19--

To

⌐   ⌐
    Wilder & Sons, Inc.   7
    3982 Redwood Drive   11
    Kansas City, KS 66112-4579   16
L   ⌐

Date	Items	Debits	Credits	Balance	
Apr. 1	Balance			684.72	20
4	Invoice J2345	146.35		831.07	25
8	Invoice J7890	371.83		1,202.90	31
10	Credit Memo 864		48.95	1,153.95	37
12	Invoice J9284	269.37		1,423.32	43
15	Payment on account		950.00	473.32	49

18	Invoice J8642	385.50			54
20	Credit Memo 891	154.37			60
26	Invoice J9136	254.17			65
28	Payment on account	500.00			71

89b ▶ 10
Review/apply communication skills: capitalization

full sheet; 1″ top margin; 74-space line

Keyboard and format as directed in 81b, p. 150.

Key: 1b. editor 2b. Left Bank 3b. Column 1 4b. ex–President

Capitalize	
1. Official titles before personal names but not occupational titles which follow personal names.	directions or compass points.
2. Words which identify specific locations or geographic regions but not general	3. Nouns followed by a number or letter except common nouns such as line, page, sentence, etc.
	4. Both parts of a hyphenated word if both initial letters are usually capitalized.

review 1a. Marion Kemper, attorney, had dinner at the home of Senator Bristol.
apply   b. Marvin Silvers, an Editor, will speak before a group of doctors.

review 2a. The Mason and Dixon Line does not extend west of the Ohio River.
apply   b. Both Houses of the French Parliament were situated on the left bank.

review 3a. All the important information is contained in line 21 of Appendix B.
apply   b. The merchandise in column 1 is less expensive than in Column 2.

review 4a. The Spanish-American War was a favorite topic of the ex-Green Beret.
apply   b. The political science students hosted ex-president Carter.

89c ▶ 35
Learn to format letters with mailing notation/attention line

1 Study the information and illustration at the right.

2 Format and type Problems 1 and 2 below and Problem 3 on p. 166 (LM pp. 25–29). Make 1 carbon copy (cc) and address an envelope for each letter.

3 Proofread and circle errors. Check correct placement of special features.

Problem 1
Letter with mailing notation/attention line

block style, open punctuation

Mailing notation in letter: If a special mailing notation (REGIS–TERED, CERTIFIED, SPECIAL DELI–VERY, etc.) is used in a letter, it is shown a double space below the dateline at the left margin of the letter in all capital letters.

Attention line: Place an attention line as the second line of the letter address. (Some companies prefer the attention line placed a double space below the letter address.)

```
Current date

SPECIAL DELIVERY

Nutech Exports Incorporated
Attention Mrs. Wilma Sullivan
2 World Trade Center
New York, NY  10047-4935

Ladies and Gentlemen
```

words

Current date | SPECIAL DELIVERY | Nutech Exports Incorporated | Attention Mrs.   16
Wilma Sullivan | 2 World Trade Center | New York, NY 10047-4935 | Ladies and   31
Gentlemen   33

(¶ 1) We at Merchants Bank of New Jersey are happy to see that your company   47
has recently discovered vast new markets overseas. We may be able to help   62
you with your business transactions.   69

(¶ 2) We are one of the nation's leading international banks, with access to an   84
international banking network spanning 40 countries. We can supply any type   99
of international banking service: international letters of credit, trade and term   116
financing, collection, foreign exchange, banker's acceptances, factoring, and   132
others.   134

(¶ 3) Think of us as an important resource for your business and provide us with   149
an opportunity to work with you. (123)   155

Sincerely | John V. Pisani | Marketing Representative | xx   166/190

Problem 2
Letter addressed to job title

modified block style; indented ¶s; mixed punctuation

Note: When a letter is addressed to a job title instead of a particular person, the job title should appear on the line above the company name in the letter ad–dress and the salutation *Dear Sir or Madam* should be used.

Current date | Purchasing Manager | Bedford Laboratories | 600 Montgomery   15
Street | San Francisco, CA 94111-6218 | Dear Sir or Madam: 26

(¶ 1) Thank you very much for your request for catalogs and prices. This mate-   41
rial will be sent to you today.   47

(¶ 2) You will find that Melrowe Distributors can supply any need you may have   62
for laboratory glassware and related supplies. We appreciate your interest in   78
our products and your giving us the opportunity to serve you. (64)   90

Sincerely, | Kevin Morgan | Sales Representative | xx   100/118

126b ▶ 45
Prepare invoices
and a memorandum
(LM pp. 143–147)

Problem 1
Invoice

Prepare the invoice given at the right; make 1 cc.

BENNETT & BENNETT SPORTING GOODS

230 ASHFORD STREET
RALEIGH, NC 27610-5723   (919) 555-9460

Invoice

	Date November 6, 19--	3
Seven Devils Ski Shop		7
1294 Wildcat Rocks Road	Our Order No. SE87304	13
Banner Elk, NC 28604-3789		18
	Cust. Order No. 3207	19
Terms 2/10, n/30	Shipped Via Mountain Express Lines	28

Quantity	Description	Unit Price	Total	
12 prs.	Beginners' skis, Stock No. 834	55.98	671.76	38
12 prs.	Beginners' skis, Stock No. 884	68.25	819.00	48
8 prs.	Intermediate skis, Stock No. 934	75.50	604.00	58
10 prs.	Intermediate skis, Stock No. 984	84.98	849.80	68
48 prs.	Fiberglass ski poles, Stock No. 329	4.15	199.20	78
24 prs.	Bindings, Stock No. 582	39.99	959.76	86
6 prs.	Bindings, Stock No. 592	46.78	280.68	96
			4,384.20	98
	Sales tax		175.37	103
			4,559.57	105

Problem 2
Invoice

Prepare an invoice, using the information at the right; make 1 cc.

SOLD TO Appalachian Ski Shop	DATE November 14, 19--	7
905 Blowing Rock Road		11
Boone, NC 28607-5348	OUR ORDER NO. SE87492	17
	CUST. ORDER NO. R83023	18
TERMS 2/10, n/30	SHIPPED VIA Speedy Express	23

(Increase the quantity of each item in Problem 1 by adding 2 to it; use the same description and unit price as in Problem 1; compute the total. Use 4% to compute sales tax.)

Total   101

Problem 3
Half-page memorandum

Compose a memo, using the information at the right.

TO: June Schmidt, Coordinator, Graphics Department
FROM: (your name), Office Administrator
DATE: (current)
SUBJECT: Request for New Invoice Forms

Request that June Schmidt have new invoice forms designed on 8½″ × 11″ paper for large orders. You will continue to use the 8½″ × 5½″ forms for regular orders. Suggest that 10,000 copies (100 pads of 100 invoice forms) be printed initially.

89c, continued

Problem 3
Letter with mailing notation/attention line

modified block style, open punctuation

words

Current date | SPECIAL DELIVERY | United Manufacturing, Inc. | Attention Mr.   16
Jack Farmer | 1724 Chestnut Street | Philadelphia, PA 19103-6423 | Ladies and   31
Gentlemen   33

(¶ 1) In response to your request, we are presently assembling a sample   46
portfolio of various insurance programs Foshee Insurance Agency can offer to   61
your corporation to meet your insurance needs. The portfolio will be sent to you   77
in a few days and will provide all the details of insurance programs relevant to   93
your company.   96

(¶ 2) Once you have had the opportunity to review the material, I will be pleased   111
to meet you at your convenience to discuss how I may be of service. (93)   125

Yours truly | Ms. Sandra Goodson | Vice President | xx   135/159

90

90a ▶ 5
Preparatory practice

each line 3 times SS (slowly, faster, slowly); DS between 3-line groups; repeat selected lines if time permits

alphabet 1   Buck's job experience and high quiz results paved the way for triumph.

fig/sym 2   Their payments totaled $9,462 ($9,305 and $337) but were 18 days late.

direct reach 3   Many large emergency units often were found to be broken or defective.

fluency 4   The city may wish to dismantle the signs; it may make problems for us.

| 1 | 2 | 3 | 4 | 5 | 6 | 7 | 8 | 9 | 10 | 11 | 12 | 13 | 14 |

90b ▶ 7
Improve keyboarding technique

each pair of lines twice SS; DS between 4-line groups; work at a controlled rate

adjacent keys 1   Her proposal was somewhat appropriate, and I'll support her positions.
2   A few union people were aware of new building and safety requirements.

double letters 3   They will soon begin to sell all books for the college summer session.
4   Our total payroll for all employees will exceed three million dollars.

long numbers 5   528; 32.07; 12/28/95; 54,076.94; 536-8853; (717) 844-6799; 189-54-8651
6   868; 45.23; 10/31/86; 23,872.39; 254-4534; (617) 010-9166; 200-30-5753

direct reach 7   I always grant maximum service on any number of my manufactured parts.
8   Branch office space must be enlarged due to increased consumer volume.

| 1 | 2 | 3 | 4 | 5 | 6 | 7 | 8 | 9 | 10 | 11 | 12 | 13 | 14 |

90c ▶ 8
Review/apply communication skills: punctuation

full sheet; 1" top margin; 74-space line

Keyboard and format as directed in 81b, p. 150.

Key: 1b. week. 2b. Alan E. Dodd, O.D. Brooks 3c. R. N., AFL–CIO, p.m.

Use a period

1. At the end of a sentence that makes a direct statement or at the end of a request expressed as a question.

2. After initials representing names.

3. After each element of an abbreviation, except for ALL-CAP abbreviations such as CIO and USPS.

review 1a. Won't you please lend your support to this good cause.
apply   b. Can you give your answer to us by the end of the next week?

review 2a. This book is by R. J. Gould with a foreword by D. K. Adler.
apply   b. Alan E Dodd wrote the play; O D Brooks adapted it for the movies.

review 3a. The 10 a.m. class on data entry will be taught by Elvin Jones, Ph.D.
review   b. The USPS has already begun implementing the 9-digit ZIP Code.
apply   c. Lou Cole, R N., joined the A.F.L.-C.I.O. meeting at 8:30 pm.

125c ▶ 30
Prepare inventories of equipment
(LM pp. 141–143)

Problem 1
Inventory of equipment

Prepare the inventory at the right.

INVENTORY OF EQUIPMENT

DEPARTMENT *Technical Services*   DATE *December 30, 19--*   7

MANAGER *Margaret Vickery*   TELEPHONE NUMBER *555-6072*   12

LOCATION	ITEM	SERIAL NUMBER	EMPLOYEE RESPONSIBLE	
10A	Electronic typewriter	2P182469	L. Bordelon	21
10A	Electronic typewriter	2P174932	L. Laborde	30
12B	Microcomputer	86284JRL	E. Gentry	37
12B	Disk drive	71490JRL	E. Gentry	43
12B	Printer	78213JRL	E. Gentry	49
14A	Copier	69083247	D. White	54
14A	Word processor	52971638	C. Jeansonne	62
14A	Transcriber	28375642	C. Jeansonne	69

Problem 2
Inventory of equipment

Use the information at the right to prepare the inventory for the Training Department. Follow the style illustrated in Problem 1.

Problem 3
Inventory of equipment

Repeat Problem 2, making these changes: Marie Snowden is now the manager, and R. Steen is responsible for Snowden's equipment.

Department: **Training** | Manager: **Dale McKee** | Date: **June 30, 19--** | 6
Telephone: **555-7000** | 8

Location: **A** | Employee Responsible: **M. Snowden** | Item: **Overhead projector,** 14
68429071; Slide projector, 29168415; Movie projector, 91652930; Video 28
recorder, 7829431; TV monitor, 37281450; Camera, 39184560 40

Location: **B** | Employee Responsible: **C. Warner** | Item: **Typewriter, 2R197638;** 47
Lettering machine, 4K261375 52

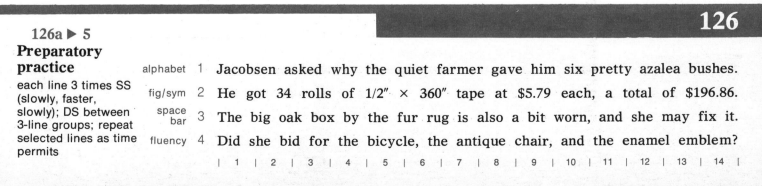

126

126a ▶ 5
Preparatory practice

each line 3 times SS (slowly, faster, slowly); DS between 3-line groups; repeat selected lines as time permits

alphabet 1 Jacobsen asked why the quiet farmer gave him six pretty azalea bushes.

fig/sym 2 He got 34 rolls of 1/2″ × 360″ tape at $5.79 each, a total of $196.86.

space bar 3 The big oak box by the fur rug is also a bit worn, and she may fix it.

fluency 4 Did she bid for the bicycle, the antique chair, and the enamel emblem?

| 1 | 2 | 3 | 4 | 5 | 6 | 7 | 8 | 9 | 10 | 11 | 12 | 13 | 14 |

Learn to format letters with subject line/reply reference notation

1 Study the information and the illustrations at the right.

2 Format and type the 3 letters that follow (LM pp. 31–35). Make 1 cc and address an envelope for each letter.

3 Proofread and circle errors. Check correct placement of special features.

Subject line: A subject line in ALL CAPS is placed a DS below salutation at left margin, at paragraph point if paragraphs are indented, or centered. It is not necessary to precede the line with the word SUBJECT.

Reply reference notation: Place the notation as you would a subject line. The word Reference or Re followed by a colon and 2 spaces may be shown before the notation.

```
Ms. Carol Valentino
Hillview Drive
Narragansett, RI  02880-4288

Dear Ms. Valentino

TAX-FREE PROFITS

Recently a Rhode Island municipal bond was
```

```
Mr. Thomas Houston
48 Broadcrest Drive
Philadelphia, PA  15235-3011

Dear Mr. Houston

Reference:  Policy #243067HP

Thank you for choosing your homeowner's insur-
```

words

Problem 1
Letter with subject line

modified block style, blocked ¶s, open punctuation; blocked subject line

Current date | Ms. Carol Valentino | Hillview Drive | Narragansett, RI 02880-4288 |	17
Dear Ms. Valentino | TAX-FREE PROFITS	24

(¶ 1) Recently a Rhode Island municipal bond was issued which returned 11 percent interest--COMPLETELY TAX FREE. — 38 / 46

(¶ 2) Unfortunately, many people did not learn of this offering until it was too late to subscribe. In addition, many people were unaware that interest earned on such securities is free from both federal and state taxes for Rhode Island residents. — 61 / 77 / 93 / 95

(¶ 3) If you would like to be notified in advance of such future offerings, please call or drop us a note to get your name on our mailing list. There is, of course, no obligation on your part. (108) — 110 / 127 / 132

Sincerely yours \| Mrs. Nancy Watson \| Investment Counselor \| xx — 144/**157**

Problem 2
Letter with reference notation

modified block style, blocked ¶s, open punctuation; blocked reply reference notation

Current date \| Mr. Thomas Houston \| 48 Broadcrest Drive \| Philadelphia, PA 15235-3011 \| Dear Mr. Houston \| Reference: Policy #243067HP — 15 / 27

(¶ 1) Thank you for choosing your homeowner's insurance policy through Foshee Insurance Agency. Your policy has been carefully designed to provide the protection you need. — 40 / 55 / 60

(¶ 2) Your policy will be mailed to you soon in a separate envelope. Please review your coverage carefully. — 74 / 80

(¶ 3) If you have any questions about your insurance, please let us know. Just contact your agent or drop by our office. We want you to be completely satisfied with your homeowner's insurance. (92) — 95 / 110 / 117

Sincerely yours \| Willard Washington \| Customer Service Agent \| xx — 130/**144**

Problem 3
Letter with subject line

modified block style, indented ¶s, mixed punctuation; centered subject line

Current date \| Dr. Jerome Davis, Director \| Western College of Optometry \| 7008 Marin Avenue \| Berkeley, CA 94708-8963 \| Dear Dr. Davis: \| OPTOMETRIC TECHNICIAN PROGRAM — 16 / 30 / 34

(¶ 1) Thank you for taking the time to talk with me last Tuesday. I want to reaffirm the interest of Babcock & Sinclair in organizing a co-op program with your Optometric Technician students. — 48 / 64 / 71

(¶ 2) In a few days, I will call you to set up a meeting time. Best wishes for a successful year. (56) — 86 / 89

Sincerely yours, \| Ms. Johanna Dickerson \| Director \| xx — 100/**120**

124c, continued

Problem 2
Purchase order

Prepare the purchase order given at the right; make 1 cc.

Problem 3
Purchase order

Repeat the purchase order given in Problem 2, making these changes:

1 Purchase Order No. **4025-3830.**

2 Date: **January 14, 19--.**

3 Double the quantity of each item; compute the total.

Office Services, Inc. 530 Montgomery Street
San Francisco, CA 94111-4225

(414) 555-3520

PURCHASE ORDER

Purchase order No.	3028-1739	2
Date	September 24, 19--	6
Terms	Net	15
Ship Via	Rapid Express	23

Custom Forms, Inc.
2438 Bay Shore Boulevard
San Francisco, CA 94134-3733

Quantity	Cat. No.	Description	Price	Total	
4 boxes	SR-253-25	Stock requisition, 6" x 9 1/2"	23.56	94.24	34
12 pads	QF-309-21	Quotation form	2.85	34.20	42
24 pads	PF-957-72	Proposal form	3.00	72.00	50
8 pads	TS-264-18	Daily professional time sheet	4.12	32.96	61
12 boxes	IS-725-41	Invoice for services	24.75	297.00	71
6 boxes	ER-284-31	Weekly expense report	37.68	226.08	81
20 boxes	TM-399-04	Telephone message pad	5.23	104.60	92
				861.08	93

By _____ Purchasing Agent

125

125a ▶ 5
**Preparatory
practice**

each line 3 times SS
(slowly, faster, slowly);
DS between 3-line
groups; repeat
selected lines
as time permits.

For Line 3, beginning at
the left margin, set 7 tab
stops 9 spaces apart.

alphabet 1 Jeffrey made his work plans, exceeded quotas, and won five big prizes.

fig/sym 2 Item #9748 now sells for $3,260.75 (a 15% price increase in 18 weeks).

tab 3 3194   2806   3714   9283   2517   5391   2649   4708159

fluency 4 The key to the theme of the rugs in the ancient chapel is in a ritual.

| 1 | 2 | 3 | 4 | 5 | 6 | 7 | 8 | 9 | 10 | 11 | 12 | 13 | 14 |

125b ▶ 15
**Preapplication drill:
prepare rules (lines);
place copy on printed
rules**

half sheet, long side up;
1" top margin

Preparing horizontal rules
Depress the shift lock and use the underline key.

Drawing vertical rules
Operate the automatic line finder. Place the point of a pencil or pen through the cardholder (or on the typebar guide above the ribbon). Roll the paper up until you have a ruling of the desired length. Remove the pen or pencil and reset the line finder.

You can also remove the paper from the typewriter and, using a pen with black ink and a ruler, draw the vertical rules.

Drill

1 Prepare a 5" horizontal rule; DS; prepare another 5" horizontal rule. Remove paper; re-insert it; align the first ruled line with the aligning scale. Place your name on the first rule and your address on the second rule. Check to see that you have placed the words close to the rule, but that you have not cut the rule.

2 Prepare three 5" horizontal rules a double space apart; draw a vertical rule 3" from the left edge of the rules; draw a second vertical rule 4" from the left edge of the rules. Place the following items on the rules:

Mike Brittan	215 lbs.	6'10"
Jimmy Foster	204 lbs.	6'10"
Duane Kendall	206 lbs.	6'11"

91a ▶ 5
Preparatory practice

each line 3 times SS (slowly, faster, slowly); DS between 3-line groups; repeat selected lines if time permits

alphabet	1	Mary went right for just six blocks and had a quiet view of the plaza.
fig/sym	2	He sold 45 luxury (3-bedroom) suites priced from $189,750 to $296,500.
double letters	3	All necessary issues must be addressed three weeks before the meeting.
fluency	4	Laurie owns a dismal shanty by the lake on the land I may wish to own.

| 1 | 2 | 3 | 4 | 5 | 6 | 7 | 8 | 9 | 10 | 11 | 12 | 13 | 14 |

91b ▶ 10
Review/apply communication skills: punctuation

full sheet; 1" top margin; 74-space line

Keyboard and format as directed in 81b, p. 150.

Key: 1c. Corporation? 2b. Fabulous! 3b. person!

Use a question mark	**Use an exclamation point**
1. At the end of a sentence that is a direct question; however, use a period after an indirect question and a request which does not give the option of refusal.	**2.** After emphatic interjections which are stated as single words, phrases, or expressions.
	3. After sentences which express strong emotions.

review 1a. Did you see seven or eight people run out of the burning building?

review   b. The director has asked when the new microcomputers will be installed.

apply   c. Have you seen the annual report of Hornbacker Corporation.

review 2a. Oh! You surprised me. Look out! That car almost hit you.

apply   b. Fabulous. What a concert.

review 3a. You have exaggerated the facts completely beyond recognition!

apply   b. I can't believe you said that to such a nice person.

91c ▶ 35
Learn to format letters with company name in closing/enclosure notation/copy notation/postscript notation

1 Study the information at the right and the Style letter on p. 169.

2 Format and type the letters that follow (LM p. 37–41). Make 1 cc and address an envelope for each letter.

3 Proofread and circle errors. Check correct placement of special features.

Problem 1
Letter with special features

Format and type the letter on page 169 illustrating company name in closing lines, enclosure notation, copy notation, and postscript. Raise the dateline 3 lines because of the special features.

Problem 2
Letter with company name in closing lines and enclosure notation

Format and type the letter given at the right in block style, open punctuation.

Company name in closing lines: When a company name is used in the closing lines, show it in ALL CAPS a DS below the complimentary close. The writer's name is then placed on the 4th line below the company name.

Enclosure notation: Place an enclosure notation a DS below the reference initials. If there is more than one enclosure, list them on succeeding lines, indented 3 spaces from the left margin:

    Enclosures
      Financial Statements
      General Information Survey

Copy notation: Show a copy notation a DS below the reference initials or enclosure notation. A cc is used to indicate a carbon copy; a pc is used to indicate a photocopy.

Postscript: Place a postscript a DS below the last item at the bottom of the letter.

	words
Current date | Dr. Susan Yamada, Director | Electronic Education Systems, Inc. |	16
200 Fifth Avenue | Seattle, WA 98121-0159 | Dear Dr. Yamada	28
(¶ 1) Enclosed are five copies of our audited financial statements for Elec-	42
tronic Education Systems, Inc., for the year ended June 30. I have also en-	57
closed three copies of the U.S. Department of Education General Information	72
Survey.	74
(¶ 2) You should forward one copy of the Department of Education General	88
Information Survey to the Department of Education after you have signed the	103
back of the form.	106
(¶ 3) If you have any questions regarding any of the enclosed items, please call	121
me. (94)	122
Sincerely | BAKER, SEXTON, AND CAVELL | Miss Cindy Sexton, CPA | xx | Enclo-	136
sures | Financial Statements | General Information Survey	147/**167**

124a ▶ 5
Preparatory practice

each line 3 times SS (slowly, faster, slowly); DS between 3-line groups; repeat selected lines as time permits.

For Line 3, beginning at the left margin, set 7 tab stops 9 spaces apart.

alphabet 1 Josefina Vazquez will spend about six days working on those documents.

figure 2 The pet shop has 149 dogs, 72 cats, 58 rabbits, 60 birds, and 93 fish.

tab 3 look   hear   talk   read   open   shut   walk   advance

fluency 4 The proficient auditors may handle the usual big problems of the city.

| 1 | 2 | 3 | 4 | 5 | 6 | 7 | 8 | 9 | 10 | 11 | 12 | 13 | 14 |

124b ▶ 15
Preapplication drill: tabulate

half sheet, long side up; 1½" top margin; 1½" left margin; set tab stops every 10 spaces, beginning at the left margin; align decimal points in decimal columns and colons in colon column; SS; DS between groups

$184.29	a.m.	23"	10 lbs.	3 5/8	25.4 mm	12:30
$178.40	p.m.	6'	8 oz.	6/2/89	2.54 cm	9:15
$350.17	FICA	75%	4 ft.	27 1/2	1.305 m	7:45
$692.53	Ph.D.	#38	7 in.	B4-53	1.61 km	6:29
$159.06	i.e.	(4)	9 ea.	n/30	4.785 l	11:27
$804.31	Inc.	12*	1 doz.	Z-104	0.47 L	6:32
$572.93	COBOL	36#	12 v.	6 1/4	0.45 kg	10:48
$831.82	No.	*90	1 tsp.	2/7/90	28.35 g	8:03

124c ▶ 30
Prepare purchase orders

(LM pp. 135–139)

Problem 1
Purchase order

A purchase order is completed by the purchasing department to order requisitioned supplies or equipment.

Prepare the purchase order given at the right; make 1 cc.

			words
King Manufacturing Co.		**PURCHASE ORDER**	
625 Allerton Avenue		Tab	
Milwaukee, WI 53221-4723 (414) 555-7225			
		Purchase order No. P-392840	2
Benchmark Supply Company		Date April 6, 19--	5
P.O. Box 3927			10
Madison, WI 53707-3906		Terms 2/10, n/30	15
			20
		Ship Via UPS	21

Quantity	Cat. No.	Description	Price	Total	words
DS 4	S2-P1046	Printwheel, Courier 10	7.25	29.00	29
4	S2-P1052	Printwheel, Courier 72	7.25	29.00	37
12	S2-R3276	Multi-strike film ribbon	5.12	61.44	46
1	F3-M8210	Anti-static chair mat, brown,			54
		Indent 3 spaces → 60" x 48" x 1/8"	170.98	170.98	60
30	S5-D7539	Flexible disk, double density	8.30	249.00	70
6	S8-3176	Disk library case	5.80	34.80	77
2	F4-7285	Adjustable turntable	31.98	63.96	86
Approximate center	Approximate center		Approximate center	DS 638.18	87

Set tab 2 spaces from rule

By _____ Purchasing Agent

Communications Design Associates

348 INDIANA AVENUE
WASHINGTON, DC 20001-1438
Tel: 1-800-432-5739

	words	in parts	total

October 15, 19--
DS · 3 · 3

Mailing notation — SPECIAL DELIVERY · 6 · 6
DS

Attention line — Search and Recruit International · 13 · 13
Attention Mr. Paul Nugent · 18 · 18
8225 Dunwood Place · 22 · 22
Atlanta, GA 30339-7239 · 27 · 27
DS

Ladies and Gentlemen · 31 · 31
DS

Subject line or reply reference — SPECIAL FEATURES IN BUSINESS LETTERS · 38 · 38
DS

Ms. Darlene Baez asked me to send you a copy of our new · 11 · 49
brochure, SPECIAL FEATURES IN BUSINESS LETTERS. This · 22 · 60
brochure describes and illustrates many of the special · 33 · 71
features that may be used in modern business letters. · 44 · 82

The special features are presented in this letter in · 55 · 93
life-size format. There are variations to the style · 65 · 103
presented here; for example, the subject line may be · 76 · 114
blocked, indented to match the paragraph indentions, or · 87 · 125
centered. · 89 · 127

The likelihood of using all these special features in a · 100 · 139
single letter is remote. However, a good typist under- · 111 · 150
stands their functions and uses good judgment as to how · 123 · 161
and when to apply them. I hope you will find the infor- · 134 · 172
mation in the enclosed brochure interesting and useful. · 145 · 183
DS

Sincerely yours · 3 · 186
DS

Company name — COMMUNICATIONS DESIGN ASSOCIATES · 8 · 191

Leona Shamura

Ms. Leona Shamura · 12 · 195
Communication Specialist · 17 · 200
DS

xx · 18 · 201
DS

Enclosure notation — Enclosure · 20 · 203
DS

Copy notation — cc Raymond Sink · 23 · 206
DS

Postscript — Additional free copies of the brochure are available. · 33 · 216
240

Style letter 6: Modified block business letter illustrating special features

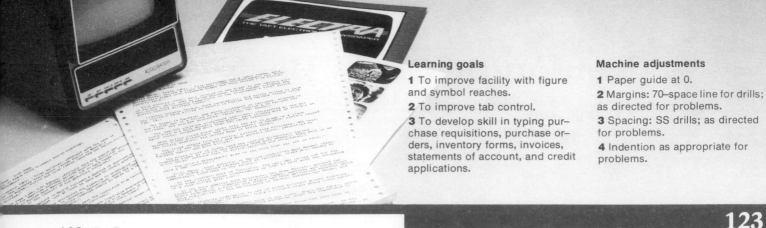

Learning goals

1 To improve facility with figure and symbol reaches.

2 To improve tab control.

3 To develop skill in typing purchase requisitions, purchase orders, inventory forms, invoices, statements of account, and credit applications.

Machine adjustments

1 Paper guide at 0.

2 Margins: 70–space line for drills; as directed for problems.

3 Spacing: SS drills; as directed for problems.

4 Indention as appropriate for problems.

123a ▶ 5
Preparatory practice

each line 3 times SS (slowly, faster, slowly); DS between 3-line groups; repeat selected lines as time permits

alphabet	1	Maxwell visited the quaint shopping plaza just sixty blocks from here.
figure	2	The waterfront lot was 147 feet wide, 239 feet deep, and cost $38,650.
fig/sym	3	I paid 25% ($3,749) down and 60% ($6,748.21) of the balance last week.
fluency	4	Jane and Sidney may both go to work for the big firm down by the lake.

| 1 | 2 | 3 | 4 | 5 | 6 | 7 | 8 | 9 | 10 | 11 | 12 | 13 | 14 |

123b ▶ 10
Study business forms

Study the illustrations of a purchase requisition (below), a purchase order (page 229), an inventory form (page 231), an invoice (page 232), a statement of account (page 233), and a credit application (page 234).

Read the following tips carefully before preparing the business forms in this section.

1 Set left margin stop for the address and first column; set tab stops for other columnar items.

2 Begin entries in the "description" or "items" column two spaces to the right of the vertical line; center the other columns under the headings.

3 If 3 or fewer entries are to be typed on a form, DS them. SS for 4 or more entries.

4 If an entry will take more than one line, indent the second and succeeding lines 3 spaces.

5 Underline the last item in a column for which a total is to be shown; DS, then type the total.

123c ▶ 35
Prepare purchase requisitions

(LM pp. 131–133)

Problem 1
Purchase requisition

A purchase requisition is completed by a department in a company that needs the supplies or equipment.

Prepare the purchase requisition given at the right; make 1 cc.

Problem 2
Purchase requisition

Reformat Problem 1, making the following changes:

1 Requisition No. **49658**.

2 Date: **February 6, 19—**.

3 Increase order for pad holders and ballpoint pens to 100.

4 Alphabetize the entries in the description column. Rearrange quantities accordingly.

words

Communications Design Associates

348 INDIANA AVENUE   WASHINGTON, DC 20001-1438

PURCHASE REQUISITION

Tab

			words
Deliver to: Starr Askew	Requisition No.	49650	5
Location: Suite 28B	Date	January 12, 19--	10
Job No. 37528	Date Required	As soon as possible	15

Quantity	Set tab 2 spaces from rule	Description	
DS			
6	Perforated pads for easel presentation		23
12	Felt-tip markers with black ink		30
6	Felt-tip markers with blue ink		36
6	Felt-tip markers with red ink		42
24	Walnut pad holders, 8 1/2" x 11"		49
24	Ballpoint pens, fine point, black ink		57
24	Clear transparencies		62

Approximate center

Requisitioned by:

91c, continued

Problem 3

Format and type in block style, open punctuation, the script letter shown at the right. Block the subject line. Make two carbon copies; make one a blind carbon copy (bcc) for *John Denby*. Address an envelope.

Blind copy notation (bcc): a blind copy notation appears only on the carbon copy of the letter. For a carbon copy, type the notation on a piece of paper held between the typewriter ribbon and the original (top) sheet of paper. Type the notation as:

bcc Ms. Linda Wilson

For a photocopy, type the *bcc* notation on the photocopy after the photocopy has been made.

	words
Current date / Mr. Thomas Fornabio, President / Dunhill	12
Container Corporation / 110 Summit Avenue / Montvale,	22
NJ 07645-2211 / Dear Mr. Fornabio / ITEMS	30
NEEDED FOR SECURITY ANALYSIS	36
(¶) In order to provide the best security analysis possible	47
for your firm, we will need several items from you. First,	59
we will need a roster of your employees, listing the hours	71
they work and the departments in which they work. We	82
will need an inventory of the number and types of	92
vehicles used for official business, along with the license	104
tag numbers of the vehicles. Also, we will need a map of	116
your plant site and facilities, showing the property	127
boundaries and all points of access to and from the site.	138
(¶) Our security analysis should be completed about two	148
weeks after we receive these items. Mr. Denby will call	159
you to discuss our findings and present our solutions	170
to your security needs.	175
(¶) You can be assured that Denby Security Systems	184
offers the finest protection systems available today.	195
The enclosed brochure describes just a few of the	205
security systems we can provide your firm. (178)	213
Sincerely yours / Ms. Carmen Zapata / Security	222
Consultant / xx / Enclosure / bcc John Denby	230/251

92a ▶ 5

Preparatory practice

each line 3 times SS (slowly, faster, slowly); DS between 3-line groups; repeat selected lines if time permits

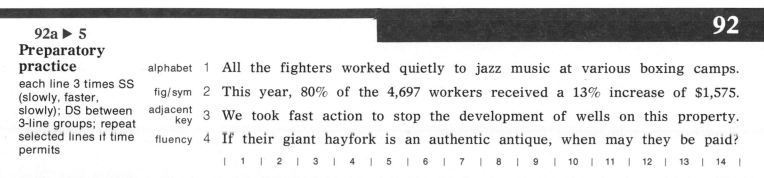

alphabet 1 All the fighters worked quietly to jazz music at various boxing camps.

fig/sym 2 This year, 80% of the 4,697 workers received a 13% increase of $1,575.

adjacent key 3 We took fast action to stop the development of wells on this property.

fluency 4 If their giant hayfork is an authentic antique, when may they be paid?

| 1 | 2 | 3 | 4 | 5 | 6 | 7 | 8 | 9 | 10 | 11 | 12 | 13 | 14 |

122b, continued

Problem 3
Ruled table with leaders

full sheet; exact vertical center; DS
body of table; 24 spaces between
Columns 1 and 2 and 6 spaces
between Columns 2 and 3

words

PROJECTED PAYMENT OF LONG-TERM DEBT

(In Thousands)

Year	Principal	Interest
1986	$41,895	$41,168
1987	48,790	39,021
1988	54,839	35,993
1989	47,036	32,872
1990	34,876	30,161
1991	46,263	31,462
1992	43,728	36,258

Source: Annual Report.

7 10 20 30 34 44 53 62 70 78 86 94 102 112 117

Problem 4
4-column table

full sheet; reading position; DS
body of table; decide spacing
between columns

SCHEDULE OF DIRECT REDUCTION OF LOAN

19--

Month	Interest	Principal	Loan Balance
January	$157.08	$59.43	$14,440.57
February	156.44	60.07	14,380.50
March	155.79	60.72	14,319.78
April	155.13	61.38	14,258.40
May	154.47	62.04	14,196.36
June	153.79	62.72	14,133.64
July	153.11	63.40	14,070.24
August	152.43	64.08	14,006.16
September	151.73	64.78	13,941.38
October	151.03	65.48	13,875.90
November	150.32	66.19	13,809.71
December	149.61	66.90	13,742.81

7 8 22 28 34 39 44 49 54 59 64 70 75 81 87

Check communication skills

full sheet; 1" top margin; 74-space line

1 Cover the answer key below. Check your answers when you have finished.

2 Read the first sentence at the right, noting errors in number usage, capitalization, and punctuation. Type the sentence correctly, including the number at the beginning.

3 DS; type the second sentence in the same way. Continue with the remaining sentences.

4 As your teacher reads the correct sentences, mark any corrections that need to be made.

5 Reformat correctly any sentence containing an error. Type the corrected sentence in the space below the incorrect sentence.

Key: 1. $9 million **2.** Army and Navy, Pete? **3.** "and, feet **4.** page 8, Chapter 2 **5.** J. D. **6.** Louisiana Territory, Napoleonic France **7.** one third, March 5. **8.** Dr., VISTA **9.** fifty-gallon **10.** immediately! **11.** 37, 42d Street **12.** Union Terminal **13.** 29th, April? **14.** consumer **15.** Senator, Republican Convention

1. A budget of $9,000,000 was voted; $10 million was projected.

2. Will you go to the army and navy game with me, Pete.

3. "Mark that spot," Valerie said, "And measure another five ft."

4. Read Page 8 for homework; outline chapter 2.

5. The works of J D Salinger are admired and sharply criticized.

6. The louisiana territory was purchased from napoleonic france.

7. Ted finished about 1/3 of his project which is due march 5th.

8. Dr Howard volunteered her services to V.I.S.T.A.

9. My order for 10 50-gallon drums and 100 ten-gallon drums is here.

10. Stop that immediately.

11. About thirty seven entries were sent to 271--Forty-second street.

12. We admired the architecture of Cincinnati union terminal.

13. Did he plan to arrive in London on the twenty-ninth of april.

14. Business must be constantly alert to changes in Consumer demands.

15. Joyce introduced senator Hunt during the republican convention.

Build sustained letter production skill

Time schedule

Assemble materials .... 3'
Timed production .... 20'
Final check; compute
   n-pram .... 7'

1 Arrange letterheads and No. 10 envelopes (LM p. 43–47), plain paper, and supplies for easy handling.

2 Make a penciled list of the following problems to be formatted and typed:

page 165, 89c, Problem 1
page 167, 90d, Problem 1
page 168, 91c, Problem 1

3 When directed to begin, format and type for 20'. Follow directions given for each problem. Move from one problem to the next quickly. As you type, correct all errors neatly. Proofread carefully each letter and envelope before removing it from the machine. If you finish all problems before time is called, redo the first problem on plain paper.

4 Compute *n-pram*:

$$\frac{\text{Gross (total words)} - \text{penalty*}}{\text{Length (in minutes) of writing**}}$$

*15 words deducted for each error
**20 minutes in this instance

Preparatory practice

each line 3 times SS (slowly, faster, slowly); DS between 3-line groups; repeat selected lines if time permits

alphabet	1	Before the judicial meeting, he quickly recognized my two proxy votes.
fig/sym	2	We must pay Invoice #4076 for $835 ($982 less 15%) to earn a discount.
direct reach	3	My firm goes to great lengths to obtain copies of any service manuals.
fluency	4	The bushel of corn and the giant box of yams may fit in my big sleigh.

| 1 | 2 | 3 | 4 | 5 | 6 | 7 | 8 | 9 | 10 | 11 | 12 | 13 | 14 |

122a ▶ 5
Preparatory practice

each line 3 times SS (slowly, faster, slowly); DS between 3-line groups; repeat selected lines as time permits

alphabet 1 Hal Jimenez fixed twelve good pancakes quickly for my breakfast today.

figure 2 They had 532 men, 498 women, and 1,067 children volunteer for 36 jobs.

outside reach 3 Polly was at the Dallas Plaza last fall; she sold Max two quilts then.

fluency 4 The key goal of the city panel is to audit the six big downtown firms.

| 1 | 2 | 3 | 4 | 5 | 6 | 7 | 8 | 9 | 10 | 11 | 12 | 13 | 14 |

122b ▶ 45
Measure production: tables

Time schedule

Assembling materials .... 5'
Timed production .... 30'
Final check; compute
n–pram .... 10'

1 Organize your supplies.

2 When directed to begin, work for 30'.

3 Erase and correct errors; proofread carefully; compute n–pram.

Problem 1
Table with leaders

half sheet, long side up; exact vertical center; SS body of table; 20 spaces between columns

ESTATE DIAMOND SOLITAIRES

		words
		5
Emerald (3.71 ct.)	$13,650	14
Pear (5.05 ct.)	23,795	22
Marquise (2.79 ct.)	9,875	30
Oval (3.04 ct.)	16,650	38
Oval (7.91 ct.)	32,495	46
Oval (1.89 ct.)	7,635	54
Heart (6.48 ct.)	27,865	62
		66

Source: Anderson Estate Jewelers.   73

Problem 2
Ruled table

full sheet; reading position; DS body of table; decide spacing between columns

REGIONAL EXPENSE ANALYSIS

(First Quarter)

Region	Travel	Entertainment	
			5
			8
			17
			26
			31
			40
Midwest	$ 48,650	$12,375	44
Northeast	41,725	10,675	48
Northwest	54,374	9,350	52
Southeast	43,679	14,795	56
Southern	44,750	13,684	60
Southwest	51,287	10,596	64
			73
Total	$284,465	$71,475	77
			86

**Build/measure
straight-copy skill**

1 Take one 1' writing on each ¶; circle errors and determine *gwam*.

2 Take one 5' writing on all ¶s combined; circle errors and determine *gwam*; compare results with 1' writings.

Difficulty index

all letters used	A	1.5 si	5.7 awl	80% hfw

gwam 1' 5'

	1'	5'
Choosing a career is one of the most important decisions affecting	13	3	68
your future. One factor that should affect your career choice is the	27	5	70
number of available jobs. Unfortunately, this is an ever-changing factor	42	8	73
that is difficult to assess, but many manpower planning studies are	56	11	76
available to help you. You owe it to yourself to learn what types of	70	14	79
jobs are likely to be available when you enter the work force. It is	84	17	82
quite reasonable to assume that many new career choices will be open in	98	20	84
the next several years in both business and government.	109	22	87
The chance to enter interesting and varied careers in business is	13	25	89
very bright for the near future. Both the natural growth of current	27	27	92
jobs and the creation of jobs in new fields will provide such a chance.	42	30	95
In the last fifteen years of this century, entirely new industries are	57	33	98
likely to develop; and they will provide many career opportunities.	69	36	101
Entirely new industries will be created because of new advances in the	84	39	103
way we do things and changes in human values that will redirect the ef-	98	41	106
forts of our culture.	102	42	107
Preparing for future jobs can best be done with the use of a system-	14	45	110
atic career plan. However, even with a career plan, you are very likely	28	48	113
to change jobs or organizations more than once during your life because	43	51	116
you alter your personal goals. Even the best of plans must be altered	57	54	119
if the facts warrant. The basic reasons people modify their career	70	56	121
plans are because they establish new goals, develop new skills, and	84	59	124
acquire new values. Each of us goes through stages of growth and un-	98	62	127
certainty in a career. The process of change goes on throughout life.	112	65	130

gwam 1' | 1 | 2 | 3 | 4 | 5 | 6 | 7 | 8 | 9 | 10 | 11 | 12 | 13 | 14 |
     5' | | 1 | | 2 | | 3 |

**Measure letter
production skill**

Time schedule

Assembling materials	3'
Timed production	25'
Final check; compute *n-pram*	5'

1 Follow time schedule shown at the left. Arrange letterheads and envelopes (LM pp. 49–53) and supplies for easy handling. Correct errors neatly as you keyboard. Address envelopes.

2 When directed to begin, format and type for 25' the problems given on page 173. If you complete the problems in less than 25', start over on plain full sheets.

3 Proofread and circle uncorrected errors found in the final check.

4 Compute *n-pram*
Deduction: 15 words per error
Time: 25'

120c, continued

Problem 2
Boxed table

full sheet; reading position; DS body of table; 6 spaces between columns; insert vertical rules

Problem 3
Boxed table

If time permits, repeat Problem 2 with 8 spaces between columns.

				words
SCHEDULED PERSONAL PROPERTY ENDORSEMENT				8
Policy 39-549718				11
				23
				35
Article	Number	Value Per Piece	Insurance	42
				54
Teaspoons	18	$ 86	$1,548	58
Dinner knives	12	90	1,080	62
Dinner forks	12	122	1,464	66
Serving spoons	4	277	1,108	71
Salad forks	12	97	1,164	75
Soup spoons	12	115	1,380	79
Meat fork	1	177	177	82
				94
Total			$7,921	96
				108

121a ▶ 5
Preparatory practice

each line 3 times SS (slowly, faster, slowly); DS between 3-line groups; repeat selected lines as time permits

alphabet	1	Quincy described two or three hazards of faking very complex injuries.
figure	2	We needed 30-, 45-, and 60-minute tapes for our Model 127893 recorder.
double letter	3	Carroll will see or call Jennifer at noon to tell her about the error.
fluency	4	Sue may make it work right if she pays Dudley to fix the handle on it.

| 1 | 2 | 3 | 4 | 5 | 6 | 7 | 8 | 9 | 10 | 11 | 12 | 13 | 14 |

121b ▶ 45
Sustained production: tables

Time schedule

Assembling materials .... 5'
Timed production .... 30'
Final check; compute
 n–pram .... 10'

1 Make a list of problems to be completed and the changes to be made in them for this assignment:
a. Page 218, 116c, Problem 1 (exact vertical center; 4 spaces between columns).
b. Page 220, 117b, Problem 3 (half sheet, long side up; SS body of table; decide spacing between columns).
c. Page 223, 119c, Problem 1 (list the companies in alphabetical or–der; reading position; 24 spaces between columns).

2 Organize your supplies for rapid handling.

3 When directed to begin, work for 30'. If you finish all problems before time is called, start over with the first problem.

4 Erase and correct errors; proofread carefully; compute n–pram.

words

Problem 1
Letter with subject line

modified block style, indented ¶s, mixed punctuation; centered subject line

Current date | Mr. John Lundstrom | 415 Lantana Avenue | Englewood, NJ 07631-2192 | Dear Mr. Lundstrom: | ADJUSTABLE RATE MORTGAGE 16 / 26

(¶ 1) As an apartment dweller, you may be interested in learning more about how an adjustable rate mortgage from Merchants Bank of New Jersey can enable you to afford your own home today. 40 / 54 / 62

(¶ 2) Merchants Bank offers a budgeted monthly payment plan with an affordable rate mortgage loan where the rate of interest changes periodically according to a preset index. Rate adjustments to the mortgage are made every six months based on the commercial bank money market certificate rate. 76 / 92 / 107 / 120

(¶ 3) Are you interested in learning more about home financing in the current economic environment? If so, please contact our Mortgage Department at 445-7834. (125) 134 / 148 / 150

Sincerely, | Mrs. Alice Rivera | Loan Advisor | xx 159/**172**

Problem 2
Letter with mailing notation, attention line, reference notation, company name in closing lines, and cc notation

block style, open punctuation

May 18, 19-- | REGISTERED | Data Information Corporation | Attention Purchasing Director | 1945 West Parnall Road | Jackson, MI 49201-1638 | Ladies and Gentlemen | Reference: Claim #5489 15 / 30 / 37

(¶ 1) Electronics Manufacturing, Inc., has agreed to make payment of $2,500 in full settlement of your claim for defective equipment purchased on January 24. 52 / 68

(¶ 2) In agreeing to this settlement, they are in no way accepting responsibility for any additional claims or damages as the result of the faulty equipment. 83 / 98

(¶ 3) Please have a representative of your firm at my office at 9 a.m. on June 1. At that time, I will present a check for $2,500 in exchange for the completion of the waiver forms. (94) 113 / 129 / 132

Sincerely yours | DONNELLY, EVERETT, AND SLOANE | Ms. Susan Everett | Attorney | xx | cc Bruce Donnelly 146 / 152/**175**

Problem 3
Letter with subject line and cc notation

modified block style, blocked ¶s, mixed punctuation; blocked subject line

Current date | Ms. Debbie Peterson | 1078 Lewis Road | Linfield, PA 19468-4353 | Dear Ms. Peterson: | METRO SERVICE 16 / 23

(¶ 1) Metro Cable TV is pleased to announce that it has been awarded the contract by the Linfield Civic Association for the installation of Metro's cable television system in your subdivision. Our installers should begin hanging cable in your neighborhood within the next month. 37 / 54 / 70 / 78

(¶ 2) The system being installed has a 35-channel capacity with 25 of the channels operational at "turn on." The system is bi-directional, permitting Metro to offer, when completed, an optional security package. 92 / 108 / 118

(¶ 3) We at Metro are excited about the opportunity to serve your neighborhood. If you wish further information or have specific questions, please call one of our service representatives at 981-6742. (136) 133 / 149 / 157

Cordially, | Robert Hartman | Vice President | xx | cc Linfield Civic Association 172/ **184**

120a ▶ 5
Preparatory practice

each line 3 times SS (slowly, faster, slowly); DS between 3-line groups; repeat selected lines as time permits

alphabet	1	Jaklynne characterized Quemoy as a very exotic paradise with big fish.
figure	2	Our income for 1975 was only $26,870; our income for 1985 was $43,275.
direct reach	3	Johnny brought a great present for Mary--a brown and grey hunting bag.
fluency	4	Eight men pay the city for the right to hang their own signs downtown.

| 1 | 2 | 3 | 4 | 5 | 6 | 7 | 8 | 9 | 10 | 11 | 12 | 13 | 14 |

120b ▶ 10
Preapplication drill: format a boxed table

half sheet, long side up; 1½″ top margin; 16 spaces be–tween columns

To insert vertical rulings, remove the page from the typewriter; use a pen with black ink and draw verti–cal lines at the midpoint between columns.

PURCHASE AGREEMENT--TRANSPARENCIES

(Price Based on Boxes Ordered)

Order Number	50-99	100+
3R20341 CL	$22.85	$19.95
3R87034 RD	24.55	21.50

120c ▶ 35
Prepare documents

Problem 1
Boxed table

full sheet; exact vertical center; DS body of table; 10 spaces between columns; insert vertical rules

words

PHOTOCOPIER RENTAL PLAN · 4

Effective January 1, 19-- Through December 31, 19-- · 14

Model	Monthly Charge	Copy Allowance	Excess Copy Charge	
				26
				38
				42
				47
				59
3170	$100	3,090	.0121	63
3405	176	5,150	.0135	66
5455	210	7,725	.0093	69
2480	150	10,300	.0051	73
3695	227	10,300	.0051	77
8280	443	41,200	.0083	81
9290	451	51,500	.0051	85
9495	529	61,500	.0043	89
9594	637	81,500	.0041	93
				105

Learning goals

1 To increase basic skill on straight, statistical, rough–draft, and script copy.
2 To improve ability to punctuate copy correctly.
3 To refine keyboarding technique.

Machine adjustments

1 Paper guide at 0.
2 Margins: 70–space line for drills and ¶ writings unless directed otherwise.
3 Spacing: SS drills; DS ¶ writings.
4 Indention: 5 spaces for ¶ writings.

94a ▶ 5
Preparatory practice

each line 3 times SS (slowly, faster, slowly); DS between 3-line groups; repeat selected lines as time permits

alphabet	1	Genevieve quickly applied zinc oxide as treatment for the bruised jaw.
fig/sym	2	With a 20% discount (until Friday), No. 1378 will sell for $49,563.90.
direct reaches	3	The brokers checked many of my account records and employment surveys.
fluency	4	The audit may be the key to the chaotic problems in the work downtown.

| 1 | 2 | 3 | 4 | 5 | 6 | 7 | 8 | 9 | 10 | 11 | 12 | 13 | 14 |

94b ▶ 12
Improve straight copy skill

1 One 1' writing on each ¶; circle errors; determine *gwam*.
2 One 5' writing on all ¶s combined; circle errors; determine *gwam*; compare results with 1' writings.

Difficulty index

all letters used	A	1.5 si	5.7 awl	80% hfw

	gwam 1'	5'

Being an effective leader is crucial to productive management. To | 13 | 3 | 50
be a good leader, one must have a fair amount of natural skill. But as | 27 | 6 | 53
useful as this talent is, there is a need for training and experience in | 42 | 9 | 56
the field of leadership. The essential job of a manager is dealing with | 57 | 12 | 59
other individuals, no matter how small or complex the enterprise is. | 71 | 15 | 62

For management to work well, a company must be properly formed and | 14 | 18 | 65
organized as a unique entity. Of course, the smaller the firm, the less | 29 | 21 | 68
the need for a formal structure. In a smaller business, the boss will | 43 | 24 | 71
probably have more direct contact with the staff. The units in a small | 57 | 27 | 74
firm are less complex. A manager may be the leader over the sales, fi- | 71 | 30 | 77
nance, personnel, and production functions. | 80 | 32 | 79

In larger firms, the role of a manager is more defined; and the | 13 | 34 | 81
channels for communication are more complex. Decision-making falls | 27 | 37 | 84
into exact domains. The financial manager must make the ultimate de- | 41 | 40 | 87
cision in money matters as the marketing manager must do in the sphere | 55 | 43 | 90
of sales. But in all these jobs, managers must be able to work well | 69 | 46 | 93
with the people in their units. | 75 | 47 | 94

gwam	1'	1	2	3	4	5	6	7	8	9	10	11	12	13	14
	5'			1				2				3			

Prepare tables

Problem 1
2-column table
with leaders

full sheet; exact vertical center; DS body of table; 30 spaces between columns

words

GULF OF MEXICO OIL LEASE BIDS

High Bidders for Tract 38*

Company	Bid
Hess and Hess Oil	$23,887,125
Webster Petroleum	23,519,250
Davis Oil Operations	23,486,175
Haskell Exploration	22,978,750
Offshore Drilling	22,864,375
Oxford Petroleum	22,739,175
Adams Drilling	22,464,375
Petro Oil	21,986,175
Fritz Exploration	21,864,375

*Bids opened November 15, 19--

words: 6, 11, 23, 35, 37, 49, 61, 73, 85, 97, 109, 121, 133, 145, 157, 169, 175

Problem 2
3-column table
with leaders

full sheet; exact vertical center; DS body of table; 24 spaces between Columns 1 and 2 and 4 spaces between Columns 2 and 3

Problem 3
2-column table
with leaders

If time permits, repeat Problem 1 with 20 spaces between columns.

ELECTRONIC TYPEWRITER PRICE UPDATE

Effective January 1, 19--

Model	Commercial	Educational
X910-86-01	$1,282.50	$1,157.50
X915-86-10	1,597.75	1,472.75
X920-86-15	2,080.00	1,930.00
X925-86-20	2,375.50	2,175.50
X930-86-25	2,625.75	2,375.75
X940-86-35	3,215.75	2,890.75
X945-86-40	3,580.50	3,230.20
X950-86-45	3,975.00	3,575.00

words: 7, 12, 24, 36, 41, 53, 63, 73, 83, 93, 103, 113, 123, 133, 145

94c ▶ 8
Improve
keyboarding
technique

each pair of lines
3 times SS at a
controlled rate;
DS between 6-line
groups

adjacent reaches	1	We quickly realized the proposed posting methods were quite effective.
	2	There are several additional copies of the weekly government booklets.
direct reaches	3	Their branch library must obtain my technical consumer service manual.
	4	My large payment for their many great services was unfortunately lost.
double letters	5	The school committee recommended that my books be shipped immediately.
	6	I am sorry your attached bill was addressed to their account in error.
long words	7	Forty representatives recommended appropriate specifications be added.
	8	We developed additional recommendations on transportation legislation.

| 1 | 2 | 3 | 4 | 5 | 6 | 7 | 8 | 9 | 10 | 11 | 12 | 13 | 14 |

94d ▶ 12
Improve script
copy skill

1 One 1' writing on each ¶;
circle errors; determine
gwam.

2 One 5' writing on all ¶s
combined; circle errors;
determine *gwam*; compare
results with 1' writings.

Difficulty index

all letters used	A	1.5 si	5.7 awl	80% hfw

gwam 1' | 5'

Forecasting is a means of generating data about such matters | 12 | 2 | 42

as the number, type, or quality of personnel, sales, or raw materials | 26 | 5 | 45

that will be available to or will be needed by a firm. Forecasts | 39 | 8 | 48

do not state ultimate facts or truths about the future. An | 51 | 10 | 50

element of uncertainty, which managers must learn to deal | 63 | 12 | 52

with and to minimize, exists in all forecasts. | 72 | 14 | 54

A high level of uncertainty wastes a great deal of both time | 12 | 16 | 56

and money. In general, the ability to control the course of | 24 | 18 | 58

events and to get reliable data on a regular basis results in | 36 | 20 | 60

a more secure feeling. Unforeseen events and inaccurate data | 48 | 22 | 70

increase uncertainty. A good rule of thumb is: the longer the | 60 | 24 | 72

time period for which plans are made, the more tentative | 71 | 26 | 74

the forecast. | 74 | 27 | 75

If ways can be found to make more informed judgments | 11 | 29 | 77

about events, we can improve the value of our forecasts. | 23 | 31 | 79

Today computers can help us to make these decisions. The | 35 | 33 | 81

ability of these machines to store and use data will be a | 47 | 35 | 83

great asset for predicting the results of our decisions. Forecasts | 61 | 38 | 86

for business activity in future decades will be more certain. | 73 | 40 | 88

118c, continued

Problem 2
4-column table
with horizontal rulings

full sheet; reading position; DS body of table; decide spacing between columns

Problem 3
3-column table
with horizontal rulings

If time permits, repeat Problem 1; SS the columnar items; decide spacing between columns.

VAN CONFERENCE CENTER

Capacity Based on Seating Arrangement

Room	Conference	Schoolroom	Auditorium
Birch	24	80	150
Cedar	18	60	110
Maple	18	60	110
Oak	12	40	65
Pecan	40	120	225
Pine	36	100	185
Walnut	20	70	135

words
4
11
23
35
42
54
56
58
60
62
64
66
69
81

119

119a ▶ 5
Preparatory practice

each line 3 times SS (slowly, faster, slowly); DS between 3-line groups; repeat selected lines as time permits

alphabet	1	Jackie said the algebra quiz was complex and was not a very fair test.
figure	2	The ZIP Code for 4591 Greene Street should be 23678 rather than 23608.
adjust key	3	Luisa was talking to excited people who were doing a very tedious job.
fluency	4	Dick and Leo make me laugh when they sit down to work on hand signals.

| 1 | 2 | 3 | 4 | 5 | 6 | 7 | 8 | 9 | 10 | 11 | 12 | 13 | 14 |

119b ▶ 10
Preapplication drill: format ruled tables with leaders

half sheet, long side up; 1½" top margin; DS body of table; 12 spaces between Columns 1 and 2 and 4 spaces between Columns 2 and 3.

Format the table with horizontal rules and leaders (alternate periods and spaces). If necessary, see page 195 to review formatting leaders.

Drill

TOP SALES AGENTS

(Southern Region)

DS

DS

DS

Agent	Sales	Percent of Budget
Amy Lee	$467,500	170%
Ted Ford	448,250	163
Pat Mee	412,500	150

SS

DS

SS

94e ▶ 13
Review/apply communication skills: punctuation

full sheet; 1″ top margin; 74-space line

Keyboard and format as directed in 81b, p. 150.

Key: 1c. museum, Chad, Togo, 2b. said, 3d. manager, Diaz, today, tomorrow, 4b. building, 5b. Roanoke, Virginia, 12, 6b. cunning, experienced, 6d. huge elm 7b. 1984, 8b. paints, scrapers, brushes, etc.,

---

Use a comma

1. After an introductory word, phrase, or clause, and to separate words in a series.
2. To set off a short direct quotation.
3. To set off appositives, words in direct address, and contrasting phrases and clauses.
4. To set off nonrestrictive clauses (not essential to the meaning of the sentence). Do not set off information with comma(s) which is essential to the designation or identification of that which is modified.
5. To separate the day from the year and the city from the state.
6. To separate coordinate adjectives in a series. Each coordinate adjective modifies the noun independently. Do not use commas to separate closely related adjectives which seem to form a single unit with the noun they modify.
7. To separate adjacent groups of figures which are unrelated and whole numbers into three digit groups. However, policy, page, room, telephone, and most serial numbers are typed without commas.
8. Before and after the abbreviation etc.

---

review 1a. After separating the socks, he folded each pair.
review   b. Yes, I do like fruits, vegetables, and cheeses.
apply   c. While touring the museum I saw exhibits from Chad Togo and Mali.

review 2a. "I shall be home early this evening," Charlotte told her mother.
apply   b. Ann said "That is the only way."

review 3a. Our mayor, Lucinda Allen, provides the leadership our city needs.
review   b. Is this the letter you wish to send, Mr. Cheng?
review   c. This book, not the one on the desk, is the one I want.
apply   d. Our manager Ms. Diaz will speak with you today not tomorrow Eve.

review 4a. Mr. Arnold Meyer, Jr., a stockbroker, handles my portfolio.
apply   b. My office, a red brick building is only 15 minutes from downtown.

review 5a. Edmund moved to Sandusky, Ohio, on June 8, 1985.
apply   b. My family reunion in Roanoke Virginia was held on April 12 1984.

review 6a. The boat disappeared in the dark, cold, icy water.
apply   b. My opponent was cunning experienced and agile.
review   c. Growing gardenias is easy along this white picket fence.
apply   d. We had a picnic under the huge, elm tree.

review 7a. During 1983, 29 maintenance calls were made to Room 312.
apply   b. In 1984 12 errors were noted and corrected on page 7 of the text.

review 8a. All books, notes, etc., should be removed from the desk.
apply   b. All paints scrapers brushes etc. were reduced for the big sale.

95a ▶ 5
Preparatory practice

each line 3 times SS (slowly, faster, slowly); DS between 3-line groups; repeat selected lines as time permits

alphabet 1 Kevin is required to recognize swiftly the major parts of both toxins.
fig/sym 2 Our Contract #496-75*, dated August 30, calls for an 18 1/2% increase.
double letters 3 The weekly sheet for all employees will be processed by noon tomorrow.
fluency 4 A key to the theme of the ancient ritual is the sign of the six goals.

| 1 | 2 | 3 | 4 | 5 | 6 | 7 | 8 | 9 | 10 | 11 | 12 | 13 | 14 |

118a ▶ 5
Preparatory practice

each line 3 times
SS (slowly, faster,
slowly); DS be-
tween 3-line
groups; repeat
selected lines
as time permits

alphabet 1 Joaquin bought a new executive desk and credenza from Polly last week.

figure 2 Write a $382 check for Invoice 4109 and a $578 check for Invoice 3926.

combination response 3 I may go with Lulu to visit the great estate on the rich reserve land.

fluency 4 Andy may pay for half of the bus, and the city may pay for half of it.

| 1 | 2 | 3 | 4 | 5 | 6 | 7 | 8 | 9 | 10 | 11 | 12 | 13 | 14 |

118b ▶ 10
Preapplication drill: horizontal rulings

Format the drill on a half sheet, long side up, according to the in-structions given at the right; leave a 1½″ top margin; 12 spaces between columns; DS column entries.

If time permits, space down 4 lines and repeat the drill with 8 spaces between columns.

Horizontal rulings

Center the heading; DS; deter-mine placement of the columns; set left and right margin stops; type first line of double ruling; operate the variable line spacer and move cylinder slightly for-ward; (electronic typewriters may have an index key that will space up ¼ line); type the second ruling. Type the body of the table. After the last item in columns has been typed, SS and type a single rul-ing. DS and type the footnote.

Drill

NEW PRODUCTS*
DS

	DS
Model	Release Date
	SS
X3836	June 2, 19--
X6837	July 7, 19--

*Low-Volume Division

118c ▶ 35
Prepare documents

Problem 1
3-column table
with horizontal rulings

full sheet; exact vertical center; DS body of table; 10 spaces between columns

SMITH COUNTY			words
			2
Sales Tax Revenue Bonds, Series A			9
			21
			33
Principal Amount	Maturity	Interest Rate	40
			52
$2,235,000	1985	8.25	56
2,415,000	1986	8.50	59
2,625,000	1987	8.75	62
2,850,000	1988	9.00	65
3,110,000	1989	9.25	68
3,395,000	1990	9.50	71
3,720,000	1991	9.75	74
4,080,000	1992	10.00	78
4,490,000	1993	10.25	82
4,950,000	1994	10.50	86
5,470,000	1995	10.75	90
			102
Source: Smith County Auditor's Records.			110

Improve statistical copy skill

1 One 1' writing on each ¶; circle errors; determine *gwam*.

2 One 5' writing on both ¶s combined; circle errors; determine *gwam*; compare results with 1' writings.

Difficulty index

all letters/figures used	A	5.7 awl	1.5 si	80% hfw

gwam 1' | 5'

Did you realize that when you purchase a house and borrow the | 12 | 2 | 54
money for 30 years to pay for it, all of the interest payments repre- | 26 | 5 | 57
sent potential deductions from your income before you pay taxes? If | 40 | 8 | 60
you are in the upper tax brackets, this purchase will make a vast dif- | 54 | 11 | 63
ference. For example, suppose you bought a $200,000 residence and were | 68 | 14 | 66
qualified to borrow $180,000. Let's say that the interest you paid on | 82 | 17 | 69
the $180,000 in the initial year amounted to $27,000. You would be | 95 | 20 | 72
eligible to deduct the entire $27,000 from your taxable income before | 109 | 23 | 75
paying your federal taxes. | 114 | 24 | 76

These deductions have definite advantages. If you were in the | 13 | 26 | 78
50-percent tax bracket, you would get a tax deduction of $18,900; the | 27 | 29 | 01
interest on the loan would, in effect, be costing you only $8,100. | 41 | 32 | 84
That is why as taxpayers get into upper-income tax brackets, it gener- | 55 | 35 | 87
ally benefits them to buy a house as opposed to renting a dwelling. | 69 | 38 | 90
Taxes and houses are related in another aspect. If you buy or construct | 84 | 41 | 93
a residence for $165,000 and sell it 4 years later for $193,000, you | 98 | 44 | 96
have gained $28,000. By not acquiring, within 18 months, another dwell- | 112 | 47 | 99
ing of equal or higher value after adjustments, you would be required | 126 | 50 | 102
to make capital gains tax payments on the $28,000 difference. | 138 | 52 | 104

gwam 1' | 1 | 2 | 3 | 4 | 5 | 6 | 7 | 8 | 9 | 10 | 11 | 12 | 13 | 14 |
      5' | 1 | 2 | 3 |

Review/apply communication skills: punctuation

full sheet; 1" top margin; 74-space line

Keyboard and format as directed in 81b, p. 150.

Key: 1b. thirty–seven 2b. short–term 3b. first–, second–, third–class 4b. time–out 5b. s-e-p-a-r-a-t-e

Use a hyphen

1. To join compound numbers from twenty-one to ninety-nine that are typed as words.

2. To join compound adjectives to the noun which is modified, unless the adjective is in the comparative or superlative form.

3. To join two or more compound words or figures with a common base which they modify as a unit. Use suspended hyphens rather than repeating the base word.

4. To form certain compound nouns.

5. To indicate the spelling of a word or a name.

review 1a. Forty-two applicants responded to the newspaper advertisement.
apply   b. About thirty seven executives attended the conference.

review 2a. The worn-out notebook was discarded.
apply   b. I obtained a short term loan at a reasonable rate of interest.

review 3a. You may respond to the items on page 55 with 1- or 2-word answers.
apply   b. Harry checked the rates on first, second, and third class mail.

review 4a. The head bolts must be torqued to approximately 75 foot-pounds.
apply   b. The officials called time out.

review 5a. The preferred spelling is e-e-r-i-e.
apply   b. Many people have difficulty spelling the word separate.

117b, continued

Problem 2
3-column table

half sheet, long side up; SS body of table; 14 spaces be—tween columns

RESIDENTIAL SALES | 4
MARCH 3-10, 19-- | 7

Listing Agent	Seling Agent	Price	
			19
Burge	Hutto	$85,900	23
Davis	Welch	104,575	27
Jeansonne	Parker	97,800	31
Le Beau	Willis	72,580	35
Long	Schultz *miller*	42,300	38
Marcote	Ellison	69,775	42
Smith	Walker	126,900	46
Martin	Tassin	73,400	50
White	Perez	198,500	54

Problem 3
4-column table

full sheet; reading position; DS body of table; 8 spaces between columns

Problem 4
3-column table

If time permits, repeat Problem 1 with 14 spaces between columns.

DANIEL MANAGEMENT CENTER | 5
Program Analysis for February | 11

Program	Income	Expenses	Profit	
C 2810	$4,820	$2,975	$1,845	27
C 2824	3,975	2,480	1,495	31
M 3612	7,655	4,375	3,280	35
M 3634	8,534	5,150	3,384	39
M 3639	6,895	4,767	2,128	43
S 4123	9,256	5,348	3,908	47
S 4130	8,850	5,025	3,825	51
S 4138	8,775	4,987	3,788	55
W 5204	5,134	3,266	1,868	59

Improve straight copy skill

1 One 1' writing on each ¶; circle errors; determine *gwam*.

2 One 5' writing on all ¶s combined; circle errors; determine *gwam*; compare results with 1' writings.

Difficulty index

all letters used	A	1.5 si	5.7 awl	80% hfw

gwam 1' | 5'

Many business people have found the new microcomputers to be a — 13 | 3 | 55
good management tool. These small computers can now be seen on the — 27 | 5 | 58
desktops of a rising number of managers. The typewriter-size tools — 40 | 8 | 61
seem well on their way to becoming as important as calculators. Micro- — 54 | 11 | 64
computer creation is a rapidly expanding field and will continue to be. — 69 | 14 | 67
In fact, sales of these new machines now amount to over a billion dol- — 83 | 17 | 69
lars a year. — 85 | 17 | 70

These machines have something for just about everyone. Business — 13 | 20 | 73
is using them to analyze, store, and locate data for tasks ranging — 26 | 22 | 75
from billing work to long-term sales projections. The machines can — 40 | 25 | 78
also develop budgets and cash-flow plans as well as follow market trends. — 55 | 28 | 81
With the computer, a telephone, and an add-on device called a modem, — 69 | 31 | 84
researchers can have contact with other data bases to get a greater — 82 | 34 | 87
amount of news or facts right off the wire services. — 93 | 36 | 89

The assets of these machines are speed, versatility, and ease of — 13 | 38 | 91
use. Tasks that previously required hours to do can be done in seconds — 27 | 41 | 94
just by tapping a few keys. In fact, with a feature called "data base — 42 | 44 | 97
management," a file can be created which can be instantly called up by — 56 | 47 | 100
using various approaches. Thus, once the proper data have been put — 69 | 50 | 102
into the data base, managers can easily summon customers' files or — 83 | 52 | 105
workers' names. — 86 | 53 | 106

gwam 1' | 1 | 2 | 3 | 4 | 5 | 6 | 7 | 8 | 9 | 10 | 11 | 12 | 13 | 14 |
5' | 1 | 2 | 3 |

95e ▶ 11
Improve skill transfer

60-space line; two 1' writings on each line; additional 1' writings on each line for which your *gwam* was less than on Line 1

words

straight copy | 1 | Executives today frequently confront the question of ethics. | 12

script | 2 | *New firms need capital to get started in the business world.* | 12

statistical | 3 | In 1989, the group will employ 43,627 workers in 105 cities. | 12

rough draft | 4 | successfull businesses set real goals so they can succeed, | 12

116c, continued

Problem 2
4-column table

full sheet; reading position; DS body of table; decide spacing between columns

Problem 3
4-column table

If time permits, repeat Problem 2 with different spacing between columns.

words

Incentive Compensation Statement 7

(Salary Suplement for Third Quarter) 14

center column heading

Sales Rep~~t.~~ resentative	Budgeted Units	Perf. ormance	Commission	words
Peter Perkins	128	225%	$ 8,575.70	42
Margaret Walters	115	212%	8,080.21	48
Tom Fernandez	130	167%	6,365.07	54
Sharon Kinser	140	156%	5,945.82	60
Doris Dunlop	120	~~114~~ 61%	5,107.30	65
~~Tom~~ Richard Robinson	110	127%	4,840.50	71
Lynn Ligon	116	63~~¢~~%	2,401.19	87
Timothy Kurtis	90	104%	3,963.~~00~~ 88	77
Yang Shih	117	85%	3,239.71	82
Jeannette Alexander	1~~4~~2	35%	1,334.00	96
Total Paid			$49,853.38	100

117

117a ▶ 5

Preparatory practice

each line 3 times SS (slowly, faster, slowly); DS between 3-line groups; repeat selected lines as time permits

alphabet 1 Jarvis knew the exact size of the pretty grey quilt he made in Pueblo.

figure 2 We planted 175 tulips, 860 daisies, 349 roses, and 824 chrysanthemums.

one-hand words 3 Phillip, in my opinion, was aware oil reserves were decreased in July.

fluency 4 She may fix the ham for us, and she may make the lamb dish for Helena.

| 1 | 2 | 3 | 4 | 5 | 6 | 7 | 8 | 9 | 10 | 11 | 12 | 13 | 14 |

117b ▶ 45

Prepare documents

Problem 1
3-column table

full sheet; exact vertical center; DS body of table; 10 spaces between columns

words

TEMPERATURES FOR SELECTED CITIES 6

November 14, 19-- 9

City	High	Low	13
Anchorage	40	31	16
Baltimore	48	36	19
Des Moines	30	11	22
Miami	83	70	24
Minneapolis	10	6	27
San Francisco	60	46	30

__________ 34

Source: United Press International. 41

96a ▶ 5
Preparatory practice

each line 3 times SS (slowly, faster, slowly); DS between 3-line groups; repeat selected lines as time permits

alphabet 1 Fay warned us to avoid a big jam by parking quickly in the sixth zone.

fig/sym 2 My bank notes (at 15% interest) will total $380,674 when paid in 1992.

adjacent reach 3 Various people quickly asked questions regarding my short buying trip.

fluency 4 The sight of the sick doe may be the sign of a problem for the island.

| 1 | 2 | 3 | 4 | 5 | 6 | 7 | 8 | 9 | 10 | 11 | 12 | 13 | 14 |

96b ▶ 12
Improve straight copy skill

1 One 1' writing on each ¶; circle errors; determine *gwam*.

2 One 5' writing on all ¶s combined; circle errors; determine *gwam*; compare results with 1' writings.

Difficulty index

all letters used | A | 1.5 si | 5.7 awl | 80% hfw

gwam 1' | 5'

Americans have always known the value of wisely managing their own 13 | 2 | 49
finances. The general rise in prosperity during the present century 27 | 5 | 52
has helped many people to build savings. People have begun to want a 41 | 8 | 55
means to gain a greater return on their money than the amount they can 55 | 11 | 58
get with just simple bank interest. One option is the buying of stock 69 | 14 | 61
in multiple firms. 73 | 15 | 62

Two basic attitudes toward the stock market exist nowadays. Some 13 | 17 | 64
people believe that the overall trend of the stock market is upward. 27 | 20 | 67
Individuals who hold this optimistic attitude about the future are 41 | 22 | 69
known as "bulls." These people buy stock with the idea that the value 55 | 25 | 72
of the stock will rise and that they will undoubtedly be able to sell 69 | 28 | 75
at a higher price than they have originally paid. 79 | 30 | 77

"Bears," on the other hand, are individuals who are not so opti- 13 | 32 | 79
mistic about stock market trends. These people feel that a decline in 27 | 35 | 82
the market is always imminent. When bears anticipate a loss on the 41 | 38 | 85
market, they quickly sell their stock in order to get back as much 54 | 40 | 87
money as they can before the drop takes place. But whether people are 68 | 43 | 90
bulls or bears, their hope is to realize a reasonable profit on their 82 | 46 | 93
personal investments. 87 | 47 | 94

gwam 1' | 1 | 2 | 3 | 4 | 5 | 6 | 7 | 8 | 9 | 10 | 11 | 12 | 13 | 14 |
5' | 1 | 2 | 3 |

96c ▶ 8
Improve keyboarding technique

each pair of lines 3 times SS at a controlled rate; DS between 6-line groups

letter response 1 As you were aware, you debated in a few cases after we were in a poll.
2 Seven million readers were in great fear after I stated a new opinion.

word response 3 Sign the right forms so the big civic panel may handle their problems.
4 The big problem with their theory is the risk to the eight lake towns.

combination response 5 Such key cases as ours are treated as secrets by a great number of us.
6 It is the duty of the big star and extras to create a loony art craze.

| 1 | 2 | 3 | 4 | 5 | 6 | 7 | 8 | 9 | 10 | 11 | 12 | 13 | 14 |

116a ▶ 5
Preparatory practice

each line 3 times SS (slowly, faster, slowly); DS between 3-line groups; repeat selected lines as time permits

alphabet 1 Max Jarwoski quickly asked if the bank gives to every organized group.

figure 2 Our company printed 6,537,318 books in 1940 and 1,264,827,302 in 1985.

shift lock 3 Do ANACOM and AMS exhibit at either the N-CBEA or the NBEA convention?

fluency 4 Susie and Alan spent their profit on a field and may dig a lake on it.

| 1 | 2 | 3 | 4 | 5 | 6 | 7 | 8 | 9 | 10 | 11 | 12 | 13 | 14 |

116b ▶ 10
Preapplication drill: use dollar signs

Format the drill on a half sheet, long side up, according to the instructions given at the right; leave a 1″ top margin; 12 spaces between columns; DS column entries.

If time permits, space down 4 lines and repeat the drill with 8 spaces between columns.

Placing dollar signs and totals

Place a dollar sign before the first amount in a column and before the total. Align the dollar sign 1 space to the left of the longest amount in the column. Indicate a total with a line under the column. DS above the total figure. Indent the word "Total" 5 spaces from the left margin.

Drill

Flight costs	$ 685.67
Per diem allowance	1,021.34
Other expenses	196.20
Total	$1,903.21

116c ▶ 35
Prepare documents

Problem 1
4-column table

full sheet; reading position; DS body of table; 4 spaces between columns

words

SALES REVENUE — 3

(Gross Sales for Third Quarter, 19--) — 10

Region	Arcade	Home Video	Microcomputer	
				24
Alaska/Canada	$ 16,123.70	$ 32,819.06	$ 102,835.42	33
Great Lakes	19,483.42	26,804.55	108,384.52	41
Gulf States	17,467.97	30,279.64	112,742.93	49
Islands	9,876.54	11,310.82	78,315.36	56
Mid-Atlantic	21,739.40	34,619.37	121,327.52	64
Midwest	18,290.41	31,214.83	118,369.02	71
Mountain Plains	10,746.35	14,987.35	90,472.41	79
New England	15,376.31	27,493.20	109,346.74	87
Northeast	22,947.63	32,617.49	120,983.45	94
Northwest	12,593.48	17,439.94	98,765.31	101
Southeast	20,639.27	33,949.31	132,659.52	108
Southwest	14,329.60	17,383.63	96,418.33	122
Totals	$199,614.08	$310,919.19	$1,290,620.53	130

96d ▶ 15
Improve rough-draft copy skill

1 Two 1' writings on each ¶; circle errors; determine *gwam*.

2 Two 3' writings on both ¶s combined; circle errors; determine *gwam*; compare results with 1' writings.

Difficulty index

all letters used	A	1.5 si	5.7 awl	80% hfw

gwam 1' | 3'

All well-managed businesses must plan for the future in   10 | 3 | 62
order to continue to be successful. Aggresive companies   22 | 7 | 66
realize that their will be changes in our society and culture,   35 | 11 | 70
and they take steps to make use of those changes. During   47 | 15 | 74
the past decade, our labor force, economy, and technology   59 | 19 | 78
have underwent rapid changes. These elements of society will   71 | 23 | 82
keep on changing. It is the job of managers to led their   83 | 27 | 86
firms to adopt to the needs of modern life.   92 | 30 | 89

In future years, the size of the labor force will grow   11 | 34 | 93
at a slower rate. But the new technology will need that   24 | 38 | 97
new types of jobs come into existance. Computer technology   36 | 42 | 101
in particular will play a large part in the type of work   47 | 46 | 105
people will be doing. the economy will increase and change   58 | 50 | 109
as hot areas of the land become population centers. Business   72 | 54 | 113
managers must view the opportunities shown by these factors   84 | 58 | 117
and find ways to take advantage of them.   92 | 59 | 118

96e ▶ 10
Review/apply communication skills: punctuation

full sheet; 1" top margin; 74-space line

Keyboard and format as directed in 81b, p. 150.

Key: 1b. reservations; 2c. implemented; con– sequently, 3b. navy; 4b. job; namely,

Use a semicolon

1. Between two independent clauses of a compound sentence when the conjunction is omitted.

2. To separate independent clauses when they are joined by a conjunctive adverb (however, therefore, consequently, etc.).

3. Before a coordinating conjunction (and, but, for, or, nor) between two independent clauses when either or both contain internal punctuation.

4. Before an expression which introduces an explanatory statement.

review **1a.** The computer course was easy; I received top grades.
apply **b.** I shall make the reservations she will provide transportation.

review **2a.** The highway was impassable; consequently, traffic was rerouted.
review **b.** I dialed the right number; however, no one answered the phone.
apply **c.** New procedures were implemented consequently efficiency was improved.

review **3a.** Yes, we ordered Beef Wellington; and they ordered Crab Imperial.
apply **b.** My skirt was brown, tan, and navy and hers was a solid color.

review **4a.** Some conditions promote effective study; for example, a quiet place.
apply **b.** He is qualified for the job namely he has training and experience.

115b ▶ 10
Preapplication drill: center columns

Format the drill on a half sheet, long side up, according to the instructions given above the drill; leave 1" top margin; 12 spaces between Columns 1 and 2 and 8 spaces between Columns 2 and 3.

If time permits, space down 4 times on the same sheet and repeat the drill.

Varying intercolumn space

Tables with long description columns look better if more space is left between the description column and the next column than between the remaining columns. If a description item is exceptionally long, break it into 2 or more lines, indenting the second and subsequent lines of the entry 3 spaces. SS these lines. To determine placement of the tables, count the spaces in the longest line of the column, whether that line is the first line of an entry or any subsequent line of the entry, including 3 spaces for indention. To center column headings, choose the longest line in each column, as you have done for single-line entries.

Drill				
Effective Writing Techniques for Executive Secretaries SS		165		92%
Productivity Under Pressure DS	12 spaces	115	8 spaces	64%
Women in Management		131		73%

115c ▶ 35
Prepare documents

Problem 1
3-column table

full sheet; exact vertical center; DS body of table; 16 spaces between Columns 1 and 2 and 10 spaces between Columns 2 and 3

			words
LEAGUE ATTENDANCE RECORD			5
19-- Season			7
Team	Average	Highest	14
Bay City Badgers	28,321	31,895	20
Big Apple City Slickers	29,174	32,386	27
Crawfish Country Cajuns	38,762	46,971	34
Everglades Froggers	39,383	42,645	40
Mississippi River Rats	31,673	32,347	47
Wild West Indians	30,694	40,765	53

Problem 2
3-column table

full sheet; exact vertical center; DS body of table; 12 spaces between Columns 1 and 2 and 8 spaces between Columns 2 and 3

Problem 3
3-column table

half sheet, long side up; SS body of table

Repeat Problem 1 with 20 spaces between Columns 1 and 2 and 12 spaces between Columns 2 and 3.

			words
FUNVISION VIDEO GAMES			4
(Games Scheduled for Release in October)			12
Game	Stock Number	Release Date	23
Big Bad BG	HV7624	October 23	28
Bronco Bull Riding	HV6187	October 15	35
Night Flier	HV9080	October 2	40
Outer Space Satellite			44
Launch and Track	HV2013	October 29	50
Weeping Weirdos	HV5189	October 17	56
Zaparoo	HV8765	October 8	60

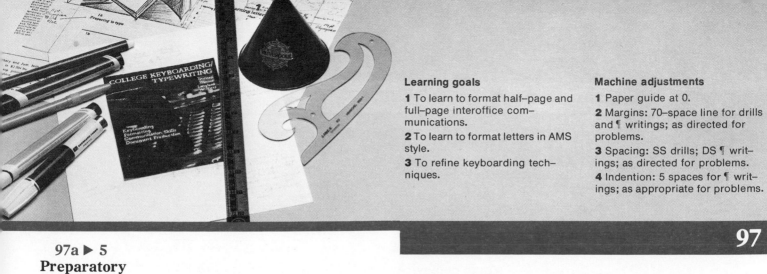

97a ▶ 5
Preparatory practice

each line 3 times SS (slowly, faster, slowly); DS between 3-line groups; repeat selected lines as time permits

alphabet	1	Sammy quickly explained it to the girl in a fuzzy brown velvet jumper.
fig/sym	2	Hunt & Dwyer's $623.75 check (Check 1489) was delivered on January 10.
double letters	3	Kelly aggressively guaranteed the current fees at the school meetings.
fluency	4	He laid the blame for the penalty on their dismal work on the problem.

| 1 | 2 | 3 | 4 | 5 | 6 | 7 | 8 | 9 | 10 | 11 | 12 | 13 | 14 |

97b ▶ 10
Align copy in columns

half sheet, long side up; 50-space line; exact vertical center; DS

1 Set tab stops according to both the key at the bottom of the table and the guides above the table. Tabs should be set to require the least forward and backward spacing.

2 Format and type the drill; repeat it if time permits.

words

margin	tab	tab	tab	
answer	592.79	I	TO:	3
brochure	24.83	I I	FROM:	7
follows	6.02	I I I	DATE:	11
technical	57.42	IV	SUBJECT:	16

key | 9 | 8 | 6 | 8 | 3 | 8 | 8 |

97c ▶ 35
Prepare memorandums

Problem 1
Half-page memorandum
(LM p. 61)

1 Read the information in the memorandum in Problem 2, p. 182.

2. Format and type the memorandum in Problem 1, shown at the right.

1″ side margins; proofread; circle errors

Note: Memorandums are often prepared on printed forms. If a printed form is not available, follow the half–page illustration on p. 182. Begin the heading on Line 7 for a half-page memo and on Line 10 for a full–page memo.

words

TO:	All Employees	3
FROM:	Bessie Arthur, Personnel Department	10
DATE:	June 30, 19--	13
SUBJECT:	Booklet on Fringe Benefits	18

Included with your next payroll check will be a booklet developed by our staff that outlines employee benefits. Of particular importance is the section relating to the changes taking place in the Social Security law and how you can make an inquiry to be sure your deductions and our contributions are being properly credited to your account. — 32 / 46 / 59 / 72 / 85 / 87

Please call me should you have any questions regarding your fringe benefits or the information contained in the booklet. — 100 / 111

xx — 112

114c, continued

Problem 2
2-column table with main and column headings

half sheet, long side up; DS body of table; 16 spaces between columns

		words
TELEPHONE DIRECTORY CHANGES		6
TS		
Employee	Telephone Number	16
	DS	
David Yoshino	787-4390	20
Maria LaGanga	251-6049	24
Jack Ruthowsky	384-5107	29
Anna Sedgwick	292-4087	34
Diane Wilson	318-6569	38

Problem 3
3-column table with main, secondary, and column headings

full sheet; reading position; DS body of table; 10 spaces between columns

			words
AVOYELLES PARISH OIL DISCOVERY			6
DS			
November, 19--			9
TS			
Company	Location	Depth	17
		DS	
Gravel Operations	Sec. 30-4N-4E	6,801	24
Jeffco Exploration	Sec. 22-1N-2W	5,985	31
Martin and Martin, Inc.	Sec. 20-2N-6E	7,448	39
Smith and Associates	Sec. 11-4N-3E	6,495	47
Long and Davis	Sec. 16-5N-3E	5,848	53
Multi-Service Drilling	Sec. 29-5N-3E	7,510	61

115a ▶ 5
Preparatory practice

each line 3 times SS (slowly, faster, slowly); DS between 3-line groups; repeat selected lines as time permits

alphabet 1   Janice was amazed at how quickly both experts verified the gains made.

figure 2   Please dial 253-8901 and ask for Extension 476 before 10:45 on May 23.

space bar 3   Jan may cut work and go down to the big city to fix the auto for them.

fluency 4   The town may risk an audit if it spent the profit on a social problem.

| 1 | 2 | 3 | 4 | 5 | 6 | 7 | 8 | 9 | 10 | 11 | 12 | 13 | 14 |

97c, continued

Problem 2
Full-page memorandum (LM p. 63)

1 Format and type the memo at the right. Assume that the copy for Eric Chang will be prepared on a photocopy machine.

2 Address a COMPANY MAIL envelope to:

Mr. Edward Davis, Director
Information Processing
Center

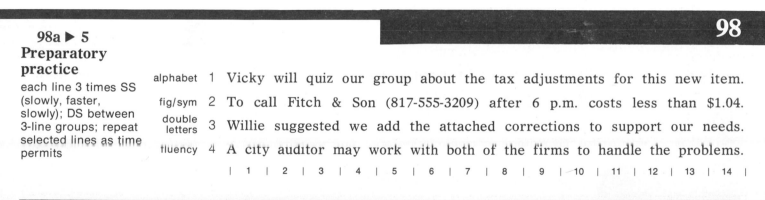

If a memorandum form is not available, use plain paper and follow the example illustrated below.

	words
TO: All Information Processors	5
FROM: Cathy Carapezzi, Director	10
DATE: December 21, 19--	13
SUBJECT: Interoffice Correspondence	18

Correspondence within a company is frequently formatted on interoffice forms, either half or full sheets, depending on the length of the message. The following points describe the features of a memorandum prepared on a printed form. — 30, 44, 56, 64

1. Space twice after the colon in the first line of the printed heading and set the left margin. The heading items and the body of the memo will begin at this point. Set the right margin stop an equal distance from the right edge. These margin adjustments will usually give you side margins of 1". — 79, 92, 105, 117, 124

2. Full addresses, the salutation, the complimentary close, and the signature are omitted. — 138, 143

3. Personal titles are usually omitted from the memo heading. They are included on the envelope, however. — 157, 164

4. TS between the last item in the heading and the body of the message. SS the paragraphs, but DS between them. DS above and below a table or a numbered list when one is included in the message. Space twice after the number in a numbered list; align the whole paragraph under the first line. — 178, 190, 203, 216, 221

5. Reference initials, enclosure notations, and copy notations are included. — 234, 236

Special colored envelopes usually are used for memorandums. Type the addressee's name, personal title, and business title or name of department for the address. Type COMPANY MAIL (in ALL CAPS) in the postage location. — 249, 263, 276, 280

xx — 281

pc Eric Chang, Assistant to the President — 289 | **300**

98

98a ▶ 5
Preparatory practice

each line 3 times SS (slowly, faster, slowly); DS between 3-line groups; repeat selected lines as time permits

alphabet 1 Vicky will quiz our group about the tax adjustments for this new item.

fig/sym 2 To call Fitch & Son (817-555-3209) after 6 p.m. costs less than $1.04.

double letters 3 Willie suggested we add the attached corrections to support our needs.

fluency 4 A city auditor may work with both of the firms to handle the problems.

| 1 | 2 | 3 | 4 | 5 | 6 | 7 | 8 | 9 | 10 | 11 | 12 | 13 | 14 |

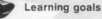

Learning goals

1 To increase your ability to format and type tables.
2 To prepare tables with rules.
3 To increase your skill in formatting tables from rough–draft and script copy.

Machine adjustments

1 Paper guide at 0.
2 Margins: 70–space line for drills and ¶ writings; as directed for problems.
3 Spacing: SS drills; DS ¶ writings; as directed for problems.
4 Indention: 5 spaces for ¶ writings; as appropriate for problems.

114a ▶ 5
Preparatory practice

each line 3 times SS (slowly, faster, slowly); DS between 3-line groups; repeat selected lines as time permits

alphabet	1	Emi Eizaburo gave Wen daily price quotations for the six major stocks.
figure	2	Please read pages 189 and 246 before you read pages 137, 150, and 239.
shift key	3	Al, Jan, Ty, and I will go to San Juan, Puerto Rico, with Rosa Martin.
fluency	4	When did they cut down the bush, and when did they hang the big signs?

| 1 | 2 | 3 | 4 | 5 | 6 | 7 | 8 | 9 | 10 | 11 | 12 | 13 | 14 |

114b ▶ 10
Preapplication drill: center columnar material

Format the 2 drills DS on a full sheet according to the instructions given at the right; leave a 2″ top margin; 10 spaces between columns for both drills; leave 8 blank lines between drills.

Recall: If an odd or leftover stroke occurs when you are back–spacing for column entries, ignore it.

Drill 1
Centering columns

Backspace from center of paper once for each 2 letters, figures, spaces, or punctuation marks in the longest line of each column; then once for each 2 spaces between columns. Set left margin. Space forward once for each character and space in the longest line of the first column and for each space between the first and second columns. Set tab. Follow the same procedure for all columns.

Drill 2
Placing column headings

Set left margin and tab stops for columns as you did in Drill 1. From the beginning of each column, space forward once for each 2 characters or spaces in the longest line of column entries or heading to get to the center of the column. From center of column, backspace once for each 2 letters in the heading or column entry. Type the heading or entry.

Drill 1

Adam	21	Senior
Linda	19	Junior
Terry	20	Junior
Wayne	20	Senior

Drill 2

Players	Team	Points
Charlie	Blue	1,028
Elizabeth	Red	1,135

114c ▶ 35
Prepare documents

Problem 1
2-column table

half sheet, long side up; DS body of table; 12 spaces between columns

words

TYPES OF LOANS OFFERED BY CITY BANK		7
(Officer Responsible for Approval) DS		14
TS		
Automobile	Sandra Hyder	19
Collateral	Glenn White	23
Commercial	Cathy Williams	29
Farm Equipment	Robert Cassidy	34

98b ▶ 10
Check communication skills

full sheet; 1" top margin; 74-space line

1 Cover the answer key below. Check your answers when you have finished the exercise.

2 Read the sentences at the right, noting errors in hyphen, comma, and semicolon usage.

3 Format and type the sentences as directed in 92b, p. 171.

Key: 1. spelling, pronunciation, **2.** December; **3.** COMPUTERS, Scheid, **4.** over–the–counter **5.** 1984, **6.** state–of–the–art **7.** late; however, 15– 20–minute **8.** people, passion;

1. Use your dictionary for spelling pronunciation and definitions.

2. Her first payment was made in December the second payment is late.

3. PERSONAL COMPUTERS written by Sue Scheid is now in the bookstore.

4. The over the counter cough syrup provided relief for my cold.

5. In 1984 45 students were enrolled in this microcomputer course.

6. The course on microcomputers had state of the art equipment.

7. I was late however I still had a 15 to 20 minute wait in line.

8. To some people football is a passion and Hal is one of those people.

98c ▶ 35
Format interoffice communications

Problem 1
Page 2 of a memorandum
(plain full sheet)

1 Format the copy at the right as page 2 of a memorandum. Begin page 2 heading SS on Line 7; use 1" side margins; TS between heading and body of memo.

2 Proofread; correct errors.

Second–page headings for memos are the same as second–page headings for letters. This memo uses block style heading.

	words
Charlene Post, Director Line 7	5
Page 2	6
February 13, 19--	9
TS	

participants who responded to our survey, 77 percent stated that they used message/reply forms. The main reasons given for adopting the message/reply form were its ease of handling and its ease of filing. **24 / 39 / 50**

A message/reply form can be used in any situation that is appropriate for a memorandum. The following procedure should be used when preparing our message/reply forms: **65 / 79 / 83**

1. The sender types a message in the left-hand section of the form, keeps the second (yellow) copy, and sends the other (white and pink) copies to the addressee. **97 / 110 / 116**

2. The addressee replies in the right-hand section of the form, keeps the third (pink) copy, and returns the original (white) copy to the sender. **130 / 144 / 145**

3. Signatures of both persons may be handwritten, or they may be typed and then initialed. **158 / 163**

4. The envelope address depends upon whether the message travels through the U.S. Postal Service or through COMPANY MAIL. The message form is creased down the center of the page and inserted into an envelope. **176 / 188 / 201 / 204**

We will begin using message/reply forms on the first of next month. Data will be collected by my office over the next six months to see how well the forms are accepted. **218 / 234 / 236**

xx **237**

LEVEL FOUR
Formatting/typing tables, forms, and reports

In Level 4, you will continue to build skill in keyboarding and in formatting communications. Emphasis is placed on communications containing statistical copy. You will learn to prepare tables with special features; frequently used business forms, including purchase requisitions, purchase orders, invoices, inventory forms, statements of account, and credit applications; technical reports; and employment communications.

In addition, you will continue to improve your communication skills and your ability to type from straight-copy, script, rough-draft, and statistical copy.

It is especially important that you learn to design and format many different kinds of business communications and that you learn to use your judgment when you are not given specific directions. In the next level, you will be asked to apply these skills in a variety of office situations.

98c, continued

Problem 2
Message/reply memo

1 On a message/reply form (LM p. 65), prepare the message and reply given at the right, using the format shown in the illustration below.
2 Address an envelope marked COMPANY MAIL.

words

TO: Jonathan Kappel | Director, Employee Development | 126 Hancock Tower   13
DATE: January 22, 19-- SUBJECT: Conference on Employee Development   23

MESSAGE: The attached brochure was received from the National Center for   36
the Advancement of Business Practices. Since employee development will be a   51
priority for us for some time, these conference topics should be relevant.   66
Please let me know your opinion.   72

SIGNED: Maria Gonzalez, Vice President   78

DATE: January 23, 19--   81

REPLY: The topics listed are timely and relevant to our long-range plans. I   95
suggest that I attend the conference in New York in March and make a formal   110
proposal to the corporate officers by April 1.   119

SIGNED: Jonathan Kappel   122 | **124**

99a ▶ 5
Preparatory practice

each line 3 times SS (slowly, faster, slowly); DS between 3-line groups; repeat selected lines as time permits

alphabet   1   A dazzling lake view just beyond the quaint farm was exciting to Paul.

fig/sym   2   A premium of $864.50 is due May 19 on Policy #32-770H, a 15% increase.

direct reach   3   Our group must agree to urge any number of new organizational changes.

fluency   4   Ruth and my neighbor may visit the ancient island city in a dirigible.

| 1 | 2 | 3 | 4 | 5 | 6 | 7 | 8 | 9 | 10 | 11 | 12 | 13 | 14 |

99b ▶ 35
Format a memo and a letter

Problem 1
AMS Simplified letter

1 On a plain full sheet, format the letter given on page 185 in the style shown, using the dateline placement and margins given. You will later format other AMS Simplified letters using the placement table given on page 162.
2 Proofread; correct errors.

Problem 2
Full-page memorandum

1 On a full-page memorandum form (LM p. 67), format the memo given at the right.
2 Proofread; correct errors.

words

TO: Regional Sales Managers FROM: Charles Harbottle, Sales Manager   11
DATE: October 3, 19-- SUBJECT: National Sales Meeting   19

(¶ 1) This memo will confirm that each of you will be participating in our   33
national sales meeting on November 3-6. We have made reservations for you to   49
stay at the Ritz-Carlton, 2100 Massachusetts Avenue, N.W., Washington, D.C.,   64
where the telephone number is (202) 555-2100. The reservations are for late   79
arrival on November 2 and departure on November 6.   89

(¶ 2) The agenda for this meeting is enclosed. The meeting will be similar to   104
recent ones in terms of workload; therefore, I would suggest that you not make   120
plans to depart Washington any earlier than midafternoon on November 6.   134

(¶ 3) Please call me should you have any questions.   143

xx | Enclosure   146

Checkup 1
Express numbers correctly

plain sheet; 70–space line; 1½″ top margin; DS; correct errors as you keyboard

The Animal Welfare Association, located at 1 Fifty-second Street, reached its annual goal of $1,000,000 dollars. Nearly 40% of the funds came from private citizens. 50% of the donations were contributed by businesses, and the remaining ten percent came from miscellaneous donors.

Only 10¢ out of every dollar goes to administrative costs. This ensures a better life for three out of every 10 domestic animals that are homeless.

All contributions received after the 1:00 p.m., April 14th deadline are added to next year's goal.

Checkup 2
Capitalize correctly

plain sheet; block style letter, open punctuation; 1½″ side margins, begin on Line 16; correct errors as you keyboard

january 7, 19-- | mr. Dwight jacobs, jr. | 3867 cromwell street | independence, mo 64055-2113 | dear mr. jacobs

(¶) the annual sales meeting of hatco, inc., will be held at the congress hotel, suite 207, in st. joseph, mo, on March 24 and 25.

(¶) because you, mr. jacobs, are one of our top sales leaders in the missouri valley district, i am asking you to participate in a panel discussion which will be presented the thursday of our conference. Panel members will discuss the topic "self-confidence and increased sales." I am enclosing a program of the conference.

(¶) barbara ellis, who is a panel member from the detroit office and vice-president of software sales, will contact you regarding this presentation. miss ellis has agreed to coordinate the panel's efforts.

(¶) i hope you will accept this challenge. our sales force could benefit from your vast knowledge and experience.

sincerely yours | jason v. morrison | sales manager | xx | enclosure

---

Checkup 3
Punctuate correctly

plain sheet; 74–space line; 1½″ top margin; type the line number before each sentence; DS between the sentences; correct errors as you keyboard

1. Was it a home run Was it fair Was it foul Who called the play?
2. J A Anderson collected forty-seven dollars 47 for the charity.
3. Hurry, Hurry, Hurry, you will miss the kick-off
4. The high level meeting was held March 12th 1984.
5. May we go to the opera La Boheme, Sue asked.
6. Ms Rose's fragile package arrived today in first rate condition.
7. These hinges are too loose therefore the barn door will not close.
8. If they accept the contract we'll make delivery early next week.
9. I plan to read "War and Peace" next summer, he will read Moby Dick.
10. Wait for the wisest of all counselors, Time. Pericles

Communications Design Associates

348 INDIANA AVENUE
WASHINGTON, DC 20001-1438
Tel: 1-800-432-5739

		words	in parts	total
Begin all major lines at left margin	May 9, 19--		2	2

Begin address 3 blank line spaces below date

Mr. William S. Rapp, Manager — 8 | 8
American Production Systems — 13 | 13
98 Clutter Mill Road — 17 | 17
Great Neck, NY 11021-4527 — 22 | 22

Omit salutation

Subject line in all capital letters with a triple space above and below it

AMS SIMPLIFIED STYLE — 26 | 26

This letter is typed in a simplified style that is recom- — 37 | 37
mended by the Administrative Management Society. It is — 48 | 48
designed to save you time. The following points outline — 59 | 59
the basic features of a letter typed in the AMS style. — 70 | 70

Begin enumerated items at left margin; indent unnumbered items 5 spaces

1. Use block format. — 4 | 74

2. Omit the salutation and the complimentary close. — 14 | 84

3. Include a subject heading in ALL CAPS a triple space — 25 | 95
    below the address; TS from the subject line to the — 35 | 105
    first line of the body. — 40 | 110

4. Begin enumerated items flush with the left margin; — 51 | 121
    indent unnumbered items five spaces. — 58 | 128

5. Place the writer's name and title in ALL CAPS on the — 69 | 139
    4th line space below the last line of the letter body. — 80 | 150

6. Place the reference initials (typist's only) a double — 92 | 162
    space below the writer's name. — 98 | 168

Correspondents in your company may like the AMS Simpli- — 12 | 180
fied letter style not only for the eye appeal it gives — 23 | 191
to letters but also for the potential reduction in letter- — 35 | 203
writing costs. — 36 | 204

Omit complimentary close

Carolyn Jackson

MRS. CAROLYN JACKSON, PRESIDENT — 42 | 210

Writer's name and title in ALL CAPS at least 3 blank line spaces below letter body

xx — 43 | 211

Style letter 7: AMS Simplified

113a ▶ 5
Preparatory practice

each line 3 times SS (slowly, faster, slowly); DS between 3-line groups; repeat selected lines as time permits

alphabet	1	Haywood may quiz eighty executives on kickbacks from false job prices.
fig/sym	2	Their Policy #856-02 is with Lee & May; we will be reimbursed $19,437.
adjacent reaches	3	A few new buyers with deposits appeared quickly when the store opened.
fluency	4	A giant penalty may make the firm dismantle the big sign in the field.

| 1 | 2 | 3 | 4 | 5 | 6 | 7 | 8 | 9 | 10 | 11 | 12 | 13 | 14 |

113b ▶ 10
Measure straight-copy skill

a 5' writing on all ¶s; circle errors; determine *gwam*

Difficulty index

all letters used | A | 1.5 si | 5.7 awl | 80% hfw |

gwam 1' 5'

If a survey were conducted of one hundred individuals and they were asked whether they had enough time to perform all the duties on their schedules, the answer from the vast majority of people would probably be a resounding no. This situation becomes critical when we realize that few people have adequate time; yet everyone has all the time that is available. Because all people have an equal amount of time, the problem becomes not how much time they have but how effectively they use time.

At some point, most people come to realize that time is a valuable resource. It cannot be accumulated like money or stockpiled like raw materials. People are forced to spend time at a definite rate of sixty seconds every minute. Time cannot be turned on and off like a machine or used like a thing. Time is irretrievable. The only control people can exercise over it is to allocate it carefully.

One essential step toward making better use of our time is to identify the items that are time wasters. When asked to identify such areas, most people will tend to point first to a list of external causes such as the telephone, meetings, visitors, and delays. However, after taking a closer look, people may also find internal sources of time loss. Failing to make plans, trying to do too much at once, being unable to say no, and listening poorly are major contributors to poor time management.

		13	3	63
		27	6	66
		41	9	69
		55	12	72
		69	15	75
		83	18	78
		97	21	81
		100	22	82
		13	25	85
		27	28	88
		41	31	91
		55	34	94
		69	37	97
		79	39	99
		13	42	102
		28	45	105
		42	48	108
		56	51	111
		70	54	114
		85	57	117
		99	60	119

gwam 1' | 1 | 2 | 3 | 4 | 5 | 6 | 7 | 8 | 9 | 10 | 11 | 12 | 13 | 14 |
5' | 1 | 2 | 3 |

113c ▶ 35
Measure communication skills

1 Complete each of the communication skills checkups (page 213) on a separate sheet.

2 Read each activity before typing it, noting the changes you must make as you keyboard.

3 Format/type each checkup, correcting errors in number expression, capitalization, and punctuation.

99c ▶ 10
Improve keyboarding technique

each pair of lines 3 times SS at a controlled rate; DS between 6-line groups

adjacent reaches	1	She quickly showed them samples of government bonds to buy or to sell.
	2	They assured the developer we would support the three required points.
double letters	3	Abbott suggested all staff personnel make an effort to arrive by noon.
	4	All classes will meet in this room to discuss the latest school offer.
direct reaches	5	A great many payments must continue to be processed until you balance.
	6	Their library recently obtained my lengthy brochure about the economy.
long words	7	Approximately eight new recommendations appeared before the committee.
	8	The opportunity to cooperate with your committee is truly appreciated.

| 1 | 2 | 3 | 4 | 5 | 6 | 7 | 8 | 9 | 10 | 11 | 12 | 13 | 14 |

100a ▶ 5
Preparatory practice

each line 3 times SS (slowly, faster, slowly); DS between 3-line groups; repeat selected lines as time permits

alphabet	1	Five backgammon experts joined together quietly to analyze some views.
fig/sym	2	The projected loss on the 36-acre site will top 24% ($87,530) by 1999.
adjacent reaches	3	Ophelia and a few friends were going to buy an oil painting for Gerry.
fluency	4	If they visit the eight big auto firms, they may do the audit on them.

| 1 | 2 | 3 | 4 | 5 | 6 | 7 | 8 | 9 | 10 | 11 | 12 | 13 | 14 |

100b ▶ 10
Review/apply communication skills: punctuation

full sheet; 1" top margin; 74-space line

Keyboard and format as directed in 81b, p. 150.

Key: 1b. (Saturday) 4c. (1783–1859) 5b. ($2,000)

Use parentheses

1. To enclose nonessential, parenthetical, or explanatory information
2. To enclose numbers or letters which identify certain sections of an outline.
3. To enclose identifying letters or figures in lists.
4. To enclose nonessential dates, times, amounts, and references.
5. To enclose figures that follow spelled amounts.

review 1a. I said I was disappointed (not crestfallen) with your decision.
apply b. Call me tomorrow Saturday during the morning.

review 2a. Rank the items in an outline I., A., 1., a., (1), (a), 1), a).

review 3a. Follow these steps: (1) Press the enter key; (2) keyboard the name.

review 4a. In the year of the merger (1972), both firms agreed to relocate.
review b. They paid the bill ($47) on Tuesday (see Invoice #22783).
apply c. Washington Irving 1783-1859 was one of America's great writers.

review 5a. Seventy-seven (77) boxes arrived at the loading dock on Friday.
apply b. The antique show nets two thousand dollars $2,000 each year.

100c ▶ 35
Build sustained production: business communications

Time schedule

Assemble materials	3'
Timed production	25'
Final check; compute n-pram	7'

1 Arrange letterheads and envelopes (LM pp. 61–73) or plain paper, as well as supplies, for easy handling.

2 Make a penciled list of the following problems to be typed:

page 181, 97c, Problem 1
page 184, 98c, Problem 2
page 184, 99b, Problem 1
page 184, 99b, Problem 2

3 When directed to begin, format and type the problems for 25'. Follow the directions given for each problem.

4 When time is called, proofread your work. Deduct 15 words from total words for each uncorrected error; divide the remainder by 25 to compute n-pram. If you finish all problems before time is called, repeat Problem 1 on plain paper.

112c, continued

Problem 1
Letter with subject line
(LM p. 125)

modified block, mixed punctuation; indented ¶s; center subject
line; address envelope

September 15, 19-- | Mr. Robert Kelsey | 300 East Joppa Road | Towson, MD	14
21204-5798 | Dear Mr. Kelsey: | SUBJECT: Reception for New Members	27

(¶ 1) The Community Action Association of Towson is pleased to invite you, as a | 42
nominee, to our reception for new members. The reception will be held at the | 58
Meridian Hotel at 5:30 p.m. on Thursday, October 9. This function will give you | 74
an orientation to the club as well as an opportunity to meet other new members. | 90

(¶ 2) We are enclosing a reply card on which you may indicate whether you will | 105
attend. Our President, Marie Carpenter, joins me in urging you to come to this | 121
important gathering. (97) | 125

Very sincerely, | Richard Johnson | Membership Director | xx | Enclosure | 139/151

Problem 2
Agenda for Meeting

plain sheet; 1½″ top margin; 1″
side margins

NATIONAL PUBLICATIONS COMPANY	6
Agenda for Meeting of Board of Directors	14
Current date	17
1. Call to Order . . . . Nicholas E. Spitznagel	30
2. Reading and Approval of Minutes . . . . James C. Weber	42
3. Reports of Officers	
President . . . . Nicholas E. Spitznagel	58
Vice President, Publications . . . . Marie Ann Ford	68
Vice President, Marketing . . . . Charles Sauder	79
Vice President, Finance . . . . Virginia L. Reed	89
4. Adjournment . . . . Nicholas E. Spitznagel	102

Problem 3
Half-page memorandum
(LM p. 127)

If a form is not available, prepare
the memo on a plain half sheet.

TO: Marsha Kendall FROM: Gerald Fitzsimmons DATE: August 26, 19-- SUB-	10
JECT: Author Conference Travel Plans	16

(¶) My travel plans are to arrive in Columbus at 6:30 p.m. on Sunday, October | 31
2. My departure time is 2:20 p.m. on October 5. | 41

(¶) I could save $115 by arriving on Saturday instead of Sunday (on the airfare, | 56
that is); however, the extra lodging and meals would probably cost at least | 71
half of that. I'm not aware of any reason that an extra day there would be | 86
beneficial, particularly on a weekend. | 94

(¶) I look forward to seeing you and the other authors. We have many new | 108
challenges to face in the development of our new edition. xx | 120

Problem 4
Business letter

plain paper; block style, open
punctuation

Reformat the letter in Problem 1.
Make the changes given at the right.
Total words: 129

1 Omit the subject line.
2 The meeting will be held on **Wednesday, October 15.**
3 The president of the club is **Howard Wilson.**
4 Miss Kay Boswell is **Membership Director.**

101a ▶ 5
Preparatory practice

each line 3 times SS (slowly, faster, slowly); DS between 3-line groups; repeat selected lines as time permits

alphabet	1	Major excavation was taking place quietly behind Zone Four on the map.
fig/sym	2	Our Invoice #58* and their Check #902 for $1,437.06 were mailed May 8.
long words	3	Arrangements were announced to honor outstanding accounting graduates.
fluency	4	When may the auditor work with the city panel to cut down on the risk?

| 1 | 2 | 3 | 4 | 5 | 6 | 7 | 8 | 9 | 10 | 11 | 12 | 13 | 14 |

101b ▶ 15
Measure straight-copy skill

1 Two 1' writings on each ¶; circle errors; determine *gwam*.

2 One 5' writing on all ¶s combined; circle errors; determine *gwam*; compare results with 1' writings.

Difficulty index

all letters used	A	1.5 si	5.7 awl	80% hfw

gwam 1' | 5'

Our economy plays a vital role in the life of each person. For 13 | 3 | 58
instance, most people must work for money to provide a living. In ad- 27 | 5 | 61
dition, people must try to raise their income so as to meet the rising 41 | 8 | 64
cost of living. Retired people living on fixed incomes often have trou- 55 | 11 | 67
ble paying their higher expenses. Taxpayers are constantly forced to 69 | 14 | 70
pay higher taxes to fund a number of government services such as national 84 | 17 | 73
defense efforts, social welfare aid, and energy research, just to mention 99 | 20 | 76
a few. 100 | 20 | 76

As a result of the impact our economy has on our daily lives, more 13 | 23 | 79
and more people are becoming aware of the structure and workings of our 28 | 26 | 82
system. By any standard, it is fair to state that the economy of our 42 | 28 | 84
nation is strong and expanding. Even the least knowledgeable person 56 | 31 | 87
realizes that the profit motive has proven to be one of the extremely 70 | 34 | 90
important factors in helping our nation become the dominant financial 84 | 37 | 93
power of the world. 87 | 38 | 94

The profit motive means that people are willing to risk their time 13 | 40 | 96
and money in a business venture with the idea that they may acquire a 27 | 43 | 99
profit. Millions of people invest money in stocks, bonds, and small 41 | 46 | 102
businesses. The profits earned in these ways offer a good flow of new 55 | 49 | 105
capital funds for more production facilities, such as new plants, machin- 70 | 52 | 108
ery, and buildings. Thus, the profit motive is the key to the operation 85 | 55 | 110
of our modern economic system. 91 | 56 | 112

gwam 1' | 1 | 2 | 3 | 4 | 5 | 6 | 7 | 8 | 9 | 10 | 11 | 12 | 13 | 14 |
5' | 1 | 2 | 3 |

112a ▶ 5
Preparatory practice

each line 3 times SS (slowly, faster, slowly); DS between 3-line groups; repeat selected lines as time permits

alphabet	1	We will fight to save the complex project and raze the bridge quickly.
fig/sym	2	The last 467 units were reduced 30% ($1,089) and were sold in 25 days.
double letters	3	I recommend a committee meet this summer to take all necessary action.
fluency	4	I may handle the usual forms for the neighbor when he signs the title.

| 1 | 2 | 3 | 4 | 5 | 6 | 7 | 8 | 9 | 10 | 11 | 12 | 13 | 14 |

112b ▶ 10
Measure straight-copy skill

a 5' writing on all ¶s; circle errors; determine *gwam*

Difficulty index

all letters used | A | 1.5 si | 5.7 awl | 80% hfw

gwam 1' | 5'

Managers are necessary in all types of companies. These important 13 | 3 | 56
positions vary from the operator of a small candy store to the head of 28 | 6 | 59
the largest manufacturing firm. But managers have many tasks in common. 42 | 8 | 62
They must plan, organize, direct, control, and coordinate the work of 56 | 11 | 65
their group. Managers must be able to train people so that they can do 71 | 14 | 68
their jobs and to motivate them so that they will want to be successful. 85 | 17 | 71

Of course, in order to do these tasks, managers must have certain 13 | 20 | 73
skills. Some skills are acquired, and others are a result of natural 27 | 23 | 76
talent; but all skills are better used once a manager has gotten some 41 | 25 | 79
experience. Conceptual skills include the ability to see how all the 55 | 28 | 82
parts of a situation fit together to form a whole. A good manager can 69 | 31 | 84
mix conceptual skills with technical knowledge related to the work of 83 | 34 | 87
the specific department. 88 | 35 | 88

Two other vital areas that a manager must master are human rela- 13 | 37 | 91
tions and communications. Human relations skill is the ability to inter- 27 | 40 | 94
act with people. And this job may best be done through the use of good 42 | 43 | 97
communication skills. All managers must relate to people; and, in trying 57 | 46 | 100
to get things done through others, they must be able to communicate. 71 | 49 | 102
The success or failure of managers is affected by their ability to use 85 | 52 | 105
these skills in daily tasks on the job. 93 | 53 | 107

gwam 1' | 1 | 2 | 3 | 4 | 5 | 6 | 7 | 8 | 9 | 10 | 11 | 12 | 13 | 14 |
5' | | 1 | | 2 | | 3 |

112c ▶ 35
Measure production on administrative communications

Time schedule

Assembling materials ...... 3'
Timed production .... 25'
Final check; compute
n-pram .... 7'

1 Follow the schedule shown at the left.

2 Arrange the letterhead and memo (LM pp. 125–127), plain sheets, and other supplies for easy handling.

3 When directed to begin, format and type the problems on page 211 for 25'. Correct errors neatly as you type. Address an envelope for the letter in Problem 1.

4 Proofread and circle uncorrected errors found in final check.

5 Compute *n-pram*.

101c ▶ 30
Measure production

Time schedule

Assembling materials ...... 3'
Timed production .... 20'
Final check; compute
  n–pram .... 7'

Problem 1
Full-page memorandum
(LM p. 75)

Format and type the full–page memorandum given at the right; proofread; correct errors; ad–dress a COMPANY MAIL envelope.

TO: Floyd Vasquez, Supervisor, Data Processing | FROM: Nancy Finch, Director 13
of Employment Programs | DATE: December 15, 19-- | SUBJECT: Educational 24
Programs 26

(¶ 1) Walton, Incorporated, has a full agenda of educational program offerings 41
planned for the coming year. Specialized sessions on estate planning, personal 57
computer systems, tax planning, gourmet cooking, literature, and much more 72
are featured. 75

(¶ 2) Enclosed is the schedule of programs, which explains many of the courses 90
to be offered. Also included are registration forms for the convenience of your 106
staff. Please inform your staff of the schedule of programs and make the regis- 122
tration forms available to them. 128

(¶ 3) Please contact me if you have any questions or if I can provide further 142
information about these course offerings. | xx | Enclosure 153 | **155**

Problem 2
AMS Simplified letter
(LM p. 77)

Format and type the letter given at the right; proofread; correct errors; address an envelope.

March 9, 19-- | Mr. Edward Fisher, President | St. Louis Business Institute | 12115 10
Lackland Road | St. Louis, MO 63141-4587 | SOFTWARE EDUCATIONAL PRO- 29
GRAMS 30

(¶ 1) If your institution is like most institutions, you have been buying com- 44
puters for educational purposes and now are face to face with the "software 59
problem": You need specific programs that will make your computers more 74
effective as educational tools. 80

(¶ 2) We may be able to help! As members of a nonprofit agency, we at Com- 94
munications Design Associates have been working on the software problem for 109
over ten years. We have reviewed and tested more than 1,000 educational pro- 124
grams and compiled a catalog of the small percentage that meet our rigid 139
standards. 149

(¶ 3) Take the time to look through the enclosed publication and consider what 164
Communications Design Associates have to offer. Order forms for instruc- 178
tional packages are included in the catalog sections, and you can get on our 193
mailing list by using the request card provided in the catalog. (168) 206

MRS. MARY G. PETERS, EDITOR | xx | Enclosure 214 | **234**

Problem 3
Message/reply memo
(LM p. 79)

Format and type the mes-sage/reply memo given at the right; proofread; correct errors; address a COMPANY MAIL en-velope.

Problem 4

If you complete the 3 problems in less than 20', start over on plain paper.

TO: Lisa Woo | Director of Operations | 190 Communications Center | DATE: 12
October 10, 19-- | SUBJECT: School Visit 18

MESSAGE: I have received a request from Linda Akers, Chairperson, Business 31
Education Department, Fall River Community College, to visit our Information 46
Processing Center on October 19. Thirty-five students would visit for approxi- 62
mately two hours. They are interested in the equipment we use and the skills 78
we require for our entry-level positions. Can we accommodate these students 93
at the time requested? SIGNED: Don Long, Director of Information 104

DATE: October 11, 19-- | REPLY: I do not see a problem with the request. Ms. 117
Akers has worked with us in the past in placing her students with us for summer 133
employment. Please let me know if you would like me to contact her to make 148
the final arrangements. | SIGNED: Lisa Woo 155 | **157**

111c ▶ 35
Measure production on administrative communications

Time schedule

Assembling materials	3'
Timed production	25'
Final check; compute n–pram	7'

Problem 1
Simplified memo

plain sheet; 1½" top margin, 1" side margins

Problem 2
Executive-size letter

(LM p. 123) or plain paper cut to size

modified block style; mixed punctuation; address envelope

Problem 3
Minutes of Meeting

plain sheet; 1½" top margin; 1" side margins; use the heading:
MINUTES OF THE MEETING
OF THE BOARD OF DIRECTORS
OF
BOSTON BUSINESS COLLEGE

December 15, 19--

Problem 4
Business letter

Reformat Problem 2 above on a plain full sheet. Use block style and open punctuation.

---

1 Follow the schedule shown at the left.
2 Arrange the executive–size letterhead (LM p. 123), plain sheets, and other supplies for easy handling.
3 When directed to begin, format and type the problems below for 25'. Correct errors neatly as you type. Address an executive–size envelope.
4 Proofread and circle uncorrected errors found in final check.
5 Compute n–pram.

words

June 15, 19-- | All Employees | RETIREMENT OF ROBERT CARY ... 11

On June 30, Bob Cary will retire after nearly 45 years of service. For more than 25 of those years, Bob has been our Director of Staff Services. Few employees have contributed to our firm in so many varied ways. In recognition of his contributions to the company and his unlimited assistance to so many of us, an informal reception will be held on June 30 at 3:00 p.m. in the main dining room. | J. D. BOBKINS, PERSONNEL DIRECTOR | xx | cc Diana Washington, President ... 23 39 53 68 84 98 100

Current date | Mr. Victor J. Goldberg | 505 King Avenue | Columbus, OH 43201-7528 | Dear Mr. Goldberg: ... 16 21

(¶ 1) At Boyd Investment Service, we believe that your retirement should be something you look forward to and not something you worry about. That is why I would like to discuss with you our IRA, Keogh, and Simplified Employee Pension retirement plans. ... 35 50 60 65

(¶ 2) Now that the tax laws have been changed, almost everyone who has earned income is eligible for one or more of the IRS-approved, tax-deferred retirement plans. ... 79 95 96

(¶ 3) An informative brochure has been mailed to you to acquaint you with the basic facts about our flexible retirement plans. I will contact you after you have had a chance to review the brochure so that we may discuss how you may receive tax relief now and financial security later. (137) ... 110 126 141 151

Sincerely, | John J. Vanderson | Senior Account Executive | xx ... 163/**175**

---

in heading 18

The Thirty-fifth Annual Meeting of the Corporate Members of Boston Business College was held at 3:00 p.m. on Monday, September 28, 19--. ... 21 35

The first order of business for the Corporate Meeting was the election of a Director of the Corporation. Upon motion duly made and seconded, it was unanimously voted: To instruct the Clerk to cast one ballot for the nominated Director, Louis F. Musco, Jr. ... 50 65 81 87

The financial reports were discussed, with action delayed until additional information could be made available. There being no further business, the meeting was adjourned at 4:00 p.m. ... 102 117 124

Respectfully submitted ... 128

_____ ... 135

Manuel Aguilar, Secretary ... 140

Learning goals

1 To learn to format various kinds of administrative communications.

2 To produce usable copy under time pressure over an extended period.

3 To improve basic proofreading skills.

Machine adjustments

1 Paper guide at 0.

2 Margins: 70–space line for drills and ¶ writings; as directed for problems.

3 Spacing: SS drills; DS ¶ writings; as directed for problems.

4 Indention: 5 spaces for ¶ writings; as appropriate for problems.

102a ▶ 5
Preparatory practice

each line 3 times SS (slowly, faster, slowly); DS between 3-line groups; repeat selected lines as time permits

alphabet	1	Megg sat by the park to relax with a cup of java on a quiet, lazy day.
fig/sym	2	Will Flight #739 leave at 10:48 p.m. and arrive in Miami at 2:56 a.m.?
shift key	3	Bob Pack, Jane Epworth, and Marie Appel will go to New York City soon.
fluency	4	They did laugh at the sight of the neighbor in the rich field of corn.

| 1 | 2 | 3 | 4 | 5 | 6 | 7 | 8 | 9 | 10 | 11 | 12 | 13 | 14 |

102b ▶ 10
Review/apply communication skills: punctuation

full sheet; 1" top margin; 74-space line

Keyboard and format as directed in 81b, p. 150.

Key: 1c. reported: 2c. report: 3c. 2:45

Use a colon

1. Following an introductory statement which causes the reader to anticipate a list, enumeration, explanation, or illustration.

2. To introduce a statement, question, or long direct quotation.

3. To separate hours and minutes when time is expressed in figures, or between numbers when used to express proportions.

review 1a. He had three books: a dictionary, a thesaurus, and a cookbook.
review b. Only one question remains to be answered: Who pays the bill?
apply c. The following students reported A. Grimley, J. Zwick, and S. Yi.

review 2a. He suddenly exclaimed: "We are out of our flight path!"
review b. This is an important question: Who will take care of the animals?
apply c. The aide gave her report "The panel will be dissolved tomorrow."

review 3a. The plane left at 12:32 a.m. and arrived in Sao Paulo at 9:15 p.m.
review b. The top lawyer won the judgeship by a 2:1 margin over her opponent.
apply c. The employees evacuated the building at 2 45 p.m.

102c ▶ 35
Format letters on executive-size stationery

Problem 1

Executive–size letter (LM p. 99) or paper cut to size (7¼″ × 10½″)

Format the letter illustrated on page 190. Use ¾″ side margins (spaces: 7 pica, 9 elite) for this letter because it is long; begin date on Line 13.

Proofread; use standard proofreader's marks to indicate needed corrections.

Problem 2

Executive–size letter (LM p. 101) or paper cut to size

Using your corrected copy, prepare a final copy of the letter in Problem 1, making the corrections indicated in your first copy. Correct errors as you type.

GUIDE FOR CORRESPONDENCE ON SPECIAL-SIZE STATIONERY		
Stationery	Margins	Date Placement
Executive–size	¾″–1″	Lines 10–16
Postal card	3 spaces	Line 3

Measurement goals

1 To measure basic skill on straight copy.

2 To measure skill and under–standing in producing business letters, simplified com–munications, and administrative communications covered in lessons of Level 3.

Machine adjustments

1 Paper guide at 0.

2 Margins: 70–space line for drills and ¶ writings; as directed for problems.

3 Spacing: SS drills; DS ¶ writings; as directed for problems.

4 Indention: 5 spaces for ¶ writings; as appropriate for problems.

111

111a ▶ 5
Preparatory practice

each line 3 times SS (slowly, faster, slowly); DS between 3-line groups; repeat selected lines as time permits

alphabet	1	Karl expects the music for the group's dance review to be quite jazzy.
fig/sym	2	The 5% discount on Invoice #394-86 amounted to a savings of $1,720.36.
direct reach	3	Why must I obtain a maximum-length mortgage and make my interest more?
fluency	4	The firm may pay eight men to cut the hay in a field down by the lake.

| 1 | 2 | 3 | 4 | 5 | 6 | 7 | 8 | 9 | 10 | 11 | 12 | 13 | 14 |

111b ▶ 10
Measure straight-copy skill

a 5' writing on all ¶s; circle errors; determine *gwam*

Difficulty index

all letters used	A	1.5 si	5.7 awl	80% hfw

gwam 1' | 5'

Many small businesses fail. Surprisingly, though, many people are · 13 | 3 | 59
still willing to take a chance on starting one of their own. A person · 27 | 5 | 62
who is willing to take the risks necessary to manage a business in order · 42 | 8 | 65
to receive the potential rewards is called an entrepreneur. In a sense, · 57 | 11 | 68
such individuals are pioneers who enjoy each step on the way to achieve- · 71 | 14 | 71
ing objectives that they have determined to be important. This type of · 85 | 17 | 74
person has had a profound impact on shaping our economy and our quality · 100 | 20 | 77
of life. · 101 | 21 | 77

What does it take to start a business venture, and what kinds of · 13 | 23 | 80
people make it work? Obviously, the desire to make money and to be · 27 | 26 | 82
one's own boss are two basic incentives; but these alone are not enough · 41 | 29 | 85
to guarantee success. Two qualifications common to most successful · 55 | 31 | 88
entrepreneurs, whatever field they are in, are an attentiveness to de- · 69 | 34 | 91
tail and a knack for solving day-to-day problems without losing sight · 83 | 37 | 94
of long-range goals. · 87 | 38 | 94

While there is a high risk in organizing any new business, the · 13 | 40 | 97
entrepreneur who is successful is seldom someone who could be con- · 26 | 43 | 100
sidered a gambler. Most gamblers expect to have the odds against them. · 40 | 46 | 103
On the other hand, a clever businessperson sees to it that the odds are · 55 | 49 | 105
as good as possible by getting all of the facts and planning carefully · 69 | 52 | 108
before going ahead. Luck helps, to be sure; but a new business enter- · 83 | 54 | 111
prise depends far more on good ideas and detailed plans. · 94 | 57 | 113

gwam 1' | 1 | 2 | 3 | 4 | 5 | 6 | 7 | 8 | 9 | 10 | 11 | 12 | 13 | 14 |
5' | 1 | 2 | 3 |

Lammey Printing & Paper Supply Co.
425 South Wabash Avenue
Chicago, IL 60605-3259   (312) 555-1503

		words	in parts	total
Line 13	August 25, 19--		5	5
	Mr. Frederick Rozier, President		11	11
	Household Products Corporation		17	17
	444 W. St. James Place		22	22
	Chicago, IL 60614-5739		27	27

Dear Mr. Rozier · 30 | 30

Thank you for your recent order for the multicolor · 40 | 40
printing of your new catalogs and manuals. We at Lam- · 51 | 51
mey Printing Company are pleased to have the opportu- · 61 | 61
nity to serve you. · 65 | 65

¾″ Sharp eyes and unfaltering attention to detail will ¾″ · 10 | 75
follow your work through every stage--from the first · 21 | 86
planning session through final production. You can · 31 | 96
depend on expert handling, conscientious proofreading, · 42 | 107
and efficient service because our employees have the · 53 | 118
same commitment to quality as you have. · 61 | 126

We know you will be impressed with the superior appear- · 11 | 137
ance of your finished catalogs and manuals. We hope · 22 | 148
that you will continue to think of our printing company · 33 | 159
whenever you need graphics work done to perfection. · 43 | 169

Sincerely yours · 46 | 172

LAMMEY PRINTING & PAPER SUPPLY CO. · 51 | 177

Richard Laramie

Richard Laramie · 54 | 180
Production Manager · 58 | 184

xx · 59 | 185

Style letter 8: Executive-size letter

110d ▶ 12
Build rough-draft skill

1 One 1' writing on each ¶; circle errors; determine *gwam*.
2 One 5' writing on both ¶s; circle errors; determine *gwam*; compare results with 1' writings.

Difficulty index

all letters used | A | 1.5 si | 5.7 awl | 80% hfw

	gwam 1'	5'

It could come as a surprize to noone that we inhabit, an *are living in*   13 | 3 | 46

age of computers. These mechanisms keep track of the flow of *machines*   25 | 5 | 48

electrical that feeds our cities, the paterns that our air- *electricity* *lights* *in which* *t*   38 | 8 | 51

planes fly, the amount of credit we gets and the balance in *can obtain,* *s*   52 | 10 | 54

our bank account. Of course, no computer does this alone, *by itself;*   64 | 13 | 56

computers are controlled by people. But not very many people *Yet few*   75 | 15 | 58

outside of the automaton industry have any real understanding   87 | 17 | 61

of how even the most simple computer works. Most people's   99 | 20 | 63

familiarity is limited to the face that they should not fold, *knowledge* *t*   111 | 22 | 66

spendle, or mutiliate there bills monthly. *i* *their*   119 | 24 | 67

Of course, computers have cometo play a big role in the opera- *central*   13 | 27 | 70

tions of government and business. But presently computers are *nowadays*   26 | 29 | 72

helping some of the most basic machines that fulfill our per- *serve*   38 | 31 | 75

sonal needs. For one thing, the engines in several of the *example,*   49 | 34 | 77

newer cars are equiped with tiny computers that control speed, *small-sized*   63 | 36 | 80

temprature, and other factures, and then ajust the spark to *e* *ors* *d*   74 | 39 | 82

get the best possibel millage for us. And we can be certain *e*   86 | 41 | 85

that more and more uses will be found for these things. *machines.*   98 | 44 | 87

110e ▶ 10
Build speed/control

1 One 1' writing on the ¶; determine *gwam*.
2 Add 4 *gwam* to your *gwam* in Step 1 for a goal rate. Take another 1' writing on the ¶, trying to equal your goal rate.
3 Two 2' writings for speed; determine *gwam*.
4 One 2' writing at this new rate for control; circle errors. Goal: 2 errors or fewer.

Difficulty index

all letters used | A | 1.5 si | 5.7 awl | 80% hfw

	gwam 1'	2'

More people are occupied today with information science than are   13 | 7 | 58

working in the huge fields of mining, production, farming, and per-   26 | 13 | 65

sonal services. This new job area is based on the creation, movement,   40 | 20 | 72

and storage of data. The vast expansion in this field in just the past   55 | 27 | 79

ten years has been quite remarkable, and this new growth will bring   68 | 34 | 86

about amazing change. We are now in an age in which the ways of com-   82 | 41 | 93

municating and learning are changing at a dizzying rate. Astute people   97 | 48 | 100

will keep up with this advance.   103 | 52 | 103

gwam 1' | 1 | 2 | 3 | 4 | 5 | 6 | 7 | 8 | 9 | 10 | 11 | 12 | 13 | 14 |
2' | | 1 | | 2 | | 3 | | 4 | | 5 | | 6 | | 7 |

Problem 3
Simplified memo
(LM p. 103)

1 Read the information in the simplified memo shown at the right.

2 Format and type the memo, following the directions in the memo.

3 Proofread; circle any errors you have made.

oei

OFFICE EFFICIENCY, INC.   35 E. South Water
EXPERTS IN OFFICE RESEARCH   Chicago, IL   60601-4737   (312) 575-2121
DS   words

January 23, 19--   3
TS

William A. Johnston, Office Manager   10
TS

SIMPLIFIED MEMORANDUM   14
TS

This is an example of the simplified memorandum you and I discussed at the   29
recent AMS meeting. Its features are listed below: 39
DS

1. The memorandum may be prepared on standard letterhead or plain paper.   53

2. It is formatted in block style with 1″ side margins, eliminating those pesky   69
   tabulator stops that some memo forms require.   78

3. The date is placed a double space below the last line of the letterhead or 1 1/2   95
   inches below the top edge of a plain sheet.   104

4. A triple space separates all major parts (date, name of recipient, subject line,   121
   body, name of originator, reference initials, enclosure notation, and copy   136
   notation).   138

5. The message is single-spaced with double spacing between paragraphs.   152

6. Enumerated items are single-spaced with either double or single spacing   167
   separating individual items.   173
   DS

Because of its uncomplicated format, the simplified memorandum can be pro-   188
cessed easily on microcomputers and other word processing equipment that   203
utilizes standard-size continuous-feed stationery or plain paper. It can also be   219
used for short messages on half sheets; but automated offices, including the   234
U.S. Government, seem to be moving rapidly toward standard 8 1/2- by 11-inch   250
stationery and plain paper for word processing operations.   261
DS

If I can be of further assistance, please let me know what I can do to help you.   277
TS

MRS. SUSAN RANDALL, MANAGER OF TECHNICAL SERVICES   287
TS

xx   288

110a ▶ 5
Preparatory practice

each line 3 times SS (slowly, faster, slowly); DS between 3-line groups; repeat selected lines as time permits

For Line 3, beginning at the left margin, set 3 tab stops 20 spaces apart.

alphabet	1	Alex judged their zither performance quickly, boldly, and very wisely.
fig/sym	2	My 25-year mortgage for $168,349 at 13% interest will be paid in 2007.
tab/cap	3	Akron Miami Dover New Albany
fluency	4	The work on the big dock may make problems for the island in the lake.

| 1 | 2 | 3 | 4 | 5 | 6 | 7 | 8 | 9 | 10 | 11 | 12 | 13 | 14 |

110b ▶ 12
Measure/compare straight-copy skill

1 One 2' writing on the first ¶ to set base rate.

2 Two 2' writings on the second ¶. Try to maintain the rate you achieved on the first ¶.

3 Two additional writings on the ¶ on which you had the lower rate. Your goal is to meet or exceed your rate on the faster ¶.

all letters used ¶1 | Difficulty index: A | 1.5 si | 5.7 awl | 80% hfw | ¶2 | Difficulty index: HA | 1.7 si | 6.0 awl | 75% hfw

	gwam 1'	2'
The tools with which office workers do their jobs are undergoing	13	7 | 49
vast changes right now. Many more changes will take place in the near	27	14 | 56
future. New tools will save both time and money. One area in which	41	21 | 63
these new devices will have an effect is in the realm of communica-	54	27 | 70
tions, especially in documents created and produced in offices. Those	69	34 | 77
who wish to maximize their chances in this area will learn this new	82	41 | 84
technology.	84	42 | 85
Today, most office workers realize that management is very eager	13	7 | 50
to cut costs. Jobs must be done less expensively, more quickly, and	27	13 | 57
with high quality. As data flows more rapidly, delays will be very	40	20 | 63
costly. Millions of new pieces of information will reach offices every	55	27 | 71
day via computers. This new material will have to be sorted, edited,	69	34 | 78
stored, retrieved, and disseminated. Efficient means must be found to	83	42 | 85
do these tasks.	86	43 | 86

gwam 1' | 1 | 2 | 3 | 4 | 5 | 6 | 7 | 8 | 9 | 10 | 11 | 12 | 13 | 14 |
2' | 1 | 2 | 3 | 4 | 5 | 6 | 7 |

110c ▶ 11
Improve keyboarding technique

each pair of lines 3 times SS at a controlled rate; DS between 6-line groups

For Line 7, beginning at the left margin, set 6 tab stops 10 spaces apart. For Line 8, set 4 tab stops 15 spaces apart.

adjacent reach	1	Yes, I buy premium goods requiring minimum service on operating parts.
	2	Twenty-three new power saws were opened quickly and serviced properly.
space bar	3	In the big city, with a map, I did go by bus to my own auto to fix it.
	4	I may work to pay for the coal, the big fur rug, and the worn oak box.
direct reach	5	An excessive number of people in my survey agreed the economy is weak.
	6	Why not obtain a large company grant from my bank to make the payment?
tab/ figures	7	$49.07 $2,365 #543-1 79,823 59-286 $39.27 9032-15768
	8	243,879 #612793 $17,985 #793-21 13,928,543

| 1 | 2 | 3 | 4 | 5 | 6 | 7 | 8 | 9 | 10 | 11 | 12 | 13 | 14 |

103a ▶ 5
Preparatory practice

each line 3 times SS (slowly, faster, slowly); DS between 3-line groups; repeat selected lines as time permits

alphabet 1 A few lazy boys parked next to the back hedge and quickly jumped.

figures 2 A new profit of $21,894,650 from a gross of $297,807,319 set a record.

fig/sym 3 Order #3950-8 (dated 6/14) must be shipped to Wells & Wall by June 27.

fluency 4 Their half of the map did make big problems for me and for the ensign.

| 1 | 2 | 3 | 4 | 5 | 6 | 7 | 8 | 9 | 10 | 11 | 12 | 13 | 14 |

103b ▶ 20
Review/apply communication skills: punctuation

full sheet; 1″ top margin; 74-space line

Keyboard and format as directed in 81b, p. 150.

Key: 1b. 4′ 2b. wasn't, o'clock 3b. i's, s's 3d. 4s 4c. dog's, nails 5c. fox's 6c. Feldcress', students' 7b. Marjorie's 7d. Alison's, Jean's 8b. virtue's

Use an apostrophe

1. As a symbol to signify feet in billings or tabulations and as a symbol for minutes.
2. To show omission of letters or figures.
3. To form the plural of most figures, numbers written as words, and letters of the alphabet using the apostrophe followed by s ('s). In market quotations, only the s is added to the figure to form the plural (5s).
4. To show possession by nouns not ending in the s or z sound by adding an apostrophe and an s ('s).
5. To show possession by singular nouns ending in the s or z sound by adding the apostrophe and s ('s) to words of one syllable and an apostrophe (') only to words of more than one syllable. Some writers use an apostrophe and s ('s) to form the possessive of a multi-syllable singular noun ending in s or z if a new syllable is formed by the pronunciation of the possessive (witness's).
6. To show possession of plural nouns or proper nouns of more than one syllable ending in the s or z sound by adding the apostrophe (') only.
7. To show joint ownership or possession after the last noun in a series of two or more persons or to indicate separate ownership after each of the nouns.
8. To indicate personification of a virtue or abstract quality by using the possessive form of the noun.

review 1a. A 20′ extension ladder will be necessary to paint the house.
apply b. The dimensions of the cabinet are 6′ × 4 × 1′.

review 2a. Aren't you a member of the Class of '85?
apply b. She wasnt in the office at one oclock.

review 3a. The 2's and the e's on this page are unclear.
apply b. How many i s and s s are in the word Mississippi?
review c. Globe Fund 3s were quoted at 19 and sold for 17 1/2.
apply d. Hershel Fund 4's sold for more than anyone anticipated.

review 4a. The car's lights reflected off the metal street sign.
review b. The children's toy box was full of broken toys.
apply c. The dogs coat was shiny, but her nail's needed to be trimmed.

review 5a. Gus's baseball bat shattered as he slammed the ball.
review b. For old times' sake, the alumnus' speech was read at the reunion.
apply c. The fox' copper coat reflected against the autumn sky.

review 6a. The babies' rattles are located in the last aisle of the store.
review b. Cornelius' party was held at the Clingenshears' home.
apply c. Mrs. Feldcress grade book is with the students tests.

review 7a. Ms. Whitney and Mr. Rainsford's book order has arrived in time.
apply b. Ruth and Marjories report was informative.
review c. Peter's and Howard's motorcycles are both red.
apply d. Both Alisons and Jeans rooms will be painted this fall.

review 8a. Spring's hand has painted the landscape a lush green.
apply b. A guilt-free conscience is virtues reward.

Improve keyboarding technique

each pair of lines 3 times SS at a controlled rate; DS between 6-line groups

hyphen usage	1	Their 10-year-growth plans were run-of-the-mill presentations at best.
	2	That 86-year-old woman gave a first-class talk to the 25-member board.
double letters	3	I will call three staff issues to his attention at the weekly meeting.
	4	One possibility is to supply small colleges in the Mississippi Valley.
long numbers	5	35,782; 901,562; #97256; 200-30-5754; (617) 448-6799; #10901; 532-2317
	6	67-091; 896,358; #52800; 120-55-7633; (412) 593-8082; #05783; 425-7981
long words	7	The representative gave membership information about the organization.
	8	Eleven outstanding members completed requirements for the association.

| 1 | 2 | 3 | 4 | 5 | 6 | 7 | 8 | 9 | 10 | 11 | 12 | 13 | 14 |

109d ▶ 12
Build statistical-copy skill

1 One 1' writing on each ¶; circle errors; determine *gwam*.

2 One 5' writing on all ¶s; circle errors; determine *gwam*; compare results with 1' writings.

Difficulty index

all letters/figures used	A	1.5 si	5.7 awl	80% hfw

gwam 1' | 5'

Inflation is defined as a continuous rise in prices for an extended — 14 | 3 | 52
period. It can also be defined as a reduction in the purchasing ability — 28 | 6 | 55
of your savings and earnings. How much impact will inflation have on — 42 | 8 | 58
your future? Plenty, if it continues to increase at the present rate! — 56 | 11 | 61
For example, let us hypothesize that the price of an average house is — 70 | 14 | 64
$85,000 in 1985 and that the rate of inflation is 10 percent annually for — 85 | 17 | 67
10 successive years. In 1986, the same house would cost $93,500; in 1991, — 100 | 20 | 70
it would cost $150,582; and in 1996, it would total a whopping $242,515. — 115 | 23 | 73
That is just one example of inflation. — 123 | 25 | 74

When comparing past salaries with present salaries, inflation again — 14 | 27 | 77
becomes a big consideration. For example, if your take-home pay in 1950 — 29 | 30 | 80
was $10,000, in 1980 you would have needed $35,659 just to equal that — 43 | 33 | 83
former spending power. Inflation becomes a startling realization when — 57 | 36 | 86
we see $25,659 eroded from our income. What will the figure be in — 71 | 39 | 88
about another 30 years, say in the year 2017? No one knows the answer — 85 | 41 | 91
to that question; however, it is a safe bet that some level of inflation — 100 | 44 | 94
will exist in the years ahead. Now may be the time to begin thinking — 114 | 47 | 97
about ways you can improve your protection against inflation. — 126 | 50 | 99

gwam 1' | 1 | 2 | 3 | 4 | 5 | 6 | 7 | 8 | 9 | 10 | 11 | 12 | 13 | 14 |
5' | 1 | 2 | 3 |

109e ▶ 10
Improve skill transfer

a 1' writing on each line; additional 1' writings on each line for which your *gwam* was less than on Line 1

words

straight copy	1	They must unite many elements to form the right combination.	12
script	2	*Our main objective is to complete the entire job by tonight.*	12
statistical	3	My band includes 97 girls, 168 boys, 350 women, and 294 men.	12
rough draft	4	if we don't try *seldom take* risks, we *will avoid useful* won't get any great opportunities.	12

103c ▶ 25
Format special messages

Problem 1
Telegraphic message

plain sheet; 2″ top margin; 60–space line; DS message; proofread and correct errors

PHONED TELEGRAM — 3

TS

Telegram — 5

July 5, 19--, 3:15 p.m. — 10
DS

Mrs. Clare Payne — 13
DS
Duffy and Larue Real Estate — 19
1500 Main Street — 22
Houston, TX 77002-5519 — 27
Phone: (713) 555-4562 — 31

Harry E. Clifford agrees to sell to Gail D. Lenehan property at 10607 Glenway — 47
DS

Drive, Houston, Texas, with cash down of $85,000 and loan of $140,000. Total — 63

sales price of $225,000. Closing date of September 3, 19--, and other terms as — 79

agreed. — 80

Harry E. Clifford — 83
DS

xx — 84
DS

Problem 2
Night letter

plain sheet; 2″ top margin; 60– space line; DS message; proofread and correct errors

Problem 3
Night letter

Format the same message used in Problem 1 as a night letter, using the current date and **6:10 p.m.** Substitute the words **Night Letter** for **Telegram** in the heading and at the left margin. Address the night letter to:

Mr. Charles Kuo
Kuo and Ryan Properties, Inc.
1802 Vine Street
Houston, TX 77002-4328
Phone: (713) 555-2800

Total words: 85

NIGHT LETTER — 2
TS

Night Letter — 4

August 13, 19--, 5:30 p.m. — 9
DS

Ms. Wendy Peters, Director — 14
DS
American Business School — 19
362 Robert Street — 22
St. Paul, MN 55115-3789 — 27

Our competitors envy our success. We take their profits and give them to you. — 43
DS

Many managers of area businesses have already switched to Vendors Ex- — 60

change. The reasons are obvious! With the Vendors Exchange program you get — 75

the advantages of keeping all your vending profits; fast, dependable local pro- — 91

duct and repair service; and new vending equipment with no investment. Call — 106

555-8100 for additional information. — 113

Peter Paulos, President — 118
DS
Vendors Exchange — 121

xx — 122
DS

109a ▶ 5
Preparatory practice

each line 3 times SS
(slowly, faster,
slowly); DS between
3-line groups; repeat
selected lines as time
permits

For Line 3, beginning at
the left margin, set 4 tab
stops 14 spaces apart.

alphabet 1 Six zany questions provoked even the cool members of the working jury.

fig/sym 2 The billing error of $295.86 (Invoice #2473) was corrected in 10 days.

tab/cap 3 Jane   Bill   Mary   Dick   Beth and James

fluency 4 The city may make the firm pay a penalty for their toxic odor problem.

| 1 | 2 | 3 | 4 | 5 | 6 | 7 | 8 | 9 | 10 | 11 | 12 | 13 | 14 |

109b ▶ 12
Build straight-copy skill

1 One 1' writing on each ¶;
circle errors; determine
gwam.

2 One 5' writing on all ¶s;
circle errors; determine
gwam; compare results
with 1' writings.

Difficulty index

all letters used | A | 1.5 si | 5.7 awl | 80% hfw

gwam 1' | 5'

Beginning typists, like other people who are first learning a   12 | 2 | 60
skill, often experience times when their progress seems to stagnate   26 | 5 | 63
and they seem to be going nowhere. It takes more than just repetition   40 | 8 | 66
or rote practice to change an amateur into a professional. Profes-   54 | 11 | 68
sionals practice not only to achieve accuracy but also to improve   67 | 13 | 71
their methods so as to overcome any setbacks. Just working on a job   81 | 16 | 74
in the same old way does not mean you will master it.   91 | 18 | 76

When people are learning to keyboard, they spell out words letter   13 | 21 | 79
by letter. This process raises a barrier to speed, and soon a plateau   27 | 24 | 81
is hit. But as the serious learners keep working, they slowly begin   41 | 27 | 84
to see words as combinations, not merely as letters. The words used   55 | 29 | 87
more often become keyboarding units rather than single strokes. It is   69 | 32 | 90
not greater finger speed but larger working units that make it possible   84 | 35 | 93
for new typists to pass each level.   91 | 37 | 94

When a plateau is encountered, it is helpful to analyze the way   13 | 39 | 97
in which a learner is working in order to find out how to improve.   26 | 42 | 99
Keyboard operators, for example, may be held at a certain level by   40 | 44 | 102
faulty techniques. It is possible that they are reading too far ahead   54 | 47 | 105
in their copy. Too many learners decide that they have achieved their   68 | 50 | 108
maximum potential at their initial plateau and quit trying too soon.   82 | 53 | 111
But these students must keep persevering. A block in progress should   96 | 56 | 113
be an opportunity to discover how to push ahead.   106 | 58 | 115

gwam 1' | 1 | 2 | 3 | 4 | 5 | 6 | 7 | 8 | 9 | 10 | 11 | 12 | 13 | 14 |
     5' | 1 | 2 | 3 |

103c, continued

Problem 4
Postal card (LM p. 105)

1 Format the message side of a postal card as illustrated in the first model at the right.

2 Format the return address and the receiver's address as shown in the second model at the right.

Problem 5
Postal card (LM p. 105)

1 Compose a response to the postal card in Problem 4.

2 Format the proper receiver's address and return address.

```
TS
  September 23, 19--
    3 spaces              TS

  Dear Miss Fordham
                        DS
  We are sorry that you were unable to keep your
  appointment.  We realize that circumstances be-
  yond your control may have prevented your visit.
                                        DS
  We would like to extend an invitation to visit
  with us at a time convenient to you.  Please
  visit or call us to arrange a suitable time for
  your informal tour.
                      DS
  Miss Susan Wong, Admissions Director
```

```
Weymouth Business Institute
196 Fulton Avenue
Hempstead, NY  11550-4725

    3 spaces

                           about 2"




        about 2"      Miss Nancy Fordham
                      6803 Lexington Avenue
                      New York, NY  10037-7658
```

104a ▶ 5
Preparatory practice

each line 3 times SS (slowly, faster, slowly); DS between 3-line groups; repeat selected lines as time permits.

alphabet	1	Excessive assignments will often jeopardize both joy and zeal quickly.
fig/sym	2	Item #30254 (pens) will cost Mack & Fox $17.89 each, less 6% discount.
shift key	3	Tommy attended Lake College; Marianne, Cooke; and Bobbie, Maine State.
fluency	4	The firms may go to the big city panel with the problem of the profit.

| 1 | 2 | 3 | 4 | 5 | 6 | 7 | 8 | 9 | 10 | 11 | 12 | 13 | 14 |

104b ▶ 10
Review/apply communication skills: punctuation

full sheet; 1" top margin; 74-space line

Keyboard and format as directed in 81b, p. 150.

Key: 1b. child—, old— 2c. problem— 3b. age.—

> **Use a dash**
> **1.** To indicate a break or change in thought.
> **2.** To indicate dramatic emphasis or pauses or hesitations in written dialogue.
> **3.** To indicate the source of a quotation.

review 1a. I decided--the choice still surprises me--to become a chemist.
apply   b. The young child about three years old stood in the doorway.

review 2a. Money--that is what they want!
review   b. She will complete the essay--well, almost finish it--by 2:30 p.m.
apply   c. There is one way to solve that problem try harder.

review 3a. Happy is the house that shelters a friend.--Ralph Waldo Emerson
apply   b. Education is the best provision for old age. Aristotle

---

Improve keyboarding technique

each pair of lines 3 times SS at a controlled rate; DS between 6-line groups

adjacent reach	1	We were assured many election polls would open quickly for all voters.
	2	The popular poplar tree was an excellent stop to build a nest quickly.
shift key	3	The Spencer Corporation is now located on South Worthington Boulevard.
	4	The Boston Red Sox will play the New York Yankees in June and October.
direct reach	5	Why must a county library go to a great expense to receive my records?
	6	Why are my treasury funds with minimum account balances charged extra?

| 1 | 2 | 3 | 4 | 5 | 6 | 7 | 8 | 9 | 10 | 11 | 12 | 13 | 14 |

108d ▶ 12

Build script-copy skill

1 One 1' writing on each ¶; circle errors; determine *gwam*.

2 One 5' writing on all ¶s; circle errors; determine *gwam*; compare results with 1' writings.

Difficulty index

all letters used	A	1.5 si	5.7 awl	80% hfw

	gwam 1'	5'
Many of us frequently go through the routine process of driv-	12	2 | 42
ing up to a computerized teller to pick up some extra cash from	25	5 | 45
our neighborhood bank. This phenomenon, a highly innovative	37	7 | 47
feature several years ago, has become a way of life. But it is	50	10 | 50
just one of many interesting banking features that are now	62	12 | 52
being developed.	65	13 | 53
All sorts of new programs are being set up that will allow	11	15 | 55
us to make contact with the electronic transfer system at the	23	18 | 58
bank without our even leaving home. For example, it is now	35	20 | 60
possible by dialing our telephones to transfer funds quickly	48	23 | 62
via a computer. We can also cause financial data and	59	25 | 65
banking instructions to show on our television screens.	70	27 | 67
The development of these new banking features will bring	11	29 | 69
about a great deal of competition among banks to lure us	23	32 | 71
consumers. And the new technology will probably help us in	35	34 | 74
making the choice. We will no doubt be able to adjust our	47	36 | 76
television screens to tell us which bank offers the	57	38 | 78
highest interest rate for savings.	64	40 | 80

108e ▶ 10

Improve keyboarding technique

each pair of lines 3 times SS at a controlled rate; DS between 6-line groups

letter response	1	Only after you started as a union steward were you regarded as a czar.
	2	As you see, a water pump you gave him was set up at a site in my area.
word response	3	The problem they wish the formal panel to handle is the key amendment.
	4	I may make a profit when I rush the eighty bushels of rye to the firm.
combination	5	My field of work may entitle me to start to save wages and halt risks.
	6	The rate panel may decree an award when they visit a few of the towns.

| 1 | 2 | 3 | 4 | 5 | 6 | 7 | 8 | 9 | 10 | 11 | 12 | 13 | 14 |

104c ▶ 35
Format schedules
plain sheets
Problem 1
Appointment schedule

1 Format and type the schedule with 2″ top margin and 1½″ side margins.
2 Center the following heading in this way:

APPOINTMENT SCHEDULE
FOR
WILMA JACKSON
DS
April 29, 19--
TS

SS appointment listings; DS below each listing.

10:15 a.m.	Paul J. Fatseas, First National Bank, and Jane Allerton,	24
	Vice President, Finance. Discuss details of financing new bonds.	37
12:15 p.m.	American Manufacturing Council. Luncheon meeting at	50
	Copley Hotel.	53
2:00 p.m.	Janet Mitchell, Mitchell Advertising Agency. Discuss adver-	67
	tising campaign for next year.	73
3:00 p.m.	Arthur Cooper, Vice President, Manufacturing. Discuss pro-	86
	duction schedules for next fiscal year and the staffing	97
	plan.	98
5:00 p.m.	Lupita Diaz, Vice President, Research and Development. Dis-	112
	cuss topic for speech at next month's luncheon meeting.	123

Problem 2
Agenda of meeting

1 Format and type the agenda, centering it both vertically and horizontally. Leave 4 spaces between columns.
2 Use spaced leaders between columns.
3 Correct errors as you type.

Typing leaders: After the first item in the first column, space once and then alternate a period and a space to a point 2 or 3 spaces short of the next column. Note whether you type the periods on odd or even line-of-writing numbers; align subsequent rows by starting them in a like manner.

APEX MANUFACTURING COMPANY 5
DS
Agenda for Meeting of the Board of Directors 14
DS
April 30, 19-- 17
TS

1. Call to Order . . . . Wilma Jackson		30
DS		
2. Reading and Approval of Minutes . . . . Alice A. William		44
3. Reports of Officers SS		49
President . . . . Wilma Jackson		61
Vice President, Marketing . . . . Matt L. Lyle		73
Vice President, Research and Development . . . . Lupita Diaz		84
Vice President, Finance . . . . Jane E. Allerton		96
Vice President, Manufacturing . . . . Arthur I. Cooper		108
4. Report of Special Actions		114
Status of the amendment to the Certificate		122
of Incorporation to eliminate preemptive		130
rights . . . . Alice A. William		142
5. Dividend Declaration . . . . Jane E. Allerton		156
6. New Business		159
Review of Long Range Objectives . . . . Lupita Diaz		170
7. Adjournment . . . . Wilma Jackson		183

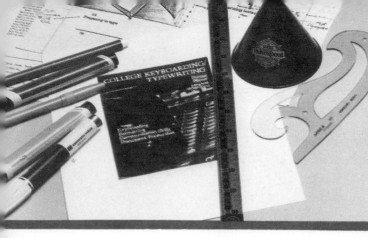

Learning goals

1 To increase basic skill on straight, statistical, rough–draft, and script copy.

2 To improve ability to punctuate copy correctly.

3 To refine keyboarding techniques.

Machine adjustments

1 Paper guide at 0.

2 Margins: 70–space line for drills and ¶ writings; as directed for problems.

3 Spacing: SS drills; DS ¶ writings; as directed for problems.

4 Indention: 5 spaces for ¶ writings; as appropriate for problems.

108a ▶ 5
Preparatory practice

each line 3 times SS (slowly, faster, slowly); DS between 3-line groups; repeat selected lines as time permits

For Line 3, beginning at the left margin, set 6 tab stops 10 spaces apart.

alphabet	1	Jagged wreckage will zoom into view quickly before the next stop sign.
fig/sym	2	Order #7066 (shipped July 31) totaled $2,985.40 (with a 9% sales tax).
tab/cap	3	Holly Teddy Carla Flynn Emily Abbot Bernadette
fluency	4	The busy auditor for the eight firms may also handle the formal visit.

| 1 | 2 | 3 | 4 | 5 | 6 | 7 | 8 | 9 | 10 | 11 | 12 | 13 | 14 |

108b ▶ 12
Build straight-copy skill

1 One 1' writing on each ¶; circle errors; determine *gwam*.

2 One 5' writing on all ¶s; circle errors; determine *gwam*; compare results with 1' writings.

Difficulty index

all letters used	A	1.5 si	5.7 awl	80% hfw

gwam 1' | 5'

Owning a home is a goal of many people in our nation today. A comfortable, attractive house is a source of pride and a good investment. But home ownership can also be a source of many financial worries. In order to make a thoughtful decision about buying a house, you should first make a conservative estimate of your dependable monthly income and then invest accordingly.

13	3	55
27	6	58
41	8	61
55	11	63
70	14	66
75	15	67

In selecting a house, as in buying any item that has an extended life expectancy, you can choose among older and newer models. In many cases, an older house may make more sense. Old residences often provide more living space for the same money than newer residences offer. On the other hand, a new house generally has fewer big maintenance problems than does a house built long ago. It is important to have your future home checked by an inspection service before you commit to it.

13	18	70
27	21	73
41	23	75
55	26	78
69	29	81
83	32	84
97	35	87

But even before you start looking for a house to buy, you must first wander through a maze of questions. For example, what is an acceptable distance to commute to your job? Is there good transportation by bus, train, or a freeway that is not congested at peak hours? Reasonable property taxes, quality schools, pleasurable shopping, and a low crime rate are only a few of the things that you must consider in your ultimate decision.

13	37	89
27	40	92
41	43	95
55	46	98
69	49	101
83	51	104
87	52	104

gwam 1' | 1 | 2 | 3 | 4 | 5 | 6 | 7 | 8 | 9 | 10 | 11 | 12 | 13 | 14 |
5' | 1 | 2 | 3 |

105a ▶ 5
Preparatory practice

each line 3 times SS (slowly, faster, slowly); DS between 3-line groups; repeat selected lines as time permits

alphabet	1	Five zebras will quietly make appearances in this dark, exotic jungle.
figures	2	Crowds of 98,194, 94,785, and 97,360 totaled a record high of 290,339.
fig/sym	3	Invoices 5423-9 and 5680-1 totaled $709.13 and were paid by Ford & Co.
fluency	4	The workbox with the worn nandle is also on the big chair by the girl.

| 1 | 2 | 3 | 4 | 5 | 6 | 7 | 8 | 9 | 10 | 11 | 12 | 13 | 14 |

105b ▶ 10
Review/apply communication skills: punctuation

full sheet; 1" top margin; 74-space line

Keyboard and format as directed in 81b, p. 150.

Key: 1b. Ethan Frome 2b. and's, but's 3b. carpe diem

Use an underline

1. With the titles of complete literary works such as books, magazines, and newspapers. Such titles may be typed in ALL CAPS without the underline.
2. To give special emphasis to words or expressions. Use an unbroken line unless each word is to be considered separately.
3. To set off a word being defined in a formal definition or to set off a foreign expression that is not part of the English language.

review 1a. I read the New York Times; she read the BOSTON GLOBE.
apply   b. Ethan Frome is one of my favorite novels by Edith Wharton.

review 2a. Insert a comma before and after an appositive.
apply   b. Omit the semicolons and add a few and's or but's.

review 3a. The term wright was used to describe someone "who worked in wood."
apply   b. The term carpe diem literally means "seize the day."

105c ▶ 35
Format minutes of a meeting and a news release

plain sheets

Problem 1
Minutes of a meeting

1½" top margin; 1" side margins, 33-space indented ¶s

Indent listed data 5 spaces from left margin

	words
SPECIAL MEETING OF BOARD OF DIRECTORS	8
BAY STATE TECHNICAL CORPORATION	14
DS	
June 30, 19--	17
TS	

Those present, being all of the Directors of Bay State Technical Corporation, today formally waived notice of the special meeting to be held June 30 and by their action acknowledged the following votes as and for the action of the Board of Directors of the Corporation: — 31 / 47 / 63 / 71

DS

Upon motion duly made and seconded, it was unanimously — 82

VOTED: To accept today the resignation of Sam Najjar as Director of said corporation. — 98 / 100

VOTED: That the President and Treasurer have the authority to execute a lease for the premises at 688 Highland Avenue in Needham, Massachusetts, for the continued operation of the corporation. — 115 / 127 / 139

DS

There being no further business to accomplish, it was then unanimously — 153

DS

VOTED: To adjourn. — 158
Adjourned accordingly. — 163
A true record. — 166

(Return 4 times)

— 170

Gerald J. Johnson, President — 176

107c ▶ 35
Measure skill on
administrative communications

Time schedule:

Assembling materials ... 3'
Timed production ...... 25'
Final check; compute
n-pram .... 7'

Problem 1
Executive-size letter
(LM p. 107)

block style, open punctuation;
date on Line 16; 1" side margins;
proofread; correct errors

words

June 30, 19-- | Ms. Dee Norton | 514 Culver Hill Drive | St. Louis, MO 63119-5768 | 16
Dear Ms. Norton 21

(¶ 1) Your "Ticket to Progress" is enclosed! Please use this ticket to attend 36
Multimedia Corporation's First Annual Computer Show to be held at St. Louis 51
Civic Auditorium. We have scheduled presentations on computer applications 66
for small businesses, exhibits and displays, and even opportunities to operate 82
the latest equipment. 86

(¶ 2) Do plan to attend the Computer Show--it's the entertaining, informative 100
way to learn more about the small business computers that will increase your 115
efficiency. 117

(¶ 3) See you at the Show! 121

Sincerely | Dan Kelly | Director, New Business Programs | xx | Enclosure 135

Problem 2
Simplified memo

plain sheet; 1½" top margin; 1"
side margins

Format/type the copy shown at
the right as a simplified memo
from **Eric Shimmel, Training
Supervisor.** Date the memo
June 30; direct it to **Janice Fox,
Word Processing Supervisor;**
use **SEMINAR/DEMONSTRATION
FOR WORD PROCESSING STAFF**
as the subject. Proofread;
correct errors.

heading 20

(¶ 1) Midwest Electronics has agreed to conduct a seminar for all members of 34
our word processing staff. The seminar will be presented twice: once on 49
July 14 at 1:30 p.m.; again on July 21 at 9:30 a.m. 59

(¶ 2) New equipment and new software packages for the processing of informa- 73
tion will be demonstrated, and new automated systems will be presented and 88
analyzed in terms of our current and future word processing needs. 101

(¶ 3) You should divide your work force into two groups and assign one group to 116
the July 14 session; the other group, to the July 21 session. In this way, total 132
work stoppage in your unit can be avoided. 140

closing lines 147

Problem 3
Night letter

plain sheet; proofread; correct
errors

NIGHT LETTER | Night Letter | November 28, 19--, 7:45 p.m. | Mr. Elbert L. Cox | 15
325 Cameron Road | Willow Grove, PA 19090-2372 24

If you act quickly, you can receive a complimentary copy of our booklet FINAN- 39
CIAL ALTERNATIVES FOR TODAY. As an investor, you will be interested in 53
finding out what we at Ferrier, McAdoo & Hancock think are timely investment 68
opportunities. We have 25 years of expertise in all areas of finance, and we 84
would like to share this knowledge with you. Call 800-555-7300 to receive this 100
important information. 104

Miss Stephanie Gutierrez, Investment Counselor | Ferrier, McAdoo & Hancock | 119
xx 120

105c, continued

Problem 2
News release

2″ top margin; 1½″ side margins;
DS the body; indent ¶s

March 1, 19--   3
DS
FOR IMMEDIATE RELEASE   7
TS

(Center) GENERAL PETROLEUM MAKES ACQUISITION   14
TS

(¶ 1) The General Petroleum Company announced today that it had reached   27
definitive terms to buy the American Oil Company of Texas for nearly $1.2   42
billion in cash and various securities.   50

(¶ 2) Analysts estimate that General Petroleum will be buying American Oil   64
Company's domestic oil and gas reserves for about $29 a barrel, or roughly 40   79
percent less than the cost of drilling for it.   88

(¶ 3) The complex provisions of the deal call for General Petroleum, the nation's   103
second-largest oil company, to pay an average of $45 a share for the 25.4 million   119
shares of American Oil, a small oil and gas company. According to Mickey M.   134
Phillips, President of General Petroleum, the transaction is in keeping with the   150
long-term objectives of the company because it improves the company's   164
reserves and production position in the United States.   175
DS
(Center) ###   176

106a ▶ 5
Preparatory practice

each line 3 times SS
(slowly, faster,
slowly); DS between
3-line groups; repeat
selected lines as time
permits

alphabet 1   The five dozen quarts of blackberry and grape juice mixture were minc.

fig/sym 2   Terms of 2/10, n/30 were listed on Invoice #416-9758 from Moore & Son.

long words 3   Marianne, Constantine, and Bernadette are outstanding representatives.

fluency 4   The theory may make big problems if they both fight for the amendment.

| 1 | 2 | 3 | 4 | 5 | 6 | 7 | 8 | 9 | 10 | 11 | 12 | 13 | 14 |

106b ▶ 10
Review/apply communication skills: punctuation

full sheet; 1″ top margin
74-space line

Keyboard and format as
directed in 81b, p. 150.

Key: 1b. "The . . . stand,"
2c. "Robots in the Office."
3c. "stoops"

Use quotation marks

1. To enclose a direct quotation.
2. To identify titles of articles and other parts of complete publications, short poems, song titles, television programs, and unpublished works such as theses and dissertations.
3. To enclose translations of foreign words, formal definitions, technical terms, coined words, humorous and ironic expressions, and purposely ungrammatical constructions.

review 1a.   "To err is human, to forgive divine," said Alexander Pope.
apply   b.   The defendant will stand, said Judge Hensley.

review 2a.   "Fog" by Carl Sandburg is filled with imagery.
review   b.   Judy Garland sang "Somewhere Over the Rainbow" in The Wizard of Oz.
apply   c.   I read an interesting article, Robots in the Office.

review 3a.   We made a faux pas, a "false step," when we met the ambassador.
review   b.   The president "interfaced" with the rest of the management team.
apply   c.   A falcon stoops when it dives to attack its prey.

107a ▶ 5
Preparatory practice

each line 3 times SS (slowly, faster, slowly); DS between 3-line groups; repeat selected lines as time permits

alphabet 1 They have excused a man who plagiarized quotes from a book or journal.

fig/sym 2 The telegram (dated 7/23) requested payment of $35,614.08 by August 9.

long words 3 Association representatives discussed suggestions regarding personnel.

fluency 4 The big lake is visible if he turns right at the end of the cornfield.

| 1 | 2 | 3 | 4 | 5 | 6 | 7 | 8 | 9 | 10 | 11 | 12 | 13 | 14 |

107b ▶ 10
Measure straight-copy skill

1 One 1' writing on each ¶; circle errors; determine *gwam*.

2 One 5' writing on all ¶s; circle errors; determine *gwam*; compare results with 1' writings.

Difficulty index

| all letters used | A | 1.5 si | 5.7 awl | 80% hfw |

gwam 1' | 5'

If you are like many individuals, you see or hear hundreds of ads 13 | 3 | 68
each day. But like most people, you probably don't recall all that is 27 | 5 | 71
flashed before your eyes on television, placed in the side columns of 41 | 8 | 74
newspapers and magazines, or played over the radio. Why is it that people 56 | 11 | 77
remember some ads and not others? This is a question of crucial interest 71 | 14 | 80
to advertisers, as well as to scientists. Even more critical is the 85 | 17 | 83
question of what kinds of advertisements work best to generate sales. 99 | 20 | 85

A great deal of research had been done to determine why individuals 14 | 23 | 88
remember certain advertisements but do not remember others. Basically, 28 | 25 | 91
research suggests that advertisements first must get people's attention. 43 | 28 | 94
This may not be so easy. If you have been looking for a good set of 57 | 31 | 97
golf clubs and you see an advertisement in the newspaper for a particu- 71 | 34 | 100
lar set of clubs, you may stop to read the ad. On the other hand, if 85 | 37 | 102
you are looking for a new automobile, chances are you will pass right 99 | 40 | 105
over the advertisement for golf clubs. Scientists explain this by say- 113 | 42 | 108
ing that individuals have to be primed, or made ready, for a message in 127 | 45 | 111
order to pay attention to it. 133 | 47 | 112

Once an ad gets attention, it then must convey a message. In order 14 | 49 | 115
to convey a message, it needs to be clear, easy to understand, and easy 28 | 52 | 118
to remember. The advertisement should also focus on the product--the 42 | 55 | 121
characteristics and images that are quite likely to appeal to the mar- 56 | 58 | 123
ket it is trying to reach. Developing a message that best summarizes 70 | 61 | 126
the advantage of a product is not easy; however, the success of a prod- 84 | 63 | 129
uct may well rest on the message that is projected. 95 | 66 | 131

gwam 1' | 1 | 2 | 3 | 4 | 5 | 6 | 7 | 8 | 9 | 10 | 11 | 12 | 13 | 14 |
5' | 1 | 2 | 3 |

Format an itinerary and a speech

plain sheets

Problem 1
Itinerary

center vertically and horizontally; DS body; 4 spaces between
columns

ITINEARY FOR WILEMA JACKSON

June 10 to June 28

DATE	FROM	DEPART	FLIGHT	TO	ARRIVE	words
						5
						9
DATE	FROM	DEPART	FLIGHT	TO	ARRIVE	22
6/10	Boston	8:00 a.m.	AA/147*	Pittsburgh	9:33 a.m.	31
6/12	Pittsburgh	3:30 p.m.	AL/189	Philadelphia	4:32 p.m.	41
6/13	Philadelphia	5:00 p.m.	AL/204**	Chicago	6:05 p.m.	51
6/15	Chicago	8:30 a.m.	DL/23*	Cincinnati	10:36 a.m.	61
6/17	Cincinnati	11:00 a.m.	DL/190	St. Louis	11:10 a.m.	71
6/18	St. Louis	4:15 p.m.	UN/132**	Houston	6:05 p.m.	81
6/19	Houston	6:00 p.m.	EA/183**	New Orleans	7:03 p.m.	91
6/20	New Orleans	4:25 p.m.	EA/153**	Miami	7:04 p.m.	101
6/21	Miami	5:15 p.m.	DL/125**	Washington	7:26 p.m.	110
6/22	Washington	8:00 p.m.	EA/241	New York	8:45 p.m.	119
6/24	New York	7:30 a.m.	AA/162*	Atlanta	9:35 a.m.	128
6/26	Atlanta	11:45 a.m.	DL/127	Denver	12:35 p.m.	137
6/27	Denver	10:45 a.m.	CO/320	Kansas City	1:09 p.m.	147
6/28	Kansas City	3:50 p.m.	AL/124**	Boston	9:50 p.m.	157

*Breakfast flight

**Dinner flight

160

163

Problem 2
Speech

1½″ top and side margins; DS the ¶s; DS twice between ¶s; indent ¶s 5 spaces

1 Place the title **RESULTS OF THIS YEAR'S OPERATIONS** a TS above the text.

2 Number the second page on Line 4 at the right margin and start the text for that page on Line 7.

3 Correct errors as you work.

words
in heading 7

Thanks for ~~coming to~~ you attending this annual stockholder's meeting   19

of Apex Manufacturing Co. I'm am going to speak very briefly   32

about the results of some of the inroads ~~we've~~ that our company has made in the   46

past ~~passed~~ 12 months.   49

During this year, advances in technology have ~~gone~~ continued   60

at a rapid pace, ~~so that we can~~ with the result that we are able to offer to our clients greater   76

~~in~~ lower productivity at ~~smaller~~ cost. This trend has led to   87

~~some~~ substantial expansion of our customers base, despite a general down-   100

turn in the economy.   104

However, ~~But~~ this economic ~~worry~~ uncertainty very likely will ~~keep on,~~ persist.   116

One factor in ~~its~~ this uncertainty is sharp changes in foreign currency rates.   130

Our gross income from rentals has been adversely affected by the pres-   145

ent exchange rates, ~~but still~~ and yet we have not benefited from   156

depreciation because ~~it's~~ that is figured at historical exchange   168

rates. In addition, gross profit margins on both sales and   180

rentals of our products somewhat have been eroded by our   191

~~big~~ major expenditures for manufacturing ~~faculties~~ facilities.   201

On the other hand, our substantial ~~But then, our big~~ investment in additional ~~items~~ capacity and   216

our development of several new channels of distribution ~~lets~~ allow   228

the company to meet the needs of its ~~consumers~~ customers more ~~quickly~~ efficiently.   242

This ability to provide greater client satisfaction   254

will ~~cause~~ assure an enduring trend of ~~much growth~~ steady improvement in business vol-   264

ume and financial performance in the coming year.   274

DS twice

Thank you for your attention. And now, Jane   283

Allerton, Vice President for Finance, will speak to you   294

about the financial outlook of Apex Manufacturing.   314

Capitalize

1 The first word of a complete sentence.

I have the final page of the report.

2 The first word of a direct quotation.

She said, "Let's work together."

3 The first and main words in titles or headings in books, poems, reports, songs, etc.

I read portions of Leaves of Grass.

4 Titles that precede personal names.

I met Major Busby and Mayor Lopez.

5 Titles of distinction that follow a personal name.

Ms. Chu is a U.S. Senator from Idaho.

6 Names of specific persons and places.

My friend Larry lives in Baltimore.

7 Words derived from the names of specific persons and places.

Barry, a Scot, wore an Edwardian costume.

8 Names of weekdays, months, holidays, and historic periods.

Thursday, November 27, is Thanksgiving.

9 Most nouns followed by identifying numbers.

Issue Check #7813 to pay Invoice 785-J.

10 The first word after a colon if it begins a complete sentence.

Notice: No running is permitted.

11 Seasons of the year if they are personified, and compass points if they designate definite regions.

The icy breath of Winter chilled the Midwest.

12 Trademarks, brand names, and names of commercial products.

My Peerless radio uses Rayovac batteries.

Do not capitalize

1 Compass points when they indicate direction.

We drove north to South Brunswick.

2 *Page* and *verse*, even when followed by a number.

The quotation is in verse 72 on page 512.

3 A title following a name that is not a title of distinction.

Rana was elected secretary of our club.

4 Commonly accepted derivatives of proper nouns.

Why not go dutch treat tonight?

5 The common noun following the name of a product.

I have a Silvertone radio; Jan has an SRE tape deck.

6 Generic terms when they appear in the plural to describe two or more names.

Meet me where Oak and Maple roads cross.

See also pages 72, 150, and 165 of the textbook.

Numbers: Type as words

1 A figure that begins a sentence.

Three of the runners were disqualified.

2 Numbers ten and lower, unless used as part of a series of figures, some of which are above ten.

I carried five books with me today.
Only 9 of the 27 ducks had been banded.

3 Expressions of time with the word *o'clock*.

Dinner will be served at seven o'clock.

4 The smaller of two numbers used together.

Buy two 5-gallon containers of gasoline.

5 Isolated fractions or indefinite amounts.

Only one third of almost six hundred members attended.

6 Names of small-numbered (ten and under) streets.

He moved from First Street to Seventh Avenue.

7 Large even numbers.

My chances of winning are one in a million.

Numbers: Type as figures

1 Numbers preceded by most nouns.

Check Column 3 of the Volume 2 appendix.

2 Expressions of time followed by a.m. or p.m. and days and years used as part of a date.

We will meet again at 2 p.m., May 5, 1989.

3 House numbers (except One) and high-numbered street names (with *d* and *th*).

Deliver the flowers to 45 East 72d Street.
My temporary address is 340-39th Street.

4 Numbers used with abbreviations, symbols, or dimensions.

For a 2% solution, add 4 tsp. salt to 4 qts. of water.

5 Dates (with *d* and *th*) that precede the month and are separated from it by words.

We signed a lease on the 23d or 24th of April.

See also pages 90-92 of the textbook.

Use a comma (followed by a single space, unless it is used internally in a large figure)

1 After introductory words, phrases, or dependent clauses.
No, I cannot answer the phone now.
If you don't answer, we may miss a call.

2 Between words or groups of words that comprise a series.
The flag is red, white, and blue.
We left home, drove to town, and saw a show.

3 To set off explanatory and descriptive words, phrases, and clauses used in a sentence.
Today, Friday, is my day off.
You did not, I know, leave early.

4 To set off words in direct address.
If you can, Betsy, write to Joan tonight.

5 To set off nonrestrictive adjective clauses (not necessary to the meaning of the sentence), but not restrictive adjective clauses (needed for meaning).
The books, some of which I read, are missing.
The guests who were late missed dinner.

6 To set off (a) a year that is used as part of a date and (b) the state when it follows a city.
On July 4, 1985, I left for Richmond, Virginia.
I saw her in Topeka, Kansas, on May 1, 1986.

7 To separate two or more parallel adjectives (adjectives that could be separated by the word *and* instead of the comma). Do not use commas to separate adjectives so closely related that they appear to form a single element with the noun they modify.
It was a frosty, windy day in March.
She sat under a green linden tree.

8 To separate (a) unrelated groups of figures that come together and (b) whole numbers into groups of three digits each (however, numbers that identify rather than enumerate are usually typed without commas).
At 5:15, 1,250 papers were sent to Room 4085.

9 To set off contrasting phrases and clauses.
People, not machines, make decisions.
See also page 176 of the textbook.

Use an apostrophe (followed by a single space unless a letter, figure, or mark of punctuation immediately follows it)

1 As a symbol for feet and *minutes.*
Take a 3' writing.
The crate measured 2' by 2' by 6'.

2 With s to form the plural of most figures, figures written as words, and letters. In market quotations, the apostrophe is not used.
2's two's C's Fourstar Fund 8s

3 To show omission of letters or figures.
Rob't Sec'y Class of '89

4 To show possession: Add the apostrophe and s to a singular noun not ending in s. If a singular noun ends in an s or z sound, add 's to form the possessive if the ending s is to be pronounced as a syllable; add the apostrophe only if the ending s would be awkward to pronounce.
book's cover horse's hoof Bess's crown box's lid species' peculiarities

5 To show possession: Add the apostrophe and s to a plural noun that does not end in s.
men's hats women's coats children's toys

6 To show possession: Add only the apostrophe after (a) plural nouns ending in s and (b) a proper noun of more than one syllable ending in s or z.
workers' cards Cortez' trip Lois' wish

7 To show possession: Add 's after the last noun in a series to indicate joint or common possession of two or more persons; however, show separate possession of two or more persons by adding 's to each noun.
Alice and Bill's anniversary
Rita's and Trevor's birthdays
See also page 192 of the textbook.

Use an exclamation point (followed by 2 spaces)

1 After emotional words or phrases.
Wow! Watch it! Hurray! Look out!

2 After exclamatory sentences.
You spilled the chemicals!
See also pages 31 and 168 of the textbook.

Use a hyphen (with no space before or after it)

1 To join compound numbers typed as words.

```
sixty-two  forty-eight  two hundred fifty-six
```

2 To join compound adjectives written *before* a noun they modify as a unit.

```
first-rate lunch  up-to-date information
```

3 After words or figures in a series that have a common ending (suspended hyphenation).

```
two-, three-, and five-minute writings
```

See also pages 36 and 177 of the textbook.

Use a dash (two consecutive hyphens with no space before or after them)

1 For emphasis, clarity, or change of thought.

```
The trees--very large trees--loomed ahead.
The trip--it was my idea--was great fun.
```

2 To show the source of a direct quotation.

```
A dash separates; a hyphen joins.--Anonymous
```

3 To indicate in written form verbal pauses.

```
Yes--er--no--oh, I don't know!
```

See also pages 35 and 194 of the textbook.

Use parentheses (with no space between them and the data they enclose)

1 To enclose explanatory, parenthetical, or nonessential material.

```
My roommate (my older sister) owns the car.
```

2 To enclose letters or figures in a listing.

```
Show your (a) name, (b) address, and (c) age.
```

3 To enclose figures that follow spelled-out amounts to give clarity or emphasis.

```
You must pay fifty dollars ($50) now.
```

See also page 186 of the textbook.

Use a colon (followed by two spaces unless it is used with integrated figures)

1 To introduce a statement or listing.

```
Order these items:  a lamp, a cord, and a plug.
This is the question:  Where is Dan?
```

2 To separate integrated figures.

```
3:1 odds  2:45 a.m.  ratio of 5:2
```

See also page 189 of the textbook.

Use a semicolon (followed by one space)

1 To separate two or more independent clauses in a compound sentence when the conjunction is omitted.

```
I came; I saw; I conquered.
```

2 To separate independent clauses joined by a conjunctive adverb (however, therefore, etc.).

```
He knows me well; however, we do not correspond.
```

3 To separate a series of word or figure groups if one or more of the groups contains a comma.

```
Bring a ball; a bat; and, of course, your mitt.
```

4 To precede an abbreviation or word(s) that introduce further explanation.

```
Myra was here; that is, I saw her earlier.
```

See also page 180 of the textbook.

Use an underline (continuously, unless each word is to be considered separately)

1 With titles of complete literary works.

```
Hamlet  The Daily News  New England Magazine
```

2 To emphasize special words or phrases.

```
Can he spell convenience?  I know he can.
```

See also page 196 of the textbook.

Use a period (followed by two spaces if it ends a sentence, one space if it ends an abbreviation)

1 To end a declaratory sentence or a request.

```
It is raining.  Will you hand me my umbrella.
```

2 With a variety of abbreviations.

```
Mr. R. E. Riaz, a CPA, called at 2 p.m.
```

See also pages 112 and 166 of the textbook.

Use quotation marks (after a comma or period, before a semicolon or colon, and after a question mark only if the quotation itself is a question)

1 To enclose a direct quotation.

```
She asked, "Who is in charge here?"
Did you hear her say, "Lex is a Gemini"?
```

2 To enclose titles and parts of publications.

```
"Storm Strikes Area"  "The Mikado"  "Trees"
```

3 To enclose special or coined words.

```
The child said he saw a "wabbit."
```

4 As a symbol for inches and seconds.

```
The board is 9" long.
The timer is set for 45".
```

See also page 197 of the textbook.

Word-division guides

A word may correctly be divided between syllables as defined in a dictionary or word-division manual. In special cases, the guidelines below will be helpful.

Short words. Do not divide words of five or fewer letters, even if they have two or more syllables.

area bonus alien aroma truth ideal

Double consonants. Divide between double consonants unless the division involves a word that ends in double con-sonants.

excel-lent call-ing win-ner add-ing

One- or two-letter syllables. Do not divide a one-letter sylla-ble at the beginning of a word.

enough ideal opened aboard ozone

Do not separate a two-letter syllable at the end of a word.

friendly shaker nickel groggy fluid

Divide after a one-letter syllable within a word; if two single-letter syllables occur together, divide between them.

tele-vision ele-ment gradu-ation idi-omatic

Hyphenated words. Divide at the hyphens only.

self-centered off-white soft-spoken

Figures. Do not divide figures presented as a unit.

2,785,321 127,100 #3290533 150/371

Avoid if possible. Try to avoid dividing proper names, dates, and the last word on a page.

See also page 43 of the textbook.

ZIP Code abbreviations

Alabama, AL	Kentucky, KY	Ohio, OH
Alaska, AK	Louisiana, LA	Oklahoma, OK
Arizona, AZ	Maine, ME	Oregon, OR
Arkansas, AR	Maryland, MD	Pennsylvania, PA
California, CA	Massachusetts, MA	Puerto Rico, PR
Colorado, CO	Michigan, MI	Rhode Island, RI
Connecticut, CT	Minnesota, MN	South Carolina, SC
Delaware, DE	Mississippi, MS	South Dakota, SD
District of Columbia, DC	Missouri, MO	Tennessee, TN
Florida, FL	Montana, MT	Texas, TX
Georgia, GA	Nebraska, NE	Utah, UT
Guam, GU	Nevada, NV	Vermont, VT
Hawaii, HI	New Hampshire, NH	Virgin Islands, VI
Idaho, ID	New Jersey, NJ	Virginia, VA
Illinois, IL	New Mexico, NM	Washington, WA
Indiana, IN	New York, NY	West Virginia, WV
Iowa, IA	North Carolina, NC	Wisconsin, WI
Kansas, KS	North Dakota, ND	Wyoming, WY

Margins/Date Placement. The average letter, business or per-sonal, fits well on an 8½" × 11" page if 1½" side margins are used. When letterhead paper is not used, type a return address on Lines 14 and 15. Type the date on Line 16, just below the return ad-dress (or alone on letterhead paper). With a short or long letter, adjust the margins in or out ½"; lower or raise the return address and date as needed. (See also let-ter placement table on page 162.)

Horizontal placement of the date varies according to letter style. In block and AMS Simplified styles, type the date at left margin; in modified block style, begin the date at center point. Other letter parts, when they are used, are formatted at left margin, unless otherwise noted.

Mailing notation: on the second line space between the date and letter address. See Letter 2 below.

Letter address: on the fourth line space below the date. Type any official title on the same line as the name or below it, whichever gives better balance. A personal title (as Ms. or Mr.) precedes an individu-al's name.

Attention line: as the second line of the letter address. The saluta-tion corresponds with the letter address, not the attention line. See Letter 1 below.

Subject line: a double space below the salutation. An introduc-tion such as Re. or SUBJECT: is optional. See Letter 3 below.

Salutation: a double space below letter address or subject line. The salutation corresponds with the first line of the letter address. If first line has no gender, use Ladies and Gentlemen or Dear Sir or Madam. See Letters 1 and 3 be-low.

Company name in closing: on the second line space below the complimentary close, in ALL CAPS, at center point for modified block style. See Letter 2 below.

Writer's typed name/official title: on the fourth line space below the complimentary close or the company name. With the exception of the AMS style, the writer's title may go on either the same line as the name or below it—whichever gives better balance. A male sig-natory may indicate personal title preference; a female does not, as Mr. is always acceptable. See Let-ters 1-4 below.

Reference initials: a double space below the name and official title in lower case. See Letters 1-4 below.

Enclosure notation: a double space below the reference initials. See Letter 2 below.

Copy notation (cc, bcc, pc): a double space below the reference initials or enclosure notation, fol-lowed by the recipient's name. See Letter 1 below.

Postscript: a double space below the last letter item, in the same style as was used for other para-graphs. The letters P.S. are rarely used. See Letter 3 below.

Multiple pages: If a letter is too long for one page, at least 2 lines of the body of the letter should be carried to the second page. Begin the sec-ond and subsequent pages on Line 7; leave two blank line spaces below page headings. Use the same side margins as the first page.

Second-page headings

block form

Leslie Moll, Inc.
Page 2
October 23, 19--
TS
and it would seem appropriate for the remainder of the shipment
to be kept in storage at the Dubuque depot until the conditions
1"

horizontal form

Leslie Moll, Inc.   2   October 23, 19--
TS
and it would seem appropriate for the remainder of the shipment
to be kept in storage at the Dubuque depot until the conditions
1"

Communications Design Associates

348 INDIANA AVENUE
WASHINGTON, DC 20001-1438
Tel: 1-800-432-5739

February 14, 19--

Sunstructures, Inc.
Attention Mr. Harvey Bell
2214 Brantford Place
Buffalo, NY 14222-5147

Ladies and Gentlemen

This letter is written in what is called "block style."
It is the style we recommend for use in your business
office for reasons detailed in the following paragraphs.

First, the style is a very efficient one. All lines
(including date) begin at the left margin, and time is
not consumed in positioning special parts of letters.

Second, the style is easy to learn. New employees will
have little difficulty learning it, and your present
staff can adjust to it without unnecessary confusion.

Third, the style is sufficiently different from most
other styles that it can suggest to clients that your
company is creative. The style gains attention.

At the request of Thomas Wray, I am enclosing his booklet about business letter styles and special features.

Sincerely

Kathryn E. Bowers

Ms. Kathryn E. Bowers
Senior Consultant

xx

pc Mr. Thomas Wray

1 Block, open

Communications Design Associates

348 INDIANA AVENUE
WASHINGTON, DC 20001-1438
Tel: 1-800-432-5739

November 28, 19--

SPECIAL DELIVERY

Mr. Otto B. Bates, President
Third Bank and Trust Company
9080 Reservoir Avenue
New Brunswick, NJ 90901-4476

Dear Mr. Bates

This letter is written in the "modified block style."
It is the style we recommend for use in your office for
reasons detailed for you in the paragraphs below.

First, the style is an efficient one that requires only
one tab setting--at center point--for positioning the
date, complimentary close, and typed signature lines.

Second, the style is easy to learn. New employees will
have little difficulty learning it, and your present
staff can adjust to it without unnecessary confusion.

Third, the style is a familiar one; it is used by more
business firms than any other. It is conservative, and
customers and companies alike feel comfortable with it.

A booklet about business letter styles and special features is enclosed. Use the reply card, also enclosed,
if you need additional information.

Sincerely yours

COMMUNICATIONS DESIGN ASSOCIATES

Kathryn E. Bowers

Ms. Kathryn E. Bowers
Senior Consultant

xx

Enclosures: 2

2 Modified block, open

Communications Design Associates

348 INDIANA AVENUE
WASHINGTON, DC 20001-1438
Tel: 1-800-432-5739

November 2, 19--

Office Manager
Ramsey Engineering, Inc.
4799 Hamner Drive
Amarillo, TX 79107-6359

Dear Sir or Madam:

Subject: Modified Block Style Letter

I am pleased to answer your letter. As you can
see, we use the modified block style, indented paragraphs, and mixed punctuation in our correspondence.
It is the style used in this letter.

The spacing from the top of the page to the date
varies with the length of the letter. Other spacing in
the letter is standard. The date, complimentary close,
and name and official title of the writer are begun at
horizontal center.

Please write to me again if I can help further.

Very truly yours,

Allen M. Woodside

Allen M. Woodside
Marketing Manager

xx

Our new LETTER STYLE GUIDE will be sent to you as
soon as it comes from the printer.

3 Modified block, indented ¶s, mixed

Communications Design Associates

348 INDIANA AVENUE
WASHINGTON, DC 20001-1438
Tel: 1-800-432-5739

May 9, 19--

Dr. William S. Rapp
Rapp, Hedgson, & Emblatt
98 Clutter Mill Road
Great Neck, NY 11021-4527

AMS SIMPLIFIED LETTER STYLE

This letter is typed in the simplified style that is
recommended by the Administrative Management Society.
The letter features the following points which are designed to save time:

1. Block format is used.

2. Salutation and complimentary close are omitted.

3. A subject heading is typed in ALL CAPS a triple
    space below the address; the first line of the body
    is typed a TS below the subject line.

4. Enumerated items begin flush with the left margin;
    unnumbered items are indented five spaces.

5. The writer's name and title are typed in ALL CAPS
    on the 4th line space below the last line of the
    body of the letter.

6. The reference initials (typist's only) are typed a
    double space below the writer's name.

Correspondents in your company may like the AMS Simplified letter style both for its eye appeal and for its
potential reduction in letter-writing costs.

Luella E. Draper

MRS. LUELLA E. DRAPER, PRESIDENT

xx

4 AMS Simplified

Ergonomics Consultants, Inc.

INTEROFFICE COMMUNICATION

TO: All Communication Processors

FROM: Rachel Darboro, Director

DATE: June 13, 19--

SUBJECT: Interoffice Memoranda

The exchange of information within a company is frequently typed on interoffice forms, either half or full sheets, depending upon the length of the message. The following points describe unique features of this form of memorandum.

1. Space twice after a printed heading; set the left margin stop for typing heading items and the body. Set the right margin stop an equal distance from the right edge. These margin adjustments will usually provide side margins of 1 inch.

2. Full addresses, the salutation, the complimentary close, and the signature are omitted.

3. Personal titles, such as Mr., are usually omitted from the memo heading. They are included on the envelope, however.

4. TS between the heading and the message; SS the paragraphs, but DS between them.

5. Reference initials, enclosure notation, and carbon copy notation are included if needed.

Special colored envelopes are often used for interoffice memos. Type the addressee's personal title, name, and business title or name of department for the address. Type COMPANY MAIL (in caps) in the postage location.

xx

pc Paul Glass, Assistant to the President

1 Interoffice memorandum

Communications Design Associates

348 INDIANA AVENUE
WASHINGTON, DC 20001-1438
Tel: 1-800-432-5739

January 11, 19--

Mr. Manuel D. Legallo
Office Manager, DGT, Inc.
4532 Mahood Drive
Huntington, WV 25705-8450

Dear Mr. Legallo

This letter is typed on executive-size stationery, a size preferred by some administrators, supervisors, and executives.

Executive-size stationery is smaller than the typical office stationery, for it measures only 7¼" x 10½". It usually carries the company letterhead and a statement identifying the office from which it originates.

When typing letters on stationery narrower than the usual 8½" by 11" paper, margins of 1" are recommended. To center long or short letters requires adjustment of the date placement, which may vary from Line 10 to Line 16. Standard letter styles and punctuation forms are used.

We hope this example letter will help to answer the questions you asked in your recent letter about the use of this special stationery.

Very truly yours

Adelle Pruitt

Mrs. Adelle Pruitt
Communications Consultant

xx

2 Letter on executive-size paper

Fairfield Manufacturing, Inc.

MESSAGE	REPLY
TO Jonathan Kappel Director, Employee Development 126 Hancock Tower	DATE: January 23, 19-- The topics listed are timely and relevant to our long-range plans. I suggest that I attend the conference in New York in March and make a formal proposal to the corporate officers by April 1.
DATE: January 22, 19-- SUBJECT: Conference on Employee Development The attached brochure was received from the National Center for the Advancement of Business Practices. Since employee development will be a priority for us for some time, these conference topics may be relevant. Please let me know your opinion.	
SIGNED: Maria Gonzalez, Vice President	SIGNED: Jonathan Kappel

3 Message/reply form

Sally Ann Dupois
123 Poinciana Road
Memphis, TN 38117-4121
(901-365-2775)

PRESENT CAREER OBJECTIVE

Eager to accept part-time position that provides opportunities for additional training and potential for full-time employment.

MAJOR QUALIFICATIONS

Knowledge of merchandising, management, inventory control, and related areas of a retail clothing store. Cheerful, outgoing personality and a dependable, cooperative worker.

EDUCATION—

Junior at Memphis State University, Memphis, Tennessee, majoring in Marketing.

AA degree (associate degree/advertising; honors), State Technical Institute, Memphis, Tennessee.

Graduate (honors), East High School, Memphis, Tennessee.

EXPERIENCE

Assistant Manager, The Toggery, 100 Madison Avenue, Memphis, TN 38103-4219, June 1985 - Present.

Inventory Clerk and Cashier, Chobie's, 1700 Poplar Avenue, Memphis, TN 38104-2176, June 1984 - September 1984.

Clerk and Assistant to the Buyer, Todds, 1450 Union Avenue, Memphis, TN 38104-5417, June 1983 - September 1983.

REFERENCES

Mrs. Evelyn J. Quinell
Manager, Chobie's
1700 Poplar Avenue
Memphis, TN 38104-2176

Professor Aldo R. MacKenzie
Marketing Department
Memphis State University
Memphis, TN 38114-3285

Ms. Lanya Roover
The Toggery
100 Madison Avenue
Memphis, TN 38103-4219

Mr. Robert E. Tindall, Jr.
Attorney-at-Law
1045 Quin Avenue
Memphis, TN 38106-4792

4 Personal data sheet

Addressing procedure

Envelope address. Set a tab stop (or margin stop if a number of envelopes are to be addressed) 10 spaces left of center for a small envelope or 5 spaces for a large envelope. Start the address here on Line 12 from the top edge of a small envelope and on Line 14 of a large one.

Style. Type the address in *block style*, single-spaced, without punctuation at the ends of lines, except when an abbreviation ends a line. Type the city name, state name or abbreviation, and ZIP Code on the last address line. The ZIP Code is usually typed 2 spaces after the state name.

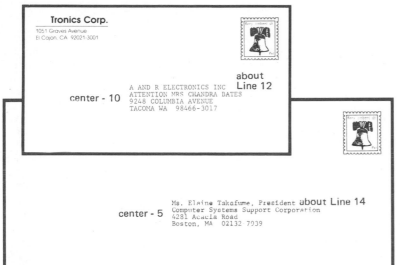

Addressee notations. Type addressee notations, such as *Hold for Arrival, Please Forward, Personal,* etc., a triple space below the return address and about 3 spaces from the left edge of the envelope. These notations may be underlined or typed in all capitals.

If an *attention line* is used, type it immediately below the company name in the address line.

Mailing notations. Type mailing notations, such as SPECIAL DELIVERY and REGISTERED, below the stamp and at least 3 line spaces above the envelope address. Type these notations in all capital letters.

Folding and inserting procedure

Small envelopes (No. 6¾, 6¼)

Step 1
With letter face up, fold bottom up to ½ inch from top.

Step 2
Fold right third to left.

Step 3
Fold left third to ½ inch from last crease.

Step 4
Insert last creased edge first.

Large envelopes (No. 10, 9, 7¾)

Step 1
With letter face up, fold slightly less than ⅓ of sheet up toward top.

Step 2
Fold down top of sheet to within ½ inch of bottom fold.

Step 3
Insert letter into envelope with last crease toward bottom of envelope.

Window envelopes (letter)

Step 1
With sheet face down, top toward you, fold upper third down.

Step 2
Fold lower third up so address is showing.

Step 3
Insert sheet into envelope with last crease at bottom.

Window envelopes (invoices and other forms)

Step 1
Place sheet face down, top toward you.

Step 2
Fold back top so address shows.

Step 3
Insert into envelope with crease at bottom.

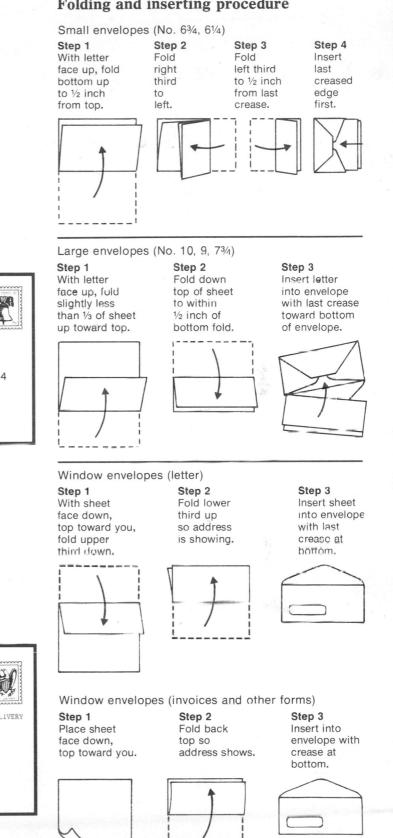

Formatting reports (See illustrations below)

Margins. Use 1" top, side, and bottom margins, except for the first page, which has a 1½" or 2" top margin.

Binding. Allow an extra ½" for side or top binding.

Spacing. Double spacing for the body of a report and 5-space paragraph indentions are usual.

Quotations. Single-space quotations of 4 or more lines and indent them 5 spaces from each margin; otherwise, enclose the quotations in quotation marks and include them double-spaced as part of the body of the report.

Ellipses. An ellipsis, an intentional omission of part of a quotation, is indicated by 3 periods with one space between each of the periods. If the omission ends a sentence, use 4 periods.

Leaders. If the report contains tabular copy, the columns may be separated by leaders. Leaders (spaced periods) can help a reader to move from one column to another. After typing the first item in the first column, space once and then alternate a period and a space to a point 2 or 3 spaces short of the next column. Note whether you type the periods on odd or even line-of-writing numbers; align subsequent rows by starting on an odd or even number as you did in the first line.

Justifying the right margin (manually). A preliminary copy must be typed to determine how many extra spaces must be added between words to insure an even right margin in a final copy. The normal procedure for the preliminary typing is to type as close to the end of each line as possible and then fill the remaining spaces with diagonals until the machine locks. Interpret diagonals as spaces to be added to each line in the final copy.

Footnotes. Footnotes may be placed at the end of a report, or they may be placed at the foot of the page on which reference to them is made.

Use a superior figure or symbol in the text of the report as reference to a footnote. Repeat the reference with the foot-note.

Separate footnotes from the body of a report with a single underline 1½" long; single-space below the last line of the report to type the underline, and double-space below the underline to begin the first line of the foot-notes.

Single-space footnotes; double-space between them. Calculate footnote placement to insure a 1" bottom margin.

Formatting outlines

Data may be reduced to a more functional form through the use of an outline. Use the following suggestions.

Separate divisions and subdivisions of various orders with 4-space indentions.

Type first order divisions in ALL CAPS; capitalize main words only in second-order divisions; capitalize only the first word in third- and subsequent-order divisions.

Use the margin release and backspacer to type all Roman numerals other than I, V, and X.

The line length chosen must accommodate the longest line but must not exceed 70 spaces.

There must be at least two parts to any division.

```
                        HEADING

                          TS

        I.  FIRST-ORDER DIVISION

                          DS
            A.  Second-Order Division
            B.  Second-Order Division
                1.  Third-order division
                2.  Third-order division
            C.  Second-Order Division

                          DS
       II.  FIRST-ORDER DIVISION

                          DS
            A.  Second-Order Division
                1.  Third-order division
                2.  Third-order division
                    a.  Fourth-order division
                    b.  Fourth-order division
                3.  Third-order division
            B.  Second-Order Division
```

PREPARING REPORTS: THE PROFESSIONAL TOUCH

Both the writer and keyboard operator, or compositor, share concern for the preparation and ultimate success of a report, but usually the writer must accept final accountability. The compositor's contribution, however, is a vital one; and she or he should proceed cautiously. For example, before starting to prepare a final copy of a report, the compositor should determine

1. the specified purpose of the report and whether some particular format is required;
2. the number, kind, and grade of copies required;[1] and
3. deadlines for completion.

The keyboard operator should be prepared to work from script, rough-draft, or printed copy and yet give the report a final presentation that is as professional as it is functional.

"Tricks of the Trade"

Those with experience in preparing reports have found that there are special procedures they can use to simplify their tasks. The following paragraphs contain samples of some procedures that can be especially helpful to a person who has not previously keyboarded reports. (Anyone who plans to prepare more than a few reports, however, should read several good books on the subject.)

Right margins. Attractive right margins result when good judgment is exercised. Using the warning bell judiciously ensures right margins that approximate left margins in width.

---

[1]For further information, see The Chicago Manual of Style, 13th ed. (Chicago: The University of Chicago Press, 1982), p. 40.

1 Unbound report, page 1

2

Reference characters. To keystroke a superior figure, turn the platen back a half line and type the figure. Asterisks and other reference symbols require no such adjustment. Keyboards with special symbol keys for report writing are available.

Page endings. A few simple guides become important whenever a report has more than one page. For example, never end a page with a hyphenated word. Further, do not leave a single line of a paragraph at the bottom of a page or at the top of a page (unless the paragraph has only one line, of course).

Footnote content. Underline titles of complete publications; use quotation marks with parts of publications. Thus, the name of a magazine will be underlined, but the title of an article within the magazine will be placed in quotation marks. Months and locational words, such as volume and number, may be abbreviated.

Penciled guides. A light pencil mark can be helpful to mark approximate page endings, planned placement of page numbers, and potential footnote locations. When the report has been finished, erase any visible pencil marks.

Conclusion

With patience and skill, the keyboard operator can give a well-written report the professional appearance it deserves. Says Lesikar[2],

> Even with the best typewriter available, the finished work is no better than the efforts of the typist. But this statement does not imply that only the most skilled typist can turn out good work. Even the inexperienced typist can produce acceptable manuscripts simply by exercising care.

---

[2]Raymond V. Lesikar, Basic Business Communication (Homewood: Richard D. Irwin, Inc., 1979), p. 364.

2 Unbound report, page 2

TRENDS IN OFFICE COMMUNICATION

Bernadette D. Blount

Northern Illinois University

January 11, 19--

3 Title page

BIBLIOGRAPHY

Blum, Lester. "Computer Generated Graphic Tutorials In Economics." Collegiate Microcomputer 4 (Winter 1983): 289-97.

Crawford, T. James, et al. Basic Keyboarding and Typewriting Applications. Cincinnati: South-Western Publishing Co., 1983.

Hess, M. Elizabeth. Printing Manager, Effective Office Systems, New Orleans, Louisiana. Interviewed by Lois Walker, March 20, 1985.

Ray, Patrick V. "Electronic Printing Applications." Class handout in BADM 487, Central University, 1984.

Toffler, Alvin. The Third Wave. New York: William Morrow and Company, Inc., 1980.

4 Bibliography

LENDING POLICY FOR COUNTY BANK

Limits of Authority

The President of the bank is authorized to make loans up to $100,000 on a secured basis and up to $50,000 on an unsecured basis. Any request for a line of credit in excess of the limit specified for the President must be approved by at least two members of the Loan Committee other than the President. These lending limits are in agreement with recommended standards (Burge, 1985).

The President shall delegate authority to make loans to the senior officers of the bank. Senior officers may approve loans up to $50,000 on a secured basis and up to $25,000 on an unsecured basis. The President may delegate authority to make loans to other officers. Authority delegated to officers other than the senior officers shall not exceed $10,000 and shall be for secured loans only. This policy is based on recommended guides (White, 1985).

REFERENCES

Burge, S. Michael. "General Lending Policy," South-Western Banking Association Report. March 12, 1985, p. 8.

White, Deborah B. "Guides for Delegating Lending Authority." Class handout in Bankers' School, Central University, 1985.

1 Reference citations

TABLE OF CONTENTS

2 Table of contents

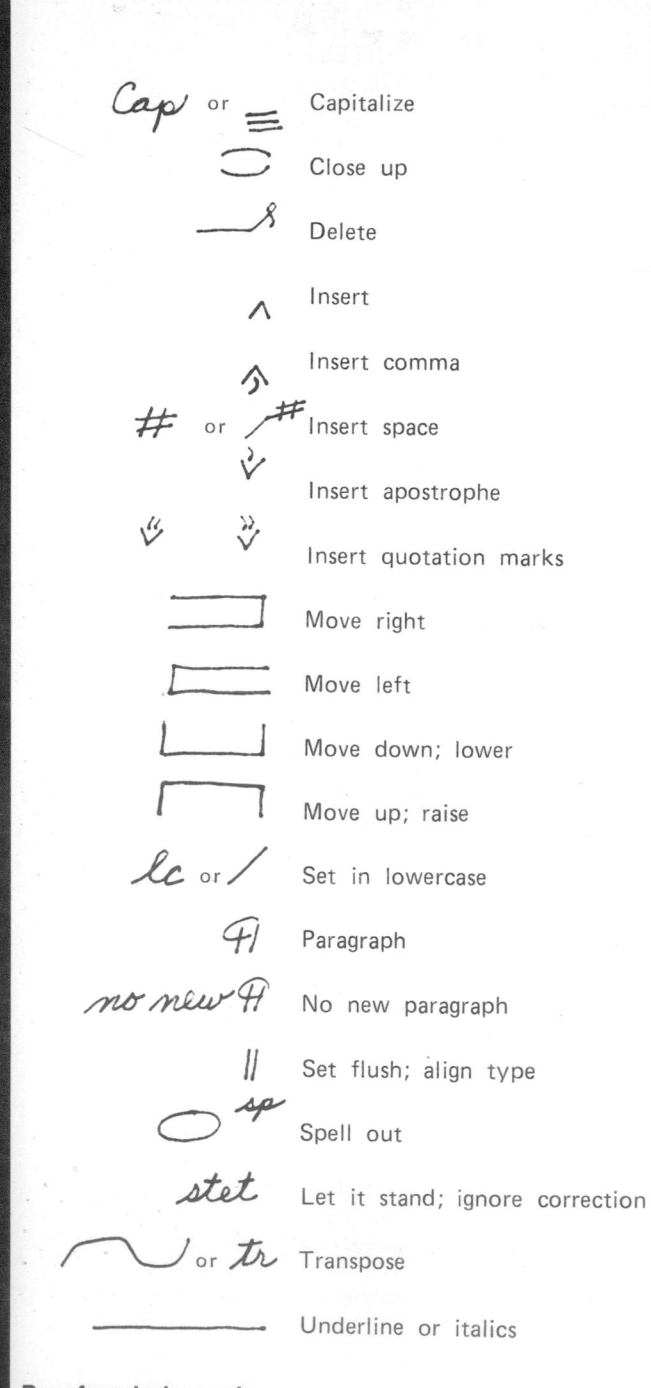

Cap or ≡	Capitalize
⊃⊂	Close up
⸜	Delete
∧	Insert
⌄	Insert comma
# or ⫽#	Insert space
⌄	Insert apostrophe
⌄⌄	Insert quotation marks
⊓	Move right
⊐	Move left
⊔	Move down; lower
⊓	Move up; raise
lc or /	Set in lowercase
¶	Paragraph
no new ¶	No new paragraph
‖	Set flush; align type
◯ sp	Spell out
stet	Let it stand; ignore correction
⌣ or tr	Transpose
___	Underline or italics

Proofreader's marks

Preliminary copy may be corrected with proofreader's marks. The typist must be able to interpret correctly these marks when retyping the corrected (rough-draft) copy. The most commonly used marks are shown above.

Correcting errors

There are several methods that can be used to correct errors, and they are explained below.

Correction paper ("white carbon")

1 Backspace to the error.

2 Place the correction paper in front of the error, coated side toward the paper.

3 Retype the error. The substance on the correction paper will cover the error.

4 Remove the correction paper; backspace; type the correction.

Rubber eraser

1 Use a plastic shield to protect surrounding and a typewriter (hard) eraser.

2 Turn the paper forward or backward in the machine to position the error for easier correction.

3 To keep bits of eraser out of the mechanism, move the carrier away from the error (or move carrier to the extreme left or right).

4 Move the eraser in one direction only to avoid cutting the paper.

Correction fluid ("liquid paper")

1 Be sure the color of the fluid matches the color of the paper.

2 Turn the paper forward or backward to ease the correction process.

3 Brush the fluid on sparingly; cover only the error, and it lightly.

4 The fluid dries quickly. Return to correction point and make the correction.

Automatic correction

If your machine is equipped with an automatic correcting ribbon, consult with your instructor or with the manufacturer's manual for operating instructions.

Horizontal centering

1 Move the margin stops to extreme ends of the scale.

2 Clear tab stops; then set a tab stop at center of paper.

3 Tabulate to the center of the paper.

4 From center, backspace once for each 2 letters, spaces, figures, or punctuation marks in the line.

5 Do not backspace for an odd or leftover stroke at the end of the line.

6 Begin to type where backspacing ends.

	Example
Scale reading at left edge of paper	0
+Scale reading at right edge of paper	102
Total ÷ 2 = Center point	102 ÷ 2 = 51

Spread headings

1 Backspace from center once for each letter, character, and space except the last letter or character in the heading. Start typing where the backspacing ends.

2 When typing a spread heading, space once after each letter or character and three times between words.

Vertical centering

Roll-back-from-center method

From vertical center of paper, roll platen (cylinder) back once for each 2 lines, 2 blank spaces, or line and blank line space. Ignore odd or leftover line.

Steps to follow:

1 To move paper to vertical center, start spacing down from top edge of paper:

  a half sheet
    down 6 TS (triple spaces)
      −1 SS (Line 17)

  b full sheet
    down 11 TS
      −1 SS (Line 34)

2 From vertical center:

  a half sheet, SS or DS; follow basic rule, back 1 for 2.

  b full sheet, SS or DS; follow basic rule, back 1 for 2; then back 2 SS for reading position.

Mathematical method

1 Count lines and blank line spaces needed to type problem.

2 Subtract lines to be used from lines available (66 for full sheet and 33 for half sheet).

3 Divide by 2 to get top and bottom margins. If fraction results, disregard it. Space down from top edge of paper 1 more than number of lines to be left in top margin.

  For reading position, which is above exact vertical center, subtract 2 from exact top margin.

Formula for vertical mathematical placement:

$$\frac{\text{Lines available} - \text{lines used}}{2} = \text{top margin}$$

Prepare

1 Insert and align paper.

2 Clear margin stops by moving them to extreme ends of the scale.

3 Clear all tab stops.

4 Decide the number of spaces to be left between columns (for intercolumns).

Plan vertical placement

Follow either of the vertical centering methods explained on page xi.

Headings. Double-space (count 1 blank line space) between main and secondary headings, when both are used. Triple-space (count 2 blank line spaces) between the last heading (either main or secondary) and the first horizontal line of column items or column headings. Double-space between column headings (when used) and the first line of the columns.

Plan horizontal placement

Backspace from center of paper 1 space for each 2 letters, figures, symbols, and spaces in the *longest item* of each column and for each 2 spaces between columns. Set the left margin stop of the longest item when backspacing, carry it forward to the next column. Ignore an extra space at the end of the last column. (See illustration below.)

An easy alternate method is to backspace for the longest item in each column first, *then* for the spaces to be left between columns.

Note. If a column heading is longer than the longest item in the column, it may be treated as the longest item in determining placement. The longest column item must then be centered under the heading, and the tab stop set accordingly.

Set tab stops. From the left margin stop, space forward 1 space for each letter, figure, symbol, and space in the longest item in the first column and for each space in the first intercolumn. Set a tab stop. Follow this procedure for each additional column to be typed.

To center column headings

Backspace-from-column-center method

From the point at which the column begins (tab or margin stop), space forward (→) once for each 2 letters, figures, or spaces in the longest item in the column. This leads to the column center point; from it, backspace (←) once for each 2 spaces in the column heading. Ignore an odd or leftover space. Type the heading at this point; it will be centered over the column.

Mathematical method

1 To the number of the cylinder (platen) or line-of-writing scale immediately under the first letter, figure, or symbol of the longest item of the column, add the number shown under the space following the last stroke of the item. Divide this sum by 2; the result will be the center point of the column. From this point on the scale, backspace to center the column heading.

—or—

2 From the number of spaces in the longest item, subtract the number of spaces in the heading. Divide this number by 2; ignore fractions. Space forward this number from the tab or margin stop and type the heading.

To type horizontal lines

Depress the shift lock; strike the underline key.

To draw vertical lines

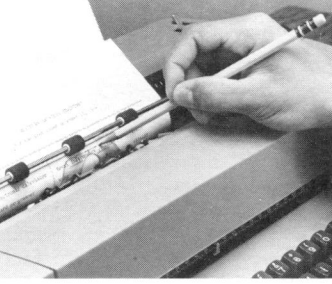

Operate the automatic line finder. Place a pencil or pen point through the cardholder (or the type bar guide above the ribbon or carrier). Roll the paper up until you have a line of the desired length. Remove the pencil or pen and reset the line finder.

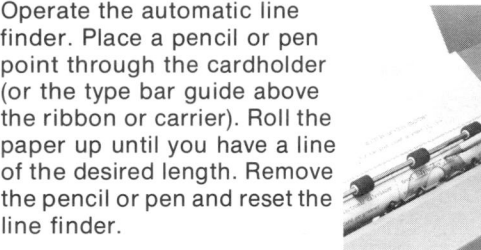

MAIN HEADING

Secondary Heading

These	Are	Column	Heads
xxxxxx	*longest*	xxxx	xxxxx
xxxx	*item*	*longest*	xxx
xxxxx	xxxxx	*item*	*longest*
longest	xxxxxx	xxxxx	*item*
item	xxxx	xxx	xxx